The U
General Knowledge Quiz Book

Geoff Tibballs

To Malcolm
We're looking forward
to hearing these questions
at Christmas!
Happy Birthday
Love
Claire + Hassan

This is a Parragon Book
This edition published in 2004

Parragon
Queen Street House
4 Queen Street
Bath BA1 1HE, UK

Produced by Magpie Books, an imprint of
Constable & Robinson Ltd, London

ISBN 1-40544-327-8

A copy of the British Library Cataloguing-in-Publication Data
is available from the British Library

Printed and bound in the UK

Cover design by Kit Rocket

Contents

Music Pot Luck 1

Answers on page 6

1. Which Angie was the subject of the Rolling Stones' track of the same name?

2. Which band took their name from the villain in Jane Fonda's 1968 film *Barbarella* since many of their early gigs were played at Barbarella's club in Birmingham?

3. Who were the first American group to top the UK charts?

4. What were the Christian names of The Everly Brothers?

5. Which Celine Dion track was the theme to *Sleepless in Seattle*?

6. Who was sacked from East 17 in 1997 after his comments about Ecstasy?

7. Which saxophonist was the Johnny of Johnny and The Hurricanes?

8. Which music paper did Chrissie Hynde used to write for?

9. Which ska prince was born Cecil Bustamante Campbell?

10. Roger Hodgson, Bob Benberg and John Helliwell were members of which Seventies band?

11. Who was lead singer with The Waterboys?

12. Which singer was an apprentice at Vauxhall Motors in Luton before leaving in 1978?

13. Which Supremes hit did Kim Wilde cover in 1986?

14. Who performed with the jazz-funk outfit Fusion before going solo?

15. Which Sixties group had what was then considered the novelty of a female drummer?

16. And what was her name?

Answers to page 6

SOUL 1: **1.** 'Papa's Got A Brand New Bag' **2.** Charles and Eddie **3.** The Chi-Lites **4.** The Bar-Kays **5.** Arthur Conley **6.** Lee Dorsey **7.** The Isley Brothers **8.** Philadelphia **9.** Archie Bell and The Drells **10.** Sam and Dave **11.** Johnny Nash **12.** (Detroit) Spinners **13.** Eddie Holman **14.** Bob Marley **15.** The Stylistics **16.** '(Sittin' On) The Dock Of The Bay'

One-Hit Wonders 1

Answers on page 7

1. Which band's only hit was the 1976 offering 'Afternoon Delight'?
2. Which twins had a UK number one with 'When' in 1958?
3. Who begged: 'Tell Laura I Love Her' in 1962?
4. Which *Neighbours* actor reached the UK top fifty just once – with 'Don't It Make You Feel Good'?
5. What was the title of Shorty Long's only UK hit?
6. 'They're Coming To Take Me Away, Ha-Haaa!' was a 1966 hit for which emperor?
7. Carly Simon provided backing vocals on 'Kissing With Confidence', a 1983 recording by which one-hit wonder?
8. Which 1969 one-hit wonders had their record banned by the BBC?
9. Which UK number one provided Kitty Kallen's moment of glory in 1954?
10. Which group's cover version of The Beatles' 'Ob-La-Di, Ob-La-Da' gave them their only hit?
11. Who had a 1969 UK top twenty hit with a medley of 'Sing A Rainbow' and 'Love Is Blue'?
12. Which instrumental got to number seven for East Of Eden in 1971?
13. Whose only UK hit was 'Gonna Make You An Offer You Can't Refuse' in 1973?
14. Who sang 'Let's Go To San Francisco' in 1967?
15. George Harrison played bass guitar on which 1974 hit for Splinter?
16. Which Australian band tasted sweet success with 'Howzat' in 1976?

Answers to page 7

COVER VERSIONS 1: **1.** 'How Deep Is Your Love' **2.** Wheatus **3.** Bananarama **4.** 'Blame It On The Boogie' **5.** The Four Preps **6.** Nicki French **7.** Little Anthony and The Imperials **8.** 'Speaking In Tongues' **9.** The Velvelettes **10.** 'Going Down To Liverpool' **11.** The Corrs **12.** The Four Seasons **13.** 'Don't Tell My Heart' **14.** Denise and Johnny **15.** 'Killing Me Softly With His Song' **16.** Betty Hutton

Soul 1

Answers on page 4

1. What was James Brown's first US top ten hit?
2. Which duo who had a worldwide hit with 'Would I Lie To You' first met on a subway train?
3. Which group had a US number one with 'Oh Girl' in 1972?
4. Four members of which band were killed along with Otis Redding in a 1967 plane crash?
5. Who had a 1967 hit with 'Sweet Soul Music'?
6. Who was 'Working In The Coalmine' in 1966?
7. O'Kelly, Rudolph and Ronald were which band of brothers?
8. In which US city were The Stylistics formed?
9. Who went on a 'Soul City Walk' in 1976?
10. Which duo had a 1969 hit with 'Soul Sister Brown Sugar'?
11. Who had hits with 'You Got Soul' and 'I Can See Clearly Now'?
12. Which US group were given the prefix 'Detroit' to distinguish them from a British folk group of the same name?
13. Whose only UK hit was the 1974 single '(Hey There) Lonely Girl'?
14. Who wrote 'Stir It Up' for Johnny Nash?
15. 'Betcha By Golly, Wow' was the first UK hit for which band?
16. Which was Otis Redding's biggest-selling single?

Answers to page 4

MUSIC POT LUCK 1: **1.** Angie Bowie **2.** Duran Duran **3.** Bill Haley and The Comets **4.** Don and Phil **5.** 'When I Fall In Love' **6.** Brian Harvey **7.** Johnny Paris **8.** *New Musical Express* **9.** Prince Buster **10.** Supertramp **11.** Mike Scott **12.** Paul Young **13.** 'You Keep Me Hangin' On' **14.** Nik Kershaw **15.** The Honeycombs **16.** Anne 'Honey' Lantree

Cover Versions 1

Answers on page 5

1. Which Bee Gees song did Take That cover in 1996?
2. Which band covered Erasure's 'A Little Respect' in 2001?
3. Which girl band covered The Beatles' 'Help!' in 1989?
4. Which song links The Jacksons and Big Fun?
5. Who originally recorded Paul Young's 'Love Of The Common People'?
6. Who covered Bonnie Tyler's 'Total Eclipse Of The Heart' in 1995?
7. Who recorded the original version of 'Tears On My Pillow', released by Kylie Minogue in 1990?
8. 'Burning Down The House' was a 1999 hit for Tom Jones and The Cardigans, but on which Talking Heads album did it originally appear?
9. Bananarama and Fun Boy Three had a hit in 1982 with 'Really Saying Something (He Was Really Sayin' Somethin')', but who originally recorded it?
10. Which song links Katrina and The Waves with The Bangles?
11. Who covered 'Dreams' by Fleetwood Mac in 1998?
12. Who originally recorded 'Bye Bye Baby', a hit for The Bay City Rollers in 1975?
13. Billy Ray Cyrus's 'Achy Breaky Heart' was originally recorded by The Marci Brothers under a different title. What was it?
14. Who covered Kylie and Jason's hit 'Especially For You' in 1998?
15. Lori Leiberman was the first to record which Roberta Flack classic?
16. Who originally recorded 'It's Oh So Quiet', a hit for Bjork in 1995?

Answers to page 5

ONE-HIT WONDERS 1: **1.** Starland Vocal Band **2.** The Kalin Twins **3.** Ricky Valance **4.** Stefan Dennis **5.** 'Here Comes The Judge' **6.** Napoleon XIV **7.** Will Powers **8.** Jane Birkin and Serge Gainsbourg ('Je T'Aime...Moi Non Plus') **9.** 'Little Things Mean A Lot' **10.** The Bedrocks **11.** The Dells **12.** 'Jig-A-Jig' **13.** Jimmy Helms **14.** The Flowerpot Men **15.** 'Costafine Town' **16.** Sherbet

Folk 1

Answers on page 10

1. As whom was Hudson Leadbetter more usually known?
2. Who released the 1975 album 'Diamonds And Rust'?
3. Who spent six months as a singer with The Strawbs before joining Fairport Convention in 1968?
4. What is Melanie's surname?
5. Whose debut album was 'The Sophisticated Beggar'?
6. Which folk group gave Paul Simon his first UK chart success with 'Someday One Day' in 1966?
7. Which group took their name from a Lincolnshire waggoner celebrated in song?
8. Craig and Charlie Reid are better known as which duo?
9. What nationality is Gordon Lightfoot?
10. Who popularised the song 'Little Boxes'?
11. Which 1968 UK top five hit by a London busker was recorded for just £8?
12. Whose second album was titled 'Ramblin' Boy'?
13. Who wrote 'If I Were A Carpenter'?
14. The million-selling single 'Amazing Grace' was taken from which Judy Collins album?
15. With whom did The Chieftains collaborate for their 1988 album 'Irish Heartbeat'?
16. Which two artists had UK hits with 'Elusive Butterfly' in 1966?

Answers to page 10

NINETIES 1: **1.** 'Firestarter' **2.** EMF **3.** 'The Chronic' **4.** Elastica **5.** 'Genie In A Bottle' **6.** Shirley Manson **7.** Texas **8.** DJ Shadow **9.** 'Hangin' Tough' by New Kids On The Block **10.** Hannon (aka Divine Comedy) wrote the theme music for *Father Ted* **11.** 'Renaissance' **12.** Teddy Pendergrass **13.** Mark Knopfler **14.** Weeks **15.** 'Automatic For The People' **16.** 'I Should Coco'

Steps 1

Answers on page 11

1. What is H's real name?
2. What was the title of Steps' first UK hit?
3. And what form of dancing did it feature?
4. Which two members of Steps were Welsh?
5. What was Steps' first UK number one?
6. Which TV talent show did Steps present?
7. Which Kylie Minogue single did Steps cover?
8. What Had A Hold On Steps' Heart?
9. Which single had an Oriental theme to the video?
10. What was the title of the other song on the double A-side with 'When I Said Goodbye'?
11. What was the title of Steps' first album?
12. Which girl band originally recorded 'Last Thing On My Mind'?
13. On which 1999 charity single in aid of the Brit Trust did Steps take part?
14. Which Steps single of March 1999 reached number two in the UK charts?
15. What was the title of Steps' second album?
16. What is Lisa's surname?

Answers to page 11

EAGLES 1: **1.** Jackson Browne **2.** 'Desperado' **3.** 'Tequila Sunrise' **4.** London **5.** Don Felder **6.** James Dean **7.** 'The Best Of My Love' **8.** 'I Wish You Peace' (Patti Reagan Davis) **9.** Timothy B. Schmit **10.** 'Hotel California' **11.** 'The Carpenters 1969–1973' **12.** Elton John **13.** Randy Meisner **14.** 'New Kid In Town' **15.** Don Felder **16.** Bruce Hornsby

Nineties 1

Answers on page 8

1. Which 1996 UK number one prompted complaints that it encouraged young people to commit arson?
2. Which band's original line-up consisted of James Atkin, Ian Dench, Zak Foley, Derry Brownson and Mark Decloedt?
3. Which Dr Dre album title is slang for marijuana?
4. Justine Frischmann left Suede to front which Indie band?
5. What was Christina Aguilera's first UK hit?
6. Who is the lead singer of Garbage?
7. Whose biggest-selling album was 'White On Blonde'?
8. What does hip hop artist Josh Davis call himself?
9. What was the first new UK number one of the Nineties?
10. What links Neil Hannon with Father Dougal?
11. Which M People single from 1994 was the theme from the BBC2 series *The Living Soap*?
12. Which soul singer was featured on the K.W.S. single 'The More I Get, The More I Want'?
13. Who played guitar on Jimmy Nail's 1995 hit 'Big River'?
14. What is Des'ree's surname?
15. From which R.E.M. album did 'Everybody Hurts' come?
16. What was the title of Supergrass's debut album?

Answers to page 8

FOLK 1: **1.** Leadbelly **2.** Joan Baez **3.** Sandy Denny **4.** Safka **5.** Roy Harper **6.** The Seekers **7.** Steeleye Span **8.** The Proclaimers **9.** Canadian **10.** Pete Seeger **11.** 'Rosie' by Don Partridge **12.** Tom Paxton **13.** Tim Hardin **14.** 'Whales And Nightingales' **15.** Van Morrison **16.** Bob Lind and Val Doonican

Eagles 1

Answers on page 9

1. Who co-wrote 'Take It Easy' with Glenn Frey?
2. Which Eagles album has a cowboy theme?
3. Which was the first single to be written by Don Henley and Glenn Frey?
4. In which city were the band's first two albums recorded?
5. Which guitarist joined The Eagles in 1974?
6. The 'On The Border' album features a track about which legendary US movie star and youth icon?
7. Which was the band's first million-selling single?
8. Which track from 'One Of These Nights' was co-written by a future US President's daughter?
9. Who replaced Randy Meisner in 1977?
10. Which single was The Eagles' only top ten UK hit?
11. Which 'Best of' album kept 'Hotel California' from the top spot in the UK?
12. Who played piano for an encore of Chuck Berry's 'Carol' when The Eagles toured Europe in 1977?
13. Who sang lead vocal on 'Take It To The Limit'?
14. Which was the first single to be released from 'Hotel California'?
15. Which Eagle played in a band with Stephen Stills at the age of 13?
16. Who played piano on Don Henley's 1989 single 'The End Of The Innocence'?

Answers to page 9

STEPS 1: **1.** Ian Watkins **2.** '5, 6, 7, 8' **3.** Line dancing **4.** H and Lisa **5.** 'Heartbeat/Tragedy' **6.** *Steps to the Stars* **7.** 'Better The Devil You Know' **8.** Love **9.** 'After The Love Has Gone' **10.** 'Summer Of Love' **11.** 'Step One' **12.** Bananarama **13.** 'Thank Abba For The Music' **14.** 'Better Best Forgotten' **15.** 'Steptacular' **16.** Scott-Lee

Rock 'n' Roll 1

Answers on page 14

1. The phrase 'That'll Be The Day' was used by which actor in the 1956 Western classic *The Searchers*?
2. From which town in Texas did The Crickets hail?
3. Whose career nearly came to an end when it emerged that he had married his 14-year-old cousin?
4. Which 1955 movie featured 'Rock Around The Clock'?
5. Who wrote 'Jailhouse Rock'?
6. What was Buddy Holly's only solo UK number one single?
7. Which was the only number one on which Cliff Richard was backed by The Drifters before they changed their name to The Shadows?
8. In which year did Adam Faith have his first UK number one?
9. And what was the title?
10. Who changed his name from Reg Smith and had a 1958 hit with 'Endless Sleep'?
11. What was Eddie Cochran's 'C'mon Everybody' originally titled?
12. Which American singer, who would resurface in the Seventies, recorded the original version of the Billy Fury hit 'Halfway To Paradise'?
13. Who wrote 'It Doesn't Matter Anymore'?
14. What was the name of Marty Wilde's backing group?
15. From which film was 'Great Balls Of Fire' taken?
16. What did The Big Bopper like in 1958?

Answers to page 14

HEAVY METAL 1: **1.** Paul Di'Anno **2.** Mötley Crüe **3.** Brian Robertson **4.** Kiss **5.** Jon Bon Jovi **6.** Ozzy Osbourne **7.** Saxon **8.** Steven Adler **9.** Sheffield **10.** Rick Allen **11.** Deep Purple **12.** Mountain **13.** 1980 **14.** Black Sabbath **15.** AC/DC **16.** Frank Beard

Film Tracks 1

Answers on page 15

1. Which Shania Twain hit was used in the 1999 film *Notting Hill*?
2. From which film was Wet Wet Wet's 'Love Is All Around'?
3. Who sang 'Up Where We Belong' from the film *An Officer and a Gentleman*?
4. Which Mama Cass song was used in the film *French Kiss* starring Meg Ryan?
5. Who sang 'Show Me Heaven' from the Tom Cruise film *Days Of Thunder*?
6. 'Brown-Eyed Girl' by Van Morrison featured in which film?
7. Who sang 'Footloose' from the film of the same name?
8. Which 1994 film featured 'Maneater' 12 years after it had been a hit for Daryl Hall and John Oates?
9. Which song by The Wannadies was used in the 1996 film *Romeo and Juliet*?
10. In which film was Kylie Minogue's hit 'Tears On My Pillow' used?
11. Which group sang the theme for the Bond movie *The Living Daylights*?
12. Who performed 'Stay (I Missed You)' from the 1994 film *Reality Bites*?
13. Who had a hit with the song 'A Life Less Ordinary' from the film of the same name starring Ewan McGregor?
14. Which film featured The Bangles' hit 'Hazy Shade Of Winter'?
15. Which Beach Boys song was used in the film *Cocktail*?
16. Blondie's 'Call Me' featured in which Richard Gere film?

Answers to page 15

MUSIC POT LUCK 2: **1.** King Crimson **2.** The line which mentioned Coca-Cola had to be changed to cherry cola **3.** 'Galveston' **4.** Phil Collins **5.** Tab Hunter (1957) and Donny Osmond (1973) **6.** Don McLean **7.** 'Do You Know The Way To San Jose?' **8.** Five Star **9.** Bev Bevan **10.** Two **11.** George Harrison **12.** The Hooters **13.** Berlin ('Take My Breath Away') **14.** Les McKeown **15.** Village People **16.** Sir Douglas Quintet

Heavy Metal 1

Answers on page 12

1. Who did Bruce Dickinson replace as singer during his first spell with Iron Maiden?
2. Which US heavy metal band was formed by Nikki Sixx in 1980?
3. Which ex-Thin Lizzy guitarist joined Motorhead in 1982?
4. Which band released a 1976 album titled 'Destroyer'?
5. As a teenager, which heavy metal frontman used to be employed making Christmas decorations?
6. And which rocker used to work as a labourer in a slaughterhouse?
7. Which English band were formerly known as Son Of A Bitch?
8. Which Guns N' Roses drummer had to be replaced temporarily after breaking his hand in a brawl?
9. Def Leppard come from which English city?
10. Which Def Leppard drummer lost his left arm in a car crash in 1984?
11. Which band were originally called Roundabout?
12. Leslie West and Felix Pappalardi were founder members of which band?
13. In which year did Motörhead release 'Ace Of Spades'?
14. Whose 1980 album was titled 'Heaven And Hell'?
15. 'Rock 'n' Roll Damnation' was which band's first UK hit?
16. Which is the only member of ZZ Top not to have a long beard?

Answers to page 12

ROCK 'N' ROLL 1: **1.** John Wayne **2.** Lubbock **3.** Jerry Lee Lewis **4.** *Blackboard Jungle* **5.** Jerry Leiber and Mike Stoller **6.** 'It Doesn't Matter Anymore' **7.** 'Living Doll' **8.** 1959 **9.** 'What Do You Want?' **10.** Marty Wilde **11.** 'Let's Get Together' **12.** Tony Orlando **13.** Paul Anka **14.** The Wildcats **15.** *Jamboree* **16.** 'Chantilly Lace'

Music Pot Luck 2

Answers on page 13

1. Robert Fripp, Mike Giles, Ian McDonald and Greg Lake were the original line-up of which band?
2. What did the BBC force The Kinks to change when they sang 'Lola' on *Top of the Pops*?
3. Which Texas town did Glen Campbell sing about in 1969?
4. Who played drums on Adam Ant's 'Puss 'n Boots'?
5. Which two artists took 'Young Love' to number one in the UK charts?
6. A performance by which singer inspired 'Killing Me Softly With His Song'?
7. Which cover of a Dionne Warwick song featured on the Frankie Goes To Hollywood album 'Welcome To The Pleasuredome'?
8. The Pearson family formed which troubled Eighties band?
9. Who was the drummer with The Move?
10. How many Marthas were there in Martha and The Muffins?
11. Who was the youngest Beatle?
12. Rob Hyman and Eric Bazilian led which American band of the Eighties?
13. Terri Nunn was the lead singer with which band who enjoyed a number one in 1986?
14. Which Bay City Roller was charged with reckless driving after killing a 75-year-old woman?
15. Which colourful Seventies group were assembled by record producer Jacques Morali?
16. Which aristocratic band's only hit was the 1965 single 'She's About A Mover'?

Answers to page 13

FILM TRACKS 1: **1.** 'You've Got A Way' **2.** *Four Weddings and a Funeral* **3.** Joe Cocker and Jennifer Warnes **4.** 'Dream A Little Dream Of Me' **5.** Maria McKee **6.** *Sleeping with the Enemy* **7.** Kenny Loggins **8.** *Runaway Bride* **9.** 'You & Me Song' **10.** *The Delinquents* **11.** a-ha **12.** Lisa Loeb and Nine Stories **13.** Ash **14.** *Less Than Zero* **15.** 'Kokomo' **16.** *American Gigolo*

Name Changes 1

Answers on page 18

1. Which British rocker changed his name from Ronald Wycherley?

2. Who was born James Jewel Osterburg?

3. Which Irish band used to be known as The Incomparable Benzini Brothers?

4. What did the ill-fated Jiles Perry Richardson change his name to?

5. Which country star was born Brenda Gail Webb?

6. Which soul singer who had a comeback hit with 'Ain't Gonna Bump No More (With No Big Fat Woman)' changed his name from Joseph Arrington Jnr?

7. Which Welsh singer with a throaty voice was born Gaynor Hopkins?

8. Who changed his name from Steven Georgiou to notch up a succession of hits in the Sixties and Seventies?

9. Which Seventies singer was previously both Bernard Jewry and Shane Fenton?

10. Which rap artist's real name is Calvin Broadus?

11. Which heavy metal band were formerly known as Atomic Mass?

12. Which reggae artist changed his name from James Chambers?

13. What is Captain Beefheart's real name?

14. What were The Box Tops previously known as?

15. Which punk band were originally called The Nightlife Thugs?

16. Which outrageous US star of the Sixties changed his name from James Smith?

Answers to page 18

SIXTIES 1: **1.** Jonathan King **2.** Brian Hyland **3.** Manfred Mann **4.** Gene Pitney **5.** The Hollies **6.** Dusty Springfield **7.** Sandie Shaw **8.** The Foundations **9.** The Herd **10.** The Casuals **11.** Billy Fury **12.** Joe Dolan **13.** The Ivy League **14.** Engelbert Humperdinck **15.** The McCoys **16.** R. Dean Taylor

Motown 1

Answers on page 19

1. Who had a 1973 hit with 'Papa Was A Rollin' Stone'?
2. Who originally recorded Diana Ross and The Supremes' 1969 hit 'Someday We'll Be Together'?
3. Which Motown group were originally called The Del-Phis?
4. Who recorded romantic duets with, in turn, Mary Wells, Kim Weston and Tammi Terrell?
5. With which Moody Blues number did The Four Tops have a top three UK hit in 1971?
6. What is Smokey Robinson's real Christian name?
7. In which year did Smokey Robinson leave The Miracles?
8. What was Gladys Knight and The Pips' last UK hit for Tamla Motown?
9. What was The Jackson Five's first UK hit?
10. Which other Jackson originally recorded The Jacksons' 'Doctor My Eyes'?
11. What was Diana Ross's first solo UK number one?
12. Which Motown classic enjoyed a new lease of life in 1986 after being featured in a TV commercial for Levi's 501 jeans?
13. Which fellow Motown band rejected 'Where Did Our Love Go', thus allowing it to become the Supremes' first major hit?
14. What was Diana Ross's last new UK hit with The Supremes?
15. And which 1970 number gave The Supremes their first UK hit without Diana Ross?
16. Who replaced Eldridge Bryant in The Temptations in 1963?

Answers to page 19

R & B 1: **1.** Three **2.** French **3.** Lisa 'Left Eye' Lopes **4.** Another Level **5.** R. Kelly **6.** 'U Know What's Up' **7.** Sisqo **8.** 'Wonderful Tonight' **9.** 2001 **10.** Whitney Houston **11.** Jennifer Lopez **12.** Monica **13.** Ireland **14.** Kelis **15.** Mel B **16.** Annie Lennox

Sixties 1

Answers on page 16

Which artists had UK hits with the following Sixties songs?

1. 'Everyone's Gone To The Moon'
2. 'Ginny Come Lately'
3. 'Oh No Not My Baby'
4. 'That Girl Belongs To Yesterday'
5. 'Bus Stop'
6. 'I Close My Eyes And Count To Ten'
7. 'Girl Don't Come'
8. 'Baby, Now That I've Found You'
9. 'From The Underworld'
10. 'Jesamine'
11. 'Jealousy'
12. 'Make Me An Island'
13. 'Tossing And Turning'
14. 'Winter World Of Love'
15. 'Hang On Sloopy'
16. 'Gotta See Jane'

Answers to page 16

NAME CHANGES 1: **1.** Billy Fury **2.** Iggy Pop **3.** Hothouse Flowers **4.** Big Bopper **5.** Crystal Gayle **6.** Joe Tex **7.** Bonnie Tyler **8.** Cat Stevens **9.** Alvin Stardust **10.** Snoop Doggy Dog **11.** Def Leppard **12.** Jimmy Cliff **13.** Don Van Vliet **14.** Ronnie & The Devilles **15.** The Boomtown Rats **16.** P.J. Proby

R & B 1

Answers on page 17

1. How many members are there in Destiny's Child?
2. What nationality is Naima of Honeyz?
3. Which member of TLC featured on Mel C's single 'Never Be The Same Again'?
4. Dane Bowers was associated with which group?
5. Which R & B solo artist released 'If I Could Turn Back The Hands Of Time'?
6. Lisa 'Left Eye' Lopes featured on which of Donell Jones's singles?
7. 'Thong Song' and 'Incomplete' are singles by which artist?
8. Which Eric Clapton song was successfully covered by Damage in 1997?
9. In which year did Usher release 'Pop Ya Collar'?
10. Which female artist got to number two in the UK charts in 1999 with 'My Love Is Your Love'?
11. Which R & B/Latino artist was voted the world's sexiest female in 2001?
12. Who did Brandy team up with on the single 'The Boy Is Mine'?
13. Which country is Samantha Mumba from?
14. Who was 'Caught Out There'?
15. Which Spice Girl released 'Feels So Good'?
16. Who provided backing vocals on Whitney Houston's 1996 single 'Step By Step'?

Answers to page 17

MOTOWN 1: **1.** The Temptations **2.** Johnny Bristol **3.** Martha and The Vandellas **4.** Marvin Gaye **5.** 'Simple Game' **6.** William **7.** 1972 **8.** 'Neither One Of Us (Wants To Be The First To Say Goodbye)' **9.** 'I Want You Back' **10.** Jackson Browne **11.** 'I'm Still Waiting' **12.** 'I Heard It Through The Grapevine' **13.** The Marvelettes **14.** 'Someday We'll Be Together' **15.** 'Up The Ladder To The Roof' **16.** David Ruffin

Punk 1

Answers on page 22

1. Why was The Stranglers' performance at a February 1977 gig at London's Rainbow Theatre cut short?
2. What was The Clash's debut single?
3. Who were the first UK punk band to play in the US?
4. Which band undertook a covert 1977 tour as Spots?
5. Who were 'Top Of The Pops' in 1978?
6. Jimmy Pursey was lead singer with which band?
7. Whose first UK top ten hit was 'Into The Valley'?
8. Johnnie Fingers, Pete Briquette and Simon Crowe were members of which punk band?
9. Which Kinks track did The Jam cover in 1978?
10. Who was singer with Generation X before branching out into a successful solo career?
11. Which band released a 1976 album called 'Teenage Depression'?
12. Which band enjoyed their only UK number one in 1991 as the result of a TV commercial for Levi's jeans?
13. Which Sex Pistols track was recorded with Great Train Robber Ronnie Biggs in Rio de Janeiro?
14. Which band stripped a heckler at Swindon in 1982 and used his bare buttocks as tom-toms during 'Golden Brown'?
15. Whose 1978 album was titled 'Another Music In A Different Kitchen'?
16. Which Barry Ryan cover gave The Damned their biggest hit?

Answers to page 22

BLUES 1: **1.** U2 **2.** B.B. – Albert King was born Albert Nelson and Freddie King was born Billy Myles **3.** Van Morrison **4.** Rufus Thomas **5.** 'Babyface' **6.** Willie Mae Thornton **7.** 43 **8.** Muddy Waters **9.** Roy Gaines **10.** The Bluesbreakers **11.** Alexis Korner's Blues Incorporated **12.** John Lee Hooker **13.** Howlin' Wolf **14.** 'Peg Leg' **15.** Peter Green **16.** Chris Farlowe

Home Towns 1

Answers on page 23

1. Which was the home city of Dave Dee, Dozy, Beaky, Mick and Tich?
2. In which city did The Spencer Davis Group start out?
3. Showaddywaddy and Engelbert Humperdinck come from which city?
4. Where is home to The Chieftains?
5. In which Merseyside town were China Crisis formed?
6. Where do Echo and The Bunnymen come from?
7. Which Nineties band are the most famous sons of Cinderford in Gloucestershire?
8. From which city do Human League hail?
9. Three-quarters of Level 42 were brought up on which island?
10. What do Ritchie Blackmore and John Cleese have in common?
11. Which punk band were formed in Chiddingford, Surrey?
12. In which Sussex town did Brett Anderson form the prototype of Suede?
13. Which city do Duran Duran come from?
14. Which Sixties group pioneered the Tottenham Sound?
15. Which new wave band sounded French but had its roots in Basildon, Essex?
16. Which London suburb is home to The Bluetones?

Answers to page 23

U2 1: **1.** Bono Vox **2.** A Miss Wet T-shirt contest **3.** 'October' **4.** 'War' **5.** 'Pride (In The Name Of Love)' **6.** 'Under A Blood Red Sky' **7.** 'Angel Of Harlem' **8.** The ballroom at Slane Castle **9.** 'A Sort Of Homecoming' **10.** 1987 **11.** Dave Evans **12.** 'Rattle And Hum' **13.** 'Desire' **14.** 'Hold Me, Thrill Me, Kiss Me, Kill Me' **15.** The Zoo Tour **16.** 'Where The Streets Have No Name'

Blues 1

Answers on page 20

1. With which band did B.B. King team up for the 1989 hit 'When Love Comes To Town'?
2. Which of the triumvirate of Kings who ruled the blues in the Sixties was the only genuine King?
3. Who released the 1968 album 'Astral Weeks'?
4. Who was 'Walking The Dog' in 1963?
5. What was Jesse Thomas's nickname?
6. Which blues singer was known as 'Big Mama'?
7. How old was Bessie Smith when she died?
8. Which blues legend was born McKinley Morganfield?
9. What was the name of Grady Gaines's guitar-playing brother?
10. What was John Mayall's famous band?
11. Charlie Watts, Long John Baldry and Jack Bruce all played with which blues band in the early Sixties?
12. Whose albums include 'Mad Man's Blues', 'Free Beer And Chicken' and 'Chill Out'?
13. To what did Chester Arthur Burnett change his name?
14. What was Joshua Howell's nickname?
15. Which future Fleetwood Mac guitarist joined John Mayall's Bluebreakers in 1965 as a temporary substitute for Eric Clapton?
16. Which British blues singer had hits with 'Out Of Time' and 'Handbags And Gladrags'?

Answers to page 20

PUNK 1: **1.** The organisers turned off the power because they objected to the four-letter word on Hugh Cornwell's T-shirt **2.** 'White Riot' **3.** The Damned **4.** The Sex Pistols (Spots = Sex Pistols On Tour Secretly) **5.** Rezillos **6.** Sham 69 **7.** The Skids **8.** The Boomtown Rats **9.** 'David Watts' **10.** Billy Idol **11.** Eddie and The Hot Rods **12.** The Clash ('Should I Stay Or Should I Go') **13.** 'No One Is Innocent (A Punk Prayer By Ronald Biggs)' **14.** The Stranglers **15.** The Buzzcocks **16.** 'Eloise'

U2 1

Answers on page 21

1. Which Dublin hearing-aid shop inspired Paul Hewson in his choice of stage name?
2. What did U2 find themselves supporting in Dallas during their 1981 US tour?
3. What was the title of U2's second album?
4. From which album was 'New Year's Day' taken?
5. Which U2 track was dedicated to Martin Luther King Jnr?
6. Which was U2's first live album?
7. Which U2 single was a tribute to Billie Holliday?
8. In which unusual setting was the album 'The Unforgettable Fire' recorded?
9. What was the first track on 'The Unforgettable Fire'?
10. In which year was 'The Joshua Tree' released?
11. What is The Edge's real name?
12. Which was U2's fourth UK number one album?
13. Which was U2's first UK number one single?
14. Which U2 single was taken from the film *Batman Forever*?
15. Which mammoth U2 tour began in 1992?
16. The video for which single was filmed on the roof of a Los Angeles building?

Answers to page 21

HOME TOWNS 1: **1.** Salisbury **2.** Birmingham **3.** Leicester **4.** Dublin **5.** Kirkby **6.** Liverpool **7.** EMF **8.** Sheffield **9.** Isle of Wight **10.** Both were raised in Weston-super-Mare **11.** The Stranglers **12.** Haywards Heath **13.** Birmingham **14.** The Dave Clark Five **15.** Depeche Mode **16.** Hounslow

FA Cup 1

Answers on page 26

1. Which Second Division team reached the FA Cup final in 1947?
2. In which year did Mansfield Town reach the sixth round of the Cup?
3. Which First Division team did they beat on the way?
4. Who defeated Leyton Orient 3–0 in the semi-finals of the Cup in 1978?
5. Who was Colchester United's two-goal hero against Leeds in 1971?
6. Who did Liverpool crush 8–0 in a third-round replay in 1990?
7. Arthur Bottom scored a Cup semi-final goal for which Third Division (North) club in 1955?
8. Who were their opponents?
9. Which Third Division club brought Blyth Spartans' 1977–8 Cup run to an end in round five?
10. Who knocked out Hereford after their memorable third-round victory over Newcastle in 1972?
11. Which Premiership team ended Morecambe's Cup run in 2001?
12. Which Sunderland player scored in every round of the Cup in 1992 except the final?
13. Which Northern Ireland winger was Luton Town's leading scorer in their 1959 Cup run?
14. Who did Manchester City lose to in the 1926 final?
15. In which year did Carlisle United reach the quarter-finals of the Cup for the first time?
16. Which London club knocked them out of the competition that year?

Answers to page 26

TRANSFER TRAIL 1: **1.** Mustapha Hadji **2.** George Eastham **3.** Anderlecht **4.** Karl-Heinz Riedle **5.** Dundee United **6.** Robert Fleck **7.** Juventus **8.** 1993 **9.** Sampdoria **10.** Walsall **11.** Wyn Davies **12.** PSV Eindhoven **13.** Steve Froggatt **14.** Northampton Town **15.** Sheffield United **16.** Paul Stewart

Whistle Happy 1

Answers on page 27

1. What was Clive Thomas's nickname?

2. What nationality was the referee of the 1998 World Cup final?

3. Which Uruguayan referee, in charge of his first international, sent off the entire Ecuador team in a 1977 match against...Uruguay?

4. Referee Ivan Robinson inadvertently deflected a wayward shot into the net to give victory to Barrow in 1968 against which opponents?

5. What nationality was referee Henning Erikstrup who was about to blow for full-time in a 1960 fixture when his dentures fell out?

6. Which referee hit trouble in 1999 for appearing to applaud a Liverpool goal?

7. Which referee did a group of Leicester City fans threaten to sue in 1997 after he had awarded a controversial penalty against City at Chelsea?

8. Who refereed the centenary FA Cup final?

9. From which Essex town does Andy D'Urso hail?

10. Which Pat refereed the 1975 FA Cup final?

11. Which cheery ref of the 1970s once gathered Leeds players around him in the centre of the pitch because the elastic in his shorts had snapped?

12. Which bald Italian refereed the final of Euro 2000?

13. Which referee allowed half-time in the crucial Serie 'A' match between Perugia and Juventus in 2000 to last 82 minutes so that surface water could be cleared from the pitch?

14. What nationality was the referee of the 1994 World Cup final?

15. Which George refereed the 1980 FA Cup final?

16. Which two refereeing Grahams have connections with Tring?

Answers to page 27

SUNDERLAND 1: **1.** Arsenal **2.** Vic Halom and Billy Hughes **3.** Six **4.** 1936 **5.** 1958 **6.** Sheffield Wednesday **7.** Terry Butcher **8.** Dennis Tueart **9.** Newcastle Road **10.** 1995 **11.** Watford **12.** Falkirk **13.** Neil Martin **14.** Aston Villa **15.** Norwich City **16.** Valencia

Transfer Trail 1

Answers on page 24

1. Which Moroccan moved from Coventry City to Aston Villa in 2001?
2. Which playmaker did Arsenal sign from Newcastle for £47,500 in 1960?
3. From which Belgian club did Chelsea sign Celestine Babayaro?
4. Which German striker, who went on to play for Liverpool and Fulham, moved from Lazio to Borussia Dortmund in 1993?
5. With which Scottish club did Duncan Ferguson make his League debut?
6. Which Scottish striker joined Norwich City from Rangers for £580,000 in December 1987?
7. Which Italian club did Roberto Baggio join for £7.7 million in May 1990?
8. In which year did Manchester United sign Roy Keane?
9. For which Italian club did Des Walker sign on leaving Nottingham Forest in 1992?
10. From which club did Bolton Wanderers sign Michael Ricketts?
11. Which Welsh international centre-forward was transferred from Bolton Wanderers to Newcastle for £85,000 in 1966?
12. Which Dutch club did Ruud Gullit leave to sign for AC Milan in 1987?
13. Which injury-riddled left-winger did Wolves buy from Aston Villa for £1 million in July 1994?
14. Who paid out what was then a club record fee of £120,000 to sign Steve Howard from Hartlepool United in 1999?
15. From which club did Leeds sign Mick Jones in 1967 for £100,000?
16. Which former Manchester City striker switched from Tottenham to Liverpool for £2.3 million in 1992?

Answers to page 24

FA CUP 1: **1.** Burnley **2.** 1969 **3.** West Ham United **4.** Arsenal **5.** Ray Crawford **6.** Swansea City **7.** York City **8.** Newcastle United **9.** Wrexham **10.** West Ham United **11.** Ipswich Town **12.** John Byrne **13.** Billy Bingham **14.** Bolton Wanderers **15.** 1975 **16.** Fulham

Sunderland 1

Answers on page 25

1. Who did Sunderland defeat 2–1 in the semi-finals of the 1973 FA Cup?
2. And who were their scorers?
3. How many times have Sunderland been crowned League Champions?
4. When did they last lift the old First Division title?
5. In which year were Sunderland relegated to Division Two after 57 years' unbroken membership of the top flight?
6. Who went down with them that year?
7. Which former England international took over as Sunderland boss in 1993?
8. Who did Sunderland sell to Manchester City for £275,000 in 1974?
9. On which ground did Sunderland play before Roker Park?
10. In which year did Peter Reid become manager?
11. From which club did Sunderland sign Kevin Phillips?
12. With which Scottish club did Alex Rae begin his professional career?
13. Which lanky striker joined Sunderland from Hibernian in 1965?
14. Who did Sunderland lose to in the 1913 FA Cup final?
15. Who did Sunderland beat in the semi-finals of the 1992 FA Cup?
16. From which Spanish club did Sunderland sign Stefan Schwarz?

Answers to page 25

WHISTLE HAPPY 1: **1.** 'The Book' **2.** Moroccan **3.** Hector Rodriguez **4.** Plymouth Argyle **5.** Danish **6.** Mike Reed **7.** Mike Reed **8.** Keith Hackett **9.** Billericay **10.** Pat Partridge **11.** Tommy Dawes **12.** Pierluigi Collina **13.** Pierluigi Collina **14.** Hungarian **15.** George Courtney **16.** Barber and Poll

European Championship 1 

Answers on page 30

1. Who did Holland beat 2–0 in the 1988 European Championship final?
2. Who were the Dutch goalscorers?
3. In which city was the 1984 final played?
4. To whom did England lose in their first qualifying match for Euro 2000?
5. And who held England to a goalless draw at Wembley in their second qualifying game?
6. What is the name of the trophy awarded to the winners of the European Championship?
7. How many times have the Germans won the European Championship?
8. On which club's ground did the final of Euro 2000 take place?
9. What was the European Championship originally known as?
10. When did England compete for the first time?
11. What device was employed to decide the 1968 semi-final between Italy and USSR?
12. How many points did England get in their group at the 1988 finals?
13. Who eliminated England from the 1964 tournament?
14. Which country prevented the Republic of Ireland from reaching the 1960 finals?
15. Which minnows did Scotland meet in the qualifying groups for both Euro 1996 and Euro 2000?
16. Who did Scotland beat 1–0 at Euro 96?

Answers to page 30

ARSENAL 1: **1.** Glenn Helder **2.** Cliff Bastin **3.** Newcastle United **4.** Leeds United **5.** 1925 **6.** Bob Wilson **7.** Senegal **8.** John Radford **9.** Middlesbrough **10.** Dennis Bergkamp **11.** FC Cologne **12.** 1987–8 **13.** Paul Vaessen **14.** Valencia **15.** Eddie Hapgood **16.** Portsmouth

Football League 1

Answers on page 31

1. Which Football League club used to be known as Boscombe St Johns?

2. Which prodigal son returned to manage Birmingham City in 1996?

3. Who won 6–0 at Burnley in a Second Division match in 1998–9?

4. Which club that has never won the League title reached the FA Cup final in 1910 and 1912?

5. Which club took over the fixtures and playing record of the expelled Leeds City in October 1919?

6. Who missed out on promotion in the Fourth Division play-offs in their debut season of 1989–90?

7. In which year did Derby County first become League Champions?

8. In 1969, which club gained promotion for the only time in their history?

9. Which prefix did Port Vale drop in 1909?

10. And which did Bournemouth acquire in 1971?

11. For which club did John Pickering make a record 367 League appearances from 1965 to 1974?

12. Harry Cripps, Barry Kitchener and Keith Stevens were long-serving stalwarts with which club?

13. In which year did Torquay United turn professional?

14. Which former Northern Ireland manager was in charge of Wigan Athletic from 1989 to 1993?

15. On whose ground did Peterborough win 9–1 in 1998–9?

16. Who beat Brentford in the 1997 Second Division play-off final?

Answers to page 31

THE WORLD GAME 1: **1.** Real Oviedo **2.** Cyprus **3.** Arie Haan **4.** Czech Republic **5.** Ghana **6.** Lilian Thuram **7.** Monaco **8.** Giovanni Trapattoni **9.** China **10.** Brussels **11.** Roma **12.** South Africa **13.** Brazil **14.** FC Porto **15.** Belgian **16.** FC Croatia Zagreb

Arsenal 1

Answers on page 28

1. Which flying Dutchman joined Arsenal from Vitesse Arnhem in 1995?
2. Whose all-time Arsenal scoring record did Ian Wright break?
3. Who defeated Arsenal in the 1930 FA Cup final?
4. Who did Arsenal pip by one point to win the League title in 1971?
5. In which year did Herbert Chapman become Arsenal manager?
6. Which former Arsenal goalkeeper's middle name is Primrose?
7. In which country was Patrick Vieira born?
8. Which prolific Arsenal marksman made his League debut for the Gunners at West Ham on 21 March 1964?
9. Who knocked Arsenal out of the League Cup in 1999–2000?
10. Who was Arsenal's top scorer in 1997–8?
11. From which German club did Arsenal sign Tony Woodcock?
12. In which season did Lee Dixon make his Arsenal debut?
13. Whose finest moment in an Arsenal shirt was scoring the winner at Juventus to put the Gunners into the 1980 European Cup-Winners' Cup final?
14. But who beat Arsenal in the final on penalties?
15. Which Arsenal legend came to Highbury in 1927 from Kettering Town and went on to make 393 League appearances for the club?
16. To which club was Peter Marinello sold in 1973?

Answers to page 28

EUROPEAN CHAMPIONSHIP 1: **1.** Soviet Union **2.** Ruud Gullit and Marco Van Basten **3.** Paris **4.** Sweden **5.** Bulgaria **6.** Henri Delaunay Cup **7.** Three **8.** Feyenoord **9.** European Nations Cup **10.** 1964 **11.** The toss of a coin **12.** None **13.** France **14.** Czechoslovakia **15.** Faroe Islands **16.** Switzerland

The World Game 1

Answers on 29

1. Which Spanish club did Stan Collymore walk out on in 2001?
2. In which country do Salamina, Anorthosis and Doxa Katokopia play?
3. Which former Dutch international did Anderlecht sack as their coach in September 1998?
4. For which country is Pavel Srnicek an international goalkeeper?
5. Who defeated Libya in the 1982 African Cup of Nations final?
6. Who scored both of France's goals in the 1998 World Cup semi-final against Croatia?
7. Who won the French Cup in 1992?
8. Which veteran Italian coach who won six titles with Juventus took charge of Fiorentina for the start of the 1998–9 season?
9. Which country's League title did Dalian Wanda win in 1998?
10. In which city do Anderlecht play their home matches?
11. Gabriel Batistuta left Fiorentina for which club in May 2000?
12. French coach Philippe Troussier led which country to the 1998 World Cup finals?
13. Full-back Cafu represents which country at international level?
14. Who plays at the Das Antas Stadium?
15. What nationality is Gilles De Bilde?
16. Who knocked Celtic out of the 1998–9 Champions' League in the second qualifying round?

Answers to page 29

FOOTBALL LEAGUE 1: **1.** Bournemouth **2.** Trevor Francis **3.** Manchester City **4.** Barnsley **5.** Port Vale **6.** Maidstone United **7.** 1972 **8.** Rochdale **9.** Burslem **10.** AFC **11.** Halifax Town **12.** Millwall **13.** 1921 **14.** Bryan Hamilton **15.** Barnet **16.** Crewe Alexandra

Which Year in Football? 1

Answers on page 34

1. In which year did Terry Paine play his last League game for Southampton?
2. In which year did Sir Matt Busby die?
3. In which year were Preston North End formed?
4. In which year did Notts County win the Anglo-Italian Cup?
5. When did Leyton Orient become plain Orient?
6. When were Hibernian last crowned Scottish League champions?
7. In which year did Watford set off on their only European campaign?
8. In which year did Coventry City finish Second Division champions?
9. When did Chesterfield reach the semi-finals of the FA Cup?
10. In which year were Rushden & Diamonds formed?
11. When did Motherwell reach their first Scottish FA Cup final?
12. When did Middlesbrough get to the FA Cup final for the first time?
13. When did Barry Fry become manager of Peterborough United?
14. In which year did Norwich City sell Chris Sutton to Blackburn?
15. In which year was John Hartson fined and given a three-match ban for kicking West Ham team-mate Eyal Berkovic in the face during training?
16. When did Wolves last win the FA Cup?

Answers to page 34

SCOTTISH SCENE 1: **1.** Trevor Steven **2.** Dunfermline Athletic **3.** Partick Thistle **4.** Alloa Athletic **5.** St Johnstone **6.** Livingston and Inverness Caledonian Thistle **7.** 1983 **8.** Celtic **9.** Hibernian **10.** Falkirk **11.** Stirling Albion **12.** Raith Rovers **13.** Paul McStay **14.** Livingston **15.** Third Lanark **16.** Four

Sharpshooters 1

Answers on page 35

1. Kevin Hector was transferred from which former League side to Derby County?
2. Which Benfica star was named European Footballer of the Year for 1965?
3. Who scored in seven successive Premiership matches between September and November 1996?
4. Who scored four goals in 13 minutes after coming on as substitute in a Premiership match in 1999?
5. Which West Ham player scored four times in 20 minutes against West Bromwich Albion in 1965?
6. Who was Chelsea's top scorer for 2000–1?
7. For which club did Graham Leggat score a three-minute hat-trick in a 10–1 thrashing of Ipswich Town on Boxing Day 1963?
8. From which club did Charlton sign John Robinson?
9. For whom did John Aldridge score 30 League goals in 1984–5?
10. Who was named BBC Sports Personality of the Year for 1998?
11. Which Chelsea and England striker moved to Southampton in March 1974?
12. As a manager, which former Liverpool striker took Swansea City into the First Division in 1981?
13. With 33 League goals, which Dundee marksman was top scorer in Scotland in 1987–8?
14. Who was Stockport County's leading scorer in 1998–9?
15. When did Marco Van Basten retire from international football?
16. Which 15-year-old made his League debut with Santos in 1956?

Answers to page 35

EUROPEAN CUPS 1: **1.** Real Madrid and Valencia **2.** Barcelona **3.** Marco Van Basten **4.** FC Zurich **5.** Liverpool **6.** Trevor Francis **7.** Munich **8.** FC Cologne **9.** Italy **10.** Alan Sealey **11.** Waterschei **12.** 5–2 **13.** Tenerife **14.** Ferencvaros **15.** Mick Jones **16.** Aberdeen

Scottish Scene 1

Answers on page 32

1. Which England international did Rangers sign from Marseille in 1992 for £2.4 million?
2. For which club did Norris McCathie make 497 League appearances between 1981 and 1996?
3. Who romped to the Scottish Second Division title in 2001–2?
4. Jock Hepburn was the only player with which club to win a full Scotland cap?
5. Who won the Scottish First Division title by 20 points in 1996–7?
6. Which two teams were promoted from the Scottish Second Division in 1998–9?
7. When did Dundee United become Scottish champions?
8. Which is the only team to have won the Scottish League Cup for five years in a row?
9. Who did Celtic beat 6–1 in the 1972 Scottish FA Cup final?
10. Which League club's ground is situated on Hope Street?
11. Who plays at the Forthbank Stadium?
12. Jimmy Nicholl managed which club to League Cup success?
13. Which Celtic starlet was voted Scotland's Young Player of the Year for 1982–3?
14. Which club are nicknamed 'The Livvy Lions'?
15. Who were beaten finalists in the 1936 Scottish FA Cup final?
16. When the club finished third in the Premier League in 1998–9, how many goals did St Johnstone's leading scorer manage that season?

Answers to page 32

WHICH YEAR IN FOOTBALL? 1: **1.** 1974 **2.** 1994 **3.** 1881 **4.** 1995 **5.** 1966 **6.** 1952 **7.** 1983 **8.** 1967 **9.** 1997 **10.** 1992 **11.** 1931 **12.** 1997 **13.** 1996 **14.** 1994 **15.** 1999 **16.** 1960

European Cups 1

Answers on page 33

1. Which Spanish clubs contested the 2000 Champions' League final?
2. Which other Spanish club also reached the semi-finals that year?
3. Who scored the only goal in the 1987 European Cup-Winners' Cup final?
4. Which Swiss club reached the semi-finals of the European Cup in 1977?
5. Who knocked them out of the competition?
6. Who scored Nottingham Forest's winning goal in the 1979 European Cup final?
7. In which city was the final played?
8. And who did Forest beat in the semi-finals that year?
9. The 1998 UEFA Cup final featured two teams from which country?
10. Who scored both West Ham goals in their 1965 European Cup-Winners' Cup final win?
11. Which Belgian club did Aberdeen beat in the semi-finals of the 1983 European Cup-Winners' Cup?
12. And what was the aggregate score?
13. Which team from the Canary Islands made it to the UEFA Cup semi-finals in 1997?
14. Which Hungarian team did Leeds United defeat in the 1968 Fairs Cup final?
15. And who scored the only goal in the two legs?
16. Which Scottish club declined the invitation to take part in the first European Cup?

Answers to page 33

SHARPSHOOTERS 1: **1.** Bradford Park Avenue **2.** Eusebio **3.** Alan Shearer **4.** Ole Gunnar Solksjaer **5.** Brian Dear **6.** Jimmy Floyd Hasselbaink **7.** Fulham **8.** Brighton & Hove Albion **9.** Oxford United **10.** Michael Owen **11.** Peter Osgood **12.** John Toshack **13.** Tommy Coyne **14.** Brett Angell **15.** 1992 **16.** Pele

Oddballs 1

Answers on page 38

1. Which footwear specialist is owner of Rushden & Diamonds?
2. Which club do Sean Connery and Texas singer Sharleen Spiteri support?
3. Which actor is such a fanatical Sheffield United supporter that he has a tattoo on his arm proclaiming: '100 per cent Blades'?
4. In which city are Glentoran based?
5. Which Argentine team won the 1986 World Club Championship?
6. Which 1999 tournament was threatened with nude protests by Nigerian prostitutes?
7. Which English youth league folded in 1999 after 44 years' competition?
8. Who won the FAI National League in 1999?
9. For which country did Alexei Lalas play?
10. In 1998–9, which Southampton defender broke his arm for the second time in a month while sweeping up garden leaves?
11. Who succeeded Bryan Hamilton as manager of Norwich City in 2000?
12. Why was the start of the 1974 World Cup final delayed?
13. Which singer attempted to kick-start the 1994 World Cup with a penalty?
14. Which two players shared the 1969 Footballer of the Year award?
15. With which three clubs did John Barnes appear in an FA Cup final?
16. Which Stockport defender is famed for his long throw?

Answers to page 38

MANAGERS 1: **1.** Sam Allardyce **2.** Bill Nicholson **3.** Holger Osieck **4.** Neil Warnock **5.** 1997 **6.** Joe Fagan **7.** Neil Warnock **8.** 11 **9.** Partick Thistle **10.** Liam Brady **11.** Martin O'Neill **12.** Ronnie Moore **13.** Lou Macari **14.** Chris Kamara **15.** Forfar Athletic **16.** Kevin Keegan

Ipswich Town 1

Answers on page 39

1. Which Ipswich defender won 53 caps with Northern Ireland in the 1970s?
2. Which Laurie kept goal when Ipswich slammed Southampton 7–0 in 1974?
3. Who moved from Tottenham to Ipswich for £1 million in June 1994?
4. Which Bulgarian forward played for Ipswich in the 1990s?
5. Who did Ipswich beat 10–0 in a 1962–3 European Cup preliminary round tie?
6. Who was Ipswich's leading scorer in 1978–9?
7. From which club did Ipswich sign Matt Holland?
8. Who were Ipswich's midfield Dutch duo in the late 1970s?
9. From which League club did Ipswich sign Paul Mariner?
10. In which year did Bobby Robson become Ipswich boss?
11. Who played 591 League games for Ipswich between 1966 and 1982?
12. To whom did Ipswich finish First Division runners-up in 1981?
13. With which League club did Mark Venus begin his career?
14. Who was Ipswich's top scorer in 2000–1?
15. Who did Ipswich beat in the semi-finals of the FA Cup in 1978?
16. Which Romeo was born in Surinam and arrived at Portman Road from West Bromwich?

Answers to page 39

PREMIERSHIP 1: **1.** Aston Villa **2.** Craig Burley **3.** Steve Gibson **4.** Steve McClaren **5.** Ade Akinbiyi **6.** Eric Cantona **7.** David Batty **8.** Francis Lee **9.** Bobby Gould **10.** Chris Armstrong **11.** Jürgen Klinsmann **12.** Leicester City **13.** Peter Beardsley **14.** Aston Villa ('Deadly' Doug Ellis) **15.** 1998 **16.** Julian Dicks

Managers 1

Answers on page 36

1. Who steered Bolton back into the Premiership in 2001?

2. Spurs 10 Everton 4 marked which White Hart Lane manager's first game in charge?

3. Which German was appointed coach of Canada in 1998?

4. Who took Scarborough into the Football League in 1987?

5. In which year did Brian Laws take over as manager of Scunthorpe United?

6. Who was named Manager of the Year for 1984?

7. Which League manager is also a qualified chiropodist?

8. How many managerial changes have Arsenal had since the war?

9. Bertie Auld, Peter Cormack and Benny Rooney have all managed which Scottish club?

10. Which former Arsenal star succeeded Barry Lloyd as Brighton boss in 1993?

11. Who was manager of Wycombe Wanderers when they won promotion to the Football League?

12. Which manager won promotion with Rotherham United in both 2000 and 2001?

13. Which manager was unable to prevent Huddersfield Town slipping into Division Two in 2001?

14. Who preceded Paul Jewell as manager of Bradford City?

15. Archie Knox, Doug Houston and Paul Hegarty were all managers of which Scottish club?

16. Who took over as Manchester City boss in summer 2001?

Answers to page 36

ODDBALLS 1: **1.** Max Griggs (Dr Martens) **2.** Celtic **3.** Sean Bean **4.** Belfast **5.** River Plate **6.** World Youth Cup **7.** South East Counties League **8.** St Patrick's Athletic **9.** USA **10.** Francis Benali **11.** Nigel Worthington **12.** There were no corner flags on the pitch **13.** Diana Ross **14.** Tony Book and Dave Mackay **15.** Watford, Liverpool and Newcastle **16.** Dave Challinor

Premiership 1

Answers on page 37

1. Who signed Hassan Kachloul from Midlands neighbours Coventry City in the summer of 2001?
2. Which nephew of George Burley played in the Premiership?
3. Who is chairman of Middlesbrough?
4. And who did he appoint as his new manager in summer 2001?
5. Which Crystal Palace striker was sent out on loan to Hereford early in his career?
6. Which Frenchman was named Footballer of the Year in 1996?
7. Who returned to Leeds for £4.4 million from Newcastle in 1998?
8. Which former player became chairman of Manchester City in 1994?
9. Which Coventry manager resigned 20 minutes after a 5–1 defeat at Queens Park Rangers in October 1993?
10. Which Crystal Palace striker failed a drugs test in 1995?
11. Who was Tottenham's top scorer in 1994–5?
12. Who went to Old Trafford and came away with a 2–2 draw on the opening day of Manchester United's treble season of 1998–9?
13. Who was Newcastle United's top scorer for 1994–5?
14. Which Premiership club has a Deadly chairman?
15. In which year did Gerard Houllier become sole manager of Liverpool?
16. Which hard man did West Ham sell to Liverpool for £1.5 million in September 1993?

Answers to page 37

IPSWICH TOWN 1: **1.** Allan Hunter **2.** Sivell **3.** Steve Sedgley **4.** Bontcho Guentchev **5.** Floriana **6.** Paul Mariner **7.** Bournemouth **8.** Arnold Muhren and Frans Thijssen **9.** Plymouth Argyle **10.** 1969 **11.** Mick Mills **12.** Aston Villa **13.** Hartlepool United **14.** Marcus Stewart **15.** West Bromwich Albion **16.** Romeo Zondervan

England 1

Answers on page 42

1. When did England first lose to continental opposition?
2. And who beat them?
3. After three draws, a 1–0 defeat against which country put England out of the 1958 World Cup finals?
4. In which year was England's match with the Republic of Ireland in Dublin abandoned because of crowd trouble?
5. Which mercurial midfielder won the first of his 57 caps against Denmark in 1989?
6. How many goals did Kevin Keegan score for England?
7. Who refused to play for England B against Chile in 1998?
8. In which year was the Home International Championship last played?
9. Who were England's final opponents in that tournament?
10. Which West Ham player won the first of his 47 caps in 1974?
11. Who was the first player to represent England at all five levels – schoolboy, youth, amateur, Under-23 and full international?
12. Which England star of the 1970s won his first three caps against Wales?
13. Who scored a hat-trick for England in a European Championship qualifier with Poland in 1999?
14. In which city did England lose 2–0 to Poland in a 1973 World Cup qualifier?
15. Which Blackburn and Everton defender won his first England cap in 1966 against Scotland?
16. Who did England thrash 9–0 at Wembley in 1982?

Answers to page 42

LIVERPOOL 1: **1.** Dean Saunders and Mark Wright **2.** Everton **3.** 1900–1 **4.** Avi Cohen **5.** Torben Piechnik **6.** Leicester City **7.** Billy Liddell **8.** Dave Hickson **9.** Chris Lawler **10.** Stan Collymore **11.** Crystal Palace **12.** Ian St John **13.** Gary Gillespie **14.** 1975 **15.** Everton and Nottingham Forest **16.** Terry McDermott

Goalkeepers 1

Answers on page 43

1. Which Aston Villa goalkeeper won his only England cap as a substitute against Austria in 1983?
2. Which keeper scored a penalty for Australia in a 13–0 win over the Solomon Islands in 1997?
3. Who replaced the sick Gordon Banks in goal for England's World Cup quarter-final with West Germany in 1970?
4. Who kept goal for Bolton Wanderers in the 1958 FA Cup final?
5. What nationality is Oliver Kahn?
6. Which Russian goalkeeper used to wear all black?
7. Which veteran was Nottingham Forest's first-choice keeper in 2000–1?
8. Which Finnish goalkeeper was a regular in Preston North End's promotion-winning side of 1999–2000?
9. What nationality is Thomas Sorensen?
10. From which club did Wolves sign Mike Stowell?
11. Which goalkeeper made his England debut while playing for Norwich City in 1985?
12. From which club did Everton sign Neville Southall?
13. Which keeper moved from Queens Park Rangers to Arsenal for £1.3 million in May 1990?
14. Who was ever present in goal for Fulham in 1998–9?
15. Which goalkeeper scored with a long clearance for Bristol City against Hull City in 1973?
16. Who was Chelsea's Russian keeper of the mid-1990s?

Answers to page 43

THE WORLD GAME 2: **1.** Mario Zagallo **2.** Zambia **3.** Valencia **4.** Nigeria **5.** 1991 **6.** Azerbaijan **7.** Australia **8.** Portuguese **9.** Georgia **10.** Partizan Belgrade **11.** Parma **12.** Costa Rica **13.** FC Cologne **14.** Argentina, Colombia and Spain **15.** Uruguay **16.** Frank Rijkaard

Liverpool 1

Answers on page 40

1. Which two Derby County players moved to Anfield in the summer of 1991?
2. For which Merseyside club did Michael Owen's father play?
3. In which season did Liverpool win their first League Championship?
4. Which Israeli did Liverpool sign in 1979?
5. Which Dane came to Anfield in 1992?
6. Who did Liverpool beat in the semi-finals of the 1974 FA Cup?
7. Who joined Liverpool in 1938 from Lochgelly Violet and went on to win 28 Scottish caps?
8. Which burly centre-forward made the short journey across Stanley Park to Anfield for £10,500 in 1959?
9. Which long-serving full-back who made his Liverpool debut in 1962 scored 11 European goals?
10. For whom did Liverpool pay Nottingham Forest £8.5 million in 1995?
11. Who beat Liverpool in the 1990 FA Cup semi-finals?
12. Who scored Liverpool's extra-time winner in the 1965 FA Cup final?
13. Which defender joined Liverpool from Coventry City for £325,000 in 1983?
14. In which year did David Fairclough make his League debut for Liverpool?
15. Who were the only two teams to beat Liverpool in the League in 1987–8?
16. Who was named Footballer of the Year in 1980?

Answers to page 40

ENGLAND 1: **1.** 1929 **2.** Spain **3.** USSR **4.** 1995 **5.** Paul Gascoigne **6.** 21 **7.** Chris Sutton **8.** 1984 **9.** Scotland **10.** Trevor Brooking **11.** Terry Venables **12.** Kevin Keegan **13.** Paul Scholes **14.** Katowice **15.** Keith Newton **16.** Luxembourg

The World Game 2

Answers on page 41

1. Who was Brazil's coach at the 1998 World Cup finals?
2. Which African nation won the Cosafa Castle Cup in 1998?
3. Which Spanish club sold Francisco Farinos to Inter Milan in 2000?
4. Thijs Libregts became coach of which national team in 1998?
5. In which year was Japan's J-League founded?
6. Which country's first international resulted in a 5–0 defeat against Malta?
7. Who hammered the Cook Islands 16–0 in the Oceania Nations Cup in 1998?
8. What nationality is Nuno Gomes?
9. For which country has Georgi Kinkladze played international football?
10. Who won the Yugoslav League in 1999?
11. Which club won the Italian Cup in 1999?
12. Colombian Francisco Maturana was appointed coach of which national team in 1998?
13. Which German team were runners-up in the 1986 UEFA Cup?
14. Which three countries did Alfredo di Stefano represent at international level?
15. Rentistas, Huracan Buceo and Bella Vista are all clubs in which country?
16. Who took over as Holland national coach in the autumn of 1998?

Answers to page 41

GOALKEEPERS 1: **1.** Nigel Spink **2.** Mark Bosnich **3.** Peter Bonetti **4.** Eddie Hopkinson **5.** German **6.** Lev Yashin **7.** Dave Beasant **8.** Teuvo Moilanen **9.** Danish **10.** Everton **11.** Chris Woods **12.** Bury **13.** David Seaman **14.** Maik Taylor **15.** Ray Cashley **16.** Dmitri Kharine

General Knowledge 1

Answers on page 46

1. What is the chemical symbol for copper?
2. Who became King of England in 1327?
3. Which movie actor starred in *From Here to Eternity, Elmer Gantry* and *Birdman of Alcatraz*?
4. Which is the third highest mountain in the world?
5. Which country's football team won the 1978 World Cup?
6. Who was the last Prime Minister of Northern Ireland before the Stormont Parliament was suspended in 1972?
7. In which song did 10cc say they'd 'had an eyeful of the tower in France'?
8. What is the state capital of Pennsylvania?
9. Which enduring character was created by Bob Clampett for the 1938 cartoon *Porky's Hare Hunt*?
10. What nationality was the artist Goya?
11. What is a kinkajou?
12. What job links Julian Clary, Carol Smillie and Chris Evans?
13. Which is the largest county in Ireland?
14. Which of these is not one of The Corrs – Andrea, Colleen, Sharon?
15. Who played the 'Man With No Name' in the 1964 film *A Fistful of Dollars*?
16. What are the only two poisonous lizards in the world?

Answers to page 46

GENERAL KNOWLEDGE 3: **1.** The Housemartins **2.** 'Fatty' Arbuckle **3.** North Yorkshire **4.** Harold Pinter **5.** The Danube **6.** Hercules **7.** The hummingbird **8.** Beethoven **9.** Piles **10.** Ernestine **11.** Estonia **12.** The Massacre of St. Bartholomew **13.** Southampton **14.** Hugh Laurie **15.** Aldersgate **16.** Photocopier

General Knowledge 2

Answers on page 47

1. Which English monarch lost the Crown Jewels in The Wash?
2. Which sport has a lane 60 ft long from the foul line to the centre of the head pin?
3. In which village does *Postman Pat* live?
4. What was the name of the eagle that famously escaped from London Zoo in 1965?
5. Who preceded John Paul II as Pope?
6. Which bird has the largest wingspan?
7. What date is St George's Day?
8. The Lempira is the national currency of which country?
9. Which composer wrote 'The Damnation Of Faust'?
10. Who won the County Cricket Championship in 2001?
11. Cranesbill is the wild form of which garden flower?
12. Which Hollywood director made a cameo appearance as the clerk who received Dan Aykroyd and John Belushi's money at the end of *The Blues Brothers*?
13. In which year did Sir Alec Douglas-Home become British Prime Minister?
14. What is the process by which green plants trap light energy and use it to form carbohydrates?
15. Which band backed singer Jimmy James?
16. In which English city did Roger Bannister become the first athlete to run a mile in under four minutes?

Answers to page 47

GENERAL KNOWLEDGE 4: **1.** Switzerland **2.** Aluminium of Canada **3.** Jerry Lewis **4.** Mud **5.** 17th **6.** Copper beech **7.** Brazil **8.** Carte blanche **9.** Papillon **10.** John Nash **11.** Louis XIX **12.** Ben Hogan **13.** 9 **14.** Joseph Priestley **15.** Arthur Ransome **16.** The Napoleonic Wars

General Knowledge 3

Answers on page 44

1. Which band's 1986 album was titled 'London 0 Hull 4'?
2. Which plumber's mate was discovered by Hollywood after being called out to unblock producer Mack Sennett's pipes?
3. Which is the largest English county?
4. Who wrote *The Birthday Party*?
5. Which river flows through Vienna, Bratislava and Belgrade?
6. What was the name of *Steptoe and Son*'s horse?
7. What is the only bird that can fly backwards?
8. Whose last words were: 'I shall hear in heaven!'
9. What did Kenneth Williams, William Wordsworth and Napoleon all suffer from?
10. What was Jane Russell's real first name?
11. Tallinn is the capital of which country?
12. Which massacre took place on 24 August 1572?
13. Which Premiership club moved to a new ground at the start of the 2001–2 season?
14. Which comedian rowed for the defeated Cambridge crew in the 1980 University Boat Race?
15. Which London Underground station had its name changed to Barbican in 1968?
16. What item of office equipment did American George C. Beidler invent in 1903?

Answers to page 44

GENERAL KNOWLEDGE 1: **1.** Cu **2.** Tenpin Bowling **3.** Burt Lancaster **4.** Kangchenjunga **5.** Argentina **6.** Brian Faulkner **7.** 'Life Is A Minestrone' **8.** Harrisburg **9.** Bugs Bunny **10.** Spanish **11.** An animal **12.** They all once worked as singing telegrams **13.** Cork **14.** Colleen **15.** Clint Eastwood **16.** Gila monster and the beaded lizard

General Knowledge 4

Answers on page 45

1. Otto Stich was President of which country in 1988 and 1994?

2. What is foil brand name Alcan an abbreviation of?

3. Which actor played seven different characters in the 1965 film *The Family Jewels*?

4. Which group had a number one hit with 'Tiger Feet'?

5. In which century was Sir Isaac Newton born?

6. Which tree has the Latin name *Fagus purpurea*?

7. In which country is the Itatinga waterfall?

8. Which phrase is taken from the French meaning 'blank sheet of paper'?

9. Which horse won the Grand National in 2000?

10. Which architect designed Brighton Pavilion?

11. Who was King of France from breakfast until tea-time on 2 August 1830?

12. Which legendary American golfer was played by Glenn Ford in the 1951 movie *Follow the Sun*?

13. Which of these is not a prime number – 5, 7, 9, 11?

14. Which English chemist discovered oxygen?

15. Who wrote *Swallows and Amazons*?

16. Which wars featured the Battle of Quatre Bras?

Answers to page 45

GENERAL KNOWLEDGE 2: **1.** King John **2.** *The Two Gentlemen of Verona* **3.** Greendale **4.** Goldie **5.** John Paul I **6.** The wandering albatross **7.** 23 April **8.** Honduras **9.** Berlioz **10.** Yorkshire **11.** Geranium **12.** Steven Spielberg **13.** 1963 **14.** Photosynthesis **15.** The Vagabonds **16.** Oxford

General Knowledge 5

Answers on page 50

1. Which Alastair is a member of the Channel 4 horse racing team?
2. The larva of which insect is known as a leatherjacket?
3. Tyre is a port in which country?
4. Who directed the 1978 film *Invasion of the Body Snatchers*?
5. In which month of the year does the Le Mans 24-Hour Race traditionally take place?
6. Which nation has Dzongkha as its official language?
7. Who was the Roman God of war?
8. Which football club used to be called Thames Ironworks?
9. In which country is Cluedo's Colonel Mustard known as Madame Curry?
10. The first sets of dentures were used in which century?
11. Which is the second-longest river in the world?
12. Who turned down the Oliver Reed role in the 1969 film *Women in Love* because of the nude wrestling scene with Alan Bates?
13. What species of animal is a vicuna?
14. Who became US President in 1928?
15. *Allium cepa* is the Latin name for which vegetable?
16. Who had Sixties hits with 'Zabadak' and 'The Legend Of Xanadu'?

Answers to page 50

GENERAL KNOWLEDGE 7: **1.** *Carry On Cowboy* **2.** Conway Twitty **3.** John Constable **4.** Corrugated iron **5.** 1961 **6.** Heard Island **7.** Melbourne **8.** 13th **9.** Pollux **10.** Idris the dragon **11.** Jonathan Aitken **12.** Gatwick **13.** Belgian **14.** Spencer Tracy **15.** Astronomer Royal **16.** Thomas

General Knowledge 6

Answers on page 51

1. What bird is also known as the 'butcher-bird'?
2. Which town is the administrative headquarters of Shropshire?
3. At which battle was James, Duke of Monmouth, defeated in 1685 as he tried to seize the English throne?
4. What was the Christian name of the newspaper cartoonist Lancaster?
5. Which Hollywood actor was born Roy Scherer Jnr?
6. What did Alfred Cruickshank claim to have seen in 1923?
7. What do Jim Bowen and Franz Schubert have in common?
8. Who became Chancellor of the Exchequer in 1990?
9. What nationality was naturalist Carolus Linnaeus?
10. HKJ is the international index mark for vehicles in which country?
11. Which girl's name means 'serpent'?
12. Who was President of France from 1981 to 1995?
13. Which Sixties pop star played Len Fairclough's son Stanley in *Coronation Street?*
14. In Argentine currency, how many australes are there in a peso?
15. Which country's national anthem is 'Inno di Mameli'?
16. What was 19 October 1987 otherwise known as in financial circles?

Answers to page 51

GENERAL KNOWLEDGE 8: **1.** Elton John **2.** West Bromwich Albion **3.** The Flagellants **4.** One sixteenth **5.** Michael Miles **6.** Johnny Rotten **7.** Burt Lancaster **8.** Dublin **9.** Flodden **10.** Two shillings **11.** 1947 **12.** Medea **13.** Norfolk **14.** Barbie **15.** Anne of Cleves **16.** Arnold Schönberg

General Knowledge 7

Answers on page 48

1. In which *Carry On* film did Richard O'Brien (of *Rocky Horror Show* fame) appear as an extra?
2. Which Fifties singer changed his name from Harold Jenkins?
3. Who painted *The Hay Wain*?
4. What material did Frenchman Pierre Carpentier invent in 1853?
5. In which year did Yuri Gagarin become the first man in space?
6. On which island is the volcanic mountain Big Ben?
7. In which city were the 1956 Olympic Games staged?
8. In which century did Marco Polo first travel to China?
9. In Greek mythology, who was the twin brother of Castor?
10. Who lived in *Ivor the Engine*'s boiler?
11. Who said of Margaret Thatcher: 'I wouldn't say she is open-minded on the Middle East, so much as empty-headed. She probably thinks Sinai is the plural of sinus'?
12. Where was the Grand National run between 1916 and 1918?
13. What nationality was the artist Magritte?
14. Who starred in *Bad Day at Black Rock* and *Guess Who's Coming to Dinner?*
15. Which title was John Flamsteed the first to hold, in 1675?
16. What was the Christian name of the furniture designer Chippendale?

Answers to page 48

GENERAL KNOWLEDGE 5: **1.** Alastair Down **2.** Crane-fly **3.** Lebanon **4.** Philip Kaufman **5.** June **6.** Bhutan **7.** Mars **8.** West Ham United **9.** Switzerland **10.** 16th **11.** Amazon **12.** Michael Caine **13.** Llama **14.** Herbert Hoover **15.** Onion **16.** Dave Dee, Dozy, Beaky, Mick and Tich

General Knowledge 8

Answers on page 49

1. Which singer released a 1974 album titled 'Caribou'?
2. Who won the 1968 FA Cup Final?
3. Which religious group whipped themselves into a frenzy in the Middle Ages?
4. What fraction of an ounce is equal to a dram?
5. Who originally presented the TV quiz *Take Your Pick*?
6. Who called Billy Idol 'the Perry Como of punk'?
7. Which Hollywood actor was born Stephen Burton?
8. Which capital city means 'black pool'?
9. At which battle of 1513 was King James IV of Scotland killed?
10. In pre-decimalisation currency, how much was a florin worth?
11. In which year did India achieve independence from Britain?
12. In Greek mythology, who was the sorceress daughter of the King of Colchis?
13. In which English county is Thetford?
14. Which female icon was created by Ruth Handler in 1959?
15. Who was known as 'The Flanders Mare'?
16. Which Austrian-born composer, who was superstitious about the number 13, died on Friday the 13th at 13 minutes to midnight?

Answers to page 49

GENERAL KNOWLEDGE 6: **1.** Shrike **2.** Shrewsbury **3.** Sedgemoor **4.** Osbert **5.** Rock Hudson **6.** Loch Ness Monster **7.** They were both schoolteachers **8.** Norman Lamont **9.** Swedish **10.** Jordan **11.** Linda **12.** François Mitterand **13.** Peter Noone (Herman's Hermits) **14.** 10,000 **15.** Italy **16.** Black Monday

General Knowledge 9

Answers on page 54

1. What is the state capital of Delaware?
2. What bird is the symbol of the United States?
3. Which sitcom starred Richard Beckinsale and Paula Wilcox as Geoffrey and Beryl?
4. What is an animal without a backbone called?
5. Which explorer has the middle name Twistleton-Wykeham?
6. Which style of architecture is distinguished by vertical lines of tall pillars, and by pointed arches?
7. How many gold medals did swimmer Mark Spitz win at the 1972 Olympics?
8. In which year did Sir Winston Churchill die?
9. Who was Poet Laureate from 1930 to 1968?
10. Who was the last King of Austria?
11. Which children's TV presenter released records as Bombalurina?
12. In which country does the Henley-on-Todd Regatta take place?
13. With which football team did Angus Deayton have trials?
14. What is rolled down Cooper's Hill in Gloucestershire?
15. Where are your metatarsals?
16. In which play did Mrs Malaprop first appear?

Answers to page 54

GENERAL KNOWLEDGE 11: **1.** Bruce Lee **2.** Sedgefield **3.** Black, red and gold **4.** Balaclava **5.** Claude **6.** Great Wall of China **7.** Gabon **8.** Vancouver **9.** Shoulder Pork and ham **10.** Henry Cooper **11.** Passenger pigeon **12.** Buckeye State **13.** Antarctica **14.** Cassandra **15.** Harold Macmillan **16.** Stravinsky

General Knowledge 10

Answers on page 55

1. What nationality is the film director Milos Forman?
2. In which county did the north-bound M1 end when it opened in 1959?
3. Which former member of The Shadows was electrocuted by his guitar?
4. Which country are the reigning Olympic rugby union champions?
5. Roughly how many islands make up the Hebrides – 100, 300, 500?
6. Which three countries make up Benelux?
7. Who did Jimmy Carter defeat in the 1976 US Presidential election?
8. What is the Chilean pine tree commonly known as?
9. What was the name of the British policewoman killed in the 1984 Libyan embassy protest?
10. Which TV sitcom originated from a stage play called *The Banana Box*?
11. Which poet and garden designer was married to Harold Nicolson?
12. In which year was the General Strike?
13. What is the world's oldest classic horse race?
14. What links Cliff Richard and Vivien Leigh?
15. What is a common spadefoot?
16. Which Irish novelist won the 1993 Booker Prize?

Answers to page 55

GENERAL KNOWLEDGE 12: **1.** Radio Caroline **2.** Michael Fagan **3.** Eucalyptus shoots **4.** Magna Carta **5.** Colonel Blood **6.** Minehead **7.** Spencer Davis Group **8.** Garrincha **9.** Cornflower **10.** Fauvism **11.** 1973 **12.** Anzac Day **13.** Eldred **14.** Mr Motivator **15.** Rochdale **16.** Alistair MacLean

General Knowledge 11

Answers on page 52

1. Which star died during filming of his movie, *Game of Death*, in 1973?
2. For which constituency is Tony Blair the MP?
3. Which three colours are in Germany's national flag?
4. During which battle did the ill-fated Charge of the Light Brigade take place?
5. What was Debussy's Christian name?
6. Which edifice was built on the orders of Shih Huang Ti?
7. Libreville is the capital of which African country?
8. In which city is the Lion's Gate Bridge?
9. What does Spam stand for?
10. Which boxer starred as prizefighter John Gully in the 1975 film *Royal Flash*?
11. Which bird, one of the commonest in the world in 1814, became extinct a century later?
12. What is the nickname of the American state of Ohio?
13. In which continent is Mt. Erebus?
14. Which yuppie banker did Rodney marry in *Only Fools And Horses*?
15. Who told electors in 1959: 'You've never had it so good'?
16. Who composed 'The Firebird'?

Answers to page 52

GENERAL KNOWLEDGE 9: **1.** Dover **2.** Eagle **3.** *The Lovers* **4.** An invertebrate **5.** Sir Ranulph Fiennes **6.** Gothic **7.** Seven **8.** 1965 **9.** John Masefield **10.** Karl I **11.** Timmy Mallett **12.** Australia **13.** Crystal Palace **14.** Cheese **15.** In your feet **16.** *The Rivals*

General Knowledge 12

Answers on page 53

1. Which was Britain's first pirate radio station?
2. Who broke into the Queen's bedroom in 1982?
3. What is the staple diet of the koala bear?
4. What was signed on 15 June 1215?
5. Which Irish adventurer attempted to steal the Crown Jewels from the Tower of London in 1671?
6. Which resort is located at the north-eastern edge of Exmoor?
7. Which group had a number one hit in 1966 with 'Keep On Running'?
8. Which Brazilian footballer was nicknamed 'Little Bird'?
9. Which plant has the Latin name *Centaurea cyanus*?
10. Which art movement originated in Paris in 1905 with the founding of the Salon d'Automne?
11. In which year did the UK join the European Union?
12. April 25 is which national holiday in Australia and New Zealand?
13. What is Gregory Peck's first name?
14. As whom was TV fitness expert Derrick Evans better known?
15. Which football club plays at Spotland?
16. Which novelist wrote *The Guns of Navarone*, *Ice Station Zebra* and *Where Eagles Dare*?

Answers to page 53

GENERAL KNOWLEDGE 10: **1.** Czech **2.** Northamptonshire **3.** John Rostill **4.** USA (they took gold in 1924 when rugby union was last an Olympic sport) **5.** 500 **6.** Belgium, the Netherlands and Luxembourg **7.** Gerald Ford **8.** Monkey puzzle **9.** Yvonne Fletcher **10.** *Rising Damp* **11.** Vita Sackville-West **12.** 1926 **13.** St Leger **14.** Both were born in India **15.** A European toad **16.** Roddy Doyle

General Knowledge 13

Answers on page 58

Answers on page 58

1. Which is the only ten-letter word that can be spelt just using the top row of letters of a keyboard?

2. In which state is Detroit?

3. Who was the first English King from the House of Lancaster?

4. The okapi is a member of which animal family?

5. Which were the five original Cinque Ports?

6. In which country could you buy a chocolate bar called Plopp?

7. The Isis is the upper stretch of which English river?

8. Which Spanish rider won the Tour de France five years in a row from 1991–5?

9. Which knight of the stage played his last-ever role, as a pub landlord in Paul McCartney's film *Give My Regards to Broad Street*?

10. As whom is Marvin Lee Aday better known?

11. Which football club held the FA Cup for eight years even though they won it only once?

12. What is a dugong?

13. Which Chinese dynasty began in AD 618 and ended in 907?

14. In which English county is Gotham?

15. How many points are scored by kicking the ball into the net in Gaelic football?

16. Who was the subject of the Neil Sedaka song 'Oh Carol'?

Answers to page 58

GENERAL KNOWLEDGE 15: **1.** Chile **2.** Stamford Bridge **3.** Ben Turpin **4.** Oscar Wilde **5.** Madrid **6.** Alexander Fleming **7.** Holland **8.** Leila Williams **9.** 'Some Might Say' **10.** Crippen **11.** Ecuador **12.** A turnip **16.** 1982

General Knowledge 14

Answers on page 59

1. In which English county is Biggin Hill airport?
2. What is the international vehicle index mark for Israel?
3. Who said: 'Hey, don't knock masturbation! It's sex with someone I love!'
4. Which law enforcers made their first appearance in London in 1960?
5. What was Bodie's first name in *The Professionals*?
6. Which letter do more capital cities start with than any other?
7. Approximately how many years ago did heated rollers first come into use for hair-styling?
8. Which Welsh town means 'Vale of the Crow'?
9. What colour are the flowers of the lily of the valley?
10. Of which political party was Benjamin Disraeli the leader?
11. What is 44 in Roman numerals?
12. What is the official language of Surinam?
13. Andy McCluskey and Paul Humphreys made up which Eighties band?
14. Who created the priestly detective Father Brown?
15. Who was Henry VIII's fifth wife?
16. How did the Roman Emperor Claudius die?

Answers to page 59

GENERAL KNOWLEDGE 16: **1.** Madonna **2.** Horse **3.** Western Australia **4.** An antelope **5.** Edgar Rice Burroughs **6.** The FA Cup Final **7.** Nancy Spungen **8.** Clark Gable **9.** Flying mower **10.** Burglar alarm **11.** Don Thompson (50 km Walk) **12.** *Amoco Cadiz* **13.** Dvorak **14.** Judy Garland **15.** Lithuania **16.** Queen Victoria

General Knowledge 15

Answers on page 56

1. In which country is the Atacama Desert?
2. What name links a London football ground with an 11th-century battle on English soil?
3. Which silent movie star was insured for $100,000 against the possibility of his eyes ever becoming normal again?
4. Who wrote *Lady Windermere's Fan*?
5. *ABC* and *Ya* are national newspapers published in which European city?
6. Who discovered penicillin?
7. In which country was gin first produced?
8. Who was the first female presenter of *Blue Peter*?
9. What was the title of Oasis's first UK number one single?
10. Which notorious killer had the first names Hawley Harvey?
11. Which country owns the Galapagos Islands?
12. What did a Bolton Wanderers fan throw in front of Wolves manager Graham Taylor in 1995 to incur a £60 fine?
13. In which English county is the Forest of Dean?
14. What did Ahmed Zewail win in 1999?
15. Which Scandinavian country is not a member of the European Union?
16. In which year was the Falklands conflict?

Answers to page 56

GENERAL KNOWLEDGE 13: **1.** Typewriter **2.** Michigan **3.** Henry IV **4.** Giraffe **5.** Sandwich, Dover, Hythe, Romney and Hastings **6.** Sweden **7.** Thames **8.** Miguel Indurain **9.** Sir Ralph Richardson **10.** Meat Loaf **11.** Portsmouth (who won the Cup in 1939, the competition not resuming until after the war) **12.** A marine mammal **13.** Tang **14.** Nottinghamshire **15.** Three **16.** Carole King

General Knowledge 16

Answers on page 57

1. Whose black bra fetched £4,600 at auction in 1997?
2. 2002 is the year of which animal in the Chinese calendar?
3. Which is the largest state in Australia?
4. What is a bushbuck?
5. Who wrote *Tarzan of the Apes*?
6. At which important event did Mr S.R. Bastard officiate in 1878?
7. What was the name of the girlfriend that The Sex Pistols' Sid Vicious was charged with murdering?
8. Which Hollywood star got his big break when, working as a telephone repair man, he went to mend the phone of drama coach Josephine Dillon who promptly took him under her wing?
9. What is 'Flymo' an abbreviation of?
10. Which safety device was invented by Edwin T. Holmes in 1858?
11. Who won Britain's only athletics gold medal at the 1960 Olympics?
12. Which tanker spilt over 200,000 tons of oil into the English Channel after drifting onto rocks off the coast of Brittany in 1978?
13. Who composed the 'New World Symphony'?
14. Which actress was born Frances Gumm?
15. Vilnius is the capital of which country?
16. Who was the last Hanoverian monarch to rule England?

Answers to page 57

GENERAL KNOWLEDGE 14: **1.** Kent **2.** IL **3.** Woody Allen in *Annie Hall* **4.** Traffic wardens **5.** William **6.** B **7.** 4000 (the ancient Egyptians used them) **8.** Cymbran **9.** White **10.** The Tories **11.** XLIV **12.** Dutch **13.** OMD **14.** G.K. Chesterton **15.** Catherine Howard **16.** He choked to death on a feather put down his throat by doctors to make him vomit

General Knowledge 17

Answers on page 62

1. After running out of ammunition at the Battle of Lepanto in 1571, with what did the Turks pelt Austrian soldiers?

2. Who were the first British group to top the US singles chart?

3. Which US presidential candidate went on *Rowan and Martin's Laugh-In* to say 'Sock it to me'?

4. Behind Greenland, what is the second largest island in the world?

5. Malaria is caused by which insect?

6. Tresco Airport is on which islands?

7. Which actor's films have included *Ricochet*, *Crimson Tide* and *Courage Under Fire*?

8. Who was the last British golfer to win the Open?

9. What does the surname of former German chancellor Helmut Kohl mean in English?

10. Whom did John Hinckley attempt to assassinate in 1981?

11. What type of commercials did ITV ban in 1965?

12. What metric unit of area is equal to 100 acres or 10,000 square metres?

13. Who wrote *Hedda Gabler*?

14. What is a teasel?

15. What links Prince Andrew and Leslie Ash?

16. Which TV crimebuster used to sign off with the words 'Keep 'em peeled'?

Answers to page 62

GENERAL KNOWLEDGE 19: **1.** Warren Beatty **2.** Safety razor **3.** Hoosiers **4.** Fremantle **5.** British Academy of Film and Television Arts **6.** Manama **7.** Bailey bridge **8.** The First Crusade **9.** Crustacean **10.** Javelin **11.** Barry **12.** 1989 **13.** H_2SO_4 **14.** Anthony Eden **15.** Group of 19th-century US writers from New York State **16.** English Civil War

General Knowledge 18

Answers on page 63

1. In which country is the Vestre Mardola waterfall?
2. The name of which European capital city means 'merchants' harbour'?
3. Of which co-star did Tony Curtis say: 'It's like kissing Hitler'?
4. Aaron Kosminski, James Maybrick and Dr Francis Tumblety were all suspected of what?
5. Which King of England died after eating a surfeit of lampreys at a banquet in France?
6. Who is the patron saint of laundry workers?
7. Which guitarist is known as 'Old Slow Hand'?
8. Who was the first foreign football manager to win the Premiership?
9. What was the name of the bear in *Rainbow*?
10. Whom did James Callaghan defeat in the 1976 Labour leadership contest?
11. Which show opened in London in 1970, promising 'an evening of elegant erotica'?
12. Which spy escaped from Wormwood Scrubs in 1966?
13. Which town is the administrative headquarters of Dyfed?
14. Which game was invented in 1875 by British army officers serving with the Devonshire Regiment in India?
15. Which resort was the setting for the first Butlin's holiday camp?
16. What is a sirocco?

Answers to page 63

GENERAL KNOWLEDGE 20: **1.** Bruce Willis **2.** Exeter City **3.** 1976 **4.** Kane **5.** Sir Walter Scott **6.** Bartholomew Diaz **7.** *Burke's Peerage* **8.** Hurricane **9.** Seven **10.** Kentucky **11.** Zebra **12.** Rowing **13.** *Doctor Who* **14.** Sri Lanka **15.** Purple **16.** St Lawrence River

General Knowledge 19

Answers on page 60

1. Which Hollywood star was once employed as a rat catcher by a theatre in Washington D.C.?
2. What was invented by King Camp Gillette in 1895?
3. What are inhabitants of Indiana known as?
4. Which Australian port is located at the mouth of the Swan River?
5. What does BAFTA stand for?
6. What is the capital of Bahrain?
7. To which World War Two device did Donald Coleman Bailey lend his name?
8. What did Peter the Hermit lead in 1095?
9. Crabs, lobsters and shrimps are all members of which class of creatures?
10. In which field event does Jan Zelezny specialise?
11. Which building worker from *Auf Wiedersehen, Pet* used to be a stalwart of the West Bromwich and District Table Tennis League?
12. In which year was the Berlin Wall dismantled?
13. What is the chemical formula for sulphuric acid?
14. Which British Prime Minister resigned following the Suez crisis?
15. Who were the Knickerbocker School?
16. In which war was the Battle of Marston Moor?

Answers to page 60

GENERAL KNOWLEDGE 17: **1.** Oranges and lemons **2.** The Tornados ('Telstar') **3.** Richard Nixon **4.** New Guinea **5.** Mosquito **6.** Scilly Isles **7.** Denzel Washington **8.** Paul Lawrie **9.** Cabbage **10.** Ronald Reagan **11.** Cigarette commercials **12.** Hectare **13.** Henrik Ibsen **14.** A prickly herb **15.** Both were born on 19 February 1960 **16.** Shaw Taylor (*Police 5*)

General Knowledge 20

Answers on page 61

1. Of whom did Cybill Shepherd say: 'His idea of a romantic kiss was to go "blaaah" and gag me with his tongue'?
2. Which Football League club are nicknamed 'The Grecians'?
3. In which year did Brotherhood of Man win the Eurovision Song Contest?
4. What is the surname of Handy Andy from *Changing Rooms*?
5. Who wrote *Ivanhoe*?
6. Who was the first European to sail around the Cape of Good Hope?
7. What is the *Genealogical and Heraldic History of the Peerage, Baronetage, and Knightage of the United Kingdom* more commonly known as?
8. What is a 'willy-willy' to Australians?
9. How many events are there in the heptathlon?
10. Which is America's Bluegrass State?
11. What breed of animal did the extinct quagga most resemble?
12. In which sport do participants compete for Doggett's Coat and Badge?
13. Which long-running British TV sci-fi series began in 1963 the day after President Kennedy's assassination?
14. Jaffna, Galle and Negombo are ports in which country?
15. What colour are the flowers of the saffron?
16. Which river does Canada's Victoria Jubilee Bridge cross?

Answers to page 61

GENERAL KNOWLEDGE 18: **1.** Norway **2.** Copenhagen **3.** Marilyn Monroe **4.** Being Jack the Ripper **5.** Henry I **6.** St Veronica **7.** Eric Clapton **8.** Arsène Wenger (1998) **9.** Bungle **10.** Michael Foot **11.** *Oh Calcutta!* **12.** George Blake **13.** Carmarthen **14.** Snooker **15.** Skegness **16.** A wind

EastEnders 1

Answers on page 66

1. Which outsize Albert Square stall-holder was famous for saying virtually nothing during his 13 years on the show?
2. Who owns the launderette?
3. Which one-hour special looked back to the Albert Square of 1942?
4. Who is Beppe di Marco's ex-wife?
5. Who was horrified to learn that his doctor flatmate was a homosexual?
6. Who was Joe Wicks's mum?
7. What was the name of the *Walford Gazette*'s ace female reporter?
8. Who played Mary Smith?
9. At what number Albert Square did the Carpenters live?
10. What was Andy O'Brien's job?
11. Who lost her fiancé in a road accident and then ran off with DI Terry Rich?
12. Who was Dirty Den's long-standing mistress?
13. Which character was played by Tommy Eytle?
14. Who married Michelle Fowler at the second attempt in 1986?
15. Who took £1,500 from the Square's Christmas Club funds to pay for his daughter's wedding?
16. What was the name of Frank Butcher's mother?

Answers to page 66

WILDLIFE 1: **1.** David Attenborough **2.** Phil Drabble **3.** Peter Scott **4.** *Zoo Time* **5.** David Grant **6.** Pekinese **7.** Conchita **8.** *Sexton Blake* **9.** Danny Daggert **10.** David Bellamy **11.** Terry Nutkins **12.** Johnny Morris **13.** *Nature Watch* **14.** *The Jetsons* **15.** *Skippy, the Bush Kangaroo* **16.** *Bellamy's Backyard Safari*

Dramas 1

Answers on page 67

1. Which pop star fell for Zoë Wanamaker in *Love Hurts*?
2. Who was the forceful female newspaper proprietor in *Lou Grant*?
3. What were Nigel Havers and Keith Barron in a 1992 ITV drama series?
4. Who is the singing secretary in *Ally McBeal*?
5. Who was the breakfast DJ on radio station KBHR in *Northern Exposure*?
6. Ash Pelham-Martyn was the British army officer hero of which series?
7. Which steamy academic saga starred Harriet Walter and Bill Nighy?
8. During which war was the first series of *The Regiment* set?
9. What was the Christian name of *Reilly – Ace of Spies*?
10. Who were the central family in *Rich Man, Poor Man*?
11. Which English king did Dermot Walsh play in a 1962 adventure series?
12. What was the name of the regiment in *Soldier, Soldier*?
13. Which actor died during the second series of *Auf Wiedersehen, Pet*?
14. Which Sixties escapist series started life as a spin-off from *Police Surgeon*?
15. E.G. Marshall and Robert Reed played father and son in which courtroom drama?
16. Which *Monty Python* star played head teacher Jim Nelson in *GBH*?

Answers to page 67

TV POT LUCK 1: **1.** Margi Clarke **2.** Ruby Wax **3.** Trish Williamson **4.** Matthew Parris **5.** Cyril Fletcher **6.** Mark Lamarr and Ulrika Jonsson **7.** Sarah Greene **8.** Rolf Harris **9.** John Thomson **10.** Joe Longthorne **11.** Percy Thrower **12.** *Monitor* **13.** Mystic Meg **14.** Good Morning Television **15.** James Mason **16.** *Did You See...?*

Wildlife 1

Answers on page 64

1. Who examined *The Life of Birds* in 1998?
2. Who presented *One Man and His Dog* for 18 years?
3. Who travelled to Oceania and the Galapagos Islands to present *Faraway Look*?
4. Harry Watt followed Desmond Morris as presenter of which series?
5. Who was the chief vet on *Animal Hospital*?
6. What breed of dog was Tricki-Woo in *All Creatures Great and Small*?
7. What was the name of the Latin cow with distinctive long eyelashes on *Pinky and Perky*?
8. Which detective owned a bloodhound called Pedro?
9. Whose dog was shot by Jack Sugden for worrying sheep in *Emmerdale*?
10. Who presented *Botanic Man*?
11. Who was the animal expert on *Pets Win Prizes*?
12. Who became a zoo-keeper to introduce *Animal Magic*?
13. Which ITV natural history series was presented by Julian Pettifer?
14. Which space-age family had a dog named Astro?
15. What was Sonny Hammond's very special pet?
16. In which series did David Bellamy shrink in size to explore back gardens?

Answers to page 64

EASTENDERS 1: **1.** Big Ron **2.** Mr Opidopoulous **3.** *Civvy Street* **4.** Sandra **5.** Mick McFarlane **6.** Lorraine **7.** Polly Becker **8.** Linda Davidson **9.** No. 3 **10.** Male nurse **11.** Debbie Wilkins **12.** Jan Hammond **13.** Jules Tavernier **14.** 'Lofty' Holloway **15.** Arthur Fowler **16.** Mo

TV Pot Luck 1

Answers on page 65

1. Which Liverpudlian actress presented *The Good Sex Guide*?
2. Which Chicago-born comedienne took part in *Hit and Run*?
3. Which Trish was an ITV weather forecaster?
4. Which former Tory MP became the presenter of *Weekend World* in 1986?
5. Who recited odd odes on *That's Life*?
6. Who were the first team captains on *Shooting Stars*?
7. Which former *Blue Peter* presenter introduced *Posh Frocks and New Trousers*?
8. Which Australian entertainer made his British TV debut on *Whirligig* in the early Fifties?
9. Which *Cold Feet* star narrated *Package Holiday 2001*?
10. Which singing impressionist was a regular on *Junior Showtime*?
11. Who presented *Gardening Club*?
12. Which BBC arts series was presented by Huw Wheldon?
13. Who was the resident soothsayer on *The National Lottery Live*?
14. What does GMTV stand for?
15. Which actor narrated the ITV series *Hollywood*?
16. What was the name of BBC2's TV review programme of the 1980s?

Answers to page 65

DRAMAS 1: **1.** Adam Faith **2.** Margaret Pynchon **3.** *The Good Guys* **4.** Elaine Vassal **5.** Chris-in-the-Morning **6.** *The Far Pavilions* **7.** *The Men's Room* **8.** Boer War **9.** Sidney **10.** The Jordaches **11.** *Richard the Lionheart* **12.** The King's Own Fusiliers **13.** Gary Holton **14.** *The Avengers* **15.** *The Defenders* **16.** Michael Palin

News 1

Answers on page 70

1. Which long-running current affairs programme was renamed *TV Eye* in 1978?

2. Which ITN newscaster presented *The Big Story*?

3. Which late-night BBC2 current affairs series began in 1980?

4. Which Corbet was a BBC newsreader?

5. Which former newsreader presided over *Treasure Hunt*?

6. Which BBC newsreader shared her surname with a Sixties' gardening guru?

7. Who quit his job as *Weekend World* frontman to become British Ambassador to the USA?

8. Which ex-BBC newsreader used to introduce *Last Night of the Proms*?

9. Who worked as a furniture store porter before joining the BBC news team in the 1950s?

10. Who is the current chairman of *Question Time*?

11. Who edited the *Daily Express* before becoming anchorman for *News at Ten*?

12. In which year did *Panorama* begin?

13. Who was the first resident interviewer on *Panorama*?

14. Which popular newsreader resigned from ITN in 1979?

15. Which programme replaced *Nationwide* in 1984?

16. Who was *Nationwide*'s regular Manchester reporter?

Answers to page 70

SCI FI 1: **1.** *Roswell* **2.** *UFO* **3.** Jeffrey Sinclair **4.** For smuggling a pregnant cat aboard his spaceship **5.** Venus **6.** Rupert Giles **7.** *Star Trek* **8.** Time And Relative Dimensions In Space **9.** Vancouver **10.** 2063 **11.** Deep Space Nine **12.** Scott Bakula **13.** John Mills **14.** Callisto **15.** Jon Pertwee **16.** Georgina Jones

Quiz & Game Shows 1

Answers on page 71

1. Who briefly replaced Paul Merton as team captain on *Have I Got News For You?*
2. Which tennis player took over from Anneka Rice on *Treasure Hunt?*
3. What was the number of the mystery box on *Take Your Pick?*
4. How many celebrities are on the panel of *Blankety Blank?*
5. Who provided the commentary for *Gladiators?*
6. Who hosted *Raise the Roof* and the revival of *Call My Bluff?*
7. Who was the resident singer on *Name That Tune?*
8. Which game show featured the Treasure Trail?
9. Robert Gladwell, Jimmy Hanley and Shaw Taylor all hosted which Fifties quiz show?
10. Which live Saturday night game show was presented by Chris Evans with musical accompaniment from Jools Holland?
11. Which quiz was the first programme to be shown on Channel 4?
12. With what subject does *Going For a Song* deal?
13. What was the name of the golfing game show presented by Jimmy Tarbuck?
14. Geoffrey Wheeler and David Dimbleby were the first questionmasters on which school quiz?
15. Which newlywed game show was hosted by Bob Monkhouse?
16. Which game show host thought everything was 'Super. Smashing. Great'?

Answers to page 71

LOCATIONS 1: **1.** *Fame* **2.** Henry Park **3.** Taransay **4.** Malibu Beach **5.** Castlefield Blues **6.** India **7.** 19 Riverbank **8.** *Vampire High* **9.** Dublin **10.** Boston **11.** *Dr Finlay's Casebook* **12.** *The Army Game* **13.** *Buffy the Vampire Slayer* **14.** *Sykes* **15.** *Sam* **16.** *The Rag Trade*

Sci Fi 1

Answers on page 68

1. Teenage space aliens Max, Michael, Isabel and Tess star in which Sky One sci fi series?
2. Which series marked Gerry and Sylvia Anderson's first attempt at human action?
3. Who was the first commander of *Babylon 5*?
4. Why was *Red Dwarf*'s Dave Lister sentenced to a period in suspended animation?
5. What was the name of Steve Zodiac's French girlfriend in *Fireball XL5*?
6. Who is the school librarian in *Buffy the Vampire Slayer*?
7. *The Cage* was the pilot episode for which classic sci fi series?
8. What does TARDIS stand for?
9. In which Canadian city was *The X Files* filmed?
10. In what year was International Rescue established?
11. Benjamin Sisko was the commander of which space station?
12. Who played Dr Sam Beckett in *Quantum Leap*?
13. Who played Professor Quatermass in the 1979 revival?
14. Who is the nemesis of *Xena: Warrior Princess*?
15. Which *Doctor Who* drove a yellow vintage car called Bessie?
16. Which young DJ rescued Adam Adamant from swinging London?

Answers to page 68

NEWS 1: **1.** *This Week* **2.** Dermot Murnaghan **3.** *Newsnight* **4.** Corbet Woodall **5.** Kenneth Kendall **6.** Debbie Thrower **7.** Peter Jay **8.** Richard Baker **9.** Michael Aspel **10.** David Dimbleby **11.** Sir Alastair Burnet **12.** 1953 **13.** Malcolm Muggeridge **14.** Reginald Bosanquet **15.** *Sixty Minutes* **16.** Stuart Hall

Locations 1

Answers on page 69

1. Which series took place at the New York High School for Performing Arts?
2. At which hospital was *Medics* set?
3. To which Scottish island were the contestants posted on *Castaway*?
4. What is the name of the beach where *Baywatch* was set?
5. What is the football team in *Playing the Field*?
6. In which country was *The Far Pavilions* set?
7. What was Victor Meldrew's address?
8. Mansbridge is the setting for which Sky One teen sci fi series?
9. In which city was *Ambassador* set?
10. In which American city does *Ally McBeal* work?
11. Arden House was home to which Sixties medical series?
12. Which military sitcom was set in Hut 29 of the Surplus Ordnance Depot at Nether Hopping?
13. Who saves souls in Sunnydale?
14. Who lived at 24 Sebastopol Terrace, Acton?
15. Which 1930s drama was set in the fictitious Yorkshire town of Skellerton?
16. Which Sixties sitcom was set at Fenner Fashions?

Answers to page 69

QUIZ AND GAME SHOWS 1: **1.** Eddie Izzard **2.** Annabel Croft **3.** 13 **4.** Six **5.** John Sachs **6.** Bob Holness **7.** Maggie Moone **8.** *Double Your Money* **9.** *Dotto* **10.** *Don't Forget Your Toothbrush* **11.** *Countdown* **12.** Antiques **13.** *Full Swing* **14.** *Television Top of the Form* **15.** *Bob's Your Uncle* **16.** Jim Bowen

Soaps 1

Answers on page 74

1. Which *EastEnders* character finally stood up to Pat Evans and told her he hated her giant ear-rings?
2. What job did Harry Clayton do in *Coronation Street*?
3. Who was Vic Lee's crooked brother in *Crossroads*?
4. What were the Christian names of the Alessi twins in *Neighbours*?
5. Who was Heather Haversham's first husband in *Brookside*?
6. And how did her second spouse, Nicholas Black, die?
7. Which British actress played Caress Morell in *Dynasty*?
8. Who was the 'Costa del Crime' villain in *Eldorado*?
9. Which ex-*Blue Peter* presenter turned up as a vet in *Emmerdale*?
10. Donald Fisher was the local headmaster in which soap?
11. Who was Ellis Cooper's boss in *The Newcomers*?
12. What business did Fiona Middleton run in *Coronation Street*?
13. Which *Dallas* character was played by Ken Kercheval?
14. In *Crossroads*, who had an affair with her stepbrother Anthony Mortimer?
15. Who was licensee of The Waterman's Arms in *Albion Market*?
16. What was the name of Dot Cotton's hopeless husband?

Answers to page 74

COMEDY 1: **1.** A mystery writer **2.** Atkins **3.** Leonard **4.** Agoraphobia **5.** Ken **6.** *Rab C Nesbitt* **7.** 12 **8.** Mike and Albie **9.** Bob Crane **10.** Charlie Drake **11.** Steve Coogan **12.** *The Cappuccino Years* **13.** *The Two Ronnies* **14.** Chris Langham **15.** Counsellor **16.** Brother Dominic

Which Year in TV? 1

Answers on page 75

In which year were the following programmes first shown in Britain?

1. *Hill Street Blues*

2. *M*A*S*H*

3. *Mork and Mindy*

4. *Compact*

5. *Absolutely Fabulous*

6. *Brush Strokes*

7. *A Question of Sport*

8. *Wish You Were Here…?*

9. *Red Dwarf*

10. *Blackadder*

11. *Birds of a Feather*

12. *Songs of Praise*

13. *The Prisoner*

14. *Prime Suspect*

15. *The Fugitive*

16. *Dee Time*

Answers to page 75

CHILDREN'S TV 1: **1.** *Sabrina the Teenage Witch* **2.** Danger Island **3.** Leslie Crowther **4.** Oxy-gum **5.** Roderick **6.** *Bizzy Lizzy* **7.** Rufus Ruffcut and Sawtooth **8.** Yellow **9.** Brian **10.** Niggling **11.** *Grange Hill* **12.** Anita Dobson **13.** Ivan Owen **14.** Hippopotamus **15.** *The Bumblies* **16.** Michael Bentine

Comedy 1

Answers on page 72

1. What was *Glynis* in the Sixties sitcom of that name?
2. What was Marmalade's surname in *Educating Marmalade*?
3. Which wealthy businessman proved a constant temptation to Ria in *Butterflies*?
4. What did Matthew suffer from in *Game On*?
5. Which *Men Behaving Badly* barman had no previous experience of pub work?
6. Which street philosopher had teenage sons named Gash and Burney?
7. How many episodes of *Fawlty Towers* were there?
8. What are Hope and Keen's Christian names?
9. Who played Col. Robert Hogan in *Hogan's Heroes*?
10. Which knockabout comedian, popular in the Fifties and Sixties, was born Charles Springall?
11. Which comedian made his standup debut in 1986 at a Law Society revue at Manchester Polytechnic?
12. Which Adrian Mole series aired in 2001?
13. Which series featured the adventures of Charley Farley and Piggy Malone?
14. Who plays the unseen Roy Mallard in *People Like Us*?
15. What is Kate's profession in *Kiss Me Kate*?
16. What was the name of Derek Nimmo's character in *Oh Brother!*?

Answers to page 72

SOAPS 1: **1.** Roy Evans **2.** Milkman **3.** Eddie **4.** Christina and Caroline **5.** Roger Huntington **6.** From a drugs overdose **7.** Kate O'Mara **8.** Marcus Tandy **9.** Tim Vincent **10.** *Home and Away* **11.** Arthur Huntley **12.** Hairdresser's **13.** Cliff Barnes **14.** Jill Harvey **15.** Ted Pilkington **16.** Charlie

Children's TV 1

Answers on page 73

1. Who owns a black cat called Salem?

2. What was the name of the adventure serial on *The Banana Splits*?

3. Which *Crackerjack* presenter was once an Ovaltiney?

4. What did *Marine Boy* chew so that he could stay underwater without oxygen?

5. What was the name of the rat in *Tales of the Riverbank*?

6. Which girl touched a wishing flower on her dress to make her dreams come true?

7. Who drove the Buzz Wagon in *Wacky Races*?

8. What colour is Fizz in *Tweenies*?

9. What was the name of *The Magic Roundabout*'s mollusc?

10. What was Nellie always doing in *Noah and Nellie*?

11. Mrs McCluskey was head teacher at which school?

12. Which landlady of the Queen Vic once presented *Play Away*?

13. Who created Basil Brush?

14. What kind of animal was *Rainbow*'s George?

15. Who were the pear-shaped creatures from the planet Bumble?

16. And which former Goon created them?

Answers to page 73

WHICH YEAR IN TV? 1: **1.** 1981 **2.** 1973 **3.** 1979 **4.** 1962 **5.** 1992 **6.** 1986 **7.** 1970 **8.** 1974 **9.** 1988 **10.** 1983 **11.** 1989 **12.** 1961 **13.** 1967 **14.** 1991 **15.** 1964 **16.** 1967

Cop Shows 1

Answers on page 78

1. Who was Neal Washington's alcoholic partner in *Hill Street Blues*?
2. What character does David Jason's brother, Arthur White, play in *A Touch of Frost*?
3. In *Cracker*, what was Fitz's nickname for DS Penhaligon?
4. Which Fifties detective worked for the Department of Queer Complaints?
5. DCI Russell was the grumpy boss of which female detective?
6. Who played Tony Clark in *Between the Lines*?
7. Which *Heartbeat* Constable devours hard-boiled eggs for lunch?
8. Pat Chappel is the senior officer in which series?
9. What was *Cannon*'s Christian name?
10. Which former *Brookside* actress plays a criminal profiler in *Waking the Dead*?
11. Which member of the Eagles made a cameo appearance in *Miami Vice*?
12. Who replaced Bobby Simone in *NYPD Blue*?
13. Who screeched around the streets of LA in a red Ford Torino?
14. Which medical examiner had a girlfriend named Lee Potter?
15. Who is the heroine of *Silent Witness*?
16. Which PC in *The Bill* was an unlikely murder suspect in 2001?

Answers to page 78

DRAMAS 2: **1.** *House of Cards* **2.** *Rumpole of the Bailey* **3.** *Moonlighting* **4.** *Medics* **5.** *The Knock* **6.** *The Jewel in the Crown* **7.** *The Human Jungle* **8.** *Howard's Way* **9.** *Crocodile Shoes* **10.** *thirtysomething* **11.** *Tutti Frutti* **12.** *A Very Peculiar Practice* **13.** *ER* **14.** *Ally McBeal* **15.** *All Creatures Great and Small* **16.** *The Hello Girls*

TV Pot Luck 2

Answers on page 79

1. Who played *The Whistle-Blower*?
2. Ortis, Trey Farley and Sarah Cawood appeared on which kids' series in 2001?
3. What was the California zip code of the Walsh family in a 1990s teen drama?
4. In which sitcom did Paul Whitehouse play a voiceover artist?
5. Who takes a peek into *Auntie's Bloomers*?
6. At whom was *The Big Breakfast* question aimed: 'Where are you Mark?'
7. Who won the first *Big Brother*?
8. Who presented *Holiday on a Shoestring*?
9. Which ITV station became Central Television in 1982?
10. Who does the building work on *Ground Force*?
11. Who reveals *TV Nightmares*?
12. Which improvisation game show was chaired by Clive Anderson?
13. Who hosted the TV version of *Trivial Pursuit*?
14. Which *New Faces* champion hosted the series when it was revived in 1986?
15. Who played Arnie Becker in *LA Law*?
16. Tris Payne lead the design team on which daytime makeover series?

Answers to page 79

EMMERDALE 1: **1.** Sam **2.** The Malt Shovel **3.** Scott Windsor **4.** Edward Peel **5.** Jackie Merrick **6.** Dee **7.** Tricia Stokes **8.** Elizabeth Feldmann **9.** Christopher Chittell **10.** Dolly Skilbeck **11.** Billy Hopwood **12.** Peggy **13.** Tate Haulage **14.** Jack Sugden **15.** Joe Sugden **16.** Her fiancé, Gavin Ferris

Dramas 2

Answers on page 76

Which series featured the following characters?

1. Francis Urquhart
2. Claude Erskine-Brown
3. Maddie Hayes
4. Ruth Parry
5. George Andreotti
6. Ronald Merrick
7. Dr Roger Corder
8. Ken Masters
9. Jed Shepperd
10. Michael Steadman
11. Danny McGlone
12. Dr Stephen Daker
13. Dr Luka Kovac
14. Richard Fish
15. Siegfried Farnon
16. Chris Cross

Answers to page 76

COP SHOWS 1: **1.** J.D. LaRue **2.** PC Ernie Trigg **3.** 'Panhandle' **4.** *Colonel March of Scotland Yard* **5.** Maggie Forbes (*The Gentle Touch*) **6.** Neil Pearson **7.** Alf Ventress **8.** *The Vice* **9.** Frank **10.** Sue Johnston **11.** Glenn Frey **12.** Danny Sorenson **13.** *Starsky and Hutch* **14.** *Quincy* **15.** Sam Ryan **16.** Reg Hollis

Emmerdale 1

Answers on page 77

1. What was the name of Matty and Dolly Skilbeck's son?
2. What is the other pub in the village besides the Woolpack?
3. Ben Freeman replaced Toby Cockerell as which character?
4. Who once played Tom Merrick before returning as Anthony Cairns?
5. Who spent five months in hospital after being knocked off his motorbike by Alan Turner's Land Rover?
6. What was the name of Eric Pollard's Filipino wife?
7. Who entered into a marriage of convenience with Jason Kirk's Australian boyfriend?
8. Who had a son called Michael and a daughter named Elsa?
9. Who plays Eric Pollard?
10. Whose maiden name was Acaster?
11. Who carried out the Post Office robbery in which Vic Windsor died?
12. What was the name of Matt Skilbeck's first wife?
13. Pete Collins and Frankie Smith were drivers for which firm?
14. Who had an affair with auctioneer Karen Moore while his wife was pregnant?
15. Who was once married to Milk Marketing Board inspector Christine Sharp?
16. Who did Bernice Blackstock find in a clinch with Jason Kirk?

Answers to page 77

TV POT LUCK 2: **1.** Amanda Burton **2.** *Live and Kicking* **3.** *Beverly Hills 90210* **4.** *Happiness* **5.** Terry Wogan **6.** Mark Lamarr **7.** Craig Phillips **8.** Kate Humble **9.** ATV **10.** Tommy Walsh **11.** Steve Penk **12.** *Whose Line Is It Anyway?* **13.** Rory McGrath **14.** Marti Caine **15.** Corbin Bernsen **16.** *Real Rooms*

Comedy 2

Answers on page 82

1. Drs Toby and Tom Latimer were father and son in which Eighties sitcom?
2. Which quiet, unsung superhero did Michael Palin play in the first series of *Monty Python's Flying Circus*?
3. Who played Dr Samuel Johnson in *Blackadder the Third*?
4. Which *Spitting Image* puppet was given a Hitler moustache?
5. What did Harry Enfield's Loadsamoney do for a living?
6. Who was the self-obsessed female newsreader on *Drop the Dead Donkey*?
7. Who was sold to Moroccan slave traders in *Absolutely Fabulous*?
8. Where were the first two series of the Spanish sitcom *Duty Free* filmed?
9. Who was the cheeky, house painter hero of *Brush Strokes*?
10. Which Seventies sitcom featured the Abbott family?
11. Who played George in *Seinfeld*?
12. What was Ken Wilberforce's finest invention?
13. Whose *Comedy Machine* won the 1972 Golden Rose of Montreux?
14. Who wrote and starred in the silent movie *The Plank*?
15. Who was the ineffectual headmaster in *Please, Sir!*?
16. What was 'Martin O'Hara' in a Sixties US sitcom?

Answers to page 82

SOAPS 2: **1.** Franky Doyle **2.** Frank and Ida **3.** Wes Parmalee **4.** *The Grove Family* **5.** *Brookside* **6.** Beth Willis **7.** Dan Sullivan **8.** Harchester United **9.** *General Hospital* **10.** The Simpsons **11.** Bill Treacher **12.** Paul Shane **13.** Jambo Bolton **14.** Phil Redmond **15.** Sid Fairgate **16.** Luke

Catchphrases 1

Answers on page 83

1. Which *Fast Show* character's excuse for his behaviour was always: 'I was very, very drunk'?
2. Which game show host tormented contestants by saying: 'Look what you would have won'?
3. Which TV cop called everyone 'Pussycat'?
4. Which Harry Enfield character announced his arrival with a cry of: 'Only me!'?
5. Which housekeeper insisted: 'You will, you will, you will, you will…'?
6. Who in *Drop the Dead Donkey* protested: 'I'm not here'?
7. Which *Fast Show* crook would say: 'I'm a geezer, a little bit whoor, a little bit waay'?
8. Who demanded: 'Look at my wad'?
9. Who called everyone 'Sweetie, darling'?
10. Which game show host offered the consolation: 'It's good, but it's not right'?
11. Who called her boyfriend 'Geoffrey Bubbles Bon Bon'?
12. Who used to say: 'Hullo, Auntie Jean'?
13. Who was 'Smarter than the average bear'?
14. Which *Blue Peter* presenter unwittingly coined the catchphrase: 'Get down, Shep'?
15. Who used to shout to her screen brother: 'Eric!'?
16. Which cat said: 'I hate these meeces to pieces'?

Answers to page 83

TV MUSIC 1: **1.** Michaela Strachan **2.** Neil Fox (formerly Dr Fox) **3.** 'Where I Find My Heaven' **4.** The Gigolo Aunts **5.** Sean Hughes and Phill Jupitus **6.** Mike Read **7.** Dave Clark **8.** ITV **9.** Jimmy Savile, Alan Freeman, Pete Murray and David Jacobs **10.** *Thank Your Lucky Stars* **11.** Sir Elton John **12.** Jools Holland **13.** Leslie Ash **14.** *The Old Grey Whistle Test* **15.** *Thank Your Lucky Stars* **16.** Pete Murray and Susan Stranks

Soaps 2

Answers on page 80

1. Who escaped from jail at the end of the first series of *Prisoner: Cell Block H*, only to be shot dead by a police officer?
2. What were the names of Ken Barlow's parents?
3. Who was the Jock Ewing impersonator in *Dallas*?
4. Which was the BBC's first adult soap?
5. Which soap used to have a character called Alan Partridge?
6. Who did Natalie Imbruglia play in *Neighbours*?
7. Who kidnapped Mel Owen in *EastEnders*?
8. What is the name of the football club in the Sky soap *Dream Team*?
9. Which afternoon medical soap premiered in 1972?
10. Which troubled family moved on to Brookside Close in 1996?
11. Which actor played Sidney the milkman in *Mrs Dale's Diary* before joining *EastEnders*?
12. Whose 45-second appearance in a 1979 episode of *Coronation Street* led to a starring role in *Hi-De-Hi*?
13. Who did Will Mellor play in *Hollyoaks*?
14. Who created *Hollyoaks* and *Brookside*?
15. Which *Knots Landing* car dealer was killed when his vehicle went over a cliff?
16. What was the name of Bernard McAllister's son in *Emmerdale*?

Answers to page 80

COMEDY 2: **1.** *Don't Wait Up* **2.** Bicycle Repair Man **3.** Robbie Coltrane **4.** Princess Michael of Kent **5.** Plasterer **6.** Sally Smedley **7.** Saffron **8.** Leeds **9.** Jacko **10.** *Bless This House* **11.** Jason Alexander **12.** *Metal Mickey* **13.** Marty Feldman **14.** Eric Sykes **15.** Mr Cromwell **16.** *My Favorite Martian*

TV Music 1

Answers on page 81

1. Who was the 'her' in *The Hitman and Her*?
2. Which former 'medic' presented his *Chart Update* on Channel 5?
3. What was the theme song to *Game On*?
4. Who had a hit with it in 1995?
5. Who are the team captains on *Never Mind the Buzzcocks*?
6. Which former Radio 1 DJ devised and presented *Pop Quiz*?
7. Which Sixties pop star later bought the rights to *Ready, Steady, Go!*?
8. Which channel screened *Supersonic*?
9. Which four DJs took it in turns to present early editions of *Top of the Pops*?
10. 'Spin a Disc' was a segment in which Sixties pop show?
11. Who presented the final edition of *TFI Friday*?
12. Who chaired *Juke Box Jury* in its 1989 revival?
13. Which nurse in *Where the Heart Is* briefly fronted *The Tube*?
14. 'Stone Fox Chase' was the theme to which music show?
15. Which pop series gave the Beatles their first national exposure?
16. Which two people were on the first and last panels of the original *Juke Box Jury*?

Answers to page 81

CATCHPHRASES 1: **1.** Rowley Birkin, QC **2.** Jim Bowen (*Bullseye*) **3.** *Kojak* **4.** Mr Don't Wanna Do It Like That **5.** Mrs Doyle (*Father Ted*) **6.** Gus Hedges **7.** Cockney Chris **8.** Loadsamoney **9.** Edina Monsoon (*Absolutely Fabulous*) **10.** Roy Walker (*Catchphrase*) **11.** Beryl in *The Lovers* **12.** *Tingha and Tucker* **13.** Yogi Bear **14.** John Noakes **15.** Hattie Jacques **16.** Mr Jinks

Music Pot Luck 3

Answers on page 86

1. Who played guitar on Kate Bush's 'Wuthering Heights'?
2. Which Paul McCartney song was banned by the BBC in 1972 for being too sexual?
3. Who was the subject of Derek and The Dominos' 'Layla'?
4. Who was sacked from her job at New York fast-food restaurant Dunkin' Donuts for squirting jam at a customer?
5. In which country was Neneh Cherry born?
6. Who recorded 'The Trumpton Riots'?
7. Who left The Buzzcocks to form Magazine?
8. Who reached number three in the UK charts with 'Boxerbeat' in 1983?
9. Who was the vocalist with Stiff Little Fingers?
10. Which band consisted solely of Matt Johnson on its formation in 1979?
11. In which year did Robbie Williams leave Take That?
12. What was Squeeze's first UK top twenty hit?
13. Which Canadian band released 'Mmmm Mmmm Mmmm' in 1994?
14. Which Eighties band recorded a song about a *Doctor Who* actor?
15. Which fruit did The Stranglers sing about in 1977?
16. Which district of London featured in a Dave Dee, Dozy, Beaky, Mick and Tich song title of 1968?

Answers to page 86

NAME CHANGES 2: **1.** Rat Scabies **2.** Georgie Fame **3.** Stuart Goddard **4.** Billy Ocean **5.** Dr John **6.** Harold Jenkins **7.** Fish **8.** Del Shannon **9.** Captain Sensible **10.** Alice Cooper **11.** Adam Faith **12.** Doris Day **13.** Sandie Shaw **14.** Paul Jones **15.** DJ Jazzy Jeff **16.** Nena

Home Towns 2

Answers on page 87

1. From which town do XTC hail?
2. Paper Lace came from which English city?
3. Tanita Tikaram was an unlikely product of which Hampshire town?
4. Where did The Jam form?
5. Which city does Joe Cocker come from?
6. Wayne Fontana and The Mindbenders came out of which city?
7. In which town was Tom Jones born?
8. Which Scottish town did Big Country come from?
9. Which Florida town was home to Lynyrd Skynyrd?
10. R.E.M. and The B-52's both come from which town in Georgia?
11. Which pair were the most famous sons of Bushey, Hertfordshire?
12. Which Eighties duo, who had two number one albums, met at school in Bath?
13. Which city was home to The Teardrop Explodes?
14. The Housemartins were based in which northern city?
15. Who is Cheshunt Secondary Modern School's most famous ex-pupil?
16. Which two successful Seventies bands had a strong Hereford influence?

Answers to page 87

GIRL BANDS 1: **1.** The Weatherman **2.** Kerry Katona **3.** Three Little Women **4.** 'I Know Where It's At' **5.** BeBe Winans **6.** 'Stop' **7.** 1992 **8.** 'Right Now' **9.** Spice Girls **10.** 7 **11.** TLC **12.** 'I Quit' **13.** Precious **14.** 12th **15.** Wyclef Jean **16.** Honeyz

Name Changes 2

Answers on page 84

1. Which punk drummer started life as Chris Miller?
2. Who was born Clive Powell?
3. What is Adam Ant's real name?
4. Which soul singer was originally known as Leslie Charles?
5. To what did Malcolm Rebennack change his name?
6. Who decided that it would be a good idea to change his name to Conway Twitty?
7. What moniker did Derek Dick adopt?
8. Which American artist of the Sixties changed his name from Charles Westover?
9. Who is Ray Burns better known as?
10. Whose real name is Vince Furnier?
11. To what did Terry Nelhams change his name?
12. Which famous actress was born Doris von Kappelhoff?
13. Who started life as Sandra Goodrich?
14. Who decided that Paul Pond was unsuitable for a stage name?
15. Who is Jeffrey Townes better known as?
16. Which German singer changed her name from Gabriela Kerner?

Answers to page 84

MUSIC POT LUCK 3: **1.** Dave Gilmour **2.** 'Hi Hi Hi' **3.** Patti Boyd **4.** Madonna **5.** Sweden **6.** Half Man Half Biscuit **7.** Howard Devoto **8.** Joboxers **9.** Jake Burns **10.** The The **11.** 1995 **12.** 'Take Me I'm Yours' **13.** Crash Test Dummies **14.** Human League ('Tom Baker') **15.** 'Peaches' **16.** Soho ('Last Night In Soho')

Girl Bands 1

Answers on page 85

1. Who did B*Witched blame it on in 1999?
2. Which member of Atomic Kitten left to have Bryan McFadden from Westlife's baby?
3. What does 3LW stand for?
4. What was All Saints' first UK single?
5. Who featured on Eternal's number one single, 'I Wanna Be The Only One'?
6. Which was the first single released by the Spice Girls not to reach number one in the UK?
7. In which year was TLC's first single 'Ain't 2 Proud 2 Beg' released?
8. What was Atomic Kitten's debut UK chart single?
9. Who made history by having their first six releases top the UK chart?
10. What number did All Saints' single 'War Of Nerves' reach in the UK charts in December 1998?
11. Whose album was called 'Crazysexycool'?
12. What was the title of Hepburn's debut single?
13. Which girl band represented the United Kingdom in the 1999 Eurovision Song Contest?
14. And where did they finish?
15. Who featured on Destiny's Child's debut single 'No No No'?
16. 'Finally Found', 'Love Of A Lifetime' and 'End Of The Line' were top ten singles for which group?

Answers to page 85

HOME TOWNS 2: **1.** Swindon **2.** Nottingham **3.** Basingstoke **4.** Woking **5.** Sheffield **6.** Manchester **7.** Pontypridd **8.** Dunfermline **9.** Jacksonville **10.** Athens **11.** Wham! **12.** Tears For Fears **13.** Liverpool **14.** Hull **15.** Cliff Richard **16.** Mott The Hoople and The Pretenders

Seventies 1

Answers on page 90

1. Which *Opportunity Knocks* winners reached number one in the UK in 1974?
2. Russell Thompkins Jnr was the lead singer with which Philly band?
3. Which two girls had barely left school in Jamaica when they topped the UK charts in February 1978?
4. Which former journalist on the *Colchester Gazette* fronted a band that had their first hit with 'Judy Teen' in 1974?
5. Which Scottish band were exposed by the *News of the World* in 1972 for backstage shenanigans involving female fans?
6. Which American band released the 1970 album 'Cosmo's Factory'?
7. Which American crooner did Mud support on a 1973 tour?
8. Which group did Olivia Newton-John join in 1970?
9. The Eagles were originally hired as the backing band to which singer?
10. Which was Barry Manilow's first UK hit?
11. Dan McCafferty was lead singer with which Seventies band?
12. Which 10cc track was named Best Beat Song at the 1974 Ivor Novello Awards?
13. Which 1972 UK number one was inspired by babysitting his manager's daughter?
14. Which Ruby and The Romantics cover gave The Carpenters a US number two in February 1972?
15. Who was the frontman of Tubeway Army?
16. Which Dusty Springfield classic gave the Bay City Rollers their last UK top ten hit?

Answers to page 90

LYRICS 1: **1.** 'Careless Whisper' (George Michael) **2.** 'Angels' (Robbie Williams) **3.** 'Especially For You' (Kylie and Jason) **4.** 'I'm A Believer' (The Monkees) **5.** 'I Will Survive' (Gloria Gaynor) **6.** 'I Say A Little Prayer' (Dionne Warwick) **7.** 'Hot Stuff' (Donna Summer) **8.** 'Lyin' Eyes' (The Eagles) **9.** 'Losing My Religion' (R.E.M.) **10.** 'House Of Fun' (Madness) **11.** 'Heaven Is A Place On Earth' (Belinda Carlisle) **12.** 'Chain Reaction' (Diana Ross) **13.** 'A New England' (Kirsty MacColl) **14.** 'You Don't Have To Say You Love Me' (Dusty Springfield) **15.** 'China In Your Hand' (T'Pau) **16.** 'I'm Still Standing' (Elton John)

Jazz 1

Answers on page 91

1. In which year did Dizzy Gillespie die?
2. With which title track of a musical did Louis Armstrong reach number four in the UK chart in 1964?
3. Who was known as 'The First Lady of Song'?
4. What was Milt Jackson's nickname?
5. In which year did Dave Brubeck chart in the UK with 'Take Five'?
6. With which instrument is Sonny Rollins usually associated?
7. Who wrote 'Dream Of Life' for Billie Holliday before finally being recognised as an outstanding jazz singer herself?
8. Which Blossom is a noted jazz singer/pianist?
9. Who began playing the trumpet when he was eight after being inspired by seeing a Louis Armstrong concert in Stockholm?
10. Which trumpet great died in a Pennsylvania car crash in 1956?
11. With which song did Billy Eckstine and Sarah Vaughan achieve their only UK chart success as a duo?
12. Which song did Billy Eckstine take to number three as a soloist in 1954?
13. In which instrument did Marian McPartland specialise?
14. George Auld, Buddy Rich and Helen Forrest were all members of whose Big Band in 1939?
15. Which big band leader formed his own experimental Innovations Orchestra?
16. In 1968 at the age of 69, which jazz icon became the oldest artist ever to top the UK charts?

Answers to page 91

ALBUMS 1: **1.** Big Country **2.** Swing Out Sister **3.** Manic Street Preachers **4.** Led Zeppelin **5.** Queen **6.** The Moody Blues **7.** Rush **8.** Electric Light Orchestra **9.** Shania Twain **10.** Curiosity Killed The Cat **11.** Chris Rea **12.** Simon and Garfunkel **13.** Paul Young **14.** Elton John **15.** Paul Weller **16.** Simple Minds

Lyrics 1

Answers on page 88

From which songs are the following lyrics taken?

1. 'I'm never gonna dance again, guilty feet have got no rhythm'
2. 'And through it all she offers me protection, a lot of love and affection'
3. 'No more dreaming about tomorrow, forget the loneliness and the sorrow'
4. 'I thought love was only true in fairytales, meant for someone else but not for me'
5. 'At first I was afraid, I was petrified'
6. 'From the moment I wake up, before I put on my make-up'
7. 'Dialled about a thousand numbers lately, almost rang the phone off the wall'
8. 'City girls just seem to find out early how to open doors with just a smile'
9. 'Every whisper of every waking hour I'm choosing my confessions'
10. 'Welcome to the lion's den, temptation's on its way'
11. 'In this world we're just beginning to understand the miracle of living'
12. 'You took a mystery and made me want it, you got a pedestal and put me on it'
13. 'I loved you then and I love you still, I put you on a pedestal, you put me on the Pill'
14. 'You don't have to stay forever, I will understand'
15. 'It was a flight on the wings of a young girl's dreams'
16. 'Looking like a true survivor, feeling like a little kid'

Answers to page 88
SEVENTIES 1: **1.** Paper Lace ('Billy Don't Be A Hero') **2.** The Stylistics **3.** Althia and Donna **4.** Steve Harley (and Cockney Rebel) **5.** Marmalade **6.** Creedence Clearwater Revival **7.** Jack Jones **8.** Toomorrow **9.** Linda Ronstadt **10.** 'Mandy' **11.** Nazareth **12.** 'Rubber Bullets' **13.** 'Clair' by Gilbert O'Sullivan **14.** 'Hurting Each Other' **15.** Gary Numan **16.** 'I Only Wanna Be With You'

Albums 1

Answers on page 89

Who released the following albums?

1. 'The Crossing' (1983)
2. 'It's Better To Travel' (1987)
3. 'This Is My Truth Tell Me Yours' (1998)
4. 'Houses Of The Holy' (1973)
5. 'A Day At The Races' (1977)
6. 'Days Of Future Passed' (1968)
7. 'Moving Pictures' (1981)
8. 'Discovery' (1979)
9. 'Come On Over' (1998)
10. 'Keep Your Distance' (1987)
11. 'Auberge' (1991)
12. 'Bookends' (1968)
13. 'No Parlez' (1984)
14. 'Caribou' (1974)
15. 'Stanley Road' (1995)
16. 'Street Fighting Years' (1989)

Answers to page 89

JAZZ 1: **1.** 1993 **2.** 'Hello Dolly' **3.** Ella Fitzgerald **4.** 'Bags' **5.** 1961 **6.** Tenor saxophone **7.** Carmen McRae **8.** Blossom Dearie **9.** Rolf Ericson **10.** Clifford Brown **11.** 'Passing Strangers' **12.** 'No One But You' **13.** Piano **14.** Artie Shaw **15.** Stan Kenton **16.** Louis Armstrong

Indie 1

Answers on page 94

1. In which city were Oasis playing when Creation boss Alan McGee spotted their potential and signed them on the spot?
2. Which Pulp single was accompanied by a short film in which celebrities were quizzed on the loss of their virginity?
3. Which band's compilation album was called 'Like You Do'?
4. In which year were Radiohead formed?
5. Whose biggest-selling album was titled 'Expecting To Fly'?
6. Rick McMurray, Tim Wheeler, Mark Hamilton and Charlotte Hatherley make up which band?
7. Tim Booth was lead singer with which band?
8. Which band's first UK chart single was 'U 16 Girls'?
9. What was Blur's first number one single in the UK?
10. Who vanished into thin air on 1 February 1995?
11. Which band split up in August 1995, only to re-form two years later and enjoy a number one album?
12. Which bassist left The La's to form Cast?
13. Which was Catatonia's first UK number one album?
14. With which Birmingham goth band did Dodgy's Nigel Clarke and Mathew Priest play in the early Eighties?
15. As which lead singer is Simon Rowbottom better known?
16. Which band took their name from a character in the novel 'To Kill A Mockingbird'?

Answers to page 94

ELVIS 1: **1.** 'All Shook Up' **2.** *The Ed Sullivan Show* **3.** 'I Need Your Love Tonight' **4.** 'All Shook Up' **5.** 'Jailhouse Rock' **6.** They were his last live performances for nearly three years because of his army call-up **7.** *GI Blues* **8.** 'Surrender' **9.** Aaron Schroeder and Wally Gold **10.** Joe Esposito **11.** 'Are You Lonesome Tonight?' **12.** The International **13.** The Jordanaires **14.** *Playboy* magazine's **15.** Bruce Springsteen **16.** 'Way Down'

Music Pot Luck 4

Answers on page 95

1. In the Seventies, which half of a famous duo saw his first two UK solo hits both go to number one, albeit at four year intervals?
2. Which B-side of Jasper Carrott's 'Funky Moped' was banned by the BBC for sexual innuendo?
3. Who played synthesiser on David Bowie's 'Space Oddity'?
4. Who had a 1954 hit with 'Gilly Gilly Ossenfeffer Katzenellen Bogen By The Sea'?
5. Which Pink Floyd track was dedicated to their erstwhile member, the reclusive Syd Barrett?
6. Which two TV shows were the subject of hits for The Firm in the Eighties?
7. Which was the best-selling UK single of 1981?
8. Which 1998 hit for All Saints was the 800th UK number one single?
9. Justin Currie and Iain Harvie formed which Scottish band in 1983?
10. Who was The Searchers' original drummer?
11. Which group were originally going to be called Daddy before deciding to take their name from the title of a 1910 book by W.H. Davies?
12. What is Roachford's Christian name?
13. What was Simple Minds' first UK number one single?
14. Who released the 1995 album 'Zeitgeist'?
15. Which backing singer on Don Henley's 1989 album 'The End Of The Innocence' has since gone on to enjoy a successful career herself?
16. Which convent-educated Sixties pop star is the daughter of an Austrian baroness?

Answers to page 95

COVER VERSIONS 2: **1.** The Bangles **2.** 'The Loco-Motion' **3.** Cleopatra **4.** 'I Have A Dream' **5.** 1985 **6.** 'Tragedy' **7.** Billy Ocean **8.** Geri Halliwell **9.** Bananarama **10.** 2 **11.** Kim Wilde **12.** Don Lang and His Frantic Five **13.** Labelle **14.** 'Hazy Shade Of Winter' **15.** 'Jackie' **16.** Bern Elliott and The Fenmen

Elvis 1

Answers on page 92

1. What was Elvis's first UK number one?
2. On which TV show was Elvis filmed from the waist up only?
3. Which track formed a double A-side with 'A Fool Such As I'?
4. Which was the only UK number one on which Elvis had a writing credit?
5. Which Elvis number achieved the distinction of being the first song to enter the UK charts at number one?
6. What was significant about Elvis's two concerts at Russwood Park, Memphis, on 15 March 1958?
7. From which Elvis film was 'Wooden Heart' taken?
8. Which Elvis hit was a revamping of an old Italian song, 'Return To Sorrento'?
9. Who wrote 'Good Luck Charm'?
10. Who was Elvis's best man at his wedding to Patricia Beaulieu in 1967?
11. What was Elvis's first UK number one of 1961?
12. At which Las Vegas hotel was 'The Wonder of You' recorded live?
13. What was the name of Elvis's regular backing singers?
14. Into which Hall of Fame was Elvis inducted in January 1968?
15. Which rock star tried to get to see Elvis on 29 April 1976 by climbing the fence at Graceland, only to be escorted off the premises by security guards?
16. Which song was a posthumous UK number one for Elvis?

Answers to page 92

INDIE 1: **1.** Glasgow **2.** 'Do You Remember The First Time?' **3.** Lightning Seeds **4.** 1991 **5.** The Bluetones **6.** Ash **7.** James **8.** Travis **9.** 'Country House' **10.** Richey Edwards (Manic Street Preachers) **11.** The Verve **12.** John Power **13.** International Velvet **14.** Three Cheers For Tokyo **15.** Sice (Boo Radleys) **16.** Boo Radleys

Cover Versions 1

Answers on page 93

1. Atomic Kitten's 2001 UK number one, 'Eternal Flame', was a 1989 hit for which other girl band?
2. Which Little Eva song did Kylie Minogue cover in 1988?
3. Which band covered The Jackson Five hit 'I Want You Back' in 1998?
4. Which cover of an Abba song did Westlife take to number one in 1999?
5. In which year did a-ha release the original version of a1's 'Take On Me'?
6. Which song was a number one for both The Bee Gees and Steps?
7. Who originally recorded Boyzone's 'When The Going Gets Tough, The Tough Get Going'?
8. 'It's Raining Men' was a number two hit for The Weathergirls in 1984, but who topped the charts with it in 2001?
9. 'Last Thing On My Mind' was an early hit for Steps, but who originally recorded it in 1992?
10. What UK chart position did Robbie Williams reach with his 1996 cover of George Michael's 'Freedom'?
11. 'You Keep Me Hangin' On' was a hit for The Supremes in 1966. Who covered it 20 years later?
12. Who recorded The Cartoons' 1999 hit 'Witch Doctor' 41 years earlier?
13. All Saints' 1998 number one 'Lady Marmalade' was a hit for which group in 1975?
14. Which Simon and Garfunkel song did The Bangles cover in 1988?
15. Scott Walker and Marc Almond both had hits with which song?
16. The Flying Lizards' 'Money' was a hit for which band in 1963?

Answers to page 93

MUSIC POT LUCK 4: **1.** Art Garfunkel ('I Only Have Eyes For You' (1975) and 'Bright Eyes' (1979)) **2.** 'Magic Roundabout' **3.** Rick Wakeman **4.** Max Bygraves **5.** 'Shine On You Crazy Diamond' **6.** *Minder* ('Arthur Daley ('E's Alright)' and *Star Trek* ('Star Trekkin'')) **7.** 'Don't You Want Me' (Human League) **8.** 'Bootie Call' **9.** Del Amitri **10.** Chris Curtis **11.** Supertramp **12.** Andrew **13.** 'Belfast Child' **14.** The Levellers **15.** Sheryl Crow **16.** Marianne Faithfull

One-Hit Wonders 2

Answers on page 98

1. Whose moment of glory was a UK number one with 'Woodstock' in 1970?
2. Who had her only hit with 'One Day At A Time' in 1979?
3. 'Together We Are Beautiful' was a hit for which singer in 1980?
4. What was Norman Greenbaum's only hit?
5. Who got to number one in 1962 with 'Nut Rocker'?
6. Who were 'Up Town Top Ranking' in 1978?
7. What was the title of Charlene's 1982 UK number one?
8. With which number did M/A/R/R/S reach the top of the UK chart in 1987?
9. Whose finest hour was 'Float On' in 1977?
10. Who failed to set the world alight after hitting number one with 'Fire' in 1968?
11. Which cartoon characters had a UK number one hit in 1969?
12. Who insisted that there was 'No Charge' in 1976?
13. Which backing singers on 'Matchstalk Men and Matchstalk Cats And Dogs' themselves became one-hit wonders two years later?
14. Who had a hit with 'Turtle Power' in 1990?
15. With which song did John Fred and His Playboy Band trouble the charts for the only time?
16. Which curious creature gave Sheb Wooley his only hit?

Answers to page 98

SINGER/SONGWRITERS 1: **1.** 'Cold Spring Harbor' **2.** Have a UK number one single ('Don't Go Breaking My Heart') **3.** k.d. lang **4.** Carole King **5.** Michael Jackson **6.** Alanis Morissette **7.** Nick Lowe **8.** 'Big Yellow Taxi' **9.** Neil Sedaka **10.** 'Only The Lonely' **11.** John Denver **12.** Pincus **13.** David Parton **14.** 'I Just Called To Say I Love You' **15.** David Gray **16.** Peter Skellern

Glam Rock 1

Answers on page 99

Answers on page 99

1. Which Sixties band did Sweet's Brian Connolly and Mick Tucker used to be with?
2. Who rejected the names Terry Tinsel, Stanley Sparkle and Vicky Vomit before choosing his stage name?
3. Which one-time T. Rex bassist co-wrote 'Grandad' for Clive Dunn?
4. Which group consisted of Alan Williams, Tony Thorpe, Bill Hurd, Mick Clarke and John Richardson?
5. What was Kenny's first UK hit?
6. Which other future star was studying at Bromley Technical High School with a young David Bowie?
7. What was the title of David Bowie's second UK number one album?
8. In which year did T. Rex get to number one with 'Metal Guru'?
9. What was Sweet's first UK hit?
10. Which famous inventor was the subject of a Sweet track?
11. What was Gary Glitter's last UK number one?
12. With which song did The Glitter Band obtain their highest UK chart position of number two?
13. On which show did Sweet make their UK TV debut in January 1971?
14. What was David Bowie's first US top twenty hit?
15. Who was Marc Bolan's other half in T. Rex?
16. In which English city did the final live T. Rex gig take place, on 20 March 1977?

Answers to page 99

DANCE 1: **1.** 'Blue' **2.** Four **3.** Darude **4.** Cassandra **5.** Kernkraft **6.** 'Chocolate' **7.** Eiffel 65 **8.** 2 **9.** Manifesto **10.** 'Start The Commotion' **11.** 'Dominoid' **12.** 'Don't Stop' **13.** Basement Jaxx **14.** Groove Armada **15.** Seven **16.** 'Astral America'

Singer/Songwriters 1

Answers on page 96

1. What was the title of Billy Joel's 1971 album?
2. What did Elton John manage with Kiki Dee that he had previously been unable to do by himself?
3. Which Canadian singer/songwriter's first names are Kathryn Dawn?
4. Whose biggest-selling album was 'Tapestry'?
5. The experience of backing which artist on his world tour is retold in Sheryl Crow's 'What I Can Do For You'?
6. Who had hits with 'Head Over Feet' and 'Thank U'?
7. Which singer/songwriter started out as bass player and vocalist with Kippington Lodge?
8. What was Joni Mitchell's only UK hit?
9. 'Stupid Cupid' was whose first major hit?
10. Which song did Roy Orbision decided to record himself after it had been rejected by both Elvis Presley and The Everly Brothers?
11. Which singer/songwriter was killed in 1997 when his private plane plunged into the Pacific?
12. What is Barry Manilow's real surname?
13. Which 'unknown' had a UK hit with Stevie Wonder's 'Isn't She Lovely'?
14. What was Stevie Wonder's only solo UK number one?
15. Who had a hit with 'Babylon' in 2000?
16. Which singer/songwriter, who charted with 'You're A Lady' and 'Hold On To Love', formed a short-lived 1984 band called Oasis with Julian Lloyd Webber and Mary Hopkin?

Answers to page 96

ONE-HIT WONDERS 2: **1.** Matthews' Southern Comfort **2.** Lena Martell **3.** Fern Kinney **4.** 'Spirit In The Sky' **5.** B Bumble and The Stingers **6.** Althia and Donna **7.** 'I've Never Been To Me' **8.** 'Pump Up The Volume' **9.** The Floaters **10.** The Crazy World Of Arthur Brown **11.** The Archies ('Sugar Sugar') **12.** J. J. Barrie **13.** St Winifred's School Choir ('There's No One Quite Like Grandma') **14.** Partners In Kryme **15.** 'Judy In Disguise (With Glasses)' **16.** 'The Purple People Eater'

Dance 1

Answers on page 97

1. Which colour was the title of an Eiffel 65 single?
2. How many members were in Vengaboys?
3. Who released 'Heart Of Asia'?
4. Who featured on Rui Da Silva's single 'Touch Me'?
5. Which German dance group released 'Zombienation'?
6. Shanks and Bigfoot had a number one hit with 'Sweet Like' what?
7. 'Europop' was an album by which dance band?
8. What number did DJ Jean's 'The Launch' reach in the UK singles charts in 1999?
9. What record label were Yomanda signed to when they released 'Synth & Strings'?
10. What was the follow-up to The Wiseguys' single 'Ooh La La'?
11. What was Moloko's first UK single?
12. What was the title of ATB's second single?
13. Whose 1999 album was titled 'Remedy'?
14. Who reached number 19 in the UK singles charts with 'At The River' in August 1999?
15. How many weeks did 'King Of My Castle' by Wamdue Project spend in the UK singles chart?
16. What was Apollo Four Forty's first UK chart single called?

Answers to page 97

GLAM ROCK 1: **1.** Wainwright's Gentlemen **2.** Gary Glitter **3.** Herbie Flowers **4.** The Rubettes **5.** 'The Bump' **6.** Peter Frampton **7.** 'Pin-Ups' **8.** 1972 **9.** 'Funny, Funny' **10.** 'Alexander Graham Bell' **11.** 'Always Yours' **12.** 'Goodbye My Love' **13.** *Lift Off* **14.** 'Space Oddity' **15.** Mickey Finn **16.** Portsmouth

Fifties 1

Answers on page 102

1. Adrian Hill worked as a fitter in a Leeds engineering works before changing his name to become which successful recording artist?
2. Which Fifties crooner once worked as a prizefighter under the name Kid Crochet?
3. Which pianist had a 1959 chart topper with 'Roulette'?
4. In which year did 'Rock Around The Clock' first enter the UK charts for Bill Haley and The Comets?
5. Who had a 1956 UK number one with 'Sixteen Tons'?
6. What was the title of Ruby Murray's first hit?
7. Concetta Franconero was better known as which Fifties singer?
8. Who had a 28-year wait between her first UK hit, 'Under The Bridges of Paris', in 1955 and her second, 'Where Is My Man', in 1983?
9. Which tune did Perez Prado and Eddie Calvert each take to number one in the UK charts in 1955?
10. Which session band became one-hit wonders in 1956 with 'It's Almost Tomorrow'?
11. What was the title of Cliff Richard's second UK number one?
12. In 1957, who became the first Liverpool act to top the UK charts?
13. What was Lonnie Donegan's real Christian name?
14. Which 1958 chart topper shot himself dead five years later?
15. Which two artists had UK number one hits with 'Singing The Blues'?
16. Which excerpt from 'The Threepenny Opera', translated into English, became a 1959 UK number one for Bobby Darin?

Answers to page 102

STAIRWAY TO HEAVEN 1: **1.** Brian Jones **2.** Sandy Denny **3.** Dennis Wilson **4.** Patsy Cline **5.** Joe Meek **6.** Clarence White **7.** Marc Bolan **8.** Jimi Hendrix **9.** Dave Prater **10.** She died in a 1985 suicide pact with her female companion, Annie Pescher **11.** Badfinger (Pete Ham in 1975 and Tom Evans in 1983) **12.** Johnny Ace **13.** Keith Relf **14.** Lynyrd Skynyrd **15.** 1985 **16.** Michael Hutchence

Chart Toppers 1

Answers on page 103

In which years did the following tracks reach number one in the UK singles chart?

1. 'Can The Can' (Suzi Quatro)

2. 'Doop' (Doop)

3. 'The Sun Ain't Gonna Shine Anymore' (Walker Brothers)

4. 'I Hear You Knocking' (Dave Edmunds Rockpile)

5. 'It's A Sin' (Pet Shop Boys)

6. 'Rose Marie' (Slim Whitman)

7. 'Cars' (Gary Numan)

8. 'Girlfriend' (Billie)

9. 'Some Might Say' (Oasis)

10. 'I Owe You Nothing' (Bros)

11. 'Sailing' (Rod Stewart)

12. 'Atomic' (Blondie)

13. 'Do It Again' (The Beach Boys)

14. 'Without You' (Nilsson)

15. 'Men In Black' (Will Smith)

16. 'Do You Love Me' (Brian Poole and The Tremeloes)

Answers to page 103

MUSIC POT LUCK 5: **1.** Chris Curtis, the ex-Searchers drummer, was one of the founders of Deep Purple but left after a few days **2.** The Cranberries **3.** Leitch **4.** The Lovin' Spoonful **5.** Modern Romance **6.** Hank Wangford **7.** Humble Pie **8.** Alison Moyet **9.** The Humblebums **10.** It is short for Refugees (two of the three were expatriate Haitians) **11.** 'He's So Fine' **12.** Clannad **13.** Eddy Grant **14.** Heather Small **15.** Mike Rutherford **16.** Rolf Harris

Stairway to Heaven 1

Answers on page 100

1. Who drowned in the swimming pool of his Sussex home in 1969?
2. Which lead singer with Fairport Convention died in 1978 after falling down stairs?
3. Which Beach Boy drowned in a boating accident off the coast of California in 1983?
4. Which female country singer died in a Tennessee plane crash in 1963?
5. Which legendary producer shot himself on 3 February 1967, the anniversary of the death of his hero, Buddy Holly?
6. Which member of The Byrds was killed by a drunk driver in 1973?
7. Who was killed near Putney on 16 September 1977?
8. Who died in a basement bedroom at the Samarkand Hotel, Notting Hill Gate, on 18 September 1970?
9. Which of Sam and Dave was killed in a 1988 road smash?
10. How did The Singing Nun die?
11. Which Seventies band lost both guiding lights to suicide?
12. Which American R & B star shot himself dead in 1954 while playing Russian roulette backstage?
13. Which former singer with The Yardbirds was electrocuted in 1976 while tuning his guitar?
14. Three members of which band were wiped out in a Mississippi plane crash in 1977?
15. In which year did Ricky Nelson die in a plane crash?
16. Who was found hanging in a Sydney hotel room in 1997?

Answers to page 100

FIFTIES 1: **1.** Ronnie Hilton **2.** Dean Martin **3.** Russ Conway **4.** 1955 **5.** Tennessee Ernie Ford **6.** 'Heartbeat' **7.** Connie Francis **8.** Eartha Kitt **9.** 'Cherry Pink And Apple Blossom Wine' **10.** The Dreamweavers **11.** 'Travellin' Light' **12.** Frankie Vaughan **13.** Anthony **14.** Michael Holliday **15.** Guy Mitchell and Tommy Steele **16.** 'Mack The Knife'

Music Pot Luck 5

Answers on page 101

1. Who linked The Searchers and Deep Purple?
2. Dolores O'Riordan is the singer with which Irish band?
3. What is Donovan's surname?
4. John Sebastian, Zal Yanovsky, Steve Boone and Joe Butler were the original members of which Sixties band?
5. Who had a 1981 hit with 'Ay Ay Ay Ay Moosey'?
6. Which country music star is a qualified gynaecologist?
7. Peter Frampton and Steve Marriott formed which supergroup in 1969?
8. Who released a 1987 album 'Raindancing'?
9. Gerry Rafferty and Billy Connolly played together as which duo?
10. How did The Fugees get their name?
11. 'My Sweet Lord' was accused of being too similar to which Chiffons hit?
12. Enya used to play the piano with which Irish band?
13. Which member of The Equals enjoyed solo success over a decade later?
14. Who was the vocalist with M People?
15. Who was the Mike of Mike and The Mechanics?
16. Which entertainer broke down in tears on breakfast TV when hearing Mike and The Mechanics' 'The Living Years'?

Answers to page 101

CHART TOPPERS 1: **1.** 1973 **2.** 1994 **3.** 1966 **4.** 1970 **5.** 1987 **6.** 1955 **7.** 1979 **8.** 1998 **9.** 1995 **10.** 1988 **11.** 1975 **12.** 1980 **13.** 1968 **14.** 1972 **15.** 1997 **16.** 1963

Who Said That? 1

Answers on page 106

1. 'I can count on the fingers of one hand ten games when we've caused our own downfall.'
2. 'Once he starts to open his legs, you've got a problem.'
3. 'I don't blame individuals – I blame myself.'
4. 'I felt a lump in my mouth as the ball went in.'
5. 'What I said to them at half-time would be unprintable on the radio.'
6. 'I'd like to think it was a case of crossing the i's and dotting the t's.'
7. 'That number 14 for Holland is a marvellous player...that Johan Strauss.'
8. 'Maradona gets tremendous elevation with his balls no matter what position he's in.'
9. 'We must have had 99 per cent of the game. It was the other three per cent that cost us the match.'
10. 'They offered me a handshake of £10,000 to settle amicably. I told them they would have to be a lot more amicable than that.'
11. 'It's easy enough to get to Ireland. It's just a straight walk across the Irish Sea as far as I'm concerned.'
12. 'It's bloody tough being a legend.'
13. 'The first ninety minutes are the most important.'
14. 'After eight and a half years, they sacked me in two minutes.'
15. 'He couldn't trap a landmine.'
16. 'We reckon he covers every blade of grass on the pitch – mainly because his first touch is crap.'

Answers to page 106

PREMIERSHIP 2: **1.** Brian Kidd **2.** Neil Lennon **3.** Mark Kennedy **4.** 14 **5.** Carlisle United **6.** Stuart Gray **7.** Swindon Town **8.** 1998 **9.** Fulham **10.** Middlesbrough **11.** Southampton **12.** Darren Peacock **13.** Ipswich Town **14.** Joe Royle **15.** 1998 **16.** Paul Merson

Goalkeepers 2

Answers on page 107

1. Which goalkeeper attributed his poor display against Newcastle in 1998 to staying up all night playing *Tomb Raider*?

2. Which former German international keeper was sacked as coach of Fortuna Köln at half-time during a match in 1999?

3. Which goalkeeper saved eight of ten penalties he faced in 1977–8?

4. At the start of 2001–2, who is the only keeper to have saved a penalty from Matthew Le Tissier?

5. Which Welsh international staged a half-time protest during a game with Leeds in 1990?

6. Which Pegguy played for Leicester and Liverpool?

7. What was Maik Taylor's first League club?

8. Which Paraguayan international keeper scored eight goals for his club in 1996?

9. Which keeper joined Liverpool from Vitesse Arnhem?

10. Which Manchester United keeper dislocated his jaw while shouting at a team-mate?

11. Which future England keeper was a member of the Birmingham City team knocked out of the FA Cup by Altrincham in 1986?

12. With which club did Peter Shilton make his 1,000th appearance?

13. For which country did Manchester United's Harry Gregg play?

14. From which club did Manchester City sign Nicky Weaver?

15. Which goalkeeper was nicknamed 'The Cat'?

16. And which was known as 'The Flying Pig'?

Answers to page 107

REPUBLIC OF IRELAND 1: **1.** 1986 **2.** David O'Leary **3.** Italy **4.** 1949 **5.** Goodison Park **6.** Liam Brady **7.** Lansdowne Road **8.** Johnny Giles **9.** Pat Bonner **10.** 19 **11.** Paul McGrath **12.** Eamon Dunphy **13.** York City and Millwall **14.** England **15.** Gerry Daly **16.** 1986

Premiership 2

Answers on page 104

1. Which manager took Blackburn Rovers down to Division One in 1999?

2. Which midfielder left Leicester City for Celtic in 2000–1?

3. Which Irish teenager did Liverpool sign from Millwall in 1995?

4. When Wimbledon were relegated in 2000, how many seasons had they spent in the top flight?

5. From whom did Derby County sign Rory Delap?

6. Who was appointed manager of Southampton in summer 2001 following a spell as caretaker boss?

7. Which club conceded 100 Premiership goals in 1993–4?

8. In which year did Gianluca Vialli become Chelsea manager?

9. Which 2001/2 Premiership team were relegated to Division Three in 1994?

10. Which Premiership club used to play at the Old Archery Ground?

11. Whom did Liverpool defeat 7–1 at Anfield in 1998–9?

12. Which defender joined Newcastle from Queens Park Rangers in 1994?

13. Which 2001/2 Premiership club joined the Football League in 1938?

14. Which former Everton striker managed the club from 1994 to 1997?

15. In which year did Dwight Yorke join Manchester United?

16. Who moved from Middlesbrough to Aston Villa in 1998 for a fee of £6,750,000?

Answers to page 104

WHO SAID THAT? 1: **1.** Joe Kinnear **2.** Howard Wilkinson (about speedy Aston Villa winger Tony Daley) **3.** Joe Royle **4.** Terry Venables **5.** Gerry Francis **6.** Dave Bassett **7.** Joe Mercer **8.** David Pleat **9.** Ruud Gullit **10.** Tommy Docherty **11.** Brian Clough **12.** Ron Atkinson **13.** Bobby Robson **14.** George Graham (leaving Arsenal) **15.** Brian Clough (on new signing Gary Megson) **16.** David Jones (on Carlton Palmer)

Republic of Ireland 1

Answers on page 105

1. In which year did Jack Charlton become Irish manager?

2. Whose penalty put the Republic into the quarter-finals of the 1990 World Cup?

3. And who knocked them out of the tournament?

4. In which year did the Republic become the first non-British team to beat England on home soil?

5. Where was that game played?

6. Which Arsenal midfield maestro won 72 caps for the Republic between 1975 and 1990?

7. Where do the Republic play home internationals?

8. Who managed the Republic from 1973 to 1980?

9. Which Celtic goalkeeper won 80 caps for the Irish between 1981 and 1996?

10. How many goals did Don Givens score for the Republic?

11. Which former Manchester United player was given permission to train intermittently because of a long-standing knee injury?

12. Which successful author won 23 caps for the Republic from 1966 to 1971?

13. And with which two clubs did he win those caps?

14. Whom did the Republic defeat in their opening match in the 1988 European Championship?

15. Who won 48 caps for the Republic as a player with Manchester United, Derby County, Coventry City, Birmingham City and Shrewsbury Town?

16. When did Tony Cascarino win his first cap?

Answers to page 105

GOALKEEPERS 2: **1.** David James **2.** Harald Schumacher **3.** Paul Cooper **4.** Mark Crossley **5.** Neville Southall **6.** Arphexad **7.** Barnet **8.** Jose Luis Chilavert **9.** Sander Westerveld **10.** Alex Stepney **11.** David Seaman **12.** Leyton Orient **13.** Northern Ireland **14.** Mansfield Town **15.** Peter Bonetti **16.** Tommy Lawrence

Whose Home? 1

Answers on page 110

1. Who plays at Bootham Crescent?
2. Which former League club used to play at Peel Park?
3. What is the name of Coventry City's ground?
4. On whose ground did the first floodlit FA Cup tie take place?
5. Whose ground is situated in Irthlingborough?
6. Which club's previous homes include Eel Brook Common, Parsons Green Lane and Captain James Field?
7. Which club's address is Clarence Road?
8. Whose temporary home is the Withdean Stadium?
9. Who plays at Moss Rose?
10. Which Scottish club plays at Love Street?
11. What is the name of Wrexham's ground?
12. Where did Stoke City play before moving to the Britannia Stadium?
13. Who plays at the McAlpine Stadium?
14. Whose home is the Stadium of Light?
15. Which former League club plays at Edgar Street?
16. What is the name of Kilmarnock's home ground?

Answers to page 110

ODDBALLS 2: **1.** Manchester City **2.** Blackburn Rovers and Bolton Wanderers **3.** Blackpool **4.** Cardiff City **5.** Preston North End **6.** Queen's Park **7.** Duncan Ferguson **8.** Wimbledon **9.** Two **10.** Ian Wright **11.** Everton **12.** Hull **13.** Boston United **14.** Six **15.** Phil Stant **16.** Jim Smith

Managers 2

Answers on page 111

1. Which former Sheffield Wednesday boss took over as manager of Wigan Athletic in summer 2001?
2. Which manager had two spells in charge at Leyton Orient from 1968 to 1971 and 1977 to 1981?
3. Who succeeded Martin O'Neill as manager of Leicester City?
4. Who was the manager of Newcastle United when they won the FA Cup in 1951 and 1952?
5. Who managed Bolton Wanderers from 1951 to 1968?
6. How many managers have West Ham appointed since the war?
7. Tom Johnston, Wilf McGuinness and Alan Little were all managers of which club?
8. In 1959, Bill Lambton was manager of which club for just three days?
9. Who succeeded Graham Taylor as Watford boss in 1987?
10. Which manager was forced to disguise himself as a steward in order to avoid the wrath of his former club's fans?
11. In 1998, which Swindon manager banned his players from supermarket shopping in the three days before a match?
12. Who was sacked as Crystal Palace manager in 2001?
13. Who followed Steve Coppell into the Maine Road hot seat in 1996?
14. When did Bill Shankly retire as Liverpool boss?
15. Which former England international had an undistinguished year in charge at Hull from 1997?
16. What nationality is Arsène Wenger?

Answers to page 111

ARSENAL 2: **1.** Luton Town **2.** George Swindin **3.** Marc Overmars **4.** Leicester City **5.** Ian Wright **6.** 184 **7.** Liberian **8.** Tottenham's **9.** Ray Kennedy **10.** Wimbledon **11.** Charles Buchan **12.** Arthur Milton **13.** 1913 **14.** Ray Parlour **15.** Romford **16.** Jim Furnell

Oddballs 2

Answers on page 108

1. Which club has a fanzine called *Bert Trautmann's Helmet*?
2. In 1971, which two teams beginning with B were relegated to Division Three for the first time in their history?
3. For which club did Jimmy Armfield make 568 League appearances?
4. Against which team did Aldershot play their final League match in 1992?
5. Which was the last Football League club to play on an artificial pitch?
6. Which is the only Scottish club to reach the FA Cup final?
7. Which footballer was known as 'Duncan Disorderly' north of the border?
8. Who are the only club to have won the FA Cup and the FA Amateur Cup?
9. How many teams are there on the Isles of Scilly?
10. Who came on as substitute and scored his first goal for England in a 1–1 draw with Poland in 1993?
11. Which was the first British club to install undersoil heating?
12. Which is the largest city in England never to have hosted top-flight football?
13. Which non-League side recorded a 6–1 away win at Derby in the 1955–6 FA Cup?
14. And how many former Derby players were in their line-up?
15. Which former soldier was sacked as manager of Lincoln City in 2001?
16. Which manager is nicknamed 'Bald Eagle'?

Answers to page 108

WHOSE HOME? 1: **1.** York City **2.** Accrington Stanley **3.** Highfield Road **4.** Kidderminster Harriers **5.** Rushden & Diamonds **6.** Fulham **7.** Hartlepool United **8.** Brighton & Hove Albion **9.** Macclesfield Town **10.** St Mirren **11.** The Racecourse Ground **12.** The Victoria Ground **13.** Huddersfield Town **14.** Sunderland **15.** Hereford United **16.** Rugby Park

Arsenal 2

Answers on page 109

1. Who defeated Arsenal in the 1988 League Cup final?
2. Who preceded Billy Wright as Arsenal manager?
3. Which winger joined Arsenal from Ajax in 1997?
4. Who beat Arsenal on penalties in the FA Cup in 2000?
5. Who is Arsenal's record goalscorer?
6. And how many goals did he score for the Gunners?
7. What nationality is Christopher Wreh?
8. On whose ground did Arsenal clinch the 1970–1 League title?
9. And who scored the winning goal?
10. From which club did Arsenal sign Nigel Winterburn?
11. Who was Herbert Chapman's first signing for Arsenal?
12. Which former Arsenal and England international footballer also played cricket for Gloucestershire and England?
13. In which year did Arsenal lose their 'Woolwich' prefix?
14. Which Arsenal player made his full League debut at Liverpool on 29 January 1992?
15. Where was Tony Adams born?
16. Which goalkeeper did Arsenal sign from Liverpool in November 1963?

Answers to page 109

MANAGERS 2: **1.** Paul Jewell **2.** Jimmy Bloomfield **3.** Peter Taylor **4.** Stan Seymour **5.** Bill Ridding **6.** Seven **7.** York City **8.** Scunthorpe United **9.** Dave Bassett **10.** Shrewsbury Town's John Bond (on his return to Burnley) **11.** Jimmy Quinn **12.** Alan Smith **13.** Frank Clark **14.** 1974 **15.** Mark Hateley **16.** French

The World Game 3

Answers on page 114

1. What is the name of Real Madrid's stadium?
2. In what colour shirts do Fiorentina play?
3. Which African country were the first to reach the quarter-finals of the World Cup?
4. What nationality is Harry Kewell?
5. Which club has won most French League titles?
6. Which Dutch international forward moved from AC Milan to Barcelona in August 1998 for £8,750,000?
7. Which Swedish goalkeeper played a record 143 times for his country?
8. Which nation's players all bleached their hair blond at the 1998 World Cup finals?
9. Which country won the 1936 Olympic soccer final?
10. From which Scandinavian club did Valencia buy John Carew?
11. For which German club did Mark Hughes play?
12. With which Danish team did Brian Laudrup win League titles in 1987 and 1988?
13. Which club won the Swedish title in 1999 despite scoring just 25 goals in 26 matches?
14. For which club did Brazilian star Zico play throughout his international career?
15. Which West German international of the 1950s had only one arm?
16. Which club supplied all 11 players for the Belgium team that played Holland in September 1964?

Answers to page 114

ON THE SPOT 1: **1.** Kazimierz Deyna **2.** 1891 **3.** Wolverhampton Wanderers **4.** John Aldridge **5.** Southend United **6.** Watney Cup **7.** 28 **8.** Deportivo La Coruña **9.** Gary McAllister **10.** Michael Gray **11.** George Mutch **12.** Notts County **13.** Tony Coton **14.** Francis Lee **15.** Mark Crossley **16.** Arnold Muhren

Football League 2

Answers on page 115

1. Which club finished bottom of the newly formed Fourth Division in 1959?
2. Which club enjoyed continuous membership of the Third Division between 1920 and 1966?
3. Who signed Darren Caskey on a Bosman free from Reading in summer 2001?
4. In 1960, which Watford player became the only player to have scored Football League hat-tricks on two successive days?
5. Which club failed to gain re-election to the League in 1977?
6. Which club used to be known as Pine Villa?
7. Which Leyton Orient player was sacked at half-time in the home match with Blackpool in 1995?
8. Who had four players sent off in a Second Division match at Wigan in 1997?
9. Which former League club were leading Gillingham 7–0 after 75 minutes of a Fourth Division match in 1961 when the game was abandoned due to bad light?
10. In which year did Crewe Alexandra gain their first promotion?
11. For whom did Sammy Collins score 204 League goals?
12. Which London club was relegated to Division Two in 2001?
13. What is the name of Kidderminster Harriers' ground?
14. Which goalkeeper went upfield to score the last-minute goal which kept Carlisle United in the League in 1999?
15. Who were Carlisle's opponents that day?
16. And who dropped out of the League instead?

Answers to page 115

EUROPEAN CUP 2: **1.** Sporting Lisbon **2.** Steaua Bucharest **3.** 1970 **4.** Gornik Zabrze **5.** Anderlecht **6.** Liverpool **7.** Alan Smith **8.** Monaco **9.** Ajax **10.** AZ 67 Alkmaar **11.** West Germany **12.** Alfredo di Stefano **13.** HJK Helsinki **14.** Kevin Keegan **15.** Glentoran **16.** Nine

On the Spot 1

Answers on page 112

1. Who missed a penalty for Poland against Argentina in the 1978 World Cup finals – on his 100th international appearance?
2. In which year was the penalty kick introduced?
3. John Heath converted the first Football League penalty. Who did he play for?
4. Who was the first player to miss a penalty in a Wembley FA Cup final?
5. Which Football League club missed seven successive penalties in 1990 and 1991?
6. In which competition was Britain's first penalty shoot-out?
7. How many penalties were needed to decide the shoot-out after a drawn Freight Rover Trophy tie between Aldershot and Fulham in 1987?
8. Miroslav Dukic's missed penalty cost who the 1994 Spanish League title?
9. Who missed a penalty for Scotland against England in Euro 96?
10. Who missed the decisive penalty for Sunderland in the shoot-out following the First Division play-off final against Charlton in 1998?
11. Whose last-minute penalty won the 1938 FA Cup final for Preston?
12. Three players from which club missed the same penalty against Portsmouth in 1973?
13. Which Birmingham City goalkeeper saved a Sunderland penalty after just 80 seconds of his debut in 1980?
14. Which Manchester City player scored 13 penalties in 1971–2?
15. Who saved Gary Lineker's penalty in the 1991 FA Cup final?
16. Who scored a penalty for Manchester United in the 1983 FA Cup final replay?

Answers to page 112

THE WORLD GAME 3: **1.** Bernabeu **2.** Purple **3.** Cameroon **4.** Australian **5.** St Etienne **6.** Patrick Kluivert **7.** Thomas Ravelli **8.** Romania **9.** Italy **10.** Rosenborg **11.** Bayern Munich **12.** Brøndby **13.** AIK Stockholm **14.** Flamengo **15.** Robert Schlienz **16.** Anderlecht

European Cup 2

Answers on page 113

1. Who knocked Manchester United out of the 1963–4 European Cup-Winners' Cup after losing the first leg 4–1?
2. Which are the only Romanian team to have won the European Cup?
3. In which year did Manchester City win the European Cup-Winners' Cup?
4. And who did they beat in the final?
5. Who did Spurs beat on penalties to lift the 1984 UEFA Cup?
6. Which English club has won most European trophies?
7. Who scored Arsenal's winning goal in the 1994 European Cup-Winners' Cup final?
8. Who knocked Manchester United out of the 1998 Champions' League?
9. Who were the last Dutch team to win the European Cup?
10. Who did Ipswich defeat in the final of the 1981 UEFA Cup?
11. All four semi-finalists in the 1980 UEFA Cup were from which country?
12. Which Real Madrid player scored 49 goals in 58 European Cup matches?
13. Which Finnish club qualified for the Champions' League in 1998–9?
14. Which Englishman played against Nottingham Forest in the 1980 European Cup final?
15. Which Irish club were the first team to lose a European Cup tie on the 'away goals' rule?
16. How many different players scored for Liverpool in the home leg against Stromgodset in the 1974–5 European Cup-Winners' Cup?

Answers to page 113

FOOTBALL LEAGUE 2: **1.** Southport **2.** Southend United **3.** Notts County **4.** Cliff Holton **5.** Workington **6.** Oldham Athletic **7.** Terry Howard **8.** Bristol Rovers **9.** Barrow **10.** 1963 **11.** Torquay United **12.** Queens Park Rangers **13.** Aggborough **14.** Jimmy Glass **15.** Plymouth Argyle **16.** Scarborough

Sharpshooters 2

Answers on page 118

1. Who scored six goals on his Newcastle debut in the 13–0 win against Newport County in 1946?
2. Who scored after 42 seconds of the 1997 FA Cup final?
3. Which Rangers player scored in the first ten Scottish Premier League games in 1997–8?
4. Which Watford player was the League's leading scorer for 1978–9?
5. Whose 'golden goal' won Euro 96 for Germany?
6. Who scored four goals in England's 6–0 victory over San Marino at Wembley in 1992?
7. In 1996, who became the first player since the war to score more than 30 top-division goals in three successive seasons?
8. From which club did Queens Park Rangers sign Rodney Marsh?
9. For whom did George Camsell score 326 League goals between 1925 and 1939?
10. Which was Marcus Stewart's first League club?
11. Graeme Jones was the League's leading marksman in 1996–7. Who did he play for?
12. Which Celtic player scored 35 goals in the Scottish Premier in 1986–7?
13. Whose hat-trick at Anfield in 1995 was the first by a visiting player for 33 years?
14. Which Wrexham player scored in nine consecutive matches in 1988?
15. Which striker joined Bolton from Wimbledon for £3.5 million in 1997?
16. Who was Rangers' leading scorer for 1998–9?

Answers to page 118

SCOTTISH SCENE 2: **1.** Queen's Park **2.** Ross County **3.** Elgin City and Peterhead **4.** Meadowbank Thistle **5.** 111 **6.** Rangers and Dumbarton **7.** Stirling Albion **8.** Glasgow **9.** Partick Thistle **10.** Leith Athletic **11.** Forfar Athletic **12.** Clyde **13.** Coatbridge **14.** Celtic **15.** Ally McCoist **16.** 1967

Non-League 1

Answers on page 119

1. Which Ryman League team are known as 'The Ducks'?
2. Which non-League team launched the career of Les Ferdinand, Cyrille Regis and Jason Roberts?
3. Who finished runners-up in the Conference to Rushden & Diamonds in 2000–1?
4. From which club did Nottingham Forest sign Ian Woan in 1989?
5. Who were the first winners of the Conference?
6. Which West Midlands Regional League side knocked Tranmere Rovers out of the FA Cup in 1975?
7. Who won the Ryman Premier League title in 2000–1?
8. What is the name of Kettering Town's ground?
9. For which Conference club did Carl Alford score 26 goals in 1998–9?
10. Former Northern Ireland international Iain Dowie was transferred to Luton from which Ryman League outfit?
11. Which former Manchester City, West Bromwich Albion, Leeds United and England winger went on to play for Northwich Victoria?
12. Which Unibond League club did Chris Waddle turn out for in 2000–1?
13. Which Beazer Homes Leaguers are known as 'The Yeltz'?
14. When was the last FA Amateur Cup competition?
15. Who beat Wimbledon in the semi-finals of the 1930 FA Amateur Cup before losing to Ilford in the final?
16. Which Conference side plays at Kingsmeadow Stadium?

Answers to page 119

LIVERPOOL 2: **1.** Ron Yeats **2.** £440,000 **3.** Rome **4.** Joe Fagan **5.** Middlesbrough Ironopolis **6.** Borussia Dortmund **7.** Chester **8.** Israeli **9.** Roger Hunt **10.** David Fairclough **11.** Bishop Auckland **12.** Joey Jones **13.** Steve McManaman **14.** 1962 **15.** Bristol Rovers **16.** Steve Heighway and Brian Hall

Scottish Scene 2

Answers on page 116

1. Which is the oldest current Scottish League club?
2. Which Scottish League team plays in Dingwall?
3. Which two clubs joined the Scottish League at the start of the 2000–1 season?
4. What was Livingston's previous name?
5. How many League goals did Kenny Dalglish score for Celtic?
6. Which two clubs shared the first Scottish League title?
7. Which club shared Stenhousemuir's ground in 1992–3?
8. In which city were Third Lanark based?
9. Which Scottish club sold Mo Johnston to Watford?
10. Which club left the Scottish League in 1953?
11. Who spent a club record fee on buying back Ian McPhee from Airdrie for £50,000 in 1991?
12. Which club moved from Glasgow to Cumbernauld?
13. In which town do Albion Rovers play?
14. Which club used to allow free admission for priests and women?
15. Who scored a hat-trick for Rangers against Celtic in the 1983–4 Scottish League Cup final?
16. In which year did Berwick Rangers sensationally knock Rangers out of the Scottish FA Cup?

Answers to page 116

SHARPSHOOTERS 2: **1.** Len Shackleton **2.** Roberto di Matteo (Chelsea) **3.** Marco Negri **4.** Ross Jenkins **5.** Oliver Bierhoff **6.** David Platt **7.** Alan Shearer **8.** Fulham **9.** Middlesbrough **10.** Bristol Rovers **11.** Wigan Athletic **12.** Brian McClair **13.** Peter Ndlovu (Coventry City) **14.** Kevin Russell **15.** Dean Holdsworth **16.** Rod Wallace

Liverpool 2

Answers on page 117

1. Which giant Liverpool centre-half joined the club from Dundee United in 1961?
2. How much did Kenny Dalglish cost when he moved to Anfield from Celtic in 1977?
3. In which city did Liverpool win the 1977 European Cup?
4. Who succeeded Bob Paisley as Liverpool manager?
5. Who were Liverpool's first opponents in a Football League fixture?
6. From which club did Liverpool sign Patrick Berger?
7. Where was Michael Owen born?
8. What nationality was Ronny Rosenthal?
9. Which Liverpool player has scored more League goals than anyone else in the club's history?
10. Who earned the nickname 'Super Sub'?
11. With which club did Bob Paisley receive an FA Amateur Cup winners' medal?
12. Which full-back joined Liverpool from Wrexham in 1975?
13. Who played 364 games for Liverpool before departing for Real Madrid?
14. When were Liverpool last promoted from Division Two?
15. From which club did Liverpool sign Larry Lloyd?
16. Which two Liverpool stars of the 1970s were university graduates?

Answers to page 117

NON-LEAGUE 1: **1.** Aylesbury United **2.** Hayes **3.** Yeovil **4.** Runcorn **5.** Altrincham **6.** Coventry Sporting **7.** Farnborough **8.** Rockingham Road **9.** Stevenage Borough **10.** Hendon **11.** Peter Barnes **12.** Worksop **13.** Halesowen Town **14.** 1973 **15.** Bournemouth Gasworks Athletic **16.** Kingstonian

Oddballs 3

Answers on page 122

1. Which club has a fanzine called *Brian Moore's Head*?
2. Which football club do comedian Jim Bowen and Foreign Secretary Jack Straw both support?
3. Rod Stewart was once a trialist with which London club?
4. Which South American country used to have a team called Liverpool?
5. Which goalkeeper who joined Leicester in summer 2001 has a father who used to manage Everton?
6. Which club in Northern Ireland has won the most trophies?
7. At which club did Steve Bruce succeed Nigel Spackman as manager in 1998?
8. Who paid Barry Town a club record £70,000 for Eifion Williams in 1999?
9. What is the nickname of Kettering Town?
10. Which Scottish club sold Paul Hartley to Millwall in 1996?
11. Which former Welsh international goalkeeper was once a dustman?
12. Which Atletico Madrid goalkeeper set a new world record by going 1,275 minutes without conceding a goal in 1990–1?
13. Which South American country used their national stadium as a prison in the 1970s?
14. Which York-born striker did Cheltenham sign from Northampton?
15. In 1957, which Midlands team became the first British club to win a match in the Soviet Union?
16. Which world statesman once proclaimed himself to be a fan of Wigan Athletic?

Answers to page 122

ENGLAND 2: **1.** Leslie Compton **2.** One **3.** 77 **4.** Paul Ince **5.** Six **6.** 22 years **7.** 1980 **8.** Two **9.** Peru **10.** 1997 **11.** Nat Lofthouse **12.** Bill Nicholson **13.** Burnley **14.** Ian Wright **15.** Czechoslovakia **16.** Crystal Palace

Transfer Trail 2

Answers on page 123

1. Which international striker moved from Juventus to Middlesbrough for £7 million in 1996?
2. Which club bought goalkeeper Shaka Hislop from Reading in 1995?
3. Which Scottish international went from Derby to Blackburn for £5.3 million in 1998?
4. Who was the first player to be transferred for £500,000 or more between two British clubs?
5. And who bought him?
6. Who was the first British player to be the subject of three £1 million transfer deals?
7. Who paid West Ham a club record £800,000 for Joey Beauchamp in 1994?
8. From which club did Leicester City sign Matt Elliott in 1997?
9. Which forward moved from Stevenage Borough to Bristol Rovers for £250,000 in 1997?
10. Who signed Justin Jackson from Morecambe in 2000 to set a record fee between non-League clubs?
11. Which Spanish club sold Albert Ferrer to Chelsea?
12. Whose transfer from Bolton to Arsenal in 1928 was the first £10,000 deal?
13. From which club did Bristol City sign midfielder Brian Tinnion?
14. Which two players joined Wimbledon from Millwall in 1994?
15. Ed de Goey joined Chelsea from which Dutch club?
16. Who paid Bolton Wanderers £4.5 million for Alan Stubbs in 1996?

Answers to page 123

WORLD CUP 1: **1.** Karim Bagheri (Iran) **2.** Sweden **3.** Algeria **4.** Garrincha **5.** Hungary **6.** Spain **7.** France **8.** Uruguay **9.** Gerd Müller **10.** Romania **11.** Bulgaria **12.** 1982 **13.** Sweden **14.** Emmanuel Petit **15.** Estonia **16.** Jimmy Greaves

England 2

Answers on page 120

1. Who won his first England cap in 1950 at the age of 38?
2. How many goals did Emlyn Hughes score for England?
3. How many England caps did Terry Butcher win?
4. Who was the first black player to captain England?
5. How many hat-tricks did Jimmy Greaves score in an England shirt?
6. How long did Stanley Matthews's international career last?
7. When did Bryan Robson win his first England cap?
8. How many England caps did Brian Clough win?
9. Against which South American country did Bobby Moore win his first England cap?
10. In which year did David Beckham win his first England cap?
11. Which 'Lion of Vienna' scored 30 goals in just 33 England appearances?
12. Which future Spurs manager scored within 30 seconds of his England debut?
13. Ray Pointer won three England caps in 1962. Which club did he play for at the time?
14. Who scored England's last goal under Graham Taylor?
15. Which country did England beat 4–2 at Wembley in 1990?
16. For which club was Kenny Sansom playing when he won his first England cap?

Answers to page 120

ODDBALLS 3: **1.** Gillingham **2.** Blackburn Rovers **3.** Brentford **4.** Uruguay **5.** Ian Walker (his father is Mike Walker) **6.** Linfield **7.** Sheffield United **8.** Torquay United **9.** 'The Poppies' **10.** Hamilton Academicals **11.** Neville Southall **12.** Abel Resino **13.** Chile **14.** Neil Grayson **15.** West Bromwich Albion **16.** Former Soviet President Mikhail Gorbachev

World Cup 1

Answers on page 121

1. Who scored 19 goals from 17 games in the qualifying competition for the 1998 World Cup?
2. In which country was the 1958 World Cup held?
3. Which African nation stunned eventual finalists West Germany by defeating them 2–1 in the first of their group matches at the 1982 World Cup finals?
4. Which Brazilian player scored twice against England in the quarter-finals of the 1962 tournament?
5. Who did West Germany beat in the 1954 World Cup final?
6. Which country did Northern Ireland defeat in the 1982 World Cup finals?
7. A player from which country scored the first ever goal in the World Cup?
8. Who did England meet in their opening match in the 1966 World Cup?
9. Who scored West Germany's winning goal in the 1974 final?
10. Who topped England's group at the 1998 World Cup finals?
11. Which country knocked Germany out of the 1994 World Cup?
12. In which year did Honduras qualify for their only World Cup finals?
13. Who did Brazil beat in the semi-finals of the 1994 World Cup?
14. Who scored France's third goal in the 1998 World Cup final?
15. Which country failed to turn up for a World Cup qualifying tie with Scotland in 1996?
16. Which English player was urinated on by a dog during the game with Brazil at the 1962 World Cup finals?

Answers to page 121

TRANSFER TRAIL 2: **1.** Fabrizio Ravanelli **2.** Newcastle United **3.** Christian Dailly **4.** David Mills **5.** West Bromwich Albion **6.** Clive Allen **7.** Swindon Town **8.** Oxford United **9.** Barry Hayles **10.** Rushden & Diamonds **11.** Barcelona **12.** David Jack **13.** Bradford City **14.** Kenny Cunningham and Jon Goodman **15.** Feyenoord **16.** Celtic

General Knowledge 21

Answers on page 126

1. Slide Mountain is the highest peak in which US mountain range?
2. Which river flows through Chester?
3. What did Charlie Chan call his eldest offspring, Barry?
4. In 1967, which golfer made the first televised hole-in-one?
5. Which is the smallest native British deer?
6. Which monster in Greek mythology had nine heads?
7. Jomo Kenyatta became the first President of which country in 1964?
8. What was Edwin Lutyens by profession?
9. Who released the 1997 album 'OK Computer'?
10. What was significant about footballer Mo Johnston's transfer to Rangers in 1989?
11. Who directed *Women in Love* and *The Devils*?
12. Which Hollywood actress was born Caryn Johnson?
13. Who designed the Clifton Suspension Bridge?
14. What colour are the flowers of a celandine?
15. Who was the first English printer?
16. Who was the commander of *Stingray*?

Answers to page 126

GENERAL KNOWLEDGE 23: **1.** David 'Kid' Jensen **2.** Thomas Hardy **3.** Mississippi **4.** *Worzel Gummidge* **5.** Ryder Cup **6.** Gary Hart **7.** In your ear **8.** Goldcrest **9.** Australia **10.** King Lear **11.** Liverpool **12.** Five **13.** Mickey Mouse ('Life Is A Minestrone') **14.** Botticelli **15.** Tom Finney **16.** South Island

General Knowledge 22

Answers on page 127

1. From which country did the chow dog originate?
2. What is the name of the area of low atmospheric pressure along the equator where calm winds can suddenly produce storms?
3. What two colours make up the flag of Portugal?
4. What was the Christian name of the German car designer Porsche?
5. On which ground do the Scotland rugby union team play home matches?
6. As which Sixties pop star did Reg Ball re-invent himself?
7. Muskie and Vince assisted which law enforcer?
8. Eboracum was the Roman name for which city?
9. What piece of furniture is a chesterfield?
10. Scottish blackface and cheviot are breeds of which animal?
11. Chesil Beach is in which English county?
12. Who went from playing a brickie to wearing 'Crocodile Shoes'?
13. Which south coast resort is host to a pre-Wimbledon tennis tournament?
14. What was the middle name of the poet Percy Shelley?
15. Which Independent candidate fought unsuccessfully against Bill Clinton in the 1992 US Presidential campaign?
16. Who is Wayne Slob's wife?

Answers to page 127

GENERAL KNOWLEDGE 24: **1.** Italian **2.** Albania **3.** A hairy-leaved plant **4.** Sandown Park **5.** Duran Duran **6.** Michael Caine (*The Caine Mutiny*) **7.** Philip II **8.** Oak tree **9.** Jordan **10.** Screaming Lord Sutch **11.** Australasia **12.** Tom Wolfe **13.** Calista Flockhart **14.** Harry Vardon **15.** Elizabeth I **16.** Coldplay

General Knowledge 23

Answers on page 124

1. Which former Radio 1 disc jockey is a descendant of Robert Louis Stevenson?
2. Who wrote *Far from the Madding Crowd*?
3. Which US state is known as the 'Magnolia State'?
4. Who lived in Ten Acre field at Scatterbrook Farm?
5. In 1985, what did Europe regain for the first time in 28 years?
6. Who withdrew from the 1988 US Presidential race following newspaper revelations about his relationship with model Donna Rice?
7. Where would you find your hammer, anvil and stirrup?
8. What is the smallest British bird?
9. In which country is the Gibson Desert?
10. Whose daughters were Goneril and Regan?
11. Which English football team achieved a European and domestic treble in 2001?
12. How many lines are there in a limerick?
13. According to 10cc, who gets more fan mail than the Pope?
14. Which 15th-century Italian artist's name means 'little barrel'?
15. Which former England international footballer was known as the 'Preston plumber'?
16. On which island of New Zealand is the city of Christchurch?

Answers to page 124

GENERAL KNOWLEDGE 21: **1.** The Catskills **2.** Dee **3.** 'Number One Son' **4.** Tony Jacklin **5.** Roe deer **6.** Hydra **7.** Kenya **8.** Architect **9.** Radiohead **10.** He was Rangers' first Catholic signing **11.** Ken Russell **12.** Whoopi Goldberg **13.** Isambard Kingdom Brunel **14.** Yellow **15.** William Caxton **16.** Troy Tempest

General Knowledge 24

Answers on page 125

1. What nationality was Christopher Columbus?

2. In the currency of which country do 100 qindarka make a lek?

3. What is comfrey?

4. On which racecourse is the Whitbread Gold Cup run?

5. Which band took their name from the villain in the film *Barbarella*?

6. Which actor took his stage name from a Humphrey Bogart movie?

7. Which Spanish King despatched the Armada?

8. What tree has the Latin name *Quercus rober*?

9. Which Formula One team sacked driver Heinz-Harald Frentzen half-way through the 2001 season?

10. Who formed the National Teenage Party in 1963?

11. In which continent does the wombat live?

12. Who wrote the novel *The Bonfire of the Vanities?*

13. Who plays *Ally McBeal*?

14. Who was the first British golfer to win the US Open?

15. Who was the last Tudor monarch?

16. Which band had hits with 'Yellow' and 'Trouble'?

Answers to page 125

GENERAL KNOWLEDGE 22: **1.** China **2.** Doldrums **3.** Green and red **4.** Ferdinand **5.** Murrayfield **6.** Reg Presley **7.** *Deputy Dawg* **8.** York **9.** Sofa **10.** Sheep **11.** Dorset **12.** Jimmy Nail **13.** Eastbourne **14.** Bysshe **15.** Ross Perot **16.** Waynetta

General Knowledge 25

Answers on page 130

1. Who pioneered birth control in London in the 1920s?
2. What do Vanessa Feltz and Tony Curtis have in common?
3. Which singer had a Bionic Woman as babysitter for his children?
4. What is a stonechat?
5. In which county is Stilton cheese traditionally made?
6. Which cathedral has the tallest spire in England?
7. Which Russian city had three different names in the course of the 20th century?
8. What took place in Chicago on 14 February 1929?
9. With what instrument was Roy Castle associated?
10. Soling, Finn and Tornado are categories in which sport?
11. Who sprinkled oofle dust?
12. As whom was Lev Davidovitch Bronstein better known?
13. When did Carole King decide it might as well rain until?
14. In which country is the fishing port of Trondheim?
15. Waverley Station is located in which British city?
16. What disease can the tsetse fly transmit to humans?

Answers to page 130

GENERAL KNOWLEDGE 27: **1.** Lord Raglan **2.** Walker Cup **3.** *Me and My Girl* **4.** Lager **5.** Radius **6.** Poll tax **7.** 15th **8.** Kate Winslet **9.** Pete Shelley was singer with The Buzzcocks and Mark Lamarr presents *Never Mind the Buzzcocks* **10.** Cross-Channel swim **11.** Coco Chanel **12.** Roald Dahl **13.** Richard Dadd **14.** Australia **15.** Senegal **16.** Norfolk

General Knowledge 26

Answers on page 131

1. What did Barbie's boyfriend Ken originally lack which other boys had?
2. Which board game was devised by unemployed heating engineer Clarence B. Darrow?
3. What is the chemical term for chalk?
4. Which Benedictine monk invented champagne?
5. At which Olympic event did David Hemery win a gold medal?
6. What was Diana Prince's alter ego?
7. Which band's best-selling album was titled 'Urban Hymns'?
8. Which writer of *The Hitch-Hiker's Guide to the Galaxy* died in 2001?
9. What is the name for a word that reads the same backwards as forwards?
10. What was the name of the lioness in *Born Free*?
11. In which English town is there a street called The Pantiles?
12. What do you call an angle which measures between 90 and 180 degrees?
13. In which forest was William II of England killed?
14. What did Wat Tyler lead in 1381?
15. On which river is Shrewsbury?
16. Who was banned from international football for a year in 1990 for insulting the French national team manager Henri Michel?

Answers to page 131

GENERAL KNOWLEDGE 28: **1.** Olga Yegorova **2.** Samantha Failsworth **3.** 1,009 **4.** Lagos **5.** Oliver Stone **6.** Guinevere **7.** Scafell Pike **8.** Jennifer Lopez **9.** Hamilton Academicals **10.** Britain **11.** Posture **12.** Browns, Seasons, Thickens-in-One **13.** Essex **14.** Kenneth Clark **15.** 1860s **16.** Sofia Coppola (daughter of Francis Ford Coppola)

General Knowledge 27

Answers on page 128

1. Which British field marshal in the Crimean War gave his name to a type of sleeve?
2. Which golf trophy did Britain and Ireland retain at Sea Island, Georgia, in August 2001?
3. Which musical features 'The Lambeth Walk'?
4. What sort of beer takes its name from the German for 'store'?
5. What is the name of the bone on the thumb side of the forearm?
6. What did the council tax replace in 1993?
7. In which century were the first reports of a Loch Ness monster?
8. Which actress split from husband Jim Threapleton in August 2001?
9. What links Pete Shelley and Mark Lamarr?
10. What was first achieved by Captain Matthew Webb in 1875?
11. Which fashion designer created the 'little black dress'?
12. Who wrote *Charlie and the Chocolate Factory*?
13. Which British painter murdered his father in 1843 and was committed to an asylum?
14. For which country did Neil Harvey play Test cricket?
15. Dakar is the capital of which African country?
16. In which county would you find the villages of Great Snoring and Little Snoring?

Answers to page 128

GENERAL KNOWLEDGE 25: **1.** Marie Stopes **2.** Both have a daughter named Allegra **3.** Glen Campbell (Lindsay Wagner) **4.** A bird **5.** Leicestershire **6.** Salisbury **7.** St Petersburg – formerly Petrograd and Leningrad **8.** St Valentine's Day Massacre **9.** Trumpet **10.** Yachting **11.** Sooty **12.** Trotsky **13.** September **14.** Norway **15.** Edinburgh **16.** Sleeping sickness

General Knowledge 28

Answers on page 129

1. Which Russian runner was booed as she won the women's 5000 metres at the 2001 World Athletics Championships?
2. Which *Coronation Street* barmaid was played by Tina Hobley?
3. What is the lowest prime number over 1,000?
4. Which city was the capital of Nigeria until 1991?
5. Who directed *Platoon* and *JFK*?
6. In Arthurian legend, what was the name of King Arthur's wife?
7. What is the highest mountain in England?
8. Which singer split up from Puff Daddy in 2001?
9. Which Scottish League football team were deducted 15 points in 2000 for refusing to fulfil a fixture at Stenhousemuir?
10. Albion was the ancient name for which country?
11. What is the Alexander technique said to improve?
12. What does Bisto stand for?
13. Where in Britain is Ugley?
14. Who popularised the history of art through the TV series *Civilisation*?
15. In which decade was the American Civil War?
16. Which daughter of a famous director won acclaim for her directorial debut, *The Virgin Suicides*?

Answers to page 129

GENERAL KNOWLEDGE 26: **1.** Genitals **2.** Monopoly **3.** Calcium carbonate **4.** Dom Pérignon **5.** 400 metres hurdles **6.** *Wonder Woman* **7.** The Verve **8.** Douglas Adams **9.** Palindrome **10.** Elsa **11.** Tunbridge Wells **12.** Obtuse **13.** New Forest **14.** Peasants' Revolt **15.** Severn **16.** Eric Cantona

General Knowledge 29

Answers on page 134

1. Which famous thespian is the mother of actress Joely Richardson?

2. Lake Tiberias is the modern name for which Biblical sea?

3. Cape Horn is at the southern tip of which group of islands?

4. What does 'ergo' mean in Latin?

5. What is a fieldfare?

6. Who was Queen of England for nine days in 1553?

7. Which spa town at the foot of the Taunus Mountains in Germany gave its name to a soft felt hat for men?

8. Action Man was the British version of which American toy doll?

9. According to medieval Christian legend, what did Jesus drink from at the Last Supper?

10. What is a koto?

11. Which cat was tormented by Pixie and Dixie?

12. Why did the BBC ban Ricky Valance's 1960 hit 'Tell Laura I Love Her'?

13. Which planet is second closest to the Sun?

14. What are kurdaitcha shoes – worn by Australian Aborigines – traditionally made from?

15. Leith is the port of which city?

16. How did Herbert Marx get his nickname of 'Zeppo'?

Answers to page 134

GENERAL KNOWLEDGE 31: **1.** Uranus **2.** 16 **3.** Mickey Dolenz **4.** New Zealander **5.** Nero **6.** Liszt **7.** Little Rock **8.** Their fathers were policemen **9.** Blue **10.** Northumberland **11.** The Dagmar **12.** Nene **13.** Australia **14.** Liam Gallagher **15.** Germany **16.** 1974

General Knowledge 30

Answers on page 135

1. What do Ronnie O'Sullivan, Keanu Reeves and Woody Harrelson have in common?
2. Edgbaston cricket ground is in which city?
3. On which island did Steve McGarrett operate?
4. Who wanted to know: 'What's The Frequency Kenneth'?
5. In 1953, which jockey finally won his first Epsom Derby at the age of 49?
6. What was installed for the first time at Barclays Bank, Enfield, on 27 June 1967?
7. Richard Hadlee played Test cricket for which country?
8. Which Hollywood actor changed his name from William Franklin Beedle Jnr?
9. What can be the position of a note in the musical scale or a sticky black substance?
10. In which county is the cathedral city of Wells?
11. In which country was the conductor Georg Solti born?
12. Who was the Greek god of dreams?
13. Which British golfer won the US Masters in 1988?
14. Which channel divides Anglesey from the Welsh mainland?
15. Edward Whymper was the first person to climb which Alpine peak?
16. For what is laser an acronym?

Answers to page 135

GENERAL KNOWLEDGE 32: **1.** Tommy Trinder **2.** P. Diddy **3.** Richard **4.** Florence **5.** Tomsk **6.** Malcolm Nash **7.** Lincolnshire **8.** Both attended the London School of Economics **9.** George Bernard Shaw **10.** Red **11.** Sumo wrestling **12.** Marlene Dietrich ('Marlene On The Wall') **13.** The bra **14.** Belisha beacon (Sir Leslie Hore-Belisha) **15.** Conner **16.** Crystal Palace

General Knowledge 31

Answers on page 132

1. Which planet was discovered by William Herschel in 1781?
2. How many weeks did Bryan Adams stay at number one in the UK in 1991 with '(Everything I Do) I Do It For You'?
3. Which of The Monkees once starred in *Circus Boy*?
4. What nationality is former speedway champion Ivan Mauger?
5. Who was said to have fiddled while Rome burned?
6. Who composed 'Transcendental Studies'?
7. What is the state capital of Arkansas?
8. What do Roger Moore, Terry Waite and Julian Clary have in common?
9. What colour does litmus paper turn in the presence of alkali?
10. In which county is Bamburgh Castle?
11. Which wine bar did James Willmott-Brown run in *EastEnders*?
12. Which river flows through Northampton?
13. In which country is the Kakadu National Park?
14. Which rock star did Robbie Williams famously challenge to a fight?
15. The Weimar Republic was established in which country in 1918?
16. In which year did Chris Evert win her first Wimbledon title?

Answers to page 132

GENERAL KNOWLEDGE 29: **1.** Vanessa Redgrave **2.** Sea of Galilee **3.** Tierra del Fuego **4.** Therefore **5.** Bird **6.** Lady Jane Grey **7.** Homburg **8.** G.I. Joe **9.** The Holy Grail **10.** A Japanese musical instrument **11.** Mr Jinks **12.** It was about death – a taboo subject **13.** Venus **14.** Emu feathers **15.** Edinburgh **16.** He was born at the time of the first zeppelins

General Knowledge 32

Answers on page 133

1. Which comedian's catchphrase was 'You lucky people'?
2. To what did Puff Daddy change his name in 2001?
3. What was the name of Hyacinth Bucket's long-suffering husband in *Keeping Up Appearances*?
4. Which city is the capital of the Tuscany region of Italy?
5. Which of the Wombles takes his name from a city in Siberia?
6. Who was the Glamorgan bowler when Nottinghamshire's Gary Sobers established a world record by hitting six sixes in one over at Swansea in 1968?
7. In which county is the resort of Ingoldmells?
8. Which seat of learning links Mick Jagger and John F. Kennedy?
9. Who wrote *Arms and the Man* and *Man and Superman*?
10. What colour beak does a shelduck have?
11. What is the national sport of Japan?
12. Which movie star was the subject of a 1986 song by Suzanne Vega?
13. What garment did Mary Phelps Jacob (aka Mrs Caresse Crosby) perfect in 1913?
14. Which flashing road safety innovation of 1934 was named after the Minister of Transport at the time?
15. What was the family surname in *Roseanne*?
16. Steve Bruce was appointed manager of which London football club in the summer of 2001?

Answers to page 133

GENERAL KNOWLEDGE 30: **1.** Their fathers have all served jail sentences **2.** Birmingham **3.** Hawaii (*Hawaii Five-O*) **4.** R.E.M. **5.** Sir Gordon Richards **6.** Cash dispenser **7.** New Zealand **8.** William Holden **9.** Pitch **10.** Somerset **11.** Hungary **12.** Morpheus **13.** Sandy Lyle **14.** Menai Strait **15.** Matterhorn **16.** Light Amplification by Stimulated Emission of Radiation

General Knowledge 33

Answers on page 138

1. Which British motor-racing team was launched by Tony Vandervell?
2. Which communications satellite was launched in 1962 to provide the first live TV transmissions between the USA and Europe?
3. Which T is one of the six counties of Northern Ireland?
4. What type of geographical feature is Skiddaw?
5. Which movie star, who separated in 2001 from his wife, was once voted Least Likely To Succeed by his classmates?
6. Which board game was the brainchild of Chris and John Haney and Scott Abbott?
7. What is a siskin?
8. Renee Zellweger and Hugh Grant starred in which Helen Fielding adaptation?
9. Which Quasimodo won the Nobel Prize for Literature in 1959?
10. In 1986, 13-year-old Sandra Kim won the Eurovision Song Contest for which country?
11. In football, which country staged the 1958 World Cup finals?
12. Au is the chemical symbol for which element?
13. What does 'décolleté' mean in the fashion world?
14. Who is the chief god in Scandinavian mythology?
15. At which London railway station would you arrive if travelling from Swindon?
16. What was special about the televised football match between Liverpool and West Ham on 15 November 1969?

Answers to page 138

GENERAL KNOWLEDGE 35: **1.** Monsoon **2.** Bob Hawke **3.** Sweden **4.** Morpeth **5.** LXXX **6.** 14 **7.** Kuala Lumpur **8.** Malawi **9.** Each have eyes of different colours **10.** REO Speedwagon **11.** Ireland **12.** Calais **13.** Hooghly **14.** Jane Tennison **15.** Russell Crowe **16.** Mia Farrow

General Knowledge 34

Answers on page 139

1. Justine Frischmann, Janet Street-Porter and Queen Noor of Jordan all studied to be what?
2. What was the name of Boycie's wife in *Only Fools And Horses*?
3. Which Football League club started the 2001–2 season playing home matches at Dorchester Town?
4. Which pen name did R.C. Lamburn use to create the adventures of a mischievous schoolboy?
5. Which duo were first to utter the corny line: 'If I Said You Have A Beautiful Body Would You Hold It Against Me'?
6. What flower is ling more commonly known as?
7. For which country does footballer Dan Petrescu play?
8. What is the female singer's equivalent of an alto voice?
9. Ownership of Jutland is divided between which two countries?
10. Arthur Stanley Jefferson achieved fame as which half of a comic duo?
11. Ascunción is the capital of which South American country?
12. Which bubble threatened to destroy the British economy in the 18th century?
13. Racehorse No Bombs was disqualified after winning a race at Ascot for eating what on the way to the races?
14. In which country was Lego invented?
15. What foodstuff was originally called an Eskimo Pie?
16. What is a liger?

Answers to page 139

GENERAL KNOWLEDGE 36: **1.** Bernie the Bolt **2.** Sarah Tisdall **3.** Richard **4.** Derbyshire, South Yorkshire, Lincolnshire and Leicestershire **5.** Supergrass **6.** Iran **7.** Australia **8.** The zip **9.** The Nile **10.** Montevideo **11.** Brian Conley **12.** Germany **13.** Hereward the Wake **14.** Ernest Hemingway **15.** Hendon **16.** Plaster of Paris

General Knowledge 35

Answers on page 136

1. What is Edina's surname in *Absolutely Fabulous*?
2. Who was Prime Minister of Australia from 1983–91?
3. Which Scandinavian country's flag is a yellow cross on a blue background?
4. Which town is the administrative centre of Northumberland?
5. What is 80 in Roman numerals?
6. How many pounds are there in a stone?
7. Which city houses the two Petronas skyscrapers, currently the tallest buildings in the world?
8. Which African country used to be called Nyasaland?
9. Which physical trait is shared by Jane Seymour and David Bowie?
10. Which US group took their name from a fire engine?
11. Which country's rugby union team plays at Lansdowne Road?
12. Which port did the French regain from English control in 1558?
13. On which river does Calcutta stand?
14. Which police officer did Helen Mirren play in *Prime Suspect*?
15. Who was the Antipodean star of the movie *Gladiator*?
16. The sister of which actress was the subject of The Beatles' 'Dear Prudence'?

Answers to page 136

GENERAL KNOWLEDGE 33: **1.** Vanwall **2.** *Telstar* **3.** Tyrone **4.** A mountain (in the Lake district) **5.** Tom Cruise **6.** Trivial Pursuit **7.** A bird **8.** *Bridget Jones's Diary* **9.** Salvatore Quasimodo **10.** Belgium **11.** Sweden **12.** Gold **13.** Low cut **14.** Odin **15.** Paddington **16.** It was the first TV game in colour

General Knowledge 36

Answers on page 137

1. Who loaded the crossbows on *The Golden Shot*?
2. Which Foreign Office clerk was jailed in 1984 for passing Cruise missile documents to the *Guardian*?
3. Which son of Oliver Cromwell succeeded him as Lord Protector?
4. Which four counties border Nottinghamshire?
5. Gaz Coombes is the singer with which band?
6. In which country are the ruins of Persepolis?
7. Which country has won most Commonwealth Games gold medals?
8. What was invented by Whitcomb L. Judson in 1893?
9. Which is the longest river in the world?
10. The name of which South American capital city means 'I see the mountain'?
11. Which British comedian and chat show host had 'No Entry' tattooed on his bottom?
12. Quark is which country's most popular cheese?
13. Who led a revolt against the Normans in 1070 from his stronghold on the Isle of Ely?
14. Who wrote *The Old Man and the Sea*?
15. Where is the Metropolitan Police Training School?
16. What is burned gypsum otherwise known as?

Answers to page 137

GENERAL KNOWLEDGE 34: **1.** Architects **2.** Marlene **3.** Bournemouth **4.** Richmal Crompton (*Just William*) **5.** Bellamy Brothers **6.** Heather **7.** Romania **8.** Contralto **9.** Denmark and Germany **10.** Stan Laurel **11.** Paraguay **12.** South Sea Bubble **13.** Mars Bar **14.** Denmark **15.** Choc ice **16.** The offspring of a lion and tigress

General Knowledge 37

Answers on page 142

1. Which Platters song was covered by Freddie Mercury in 1987?
2. On which racecourse is the Royal Hunt Cup run?
3. What did Adam push up his bottom to woo Rachel in *Cold Feet*?
4. Ipswich is located at the estuary of which river?
5. Who played The Joker in the 1989 *Batman* movie?
6. Which flower is the national emblem of Japan?
7. Which Archbishop of Canterbury declared Henry VIII's marriage to Catherine of Aragon null and void?
8. Which Liverpool footballer was nicknamed 'Crazy Horse'?
9. Corfu is an island in which sea?
10. The dong is the currency of which country?
11. In which American state is Key West?
12. Which singer with The Moody Blues later joined Wings?
13. Choo Choo and Spook were members of whose gang?
14. What do you fear if you suffer from linonophobia?
15. Which British comedian used to drive a hearse for Co-op Funerals?
16. Which 1980 TV programme caused diplomatic relations to be broken off between Britain and Saudi Arabia?

Answers to page 142

GENERAL KNOWLEDGE 39: **1.** Robert Mitchum **2.** The Mamas and The Papas **3.** A ship **4.** Somerset **5.** Dick Tracy **6.** Somerset Maugham **7.** Dusty Springfield **8.** Stanley Matthews **9.** Mauritius **10.** *ER* **11.** Viscount Palmerston **12.** Mel Brooks **13.** Black, yellow and red **14.** Tracy Chapman **15.** Rugby **16.** Mount Rushmore

General Knowledge 38

Answers on page 143

1. What is the connection between Winnie the Pooh and The Rolling Stones?
2. What is the sign of Sagittarius?
3. Between which two towns did the world's first railway run?
4. What type of musical instrument is a triangle?
5. For what crime was Al Capone eventually brought to justice?
6. Who did Muhammad Ali beat in the 'thriller in Manila' to retain his World Heavyweight title?
7. Which river does Balmoral Castle overlook?
8. Which golfer won the British Open in 1979, 1984 and 1988?
9. Who was Lucille Ball's husband on and off screen in the 1950s?
10. What does PLO stand for?
11. And what did ELO stand for?
12. In which sea are the Aland Islands?
13. What is the capital of New York state?
14. Who solved crimes in St Mary Mead?
15. Which playwright wrote *Entertaining Mr Sloane* and *Loot*?
16. Who was the Roman goddess of chastity and hunting?

Answers to page 143

GENERAL KNOWLEDGE 40: **1.** Flemish **2.** Blue **3.** Norwich City **4.** Five ('Slam Dunk (Da Funk)') **5.** Never Say Die **6.** Michael Keaton (who played Batman in the original movie) was born Michael Douglas **7.** Damon Hill **8.** Coventry **9.** 15 July **10.** He invented plasticine **11.** Oklahoma City **12.** Paul **13.** Massachusetts **14.** It is the only mammal which dies automatically after mating **15.** Jean Acker **16.** Gerald Durrell

General Knowledge 39

Answers on page 140

1. Which fellow actor said: 'A Steve McQueen performance just naturally lends itself to monotony. Steve doesn't bring much to the party'?
2. Who sang about 'Creeque Alley'?
3. What is a dhow?
4. Jamie Cox was the captain of which county cricket team in 2001?
5. Which cartoon hero was created by Chester Gould?
6. Who wrote *Of Human Bondage* and *The Moon and Sixpence*?
7. Which Sixties singer was born Mary O'Brien?
8. In 1956, who was voted the first European Footballer of the Year?
9. Port Louis is the capital of which Indian ocean island?
10. Which medical drama is set in Chicago's Cook County General Hospital?
11. Which British Prime Minister is said to have died from a heart attack while having sex with a parlour maid on his private billiard table?
12. Which movie director changed his name from Melvin Kaminsky?
13. What colours are the three stripes on the Belgian national flag?
14. 'Fast Car' was a 1988 hit for which artist?
15. Which sport was invented by schoolboy William Webb Ellis?
16. On the face of which mountain are carved giant portrait heads of four former US Presidents?

Answers to page 140

GENERAL KNOWLEDGE 37: **1.** 'The Great Pretender' **2.** Ascot **3.** A rose **4.** Orwell **5.** Jack Nicholson **6.** Chrysanthemum **7.** Thomas Cranmer **8.** Emlyn Hughes **9.** Ionian Sea **10.** Vietnam **11.** Florida **12.** Denny Laine **13.** Top Cat **14.** String **15.** Russ Abbot **16.** *Death of a Princess*

General Knowledge 40

Answers on page 141

1. What nationality was the artist Rubens?
2. What colour is azure?
3. Which English football team plays at Carrow Road?
4. Which boy band topped the charts with a basketball term?
5. On which horse did 18-year-old Lester Piggott become the youngest jockey to win the Epsom Derby?
6. What links Batman and Catherine Zeta-Jones?
7. Which former world motor-racing champion's middle names are Ernest Deveraux?
8. Through which English city did Lady Godiva ride naked?
9. What date is St Swithin's Day?
10. Why do Wallace & Gromit owe their lives to William Harbutt?
11. In which city were parking meters first introduced?
12. Who is Sindy's boyfriend?
13. Which American state did The Bee Gees sing about in 1967?
14. What is unique – and unfortunate – about the male swamp antechinus, a mouse-like marsupial from Australia?
15. Which actress left Rudolph Valentino on their wedding night?
16. Which author wrote *My Family and Other Animals* about his experiences growing up on Corfu?

Answers to page 141

GENERAL KNOWLEDGE 38: **1.** Brian Jones bought A.A. Milne's old house **2.** The archer **3.** Stockton and Darlington **4.** Percussion **5.** Tax evasion **6.** Joe Frazier **7.** Dee **8.** Severiano Ballesteros **9.** Desi Arnaz **10.** Palestinian Liberation Organisation **11.** Electric Light Orchestra **12.** Baltic **13.** Albany **14.** *Miss Marple* **15.** Joe Orton **16.** Diana

EastEnders 2

Answers on page 146

1. What was Carmel Jackson's job?
2. Who lost her virginity to Michael Rose?
3. Who floored Ian Beale in the Queen Vic because he had left her boy to die?
4. Who inadvertently killed his own son by tampering with Mark Fowler's motorbike?
5. Who sharpened her claws on Dr Anthony Trueman?
6. Which family opened an Italian restaurant?
7. What was the restaurant called?
8. What was Sonia Jackson's favourite musical instrument?
9. Who made Carol Branning pregnant at 14?
10. What is the name of Steve Owen's weird sister?
11. Which female lecturer took Michelle Fowler in as a lodger?
12. Which Walford villain was played by William Boyde?
13. What was the name of Mehmet Osman's wife?
14. Which chubby barrowboy was Colin Russell's partner?
15. Who sold his half of the Queen Vic to Dan Sullivan for £5?
16. Who framed Arthur Fowler?

Answers to page 146

WESTERNS 1: **1.** John Wayne **2.** Johnny Cash **3.** Tombstone **4.** *Maverick* **5.** Charlie Wooster **6.** Rex Allen **7.** Andy **8.** *Dr Quinn, Medicine Woman* **9.** Joshua Smith **10.** Chuck Connors **11.** Victoria Barkley **12.** Lofty Craig **13.** Jimmy Smits **14.** *The Lone Ranger* **15.** El Toro **16.** Eric Fleming (Gil Favor)

Which Year in TV? 2

Answers on page 147

In which year did the following programmes begin in the UK?

1. *Clangers*
2. *Tenko*
3. *Howard's Way*
4. *Dixon of Dock Green*
5. *Emmerdale Farm*
6. *The Generation Game*
7. *The Avengers*
8. *Rising Damp*
9. *The Big Breakfast*
10. *Casualty*
11. *Only Fools and Horses*
12. *Pinky and Perky*
13. *Danger Man*
14. *Minder*
15. *Desmond's*
16. *Colditz*

Answers to page 147

TV POT LUCK 3: **1.** Carol Vorderman **2.** ITV **3.** Mary Nightingale **4.** Carol Smillie **5.** Denise Robertson **6.** Principal Skinner **7.** Jeremy Paxman and Jeremy Vine **8.** Adrian Mole **9.** Michael Barrymore **10.** Mike Reid **11.** *Streetmate* **12.** Danny Blanchflower **13.** *Your Life in Their Hands* **14.** Barbara Woodhouse **15.** Fred Dibnah **16.** Raymond Baxter

Westerns 1

Answers on page 144

1. Who turned down the role of Matt Dillon in *Gunsmoke* because he was contracted to movies?
2. Which singer played Davy Crockett in a 1990s remake of the series?
3. Wyatt Earp was the marshal of which town in Arizona?
4. Which surname was shared by Bret, Bart, Beau and Brent?
5. What was the name of the cook in *Wagon Train*?
6. Who starred as Dr Bill Baxter in *Frontier Doctor*?
7. Who was Slim Sherman's younger brother in *Laramie*?
8. Which Western heroine was played by Jane Seymour?
9. What was Hannibal Hayes' alias?
10. Who played Jason McCord in *Branded*?
11. Who owned the cattle ranch in *The Big Valley*?
12. Which deputy sheriff had a crush on *Annie Oakley*?
13. Which *NYPD Blue* star played *The Cisco Kid* in a 1993 version of the Fifties classic?
14. Which Western hero never removed his mask?
15. Who was Kit Carson's Mexican sidekick?
16. Which *Rawhide* actor drowned in 1966 while filming a movie on location in South America?

Answers to page 144

EASTENDERS 2: **1.** Health visitor **2.** Lisa Shaw **3.** Peggy Butcher **4.** Nick Cotton **5.** Kat Slater **6.** The di Marcos **7.** Guiseppe's **8.** Trumpet **9.** David Wicks **10.** Jackie **11.** Rachel Kominski **12.** James Willmott-Brown **13.** Guizin **14.** Barry Clark **15.** Phil Mitchell **16.** Willy Roper

TV Pot Luck 3

Answers on page 145

1. Who presents *Stars and Their Lives*?
2. On which channel would you encounter *Neighbours From Hell, Salesmen From Hell* and *Garages From Hell*?
3. Who announced in 2002 that she was giving up *Wish You Were Here...?* to spend more time with her family?
4. Which former *Wheel of Fortune* hostess keeps order in *Changing Rooms*?
5. Who is the resident agony aunt on *This Morning*?
6. What is the name of the school principal in *The Simpsons*?
7. Which two Jeremys present *Newsnight*?
8. Which character talked us through *The Cappuccino Years* in 2001?
9. Who hosted *My Kind of Music* before finding himself in all kinds of trouble?
10. Which actor/comedian showed clips from his *Late Home Video Show*?
11. Which Channel 4 match-making show was hosted by Davina McCall?
12. Which footballer was the first person to walk out on *This Is Your Life*?
13. Which BBC medical documentary series of the Fifties was accused by the BMA of 'pandering to the morbid'?
14. Which intimidating dog trainer received 300 fan letters a day?
15. Who was TV's first celebrity steeplejack?
16. Who was the first presenter of *Tomorrow's World*?

Answers to page 145

WHICH YEAR IN TV? 2: **1.** 1969 **2.** 1981 **3.** 1985 **4.** 1955 **5.** 1972 **6.** 1971 **7.** 1961 **8.** 1974 **9.** 1992 **10.** 1986 **11.** 1981 **12.** 1957 **13.** 1960 **14.** 1979 **15.** 1989 **16.** 1972

Wildlife 2

Answers on page 150

1. Who introduced his *Amazing World of Animals*?
2. Which vet travelled the world in search of *Ultimate Killers*?
3. Who presented *Nature Watch*?
4. Which series was presented by Wendy Turner and Mark Evans?
5. What nationality is Steve Irwin?
6. Which bearded wildlife expert hunted down *Dangerous Reptiles*?
7. Which Charlotte made films about chimps and gorillas in Africa?
8. Who used to be 'wide awake' but is now 'really wild'?
9. Which Simon is a well-known wildlife photographer?
10. Which German husband-and-wife diving team popularised undersea programmes in the Fifties and Sixties?
11. Which was David Attenborough's first major series?
12. Which popular wildlife series ran for 11 years from 1958?
13. Which ITV company made *Survival*?
14. Who narrates *Wildlife On One*?
15. Who presented *Animal Magic*?
16. Which *Emmerdale* character has a dog named Batley?

Answers to page 150

CHILDREN'S TV 2: **1.** Sabrina **2.** *Tweenies* **3.** John Ryan **4.** Roderick the Rat **5.** Aardvark **6.** Australia **7.** *Teletubbies* **8.** *Bob the Builder* **9.** Sam Bacon **10.** Roger Moore **11.** Robert Harbin **12.** Mr Clamp **13.** Peter Glaze **14.** *Top Cat* **15.** Duck **16.** Billy Bunter

Dramas 3

Answers on page 151

1. What was Gambit's first name in *The New Avengers*?
2. Stephen Crane was the opportunist hero of which series?
3. Which British movie star played restaurateur Maurice Allington in *The Green Man*?
4. What job did *Casualty*'s Josh Griffiths do?
5. What is Stuart Mackenzie's nickname in *London's Burning*?
6. Who gave up her hairdressing salon in Weatherfield for a career in nursing at *Holby City*?
7. Which notorious *Bad Girls* inmate is played by Debra Stephenson?
8. Ben Manfred was the leader of which gang of adventurers?
9. For which organisation did *Bognor* work?
10. Which series features investigators from HM Customs and Excise?
11. Which *This Life* actor changed career to become one of Channel 4's *Teachers*?
12. Amanda Holden and Adrian Lukis starred in which two-part rural drama?
13. Who plays Dr John Carter in *ER*?
14. Who was the managing director of *Mogul*?
15. What was the name of the shipyard in *Howard's Way*?
16. Which period drama featured bustling heroine Louisa Trotter?

Answers to page 151

COMEDY 3: **1.** Lee Evans **2.** Frank Finlay **3.** *The Odd Couple* **4.** Harry 'Snapper' Organs **5.** Chandler **6.** 1940s **7.** Lewis Collins **8.** Edgar Briggs **9.** Stan Butler **10.** Norma **11.** Julian Clary **12.** George and Anthea **13.** *The Lovers* **14.** Syd Little **15.** *KYTV* **16.** Warrender

Children's TV 2

Answers on page 148

1. Who is TV's teenage witch?

2. Jake, Milo, Bella and Fizz are better known as what?

3. Who created *Sir Prancelot*?

4. Who was the concert pianist on *Tales of the Riverbank*?

5. What kind of creature is *Arthur*?

6. Which country produces *Round the Twist*?

7. 'Over the hills and far away', who come to play?

8. Which animated character had a surprise hit at Christmas 2000?

9. Which *Grange Hill* character was nicknamed 'Cracker'?

10. Who links *Ivanhoe* and James Bond?

11. Which magician taught *Origami* in the 1960s?

12. Who was *Trumpton*'s greengrocer?

13. Which member of the *Crackerjack* team was a reserve for The Crazy Gang?

14. Which cartoon character lives in a dustbin?

15. Who is Dog's friend?

16. Which outsize schoolboy was played by Gerald Campion?

Answers to page 148

WILDLIFE 2: **1.** Rolf Harris **2.** Steve Leonard **3.** Julian Pettifer **4.** *Pet Power* **5.** Australian **6.** Mark O'Shea **7.** Charlotte Uhlenbroek **8.** Michaela Strachan **9.** Simon King **10.** Hans and Lotte Hass **11.** *Zoo Quest* **12.** *On Safari* **13.** Anglia **14.** David Attenborough **15.** Johnny Morris **16.** Edna Birch

Comedy 3

Answers on page 149

1. Which knockabout comedian asked *So What Now*?
2. Who played Patrick Kelly in the pilot episode of *Never Mind the Quality, Feel the Width*?
3. What were Felix Unger and Oscar Madison?
4. Which intrepid policeman pursued the Piranha Brothers in *Monty Python's Flying Circus*?
5. Which Friend proposed to Monica?
6. To which decade was Gary Sparrow transported back in time in *Goodnight Sweetheart*?
7. Which Professional played Gavin Rumsey in *The Cuckoo Waltz*?
8. Which David Jason character worked for the Secret Intelligence Service?
9. Who drove a bus for the Luxton and District Traction Company?
10. What is Nana's name in *The Royle Family*?
11. Who was ostracised from television for a while after making a tasteless remark about Norman Lamont at the Comedy Awards?
12. Who were Gary's two work colleagues in *Men Behaving Badly*?
13. In Jack Rosenthal's 1970 comedy, what were Beryl and Geoffrey?
14. Which half of a comedy double act was born Cyril Mead?
15. Anna Daptor and Mike Channel worked for which television company?
16. What was Penny's surname in *Just Good Friends*?

Answers to page 149

DRAMAS 3: **1.** Mike **2.** *Chancer* **3.** Albert Finney **4.** Paramedic **5.** 'Recall' **6.** Angela Griffin **7.** Shell Dockley **8.** *The Four Just Men* **9.** The Board of Trade **10.** *The Knock* **11.** Andrew Lincoln **12.** *The Hunt* **13.** Noah Wyle **14.** Brian Stead **15.** The Mermaid **16.** *The Duchess of Duke Street*

Commercials 1

Answers on page 154

1. Who plays Prunella Scales' long-suffering daughter in the Tesco ads?
2. Which sweets taste 'unbelievably' of strawberries and cream?
3. Which *Last of the Summer Wine* star advertises chair-lifts?
4. Which footballer has ''ealthy looking 'air'?
5. Which cat goes clubbing for Bacardi Breezer?
6. Who famously tipped a Cinzano over Leonard Rossiter?
7. Who makes 'exceedingly good cakes'?
8. In which English county is Bernard Matthews based?
9. Which bottled beer 'worked wonders'?
10. Which product cleaned 'a big, big carpet for less than half a crown'?
11. Which actress insisted that the chocolates 'aren't Terry's, they're mine'?
12. What does Just For Men remedy?
13. What was the Brooke Bond chimp's reply to the question: 'Dad, do you know the piano's on my foot'?
14. Which comedian promotes second-hand cars 'with no questions asked'?
15. According to the adverts, what did Pal stand for?
16. Which cigarette were you never alone with?

Answers to page 154

QUIZ & GAME SHOWS 2: **1.** Ian Wright **2.** Nick Weir **3.** *Survivor* **4.** Simon Mayo **5.** Channel 5 **6.** *Blockbusters* **7.** John Leslie **8.** *Take Your Pick* **9.** *The Golden Shot* **10.** 15 **11.** Robert Robinson **12.** *Through the Keyhole* **13.** Lily Savage **14.** *Play Your Cards Right* **15.** *Bullseye* **16.** *Trick or Treat*

Soaps 3

Answers on page 155

1. Who was *Neighbours*' biker chick?

2. Which Summer Bay girl got married in August 2001?

3. Which fictitious country was the scene of a wedding-day bloodbath in *Dynasty*?

4. Who became the Rovers' new barmaid in the summer of 2001?

5. In *Crossroads*, what was the name of Glenda Brownlow's seafaring brother?

6. Which promising young Walford Town footballer's career was ended by a knee injury in 1993?

7. And which actor who played him left *EastEnders* to pursue a singing career?

8. In *Brookside*, which family placed Mandy Jordache in a 'safe house'?

9. Which *Emmerdale* old lag was Jack Sugden's cell-mate?

10. Which Sixties soap centred around the Cooper family?

11. Which daytime soap of the Eighties was set in the Covent Garden rag trade?

12. Who took over from Barbara Bel Geddes as Miss Ellie in *Dallas*?

13. Which Weatherfield resident married Myra Dickinson in 1963?

14. Which actor played Norman Crabtree in *Coronation Street* and Sid Hooper in *Crossroads*?

15. Which Ramsay Street character died of cancer in 2001?

16. Who is Paddy Kirk's gay cousin in *Emmerdale*?

Answers to page 155

DOCUSOAPS 1: **1.** The Adelphi **2.** Maureen Rees **3.** *Clampers* **4.** *The House* **5.** *Airline* **6.** Blackpool **7.** *Airport* **8.** Norwegian **9.** The Wilkins **10.** Reading **11.** Roger Graef **12.** Sunderland **13.** *Paddington Green* **14.** *Doctors' Orders* **15.** Emma and Joe Inglis **16.** *Blues and Twos*

Quiz & Game Shows 2

Answers on page 152

1. Which ex-footballer became the new presenter of *Friends Like These?*
2. Who spent the first series of *Catchphrase* on crutches after tripping down the studio stairs?
3. What is the title of ITV's much-hyped, desert island game show?
4. Which former Radio I disc jockey used to present *National Lottery: Winning Lines?*
5. On which channel is *One to Win?*
6. Which quiz show encouraged contestants to 'go from gold to gold in 60 seconds or less'?
7. Which former *Blue Peter* presenter went on to watch over the *Wheel of Fortune?*
8. Which game show featured the treasure chest?
9. Princess Grace of Monaco was a contestant on which Sixties game show?
10. How many questions have to be answered correctly to win the ultimate prize on *Who Wants To Be a Millionaire?*
11. Who asked the questions on *Ask the Family?*
12. Which afternoon panel game snoops around celebrities' homes?
13. Which sharp-tongued Scouser is the latest host of *Blankety Blank?*
14. On which game show would you find contestants' row?
15. Which game show offered consolation prizes made of tungsten?
16. Which game show was presented by Julian Clary and Mike Smith?

Answers to page 152

COMMERCIALS I: **1.** Jane Horrocks **2.** Campino **3.** Dame Thora Hird **4.** David Ginola **5.** Tom **6.** Joan Collins **7.** Mr Kipling **8.** Norfolk **9.** Double Diamond **10.** 1001 **11.** Dawn French **12.** Grey hair **13.** 'You hum it, son, I'll play it.' **14.** Jim Davidson **15.** Prolongs Active Life **16.** Strand

Docusoaps 1

Answers on page 153

1. Which Liverpool establishment was under scrutiny in *Hotel*?
2. Who was the star turn on *Driving School*?
3. Which docusoap followed a team of traffic wardens?
4. PR man Keith Cooper was portrayed as the villain of which fly-on-the-wall series?
5. Easyjet's operations have been featured in which series?
6. *Pleasure Beach* looked at which resort's amusement park?
7. Russell and Steve are the press pack in which docusoap?
8. What nationality is Trude Mostue, one of the subjects of *Vets in Practice*?
9. Which clan were the subject of the Seventies' series *The Family*?
10. In which town did they live?
11. Which documentary-maker was responsible for *Police*?
12. Which football club was the subject of *Premier Passions*?
13. Which district of London has its own series?
14. Which docusoap was filmed at the Inham Lodge surgery in Somerset?
15. Which *Vets in Practice* couple split up in 2001?
16. Which series with a rhyming title tracked the work of the emergency services?

Answers to page 153

SOAPS 3: **1.** Steph Scully **2.** Sally Fletcher **3.** Moldavia **4.** Shelly Unwin **5.** Ron **6.** Aidan Brosnan **7.** Sean Maguire **8.** The Shackletons **9.** Harry **10.** *The Newcomers* **11.** *Gems* **12.** Donna Reed **13.** Jerry Booth **14.** Stan Stennett **15.** Madge Bishop **16.** Jason

TV Pot Luck 4

Answers on page 158

1. Which star of *The Sweeney* introduced the nostalgic *I Love 1975*?
2. Which breakfast DJ presents *Points of View*?
3. Which former Saturday morning regular presents *Countryfile*?
4. Which Channel 5 show brings the latest entertainment news?
5. Which Sunday teatime show is presented by Pam Rhodes?
6. Who was dropped after the first series of *Surprise Surprise!*?
7. Who starred in *Highway to Heaven*?
8. Which religious presenter was nicknamed 'The Bishop'?
9. Which series encourages celebrities to spend the night in someone else's home?
10. Which wine buff attempted to become a ski guide in *Danger: Celeb at Work*?
11. Who presented *Ratrap*?
12. Which landmark series of 1969 visited 118 museums and 18 libraries in 11 different countries?
13. Which science series was presented by Miriam Stoppard and Rob Buckman?
14. Which Geordie lass says *She's Gotta Have It*?
15. Which distress signal do Lowri Turner and Nick Knowles answer?
16. What was the name of the character played by Todd Carty in *Grange Hill*?

Answers to page 158

SPORT 1: **1.** Clare Balding **2.** Mark Lawrenson **3.** Golf **4.** Channel 4 **5.** Australian **6.** Motor racing **7.** Suzi Perry **8.** Gabby Logan **9.** Ian Bishop **10.** Peter Dimmock **11.** David Vine **12.** *They Think It's All Over* **13.** Peter Alliss **14.** Bob Colston **15.** Kent Walton **16.** James Richardson

Cop Shows 2

Answers on page 159

1. Which crime-fighter, played by Don Johnson, is an inspector with the Special Investigations Unit of the San Francisco Police Department?
2. Samantha Janus starred in which police series?
3. Which ex-*Brookside* actor plays Sun Hill's new recruit Des Taviner?
4. Which female pathologist caught the eye of *Inspector Morse*?
5. Who was *Hooperman*'s female boss?
6. Which gang leader got to call Captain Furillo 'Frankie' in *Hill Street Blues*?
7. Who played *Delvecchio*?
8. What was the name of Ken Boon's team of motorcycle despatch riders?
9. Which TV cop first appeared in a TV movie *The Marcus-Nelson Murders*?
10. Which TV detective wore an eye-patch?
11. Comedian Alan Davies plays which magical mystery solver?
12. What was the name of Marty Hopkirk's widow?
13. Jake Styles assisted which detective?
14. Who replaced Twentyman as desk sergeant in *Z Cars*?
15. Who plays Greg Medavoy in *NYPD Blue*?
16. In which century was *Sergeant Cork* set?

Answers to page 159

EMMERDALE 2: **1.** Scott Windsor **2.** Marlon **3.** Frankie **4.** Jan **5.** Richie Carter **6.** Dolly Skilbeck **7.** Peter Amory **8.** Steve Merchant **9.** Australia **10.** Helicopter **11.** Tina Dingle **12.** Britt **13.** Amos Brearly **14.** Vicar **15.** Butch **16.** Diane Blackstock

Sport 1

Answers on page 156

1. Who is the feminine face of the BBC's horse racing coverage?

2. Which former Oxford United manager is a laconic BBC soccer pundit?

3. Ken Brown offers commentary on which sport?

4. Which channel has a Saturday morning show called *Gazzetta Football Italia*?

5. What nationality is BBC horse racing commentator Jim McGrath?

6. For which sport does Louise Goodman conduct interviews?

7. Who is the glamorous presenter of the World Superbike series?

8. Which daughter of a former Wales team manager presents *On the Ball*?

9. Which ex-West Indian fast bowler is a Channel 4 cricket commentator?

10. Who was the first presenter of *Grandstand*?

11. Who recently stepped down as the BBC's chief snooker presenter?

12. David Gower and Gary Lineker are the team captains on which show?

13. Who is the BBC's voice of golf?

14. Who used to read the football results on *World of Sport*?

15. Who was ITV's wrestling commentator?

16. Who presents *Football Italia*?

Answers to page 156

TV POT LUCK 4: **1.** Dennis Waterman **2.** Terry Wogan **3.** John Craven **4.** *Exclusive* **5.** *Songs of Praise* **6.** Christopher Biggins **7.** Michael Landon **8.** Jess Yates **9.** *Celebrity Sleepover* **10.** Jilly Goolden **11.** Mary Nightingale **12.** *Civilisation* **13.** *Where There's Life* **14.** Jayne Middlemiss **15.** *DIY SOS* **16.** Tucker Jenkins

Emmerdale 2

Answers on page 157

1. Who had an incestuous relationship with his sister?
2. Which Dingle is a chef?
3. What was the name of Zoë Tate's trucker girlfriend?
4. Which member of the Glover family went loopy?
5. Which computer whizz-kid was Sarah Sugden's lover?
6. Which character was played first by Katharine Barker and then by Jean Rogers?
7. Who plays Chris Tate?
8. Who ended up in jail after helping Kim Marchant kidnap a horse?
9. In which country did Nick Bates's daughter Alice go to live?
10. By what mode of transport did Kim Marchant flee Emmerdale?
11. Who did Jacqueline Pirie play in *Emmerdale*?
12. What was the name of Terry Woods's wife?
13. Which *Woolpack* landlord was a correspondent for the *Hotten Courier*?
14. What post did Donald Hinton once occupy in the village?
15. Which Dingle was killed in a minibus crash?
16. Who rejected Alan Turner in favour of Jack Sugden?

Answers to page 157

COP SHOWS 2: **1.** Nash Bridges **2.** *Liverpool One* **3.** Paul Usher **4.** Dr Grayling Russell **5.** Captain C.Z. Stern **6.** Jesus Martinez **7.** Judd Hirsch **8.** The Texas Rangers **9.** Theo Kojak **10.** *Colonel March of Scotland Yard* **11.** *Jonathan Creek* **12.** Jean **13.** J.L. McCabe in *Jake and the Fatman* **14.** Blackett **15.** Gordon Clapp **16.** 19th

Comedy 4

Answers on page 162

1. What is Geraldine Granger better known as?
2. Who were the first American sitcom couple allowed to be seen regularly sharing a bed?
3. The 'Dagenham Dialogues' were a regular feature of which Sixties series?
4. Which company did Nellie and Eli inherit in *Nearest and Dearest*?
5. With whom was 'Hotlips' Houlihan conducting a discreet affair in *M*A*S*H*?
6. Which Seventies sitcom starred Derek Nimmo and Rosemary Leach as Chris and Katy Bunting?
7. Who plays Linda La Hughes in *Gimme Gimme Gimme*?
8. Which ex-Modern Romance singer wrote *Babes in the Wood*?
9. Which two shows were spin-offs from *Man About the House*?
10. Which soldier used the phrase 'It ain't half hot mum' in letters home?
11. What was Daisy Jackson's job in *Foxy Lady*?
12. What is the name of *Frasier*'s son?
13. Which residential establishment does Harry Springer run?
14. In *The Simpsons*, which pillar of the community was shot in 2000?
15. Who played the brothers in *Sink or Swim*?
16. In *Ripping Yarns*, how did a British expedition cross the Andes?

Answers to page 162

WHICH YEAR IN TV? 3: **1.** 1978 **2.** 1984 **3.** 1970 **4.** 1964 **5.** 1988 **6.** 1956 **7.** 1995 **8.** 1982 **9.** 1973 **10.** 1965 **11.** 1950 **12.** 1962 **13.** 1983 **14.** 1979 **15.** 1994 **16.** 1982

Catchphrases 2

Answers on page 163

1. On which show do contestants say: 'Tonight, Matthew, I'm going to be...'?
2. Which dim couple used to say: 'Ooh, Ron.' 'Ooh, Eth'?
3. Whose favourite expletive is 'My arse!'?
4. Whose catchphrase was: 'Don't embawass me'?
5. Who said: 'Let's meet the eight who are going to generate'?
6. What was Victor Meldrew's catchphrase?
7. Who used to enthuse: 'Goody, goody gumdrops'?
8. Who would tell his partner: 'Get out of that'?
9. Who tells us: 'Don't have nightmares'?
10. Who habitually referred to his son-in-law as a 'randy Scouse git'?
11. Who would scream at the start of a motor race: 'It's go, go, go!'?
12. In which sitcom was the cry regularly heard: 'Everybody Out!'?
13. Which caring mother told her kids: 'Go play with the traffic'?
14. Who referred to his father as 'You dirty old man'?
15. Who used to stutter: 'Gr-Gr-Granville'?
16. Who frequently despaired of his brother: 'You plonker!'?

Answers to page 163

DRAMAS 4: **1.** *Moody and Pegg* **2.** Preston **3.** *Jesus of Nazareth* (Olivia Hussey and Robert Powell) **4.** The Channel Islands **5.** *Kavanagh Q.C.* **6.** *The Irish RM* **7.** *Badger* **8.** Suzi Kettles **9.** Novelist **10.** *Playing the Field* **11.** THRUSH **12.** John Hurt **13.** Hazel **14.** Richard **15.** *Making Out* **16.** Dennis Potter

Which Year in TV? 3

Answers on page 160

In which year did the following programmes begin in the UK?

1. *Rumpole of the Bailey*
2. *'Allo, 'Allo*
3. *The Goodies*
4. *Crossroads*
5. *Red Dwarf*
6. *Opportunity Knocks*
7. *Friends*
8. *The Tube*
9. *Are You Being Served?*
10. *Thunderbirds*
11. *Andy Pandy*
12. *The Saint*
13. *Treasure Hunt*
14. *To the Manor Born*
15. *The Vicar of Dibley*
16. *Countdown*

Answers to page 160

COMEDY 4: **1.** *The Vicar of Dibley* **2.** Herman and Lily Munster **3.** *Not Only...But Also* **4.** Pledge's Purer Pickles **5.** Frank Burns **6.** *Life Begins at Forty* **7.** Kathy Burke **8.** Geoff Deane **9.** *George and Mildred* and *Robin's Nest* **10.** Gunner Parkins **11.** Newspaper editor **12.** Frederick **13.** *Heartbreak Hotel* **14.** Mr Burns **15.** Peter Davison and Robert Glenister **16.** By frog

Dramas 4

Answers on page 161

1. Which 1974 comedy/drama starred Derek Waring and Judy Cornwell?
2. On which front was it all quiet in Tim Firth's territorial army series?
3. In which production was the Virgin Mary nine years younger than Jesus, her son?
4. Which islands were the setting for the Second World War series *Enemy at the Door*?
5. Which series features Jeremy Aldermarten and Peter Foxcot?
6. Played by Peter Bowles, what did Major Sinclair Yeates leave England to become?
7. Which conservation drama starred Jerome Flynn as Tom McCabe?
8. In *Tutti Frutti*, who was Danny McGlone's old flame?
9. What was Mary Fisher's career in *The Life and Loves of a She-Devil*?
10. Which series is centred around a women's football team?
11. Which organisation was the sworn enemy of UNCLE?
12. Who played Caligula in *I, Claudius*?
13. What was the name of *Budgie*'s girlfriend?
14. What was *Crane*'s first name in the 1960s adventure series?
15. Which 1989 comedy/drama series starring Margi Clarke was set at Lyne Electronics?
16. Who wrote *The Singing Detective*?

Answers to page 161

CATCHPHRASES 2: **1.** *Stars in Their Eyes* **2.** *The Glums* **3.** Jim Royle **4.** Lenny the Lion **5.** Bruce Forsyth (on *The Generation Game*) **6.** 'I don't believe it!' **7.** Humphrey Lestocq **8.** Eric Morecambe **9.** Nick Ross **10.** Alf Garnett **11.** Murray Walker **12.** *The Rag Trade* **13.** *Roseanne* **14.** Harold Steptoe **15.** Arkwright **16.** Del Boy

Name Changes 3

Answers on page 166

1. Which Eighties band changed their name from Caviar?

2. Which rap artist was born Tracy Marrow?

3. Which band were previously called Kippington Lodge?

4. Which punk rocker started life as William Broad?

5. What were Idle Race once known as?

6. Which guitar legend was born Brian Rankin?

7. Which band were formerly known as The Spectres?

8. Caesar and Cleo found fame as which duo?

9. Which band changed their name from The New Yardbirds?

10. Who came up with a better name than The Golliwogs?

11. Which Liverpool group were originally known as The Mavericks?

12. Which famous half of a comedy duo was christened Norvell?

13. Which Sixties girl band used to be called The Primettes?

14. Which band started out as Angel and The Snakes?

15. To what did The New Journeymen change their name in the Sixties?

16. Which girl band sensibly decided to dispense with their name of The Bangs?

Answers to page 166

CHRISTMAS HITS 1: **1.** 'Christmas Alphabet' **2.** Dickie Valentine **3.** Greg Lake **4.** 'Long Haired Lover From Liverpool' **5.** The Goodies **6.** 1973 **7.** Twiggy **8.** 'Lonely This Christmas' **9.** 4 **10.** 'Bohemian Rhapsody' **11.** The Flying Pickets ('Only You') **12.** Shakin' Stevens **13.** 'Earth Song' **14.** 'Mull Of Kintyre' **15.** Johnny Mathis **16.** Johnny Hammer

Eighties 1

Answers on page 167

1. Which chart-topping duo were the Appleby sisters better known as?
2. Which was the biggest-selling UK single of 1984?
3. Which three posthumous UK number one hits did John Lennon have?
4. Who wrote 'Chain Reaction' for Diana Ross?
5. Which was the first R.E.M. single to chart in the UK?
6. Who produced Feargal Sharkey's 'A Good Heart'?
7. Which 1981 chart topper was a cover version of a 1954 Rosemary Clooney hit?
8. Which duo with a combined age of 80 reached number one in the UK charts in September 1985 with a cover version of a Sixties classic?
9. Who sang lead vocal on The Cars' 'Drive'?
10. Who won Best British Group at the 1983 Brit Awards?
11. Which re-release that featured in a TV commercial for Miller Lite lager gave The Hollies an unexpected number one in 1988?
12. What was Depeche Mode's first UK top ten hit?
13. What nationality were a-ha?
14. Which ex-Clash member fronted Big Audio Dynamite?
15. Who had a 1987 hit with a cover of Bread's 'Everything I Own'?
16. Which 1989 hit was Cliff Richard's 100th single?

Answers to page 167

FILM TRACKS 2: **1.** 'When You Say Nothing At All' **2.** *The Full Monty* **3.** 'Turn Back Time' **4.** *Dirty Dancing* **5.** Diana King **6.** *Top Gun* **7.** *When Harry Met Sally* **8.** The Foundations **9.** *Up Close and Personal* **10.** Christopher Cross **11.** *Pulp Fiction* **12.** Boy Meets Girl **13.** 'Unchained Melody' **14.** *Godzilla* **15.** *Mermaids* **16.** The Cardigans

Christmas Hits 1

Answers on page 164

1. Which 1955 song was the first record made specifically for the Christmas market to reach number one in the UK charts?
2. And who sang it?
3. Who reached number two in 1975 with 'I Believe In Father Christmas'?
4. What was the 1972 Christmas number one?
5. Who released 'Father Christmas Do Not Touch Me' in 1974?
6. In which year was 'Merry Xmas Everybody' a monster hit for Slade?
7. Which former model originally recorded Cliff Richard's 'Mistletoe And Wine'?
8. What was Mud's Christmas offering for 1974?
9. What number did Wizzard's 'I Wish It Could Be Christmas Everyday' reach in the UK charts in 1973?
10. Which song was the UK Christmas number one in both 1975 and 1991?
11. Red Stripe was a member of which band that had the 1983 Christmas number one?
12. Which artist formerly known as Michael Barrett enjoyed a 1985 yuletide chart topper, 'Merry Christmas Everyone'?
13. What was the 1995 UK Christmas number one?
14. Which Christmas number one was composed out of a perceived need to give Scotland a contemporary anthem?
15. Who had a 1976 Christmas hit with 'When A Child Is Born'?
16. According to Scaffold's 1968 Christmas number one, 'Lily The Pink', who had a terrible s-s-s-s-stammer?

Answers to page 164

NAME CHANGES 3: **1.** Bros **2.** Ice-T **3.** Brinsley Schwarz **4.** Billy Idol **5.** The Nightriders **6.** Hank Marvin **7.** Status Quo **8.** Sonny and Cher **9.** Led Zeppelin **10.** Creedence Clearwater Revival **11.** The Merseybeats **12.** Oliver Hardy **13.** The Supremes **14.** Blondie **15.** The Mamas and The Papas **16.** The Bangles

Film Tracks 2

Answers on page 165

1. Which Ronan Keating song was used in the 1999 film *Notting Hill*?
2. Which film featured 'You Sexy Thing' by Hot Chocolate?
3. Which Aqua hit was heard in the 1998 film *Sliding Doors*?
4. Which film featured '(I've Had) The Time Of My Life' by Bill Medley and Jennifer Warnes?
5. Who performed 'I Say A Little Prayer' for *My Best Friend's Wedding*?
6. Berlin's 'Take My Breath Away' came from which Tom Cruise film?
7. 'It Had To Be You' by Harry Connick Jnr featured in which Meg Ryan film?
8. Which Sixties band recorded 'Build Me Up Buttercup' which was used in the 1998 comedy *There's Something About Mary* starring Cameron Diaz?
9. Which film featured Celine Dion's 'Because You Loved Me'?
10. Who sang 'Arthur's Theme (Best That You Can Do)' from the 1981 film *Arthur*?
11. 'Son Of A Preacher Man' by Dusty Springfield was used in which film directed by Quentin Tarantino?
12. Who performed 'Waiting For A Star To Fall' from the film *Three Men and a Little Lady*?
13. Which song by The Righteous Brothers was used in the 1990 film *Ghost*?
14. 'Deeper Underground' by Jamiroquai featured in which 1998 film?
15. Cher's 'The Shoop Shoop Song (It's In His Kiss)' was used in which film?
16. Who performed 'Lovefool' in *Romeo and Juliet*, starring Leonardo DiCaprio?

Answers to page 165

EIGHTIES 1: **1.** Mel and Kim **2.** 'Do They Know It's Christmas'? **3.** '(Just Like) Starting Over', 'Imagine' and 'Woman' **4.** The Bee Gees **5.** 'The One I Love' **6.** Dave Stewart **7.** 'This Ole House' (Shakin' Stevens) **8.** David Bowie and Mick Jagger ('Dancing In The Street') **9.** Benjamin Orr **10.** Dire Straits **11.** 'He Ain't Heavy, He's My Brother' **12.** 'Just Can't Get Enough' **13.** Norwegian **14.** Mick Jones **15.** Boy George **16.** 'The Best Of Me'

Albums 2

Answers on page 170

1. Which track from Dire Straits' 'Brothers In Arms' featured vocals by Sting?
2. Which was the biggest-selling UK album of 1992?
3. Whose best-selling album was titled 'The Lexicon Of Love'?
4. Who released the album 'Arrival' in 1976?
5. Which former husband of Kirsty MacColl produced U2's debut album, 'Boy'?
6. Whose albums have included 'The Lion And The Cobra' and 'Universal Mother'?
7. Which Phil Collins album was the UK best-seller of 1990?
8. Which was the first Led Zeppelin album to be given a proper title instead of merely a number?
9. What was the title of Elton John's second album?
10. In 1996, which album had the shortest title ever to top the UK chart?
11. Which was Roxy Music's first UK number one album?
12. Who were in 'Cloudcuckooland' in 1990?
13. Which band's albums have included 'Black Sea', 'English Settlement' and 'Mummer'?
14. Whose debut album in 1987 was titled 'Raintown'?
15. Which album spent a total of 303 weeks in the UK album charts from 1970?
16. What was Rod Stewart's first UK number one album?

Answers to page 170

SOLO ARTISTS 1: **1.** 'Dizzy' **2.** Maria Muldaur **3.** Chris Rea **4.** 'Reach Out And Touch (Somebody's Hand)' **5.** Dusty Springfield **6.** 1979 **7.** Kylie Minogue **8.** Chaka Khan **9.** Robert **10.** Toni Braxton **11.** Neil Sedaka **12.** His then girlfriend, Christie Brinkley **13.** Because he is related to Herman Melville, author of *Moby Dick* **14.** David Essex **15.** Peter Frampton ('Frampton Comes Alive') **16.** 'An Englishman In New York'

Music Pot Luck 6

Answers on page 171

1. What was significant about The Johnston Brothers' 1955 number one 'Hernando's Hideaway'?

2. Which Annie Lennox number was the first hit single in the CD age not to be available on vinyl?

3. Which 1972 Paul McCartney track was banned by the BBC for being too political?

4. Which Eighties band were named after Mr Spock's Vulcan friend in *Star Trek*?

5. Who was the female member of New Order?

6. What is Seal's full name?

7. Which film track kept Squeeze's 'Cool For Cats' from number one in 1979?

8. Steve Winwood, Dave Mason, Chris Wood and Jim Capaldi were the original line-up for which Sixties band?

9. As a 15-year-old, which musical giant was jailed for three months in 1960 for stealing 300 tyres from a Los Angeles car dealer?

10. Which female rocker left school in Detroit in 1964 and formed The Pleasure Seekers with her three sisters?

11. Who played harmonica and guitar on Bill Wyman's album 'Stone Alone'?

12. How many Red Balloons did Nena have?

13. Who duetted with Paul McCartney on the 1982 hit 'The Girl Is Mine'?

14. With which band did Midge Ure have his first UK number one?

15. Which Jamaican group reached the charts with 'Black And White' in 1971?

16. Where was Roger Whittaker leaving in 1969?

Answers to page 171

EUROVISION 1: **1.** 'La La La' (1968) **2.** Spain **3.** The Allisons **4.** Nicki French **5.** Co-Co **6.** 1969 **7.** Sweden **8.** 1997 **9.** 'Love Games' **10.** 1956 **11.** 'Knock Knock Who's There' **12.** Johnny Logan **13.** 13 **14.** The construction of a hydro-electric power station **15.** He received *nul points* for Norway in 1978 with 'Mil Etter Mil' **16.** Gina G

Solo Artists 1

Answers on page 168

1. Which song links Tommy Roe with Vic Reeves?

2. Who spent 'Midnight At The Oasis' in 1974?

3. Which Middlesbrough-born artist saved up to buy his first guitar by working in his family's ice-cream parlour?

4. Which was Diana Ross's debut solo single?

5. Which British girl singer was deported from South Africa in December 1964 for singing to a multi-racial audience at a cinema near Cape Town?

6. In which year did Joe Jackson record 'Is She Really Going Out With Him'?

7. Which singer once played Charlotte Kernow in the TV series *The Hendersons*?

8. What did Yvette Stevens change her name to?

9. What does the R. stand for in R. Kelly?

10. Who reached number two in the UK charts in 1994 with 'Breathe Again'?

11. Which singer/songwriter contributed the whistling to the 1957 Pat Boone hit 'Love Letters In The Sand'?

12. About whom did Billy Joel write 'Uptown Girl'?

13. Why did Richard Melville Hall decide to call himself Moby?

14. Whose 1975 album was called 'All The Fun Of The Fair'?

15. Whose is the biggest-selling live album of all time?

16. Which Sting single was written about Quentin Crisp?

Answers to page 168

ALBUMS 2: **1.** 'Money For Nothing' **2.** 'Stars' by Simply Red **3.** ABC **4.** Abba **5.** Steve Lillywhite **6.** Sinead O'Connor **7.** '...But Seriously' **8.** 'Houses Of The Holy' **9.** 'Elton John' **10.** 'K' by Kula Shaker **11.** 'Stranded' **12.** Lightning Seeds **13.** XTC **14.** Deacon Blue **15.** 'Bridge Over Troubled Water' (Simon and Garfunkel) **16.** 'Every Picture Tells A Story'

Eurovision 1

Answers on page 169

1. Which Eurovision Song Contest winner had no fewer than 138 la's?
2. And which country was responsible for it?
3. Which male duo came second for the UK in the 1961 contest with 'Are You Sure'?
4. 'Don't Play That Song Again' prophetically came a lowly 16th for the UK in 2000 for which singer?
5. With which group had Cheryl Baker of Bucks Fizz previously represented the UK in the Eurovision?
6. Which year's contest ended in a four-way tie?
7. Which country won in 1984 with 'Diggy Loo Diggy Ley'?
8. In which year were Katrina and The Waves triumphant with 'Love Shine A Light'?
9. Which 1984 UK entry by Belle and The Devotions was booed after newspaper stories in Holland claimed the song was similar to an old Supremes number?
10. In which year was the first Eurovision Song Contest?
11. With which song did Mary Hopkin come second in 1970?
12. Who was the first singer to win the Eurovision twice?
13. How old was Belgium's 1986 Eurovision winner, Sandra Kim?
14. What was the subject of Norway's 1980 entry?
15. What is Jahn Teigen's claim to Eurovision fame?
16. Who came eighth for the UK in 1996 with 'Ooh Aah…Just A Little Bit'?

Answers to page 169

MUSIC POT LUCK 6: **1.** They were the first set of unrelated brothers to top the UK chart **2.** 'Cold' **3.** 'Give Ireland Back To The Irish' **4.** T'Pau **5.** Gillian Gilbert **6.** Sealhenry Samuel **7.** 'Bright Eyes' (Art Garfunkel) **8.** Traffic **9.** Barry White **10.** Suzi Quatro **11.** Van Morrison **12.** 99 **13.** Michael Jackson **14.** Slik **15.** Greyhound **16.** 'Durham Town'

Rolling Stones 1

Answers on page 174

1. Which number did the Stones perform on the very first edition of *Top of the Pops*?
2. Charlie Watts's book, 'Ode To A High Flying Bird', was a tribute to which jazz great?
3. Which Stones single of 1963 had previously been recorded by The Beatles?
4. Which was the only Stones number one on which Mick Taylor played?
5. On which Stones double A-side did Lennon and McCartney provide backing vocals?
6. Which was the first number one to be written by Jagger and Richard?
7. Who designed the sleeve of 'Sticky Fingers'?
8. Which live album was recorded at New York's Madison Square Garden in November 1969?
9. What was the B-side to 'Honky Tonk Women'?
10. Who was the first Stone to release a solo album?
11. Which was the Stones' last top ten UK single?
12. On which Stones track was Jagger portrayed as the Boston Strangler?
13. Which Stone was once part of a school choir that sang Handel's *Messiah* at Westminster Abbey in the presence of the Queen?
14. In which year did 'Get Off of My Cloud' reach number one in the UK?
15. Who joined Jagger on stage in Tokyo in March 1988, duetting with him on 'Brown Sugar' and 'It's Only Rock 'n' Roll'?
16. Which Stone accidentally set himself on fire after falling asleep in his room at the Londonderry House Hotel, Hyde Park, in 1973?

Answers to page 174

SEVENTIES 2: **1.** Clodagh Rodgers **2.** C.W. McCall **3.** Gloria Gaynor **4.** The Pretenders **5.** Status Quo **6.** Gerry Monroe **7.** Guys and Dolls **8.** Don Williams **9.** Sham 69 **10.** Demis Roussos **11.** Isley Brothers **12.** Dr Hook **13.** Jethro Tull **14.** Peter Gabriel **15.** Three Degrees **16.** John Paul Young

Classical Gas 1

Answers on page 175

1. In which German city was Beethoven born?
2. Who wrote *The Barber of Seville*?
3. What nationality was Haydn?
4. How old was Mozart when he died?
5. Who composed the 'Brandenburg Concertos'?
6. Which Puccini opera of 1926 was never finished?
7. What nationality was Sibelius?
8. Who composed 'A German Requiem'?
9. In which year did Tchaikovsky compose *The Nutcracker*?
10. At what age did Chopin make his debut as a pianist?
11. Which German composer claimed that his best ideas came from two imaginary companions, Florestan and Eusebius?
12. Which composer was paid an annual allowance by wealthy widow Nadezhda von Meck on condition that they never met?
13. What was Debussy's Christian name?
14. Who wrote the music for *The Firebird*?
15. Who composed *Tales From The Vienna Woods*?
16. Which composer died at Bayreuth in Germany in 1886?

Answers to page 175

MUSIC POT LUCK 7: **1.** Joe Cocker **2.** 'Memory' **3.** Shirley Manson **4.** 'Spirit In The Sky' (Norman Greenbaum and Dr and The Medics) **5.** The Gap Band **6.** Whigfield **7.** 'Saturday Night' **8.** 'Just What I Always Wanted' **9.** 'Enola Gay' (Orchestral Manoeuvres In The Dark) **10.** Cher **11.** Patrick Macnee and Honor Blackman ('Kinky Boots') **12.** 'Call Me' **13.** 'Hey Child' **14.** David Bowie **15.** Mel Smith and Kim Wilde **16.** Manic Street Preachers

Seventies 2

Answers on page 172

Which artists had hits with the following tracks in the Seventies?

1. 'Jack In The Box' (1971)
2. 'Convoy' (1976)
3. 'Never Can Say Goodbye' (1974)
4. 'Stop Your Sobbing' (1979)
5. 'Mystery Song' (1976)
6. 'Sally' (1970)
7. 'There's A Whole Lot Of Loving' (1975)
8. 'I Recall A Gypsy Woman' (1976)
9. 'If The Kids Are United' (1978)
10. 'Happy To Be On An Island In The Sun' (1975)
11. 'Harvest For The World' (1976)
12. 'Sylvia's Mother' (1972)
13. 'The Witch's Promise' (1970)
14. 'Solsbury Hill' (1977)
15. 'Take Good Care Of Yourself' (1975)
16. 'Love Is In The Air' (1978)

Answers to page 172

ROLLING STONES 1: **1.** 'I Wanna Be Your Man' **2.** Charlie Parker **3.** 'I Wanna Be Your Man' **4.** 'Honky Tonk Women' **5.** 'We Love You'/ 'Dandelion' **6.** 'The Last Time' **7.** Andy Warhol **8.** 'Get Yer Ya-Ya's Out' **9.** 'You Can't Always Get What You Want' **10.** Bill Wyman **11.** 'Start Me Up' **12.** 'Midnight Rambler' **13.** Keith Richards **14.** 1965 **15.** Tina Turner **16.** Keith Richards

Music Pot Luck 7

Answers on page 173

1. Which singer worked as an apprentice fitter with the East Midlands Gas Board in Sheffield in 1960?
2. Which song from the musical *Cats* gave Elaine Paige a UK top ten hit in 1981?
3. Who once said that the Spice Girls should be 'tarred and feathered'?
4. Which song was a UK number one hit for different artists in 1970 and 1986?
5. Which Eighties band took their name from the initials of three streets in their home town of Tulsa, Oklahoma?
6. Who was the first new artist to go straight in at number one on the UK singles chart?
7. And what was the title of the song?
8. Which was Mari Wilson's most successful single?
9. Which 1980 hit was named after the plane that dropped the atomic bomb on Hiroshima?
10. Which female singer did uncredited vocals on Meat Loaf's 'Dead Ringer For Love'?
11. Which duo's combined age totalled 132 when they charted in 1990?
12. Which Blondie hit was taken from the film *An American Gigolo*?
13. Which East 17 single was written for Tony Mortimer's daughters Atlanta and Ocean?
14. Who did backing vocals on Mott The Hoople's 'All The Young Dudes'?
15. Who were Mel and Kim for Comic Relief in 1987?
16. Whose 1992 album was called 'Generation Terrorists'?

Answers to page 173

CLASSICAL GAS 1: **1.** Bonn **2.** Rossini **3.** Austrian **4.** 35 **5.** Bach **6.** *Turandot* **7.** Finnish **8.** Brahms **9.** 1892 **10.** Eight **11.** Schumann **12.** Tchaikovsky **13.** Claude **14.** Stravinsky **15.** Johann Strauss the Younger **16.** Liszt

Backstreet Boys 1

Answers on page 178

1. Who was the oldest member of Backstreet Boys?
2. What was the title of the band's first UK number one single?
3. What was the first single released off the 'Black And Blue' album?
4. Which two members are cousins?
5. What is A.J.'s full name?
6. Which member used to be a ventriloquist?
7. In which state was Nick Carter born?
8. Who has a younger brother called Aaron?
9. Which band member helped to write 'Larger Than Life'?
10. In which year did Backstreet Boys have their first UK top ten hit?
11. And what was the title of the single?
12. What was the title of the band's second album?
13. What was the band's record label?
14. Which Backstreet Boy had a role in *Edward Scissorhands*?
15. What number did 'Millennium' reach in the UK album charts?
16. What was the band's only UK single release of 1998?

Answers to page 178

COUNTRY AND WESTERN 1: **1.** The Scottsville Squirrel Barkers (Chris Hillman and Bernie Leadon) **2.** Earl Scruggs **3.** Mel Tillis **4.** Otis Dewey Whitman Jnr **5.** The First Edition **6.** Jimmie Rodgers **7.** The Mavericks **8.** Mutt Lange **9.** He stuck pins in a map and paired a town in Arkansas with one in Texas **10.** Bill Monroe **11.** Hank Mizell **12.** Emmylou Harris **13.** 'I Can't Help It If I'm Still in Love With You' **14.** Merle Haggard **15.** The Flying Burrito Brothers **16.** Patsy Cline

Duos 1

Answers on page 179

1. On the platform of which English railway station did Paul Simon write 'Homeward Bound'?
2. Daryl Dragon is the male half of which duo?
3. Which Seventies middle-of-the-road duo achieved fame via the TV talent show *Opportunity Knocks*?
4. What was the title of Windsor Davies and Don Estelle's hit album of 1976?
5. Which Beatles cover version was The Carpenters' debut single?
6. What nationality were Nina and Frederick?
7. And which children's favourite did they take to number three in the UK charts in 1960?
8. Who recorded the original version of Soft Cell's 'Tainted Love'?
9. Where did Soft Cell play their first gig?
10. Which duo comprised Alison Moyet and Vince Clarke?
11. Which duo first met when she waited on his table at Pippins restaurant in Hampstead?
12. Which pair won the Best British Group category at the 1989 Brit Awards?
13. What was the title of Daryl Hall and John Oates's first UK top ten single?
14. Which Simon and Garfunkel classic was the first disc played by Capital Radio?
15. Which song kept The Eurythmics' 'Sweet Dreams (Are Made Of This)' off the top of the UK charts in March 1983?
16. Which duo evolved from a Californian group called The Paramours?

Answers to page 179

CHART TOPPERS 2: **1.** Middle Of The Road **2.** 'Kung Fu Fighting' **3.** 'The Power Of Love' (Frankie Goes To Hollywood and Jennifer Rush) **4.** 'Parallel Lines' **5.** Jimmy Nail **6.** 'Killing Me Softly' (The Fugees) **7.** Steve and Muff Winwood **8.** John Leyton ('Johnny Remember Me') **9.** Brotherhood Of Man ('Angelo') **10.** Sweet Sensation **11.** Falco **12.** 'Rock Me Amadeus' **13.** Chrissie Hynde **14.** Herman's Hermits **15.** 'I'm Into Something Good' **16.** Pussycat ('Mississippi')

Country and Western 1

Answers on page 176

1. Which bluegrass band – also known as The Kentucky Mountain Boys – had a future Byrd and a future Eagle among its members?
2. Which country artist recorded the 1972 album 'I Saw The Light With Some Help From My Friends'?
3. Which country singer/songwriter, who penned 'Ruby, Don't Take Your Love To Town', was left with a permanent stutter after contracting malaria at the age of three?
4. What is Slim Whitman's real name?
5. Which group backed Kenny Rogers on his first two UK hits?
6. Who was known as 'The Singing Brakeman'?
7. Raul Malo is the lead singer with which country rock band?
8. To which successful record producer is Shania Twain married?
9. How did Conway Twitty come by his stage name?
10. Who was generally regarded as the 'father of bluegrass music'?
11. Who had a 1976 UK hit with 'Jungle Rock' – 19 years after the track was recorded?
12. Whose debut album was 'Gliding Bird'?
13. Which 'Heart Like A Wheel' track won Linda Ronstadt a Grammy Award for Best Female Country Vocal?
14. Who did President Nixon say was his favourite country singer?
15. Ex-Byrds Gram Parsons and Chris Hillman were instrumental in forming which country rock band in 1968?
16. Which country star was born Virginia Patterson Hensley?

Answers to page 176

BACKSTREET BOYS 1: **1.** Kevin Richardson **2.** 'I Want It That Way' **3.** 'Shape Of My Heart' **4.** Brian and Kevin **5.** Alexander James McLean **6.** A.J. **7.** New York State **8.** Nick **9.** Brian Littrell **10.** 1996 **11.** 'We've Got It Goin' On' **12.** 'Backstreet's Back' **13.** Jive **14.** Nick Carter **15.** 2 **16.** 'All I Have To Give'

Chart Toppers 2

Answers on page 177

1. Sally Carr was lead singer with which 1971 UK chart toppers?
2. Which 1974 hit about martial arts was recorded in ten minutes and went on to sell 10 million copies worldwide?
3. Which title made UK number one twice in the space of a year in the mid-Eighties, but with completely different songs?
4. From which Blondie album was the 1979 hit 'Sunday Girl' taken?
5. Which actor/singer reached number one in July 1992 with 'Ain't No Doubt'?
6. Which cover of a Roberta Flack song became the biggest-selling single of 1996?
7. Which two brothers were members of The Spencer Davis Group?
8. Which 1961 UK chart topper was best known for playing Biggles on TV?
9. Who took a sad song about a Mexican shepherd boy to the top of the UK charts in 1977?
10. Which *New Faces* winners had a 1974 number one with 'Sad Sweet Dreamer'?
11. Which 1986 chart topper was born in Vienna as Johann Holzel?
12. And with which song about a famous composer did he taste fame?
13. Who was guest vocalist on UB40's 'I Got You Babe'?
14. Which Manchester-based Sixties group had one number one in the UK but two in America?
15. And what was their British success?
16. Which were the first Dutch group to have a UK number one?

Answers to page 177

DUOS 1: **1.** Widnes **2.** Captain and Tennille **3.** Peters and Lee **4.** 'Sing Lofty' **5.** 'Ticket To Ride' **6.** Danish **7.** 'Little Donkey' **8.** Gloria Jones **9.** Leeds Polytechnic **10.** Yazoo **11.** The Eurythmics (Annie Lennox and Dave Stewart) **12.** Erasure **13.** 'I Can't Go For That (No Can Do)' **14.** 'Bridge Over Troubled Water' **15.** 'Total Eclipse Of The Heart' (Bonnie Tyler) **16.** The Righteous Brothers

Reggae 1

Answers on page 182

1. Which reggae artist, who charted in 1986 with 'Hello Darling', also teamed up with Arsenal FC for their 1993 Cup Final song?
2. With which song did Desmond Dekker get to number two in the UK in 1970?
3. Frederick 'Toots' Hibbert was leader of which band?
4. What does Everton Brown prefer to call himself?
5. Which British reggae band named themselves after the form issued to unemployed people so that they can claim benefit?
6. What was Bob Marley's only UK hit of 1983?
7. Why were Alex Hughes's records never heard on radio?
8. Who had a 1974 hit with his version of 'Help Me Make It Through The Night'?
9. Who topped the UK charts in 1974 with a cover of a Bread song?
10. Which Bob Marley track reached number five in the UK in 1992?
11. Who had a 1979 hit with 'Reggae For It Now'?
12. Which infamous Max Romeo track managed to reach the UK top ten despite a total radio ban?
13. Who is Orville Richard Burrell better known as?
14. Who sang about 'Ram Goat Liver' in 1976?
15. Which reggae band reached number five in the UK singles chart in 1969 with 'Return Of Django'?
16. With which song did Shaggy top the charts in 1993?

Answers to page 182

MADONNA 1: **1.** The Breakfast Club **2.** 'Into The Groove' **3.** 'Crazy For You' and 'Gambler' **4.** 'The Virgin Tour' **5.** Bette Midler **6.** 1987 **7.** Michael Jackson **8.** 1991 **9.** 'Frozen' **10.** 'Erotica' **11.** 'Bedtime Story' **12.** *Top of the Pops* **13.** Gothenburg **14.** 'True Blue' **15.** Babyface **16.** 'Like A Prayer'

Sixties 2

Answers on page 183

1. Which band did Peter Frampton join as a 16-year-old?
2. In which year were Fleetwood Mac formed?
3. Who had a hit with the ethereal 'Kites'?
4. What was The Move's first single?
5. Which supergroup started out in the Sixties as The Architectural Abdabs?
6. Which Troggs single was banned in Australia on account of its suggestive lyrics?
7. What was Screaming Lord Sutch's backing band?
8. Which Monkees hit was originally called 'Randy Scouse Git'?
9. Which Dusty Springfield song was the first-ever to be played on *Top of the Pops*?
10. Who played piano on The Hollies' 1969 hit 'He Ain't Heavy...He's My Brother'?
11. Whose hits included 'I Love My Dog' and 'I'm Gonna Get Me A Gun'?
12. Who had a 1968 hit with 'Everything I Am'?
13. What did Brian Poole become for a while after splitting from The Tremeloes?
14. Which group changed their name from Bag Of Blues?
15. Who was the driving force behind Family Dogg?
16. Which Australian band of the Sixties, who had a hit with 'Friday On My Mind', were the forerunners of AC/DC?

Answers to page 183

LYRICS 2: **1.** 'Maneater' (Hall and Oates) **2.** 'The Air That I Breathe' (The Hollies) **3.** 'Rave On' (Buddy Holly) **4.** 'Against All Odds (Take A Look At Me Now)' (Phil Collins) **5.** 'Dancing Girls' (Nik Kershaw) **6.** 'Everything I Do (I Do It For You)' (Bryan Adams) **7.** 'Delilah' (Tom Jones) **8.** 'From Me To You' (The Beatles) **9.** 'Can't Stand Losing You' (The Police) **10.** 'Invisible Touch' (Genesis) **11.** 'Country House' (Blur) **12.** 'Song For Whoever' (The Beautiful South) **13.** 'Heart Of Glass' (Blondie) **14.** 'Peaceful Easy Feeling' (The Eagles) **15.** 'Summer Holiday' (Cliff Richard) **16.** 'I Can't Control Myself' (The Troggs)

Madonna 1

Answers on page 180

1. Which band did Madonna form with then boyfriend Dan Gilroy?

2. What was Madonna's first UK number one?

3. Which two singles were taken from the film *Vision Quest*?

4. Which tour did Madonna begin in April 1985?

5. Who said that Madonna is 'a woman who pulled herself up by her bra straps'?

6. In which year did Madonna tour Britain for the first time?

7. Who was Madonna's escort for the 1991 Oscars?

8. In which year did *In Bed With Madonna* premiere in London?

9. Which 1998 hit was Madonna's first UK number one for eight years?

10. Which single sampled 'Jungle Boogie' by Kool and The Gang?

11. Which 1995 release ended Madonna's run of 32 consecutive US top forty singles hits?

12. On 2 November 1995 Madonna made her first appearance for 11 years on which show?

13. In which city did Madonna begin the European leg of her 'Blonde Ambition' tour in 1990?

14. What was the title of Madonna's second UK number one album?

15. Who did backing vocals on 'Take A Bow'?

16. Which Madonna video was banned by the Vatican on grounds of blasphemy?

Answers to page 180

REGGAE 1: **1.** Tippa Irie **2.** 'You Can Get It If You Really Want' **3.** The Maytals **4.** Mad Cobra **5.** UB40 **6.** 'Buffalo Soldier' **7.** He was better known as Judge Dread whose singles were banned for being sexually explicit **8.** John Holt **9.** Ken Boothe ('Everything I Own') **10.** 'Iron Lion Zion' **11.** Bill Lovelady **12.** 'Wet Dream' **13.** Shaggy **14.** Pluto Shervington **15.** The Upsetters **16.** 'Oh Carolina'

Lyrics 2

Answers on page 181

From which songs are the following lyrics taken?

1. '(Oh-oh here she comes) Watch out boy, she'll chew you up'
2. 'Peace came upon me and it leaves me weak'
3. 'The way you dance and hold me tight, the way you kiss and say goodnight'
4. 'And there's nothing left here to remind me, just the memory of your face'
5. 'Take off the twilight and the skies so grey'
6. 'You can't tell me it's not worth dying for'
7. 'I saw the flickering shadows of her love on her blind'
8. 'I've got everything that you want, like a heart that is oh-so true'
9. 'I guess you'd call it cowardice, but I'm not prepared to go on like this'
10. 'She reaches in and grabs right hold of your heart'
11. 'I'm paying the price of living life at the limit'
12. 'I love you from the bottom of my pencil case'
13. 'Once I had a love and it was divine'
14. 'I like the way your sparkling earrings lay against your skin, so brown'
15. 'We're going where the sun shines brightly'
16. 'Your slacks are low and your hips are showing'

Answers to page 181

SIXTIES 2: **1.** The Herd **2.** 1967 **3.** Simon Dupree and The Big Sound **4.** 'Night Of Fear' **5.** Pink Floyd **6.** 'I Can't Control Myself' **7.** The Savages **8.** 'Alternate Title' **9.** 'I Only Want To Be With You' **10.** Elton John **11.** Cat Stevens **12.** Plastic Penny **13.** A butcher **14.** Jethro Tull **15.** Steve Rowland **16.** The Easybeats

Managers 3

Answers on page 186

1. Which Frenchman guided Fulham into the Premiership in 2001?
2. Which larger-than-life character had two spells in charge of both Manchester City and Plymouth Argyle?
3. Which former Sunderland and Republic of Ireland centre-half managed Reading in the 1970s?
4. Who was joint manager of Liverpool with Gerard Houllier?
5. Eddie Firmani, Theo Foley and Andy Nelson were all managers of which London club?
6. Which Yorkshire club did George Kirby manage twice in the 1970s?
7. Which club offered Peter Shilton his first chance in management?
8. With which club did Don Revie earn an FA Cup winners' medal as a player?
9. How many managers have Manchester United had since the war?
10. Which two managerial greats both spent just 44 days in charge of Leeds United?
11. Which former Chelsea and England forward was sacked as boss of Doncaster Rovers just 12 days into the 1997–8 season?
12. Who did Alan Ball succeed as boss of Stoke City in 1989?
13. In 1986–7 who had spells in charge of both Manchester City and Aston Villa, two of the teams that were relegated from Division One at the end of that season?
14. Which club did Dario Gradi manage from 1978 to 1981?
15. Who briefly managed Chelsea between Ian Porterfield and Glenn Hoddle?
16. Who was sacked as boss of Bristol Rovers in 2000–1?

Answers to page 186

WHICH YEAR IN FOOTBALL? 2: **1.** 1949 **2.** 1961 **3.** 1928 **4.** 1981 **5.** 1996 **6.** 1950 **7.** 1985 **8.** 1987 **9.** 1991 **10.** 1965 **11.** 1997 **12.** 1960 **13.** 1961 **14.** 1993 **15.** 1968 **16.** 1978

FA Cup 2

Answers on page 187

1. In which year did Walsall create a sensation by knocking Arsenal out of the FA Cup?
2. Who won the Cup in 1987 for the first time in their history?
3. Who scored both West Ham goals when they beat Fulham in the 1975 final?
4. Who was just 18 when he turned out for Manchester United against Brighton in the 1983 Cup final?
5. Which Sussex County League side were Colchester United's first Cup victims in 1970–1, the year they went on to beat Leeds in the fifth round?
6. And who finally brought Colchester's run to an end in the quarter-finals?
7. Which eventual Cup winners did Tooting & Mitcham take to a third-round replay?
8. Who was in goal for Queens Park Rangers in the 1982 final?
9. Who played for different clubs in two finals against Spurs in the 1980s?
10. When was the first all-London FA Cup final?
11. Which non-League club reached the last 16 of the Cup in 1985?
12. Which Southern League team knocked the League champions out of the Cup in 1900?
13. Which club was unable to compete in the 1921–2 competition because they forgot to post the entry forms?
14. Who scored Manchester United's winning goal in the 1990 Cup final replay against Crystal Palace?
15. Who ended Sutton United's 1988–9 Cup run to the tune of 8–0?
16. Who did Newcastle beat in the semi-finals in 1999?

Answers to page 187

RANGERS 1: **1.** Sam English **2.** John Greig **3.** Lazio **4.** Willie Henderson **5.** Alex Ferguson **6.** John Greig **7.** Sunderland **8.** Hearts **9.** Tom Forsyth **10.** Aberdeen **11.** Andrei Kanchelskis **12.** Queen's Park **13.** 1991 **14.** Arbroath **15.** Jimmy Millar **16.** Davie Cooper

Which Year in Football? 2

Answers on page 184

1. When did Leicester City reach their first FA Cup final?
2. When did England beat Scotland 9–3 at Wembley?
3. When were numbered shirts first worn in the Football League?
4. When did Queens Park Rangers become the first British club to install an artificial pitch?
5. When did Arsène Wenger become Arsenal manager?
6. When was the last time that Portsmouth were League champions?
7. When did Aberdeen last win the Scottish title?
8. When did Ian Rush leave Liverpool for Juventus?
9. When did Manchester United win the European Cup-Winners' Cup?
10. When did Charlton's Keith Peacock become the first substitute to be used in a Football League match?
11. When did Middlesbrough lose both the FA Cup final and the Coca-Cola Cup final?
12. When did Alfredo di Stefano score a hat-trick for Real Madrid in the European Cup final against Eintracht Frankfurt?
13. When was the players' maximum wage abolished?
14. When did Arsenal win the FA Cup and the Football League Cup in the same year?
15. When did Dunfermline Athletic last win the Scottish FA Cup?
16. When were Nottingham Forest League champions for the only time?

Answers to page 184

MANAGERS 3: **1.** Jean Tigana **2.** Malcolm Allison **3.** Charlie Hurley **4.** Roy Evans **5.** Charlton Athletic **6.** Halifax Town **7.** Plymouth Argyle **8.** Manchester City **9.** Eight **10.** Brian Clough and Jock Stein **11.** Kerry Dixon **12.** Mick Mills **13.** Billy McNeill **14.** Wimbledon **15.** David Webb **16.** Ian Holloway

Rangers 1

Answers on page 185

1. Which ironically named player holds the record for scoring most League goals in a season for Rangers?
2. Whose tenure as manager at Ibrox was sandwiched between two stints by Jock Wallace?
3. To whom did Rangers pay £4.3 million for Paul Gascoigne in 1995?
4. Which Rangers winger was nicknamed 'Scotland's Garrincha'?
5. Which Rangers striker played his last game for the club in the 1969 Scottish FA Cup final defeat by Celtic after being blamed for one of the goals?
6. Who played 857 games for Rangers between 1961 and 1978?
7. From which English club did Rangers sign Ally McCoist?
8. Who knocked Rangers out of the Scottish FA Cup in 1994–5?
9. Which defender, signed from Motherwell in 1972, played 29 games in domestic competition for Rangers before finishing on the losing side?
10. Who did Rangers beat in the 1953 Scottish FA Cup final after a replay?
11. Who joined Rangers for £5.5 million from Fiorentina in 1998?
12. From which other Glasgow club did Rangers sign Alan Morton in 1920?
13. In which year did Walter Smith become Rangers manager?
14. Who beat Rangers in the 1884–5 Scottish FA Cup, only to have to replay the tie because their pitch was ruled too narrow?
15. Who scored both Rangers goals in the 1960 Scottish FA Cup final victory over Kilmarnock?
16. Which tricky Clydebank winger was signed by Rangers after giving them a torrid time in a 1976–7 Scottish League Cup tie?

Answers to page 185

FA CUP 2: **1.** 1933 **2.** Coventry City **3.** Alan Taylor **4.** Norman Whiteside **5.** Ringmer **6.** Everton **7.** Nottingham Forest (1959) **8.** Peter Hucker **9.** Dave Bennett (for Manchester City in 1981 and for Coventry City in 1987) **10.** 1967 **11.** Telford United **12.** Millwall Athletic (they beat Aston Villa) **13.** Birmingham City **14.** Lee Martin **15.** Norwich City **16.** Spurs

Football League 3

Answers on page 190

1. Who finished runners-up to Tottenham in the 1960–1 First Division table?
2. Which club used to be known as Heaton Norris Rovers?
3. Which current club has played the most Football League games without ever winning a major trophy?
4. Which three teams lost out in the Second Division play-offs at the end of 2000–1?
5. For which club did Reg Jenkins score a record 119 League goals between 1964 and 1973?
6. Which Yorkshire club did Emlyn Hughes manage between 1981 and 1983?
7. Which club joined the League in 1989, only to resign three years later?
8. Which future FA Cup winners lifted the Fourth Division title in 1983?
9. Who were relegated to the Fourth Division for the first time in their history in 1986?
10. Which London club used to play at The Nest?
11. In which year did York City join the Football League?
12. Who finished Second Division runners-up to Fulham in 1998–9?
13. Which club's announcer was sacked at half-time during a match with Bolton in 1995 for criticising the referee?
14. Which club painted the away dressing-room 'sleepy pink' in 1992–3 in the hope of lulling opponents into a state of drowsiness?
15. Who won the Second and First Division titles in successive seasons in 1931 and 1932?
16. Which club used to be known as Belmont FC?

Answers to page 190

WHOSE HOME? 2: **1.** 1991 **2.** The Old Showground **3.** Fulham **4.** Portsmouth **5.** Airdrie **6.** Darwen **7.** 1912 **8.** Darlington **9.** Villa Park **10.** Stranraer **11.** Atletico Madrid **12.** Charlton Athletic **13.** Macclesfield Town **14.** Sao Paulo **15.** Southend United **16.** Bath City

The World Game 4

Answers on page 191

1. Who moved from Juventus to Real Madrid for a world record £48 million in the summer of 2001?
2. Which is Poland's oldest club?
3. In which country are Principat the most successful club side?
4. Who won the Portuguese Cup for the first time in their history in 1998–9 but were relegated in the same season?
5. Who gave up his job as a bank clerk when he was transferred to Bayern Munich in 1974?
6. In which South American city do Vasco da Gama play?
7. Who won the first World Club Championship?
8. Who are the most successful club in Cyprus?
9. Which club lifted the Spanish League title in the closing minutes of the last day of the season for three successive years in the 1990s?
10. In which country did IBV defeat Leiftur in the 1998 Cup final?
11. What is the Stadio Giuseppe Meazza more commonly known as?
12. Who met in the final of the 2000 African Nations Cup?
13. Which team has won more Moldovan League titles than any other?
14. At what age did Diego Maradona makes his international debut for Argentina?
15. Which world figure was enrolled as member No. 108000 at Barcelona?
16. Which club signed Hernan Crespo from Parma for £36 million in July 2000?

Answers to page 191

EARLY BATHS 1: **1.** Graeme Souness **2.** Ray Wilkins **3.** Frank Saul **4.** 21 **5.** Matt Elliott **6.** Hereford United **7.** Dave Higgins **8.** Georghe Hagi **9.** Crewe Alexandra **10.** Justin Edinburgh **11.** Billy Bremner and Kevin Keegan **12.** Dave Wagstaffe (Blackburn Rovers) **13.** Alan Mullery **14.** Kevin Moran **15.** Hristo Stoichkov **16.** Dave Caldwell

Whose Home? 2

Answers on page 188

1. When did Wimbledon play their last game at Plough Lane?
2. Where was Scunthorpe United's home from 1899 to 1988?
3. Which current Premiership side did not install floodlights at their ground until 1962?
4. Who plays at Fratton Park?
5. Which Scottish team used to play at Old Mavisbank?
6. Which former Football League club played at Barley Bank?
7. In which year were the last horse races run at Wrexham's Racecourse Ground?
8. Which current English Third Division club have played at the same ground since 1883?
9. Which Premiership ground was built on the site of a Victorian amusement park?
10. Stair Park is the home of which Scottish club?
11. Which Spanish club plays at Vicente Calderon?
12. Which London club used to play at Siemens Meadow?
13. Whose ground did Chester City share before moving to the Deva Stadium?
14. In which city is the Morumbi Stadium?
15. Who plays at Roots Hall?
16. On which club's ground did Bristol Rovers play home matches between 1986 and 1996?

Answers to page 188

FOOTBALL LEAGUE 3: **1.** Sheffield Wednesday **2.** Stockport County **3.** Crewe Alexandra **4.** Reading, Stoke City and Wigan Athletic **5.** Rochdale **6.** Rotherham United **7.** Maidstone United **8.** Wimbledon **9.** Wolverhampton Wanderers **10.** Crystal Palace **11.** 1929 **12.** Walsall **13.** Swindon Town **14.** Torquay United **15.** Everton **16.** Tranmere Rovers

Early Baths 1

Answers on page 189

1. Who was sent off in his first game as player-manager of Rangers in 1986?
2. Which England player was sent off at the 1986 World Cup?
3. Whose 1965 sending-off made him the first Spurs player to be dismissed in a League game for 37 years?
4. How many times was Scottish bad boy Willie Johnston sent off in his career?
5. Which Scotland player was sent off against the Faroe Islands in 1999?
6. Which club had four players sent off during a Third Division match with Northampton in 1992?
7. Which Tranmere defender was sent off twice at West Bromwich in the space of 12 days in April 1995?
8. Which Romanian international was sent off in the 2000 UEFA Cup final against Arsenal?
9. For which club was goalkeeper Mark Smith playing when he was sent off after 19 seconds of a Third Division game at Darlington in 1994?
10. Which Tottenham player was sent off in the 1999 League Cup final?
11. Which two players were sent off in the 1974 Charity Shield?
12. In 1976 who became the first Football League player to be shown a red card?
13. Who was the first England player to be sent off in a full international?
14. Who was the first player to be sent off in an FA Cup final?
15. Which Barcelona forward was banned for six months in 1990 for stamping on the referee's foot after being sent off?
16. Which Chesterfield and Torquay player was sent off five times in 1987–8?

Answers to page 189

THE WORLD GAME 4: **1.** Zinedine Zidane **2.** Cracovia **3.** Andorra **4.** Beira Mar **5.** Karl Heinz Rummenigge **6.** Rio de Janeiro **7.** Real Madrid **8.** Apoel **9.** Barcelona **10.** Iceland **11.** The San Siro **12.** Nigeria and Cameroon **13.** Zimbru Chisinau **14.** 16 **15.** Pope John Paul II **16.** Lazio

Wales 1

Answers on page 194

1. With which three clubs did Ivor Allchurch win 68 Welsh caps?
2. On which ground did Wales beat Spain 3–0 in a 1985 World Cup qualifier?
3. Against whom did Wales record their record score of 11–0 in 1888?
4. With which club was Dean Saunders a player when he won his first Welsh cap?
5. How many goals did John Toshack score for Wales?
6. Who won the last of his 48 Welsh caps at the age of 45?
7. Who defeated Wales 2–0 at Liverpool in a European Championship qualifier in 1999?
8. Which combative midfield player who began his career with Crystal Palace won 73 Welsh caps from 1979 to 1992?
9. Who thrashed Wales 7–1 in a World Cup qualifier in 1997?
10. Who succeeded Mike Smith as manager of Wales in 1980?
11. Which Jack was an Arsenal and Wales goalkeeper of the 1950s and early 1960s?
12. Malcolm Page won 28 Welsh caps between 1971 and 1979. For which English club did he play during that period?
13. Against which country did Ryan Giggs win his first Welsh cap?
14. And in which year?
15. Which club supplied five of the Welsh team for the inaugural international with Scotland in 1876?
16. With whom did Wales draw 4–4 in a European Championship qualifier in 1982?

Answers to page 194

PREMIERSHIP 3: **1.** Jimmy Floyd Hasselbaink **2.** Crystal Palace **3.** 20th **4.** Three **5.** Eric Cantona **6.** Ten **7.** John Burridge **8.** West Ham United **9.** Iwan Roberts **10.** Queens Park Rangers **11.** Southampton **12.** Coventry City **13.** Crystal Palace and Nottingham Forest **14.** Benito Carbone **15.** David Beckham **16.** Sheffield Wednesday

Nicknames 1

Answers on page 195

1. Who are known as 'The Terriers'?
2. What is Macclesfield Town's nickname?
3. Which team are nicknamed 'The Chairboys'?
4. Which two Lancashire clubs are called 'The Latics'?
5. Which Scottish club are known as 'The Red Lichties'?
6. What are Barry Town called?
7. What is the nickname of Roma?
8. Who are 'The Valiants'?
9. Which London club are popularly known as 'The 'Addicks'?
10. Which Scottish team are called 'The Honest Men'?
11. Which international team's nickname is 'The Azzurri'?
12. Which two English clubs share the nickname 'The Magpies'?
13. What is the nickname of Stenhousemuir?
14. Who are 'The Saddlers'?
15. What is the nickname of Napoli?
16. Which club are known as 'The Eagles'?

Answers to page 195

GOALKEEPERS 3: **1.** Dave Beasant **2.** Austrian **3.** Jim Standen **4.** Kevin Poole **5.** René Higuita **6.** Steve Ogrizovic **7.** Tooting & Mitcham **8.** Estonian **9.** Alexander Morton **10.** Chris Woods **11.** Pat Jennings **12.** Tony Read **13.** Mark Bosnich **14.** Andy Goram **15.** Gordon West **16.** PSV Eindhoven

Premiership 3

Answers on page 192

1. Which Leeds player was joint top scorer in the Premiership in 1998–9?
2. Which London club were relegated to the First Division in 1995?
3. Where did Nottingham Forest finish on their first season back in the Premiership in 1998–9?
4. How many League matches did Manchester United lose in 1999–2000?
5. Who was PFA Player of the Year for 1993–4?
6. By how many points did Manchester United win the title in 1992–3?
7. Who turned out in goal for Manchester City against Newcastle in 1995 even though he was employed at the time as goalkeeping coach to Newcastle?
8. Which London club finished fifth in the Premiership in 1998–9?
9. Who was Leicester's leading scorer in their relegation season of 1994–5?
10. Where did Swindon gain their solitary away win in 1993–4?
11. Who lost 7–2 at White Hart Lane in 1999–2000?
12. Who dropped out of the top flight for the first time since 1967 at the end of 2000–1?
13. Which two teams have been relegated three times from the Premiership?
14. Who was Sheffield Wednesday's top scorer in 1998–9?
15. Which promising Manchester United youngster was sent on loan to Preston North End in 1995 and found himself playing at Exeter on a Tuesday night?
16. Who lost 7–1 at home to Nottingham Forest in April 1995?

Answers to page 192

WALES 1: **1.** Swansea Town, Newcastle United and Cardiff City **2.** Wrexham **3.** Ireland **4.** Brighton & Hove Albion **5.** 12 **6.** Billy Meredith **7.** Denmark **8.** Peter Nicholas **9.** Holland **10.** Mike England **11.** Kelsey **12.** Birmingham City **13.** Germany **14.** 1992 **15.** Druids **16.** Yugoslavia

Goalkeepers 3

Answers on page 193

1. Which goalkeeper was put out of action after dropping a jar of salad cream on his toe?
2. What nationality is Alex Manninger?
3. Who kept goal for West Ham in the 1964 FA Cup final?
4. Which goalkeeper dropped a cut-glass rose bowl...moments after being presented with it as Leicester City's player of the year for 1995–6?
5. Which Colombian keeper pulled off the famous 'scorpion' save at Wembley in 1995?
6. Which goalkeeper played for Coventry at the age of 42 in 1999–2000?
7. With which non-League club did Alex Stepney begin his career?
8. What nationality is Mart Poom?
9. Who was the first goalkeeper to captain England?
10. Which Rangers goalkeeper went 1,196 minutes without conceding a goal in 1986–7?
11. Which Spurs goalkeeper scored with a clearance from his own area in the 1967 Charity Shield?
12. Which Luton Town goalkeeper scored a hat-trick in 1965 after being moved up front because of an injury crisis?
13. Which goalkeeper was fined for appearing to give a Nazi salute at White Hart Lane?
14. Which Hibernian keeper scored with a drop-kick against Morton in 1988?
15. Who kept goal for Everton in the 1966 FA Cup final?
16. From which Dutch club did Tranmere sign John Achterberg?

Answers to page 193

NICKNAMES 1: **1.** Huddersfield Town **2.** 'The Silkmen' **3.** Wycombe Wanderers **4.** Wigan Athletic and Oldham Athletic **5.** Arbroath **6.** 'The Dragons' **7.** I Lupi (The Wolves) **8.** Port Vale **9.** Charlton Athletic **10.** Ayr United **11.** Italy **12.** Newcastle United and Notts County **13.** 'The Warriors' **14.** Walsall **15.** Bluerchiati **16.** Crystal Palace

Transfer Trail 6

Answers on page 198

1. Who moved from Barcelona to Real Madrid for £37.5 million in July 2000?
2. Who paid Southampton £7.25 million for Kevin Davies in June 1998?
3. Which club sold goalkeeper Andy Goram to Rangers in 1991?
4. Which Italian club signed Enrico Chiesa from Parma for £10.2 million in June 1999?
5. Who signed David Healy from Manchester United in 2000–1?
6. From which club did Tottenham sign Justin Edinburgh?
7. From which Scottish club did Liverpool sign Alan Hansen?
8. Which was Chris Bart-Williams's first League club?
9. Who moved from Fiorentina to AC Milan for £24.5 million in July 2001?
10. From which Scottish club did Arsenal sign Ian Ure?
11. Who paid Barcelona £18 million for Ronaldo in 1997?
12. Which Chelsea defender started his professional career with Nantes?
13. Who sold Eoin Jess to Coventry City for £1.75 million in 1996?
14. Which Parma star moved to Juventus for £32 million in 2001?
15. From which club did Derby County sign defender Craig Short for £2.5 million in 1992?
16. Who sold goalkeeper Pat Jennings to Tottenham?

Answers to page 198

LEAGUE CUP 1: **1.** 1961 **2.** Rotherham United **3.** Clive Clark **4.** The Milk Cup **5.** Allan Nielsen **6.** Swindon Town **7.** 1986 **8.** 1993 **9.** Nottingham Forest **10.** Rochdale **11.** George Eastham **12.** Liverpool **13.** Steve Claridge **14.** Birmingham City **15.** 1994 **16.** Ralph Coates

Oddballs 4

Answers on page 199

1. What did Stuart Pearce train as before becoming a professional footballer?
2. Which Third Division team does TV sports presenter John Inverdale support?
3. How many hat-tricks did Geoff Hurst score for England?
4. Snooker player Ronnie O'Sullivan was a young left-winger on the books of which London club?
5. Which football presenter used to play at full-back for Tranmere Rovers Reserves?
6. Which son of a Manchester United player starred as a footballer gone to ruin in the film *Yesterday's Hero*?
7. Which actor named his dog Wagstaff after Hull City legend Ken Wagstaff?
8. Which footballer was known as 'The Black Panther'?
9. Which 1960s soccer star advertised Fore grooming aids for men?
10. Which club has a fanzine called *Load of Bull*?
11. Who used to play at The Cow Pat?
12. Which French keeper was transferred to Sunderland in 1996?
13. Which Scottish club was once known as Excelsior FC?
14. Which club does Jeffrey Archer support?
15. Which two teams featured on the first edition of *Match of the Day*?
16. And what was the score?

Answers to page 199

CHELSEA 1: **1.** Stuttgart **2.** Gianfranco Zola **3.** East Stirlingshire **4.** John Hollins **5.** Peter Osgood **6.** Ian Porterfield, David Webb and Glenn Hoddle **7.** Stockport County **8.** William 'Fatty' Foulke **9.** Leicester City **10.** Manchester City **11.** Six **12.** Slough Town **13.** Ron Harris **14.** Pierluigi Casiraghi **15.** 1911 **16.** Zenith Data Systems Cup

League Cup 1

Answers on page 196

1. In which year was the Football League Cup competition first staged?
2. Which Second Division club reached the final?
3. Which player scored twice but finished on the losing side in the 1967 final?
4. What was the competition called between 1982 and 1986?
5. Who scored Tottenham's winner in the 1999 Worthington Cup final?
6. Which Third Division team shocked Arsenal in the 1969 final?
7. In which year did Oxford United win the competition?
8. When did the competition become known as the Coca-Cola Cup?
9. Which club won the League Cup in 1978 and 1979?
10. Which Fourth Division club reached the 1962 final?
11. Which veteran campaigner scored Stoke City's winner in the 1972 final?
12. Who won the competition for three successive years in the early 1980s?
13. Who was Leicester City's matchwinner in the 1997 final against Middlesbrough?
14. Who reached their first League Cup final for 38 years in 2001?
15. When was Manchester United's last appearance in a League Cup final?
16. Who scored Tottenham's winning goal against Norwich City in the 1973 final?

Answers to page 196

TRANSFER TRAIL 3: **1.** Luis Figo **2.** Blackburn Rovers **3.** Hibernian **4.** Fiorentina **5.** Preston North End **6.** Southend United **7.** Partick Thistle **8.** Leyton Orient **9.** Rui Costa **10.** Dundee **11.** Inter Milan **12.** Marcel Desailly **13.** Aberdeen **14.** Gianluigi Buffon **15.** Notts County **16.** Watford

Chelsea 1

Answers on page 197

1. Who did Chelsea defeat in the 1998 European Cup Winners' Cup final?
2. And who scored the only goal of the game?
3. From which Scottish club did Chelsea sign Eddie McCreadie?
4. Which former Blues player was manager from 1985 to 1988?
5. Which Chelsea forward is the only player to have scored in every round of the FA Cup?
6. Which three Chelsea managers of the 1990s had all scored winning goals in FA Cup finals?
7. Who were Chelsea's first-ever opponents in the Football League?
8. Which legendary Chelsea goalkeeper weighed over 20 stone?
9. Who bought Dennis Wise from Chelsea in the summer of 2001?
10. Who did Chelsea beat in 1986 to become the first winners of the Full Members' Cup?
11. How many times have Chelsea been relegated from the top division of the League?
12. From which non-League club did Chelsea sign Micky Droy?
13. Which Chelsea hard man made 655 League appearances for the club between 1962 and 1980?
14. Which forward moved from Lazio to Stamford Bridge for £5.4 million in May 1998?
15. In which year did Chelsea reach their first FA Cup semi-final?
16. Which trophy did Chelsea win in 1990?

Answers to page 197

ODDBALLS 4: **1.** Electrician **2.** Lincoln City **3.** Two **4.** Tottenham Hotspur **5.** Ray Stubbs **6.** Ian McShane **7.** Tom Courtenay **8.** Eusebio **9.** George Best **10.** Wolverhampton Wanderers **11.** Lincoln City **12.** Lionel Perez **13.** Airdrie **14.** Bristol Rovers **15.** Liverpool and Arsenal **16.** Liverpool 3 Arsenal 2

Managers 4

Answers on page 202

1. Which Tottenham manager pioneered the 'push and run' style?
2. Which manager steered Portsmouth to their two League Championship wins?
3. Which former Dundee manager took the reins at Notts County in 2000?
4. Who succeeded Steve Parkin as Mansfield Town manager in 1999?
5. Who was manager of Exeter City for just seven days in 1953?
6. Who followed Lawrie McMenemy as Sunderland manager?
7. Jimmy Hagan, Alan Ashman and Ronnie Allen have all been managers of which English League club?
8. Who took over from Liam Brady as manager of Celtic?
9. Alan Buckley became manager of which club in spring 2001?
10. Who guided Nottingham Forest to their FA Cup triumph in 1959?
11. Which manager moved from Gillingham to Bristol City to Portsmouth between 1999 and 2000?
12. Which manager scaled the walls of Colchester Castle following his club's famous FA Cup defeat of Leeds United?
13. Which Italian club did Graeme Souness manage?
14. Which Charlton, Middlesbrough, Luton and Grimsby manager never played League football?
15. Which manager had three spells in charge of Carlisle United?
16. Who was the first black manager of an English League club?

Answers to page 202

FA CUP 3: **1.** Nicolas Anelka **2.** Jesper Olsen **3.** Joe Smith **4.** Arsenal and Sheffield Wednesday **5.** Les Allen (1961) and Paul Allen (1987) **6.** Preston North End **7.** Bobby Moore **8.** Paul Bracewell **9.** Teddy Sheringham **10.** Bedford Town **11.** Nigel Callaghan (Watford) and Eric Young (Wimbledon) **12.** Bobby Johnstone **13.** Blyth Spartans **14.** Tottenham Hotspur **15.** 1986 **16.** Dave Whelan

Which Year in Football? 3

Answers on page 203

1. When were Cambridge United elected to the Football League?
2. In which year was the FA Cup final first played at Crystal Palace?
3. In which year did the European Cup winners first come from outside the Iberian peninsular?
4. When were Leeds City expelled from the Football League?
5. In which year was the FA Cup final first televised?
6. In which year did the first-ever floodlit match take place, at Bramall Lane, Sheffield?
7. In which year was Paul Scholes sent off for England against Sweden?
8. In which year did Manchester United complete their first League and FA Cup double?
9. When did Aberdeen become the first British club to provide all-seater accommodation?
10. In which year did a foreign manager lift the FA Cup for the first time?
11. In which year did the white ball come into official use?
12. In which year were end-of-season play-offs introduced by the Football League?
13. In which year did goal difference replace goal average in the Football League?
14. In which year did Neil Young win the FA Cup for Manchester City?
15. In which year did Jimmy Hill act as replacement linesman at Highbury in a First Division match?
16. In which year did the Germans win their first World Cup?

Answers to page 203

SCOTTISH SCENE 3 1: **1.** Kenny Dalglish and Denis Law **2.** Sunderland **3.** Yugoslavia **4.** Oldham Athletic **5.** Ninian Park, Cardiff **6.** Willie Ormond **7.** Peru **8.** Alan Morton **9.** Norway **10.** Zaire **11.** Lawrie Reilly **12.** Romania **13.** Jim Leighton **14.** Willie Johnston **15.** Alex Ferguson **16.** Sweden

FA Cup 3

Answers on page 200

1. Which Frenchman scored for Arsenal in their 1998 Cup triumph?

2. Who was the first Dane to play in an FA Cup final?

3. Who won two Cup winners' medals with Bolton as a player in 1923 and 1926 and then managed the victorious Blackpool team of 1953?

4. Which two teams fought out a third-round tie in 1979 that went to five games?

5. Which uncle and nephew picked up Cup winners' medals with Spurs?

6. Which was the only non-First Division team to reach the Cup final in the 1960s?

7. Who played for West Ham in the 1964 final and against them in the 1975 final?

8. Who finished a Cup final loser three times with Everton and once with Sunderland?

9. Who scored Manchester United's first goal in the 1999 final?

10. Which Southern League team won 2–1 at Newcastle in a third-round tie in 1964?

11. Which two Singapore-born players have appeared in Cup finals?

12. Which player scored in successive finals for Manchester City in the 1950s?

13. Which non-League club reached the fifth round of the Cup in 1977–8?

14. Which team went unbeaten for 18 FA Cup ties between January 1981 and February 1983?

15. In which year was the first all-Merseyside final?

16. Which Blackburn player broke a leg in the 1960 Cup final?

Answers to page 200

MANAGERS 4: **1.** Arthur Rowe **2.** Bob Jackson **3.** Jocky Scott **4.** Bill Dearden **5.** Tim Ward **6.** Denis Smith **7.** West Bromwich Albion **8.** Lou Macari **9.** Lincoln City **10.** Billy Walker **11.** Tony Pulis **12.** Dick Graham **13.** Torino **14.** Lennie Lawrence **15.** Bob Stokoe **16.** Keith Alexander (at Lincoln)

Scottish Scene 3

Answers on page 201

1. Which two players have scored the most international goals for Scotland?
2. With which English club did Jim Baxter win ten of his Scottish caps?
3. Who did Scotland crush 6–1 at Hampden Park in 1984?
4. For which club was Andy Goram playing when he won his first cap?
5. On which ground did Jock Stein collapse and die in 1985?
6. Who became manager of Scotland in 1973?
7. Who beat Scotland in the opening match of the 1978 World Cup finals in Argentina?
8. Which Scottish international of the 1920s was known as the 'Wee Blue Devil'?
9. Who were Scotland's first continental opponents in an international match?
10. Which nation did Scotland meet for the only time at the 1974 World Cup finals?
11. Which Hibernian forward of the 1950s won 38 Scottish caps?
12. Against which country did Kenny Dalglish win his 100th cap?
13. Which goalkeeper won his first Scotland cap while playing for Aberdeen in 1983?
14. Who was sent home in disgrace from the 1978 World Cup finals?
15. Who acted as caretaker-manager for Scotland at the 1986 World Cup finals?
16. Against whom did Scotland record their only success at the 1990 World Cup finals?

Answers to page 201

WHICH YEAR IN FOOTBALL? 3: **1.** 1970 **2.** 1895 **3.** 1963 **4.** 1919 **5.** 1937 **6.** 1878 **7.** 1999 **8.** 1994 **9.** 1978 **10.** 1997 (Ruud Gullit) **11.** 1951 **12.** 1987 **13.** 1976 **14.** 1969 **15.** 1972 **16.** 1954

General Knowledge 41

Answers on page 206

1. In which county is Beamish open-air industrial museum?
2. Who rode Shergar to victory in the Epsom Derby?
3. Which city is the administrative headquarters of Tayside?
4. Who recorded 'Earth Song'?
5. What nationality is tennis player Ivan Lendl?
6. Which creatures sometimes hurl themselves to their deaths over cliffs during mass migrations?
7. What is the chemical formula for table salt?
8. What is the first day of Lent?
9. Who starred in *Hudson Hawk* and *The Last Boy Scout*?
10. What is the state capital of New Mexico?
11. According to the Irish proverb, what do bare walls make?
12. What is nephelophobia?
13. Which model starred in the film *The Boyfriend*?
14. The quetzal is the currency of which country?
15. In Greek mythology, who was the mother of Artemis and Apollo?
16. David Bryant was an English champion at which sport?

Answers to page 206

GENERAL KNOWLEDGE 43: **1.** The Monkees **2.** Canberra **3.** John Surtees **4.** 1,001 **5.** Tawe **6.** Society Islands **7.** Tennis **8.** Libra, Aquarius and Gemini **9.** Cormorant **10.** 4 July **11.** Desert Orchid **12.** March and September **13.** Tagus **14.** Charles II **15.** Afghanistan **16.** *Bright Eyes*

General Knowledge 42

Answers on page 207

1. Which playing card was a hit with Motörhead?
2. What string of beads is used in a Catholic prayer?
3. *Salvia officianalis* is better known as which herb?
4. Who was Noggin the Nog's wicked uncle?
5. Where do barnacles have their ovaries?
6. In 1984, who called the National Gallery extension a 'monstrous carbuncle'?
7. Which human organ contains the smallest bones?
8. By what colour is the District Line depicted on London Underground maps?
9. Sir Walter Tyrrel inadvertently killed which English king?
10. Which Hollywood entertainer was born Frederick Austerlitz?
11. Who was appointed Poet Laureate in 1968?
12. What does 'scherzo' mean in music?
13. Where is Cape Wrath?
14. Which controversial product went on sale in Britain for the first time in 1961 although it was not available on prescription for another two years?
15. What nationality is tennis player Martina Hingis?
16. Which *Big Breakfast* presenter appeared in *Byker Grove*?

Answers to page 207

GENERAL KNOWLEDGE 44: **1.** Lord Byron **2.** *Mansfield Park* **3.** Blue **4.** Pretenders to the throne in the reign of Henry VII **5.** Albania and Italy **6.** Ostrich **7.** The Jam **8.** Trevor Jordache **9.** Joan Crawford **10.** Addis Ababa **11.** Jack Taylor **12.** James **13.** Dopey **14.** On a tennis court **15.** Terrier **16.** Long John Silver's

General Knowledge 43

Answers on page 204

1. For which band did Stephen Stills unsuccessfully audition?
2. What is the capital of Australia?
3. Who is the only person to have won world titles on two and four wheels?
4. How many nights are there in the *Arabian Nights*?
5. Swansea is situated at the mouth of which river?
6. Tahiti is the largest of which group of islands?
7. At which sport do countries compete for the Davis Cup?
8. What are the three air signs of the zodiac?
9. A shag is a small species of which sea bird?
10. What date is Independence Day in the USA?
11. Which racehorse was affectionately known as 'Dessie'?
12. Which two months have equinoxes?
13. Which river rises in Aragon, Spain, and reaches the Atlantic at Lisbon, Portugal?
14. Orange-seller Nell Gwynne was a mistress of which English monarch?
15. Which country forms the southern border of Tajikistan?
16. In which film did Shirley Temple sing 'On The Good Ship Lollipop'?

Answers to page 204

GENERAL KNOWLEDGE 41: **1.** Durham **2.** Walter Swinburn **3.** Dundee **4.** Michael Jackson **5.** Czech **6.** Lemmings **7.** NaCl (sodium chloride) **8.** Ash Wednesday **9.** Bruce Willis **10.** Santa Fe **11.** Giddy housekeepers **12.** Fear of clouds **13.** Twiggy **14.** Guatemala **15.** Leto **16.** Bowls

General Knowledge 44

Answers on page 205

1. Which poet kept a pet bear at Cambridge University because dogs weren't allowed?
2. Fanny Price was a character in which Jane Austen novel?
3. What colour is a lobster's blood?
4. Who were Lambert Simnel and Perkin Warbeck?
5. The Strait of Otranto separates which two countries?
6. What bird lays the largest egg?
7. Who sang about a 'Town Called Malice'?
8. Who was buried under the patio of 10 Brookside Close?
9. Which actress called Elizabeth Taylor 'a spoiled, indulgent child, a blemish on public decency'?
10. The name of which capital city means 'new flower'?
11. Which British referee awarded a penalty inside the first minute of the 1974 World Cup Final?
12. Tim Booth is the singer with which band?
13. Which is the only one of the Seven Dwarfs without a beard?
14. Where would you find tramlines on grass?
15. Cairn, Sealyham and Bedlington are all types of what?
16. Whose shoulder did Captain Flint perch on?

Answers to page 205

GENERAL KNOWLEDGE 42: **1.** 'Ace Of Spades' **2.** Rosary **3.** Sage **4.** Nogbad the Bad **5.** In their heads **6.** Prince Charles **7.** The ear **8.** Green **9.** William Rufus **10.** Fred Astaire **11.** Cecil Day Lewis **12.** Lively **13.** Scotland **14.** The Pill **15.** Swiss **16.** Donna Air

General Knowledge 45

Answers on page 210

1. What stage name did Thomas Terry Hoar Stevens adopt?
2. How many faces does a tetrahedron have?
3. The Jumna is a tributary of which Indian river?
4. Alex Kingston, Patsy Palmer and Letitia Dean have all appeared in which TV series?
5. Alec Stewart and Mark Butcher played cricket for which English county in 2001?
6. What would Alan Titchmarsh do if confronted with a red-hot poker?
7. Who weren't afraid of the Big Bad Wolf?
8. What is the oldest known vegetable?
9. Which American singer took a 'Walk On The Wild Side' in 1973?
10. Who is St Elmo the patron saint of?
11. What is the only mammal with four knees?
12. The San Andreas fault runs through which American state?
13. What is another name for potassium nitrate?
14. Which ball game occupies the largest playing area?
15. Which city is the administrative capital of South Africa?
16. Who starred opposite Dustin Hoffman in *Kramer vs Kramer*?

Answers to page 210

GENERAL KNOWLEDGE 47: **1.** Dylan Thomas **2.** Helga **3.** Orion **4.** *Platoon* **5.** Eros **6.** Michael Stich **7.** Ethiopia **8.** 42 **9.** The Clash **10.** Y-fronts **11.** Potato **12.** On the fruit counter – it's a variety of apple **13.** Pompeii **14.** Dutch **15.** Maxine Peacock **16.** Billie Jean Moffitt

General Knowledge 46

Answers on page 211

1. What is the name for the male reproductive organ of a flower?
2. Which band's 1998 album was titled 'This Is Hardcore'?
3. Whereabouts on a cricket pitch would you find a chain?
4. What letter is at the bottom right end of a standard keyboard?
5. Cannock Chase is in which English county?
6. Who appeared as King Arthur in the film *Camelot* with a piece of Elastoplast visible on his neck?
7. Which Cornish detective was created by W.J. Burley?
8. When was the only time all four home international football countries qualified for the World Cup finals?
9. Which American novelist wrote *Of Mice and Men*?
10. What is the Taoiseach?
11. What colour are the flowers of wild garlic?
12. The Aleutian Islands are part of which American state?
13. Which Formula One team are based at Maranello?
14. What was the name of the romantic car salesman on *The Fast Show*?
15. In which century did the Thirty Years' War take place in Europe?
16. Which plant is sometimes known as thrift?

Answers to page 211

GENERAL KNOWLEDGE 48: **1.** Robin Williams **2.** *Friends* **3.** Theodore Roosevelt **4.** Copenhagen **5.** Once **6.** An onion **7.** Hawaii **8.** Octopus **9.** Strathclyde **10.** Leslie Charteris **11.** An Indian tree **12.** Dick Emery **13.** Manila **14.** New Deal **15.** Cod **16.** Guy Ritchie

General Knowledge 47

Answers on page 208

1. Who wrote *Under Milk Wood*?
2. Who was Herr Flick's right-hand woman in *'Allo 'Allo*?
3. What constellation depicts a hunter with club and shield?
4. Which Oliver Stone movie won an Oscar for Best Picture in 1986?
5. Who was the Greek god of love?
6. Which German won the men's singles at Wimbledon in 1991?
7. In which country is Dallol, the hottest place in the world?
8. How many dots are there on a pair of dice?
9. Which band asked: 'Should I Stay Or Should I Go'?
10. Inspired by a photo of a pair of swimming trunks on the French Riviera, what did underwear manufacturers Coopers introduce to the market in 1934?
11. Which vegetable was used as a windscreen wiper in the early days of motoring?
12. Where might you find a Beauty of Bath at the supermarket?
13. Which town was destroyed by Vesuvius in 79BC?
14. What nationality was the painter Vermeer?
15. Which *Coronation Street* hairdresser cheated on her husband with the local doctor in 2001?
16. Under what name did Billie Jean King first compete at Wimbledon?

Answers to page 208

GENERAL KNOWLEDGE 45: **1.** Terry-Thomas **2.** Four **3.** Ganges **4.** *Grange Hill* **5.** Surrey **6.** Grow it (it's a perennial plant) **7.** The Three Little Pigs **8.** The pea **9.** Lou Reed **10.** Sailors **11.** Elephant **12.** California **13.** Saltpetre **14.** Polo **15.** Pretoria **16.** Meryl Streep

General Knowledge 48

Answers on page 209

1. Who played the title role in the film *Popeye*?
2. George Clooney, the Duchess of York and June Whitfield have all guested on which sitcom?
3. Who was the first teddy bear named after?
4. Which European city did Danny Kaye think was 'wonderful, wonderful'?
5. How many times a year does a penguin mate?
6. The ancient Egyptians believed that mixing half of what with beer foam would ward off death?
7. Which American state supplies over a third of the world's commercial pineapples?
8. Which sea creature sometimes eats itself if it becomes unduly stressed?
9. In which Scottish county is Troon golf course?
10. Who created *The Saint*?
11. What is a chaulmoogra?
12. Which comedian's characters included Lampwick, College and Hetty?
13. What is the capital of the Philippines?
14. Which programme did President Franklin Roosevelt introduce in 1933 to counter the depression?
15. A pollack is a member of which family of fish?
16. Which British film director married Madonna?

Answers to page 209

GENERAL KNOWLEDGE 46: **1.** Stamen **2.** Pulp **3.** Between the wickets (a chain equals 22 yards) **4.** M **5.** Staffordshire **6.** Richard Harris **7.** Wycliffe **8.** 1958 **9.** John Steinbeck **10.** The Gaelic name for the Prime Minister of the Irish Republic **11.** White **12.** Alaska **13.** Ferrari **14.** Swiss Toni **15.** 17th **16.** Sea pink

General Knowledge 49

Answers on page 214

1. How much of an iceberg is visible above water?
2. Who was manager of Whitbury Newtown leisure centre?
3. What sort of drum is a tympanum?
4. What is a twite?
5. Which Michael was thwarted in his attempts to become Conservative Party leader in 2001?
6. What nationality is the soprano Joan Sutherland?
7. Which Shakespeare play featured Banquo?
8. What is the capital of Syria?
9. How many points are needed to win a game of table tennis?
10. What essential item was invented by Joseph Gayetty in 1857?
11. Tom Bailey and Alannah Currie were members of which Eighties band?
12. What does a tachometer record?
13. What is vestiphobia a fear of?
14. Who wrote *The Chronicles of Narnia*?
15. In which American state is Tampa?
16. Which county cricket team's home ground is Trent Bridge?

Answers to page 214

GENERAL KNOWLEDGE 51: **1.** Cannes **2.** Pear **3.** Wales **4.** The Kennedy Space Center **5.** Livy **6.** San Francisco Bay **7.** Burt Lancaster **8.** Pickles **9.** Richard Trevithick **10.** Yellow **11.** Snuff users **12.** Three seconds **13.** *The Bill* **14.** 'Tragedy' **15.** Aries **16.** A litre

General Knowledge 50

Answers on page 215

1. Which character was the lovesick young hero of *Titanic*?
2. Which golfing accessory was patented by George Grant in 1899?
3. The Great Barrier Reef lies off the coast of which Australian state?
4. In which war was the Battle of the Bulge?
5. In which year did Simple Minds top the UK singles chart with 'Belfast Child'?
6. What is worsted?
7. What colour is amethyst?
8. What did Queen Ranavalona of Madagascar do to any of her subjects who appeared in her dreams?
9. How many letters are there in the Hawaiian alphabet?
10. Which port is opposite Harwich on the Suffolk side of the Stour estuary?
11. What was the name of the dinosaur on *Multi-Coloured Swap Shop*?
12. Who released the album 'Tuesday Night Music Club'?
13. Who won the County Cricket Championship in 1996 and 1998?
14. Of whom did Howard Hughes say: 'His ears make him look like a taxi-cab with both doors open'?
15. What was the name of the schooner in the TV series *The Onedin Line*?
16. Who wrote *Lucky Jim*?

Answers to page 215

GENERAL KNOWLEDGE 52: **1.** Sir Robert Peel **2.** Harry S. Truman **3.** Eddie Kelly (Arsenal, 1971) **4.** 'Luton Airport' **5.** Robert Maxwell **6.** Gumshield **7.** Four – Robert, Kenneth, Anne and Tony **8.** They all only reached number two in the UK singles chart **9.** Cheyenne **10.** Italy **11.** The Malvinas **12.** Last Suspect **13.** Lloyd Honeyghan **14.** *Man About the House* **15.** Aqua **16.** Hair

General Knowledge 51

Answers on page 212

1. In which French resort is an international film festival held annually?
2. Conference is a type of which fruit?
3. For which country does Ryan Giggs play international football?
4. What is located on Merritt Island near Florida?
5. Which ancient scholar wrote *A History of Rome*?
6. In what bay is Alcatraz Island?
7. And who starred as the *Birdman of Alcatraz*?
8. What was the name of the dog that found the Jules Rimet Trophy in 1966?
9. Who built the first steam engine to run on rails?
10. What colour blood do insects have?
11. What did Pope Urban VIII threaten to excommunicate in 1924?
12. How long is the memory span of a goldfish?
13. Tony Stamp and Reg Hollis are characters in which TV series?
14. Which Bee Gees song gave Steps a number one in 1998?
15. Which zodiac sign has the symbol of the ram?
16. What does 1.76 pints equal?

Answers to page 212

GENERAL KNOWLEDGE 49: **1.** One ninth **2.** Gordon Brittas **3.** Ear-drum **4.** A bird **5.** Michael Portillo **6.** Australian **7.** *Macbeth* **8.** Damascus **9.** 21 **10.** Toilet paper **11.** The Thompson Twins **12.** A vehicle's speed **13.** Wearing clothes **14.** C.S. Lewis **15.** Florida **16.** Nottinghamshire

General Knowledge 52

Answers on page 213

1. Whose name led to policemen being christened 'bobbies'?
2. Who became President of the United States in 1945?
3. Who was the first substitute to score in an FA Cup Final?
4. Which airport did Cats U.K. sing about in 1979?
5. Who was nicknamed 'The Bouncing Czech'?
6. What boxing aid was invented by Jack Marks in 1902?
7. How many Robinsons have presented *Points of View*?
8. What do 'Brown Sugar', 'Heartbreak Hotel', 'Let It Be' and 'Vienna' have in common?
9. What is the state capital of Wyoming?
10. In which country is the Great Appenine railway tunnel?
11. What is the Argentine name for the Falklands?
12. Which horse owned by the Duchess of Westminster won the 1985 Grand National?
13. Which London boxer became World Welterweight Champion in September 1986?
14. *Robin's Nest* was a spin-off from which TV sitcom?
15. Who topped the charts in 1998 with 'Doctor Jones'?
16. What is a rhinoceros horn made of?

Answers to page 213

GENERAL KNOWLEDGE 50: **1.** Jack Dawson **2.** The tee **3.** Queensland **4.** World War Two **5.** 1989 **6.** A stiff woollen fabric **7.** Violet **8.** She executed them **9.** 12 **10.** Felixstowe **11.** Posh Paws **12.** Sheryl Crow **13.** Leicestershire **14.** Clark Gable **15.** *Charlotte Rhodes* **16.** Kingsley Amis

General Knowledge 53

Answers on page 218

1. What are the only two countries whose names start with an 'A' but don't end with an 'A'?
2. In which Australian city are there more Maltese people than in Malta itself?
3. Which is India's largest city?
4. Which singer had a 'Perfect Moment' in 1999?
5. Who preceded Bobby Robson as manager of the England football team?
6. What games room features on a Cluedo board?
7. In which county would you find Looe?
8. Patrick and Pippa lived next door to which sitcom couple?
9. Which swimmer is nicknamed 'Thorpedo'?
10. Which animal's fur is brown in summer and white in winter?
11. Which young actor died while shooting the 1993 film *Dark Blood*?
12. In Greek mythology, who was carried off to the underworld as the bride of Pluto?
13. Who were Huey, Dewey and Louie?
14. Which table sets out the classification of chemical elements?
15. Which Football League club are nicknamed 'The Tigers'?
16. Which English town is known to the locals as 'Pompey'?

Answers to page 218

GENERAL KNOWLEDGE 55: **1.** He threw an egg at John Prescott and was punched for his pains **2.** The Pet Shop Boys **3.** Munich **4.** Oliver Cromwell **5.** Johansson **6.** Tesco **7.** Laissez-faire **8.** Glenn Roeder **9.** Skip **10.** Alan Davies **11.** Artificial Intelligence **12.** A small-scale railway **13.** Pekingese **14.** Juan Veron **15.** Loire **16.** *The Persuaders*

General Knowledge 54

Answers on page 219

1. What is the most common name in the world?
2. Who was President of France from 1969–74?
3. What day of the week did Chairmen of the Board say everything was in 1971?
4. Over how many holes are most championship golf tournaments contested?
5. Which Welsh long-jumper was known as 'Lynn the leap'?
6. What colour cats are always female except for the occasional sterile male?
7. What drink consists of pineapple, rum and coconut milk?
8. Zanzibar is an island region of which mainland country?
9. Which US actor was nicknamed 'Duke'?
10. Who did Nicholas Lyndhurst play in *Goodnight Sweetheart*?
11. In what does an archer carry his arrows?
12. What is the name for an auctioneer's hammer?
13. Who composed the 'Four Seasons'?
14. Who was the falsetto singer with the Four Seasons?
15. Which is the longest river in Europe?
16. What colour is the gem peridot?

Answers to page 219

GENERAL KNOWLEDGE 56: **1.** The Fosbury Flop **2.** Seal **3.** Sculpture **4.** A harvesting tool **5.** The Siegfried Line **6.** Spectrum **7.** Fenchurch Street, Kings Cross, Liverpool Street and Marylebone **8.** 'Albatross' **9.** Liza Minnelli (Judy Garland) **10.** Deuce **11.** Shropshire **12.** 1988 **13.** Green **14.** Very loud **15.** The science of language **16.** Esk

General Knowledge 55

Answers on page 216

1. What was Craig Evans's contribution to the 2001 General Election?
2. As whom are Neil Tennant and Chris Lowe better known?
3. Which German city is famous for its Oktoberfest?
4. Who declared Britain a republic in 1649?
5. What is the most common surname in Sweden?
6. Sir John Cohen founded which chain of supermarkets?
7. What policy of minimal governmental interference takes its name from the French for 'allow to do'?
8. Who was appointed manager of West Ham United in summer 2001?
9. What can be a large receptacle for builders' rubble or the captain of a bowls foursome?
10. Which comedian played Lesley Sharp's gay boyfriend in the TV series *Bob and Rose?*
11. What did *A.I.* stand for in the title of a Steven Spielberg film?
12. What is the Romney, Hythe and Dymchurch?
13. What is the royal dog of China?
14. Who did Manchester United sign from Lazio for £28.1 million in 2001?
15. Muscadet, Vouvray and Sancerre are all wines from which region of France?
16. Danny Wilde and Lord Brett Sinclair formed which pair of TV crime-fighters?

Answers to page 216

GENERAL KNOWLEDGE 53: **1.** Afghanistan and Azerbaijan **2.** Melbourne **3.** Bombay **4.** Martine McCutcheon **5.** Ron Greenwood **6.** Billiard room **7.** Cornwall **8.** The Meldrews (*One Foot in the Grave*) **9.** Ian Thorpe **10.** Stoat **11.** River Phoenix **12.** Persephone **13.** Donald Duck's nephews **14.** Periodic table **15.** Hull City **16.** Portsmouth

General Knowledge 56

Answers on page 217

1. What technique revolutionised high jumping following the 1968 Olympics?
2. Which marine mammal had a 1990 hit with 'Crazy'?
3. Barbara Hepworth practised in which field of the arts?
4. What is a sickle?
5. On what line were British women jokingly asked to hang out their washing during the Second World War?
6. For which security organisation did Captain Scarlet work?
7. What are the four London stations on a Monopoly board?
8. Which bird gave Fleetwood Mac a number one hit?
9. Which actress called her mother 'the real-life Wicked Witch of the West'?
10. What is the score 40-40 called in tennis?
11. In which English county is the world's first iron bridge?
12. In which year did Kylie and Jason reach number one with 'Especially For You'?
13. What colour was Coca-Cola originally?
14. What does 'fortissimo' mean in music?
15. What is philology?
16. Which river flows into the sea at Whitby?

Answers to page 217

GENERAL KNOWLEDGE 54: **1.** Mohammed **2.** Georges Pompidou **3.** Tuesday **4.** 72 **5.** Lynn Davies **6.** Tortoiseshell **7.** Pina colada **8.** Tanzania **9.** John Wayne **10.** Gary Sparrow **11.** A quiver **12.** Gavel **13.** Vivaldi **14.** Frankie Valli **15.** Volga **16.** Pale green

General Knowledge 57

Answers on page 222

1. In which country was St Patrick born?
2. Old Father Time perches above which English cricket ground?
3. 'And' or 'but' are examples of which type of word?
4. Milly and Egg were characters in which TV series?
5. What did Darius Perkins do before Jason Donovan?
6. Which actor played three roles in the 1959 film *The Mouse That Roared*?
7. What are Euroglider, Happy Face and Billy Boy?
8. Which London Underground station was called Enfield West until 1934?
9. From which continent does the banana originate?
10. Which girl's name means 'hay-meadow'?
11. 'Me Duck' is a term of endearment in which part of England?
12. Who wore a 'Bullet Bra' on tour in 1990?
13. What is triskaidekaphobia?
14. What number is at six o'clock on a dartboard?
15. Which jockey completed a hat-trick of wins in the Prix de l'Arc de Triomphe 1996–8?
16. The Pas-de-Calais is the French name for which stretch of water?

Answers to page 222

GENERAL KNOWLEDGE 59: **1.** 1970 **2.** The Kray twins **3.** Nottinghamshire **4.** Eisteddfod **5.** Portugal **6.** Eleanor of Aquitaine **7.** Nancy Mitford **8.** Pakistan and Afghanistan **9.** Lloyd's **10.** Middle of the Road **11.** Loch Ness Monster **12.** A tail **13.** Gérard de Nerval **14.** *The Woodentops* **15.** Turkey **16.** Rabbits

General Knowledge 58

Answers on page 223

1. Who bought the car numberplate COM 1C?
2. To which family of birds would something 'corvine' be related?
3. Which *Superman* committed suicide?
4. Which city staged the 1980 Olympic Games?
5. Who created master-thief Raffles?
6. Curt Smith and Roland Orzabal made up which musical duo?
7. Which Steven Spielberg film won the Oscar for Best Picture in 1993?
8. Which treaty ended the War of Spanish Succession?
9. Which capital city stands where the rivers Sava and Danube meet?
10. How many months does it take the Moon to revolve around the Earth?
11. In physics, what is UV an abbreviation for?
12. On which Dutch football club's ground did the final of Euro 2000 take place?
13. Which Jane Austen novel featured Captain Wentworth?
14. Who was the first Prime Minister of India?
15. What three colour bands make up the flag of Ethiopia?
16. In which year did Queen Victoria die?

Answers to page 223

GENERAL KNOWLEDGE 60: **1.** In Spanish 'no va' means 'doesn't go' **2.** Vitamin C **3.** Rugby **4.** Shakin' Stevens **5.** Professor Moriarty **6.** Vanessa Kensington **7.** Columbia Broadcasting System **8.** *Naked Video* **9.** Lincoln **10.** Amanda Barrie **11.** A wild sheep **12.** Kilt **13.** King Alfred **14.** Four **15.** Gibraltar **16.** Gerry Marsden (Gerry and The Pacemakers)

General Knowledge 59

Answers on page 220

1. In which year did The Beatles break up?
2. Whose 1969 trial lasted nine months?
3. In which county is Newark?
4. What is the name of the traditional Welsh arts gathering?
5. Against which nation did England concede their first goal at the 1966 World Cup finals?
6. Which Eleanor was wife of Henry II?
7. Who wrote *Love in a Cold Climate*?
8. The Khyber Pass links which two countries?
9. What is the name of the international register of shipping?
10. Who had a hit in the Seventies with 'Chirpy Chirpy Cheep Cheep'?
11. Which probable myth is worth some £30 million a year to Scottish tourism?
12. What does a Manx cat lack?
13. Which 19th-century French poet, who used to walk a pet lobster on a lead, eventually took his own life by hanging himself from a lamp-post?
14. Who owned Spotty Dog?
15. In which country was Aristotle Onassis born?
16. What animals live in a warren?

Answers to page 220

GENERAL KNOWLEDGE 57: **1.** Wales **2.** Lord's **3.** Conjunction **4.** *This Life* **5.** Play Scott Robinson in *Neighbours* **6.** Peter Sellers **7.** Brands of condom **8.** Oakwood **9.** Asia **10.** Hayley **11.** East Midlands **12.** Madonna **13.** Fear of the number 13 **14.** Three **15.** Olivier Peslier **16.** Strait of Dover

General Knowledge 60

Answers on page 221

1. Why did the Chevrolet Nova fail to sell well in Spain?
2. A lack of which vitamin can cause scurvy?
3. In which sport do you need a hooker and a prop?
4. In 1987 who sang about 'A Little Boogie Woogie In The Back Of My Mind'?
5. Who was Sherlock Holmes's arch enemy?
6. Who did Elizabeth Hurley play in *Austin Powers: International Man Of Mystery*?
7. What does CBS stand for?
8. On which sketch show did Rab C. Nesbitt first appear?
9. Lindum was the Roman name for which British city?
10. Which *Coronation Street* actress, whose character met an untimely end in 2001, was born Shirley Ann Broadbent?
11. What breed of animal is a moufflon?
12. What is a filibeg another name for in Scotland?
13. Which English king burnt the cakes?
14. How many points is a letter 'V' worth in Scrabble?
15. Where do vehicles bearing the international index mark GBZ come from?
16. Which singer was barely 20 when he acquired a Pacemaker?

Answers to page 221

GENERAL KNOWLEDGE 58: **1.** Jimmy Tarbuck **2.** Crow **3.** George Reeves **4.** Moscow **5.** E.W. Hornung **6.** Tears For Fears **7.** *Schindler's List* **8.** Treaty of Utrecht **9.** Belgrade **10.** One **11.** Ultraviolet **12.** Feyenoord **13.** *Persuasion* **14.** Nehru **15.** Green, yellow and red **16.** 1901

Soaps 4

Answers on page 226

1. With which Spanish chef did vicar's wife Bernice have an affair in *Emmerdale*?
2. Which soap returned to ITV in 2001 after a 13-year absence?
3. Whose children in *EastEnders* owned a snake called Crush?
4. Which actress quit playing Louise Hope in *Brookside*, only to be killed off in *Holby City*?
5. Which three wise men bought The Rovers Return from Natalie Barnes?
6. Who is Karl Kennedy married to in *Neighbours*?
7. *Oil* was the original working title for which American soap?
8. Which former mayor of Weatherfield died in his chair at a New Year's party?
9. Who killed Josh Matthews in *Family Affairs* but let his wife take the rap?
10. What was George Holloway's nickname in *EastEnders*?
11. Which ill-fated soap was launched with the promise of 'sun, sand, sangria and sex'?
12. Which resident of Brookside Close saw his son go off to be a policeman in 2001?
13. Which 1980s soap was set among a group of Manchester stallholders?
14. Who did the widowed Viv Windsor marry in *Emmerdale*?
15. Which soap was created by doctor's daughter Tessa Diamond?
16. Which soap introduced a fourth weekly episode in August 2001?

Answers to page 226

DRAMAS 5: **1.** Alex Kingston **2.** Michael Cashman **3.** *The Onedin Line* **4.** Susannah Doyle (daughter of Tony Doyle) **5.** 'Gracie' **6.** *Mrs Thursday* **7.** Paul McGann **8.** 1920s **9.** Alan Bleasdale **10.** *The District Nurse* **11.** Shane Longman **12.** Lee Remick **13.** Ioan Gruffudd **14.** Evan **15.** Shelly Tambo **16.** *Danger Man*

Comedy 5

Answers on page 227

1. Which *Cold Feet* actress played Ross's English girlfriend in *Friends*?

2. What is the name of the hideous boss in *The Office*?

3. In which sitcom would you meet John Fuller-Carp?

4. Who are the two stars of *Life As We Know It*?

5. Who was the 'I' in *I, Lovett*?

6. Which comedy icon was given a 75th birthday tribute by the BBC in July 2001?

7. What was the chosen profession of Simon Peel and Oliver Smallbridge?

8. Who was *Seinfeld*'s manic neighbour?

9. Who plays the title role in *Barbara*?

10. Which fake member of the aristocracy duped Basil Fawlty?

11. Which actress helped Alistair McGowan make a *Big Impression*?

12. In which BBC sitcom did Mel Smith play a British Rail office clerk?

13. Which brassy Liver bird is Paul O'Grady's alter ego?

14. Who owned a hamster called SPG?

15. Which of *The Monkees* invariably wore a woolly hat?

16. Which *Morecambe and Wise* guest was always waiting to be paid?

Answers to page 227

CHILDREN'S TV 3: **1.** Tinky Winky **2.** Sally Field **3.** Professor Yaffle **4.** Neil Buchanan **5.** Chums **6.** *Crackerjack* **7.** Buttercup **8.** Bernard Cribbins **9.** Rosco P. Coltrane **10.** Simon Thomas **11.** *Rosie and Jim* **12.** The Hood **13.** Fish **14.** Professor Pat Pending **15.** *The Buccaneers* **16.** *The Daily Slate*

Dramas 5

Answers on page 224

1. Which English actress was heavily pregnant as Dr Elizabeth Corday in *ER*?
2. Which gay *EastEnder* used to be one of *The Sandbaggers*?
3. Which Seventies seafaring saga starred Peter Gilmore?
4. Which daughter of a late *Ballykissangel* star joined the series as Avril?
5. What is Sally Fields' nickname in *London's Burning*?
6. Which Sixties charlady inherited a fortune?
7. Who played *The Monocled Mutineer*?
8. In which decade was the first series of *The House of Eliott* set?
9. Who wrote *GBH*?
10. What was Megan Roberts better known as?
11. What was the name of the international bank in *Capital City*?
12. Which American actress starred as *Jennie, Lady Randolph Churchill*?
13. Who played Phillip Bosinney in ITV's 2002 remake of *The Forsyte Saga*?
14. Who was the aspiring author in the Australian series *The Secret Life of Us*?
15. Which character in *Northern Exposure* was a former Miss Northwest Passage?
16. Whose name was 'Drake, John Drake'?

Answers to page 224

SOAPS 4: **1.** Carlos Diaz **2.** *Crossroads* **3.** Mehmet Osman **4.** Lisa Faulkner **5.** Duggie Ferguson, Fred Elliott and Mike Baldwin **6.** Susan **7.** *Dynasty* **8.** Alf Roberts **9.** Pete Callan **10.** Lofty **11.** *Eldorado* **12.** Mick Johnson **13.** *Albion Market* **14.** Bob Hope **15.** *Emergency – Ward 10* **16.** *EastEnders*

Children's TV 3

Answers on page 225

1. Which is the purple Teletubby?

2. Which Hollywood star used to play *The Flying Nun*?

3. What was the name of the wooden woodpecker bookend in *Bagpuss*?

4. Who hosts *Art Attack*?

5. What was the title of *SM:TV Live*'s send-up of *Friends*?

6. Eamonn Andrews was the first presenter of which long-running children's show?

7. Which cow was *The Woodentops*' principal source of milk?

8. Who was the original narrator of *The Wombles*?

9. What was the name of the sheriff in *The Dukes of Hazzard*?

10. Which Simon is a current *Blue Peter* presenter?

11. Which ragdolls live on a canal boat?

12. Who is Kyrano's villainous half-brother in *Thunderbirds*?

13. What did Mr Carraway sell in *Camberwick Green*?

14. Which Wacky Racer drove The Convert-A-Car?

15. Which series featured the swashbuckling adventures of Dan Tempest?

16. What is the name of *The Flintstones*' daily newspaper?

Answers to page 225

COMEDY 5: **1.** Helen Baxendale **2.** David Brent **3.** *Chambers* **4.** Richard Wilson and Stephanie Cole **5.** Norman Lovett **6.** Stanley Baxter **7.** Antiques dealers **8.** Kramer **9.** Gwen Taylor **10.** Lord Melbury **11.** Ronni Ancona **12.** *Colin's Sandwich* **13.** Lily Savage **14.** *The Young Ones* **15.** Mike Nesmith **16.** Peter Cushing

TV Pot Luck 5

Answers on page 230

1. Which *Tomorrow's World* presenter is *Barking Mad*?
2. Whose TV existence is made up of a succession of *Weird Weekends*?
3. Who was the very first presenter of *Holiday*?
4. How many days are the *Ground Force* team given to carry out their makeovers?
5. *Jeux Sans Frontieres* was the European version of which British contest?
6. Which comedian was a natural choice to host *Small Talk*?
7. Who studied *The Human Face* in 2001?
8. Which Angus Deayton series shows clips of celebrities when they were still unknowns?
9. Which *Doctor in the House* star also had a stint on *That's Life*?
10. Don Arrol, Norman Vaughan and Des O'Connor all hosted which long-running entertainment show?
11. Which quartet were *Game For a Laugh*?
12. Who was the first female presenter of *Crimewatch UK*?
13. Which husband and wife team quit *This Morning* in 2001?
14. Syd Perkins and Edna Duffield were early champions on which show?
15. Where would you book into in order to meet Jamie Theakston and Zoe Ball on Channel 4?
16. Who took over from Hugh Scully as presenter of *Antiques Roadshow*?

Answers to page 230

WHICH YEAR IN TV? 4: **1.** 1970 **2.** 1987 **3.** 1990 **4.** 1953 **5.** 1962 **6.** 1982 **7.** 1993 **8.** 1969 **9.** 1958 **10.** 1991 **11.** 1973 **12.** 1990 **13.** 1965 **14.** 1981 **15.** 1987 **16.** 1995

Quiz & Game Shows 3

Answers on page 231

1. Who was the first person to win £1 million on the British version of *Who Wants To Be a Millionaire*?
2. Who was the chirpy Cockney sidekick on *Double Your Money*?
3. Which game show features Mr Chips?
4. Who presented *Steal*?
5. On which show are team members invited to 'feel the sportsman'?
6. Which *News Huddlines* stalwart was a regular on *3-2-1*?
7. Who is the woman in black on *The Weakest Link*?
8. Which game show offers a much-coveted cheque book and pen?
9. Who played the organ on *Sale of the Century*?
10. Who asks the questions on *University Challenge*?
11. On which quiz are Lorraine Kelly and Rowland Rivron the two team captains?
12. Who succeeded Bob Monkhouse as host of *Family Fortunes*?
13. Which magician insisted that *Every Second Counts*?
14. Which diddy disc jockey was *All Clued Up*?
15. Which Channel 5 quiz show has no host?
16. On which game show did Tony Green keep the scores?

Answers to page 231

COP SHOWS 3: **1.** Patsy Palmer **2.** *Homicide: Life on the Street* **3.** *Mersey Beat* **4.** *Murder Bag* **5.** Dr Robert Astin **6.** Kris **7.** Five **8.** Barry Newman **9.** *Waking the Dead* **10.** Lt Arthur Fancy **11.** Benton Fraser **12.** Dorothy L. Sayers **13.** Don Beech **14.** Geoffrey Hayes (DC Scatliff) **15.** 714 **16.** Dora

Which Year in TV? 4

Answers on page 228

In which year did the following programmes begin in the UK?

1. *A Question of Sport*
2. *Porterhouse Blue*
3. *One Foot in the Grave*
4. *Panorama*
5. *Steptoe and Son*
6. *Brookside*
7. *Peak Practice*
8. *Monty Python's Flying Circus*
9. *Blue Peter*
10. *Soldier, Soldier*
11. *Last of the Summer Wine*
12. *Keeping Up Appearances*
13. *Call My Bluff*
14. *Brideshead Revisited*
15. *Inspector Morse*
16. *Kavanagh Q.C.*

Answers to page 228

TV POT LUCK 5: **1.** Philippa Forrester **2.** Louis Theroux **3.** Cliff Michelmore **4.** Two **5.** *It's a Knockout* **6.** Ronnie Corbett **7.** John Cleese **8.** *Before They Were Famous* **9.** George Layton **10.** *Sunday Night at the London Palladium* **11.** Matthew Kelly, Henry Kelly, Sarah Kennedy and Jeremy Beadle **12.** Sue Cook **13.** Richard Madeley and Judy Finnigan **14.** *Come Dancing* **15.** *The Priory* **16.** Michael Aspel

Cop Shows 3

Answers on page 229

1. Which ex-*EastEnder* stars in *McCready and Daughter*?
2. Which US police series featured Detectives John Munch and Meldrick Lewis?
3. What beat does Haydn Gwynne oversee as Superintendent Susan Blake?
4. Which was the first series to feature Superintendent Lockhart?
5. Who was the long-suffering boss of *Quincy, M.E.*?
6. In *Charlie's Angels*, what was the name of Jill Munroe's younger sister?
7. For how many years had Jim Rockford been wrongly imprisoned?
8. Who played *Petrocelli*?
9. Which 2001 police drama starring Trevor Eve investigated 'cold cases'?
10. Who is the precinct commander in *NYPD Blue*?
11. Which Mountie headed *Due South*?
12. Who created aristocratic sleuth Lord Peter Wimsey?
13. Which bent copper killed DS John Bolton in *The Bill*?
14. Who left *Z Cars* to join *Rainbow*?
15. What was Joe Friday's badge number?
16. What was the name of Reg Wexford's wife?

Answers to page 229

QUIZ & GAME SHOWS 3: **1.** Judith Keppel **2.** Monica Rose **3.** *Catchphrase* **4.** Mark Walker **5.** *They Think It's All Over* **6.** Chris Emmett **7.** Anne Robinson **8.** *Blankety Blank* **9.** Peter Fenn **10.** Jeremy Paxman **11.** *A Question of TV* **12.** Max Bygraves **13.** Paul Daniels **14.** David Hamilton **15.** *100 Per Cent* **16.** *Bullseye*

Corrie 1

Answers on page 234

1. Which odd couple went on the run with Wayne in 2001?
2. How did Albert Tatlock get his allotment dug over by Eddie Yeats and Stan Ogden?
3. What are the names of the Webster girls?
4. Which cousin of Alma Baldwin's took a shine to Gail Platt?
5. Who did Elsie Tanner marry in 1967?
6. Who played Jenny Bradley?
7. With whom did Ken Barlow have an affair in 1989, causing Deirdre to throw him out?
8. Who went to France in 2000 to visit his daughter Alice?
9. What relation is Fred Elliott to Ashley Peacock?
10. Which blue-rinsed battleaxe had the hots for Percy Sugden?
11. With which store detective did Reg Holdsworth have a fling?
12. Who ran off to Milton Keynes with her husband's physiotherapist?
13. What was the name of Len Fairclough's troubled son?
14. And which Sixties pop star played him?
15. What was Emily Bishop's maiden name?
16. Who is Weatherfield's 'queen of the hotpot'?

Answers to page 234

COMEDY 6: **1.** Roy Mallard **2.** Glenn Ponder **3.** *World of Pub* **4.** Martin Bryce **5.** *Happy Ever After* **6.** *Mister Ed* **7.** A.P. Herbert **8.** Road accident **9.** *TV To Go* **10.** Thermoman **11.** *Luv* **12.** Elliott Bay Towers **13.** Charlie Drake **14.** Tracey Ullman **15.** Rigsby **16.** Librarian

Sport 2

Answers on page 235

1. Which former Hampshire captain is anchor man for Channel 4's cricket coverage?
2. Which trainer's wife is the feminine face of the Channel 4 racing team?
3. Which broadcasting legend commentated on his final Grand Prix in 2001?
4. Which midweek sports programme did Peter Dimmock present?
5. Who is the BBC's rowing commentator?
6. Which men's 400-metre champion is now a mainstay of the BBC athletics team?
7. Which BBC horse-racing expert has to stand on a box?
8. Which ill-fated new channel screened live Nationwide League football matches in season 2001–2?
9. Which Alex is part of the BBC's golf commentary team?
10. Which Saturday afternoon sports show was presented by Dickie Davies?
11. Which former breakfast TV presenter – once described as the hairiest man on television – is a football fixture at Sky?
12. Who read the football results for over 30 years on *Grandstand*?
13. What nationality was he?
14. On which sport does Ray French commentate?
15. Which former Tottenham player asks profound questions on *Football Focus*?
16. Which Champion moved to ITV from BBC in 2001?

Answers to page 235

DRAMAS 6: **1.** Jerome Flynn **2.** Double-glazing **3.** *The Protectors* **4.** South Worfordshire **5.** William Ivory **6.** Leslie Ash **7.** Richard E. Grant **8.** Africa **9.** Richard **10.** Derek Thompson **11.** Janet **12.** *Bluebell* **13.** The Braithwaites **14.** *In a Land of Plenty* **15.** *The Wednesday Play* **16.** Cathy Gale

Comedy 6

Answers on page 232

1. What is the name of the inept interviewer in *People Like Us*?
2. Who was the band leader on *Knowing Me, Knowing You... With Alan Partridge*?
3. On which show might you be served by Dodgy Phil?
4. Who did Richard Briers play in *Ever Decreasing Circles*?
5. Which domestic sitcom begat *Terry And June*?
6. What was TV's talking horse called?
7. Who was the creator of *Misleading Cases*?
8. In what surprisingly ordinary manner was Victor Meldrew killed?
9. Which sketch show features the househusbands?
10. Which superhero does Ardal O'Hanlon turn into?
11. Which Carla Lane sitcom featured the Craven family?
12. In which apartment block does Frasier live?
13. Who was *The Worker*?
14. Who played Candice in *Girls On Top*?
15. Who owned a cat called Vienna?
16. What did Timothy Lumsden do for a living?

Answers to page 232

CORRIE 1: **1.** Roy and Hayley **2.** By telling them that he had found ancient coins on his plot **3.** Rosie and Sophie **4.** Richard Hillman **5.** Steve Tanner **6.** Sally Ann Matthews **7.** Wendy Crozier **8.** Curly Watts **9.** Father **10.** Phyllis Pearce **11.** Renee Dodds **12.** Liz McDonald **13.** Stanley **14.** Peter Noone **15.** Nugent **16.** Betty Turpin

Dramas 6

Answers on page 233

1. Who played Paddy Garvey in *Soldier, Soldier*?
2. What type of firm did John Thaw run in *The Glass*?
3. Harry Rule, Contessa di Contini and Paul Buchet were better known as which crime fighters?
4. For which constituency was Sir Giles Lynchwood the MP in *Blott on the Landscape*?
5. Which former dustman wrote *Common as Muck*?
6. Who stopped *Behaving Badly* as a nurse in *Where the Heart Is*?
7. Who played Sir Percy Blakeney in the most recent TV adaptation of *The Scarlet Pimpernel*?
8. In which country had Dr Jack Kerruish been practising before returning to England for *Peak Practice*?
9. What was *Hannay*'s first name?
10. Which *Casualty* mainstay played a ruthless terrorist in *The Price*?
11. What was the name of the housekeeper in *Dr Finlay's Casebook*?
12. Which dancer was Margaret Kelly otherwise known as?
13. Which family won the lottery in 2000?
14. Which 2001 drama series followed the fortunes of the Freeman family?
15. *Up the Junction* was a strand of which innovative BBC series of the Sixties?
16. Who was John Steed's first female sidekick?

Answers to page 233

SPORT 2: **1.** Mark Nicholas **2.** Lesley Graham **3.** Murray Walker **4.** *Sportsview* **5.** Gary Herbert **6.** Roger Black **7.** Willie Carson **8.** ITV Sport **9.** Alex Hay **10.** *World of Sport* **11.** Richard Keys **12.** Len Martin **13.** Australian **14.** Rugby League **15.** Garth Crooks **16.** Jon Champion

TV Chefs 1

Answers on page 238

1. Who was the 'crafty cook' on *Food and Drink*?
2. Who was the original presenter of *Masterchef*?
3. Which spiky-haired chef took over from him?
4. Which 'pukka' TV chef does adverts for Sainsbury's?
5. Which TV chef is on the board of Norwich City Football Club?
6. Which chef was popularly known as *The Galloping Gourmet*?
7. Which chef is famed for his seafood recipes?
8. Who was appalled at being presented with nothing more than £5 worth of potatoes with which to prepare a meal on *Ready Steady Cook*?
9. Which GMTV presenter was the unimaginative shopper on that edition of *Ready Steady Cook*?
10. Who was *The Man in the Kitchen*?
11. Which TV chef is Fern Britton's partner?
12. Which Brian was a regular on *This Morning*?
13. Which Fifties cook was renowned for his monocle?
14. Which Zena was a TV cook of the Sixties?
15. Which lively character is the new host of *Ready Steady Cook*?
16. Which TV cook 'bites' on Channel 4?

Answers to page 238

SOAPS 5: **1.** Starry **2.** Channel 5 **3.** In a blazing barn **4.** Hattie **5.** Ruth **6.** Ray Krebbs **7.** 'Tinhead' **8.** Cyril **9.** The Harts **10.** Marcus Christie **11.** Angie Reynolds **12.** Irene and Terry Raymond **13.** Frank Adam **14.** Ernest Bishop **15.** *Compact* **16.** John James

TV Pot Luck 6

Answers on page 239

1. Who was the first person to be evicted on *Celebrity Big Brother*?
2. Who escaped from *Black Adder*'s service to present *Time Team*?
3. Which TV presenter upset the Welsh with her remarks on *Room 101*?
4. Who was our tour guide on *A History of Britain*?
5. Who took over from Jeremy Beadle as presenter of *You've Been Framed*?
6. Who was the original chairman of the talent show *New Faces*?
7. Which Eileen was television's first keep fit expert?
8. Which series celebrated the Queen's Silver Jubilee by taking viewers inside various royal residences?
9. What is *Montel*'s surname?
10. Which star of *Goodness Gracious Me* went in search of the Kama Sutra?
11. What is the title of Channel 4's programme about compulsive collectors?
12. *Escape to the Sun* followed British expats in which Mediterranean resort?
13. Which garden designer set out to explore *Planet Patio*?
14. *Seeing Stars* was a junior version of which long-running programme?
15. Who targets the public in *Trigger Happy TV*?
16. Which TV magicians lived in an unpleasant world?

Answers to page 239

LOCATIONS 2: **1.** Crete **2.** Charnham **3.** *Shortland Street* **4.** Boston **5.** Cicely **6.** *Bad Girls* **7.** Reg Wexford **8.** Seven Dials **9.** *Brookside* **10.** The E20 **11.** Derbyshire **12.** Mavis Wilton **13.** *In Loving Memory* **14.** Toronto **15.** Melbourne **16.** Ansons Corner

Soaps 5

Answers on page 236

1. What was the name of Benny's goat in *Crossroads*?
2. Which channel re-introduced *Home and Away* in 2001?
3. How did Sarah Sugden die in *Emmerdale*?
4. In *EastEnders* who was Lloyd Tavernier's twin sister?
5. Who was Lance and Anne Wilkinson's mother in *Neighbours*?
6. Which *Dallas* ranch-hand turned out to be Jock Ewing's illegitimate son?
7. What was Timothy O'Leary's nickname in *Brookside*?
8. What was the name of Betty Turpin's policeman husband in *Coronation Street*?
9. Which family was wiped out by a boat explosion in *Family Affairs*?
10. In *EastEnders*, what is the name of Phil Mitchell's dubious solicitor?
11. Which *Emmerdale* character does Freya Copeland play?
12. Which Albert Square couple owned the First Till Last shop?
13. Which struggling film star got *Crossroads* waitress Diane Lawton pregnant?
14. Which Weatherfield resident was killed during a 1978 wages snatch?
15. Which Sixties soap was set on a woman's magazine?
16. Who played Jeff Colby in *Dynasty*?

Answers to page 236

TV CHEFS 1: **1.** Michael Barry **2.** Loyd Grossman **3.** Gary Rhodes **4.** Jamie Oliver **5.** Delia Smith **6.** Graham Kerr **7.** Rick Stein **8.** Kevin Woodford **9.** Fiona Phillips **10.** Philip Harben **11.** Phil Vickery **12.** Brian Turner **13.** Johnnie Cradock **14.** Zena Skinner **15.** Ainsley Harriott **16.** Nigella Lawson

Locations 2

Answers on page 237

1. Which island was the setting for the drama series *The Lotus Eaters*?
2. In which fictional town is *Family Affairs* set?
3. Which medical drama is set in New Zealand?
4. In which American city was *Cheers* set?
5. What was the name of the town in *Northern Exposure*?
6. Which drama series is set in Larkhall women's prison?
7. Which TV detective was based in Kingsmarkham?
8. What was the police station called in *The Gentle Touch*?
9. In which soap do the regulars drink at Bev's Bar?
10. What is the name of Albert Square's local nightclub?
11. In which county is *Peak Practice* set?
12. Which *Coronation Street* character went off to live in Cartmel?
13. Which funereal sitcom was set in the fictional Lancashire mill town of Oldshaw?
14. In which city was *Due South* filmed?
15. Which Australian city's police force provided the stories for *Homicide*?
16. Which corner is a neighbouring district of Erinsborough?

Answers to page 237

TV POT LUCK 6: **1.** Chris Eubank **2.** Tony Robinson **3.** Anne Robinson **4.** Simon Schama **5.** Lisa Riley **6.** Derek Hobson **7.** Eileen Fowler **8.** *Royal Heritage* **9.** Williams **10.** Sanjeev Bhaskar **11.** *Collectors' Lot* **12.** Benidorm **13.** Diarmuid Gavin **14.** *The Sky at Night* **15.** Dom Joly **16.** Penn and Teller

TV Music 2

Answers on page 242

1. Which former dancer became known as 'Nasty Nigel' on *Popstars*?
2. Which chart show follows on from *SM:TV Live*?
3. Who are the team captains on *A Question of Pop*?
4. Which Saturday morning favourite presented Channel 4's *Top Ten: Teen Idols*?
5. With which long-running music show was 'Whispering' Bob Harris associated?
6. Which former *Playboy* centrefold presented *The Word* at the age of 17?
7. Which American crooner – who enjoyed a recent renaissance – ended each of his shows by singing 'May Each Day'?
8. Which band frontman vetoed an entire set he had recorded for *The Tube* because he didn't think any of the numbers were up to standard?
9. Who was a £10-a-week secretary when she answered an ad to appear on *Ready, Steady, Go!*?
10. Which music show is due to celebrate its 40th birthday in 2004?
11. Which Fifties show featured Welsh tenor Ivor Emmanuel?
12. Which music quiz featured a dummy keyboard?
13. Which *Never Mind the Buzzcocks* presenter no longer looks like a Fifties throwback?
14. Who hosted *Juke Box Jury* on its return in 1979?
15. Which singer's doppel-ganger won the 2001 series of *Stars in Their Eyes*?
16. Why did the Rolling Stones refuse to get on the famous revolving stage at the end of *Sunday Night at the London Palladium*?

Answers to page 242

COMEDY 7: **1.** *The Golden Girls* **2.** *I Didn't Know You Cared* **3.** *My Three Sons* **4.** *Dad's Army* **5.** *Birds of a Feather* **6.** *Happy Days* **7.** *Not In Front of the Children* **8.** *The Fall and Rise of Reginald Perrin* **9.** *Hugh and I* **10.** *Citizen Smith* **11.** *Car 54, Where Are You?* **12.** *Caroline in the City* **13.** *Father, Dear Father* **14.** *Hark at Barker* **15.** *Whoops Apocalypse* **16.** *One Foot in the Grave*

Cop Shows 4

Answers on page 243

1. Who resigned as Superintendent at Sun Hill in 2000?
2. Under what burden does DCI Ross Tanner operate?
3. Who plays Dalziel in *Dalziel and Pascoe*?
4. Which series featured the work of fictional celebrity attorney Theodore 'Teddy' Hoffman?
5. TV John was a regular character in which police series?
6. Why was *Hazell* invalided out of the police force?
7. What was the name of Quincy's houseboat?
8. Who was Sid Halley's sidekick in *The Racing Game*?
9. In *NYPD Blue*, what was the profession of John Kelly's wife?
10. Which detective investigates *Midsomer Murders*?
11. Who laid out Chief Daniels in the final episode of *Hill Street Blues*?
12. Which bumbling detective was played by David Rasche?
13. Who was frequently aided and abetted by Stick?
14. Which TV policeman finally retired in 1976 at the age of 80?
15. Which law enforcer strode the moors with a dog called Clive?
16. What kind of establishment did Diamante Lil run in *Bergerac*?

Answers to page 243

SCI FI 2: **1.** Zaphod Beeblebrox **2.** A comet **3.** Toby Wren **4.** Jack McGee **5.** *The Invisible Man* **6.** Gauda Prime **7.** Athena **8.** The Sterlings **9.** Jose Chung's From Outer Space **10.** Victor Carroon **11.** Ed Bishop **12.** Harry Mudd **13.** Australian **14.** Number Two **15.** *Man From Atlantis* **16.** Patrick Allen

Comedy 7

Answers on page 240

In which sitcoms would you find the following characters?

1. Dorothy Zbornak
2. Carter Brandon
3. Steve Douglas
4. Maurice Yateman
5. Tracey Stubbs
6. Ralph Malph
7. Jennifer Corner
8. Tony Webster
9. Arthur Wormold
10. Harry Fenning
11. Francis Muldoon
12. Caroline Duffy
13. Patrick Glover
14. Mildred Bates
15. Kevin Pork
16. Nick Swainey

Answers to page 240

TV MUSIC 2: **1.** Nigel Lythgoe **2.** *CD: UK* **3.** Noddy Holder and Suggs **4.** Cat Deeley **5.** *The Old Grey Whistle Test* **6.** Amanda de Cadenet **7.** Andy Williams **8.** Robert Plant (Led Zeppelin) **9.** Cathy McGowan **10.** *Top of the Pops* **11.** *Land of Song* **12.** *Face the Music* **13.** Mark Lamarr **14.** Noel Edmonds **15.** Dusty Springfield **16.** They didn't think it would fit their rebellious image

Sci Fi 2

Answers on page 241

1. In *The Hitch-Hiker's Guide to the Galaxy*, who created the Pan Galactic Gargle Blaster?
2. What blinded most of the people in *The Day of the Triffids*?
3. Which *Doomwatch* hero was killed trying to defuse a bomb?
4. Which intrepid reporter was keen to expose *The Incredible Hulk*?
5. What was Peter Brady otherwise known as?
6. In the final episode of *Blake's 7*, on which lawless planet did Blake meet up again with his crew?
7. Who was Adama's daughter in *Battlestar Galactica*?
8. Which 'typical Southern Californian family' became lost in another dimension in *Otherworld*?
9. In which episode of *The X Files* did Mulder and Scully appear as Men in Black?
10. Who was the sole survivor from the spaceship in *The Quatermass Experiment*?
11. Who was the voice of Captain Blue in *Captain Scarlet and the Mysterons*?
12. Who surprised Captain Kirk with his illicit human cargo of three glamorous girls?
13. What nationality was Pal Kenzy in *Star Cops*?
14. Which Number in *The Prisoner* was served by a mute dwarf butler?
15. Whose life did Dr Elizabeth Merrill save?
16. Who played Luther Ames in *Journey to the Unknown*?

Answers to page 241

COP SHOWS 4: **1.** Charles Brownlow **2.** His eyesight is deteriorating rapidly **3.** Warren Clarke **4.** *Murder One* **5.** *Hamish Macbeth* **6.** Ankle injury **7.** *Fiji* **8.** Chico Barnes **9.** Attorney **10.** Chief Inspector Barnaby **11.** Norm Buntz **12.** *Sledge Hammer!* **13.** *Spender* **14.** George Dixon **15.** *Cluff* **16.** Restaurant

Music Pot Luck 8

Answers on page 246

1. With which group did Belinda Carlisle sing lead vocals before going solo in 1985?
2. Which legendary blues artist was born McKinley Morganfield?
3. Which band's debut single was 'Caught By The Fuzz'?
4. Who played guitar under the name L'Angelo Mysterioso on Cream's 'Badge'?
5. Which 17-year-old unknown replaced guitarist Bernard Butler in Suede?
6. Which duo had a hit with 'Only One Woman' in 1968?
7. Who sang the Crowded House number 'Don't Dream It's Over' at the Nelson Mandela concert at Wembley Stadium in 1988?
8. Which singer did The Nice back in their early days?
9. What was S Club 7's first number one?
10. Who wrote the soundtrack for the film of Nick Hornby's book *About a Boy*?
11. To what did The Farinas change their name in the Sixties?
12. Which band reached number eight in the charts in 1985 with 'Johnny Come Home'?
13. In what year were Radiohead formed?
14. In which city were Super Furry Animals founded?
15. In which band did Dave Stewart and Annie Lennox first enjoy chart success?
16. Who released a 1987 album called 'Document'?

Answers to page 246

EIGHTIES 2: **1.** 'True' **2.** Nine **3.** Everything But The Girl **4.** Deborah Harry **5.** Frankie Goes To Hollywood **6.** Chris de Burgh ('Lady In Red') **7.** Forties **8.** Orchestral Manoeuvres In The Dark **9.** 'The Model' **10.** 1981 **11.** 'Morning Train' **12.** 'Don't You Want Me' (Human League) **13.** It was the first new UK number one of the Eighties **14.** Soft Cell **15.** Def Leppard **16.** 1984

R & B 2

Answers on page 247

1. Which group released 'Ghetto Romance'?
2. Which Destiny's Child single was the soundtrack to the Charlie's Angels movie?
3. The album 'Fanmail' was by which band?
4. Sisqo used to be the lead singer of which group?
5. Who had a recent hit with 'Money'?
6. Who made the album 'TP-2.COM'?
7. Who released 'Things I've Seen'?
8. Stargate remixed for Sisqo, but in which country are their studios?
9. What record label are Fierce signed to?
10. What was the title of Shola Ama's first UK single?
11. What was Honeyz first album called?
12. What was Another Level's first UK number one single?
13. Which other solo artist sang on R. Kelly's hit 'I'm Your Angel' in November 1998?
14. Whitney Houston's 'I Will Always Love You' was recorded by which artist in 1974?
15. What is Usher's record label?
16. What was Jennifer Lopez's first single?

Answers to page 247

NAME CHANGES 4: **1.** Blur **2.** Radiohead **3.** The Bay City Rollers **4.** Simon and Garfunkel **5.** Marmalade **6.** Madness **7.** Depeche Mode **8.** Middle Of The Road **9.** The Who **10.** Blondie **11.** Johnny Kidd and The Pirates **12.** The Beach Boys **13.** Talking Heads **14.** Procol Harum **15.** Kajagoogoo **16.** The Byrds

Eighties 2

Answers on page 244

1. What was Spandau Ballet's only number one?
2. How many weeks did Dire Straits' 'Brothers In Arms' spend at the top of the US album charts?
3. Who had a 1988 hit with their version of Danny Whitten's 'I Don't Want To Talk About It'?
4. Whose debut solo album was 'Koo Koo' in 1981?
5. Nasher Nash, Mark O'Toole and Peter Gill were members of which band?
6. Which singer, born Christopher John Davidson, spent three weeks at number one in August 1986 with a song he wrote for his wife?
7. In which decade was Mark Knopfler born?
8. Who reached number three in the UK album charts with 'Architecture And Morality'?
9. Which Kraftwerk number one was officially the B-side of 'Computer Love'?
10. In which year did Bucks Fizz win the Eurovision Song Contest?
11. What was Sheena Easton's '9 To 5' re-titled in the US?
12. What was the biggest-selling UK single of 1981?
13. What was significant about The Pretenders' 'Brass In Pocket'?
14. David Ball was the less flamboyant member of which duo?
15. Who released the 1987 album 'Hysteria'?
16. In which year did Madonna first enter the UK singles charts?

Answers to page 244

MUSIC POT LUCK 8: **1.** The Go-Go's **2.** Muddy Waters **3.** Supergrass **4.** George Harrison **5.** Richard Oakes **6.** Marbles **7.** Paul Young **8.** P.P. Arnold **9.** 'Bring It All Back' **10.** Badly Drawn Boy **11.** Family **12.** Fine Young Cannibals **13.** 1991 **14.** Cardiff **15.** The Tourists **16.** R.E.M.

Name Changes 4

Answers on page 245

1. Which band used to be called Seymour?
2. Who were once known as On A Friday?
3. Which teenybop favourites were formerly called The Saxons?
4. Who changed their name from Tom and Jerry?
5. Who wisely decided to dispense with the name Dean Ford and The Gaylords?
6. Which band were previously called The Invaders?
7. Who were once called Composition Of Sound?
8. To what did Los Caracas change their name?
9. Which Sixties band used to be called The High Numbers?
10. Which American band were once known as The Stilettos?
11. What did Freddie Heath and The Nutters Become?
12. Who were formerly known as Carl and The Passions?
13. Who changed their name from The Artistics?
14. Which Sixties band chose something more Latin than The Paramounts?
15. Who used to be known as Art Nouveau?
16. Who were once called The Beefeaters?

Answers to page 245

R & B 2: **1.** Damage **2.** 'Independent Women' **3.** TLC **4.** Dru Hill **5.** Jamelia **6.** R. Kelly **7.** Spooks **8.** Norway **9.** Wildstar **10.** 'You Might Need Somebody' **11.** 'Wonder No. 8' **12.** 'Freak Me' **13.** Celine Dion **14.** Dolly Parton **15.** LaFace **16.** 'If You Had My Love'

Chart Toppers 3

Answers on page 250

1. Which singer reached number one in 1973 with 'Get Down'?
2. In which year did Shakespear's Sister get to number one with 'Stay'?
3. Which group's only number one was 'All Or Nothing'?
4. What was the first reggae record to top the UK charts?
5. For which artist was Kelly Marie's 'Feels Like I'm In Love' originally intended?
6. Which band topped the singles charts in 1999 – 19 years after their previous number one?
7. Which two artists took 'Mary's Boy Child' to number one in the UK?
8. How many number ones did B*Witched have in 1998?
9. With which song did The Bee Gees top the UK charts in October 1967?
10. Which female artist went 'All Around The World' in 1989?
11. Who reached number one in September 1956 with 'Lay Down Your Arms'?
12. What was Christie's only UK number one?
13. From which Boomtown Rats album did 'Rat Trap' come?
14. Who took a Rodgers and Hammerstein song to number one in 1982?
15. Who asked 'Would I Lie To You' in 1992?
16. Which was the first official Stock/Aitken/Waterman production to top the UK charts?

Answers to page 250

BOY BANDS 1: **1.** Blue **2.** RCA **3.** 'Love Me For A Reason' **4.** *North Hollywood High* **5.** Ten **6.** 1995 **7.** *Bean: The Movie* **8.** Mark **9.** 'Do We Rock' **10.** 1996 **11.** Shane Lynch **12.** Two **13.** O-Town **14.** The Moffatts **15.** 'Promises' **16.** 'Relight My Fire'

Albums 3

Answers on page 251

1. Which distinctive-looking band released 'Kimono My House'?
2. Which Scottish band topped the UK album charts in 1989 with 'When The World Knows Your Name'?
3. The single 'Pride (In The Name Of Love)' was taken from which U2 album?
4. What was the title of Prince's first number one UK album?
5. Who were 'Nicely Out Of Tune' in 1970?
6. Who had a number one album in 1989 with 'Crossroads'?
7. Which Pulp album spawned 'Common People'?
8. Which Simple Minds album spent a total of 83 weeks in the UK charts?
9. Which two bands made albums called 'Raising Hell'?
10. Which Lou Reed album was re-issued for a second time in 1998?
11. Which Rolling Stones album topped the UK charts in September 1973?
12. Whose second album was titled 'Meat Is Murder'?
13. Which boy band's 1993 number one album reminded them of their home town?
14. Which former soap star's debut album was called 'Ten Good Reasons'?
15. Whose greatest hits album was titled 'Sex Machine'?
16. Whose best-selling album was the 1989 offering 'The Twelve Commandments Of Dance'?

Answers to page 251

SOLO ARTISTS 2: **1.** Harry Chapin **2.** Bill Withers **3.** Eddi Reader **4.** Slim Whitman **5.** 'She's The One' **6.** Freda Payne **7.** Sinitta **8.** Gary Moore **9.** Gladys Knight **10.** Gene Pitney **11.** 'In The Air Tonight' **12.** Cuba **13.** Celine Dion **14.** Randy Crawford **15.** Jacques Brel **16.** 14

Boy Bands 1

Answers on page 248

1. Which group released the single 'All Rise' in 2001?
2. What is Westlife's record label?
3. What was the title of Boyzone's first single?
4. Which Channel 4 TV programme featured 'Bomb Diggy' by Another Level?
5. What number did Five's first single get to in the UK charts?
6. In which year did Backstreet Boys release their first single?
7. From which film was Boyzone's 'Picture Of You'?
8. Which member of a1 played the piano in the performances of 'Everytime'?
9. What was the title of Point Break's first UK single?
10. In which year was 911's first UK single released?
11. Which member of Boyzone was studying an architecture course when he was recruited for the band?
12. What number in the UK charts did the album 'Westlife' reach?
13. Trevor, Ashley and Jacob are members of which boy band?
14. 'Chapter 1: A New Beginning' was which group's debut album?
15. What was the title of Take That's first single?
16. Which Take That single featured Lulu?

Answers to page 248

CHART TOPPERS 3: **1.** Gilbert O'Sullivan **2.** 1992 **3.** The Small Faces **4.** 'Israelites' (Desmond Dekker) **5.** Elvis Presley **6.** Blondie ('Maria') **7.** Harry Belafonte and Boney M **8.** Three – 'C'est La Vie', 'Rollercoaster' and 'To You I Belong' **9.** 'Massachusetts' **10.** Lisa Stansfield **11.** Anne Shelton **12.** 'Yellow River' **13.** 'Tonic For The Troops' **14.** Captain Sensible ('Happy Talk') **15.** Charles & Eddie **16.** 'Respectable' (Mel and Kim)

Solo Artists 2

Answers on page 249

1. Who directed the Oscar-nominated film *Legendary Champions* in 1968 before turning to music?
2. Which American soul singer used to be employed producing toilet seats for Boeing 747s at a Los Angeles aerospace factory?
3. Which former session singer went solo after Fairground Attraction disbanded?
4. Which American artist had 1955 hits with 'Rose Marie' and 'Indian Love Call'?
5. Which Robbie Williams hit was originally recorded by World Party on their 1997 album 'Egyptology'?
6. Whose only number one was 'Band Of Gold'?
7. Which female singer had a hit with 'So Macho' in the 1980s?
8. Which former Thin Lizzy guitarist enjoyed solo success with 'Empty Rooms'?
9. Which Motown artist made her acting debut in the 1976 movie *Pipedream*?
10. 'That Girl Belongs To Yesterday' was a 1964 hit for which American artist?
11. What was Phil Collins's first solo hit?
12. In which country was Gloria Estefan born?
13. Which Canadian chanteuse is the youngest in a family of 12?
14. Who sang with The Crusaders before going solo?
15. Who wrote Terry Jacks's 1974 UK number one 'Seasons In The Sun'?
16. How old was Helen Shapiro when she topped the charts in 1961 with 'You Don't Know'?

Answers to page 249

ALBUMS 3: **1.** Sparks **2.** Deacon Blue **3.** 'The Unforgettable Fire' **4.** 'Lovesexy' **5.** Lindisfarne **6.** Tracy Chapman **7.** 'Different Class' **8.** 'Once Upon A Time' **9.** Fatback Band and Run D.M.C. **10.** 'Transformer' **11.** 'Goat's Head Soup' **12.** The Smiths **13.** East 17 ('Walthamstow') **14.** Jason Donovan **15.** James Brown **16.** London Boys

Sixties 3

Answers on page 254

1. Which Beatles number gave Peter and Gordon their first hit?
2. Which 17-year-old landed a recording contract after singing to Adam Faith in his dressing-room?
3. Which Sixties singer was famous for his ability to yodel?
4. Art Sharp, John Allen, Pete Shannon, John Hawken, Ray Phillips and Barry Jenkins were the original line-up for which UK band?
5. Which was the last UK number one of the Sixties?
6. Which American singer hit the UK charts with the sinister 'Ode To Billy Joe'?
7. Which Kinks song satirised Carnaby Street narcissism?
8. Athol Guy played the double bass in which Australian band?
9. Which British group – closely modelled on The Rolling Stones – had their only top ten hit with 'Don't Bring Me Down' in 1964?
10. Who were 'Living In The Past' in 1969?
11. Which Manchester band was formed by a merger of The Deltas and The Dolphins?
12. Which complex 1966 number one was recorded over six months during 17 sessions in four studios?
13. Who reached number 12 in the charts with 'Sunny' in September 1966?
14. Who had a hit with 'Three Steps To Heaven' shortly after being killed in a car crash?
15. What was Jimi Hendrix's first UK hit?
16. What was the title of the only hit by the 1910 Fruitgum Co.?

Answers to page 254

MUSIC POT LUCK 9: **1.** George Michael **2.** Pete Shelley **3.** The Belmonts **4.** Chumbawamba **5.** Timmy Mallett **6.** 'Annie's Song' **7.** Nik Kershaw **8.** The Netherlands **9.** Bobby Goldsboro **10.** Mungo Jerry **11.** The Goombay Dance Band **12.** 'Calling Occupants Of Interplanetary Craft (The Recognised Anthem Of World Contact Day)' **13.** 'Margate' **14.** Rita Coolidge **15.** Eighth Wonder **16.** Shanks & Bigfoot

Stairway to Heaven 2

Answers on page 255

1. Which two members of the same band were killed in separate motorbike crashes in Macon, Georgia, a year and three blocks apart?
2. Whose last words were 'Don't worry, it's not loaded' before shooting himself dead during a 1978 game of Russian roulette?
3. Which former Shadows member was electrocuted by his guitar in 1973?
4. How did Mama Cass Elliot die in 1974?
5. And who died from an accidental drug overdose in the same London flat four years later?
6. In which year was Jim Croce killed in a plane crash?
7. Which singer with Joy Division hanged himself in 1980?
8. Which American singer shot himself dead in his Californian home in 1990?
9. Which legendary soul singer was shot dead by his father during a blazing row in 1984?
10. Which drummer, who tasted chart success with 'Dance With The Devil', was killed in a road smash in 1998?
11. Where was Eddie Cochran killed?
12. How did Graham Bond die in 1974?
13. Who died in a fire at his home in Arkesden, Essex, in 1991?
14. In which year was Otis Redding killed in a plane crash?
15. Which US blues guitarist hanged himself in a prison cell in 1988 following his arrest for drunken behaviour?
16. Which drummer with Booker T and The MGs was shot dead by burglars in 1975?

Answers to page 255

ONE-HIT WONDERS 3: **1.** Jeannie C. Riley ('Harper Valley P.T.A.') **2.** Barry McGuire **3.** 'Michelle' **4.** 'Shaddup You Face' **5.** Joe Dolce Music Theatre **6.** 'Matchstalk Men And Matchstalk Cats And Dogs' **7.** Steam **8.** Toni Basil **9.** Phyllis Nelson **10.** The Simon Park Orchestra **11.** 'Eye Level' **12.** The Lemon Pipers **13.** 'In The Year 2525 (Exordium And Terminus)' **14.** Barbados **15.** 'Up Town Top Ranking' **16.** Joe Simon

Music Pot Luck 9

Answers on page 252

1. Which future international star was sacked from his Saturday job at British Home Stores for not wearing a shirt and tie in the stockroom?
2. Which Pete was lead singer with The Buzzcocks?
3. What was the name of Dion's backing group?
4. Danbert Nobacon was a member of which Nineties band?
5. Which children's TV presenter hid behind the name of Bombalurina?
6. With which John Denver tune did flautist James Galway enjoy his only UK hit?
7. Whose debut single was 'I Won't Let The Sun Go Down On Me'?
8. From which country did Golden Earring originate?
9. Which US singer, who had an international 'weepie' hit in 1968, had first made his name as a guitarist in Roy Orbison's touring band?
10. Ray Dorset was the lead singer with which early Seventies chart band?
11. Who reached number one in 1982 with 'Seven Tears'?
12. Which Carpenters single had 73 letters in its title?
13. Which seaside resort did Chas and Dave sing about in 1982?
14. About whom did Leon Russell supposedly write 'Delta Lady'?
15. What was the name of Patsy Kensit's band?
16. Who reached number one with 'Sweet Like Chocolate' in May 1999?

Answers to page 252

SIXTIES 3: **1.** 'World Without Love' **2.** Sandie Shaw **3.** Frank Ifield **4.** The Nashville Teens **5.** 'Two Little Boys' (Rolf Harris) **6.** Bobbie Gentry **7.** 'Dedicated Follower Of Fashion' **8.** The Seekers **9.** The Pretty Things **10.** Jethro Tull **11.** The Hollies **12.** 'Good Vibrations' **13.** Bobby Hebb **14.** Eddie Cochran **15.** 'Hey Joe' **16.** 'Simon Says'

One-Hit Wonders 3

Answers on page 253

1. Which female American country singer's only hit was a 1968 ditty about a parent teacher association?
2. Which former member of the New Christy Minstrels enjoyed his only hit with the 1965 protest song 'Eve Of Destruction'?
3. With which Beatles song did The Overlanders reach number one in 1966?
4. Which novelty hit famously kept Ultravox's 'Vienna' from the number one spot in 1981?
5. And who sang it?
6. Which 1978 hit was a tribute to painter L.S. Lowry?
7. Whose only UK hit was 'Na Na Hey Hey Kiss Him Goodbye' in 1970?
8. Whose top 50 career began and ended with 'Mickey' in 1982?
9. Whose only hit was the 1985 UK number one 'Move Closer'?
10. Who had a hit with the theme music from the TV detective series *Van Der Valk*?
11. And what was the title of the track?
12. Who reached the top of the American charts in 1968 with 'Green Tambourine'?
13. Which prophetic number one of 1969 brought fleeting fame for Zager and Evans?
14. About which island did Typically Tropical sing in 1975?
15. What was the title of Althia and Donna's only hit?
16. Which American singer's only UK hit was 'Step By Step' in 1973?

Answers to page 253

STAIRWAY TO HEAVEN 2: **1.** Duane Allman and Berry Oakley (Allman Brothers Band) **2.** Terry Kath (Chicago) **3.** John Rostill **4.** Heart attack **5.** Keith Moon **6.** 1973 **7.** Ian Curtis **8.** Del Shannon **9.** Marvin Gaye **10.** Cozy Powell **11.** Chippenham, Wiltshire **12.** He mysteriously fell to his death under a tube train at Finsbury Park Station **13.** Steve Marriott **14.** 1967 **15.** Roy Buchanan **16.** Al Jackson

Punk 2

Answers on page 258

1. Which band started out supporting The Sex Pistols on their 'Anarchy' tour?
2. Which Police single reached number two in the UK charts in July 1979 – nine months after its first entry?
3. Which band named after a TV detective show asked: 'Is Vic There'?
4. Which Sham 69 song revealed the group's geographical origins?
5. Who were banned from appearing at the European Punk Rock Festival in France in August 1976?
6. Who was drummer with The Jam?
7. Whose first album was 'New Boots And Panties!'?
8. What were The Skids working for in 1979?
9. Susan Dallion was working as a waitress in Chislehurst, Kent, when she changed her name to which punk princess?
10. Which was X-Ray Spex's biggest UK hit?
11. Who had a hit in 1979 with 'Back Of My Hand'?
12. Which band were forced to pull out at the last minute of a 1976 interview with Bill Grundy on the *Today* TV show, thereby allowing The Sex Pistols to take their place and make front-page headlines?
13. Which of The Stranglers was once an ice-cream salesman?
14. Which TV presenter was a member of Jet Bronx and The Forbidden?
15. What was Brenda Spencer's role in the history of The Boomtown Rats?
16. 'Oliver's Army' was taken from which album by Elvis Costello and The Attractions?

Answers to page 258

COUNTRY AND WESTERN 2: **1.** Shania Twain **2.** Trisha Yearwood **3.** Dolly Parton **4.** Maurice **5.** Slim Dusty **6.** She had divorced husband George Jones two months before it reached number one in the UK **7.** Loretta Lynn **8.** 30 **9.** England Dan (real name Dan Seals) **10.** Daniel O'Donnell **11.** The Korean War **12.** Roger Miller **13.** Kitty Wells **14.** Crystal Gayle **15.** k.d. lang **16.** Charley Pride

Merseybeat 1

Answers on page 259

1. Ray Ennis, Ralph Ellis, Les Braid and Norman Kuhlke were the original line-up of which Merseybeat group?
2. Which group reached number one in August 1963 with a cover of an old Drifters number?
3. And what was the title of the song?
4. Which group's debut single was 'Hello Little Girl'?
5. Which brothers used to be in a band called The Mars Bars?
6. Which group took their name from the title of a 1956 John Wayne movie?
7. Which Liverpool band did Ringo Starr leave to join The Beatles?
8. Which Merseybeat frontman was born William Ashton?
9. What was inscribed on the drum kit of The Merseybeats' John Banks?
10. Why was Paul McCartney absent when The Quarry Men made their Cavern club debut in August 1957?
11. Which was Billy J. Kramer and The Dakotas' first number one?
12. Which band were voted second behind The Beatles in *Mersey Beat* magazine's first group popularity poll in January 1962?
13. Who reached number three in the UK charts with 'You're No Good' in 1964?
14. Who walked out of The Merseybeats in 1964?
15. Which was The Beatles' fifth consecutive UK number one?
16. Which backing band had an instrumental hit with 'The Cruel Sea' in 1963?

Answers to page 259

NINETIES 2: **1.** Shamen **2.** Mariah Carey **3.** 'Doctor Jones' **4.** Sean Moore **5.** Right Said Fred **6.** Portishead **7.** Massive Attack **8.** 'Dreams' **9.** Four **10.** Kula Shaker ('Hush') **11.** Outhere Brothers **12.** 'Things Can Only Get Better' **13.** Johnny Marr and Bernard Sumner **14.** EMF **15.** Mark Morrison **16.** Canadian

Country and Western 2

Answers on page 256

1. Which country beauty named her son Eja?
2. Who sang backing vocals on the Garth Brooks album 'No Fences' before becoming a star in her own right?
3. Which voluptuous female artist is one of a family of 12?
4. What was Tex Ritter's real Christian name?
5. Which country star was born David Gordon Kirkpatrick in 1927?
6. What was ironic about Tammy Wynette's 'Stand By Your Man'?
7. Who had a US country number one with the autobiographical 'Coal Miner's Daughter' in 1970?
8. How old was Patsy Cline when she died?
9. Who came from a family of performing Seals?
10. Who released a 1987 album entitled 'The Boy From Donegal'?
11. 'Ruby, Don't Take Your Love To Town' was based on a true incident following which war?
12. Who had a US top ten hit in 1964 with 'Dang Me'?
13. Who was the first female singer to reach number one in the US country charts?
14. Which country singer is a younger sister of Loretta Lynn?
15. Whose debut album was 'A Truly Western Experience'?
16. Who took just 15 minutes to learn and record 'Is Anybody Goin' To San Antone'?

Answers to page 256

PUNK 2: **1.** The Clash **2.** 'Can't Stand Losing You' **3.** Department S **4.** 'Hersham Boys' **5.** The Sex Pistols **6.** Rick Buckler **7.** Ian Dury and The Blockheads **8.** 'Working For The Yankee Dollar' **9.** Siouxsie **10.** 'Germ Free Adolescence' **11.** The Jags **12.** Queen **13.** Jet Black **14.** Loyd Grossman **15.** She shot dead several of her San Diego schoolfriends in 1979, citing as her reason: 'I don't like Mondays' **16.** 'Armed Forces'

Nineties 2

Answers on page 257

1. Who reached number one with 'Ebeneezer Goode' in 1992?

2. Who won 1991 Grammies for Best Female Vocalist and Best New Artist?

3. What was Aqua's second UK number one?

4. Who is the youngest of the Manic Street Preachers?

5. Which band was named after a Bernard Cribbins novelty hit of 1962?

6. Which band were named after the place in south-west England where Geoff Barrow spent his teens?

7. Whose 1998 number one album was titled 'Mezzanine'?

8. Which was The Corrs' first top ten hit in the UK?

9. How many number one singles did Westlife have in 1999?

10. Which band changed their name from The Lovely Lads and hit number two in the UK charts in March 1997 with their version of a Deep Purple song?

11. Who had a 1995 hit with 'Boom Boom Boom'?

12. Which 1994 number one was adopted by the Labour Party as its theme song for the 1997 General Election?

13. Which duo made up Electronic?

14. Whose first hit in 1990 was 'Unbelievable'?

15. Which UK chart topper fell foul of the law again after getting an impostor to do his community service?

16. What nationality is Alanis Morissette?

Answers to page 257

MERSEYBEAT 1: **1.** The Swinging Blue Jeans **2.** The Searchers **3.** 'Sweets For My Sweet' **4.** The Fourmost **5.** Gerry and Freddie Marsden **6.** The Searchers **7.** Rory Storm and The Hurricanes **8.** Billy J. Kramer **9.** 'Free Love' **10.** He was away at a scout camp in Derbyshire **11.** 'Bad To Me' **12.** Gerry and The Pacemakers **13.** The Swinging Blue Jeans **14.** Billy Kinsley **15.** 'A Hard Day's Night' **16.** The Dakotas

Beatles 1

Answers on page 262

1. On which regional show did The Beatles make their TV debut in October 1962?
2. Which was the first Beatles song to enter the US charts?
3. Which Lennon and McCartney composition knocked 'Can't Buy Me Love' off the top of the UK chart in April 1964?
4. Who was the first artist to chart in the UK with a cover of a Beatles single?
5. Who did The Beatles meet for the only time on 27 August 1965 in Bel Air, California?
6. Which comedy actor recorded a version of 'A Hard Day's Night' in the guise of Sir Laurence Olivier reciting the song as Richard III?
7. At which Buckinghamshire school did The Beatles appear in April 1963 for £100 at the request of schoolboy Dave Moores?
8. To whom did Paul McCartney become engaged on Christmas Day 1967?
9. Which chart-topping group supported The Beatles on their final UK tour, in December 1965?
10. Which famous photograph was taken at 10am on 8 August 1969?
11. Which track topped the US charts for one week in March 1967?
12. Which venture opened at 94 Baker Street, London, on 7 December 1967?
13. In December 1961, where did The Beatles play their first gig in the south of England?
14. What number did 'Love Me Do' reach in the UK charts?
15. What was the group's last UK number one?
16. For how many weeks did 'From Me To You' remain a UK number one?

Answers to page 262

HEAVY METAL 2: **1.** Megadeth **2.** Israel **3.** His school uniform **4.** 1991 **5.** Metallica **6.** 'Race With The Devil' **7.** Michael Moorcock **8.** Ian Kilmister **9.** Mammoth **10.** Deep Purple **11.** Black Sabbath **12.** The Blackhearts **13.** Jo Jo Gunne **14.** 'Sweet Child O' Mine' **15.** Steppenwolf **16.** Axl Rose

Chart Toppers 4

Answers on page 263

Which artists topped the UK charts with the following tracks?

1. 'Japanese Boy' (1981)
2. 'Beetlebum' (1997)
3. 'Mouldy Old Dough' (1972)
4. 'Tower Of Strength' (1961)
5. 'Ring My Bell' (1979)
6. 'Show Me Heaven' (1990)
7. 'Star Trekkin'' (1987)
8. 'This Is My Song' (1967)
9. 'Son Of My Father' (1972)
10. 'I Don't Wanna Dance' (1982)
11. 'Young At Heart' (1993)
12. 'King Of My Castle' (1999)
13. 'Whole Lotta Woman' (1958)
14. 'Tired Of Waiting For You' (1965)
15. 'Rock Me Amadeus' (1986)
16. 'So You Win Again' (1977)

Answers to page 263

NOVELTY NUMBERS 1: **1.** St Winifred's School Choir **2.** 'Don't Jump Off The Roof Dad' **3.** 51 **4.** 'Gossip Calypso' **5.** 1993 **6.** Brian and Michael **7.** 'Tie Me Kangaroo Down, Sport' **8.** A council flat ('My Old Man's a Dustman') **9.** 'The Fastest Milkman In The West' **10.** Renée and Renato **11.** 1986 **12.** Mike Sarne **13.** The Wombles **14.** Bernard Bresslaw **15.** The Singing Nun **16.** The Singing Dogs

Heavy Metal 2

Answers on page 260

1. Which thrash metal quartet was founded in San Francisco in 1983 by guitarist Dave Mustaine?
2. In which country was Gene Simmons of Kiss born?
3. What does AC/DC's Angus Young like to wear on stage?
4. In which year did Nirvana's 'Smells Like Teen Spirit' hit the UK charts?
5. Which band's first demo was titled 'No Life Til' Leather'?
6. Which Adrian Gurvitz number gave Girlschool their first taste of UK chart action?
7. Which science-fiction writer used to be a part-time member of Hawkwind?
8. What is Lemmy's real name?
9. Which UK band of the late Eighties imposed a minimum weight of 20 stone for any potential members?
10. Who entered the *Guinness Book of Records* in 1972 as the loudest band of their time?
11. Who released the 1976 album 'We Sold Our Soul For Rock 'n' Roll'?
12. Ricky Byrd, Gary Ryan and Lee Crystal were which original backing band?
13. Whose debut single, 'Run Run Run', reached number six in the UK charts?
14. Axl Rose's then girlfriend Erin Everly was the subject of which Guns N' Roses track?
15. Who took their name from a novel by cult author Herman Hesse?
16. Who was born William Bailey but changed his name to be an anagram of Oral Sex?

Answers to page 260

BEATLES 1: **1.** *People and Places* **2.** 'I Want To Hold Your Hand' **3.** 'World Without Love' (Peter and Gordon) **4.** Ella Fitzgerald ('Can't Buy Me Love') **5.** Elvis Presley **6.** Peter Sellers **7.** Stowe School **8.** Jane Asher **9.** The Moody Blues **10.** The zebra crossing photo for the cover of 'Abbey Road' **11.** 'Penny Lane' **12.** The Apple Boutique **13.** The Palais Ballroom, Aldershot **14.** 17 **15.** 'The Ballad of John and Yoko' **16.** Seven

Novelty Numbers 1

Answers on page 261

1. Who thought there was 'No One Quite Like Grandma' in 1980?
2. What was Tommy Cooper's only UK hit?
3. How old was Clive Dunn when he reached number one with 'Grandad'?
4. What was Bernard Cribbins's third – and final – UK hit of 1962?
5. In which year did Mr Blobby have the Christmas number one?
6. Kevin Parrott and Mick Coleman are better known as which 1978 UK chart toppers?
7. What was Rolf Harris's first UK hit?
8. Where did Lonnie Donegan's old man live in a 1960 UK number one?
9. What was Ernie, to complete the title of Benny Hill's 1971 hit?
10. Hilary Lefter was one half of which supposedly Italian duo of the Eighties?
11. In which year did Cliff Richard team up with The Young Ones for a re-make of 'Living Doll'?
12. Who asked Wendy Richard to 'Come Outside'?
13. Which creatures were Britain's biggest-selling chart act of 1974?
14. Which gormless actor from the TV sitcom *The Army Game* wanted to make 'Mad Passionate Love' in 1958?
15. Who had a hit with 'Dominique' in 1963?
16. Which canine vocal group reached number 13 in the UK charts in 1955 with a medley including 'Three Blind Mice' and 'Jingle Bells'?

Answers to page 261

CHART TOPPERS 4: **1.** Aneka **2.** Blur **3.** Lieutenant Pigeon **4.** Frankie Vaughan **5.** Anita Ward **6.** Maria McKee **7.** The Firm **8.** Petula Clark **9.** Chicory Tip **10.** Eddy Grant **11.** Bluebells **12.** Wamdue Project **13.** Marvin Rainwater **14.** The Kinks **15.** Falco **16.** Hot Chocolate

Sharpshooters 3

Answers on page 266

1. Who scored nine goals and missed a penalty for Tranmere Rovers against Oldham Athletic in a Third Division (North) fixture on Boxing Day, 1935?
2. Who scored five times for Dundee United against Morton in a Scottish Premier League game in 1984?
3. For which English club did Craig Madden score 35 League goals in 1981–2?
4. Which was Chris Armstrong's first League club?
5. Which 1960s striker scored hat-tricks on his debuts for both Rotherham United and Bristol City?
6. Which Spanish club signed Nicolas Anelka from Arsenal in 1999?
7. Which Wrexham player was the Football League's leading scorer for 1969–70?
8. Which Arsenal player was the top scorer at Euro 2000?
9. Which Sunderland striker netted four times against Millwall in a First Division game in 1995–6?
10. For which English club is Jim Hall the record League scorer?
11. For which two Scottish clubs did Bob McPhail score 306 League goals between 1923 and 1939?
12. For which Spanish club did John Aldridge play?
13. Who was Walsall's leading marksman in 2000–1?
14. From which Scottish club did Tottenham sign Alan Gilzean?
15. Which former Albion Rovers striker became a prolific goalscorer for Middlesbrough in the 1990s and a Republic of Ireland international?
16. Who has scored the most League goals for Chelsea?

Answers to page 266

THE WORLD GAME 5: **1.** Borislav Mikhailov **2.** Rudi Völler **3.** Spain **4.** Jean-Pierre Papin **5.** Iran **6.** Palmeiras **7.** Salvatore Schillaci **8.** Uruguay **9.** Berne **10.** Napoli **11.** Saint Etienne **12.** Atalanta **13.** Brescia **14.** San Marino **15.** Shamrock Rovers **16.** Austria

Who Said That? 2

Answers on page 267

1. Which country's coach said in 1998: 'We are the Cinderellas of the World Cup. Our mission is to postpone midnight for as long as possible'?
2. Which England manager said: 'Napoleon wanted his generals to be lucky. I don't think he would have wanted me'?
3. Which Everton manager moaned in 1994: 'I must have broken a lot of mirrors and run over a few black cats'?
4. Who said in 1982: 'Watford are setting football back ten years'?
5. Who described Maradona as 'the best one-footed player since Puskas'?
6. Who said: 'I wanted to be the England manager, but I swear too much'?
7. Which Dutch coach, criticised for losing to Austria in the run-up to the 1990 World Cup, complained: 'They do not judge Pavarotti by how he sings in the shower. They wait until he is on stage'?
8. Which coach said in 1998: 'If Barça come second, that's failure'?
9. Which fellow player called Kevin Keegan 'the Julie Andrews of football'?
10. Which manager of a struggling Scottish club said in 1995: 'I'd hang myself, but we can't afford the rope'?
11. Who said: 'Anfield without European football is like a banquet without wine'?
12. Which Newcastle boss said: 'It's not like the brochures'?
13. Who said: 'Football hooligans? There are ninety-two club chairmen for a start'?
14. Which Oxford United manager said: 'My chairman, Robert Maxwell, they ought to let him run football'?
15. Which Wales manager said: 'I know that my vultures are out there'?
16. Who said in 1988: 'I like to upset anybody I play against'?

Answers to page 267

FOOTBALL LEAGUE 4: **1.** Millwall **2.** Rotherham United **3.** Wolverhampton Wanderers **4.** Swindon Town **5.** Alf Wood **6.** Preston North End **7.** Blackpool **8.** Scarborough **9.** Hartlepool United **10.** Harry Hardy **11.** Manchester United **12.** Walsall **13.** Scunthorpe United **14.** Gillingham **15.** 1952 **16.** Queens Park Rangers

The World Game 5

Answers on page 264

1. Which Bulgarian international goalkeeper was bald at the 1994 World Cup but had luxuriant hair when playing for Reading a few weeks later?
2. Who became national coach of Germany for their 2002 World Cup qualifying campaign?
3. Which country won both the 1952 and 1954 International Youth Championships on the toss of a coin?
4. Which striker moved from Marseille to AC Milan in June 1992 for £10 million?
5. Who beat the Maldives 17–0 in a World Cup qualifier in 1997?
6. Who won the 1999 Copa Libertadores on penalties?
7. Which Italian striker was top scorer at the 1990 World Cup?
8. Which South American national team play in sky blue shirts and black shorts?
9. Young Boys play in which Swiss city?
10. Which Italian club signed Diego Maradona in June 1984?
11. Which French team play at the Geoffroy-Guichard Stadium?
12. With which Italian club did Gaetano Scirea begin his career?
13. Which Italian club signed Gheorghe Hagi in July 1992 for £4 million?
14. Which country's Cup competition has been won by Faetano, Libertas and Cosmos?
15. In terms of trophies, which is the most successful club in the Republic of Ireland?
16. In which country do Stürm Graz play?

Answers to page 66

SHARPSHOOTERS 3: **1.** Robert 'Bunny' Bell **2.** Paul Sturrock **3.** Bury **4.** Wrexham **5.** John Galley **6.** Real Madrid **7.** Albert Kinsey **8.** Thierry Henry **9.** Craig Russell **10.** Peterborough United **11.** Airdrie and Rangers **12.** Real Sociedad **13.** Mark Robins **14.** Dundee United **15.** Bernie Slaven **16.** Bobby Tambling

Football League 4

Answers on page 265

1. Victory over which club on the final day of the 1933–4 season saved Manchester United from dropping into Division Three?

2. Which club used to be known as Thornhill United?

3. For which club did Derek Parkin make 501 League appearances between 1967 and 1982?

4. Who beat Leicester City 4–3 in the 1993 First Division play-off final?

5. Which Shrewsbury Town player scored five times against Blackburn in a Third Division match in 1971?

6. Which club sold Kevin Kilbane to West Bromwich Albion in 1997?

7. Who won the 2000–1 Third Division play-off final?

8. Which former League club was banned from wearing shirts advertising Black Death vodka on the grounds of bad taste?

9. Before relegation to the Conference was introduced, which League club made most applications for re-election?

10. Who was the only Stockport County player to win a full England cap?

11. Based on final League placings, which was the most successful League club of the 1950s?

12. And which was the least successful?

13. For which soccer club did cricketer Ian Botham make a substitute's appearance in 1980?

14. Who lost to Manchester City in the 1999 Division Two play-off final?

15. When did Johnny Haynes make his Fulham debut?

16. Which club was originally known as St Jude's?

Answers to page 67

WHO SAID THAT? 2: **1.** Jamaica **2.** Graham Taylor **3.** Mike Walker **4.** Terry Venables **5.** Sir Stanley Matthews **6.** Barry Fry **7.** Leo Beenhakker **8.** Louis Van Gaal **9.** Duncan McKenzie **10.** Iain Munro **11.** Roy Evans **12.** Kevin Keegan **13.** Brian Clough **14.** Jim Smith **15.** Bobby Gould **16.** Vinnie Jones

European Championship 2

Answers on page 270

1. Which nation won the 1992 European Championship despite not qualifying for it?
2. And who did they beat in the final?
3. Who did Germany beat in the final of Euro 96?
4. Who scored in all five games for France in the 1984 tournament?
5. Where was the opening game of Euro 2000 played?
6. Who went into their final qualifying group match in 1983 needing to beat Malta by 11 clear goals to qualify, and won 12–1?
7. Who scored West Germany's two goals in the 1980 final?
8. Who were the first winners of the competition?
9. And who did they beat in the final?
10. Whose last-minute penalty miss for Spain in the quarter-finals of Euro 2000 allowed France to win 2–1?
11. Where was the 1976 final held?
12. Who were the only team that failed to score in Euro 96?
13. Who did Italy beat in the semi-finals of Euro 2000?
14. Who scored twice in the 1972 final?
15. Which two grounds staged the semi-finals of Euro 96?
16. How many host nations have won the European Championship?

Answers to page 270

ODDBALLS 5: **1.** Doncaster Rovers **2.** Stan Lynn **3.** Manchester City **4.** Chris Balderstone **5.** Ruud Gullit **6.** Ramon Quiroga **7.** Southend United **8.** Namibia **9.** Crystal Palace **10.** Danny Blanchflower **11.** Kenny Miller **12.** 1990 **13.** Walsall **14.** Queen's Park **15.** Congo **16.** Cambridge United

Newcastle United 1

Answers on page 271

1. From which club did Newcastle sign Nolberto Solano?
2. Who scored a club record 177 League goals for Newcastle?
3. Which former schoolteacher was Magpies manager for less than a year in 1977?
4. Which cup competition did Newcastle win in 1974 and 1975?
5. Who did Newcastle beat in the 1969 Inter-Cities Fairs Cup final?
6. What nationality was Temuri Ketsbaia?
7. Which club prevented Newcastle from doing the League and Cup double in 1905?
8. When did Newcastle last win the League championship?
9. Who was in goal for Newcastle in the 1999 FA Cup final?
10. Who succeeded Jim Smith as Newcastle manager in 1991?
11. Who was just 16 when making his League debut against Wolves in 1990?
12. Which two clubs were relegated from Division One along with Newcastle in 1989?
13. Who moved from Newcastle to Bolton for £2.2 million in July 1997?
14. From which French club did Stephane Guivarc'h join Newcastle?
15. In which year did Newcastle first play at St James' Park?
16. Who did Newcastle beat in the 1951 FA Cup final?

Answers to page 271

SCOTTISH SCENE 4: **1.** Nine **2.** East Stirlingshire **3.** Clyde **4.** Motherwell **5.** Dundee **6.** Celtic **7.** Aberdeen **8.** Forfar Athletic **9.** Dunfermline Athletic **10.** Dumbarton **11.** Kilmarnock **12.** Dundee United **13.** Eyemouth United **14.** Ronnie Corbett **15.** Motherwell **16.** Gordon Dalziel

Oddballs 5

Answers on page 268

1. Which former League club's first competitive game was against the Yorkshire Institution for the Deaf?
2. Which Birmingham City full-back finished as the club's top scorer in 1964–5 thanks mainly to his penalty-taking expertise?
3. Which club has a fanzine called *Chips and Gravy*?
4. Who spent the day of 15 September 1975 playing cricket for Leicestershire against Derbyshire at Chesterfield before dashing to Doncaster to play in Rovers' evening kick-off against Brentford?
5. Which former Chelsea manager used to do TV commercials for Pizza Hut?
6. Which Peruvian goalkeeper was christened 'El Loco' by team-mates?
7. Which club does singer Alison Moyet support?
8. Which nation boasts a football team called Bingo?
9. Which London club reached number 50 in the charts with their version of The Dave Clark Five's 'Glad All Over' in 1990?
10. Which former Spurs captain made a cameo appearance in the 1983 film *Those Glory, Glory Days*?
11. Who was Scotland's Young Player of the Year for 2000?
12. In which year was Tony Adams jailed for drink-driving?
13. Which club left Fellows Park in 1990?
14. Which Scottish club didn't concede a goal in the first seven years of their history?
15. Which national team are nicknamed 'The Leopards'?
16. Which English club used to be known as Abbey United?

Answers to page 268

EUROPEAN CHAMPIONSHIP 2: **1.** Denmark **2.** Germany **3.** Czech Republic **4.** Michel Platini **5.** Brussels **6.** Spain **7.** Horst Hrubesch **8.** Soviet Union **9.** Yugoslavia **10.** Raul **11.** Belgrade **12.** Turkey **13.** Holland **14.** Gerd Müller **15.** Wembley and Old Trafford **16.** Three

Scottish Scene 4

Answers on page 269

1. How many Scottish League titles did Rangers win in the 1990s?
2. Which Scottish League club used to be known as Bainsford Britannia?
3. With which club did Craig Brown first make his name as a manager?
4. Who bought John Spencer from Everton for £500,000 in 1999?
5. Who beat Hearts on the final day of the 1985–6 season to deprive the Edinburgh club of the League title?
6. Who were crowned champions instead?
7. And who crushed Hearts 3–0 in the Scottish FA Cup final a week later?
8. Which team reached the semi-finals of the Scottish FA Cup in 1982 for the only time in their history?
9. From which Scottish club did Aston Villa sign defender Allan Evans?
10. Who were the first outright winners of the Scottish League championship?
11. Who finished runners-up in the Scottish League four times in five years between 1960 and 1964?
12. For which club did David Narey make 612 League appearances between 1973 and 1994?
13. Which non-League team reached the quarter-finals of the Scottish FA Cup in 1960?
14. Which comedian once had a trial with Hearts but was rejected because he was too small?
15. With which Scottish club did Gary McAllister begin his professional career?
16. Who scored 154 League goals for Raith Rovers between 1987 and 1994?

Answers to page 269

NEWCASTLE UNITED 1: **1.** Boca Juniors **2.** Jackie Milburn **3.** Richard Dinnis **4.** Texaco Cup **5.** Ujpest Dozsa **6.** Georgian **7.** Aston Villa **8.** 1926–7 **9.** Steve Harper **10.** Osvaldo Ardiles **11.** Steve Watson **12.** Middlesbrough and West Ham **13.** Robbie Elliott **14.** Auxerre **15.** 1892 **16.** Blackpool

Whose Home? 3

Answers on page 274

1. Which English League club played at Cassio Road before moving to their present home?
2. In which year did Wycombe Wanderers move to Adams Park?
3. Which Scottish club plays at Almondvale Stadium?
4. What was Belgium's Stade du Roi Baudouin previously known as?
5. Who plays at Gay Meadow?
6. What is the name of Clyde's home ground?
7. And who shared it in 1994–5?
8. Which German team moved from the Grünwalder Stadium in 1972?
9. In which country would you find the Rungnado Stadium?
10. Which Yorkshire club used to play at Sandhall?
11. Who plays at Gigg Lane?
12. In which year did Millwall move to the New Den?
13. What is Mexico's Estadio Guillermo Caledo more usually known as?
14. Which Scottish club plays in Kirkcaldy?
15. Which former Football League team plays at The Recreation Ground?
16. What is the name of Wigan Athletic's ground?

Answers to page 274

WHISTLE HAPPY 2: **1.** Paul Alcock **2.** Jim Finney **3.** Treorchy **4.** Philip Don **5.** Roger Kirkpatrick **6.** David Elleray **7.** Norman Burtenshaw **8.** Mervyn Griffiths **9.** Denis Howell **10.** Arthur Ellis **11.** Swiss **12.** S.R. Bastard **13.** Gary Willard **14.** Paul Durkin **15.** 1966 **16.** Uriah Rennie

World Cup 2

Answers on page 275

1. Who did Germany beat 1–0 in the opening match of the 1994 World Cup finals?
2. Who was top scorer at the 1998 World Cup finals?
3. Who was Argentina's victorious coach in 1978?
4. In which city was the 1934 World Cup final played?
5. Which nation finished third in the 1998 tournament?
6. Which Brazilian was leading scorer at the 1938 World Cup finals?
7. Which nation had never previously won a game in the World Cup finals before going on to reach the last four in 1994?
8. Whose only appearance in the final stages of the World Cup saw them lose 6–0 to Hungary in 1938?
9. Which country turned down an invitation to the 1950 World Cup finals because they had only finished runners-up in the Home International Championship?
10. Which club, a month after being relegated to the Third Division of the Football League, provided one of the venues for the 1966 World Cup?
11. Who was France's two-goal hero in the 1998 World Cup final?
12. Who knocked Spain out of the 1994 World Cup?
13. Which two African countries made their first appearances at the final stages in the 1982 tournament?
14. Who were runners-up in 1950?
15. How many clean sheets did Brazil keep in the 1994 finals?
16. Who was top scorer at the 1986 finals?

Answers to page 275

TRANSFER TRAIL 4: **1.** PSV Eindhoven **2.** Anderlecht **3.** Crystal Palace **4.** Luca Marchegiani **5.** Bixente Lizarazu **6.** Bari **7.** Hearts **8.** Phil Parkes **9.** Wimbledon **10.** Portsmouth **11.** Queen of the South **12.** Lou Macari **13.** Peter Schmeichel **14.** Sporting Lisbon **15.** Tommy Lawton **16.** Blackpool

Whistle Happy 2

Answers on page 272

1. Which referee was sent sprawling by Paolo Di Canio?
2. Who was the first referee to take charge of an FA Cup final and a League Cup final at Wembley?
3. From which Welsh town did Clive Thomas hail?
4. Which English referee officiated in that capacity at the 1994 World Cup finals?
5. Which 1970s referee was nicknamed 'Mr Pickwick' for his bushy sideburns?
6. Which referee is a Harrow schoolmaster?
7. Which referee was attacked by a supporter at Millwall in 1967?
8. Which Welsh referee officiated at all three World Cup finals in the 1950s?
9. Which referee later became Minister for Sport?
10. Which Yorkshire-based referee kept order on TV's *It's a Knockout*?
11. What was the nationality of the referee at the 1966 World Cup final?
12. What was the unfortunate name of the referee at the 1878 FA Cup final?
13. Which referee walked off during a 1998 match between Barnsley and Liverpool?
14. Which referee was hit by a hot dog thrown from the crowd at Oldham in 1998?
15. In which year did Jack Taylor referee the FA Cup final?
16. Who was the first black referee to be appointed to the Premiership list?

Answers to page 272

WHOSE HOME? 3: **1.** Watford **2.** 1990 **3.** Livingston **4.** Heysel Stadium **5.** Shrewsbury Town **6.** Broadwood Stadium **7.** Airdrie **8.** Bayern Munich **9.** North Korea **10.** Halifax Town **11.** Bury **12.** 1993 **13.** Aztec Stadium **14.** Raith Rovers **15.** Aldershot **16.** JJB Stadium

Transfer Trail 4

Answers on page 273

1. From which club did Manchester United sign Ruud Van Nistelrooy in 2001?
2. For which Belgian club did Duncan McKenzie play on leaving Leeds?
3. Who paid Watford £1.1 million for teenager Bruce Dyer in March 1994?
4. Whose £6 million move from Torino to Lazio in July 1993 established what was then a record fee for a goalkeeper?
5. Which French international full-back played for Bayern Munich in 2000–1?
6. For which Italian club did Gordon Cowans make 94 appearances?
7. From which Scottish club did Tottenham sign Dave Mackay?
8. Which goalkeeper moved from Queens Park Rangers to West Ham for a then world record fee of £565,000 in 1979?
9. Who paid a club record £7.5 million to buy John Hartson from West Ham in January 1999?
10. What was Kevin Ball's first League club?
11. Which Scottish club sold Andy Thomson to Southend in 1994?
12. Which diminutive forward moved from Celtic to Manchester United for £200,000 in 1973?
13. Which great Dane returned to English football with Aston Villa in July 2001?
14. And for which Portuguese club had he been playing?
15. In 1947, who became the first British player to be transferred for £20,000?
16. From which club did Emlyn Hughes join Liverpool in 1967?

Answers to page 273

WORLD CUP 2: **1.** Bolivia **2.** Davor Suker **3.** Cesar Menotti **4.** Rome **5.** Croatia **6.** Leonidas da Silva **7.** Bulgaria **8.** Dutch East Indies **9.** Scotland **10.** Middlesbrough **11.** Zinedine Zidane **12.** Italy **13.** Algeria and Cameroon **14.** Brazil **15.** Five **16.** Gary Lineker

European Cups 3

Answers on page 278

1. Which Armenian team reached the quarter-finals of the 1975 European Cup?
2. Where was the 1998 Champions' League final played?
3. For which player did Teddy Sheringham come on as substitute during the 1999 European Champions' League final?
4. Which Belgian side won the 1988 European Cup-Winners' Cup?
5. Which team won the 2000 Champions' League despite losing three times to Bayern Munich en route to the final?
6. Which English club were beaten finalists in the first UEFA Cup in 1972?
7. Which team from the Republic of Ireland did Dynamo Tbilisi defeat on their way to winning the 1981 European Cup-Winners' Cup?
8. Which French team were beaten on penalties in the 1991 European Cup final?
9. Which Liverpool defender scored in two of their European Cup final victories?
10. Who scored Nottingham Forest's winning goal in the 1980 European Cup final?
11. Which German team were beaten by IFK Gothenburg in the 1982 UEFA Cup final?
12. Who won the UEFA Cup in 2000?
13. And who did they beat in the final?
14. Who were beaten finalists in the 1999 European Cup-Winners' Cup?
15. Who did Celtic beat in the semi-finals of the 1967 European Cup?
16. Which Portuguese team won the European Cup in 1987?

Answers to page 278

MANAGERS 5: **1.** David Platt **2.** Paul Hart **3.** Queens Park Rangers **4.** Sporting Lisbon and Porto **5.** Arsène Wenger **6.** Paul Futcher **7.** Mark McGhee **8.** Wim Jansen **9.** Strasbourg **10.** Hibernian **11.** Frank O'Farrell **12.** Tony Waddington **13.** Harry Gregg **14.** Barnet **15.** Roy McDonough (his father-in-law was club chairman Gordon Parker) **16.** 1999

Non-League 2

Answers on page 279

1. Who were the first GM Vauxhall Conference champions?
2. Which was the only club to have entered the FA Cup every year throughout the first 100 years of the competition?
3. For which Staffordshire team did Mark Bright play before moving into League football?
4. On whose ground did a three-foot-deep hole suddenly appear during a Conference match in 1997, causing the game to be abandoned?
5. In which county do Forest Green Rovers play?
6. Which non-League side knocked Liverpool out of the FA Cup in 1959?
7. Which Conference club plays at Broadhall Way?
8. Which club are nicknamed 'The Missioners'?
9. Which Welsh team had three players named Denis Wilson on their books in the 1956–7 season?
10. Who were the first winners of the FA Trophy?
11. Which Derbyshire team won the FA Trophy in 1975 – their only appearance in the final?
12. Which former Arsenal player took over as manager at Yeovil in 2000–1?
13. Which prolific striker joined Portsmouth from Dorchester Town in 1981?
14. Which current Premiership team won the FA Amateur Cup in 1895 and 1898?
15. Which team won the Amateur Cup a record ten times?
16. What is the name of Barrow's ground?

Answers to page 279

ASTON VILLA 1: **1.** 1897 **2.** Vic Crowe **3.** Gareth Southgate **4.** Czech **5.** Real Zaragoza **6.** Northampton Town **7.** Millwall **8.** Charlie Aitken **9.** 14 **10.** Wolves **11.** Port Vale **12.** Tony Hateley **13.** Aldershot **14.** Ray Graydon **15.** Gerry Hitchens **16.** Blackpool

Managers 5

Answers on page 276

1. Which manager left Nottingham Forest in July 2001 to take charge of the England Under-21 team?
2. And who succeeded him at the City Ground?
3. Trevor Francis and Gerry Francis were both managers of which club?
4. Which two Portuguese teams have been managed by Bobby Robson?
5. Who was voted Manager of the Year in 1998?
6. After taking over in 1995, which Darlington boss had to wait eight games before seeing his side score?
7. Who became manager of Millwall in September 2000?
8. Which Celtic boss was named Scottish Manager of the Year in 1998?
9. At which club did Arsène Wenger take over as youth team coach in 1981?
10. Eddie Turnbull, Willie Ormond and Bertie Auld all managed which Scottish club?
11. Who succeeded Matt Gillies as Leicester City manager in 1968?
12. Which manager steered Stoke City to their 1972 Football League Cup triumph?
13. As manager of Shrewsbury Town, which former Old Trafford goalkeeper sold Jim Holton to Manchester United?
14. Which former League club was managed by Ray Clemence from 1994 to 1996?
15. Which Colchester United manager was sacked by his father-in-law in 1994?
16. When did Lawrie Sanchez take over as manager of Wycombe Wanderers?

Answers to page 276

EUROPEAN CUPS 3: **1.** Ararat Yerevan **2.** Amsterdam **3.** Jesper Blomqvist **4.** Mechelen **5.** Real Madrid **6.** Wolverhampton Wanderers **7.** Waterford **8.** Marseille **9.** Phil Neal **10.** John Robertson **11.** SV Hamburg **12.** Galatasaray **13.** Arsenal **14.** Real Mallorca **15.** Dukla Prague **16.** FC Porto

Aston Villa 1

Answers on page 277

1. In which year did the club move to Villa Park?
2. Who managed Villa between 1970 and 1974?
3. Which defender moved to Middlesbrough for £6.5 million in July 2001?
4. What nationality was Villa boss Dr Jozef Venglos?
5. Which Spanish club did Savo Milosevic join in 1998?
6. From which club did Villa sign John Gregory as a player?
7. To whom did Villa finish runners-up in the Second Division in 1987–8?
8. Which player made a record 561 League appearances for the club between 1961 and 1976?
9. How many players did Ron Saunders use during Villa's Championship-winning season of 1980–1?
10. Against whom did Villa play their first Football League game, in 1888?
11. What was Ian Taylor's first League club?
12. Who moved from Villa to Chelsea for £100,000 in October 1966?
13. Who knocked Villa out of the FA Cup in 1964 in a third-round replay?
14. Who scored Villa's winner in the 1975 League Cup final?
15. Which forward scored five times against Charlton in a Second Division match in 1959?
16. With which club did Alan Wright make his Football League debut?

Answers to page 277

NON-LEAGUE 2: **1.** Altrincham **2.** Marlow **3.** Leek Town **4.** Woking **5.** Gloucestershire **6.** Worcester City **7.** Stevenage Borough **8.** Hayes **9.** Rhyl Athletic **10.** Macclesfield Town **11.** Matlock Town **12.** Colin Addison **13.** Trevor Senior **14.** Middlesbrough **15.** Bishop Auckland **16.** Holker Street

Northern Ireland 1

Answers on page 282

1. Who scored Northern Ireland's winner against Spain at the 1982 World Cup finals?

2. With which club did Danny Blanchflower win his first Irish cap?

3. How many goals did George Best score for Northern Ireland?

4. By what score did the Irish lose at home to England in their first-ever international?

5. Who scored the winner against Finland in a Euro 2000 qualifier in Belfast?

6. How many caps did Jimmy Quinn win?

7. Who has enjoyed two spells as Northern Ireland manager?

8. On which ground do Northern Ireland play home matches?

9. Who won a record 119 caps for Northern Ireland?

10. Who played for Northern Ireland in 1949 and then for the USA in 1953?

11. Who did Ireland beat 7–0 at Belfast in 1930?

12. With which club did Jim Magilton win his first Irish cap?

13. Which player/manager scored the winning goal against England at Wembley in 1972?

14. Who did Northern Ireland beat in their opening match at the 1958 World Cup finals?

15. Who knocked Ireland out of the 1958 World Cup?

16. Which Luton, Manchester United and Chelsea defender won 91 caps for Northern Ireland?

Answers to page 282

WHICH YEAR IN FOOTBALL? 4: **1.** 1988 **2.** 1969 **3.** 1995 **4.** 1982 **5.** 1976 **6.** 1992 **7.** 1981 **8.** 1945 **9.** 1974 **10.** 1991 **11.** 1970 **12.** 1986 **13.** 1959 **14.** 1978 **15.** 1989 **16.** 1982

The World Game 6

Answers on page 283

1. Which Icelandic international came on for his father during a 1996 international with Estonia?
2. Which two clubs share Italy's Luigi Ferraris Stadium?
3. Bursapor, Kocaeli and Sakaryaspor have all won the Cup competition of which country?
4. Which Oceanic national team play in royal blue shirts and white shorts?
5. Which Italian defender was nicknamed 'The Emperor of Milan'?
6. Which was the only country to defeat Hungary in 48 internationals between 1950 and 1956?
7. Which two countries have teams called Nacional which have won the Copa Libertadores?
8. Who was the first non-German manager to win the Bundesliga?
9. Who was voted European Footballer of the Year for 1997?
10. Which country's goalkeeper has been known to wear a bobble hat during matches?
11. Who won the German Cup in 1999?
12. Which club won the Norwegian League for the seventh successive year in 1999?
13. How many times did Porto win the Portuguese title during the 1990s?
14. Skonto Riga won the 1998 championship of which country?
15. Colo Colo, beaten Copa Libertadores finalists in 1973, hailed from which South American country?
16. Which Italian club did Alen Boksic join from Marseille in October 1993?

Answers to page 283

FA CUP 4: **1.** Port Vale **2.** David Herd **3.** Roger Osborne **4.** Millwall **5.** Liverpool, Swansea City and Crewe Alexandra **6.** Leicester City **7.** West Bromwich Albion **8.** Nottingham Forest **9.** Bob Thomson **10.** Arthur Turner **11.** Malcolm Macdonald **12.** Norwegian (Erik Thorstvedt) **13.** Leicester City **14.** Leeds United **15.** Bill Slater **16.** Wolves

Which Year in Football? 4

Answers on page 280

1. When did the Football League celebrate its centenary?
2. When did Mansfield Town reach the sixth round of the FA Cup for the only time in their history?
3. When did Les Ferdinand join Newcastle from Queens Park Rangers?
4. When did Allan Ball retire as goalkeeper following 20 years with Queen of the South?
5. In which year did East Germany win the Olympic soccer tournament?
6. In which year did Wrexham defeat Arsenal 2–1 in the third round of the FA Cup?
7. When did the Football League introduce three points for a win?
8. When was the inaugural Scottish League Cup competition?
9. When was Sir Alf Ramsey sacked as England manager?
10. In which year was an FA Cup semi-final first staged at Wembley?
11. When did Howard Kendall win a League Championship medal as a player with Everton?
12. When did Liverpool achieve the League and Cup double?
13. When did Billy Wright win his last England cap?
14. In which year did Ipswich Town win the FA Cup?
15. In which year did Rangers sign their first Catholic player, Mo Johnston?
16. When did Bryan Robson score after just 27 seconds for England against France in the World Cup finals?

Answers to page 280

NORTHERN IRELAND 1: **1.** Gerry Armstrong **2.** Barnsley **3.** Nine **4.** 13–0 **5.** Keith Rowland **6.** 46 **7.** Billy Bingham **8.** Windsor Park **9.** Pat Jennings **10.** Cecil Moore **11.** Wales **12.** Oxford United **13.** Terry Neill **14.** Czechoslovakia **15.** France **16.** Mal Donaghy

FA Cup 4

Answers on page 281

1. Which Second Division team were beaten by Ryman Leaguers Canvey Island in the 2000–1 FA Cup?
2. Who scored twice for Manchester United in their 1963 FA Cup final victory over Leicester City?
3. Who scored Ipswich Town's winning Cup final goal against Arsenal?
4. Which London League club was put out of the FA Cup four times by non-League opponents between 1958 and 1965?
5. For which three clubs did Ian Callaghan play in the FA Cup?
6. Which team finished a lowly 19th in Division Two in 1948–9 but still reached that year's Cup final?
7. For which club did Jeff Astle score in every round in 1968?
8. Who are the only Football League club to have played FA Cup ties in all four home countries?
9. Which Chelsea player was the only one-eyed man ever to appear in an FA Cup final?
10. Who earned an FA Cup winners' medal with Charlton Athletic but never played a League game for the club?
11. Who scored Newcastle's goal in their 2–1 defeat by Hereford in 1972?
12. What nationality was Tottenham's goalkeeper in the 1991 final?
13. Which club lost three FA Cup finals in the 1960s?
14. Who went 16 FA Cup ties without a win between 1952 and 1963?
15. Which member of the 1951 Blackpool Cup final side was still an amateur?
16. And which side did he captain to victory nine years later?

Answers to page 281

THE WORLD GAME 6: **1.** Eidur Gudjohnsen **2.** Genoa and Sampdoria **3.** Turkey **4.** Western Samoa **5.** Franco Baresi **6.** West Germany **7.** Uruguay and Colombia **8.** Giovanni Trapattoni **9.** Ronaldo **10.** Faroe Islands **11.** Werder Bremen **12.** Rosenborg Trondheim **13.** Eight **14.** Latvia **15.** Chile **16.** Lazio

General Knowledge 61

Answers on page 286

1. Who were the first club to score 1,000 Football League goals?

2. Who starred in *Breakfast at Tiffany's* and *My Fair Lady*?

3. What nationality was playwright Samuel Beckett?

4. Which foodstuff was invented by Frenchman Hippolyte Mège-Mouries in 1868?

5. What is the chemical symbol for iron?

6. Which European country has the international vehicle index mark CH?

7. Which boy's name means 'small' in Latin?

8. What is the capital of Uzbekistan?

9. Who sang about a 'Stupid Girl' in 1996?

10. And who did Captain Mainwaring think was a 'stupid boy'?

11. Which town is the administrative centre of Essex?

12. What is the name of an otter's home?

13. Which camp TV presenter was named after the tough-guy actor who starred in *Tales of Wells Fargo*?

14. Dar es Salaam is the chief seaport in which country?

15. Which Australian golfer won the British Open in 1991?

16. Which is the world's largest inland sea?

Answers to page 286

GENERAL KNOWLEDGE 63: **1.** *The Color of Money* **2.** Alfred **3.** Bayeux Tapestry **4.** Montrose **5.** Thermos flask **6.** North Sea **7.** Liverpool **8.** Bangladesh **9.** Pat Eddery **10.** John Adams **11.** Supermarket **12.** A small whirlpool **13.** Catkins **14.** Derek Fowlds (*The Basil Brush Show* to *Yes, Minister*) **15.** Eldred **16.** Lynn Davies and Mary Rand

General Knowledge 62

Answers on page 287

1. Which former England football manager was named after an ill-fated bandleader?
2. Britney Spears appeared in which TV series about a girl with supernatural powers?
3. Saintpaulia is the Latin name for which popular house plant?
4. Which musical instrument was invented by Cyrill Damien in 1829?
5. Who directed *Dances With Wolves*?
6. Which country used to be called Kampuchea?
7. Georgetown is the capital of which South American country?
8. In which year was the Gunpowder Plot?
9. Who was head of the Gestapo from 1936?
10. For which county did Len Hutton play cricket?
11. A gumtree is the common name for which tree?
12. In which county is Caernarvon?
13. What is the state capital of Idaho?
14. Which Belgian punk had a 1978 hit with 'Ça Plane Pour Moi'?
15. With what physical handicap was Dudley Moore born?
16. Which comedian's real name is Jim Moir?

Answers to page 287

GENERAL KNOWLEDGE 64: **1.** Violet **2.** Green, white and orange **3.** Four – France, The Netherlands, Germany and Luxembourg **4.** Peter Dimmock **5.** Paul Nicholas **6.** Subbuteo (*Falco subbuteo* is the Latin name for the hobby) **7.** Haiti **8.** Hercule Poirot **9.** The Thompson Twins **10.** Ben Kingsley **11.** The Oaks **12.** *Henry VIII* **13.** Stephen Fry **14.** Fencing **15.** A small flute **16.** Greek

General Knowledge 63

Answers on page 284

1. For which film did Paul Newman win an Oscar for Best Actor in 1986?
2. What is the name of Batman's butler?
3. Which tapestry gives a vivid pictorial record of the Norman Conquest?
4. Which Scottish League football team are nicknamed the 'Gable Endies'?
5. What type of flask was originally called a Dewar Vessel in honour of its inventor?
6. The Dogger Bank is a submerged sandbank in which sea?
7. Which city were both Katrina and The Waves and The Bangles going down to?
8. Which country was formerly known as East Pakistan?
9. Which Irish jockey recorded a hat-trick of wins in the Prix de L'Arc de Triomphe from 1985-7?
10. Who was the second US President after George Washington?
11. An early example of what was called a 'Piggly Wiggly'?
12. What is an eddy?
13. What are the flowers of willows, poplars and birches called?
14. Which actor went from straight man to a puppet fox to a job as Private Secretary to the Prime Minister?
15. What is Gregory Peck's real Christian name?
16. Which two British athletes won long jump gold medals at the 1964 Tokyo Olympics?

Answers to page 284

GENERAL KNOWLEDGE 61: **1.** Aston Villa **2.** Audrey Hepburn **3.** Irish **4.** Margarine **5.** Fe **6.** Switzerland **7.** Paul **8.** Tashkent **9.** Garbage **10.** Pike **11.** Chelmsford **12.** Holt **13.** Dale Winton (named after Dale Robertson) **14.** Tanzania **15.** Ian Baker-Finch **16.** Caspian Sea

General Knowledge 64

Answers on page 285

1. What is the colour of mourning in Turkey?
2. What three colours are on the flag of the Republic of Ireland?
3. How many countries border Belgium?
4. Who was the first presenter of *Grandstand*?
5. Which singer/actor was born Paul Beuselinck?
6. Which game takes its name from the Latin for a bird of prey?
7. The gourde is the currency of which country?
8. Whose companion was Captain Hastings?
9. Which Eighties band took their name from two bowler-hatted secret service agents in *Hergé's Adventures of Tintin*?
10. Which star of *Gandhi* once chatted up Irma Barlow in *Coronation Street*?
11. In horse racing, what is the fillies' version of the Derby?
12. What was Shakespeare's last play?
13. Which actor suffered such bad stage fright during a production of *Cell Mates* that he left the country?
14. Foil, épee and sabre are the three types of weapon used in which sport?
15. What kind of musical instrument is a fife?
16. What nationality was the physician Galen?

Answers to page 285

GENERAL KNOWLEDGE 62: **1.** Glenn Hoddle (after Glenn Miller) **2.** *Sabrina the Teenage Witch* **3.** African violet **4.** Accordion **5.** Kevin Costner **6.** Cambodia **7.** Guyana **8.** 1605 **9.** Heinrich Himmler **10.** Yorkshire **11.** Eucalyptus **12.** Gwynedd **13.** Boise **14.** Plastic Bertrand **15.** A club foot **16.** Vic Reeves

General Knowledge 65

Answers on page 290

1. Who searched for the one-armed man in *The Fugitive*?

2. Mike Barson was the chief songwriter with which Eighties band?

3. What does EMU stand for?

4. What is a smolt?

5. What is the Japanese wine saké made from?

6. Which Fulke was a well-known racehorse trainer?

7. What was the name of *Perry Mason*'s secretary?

8. Which group backed Johnny Kidd?

9. What was St Vitus the patron saint of?

10. The London Promenade Concerts are named after which conductor?

11. For which film did Emma Thompson win an Oscar for Best Actress in 1992?

12. Which Formula One Grand Prix takes place at Interlagos?

13. A bombardon is a member of which group of musical instruments?

14. What was the first name of the German dramatist Brecht?

15. Who was the youngest of the three Brontë sisters?

16. Who wrote *Hotel du Lac*?

Answers to page 290

GENERAL KNOWLEDGE 67: **1.** Johnny Nash **2.** Willie Johnston **3.** Italy **4.** Queen Anne **5.** 23 Railway Cuttings, East Cheam **6.** Denmark **7.** Apollo XI **8.** Pierce **9.** Ruby Murray **10.** *Play Misty For Me* **11.** Mick Jagger **12.** South America **13.** Fulham Broadway **14.** Marylebone **15.** Japan **16.** Crossword puzzle

General Knowledge 66

Answers on page 291

1. Which hero of spaghetti Westerns is allergic to horses?
2. What did Arsenal and Chelsea have on 25 August 1928 that no other team did?
3. Who was the first woman in space?
4. What were the young men of Britain no longer required to perform after 1960?
5. Whose 1995 album was 'Different Class'?
6. In which Irish county is Connemara?
7. Who announced that he was going to leave old Durham town?
8. Who composed the 'Brandenburg Concertos'?
9. What animal lives in a sett?
10. To what family of birds does the blackcap belong?
11. What were followers of Oswald Mosley's British Union of Fascists commonly known as?
12. Which romantic novelist's first book was *Jigsaw*, published in 1921?
13. In which Dublin park were two prominent members of the British government murdered in 1882?
14. Who was Starsky and Hutch's jive-talking informant?
15. Who invented the Polaroid camera?
16. In which US state does the Rio Grande river rise?

Answers to page 291

GENERAL KNOWLEDGE 68: **1.** 6th century BC **2.** Dissolvable aspirin **3.** Mr Black **4.** Botswana **5.** Bangkok **6.** Chickens **7.** Incontinence **8.** Mexico **9.** Those fascinated by handwriting **10.** *Longstreet* **11.** Northampton Town **12.** Pregnant **13.** Anita Dobson **14.** Denis Healey **15.** Michael Palin **16.** Algeria

General Knowledge 67

Answers on page 288

1. Whose only UK number one single was 'Tears On My Pillow'?
2. Which Scottish international footballer was sent home in disgrace from the 1978 World Cup finals after testing positive for drugs that were contained in a cold remedy?
3. In which country is the resort of Rimini?
4. Who was the last Stuart sovereign of England?
5. Where did Tony Hancock live in *Hancock's Half-Hour*?
6. Which country rules the Faeroe Islands?
7. Which American space mission took Neil Armstrong and Buzz Aldrin to the Moon?
8. What was the surname of 'Hawkeye' in *M*A*S*H*?
9. Who had five hits in the Top Twenty at the same time in 1955?
10. On which film did Clint Eastwood make his debut as a director?
11. Which Rolling Stone once worked as a porter at a mental hospital?
12. From which continent does the potato originate?
13. Which London Underground station was called Walham Green until 1952?
14. Which London railway terminus is at the end of the Chiltern Line?
15. Which country uses more condoms than any other?
16. What pastime did Arthur Wynne invent in 1913?

Answers to page 288

GENERAL KNOWLEDGE 65: **1.** Dr Richard Kimble **2.** Madness **3.** European Monetary Union **4.** A young salmon **5.** Rice **6.** Fulke Walwyn **7.** Della Street **8.** The Pirates **9.** Dancers **10.** Henry Wood **11.** *Howard's End* **12.** Brazilian **13.** Brass **14.** Bertolt **15.** Anne **16.** Anita Brookner

General Knowledge 68

Answers on page 289

1. In which century did the first known dictionary appear?
2. What is Disprin short for?
3. Who is the perpetual victim in Cluedo?
4. Which country used to be known as Bechuanaland?
5. Which Oriental capital city means 'wild plum village'?
6. Alektorophobia is a fear of what?
7. According to medieval beliefs, what was urinating on an open grave supposed to cure?
8. In which country do they celebrate the Day of the Dead on 2 November?
9. For what does the Cheirological Society cater?
10. Who was TV's first blind detective?
11. Which Football League team are nicknamed the 'Cobblers'?
12. What perfectly natural word was Lucille Ball banned from saying in *I Love Lucy*?
13. Which future landlady of the Queen Vic appeared on *Play Away*?
14. Who was the only human to appear on *Spitting Image*?
15. Which member of the *Monty Python* team once appeared as a surfer on *Home and Away*?
16. Which country achieved independence from France in 1962?

Answers to page 289

GENERAL KNOWLEDGE 66: **1.** Clint Eastwood **2.** Numbered shirts **3.** Valentina Tereshkova **4.** National service **5.** Pulp **6.** Galway **7.** Roger Whittaker **8.** Bach **9.** Badger **10.** Warbler **11.** Blackshirts **12.** Dame Barbara Cartland **13.** Phoenix Park **14.** Huggy Bear **15.** Dr Edwin Land **16.** South Colorado

General Knowledge 69

Answers on page 294

1. Which jockey won all seven races on the card at Ascot in 1996?
2. With which style of music is Scott Joplin associated?
3. How many points is the green ball worth in snooker?
4. In which county is Carlyon Bay where Tony Blair and his family went on holiday in 2001?
5. Which animal symbolises the zodiac sign Capricorn?
6. Which Swedish novelist was the first woman to win the Nobel Prize for Literature?
7. What nationality are rock band The Cardigans?
8. What is the name of *Frasier*'s father?
9. Which country inflicted Sven Goran Eriksson's first defeat as England football manager?
10. In which city was actress Angela Lansbury born?
11. Who was Britain's first Labour Prime Minister?
12. What is a prickly pear?
13. Where is Prince William Sound?
14. What were Vince and Penny in John Sullivan's sitcom?
15. Who wrote *The Railway Children*?
16. What are the names of Thomas the Tank Engine's two carriages?

Answers to page 294

GENERAL KNOWLEDGE 71: **1.** Species of toad **2.** 16 **3.** Lambeth Bridge **4.** Flying **5.** Cane toads **6.** Deep Blue Something **7.** South Wales **8.** Delft **9.** Anthony Hopkins **10.** Dennis Potter **11.** Kirk Douglas **12.** Douglas **13.** Coypu **14.** Great Bear **15.** Breed of pig **16.** Aldous Huxley

General Knowledge 70

Answers on page 295

1. In *Coronation Street*, which Battersby daughter was briefly married to Nick Tilsley?
2. Which heavy metal band took a ride on a 'Silver Machine'?
3. Which English city was called Glevum by the Romans?
4. Who won the Academy Award for Best Actor in 1996 for the film *Shine*?
5. In cricket, is the fielding position of extra cover situated on the off or the on side of the wicket?
6. Which is the smallest but most densely populated Central American country?
7. Ray Alan put words into the mouth of which mischievous schoolboy?
8. What type of bird is a pintail?
9. In which city would you find the Clifton Suspension Bridge?
10. Which wild flower has the Latin name *digitalis*?
11. What does the fourth estate refer to?
12. Who succeeded Stephen as King of England in 1154?
13. What was Buddy Holly's real Christian name?
14. In which country does the Indus river rise?
15. What nationality is athlete Eunice Barber?
16. With which sport is Dennis Rodman associated?

Answers to page 295

GENERAL KNOWLEDGE 72: **1.** Jacobite **2.** *Brookside* (an actor named Vincent Price played Jason Shadwick) **3.** German **4.** 'Seven Seas Of Rhye' **5.** Bulgaria **6.** Albania **7.** Mel Blanc **8.** Cyprus **9.** A small antelope **10.** Rugby union **11.** *Kojak* **12.** Clement Attlee **13.** Spain **14.** Medical **15.** Potato **16.** Czech Republic

General Knowledge 71

Answers on page 292

1. What is a natterjack?
2. How many Popes have been called Gregory?
3. Heading west, what is the next London bridge after Westminster Bridge?
4. What is footballer Dennis Bergkamp afraid of?
5. What repellent animals were introduced into Australia in 1935 to control the numbers of cane beetles?
6. Which band had a number one hit in 1996 with 'Breakfast At Tiffany's'?
7. Where are the Mumbles?
8. Which town in the Netherlands is famous for its pottery and porcelain?
9. Who starred in *Remains of the Day* and *Shadowlands*?
10. Which playwright's last TV dramas were *Karaoke* and *Cold Lazarus*?
11. Which actor was born Issur Danielovitch Demsky?
12. What is the capital of the Isle of Man?
13. Nutria is the fur of which animal?
14. What is the popular name for the constellation Ursa Major?
15. What is a Gloucester Old Spot?
16. Who wrote the science fiction novel *Brave New World*?

Answers to page 292

GENERAL KNOWLEDGE 69: **1.** Frankie Dettori **2.** Ragtime **3.** Three **4.** Cornwall **5.** Goat **6.** Selma Lagerlof **7.** Swedish **8.** Martin **9.** Holland **10.** London **11.** Ramsay MacDonald **12.** Cactus **13.** The Gulf of Alaska **14.** *Just Good Friends* **15.** E. Nesbit **16.** Annie and Clarabel

General Knowledge 72

Answers on page 293

1. Which uprising led to the Battle of Killiecrankie in 1689?
2. Vincent Price has appeared in which British soap?
3. What nationality was St Bruno?
4. What was the title of Queen's first hit?
5. Sofia is the capital of which European country?
6. Who did England's footballers beat in another World Cup qualifier four days after trouncing Germany in September 2001?
7. Who provided the voice of Bugs Bunny but was allergic to carrots?
8. Larnaca and Kyrenia are ports on which island?
9. What is a dik-dik?
10. At which sport did Gareth Edwards excel for Wales?
11. Whose catchphrase was 'Who loves ya, baby'?
12. Who succeeded Winston Churchill as British Prime Minister in 1945?
13. In which country is Cape Finisterre?
14. Which profession takes the Hippocratic Oath?
15. The Colorado Beetle preys on which plant in particular?
16. Which country were world ice hockey champions in 1999 and 2000?

Answers to page 293

GENERAL KNOWLEDGE 70: **1.** Leanne **2.** Hawkwind **3.** Gloucester **4.** Geoffrey Rush **5.** Off **6.** El Salvador **7.** Tich **8.** Duck **9.** Bristol **10.** Foxglove **11.** The press **12.** Henry II **13.** Charles **14.** Tibet **15.** French **16.** Basketball

General Knowledge 73

Answers on page 298

1. Which US comedy actor was once offered a trial with the Green Bay Packers American Football team?
2. What links Sharon Stone, Nigel Mansell and John Fashanu?
3. What was the Manic Street Preachers' first UK number one?
4. In which year did the state of Israel come into being?
5. Which Beach Boy drowned in a boating accident off California in 1983?
6. What was the name of the *Monty Python* character who had a knotted handkerchief on his head?
7. Who resigned as West German Chancellor in 1974 after an East German spy was discovered working in his office?
8. Which is the most recent county to join the County Cricket Championship?
9. What is a mistral?
10. What colour are the flowers of mimosa?
11. Mahon and Ciudadela are towns on which Mediterranean island?
12. The monstera is better known as which indoor climbing plant?
13. What form of gambling was introduced to Britain in 1922?
14. On which racecourse is the Welsh Grand National run?
15. What was Susan Brown's claim to fame in the world of rowing?
16. What was the Christian name of TV detective *Cannon*?

Answers to page 298

GENERAL KNOWLEDGE 75: **1.** Henry Cooper **2.** Bruce Jenner **3.** Coleridge **4.** Colchester **5.** Freetown **6.** Superman **7.** The Hollies **8.** Terns **9.** Percussion **10.** Cycling **11.** Cumbria **12.** Tracey in *Birds of a Feather* **13.** Apollo **14.** 2004 **15.** Minnesota **16.** Cheesemaking

General Knowledge 74

Answers on page 299

1. In 1978, which woman was accused of kidnapping and sexually abusing a Mormon?
2. Whose motto was 'spend, spend, spend'?
3. Which boy band's 1993 album was titled 'Walthamstow'?
4. For which country does Jason McAteer play international football?
5. Who was named Best Actress at the 1999 Academy Awards for *Boys Don't Cry*?
6. A convalescent visit by which king gave Bognor its suffix of Regis?
7. Who directed *Casablanca*?
8. On which English moor would you come across Brown Willy?
9. Who was defeated by Ronald Reagan in the 1980 US Presidential election?
10. Which US secretary of state won the Nobel Peace Prize in 1973?
11. Who did Robson Green play in *Soldier, Soldier*?
12. On which river does Mainz stand?
13. Who were the two principal families in *Soap*?
14. Which football team plays at Pittodrie?
15. Who composed the operas *Manon* and *Le Cid*?
16. What is an orfe?

Answers to page 299

GENERAL KNOWLEDGE 76: **1.** Velcro **2.** 'January February' **3.** Poethlyn (1918, 1919) **4.** Waldo **5.** Cherries **6.** St Helena **7.** Seville **8.** Lillehammer **9.** Wild ass **10.** Dorothy Parker **11.** Cher **12.** Lee **13.** Ayr **14.** Gwyneth Paltrow **15.** Harold Robbins **16.** River Lossie

General Knowledge 75

Answers on page 296

1. Who was the first person to be named BBC Sports Personality of the Year twice?
2. Which 1976 Olympic gold medallist went on to star in *CHiPS*?
3. Whose poems included 'The Ancient Mariner' and 'Kubla Khan'?
4. Camulodunum was the Roman name for which English town?
5. What is the capital of Sierra Leone?
6. Which superhero was created by Jerome Siegel and Joseph Shuster?
7. Which group had hits with 'Sorry Suzanne' and 'I Can't Tell The Bottom From The Top'?
8. What can be common, Arctic or sooty?
9. To what group of musical instruments does the vibraphone belong?
10. At which sport was Englishman Tommy Simpson a champion?
11. In which county is Whitehaven?
12. Which sitcom character had a son called Garthy?
13. Who was the Roman god of the sun?
14. When is the next Chinese year of the monkey?
15. Which American state is known as the Gopher State?
16. Whey is the watery by-product of which process?

Answers to page 296

GENERAL KNOWLEDGE 73: **1.** Bill Cosby **2.** All are black belts at karate **3.** 'If You Tolerate This Your Children Will Be Next' **4.** 1948 **5.** Dennis Wilson **6.** Mr Gumby **7.** Willy Brandt **8.** Durham **9.** A wind **10.** Yellow **11.** Menorca **12.** Swiss cheese plant **13.** Football pools **14.** Chepstow **15.** She was the first woman cox in the University Boat Race **16.** Frank

General Knowledge 76

Answers on page 297

1. What was invented by Georges de Mestral after taking his dog for a walk in the woods?
2. Which two months did Barbara Dickson sing about in 1980?
3. Which was the first horse to win the Grand National twice in the 20th century?
4. What was the name of Mr Magoo's nephew?
5. From which fruit is the spirit kirsch made?
6. On which island did Napoleon die?
7. Which Spanish city was the birthplace of the artists Murillo and Velázquez?
8. In which Norwegian town were the 1994 Winter Olympics held?
9. What is an onager?
10. Which Parker was an American writer and wit?
11. Which 52-year-old topped the singles charts in 1998?
12. What is Miss Piggy's surname?
13. On which racecourse is the Scottish Grand National run?
14. About whom was Sharon Stone speaking when she said: 'She lives in rarefied air that's a little thin. It's like she's not getting quite enough oxygen'?
15. What pseudonym was used by novelist Francis Kane?
16. On which river does Elgin stand?

Answers to page 297

GENERAL KNOWLEDGE 74: **1.** Joyce McKinney **2.** Viv Nicholson **3.** East 17 **4.** Republic of Ireland **5.** Hilary Swank **6.** George V **7.** Michael Curtiz **8.** Bodmin Moor **9.** Jimmy Carter **10.** Henry Kissinger **11.** Dave Tucker **12.** Rhine **13.** The Tates and the Campbells **14.** Aberdeen **15.** Jules Massenet **16.** A fish

General Knowledge 77

Answers on page 302

1. For which Jersey police department did Jim Bergerac work?
2. Which acid occurs in stinging ants?
3. Which Seventies rock star was born Vince Furnier?
4. What was the name of the milkman in *Camberwick Green*?
5. Which West End musical star once played Caroline Winthrop in *Crossroads*?
6. How many yards are there in a furlong?
7. What are Razor strop and Jew's ear types of?
8. Which music-hall comedian made famous the song 'I Belong To Glasgow'?
9. Which one-hit wonder had a 1980 chart-topper with 'Together We Are Beautiful'?
10. In which year did British wartime rationing end on butter, bacon and meat?
11. What do gibbons, foxes and swans have in common?
12. Which venomous spider gets its name from a town in Italy?
13. What is Rupert Murdoch's first name?
14. Which US President was known as 'The Accidental President'?
15. Which Australian Prime Minister played himself in Barry Humphries' 1974 film *Barry McKenzie Holds His Own*?
16. Which country's rugby union team are called the Springboks?

Answers to page 302

GENERAL KNOWLEDGE 79: **1.** Isotope **2.** *Peak Practice* **3.** Spa-Francorchamps **4.** Windward Islands **5.** The Rebel Rouser **6.** Colombo **7.** Portuguese **8.** They're all green **9.** Michael, Peter and Tom **10.** Centaur **11.** Tutankhamen **12.** Archimedes **13.** Napoleon **14.** A freshwater fish **15.** St Mary's **16.** Kajagoogoo

General Knowledge 78

Answers on page 303

1. Who wrote *Hay Fever* and *Private Lives*?
2. Who had a 1998 number one with 'Brimful Of Asha'?
3. What is a cowrie?
4. From what were London, Durham and Winchester omitted in 1086?
5. Which author of a book of British battleaxes is married to the former MP for Tatton?
6. What does 'Dodecanese' mean, as in the group of Greek islands?
7. What is the chemical symbol for carbon dioxide?
8. In which county is Wookey Hole?
9. What was the name of the poet William Wordsworth's sister?
10. What is the name of the pub in *Emmerdale*?
11. Which Football League team plays at Sincil Bank?
12. Who founded the Amstrad electronics company?
13. Which British acting knight was born Lewis Ernest Watts?
14. Which blockbuster won the Oscar for Best Film in 1997?
15. In which book did Ian Fleming introduce James Bond?
16. What did Hugh Hefner launch in 1953?

Answers to page 303

GENERAL KNOWLEDGE 80: **1.** Germany **2.** Mullard Furniture Industries **3.** Jack Benny **4.** *Campion* **5.** He was the first substitute to be used in a Football League game **6.** Frisian Islands **7.** A nocturnal bird **8.** They're all carnivorous plants **9.** South Africa **10.** Crowded House **11.** Treaty of Versailles **12.** Whitehorse **13.** A small, triangular bone at the base of the human spine **14.** Denny Hulme **15.** Keats **16.** 17th

General Knowledge 79

Answers on page 300

1. What term in physics was first coined by Frederick Soddy?
2. Which TV medical drama is set in Cardale?
3. In Formula One, on which circuit is the Belgian Grand Prix staged?
4. Which group of islands are known as the 'Iles du Vent' by the French?
5. Which group backed Cliff Bennett in the 1960s?
6. What is the capital of Sri Lanka?
7. What is the official language of Brazil?
8. What do Kermit, Orville and Dipsy have in common?
9. Which three generations of the Scudamore family have become National Hunt jockeys?
10. Which creature in Greek mythology was half-human and half-horse?
11. Whose tomb was opened in 1922?
12. Who shouted 'Eureka' over what he had discovered in the bath?
13. Who defeated Russian Tsar Alexander I at Austerlitz in 1805?
14. What is a barbel?
15. Which is the largest of the Isles of Scilly?
16. Which band were 'Too Shy' in 1983?

Answers to page 300

GENERAL KNOWLEDGE 77: **1.** Bureau des Etrangers **2.** Formic acid **3.** Alice Cooper **4.** Thomas Tripp **5.** Elaine Paige **6.** 220 **7.** Fungi **8.** Will Fyffe **9.** Fern Kinney **10.** 1954 **11.** They all mate for life **12.** Tarantula (Taranto) **13.** Keith **14.** John Tyler **15.** Gough Whitlam **16.** South Africa

General Knowledge 80

Answers on page 301

1. In which country was the world's first motorway?
2. What does MFI stand for?
3. Of which US comedian did Fred Allen once say: 'He couldn't ad-lib a belch after a goulash'?
4. Which TV detective had a manservant by the name of Magersfontein Lugg?
5. What landmark was created by Charlton Athletic footballer Keith Peacock on 21 August 1965?
6. Texel is the largest of which group of islands?
7. What is a frogmouth?
8. What do the bladderwort, sundew and pitcher plant have in common?
9. In which country is Sun City?
10. Which band took their name from a cramped apartment they once shared?
11. Which 1919 peace treaty between the Allies and Germany officially ended the First World War?
12. What is the capital of Canada's Yukon territory?
13. What is a coccyx?
14. Which New Zealand driver was Formula One World Champion in 1967?
15. Which poet wrote 'Endymion'?
16. In which century did Sir Isaac Newton formulate his theory of gravitation?

Answers to page 301

GENERAL KNOWLEDGE 78: **1.** Noel Coward **2.** Cornershop **3.** A marine snail **4.** The Domesday Book **5.** Christine Hamilton **6.** 'Twelve islands' **7.** CO2 **8.** Somerset **9.** Dorothy **10.** The Woolpack **11.** Lincoln City **12.** Alan Sugar **13.** Sir John Mills **14.** *Titanic* **15.** *Casino Royale* **16.** *Playboy*

Cop Shows 5

Answers on page 306

1. Which series starred Edward Woodward as mystery writer Max Beckett?

2. Who tried to solve the killing of Laura Palmer in *Twin Peaks*?

3. Who is Jack Frost's boss?

4. What was the name of *Taggart*'s wheelchair-bound wife?

5. What was Kookie's full name in *77 Sunset Strip*?

6. *Remington Steele* was a figment of whose imagination?

7. Which comedians revived *Randall & Hopkirk (Deceased)* in 1999?

8. Which loner private eye was originally called Frank Marvin?

9. *Fitz* was the US version of which British detective series?

10. Which gangster was Michael Torello's arch enemy in *Crime Story*?

11. Joe Dominguez partnered which police detective?

12. Which *Hill Street Blues* officer suffered a fatal coronary while having sex with a merry widow?

13. What was Makepeace's Christian name in *Dempsey and Makepeace*?

14. Who created *Maigret*?

15. What was the rank of Stewart McMillan in *McMillan and Wife*?

16. *Last Bus to* where was the title of an *Inspector Morse* case?

Answers to page 306

DRAMAS 7: **1.** *Fortunes of War* **2.** *The Charmer* **3.** Burt Kwouk **4.** Birmingham **5.** *Secret Army* **6.** *Bad Girls* **7.** Andrea Newman **8.** *Raffles* **9.** *The Mallens* **10.** Gabriella Benson **11.** Peter Bowles and Bryan Murray **12.** Marietta **13.** Alexei Sayle **14.** Hari Kumar **15.** Alan Bennett **16.** *The Sovereign*

Wildlife 3

Answers on page 307

1. Which series chronicled the adventures of Big Al?
2. Who narrates *Vets in Practice*?
3. Which 1979 series was more than three years in the making?
4. Which *Survival* film-maker was trapped on South Georgia in 1982 when Argentine troops invaded the island during filming?
5. Who kept a *Big Cat Diary*?
6. Which ex-Goodie went wild in 2001?
7. Which Shauna was a presenter of *Animal Hospital*?
8. What kind of animal is Archibald?
9. Which channel screens *Vets Abroad*?
10. What was the name of *Jungle Boy*'s pet lion?
11. In which city was Michaela Denis born?
12. Which bearded botanist was one of the trio of experts on *Don't Ask Me*?
13. What was the title of David Attenborough's 1990 series which looked at animal behaviour?
14. From which zoo did Chris Kelly present *Zoo Time* in 1967?
15. What breed of animal was Flicka?
16. In which series did Hans and Lotte Hass explore underwater life in the Indian Ocean from the marine research vessel *Xarifa*?

Answers to page 307

SOAPS 6: **1.** Barber's **2.** Brenna Jordache **3.** *The Bold and the Beautiful* **4.** Robert Sugden **5.** Annie Miles **6.** Vera Downend **7.** The Hot Biscuit **8.** The Flying Horse **9.** Alexis Rowan **10.** Libby **11.** Roy Farmer **12.** Rosie **13.** Elliot Carson **14.** Michelle Fowler **15.** Adele Silva **16.** Ashley Peacock

Dramas 7

Answers on page 304

1. Which series starred Kenneth Branagh and Emma Thompson as Guy and Harriet Pringle?
2. As played by Nigel Havers, what was Ralph Gorse better known as?
3. Who played Captain Yamuchi in *Tenko*?
4. In which city is *Doctors* set?
5. *Kessler* was a spin-off from which wartime series?
6. Karen Betts is the prison governor in which series?
7. Who wrote *A Bouquet of Barbed Wire*?
8. Which master thief's companion was Bunny Manners?
9. Which family, created by Catherine Cookson, had a distinctive silver streak in their hair?
10. What was the name of *The Manageress*?
11. Which two actors starred together in *The Irish RM* and *Perfect Scoundrels*?
12. Who was Ma and Pop Larkin's eldest daughter in *The Darling Buds of May*?
13. Which anarchic comedian played the forger of the Hitler diaries in *Selling Hitler*?
14. Who was Daphne Manners' lover in *The Jewel in the Crown*?
15. Who created *Talking Heads*?
16. What was the name of the aircraft being manufactured by *The Plane Makers*?

Answers to page 304

COP SHOWS 5: **1.** *Over My Dead Body* **2.** Agent Dale Cooper **3.** Superintendent Mullett **4.** Jean **5.** Gerald Lloyd Kookson III **6.** Laura Holt **7.** Vic Reeves and Bob Mortimer **8.** Frank Marker **9.** *Cracker* **10.** Ray Luca **11.** *Nash Bridges* **12.** Sgt Phil Esterhaus **13.** Harriet **14.** Georges Simenon **15.** Commissioner **16.** *Woodstock*

Soaps 6

Answers on page 305

1. What sort of shop did Felix Kawalski run in Walford?
2. Who tried to poison *Brookside*'s Mandy Jordache shortly before her wedding day?
3. Which soap did *Home and Away* replace on Channel 5?
4. Which *Emmerdale* character went to stay with his grandmother in Spain and came back with a new head?
5. Which actress played Sue Sullivan in *Brookside* and Maria Simons in *Family Affairs*?
6. Which *Crossroads* hairdresser lived on a barge?
7. What was the name of the diner where Lucy Ewing worked in *Dallas*?
8. Which rival ale house took part in a pub Olympics against the Rovers Return in 1984?
9. Who caused Krystle Carrington to suffer a miscarriage in *Dynasty*?
10. Which member of the Kennedy family has worked on the *Erinsborough News*?
11. Who owns the cybercafe in *Family Affairs*?
12. Which character did Anne Haddy play in *Sons and Daughters*?
13. Who ran *Peyton Place*'s local newspaper?
14. Who lost her virginity at 16 to 'Dirty Den'?
15. Who played Kelly Glover in *Emmerdale*?
16. Which Weatherfield sausage champion had a low sperm count?

Answers to page 305

WILDLIFE 3: **1.** *Walking With Dinosaurs* **2.** Christopher Timothy **3.** *Life on Earth* **4.** Lucinda Buxton **5.** Jonathan Scott **6.** Bill Oddie **7.** Shauna Lowry **8.** Koala bear **9.** Channel 5 **10.** Simba **11.** London **12.** David Bellamy **13.** *The Trials of Life* **14.** Chester **15.** Horse **16.** *Adventure*

Comedy 8

Answers on page 310

1. Which series starred Miriam Karlin as the ghostly Yetta Feldman?
2. Who had sisters called Rose and Daisy?
3. What was the name of the psychopathic PE teacher played by Brian Conley in *The Grimleys*?
4. Who is Paul Calf's overweight mate?
5. Which Scottish comedian started out in a folk group called the Humblebums?
6. What was Gareth Blackstock's profession?
7. Which Roman romp was the first series to be made by Hat Trick Productions?
8. What was the name of Ria Parkinson's husband in *Butterflies*?
9. Who played *Andy Capp* in the TV version of the cartoon strip?
10. Which Irish comic was born David Tynan O'Mahony?
11. Who achieved cult comic status after changing his name from Matthew Hall?
12. What was Foggy's surname in *Last of the Summer Wine*?
13. Desmond 'Olivier' Dingle is the leading light in which company?
14. Mark Gatiss and Reece Shearsmith are members of which comedy team?
15. What was the name of the school caretaker in *Please, Sir!*?
16. Who played Max Wild in the 1987 sitcom *Running Wild*?

Answers to page 310

QUIZ AND GAME SHOWS 4: **1.** Julian Pettifer **2.** Les Dawson **3.** Anne Robinson **4.** Cilla Black **5.** Jonathan Pearce **6.** *Through the Keyhole* **7.** *Bare Necessities* **8.** *Play Your Cards Right* **9.** New Zealander **10.** Kenny Everett **11.** *You Bet!* **12.** *Shooting Stars* **13.** Bradley Walsh **14.** *The Generation Game* **15.** *Take Your Pick* **16.** Jonathan Ross

TV Pot Luck 7

Answers on page 311

1. Who trained as a dental nurse before joining *Blue Peter*?
2. What was the sequel to *Fresh Fields*?
3. Who presents *Star For a Night*?
4. What is Nick's profession in *Beast*?
5. Which pair of comedians did a live, unscripted series in 2001?
6. What is the title of the US version of *Scrapheap Challenge*?
7. Who creates *Fantasy Rooms*?
8. On which show did muscleman Tony Holland flex his biceps to the tune of the 'Wheels Cha-Cha'?
9. What was aerobics queen Diana Moran better known as?
10. What did Bert Ford do on TV in the 1970s?
11. What was the name of the chief scientist on *The Muppet Show*?
12. Who starred in *Me Mammy*?
13. Who set off in search of lost tribes in *Disappearing World*?
14. The 1959 series *On the Bright Side* marked the TV breakthrough of which comedian?
15. Which *That Was The Week That Was* regular was called a 'thick-lipped Jewboy' by a Cheshire vicar?
16. Who was the first host of *Candid Camera*?

Answers to page 311

EMMERDALE 3: **1.** Matt and Dolly Skilbeck **2.** Granddaughter **3.** Elizabeth Estensen **4.** 18 **5.** Nick Bates **6.** Jacob **7.** Cain Dingle **8.** Carol Wareing **9.** Graham Clark **10.** Two – Jackie Merrick and Dave Glover **11.** Patrick Mower **12.** Chez Marlon **13.** Bob Hope **14.** Emily Symons **15.** Danny **16.** The plane crash

Quiz & Game Shows 4

Answers on page 308

1. Which Julian presented *Busman's Holiday*?
2. Who took over from Terry Wogan as host of *Blankety Blank*?
3. Who says: 'You are the weakest link. Goodbye'?
4. Who hosts *The Moment of Truth*?
5. Who describes the action on *Robot Wars*?
6. Loyd Grossman is the house detective on which show?
7. Which survival game show pits two professions against each other?
8. Which game show featured the Dolly Dealers?
9. What nationality was Michael Miles?
10. Which former disc jockey hosted *Brainstorm*?
11. Which game show has been hosted by Bruce Forsyth, Matthew Kelly and Darren Day?
12. On which show did the Dove from Above appear?
13. Who succeeded Nicky Campbell as host of *Wheel of Fortune*?
14. Which game show originated from a Dutch programme called *Een Van De Aacht* ('One out of Eight')?
15. Which show always had three booby prizes?
16. Who is the chairman on *It's Only TV... But I Like It*?

Answers to page 308

COMEDY 8: **1.** *So Haunt Me* **2.** Hyacinth Bucket **3.** Doug Digby **4.** Fat Bob **5.** Billy Connolly **6.** *Chef!* **7.** *Chelmsford 123* **8.** Ben **9.** James Bolam **10.** Dave Allen **11.** Harry Hill **12.** Dewhurst **13.** The National Theatre of Brent **14.** The League of Gentlemen **15.** Norman Potter **16.** Ray Brooks

Emmerdale 3

Answers on page 309

1. Which couple inherited Crossgill after the owner shot himself?
2. What relation is Tricia Stokes to Alan Turner?
3. Which former Liver Bird plays Diane Blackstock?
4. How old was Joe Sugden when *Emmerdale Farm* began?
5. Who was sent to jail for shooting a poacher?
6. What was the name of Annie Sugden's husband?
7. With whom did Angie Reynolds have an affair in 2001?
8. Which friend of Viv Windsor's stole the B & B from under her nose?
9. Which mad schoolteacher killed Rachel Hughes?
10. How many husbands have died on Kathy Glover?
11. Which Seventies heart-throb joined the cast in 2001 as Rodney Blackstock?
12. In which restaurant did Rodney soon become a partner?
13. Which character is a salesman of Naughty Nylons?
14. Which former *Home and Away* actress turned up as the Woolpack's new barmaid?
15. What is the name of Cynthia Daggert's son?
16. Archie Brooks and Mark Hughes were among those killed in which *Emmerdale* disaster?

Answers to page 309

TV POT LUCK 7: **1.** Yvette Fielding **2.** *French Fields* **3.** Jane McDonald **4.** Vet **5.** Frank Skinner and David Baddiel **6.** *Junkyard Wars* **7.** Laurence Llewelyn-Bowen **8.** *Opportunity Knocks* **9.** The Green Goddess **10.** BBC weatherman **11.** Dr Bunsen Honeydew **12.** Milo O'Shea **13.** Brian Moser **14.** Stanley Baxter **15.** Bernard Levin **16.** Bob Monkhouse

Westerns 2

Answers on page 314

1. Which future Hollywood star was *Wanted: Dead or Alive*?

2. Who played Wishbone in *Rawhide*?

3. Slim Sherman and Jess Harper were the principals in which Western?

4. Which Western was based on Owen Wister's 1902 novel of the same name?

5. Who switched from playing *Davy Crockett* to *Daniel Boone*?

6. Which series starred Robert Horton as an amnesiac in search of his identity?

7. Who won a railroad in a poker game in *The Iron Horse*?

8. Who played *Shane*?

9. Which family owned *The High Chaparral*?

10. In *Kung Fu*, who stayed with Kwai Chang Caine in spirit after being killed in a fight?

11. The Ingalls family were the central characters in which domestic Western?

12. In which town did gunfighter Ethan Allen Cord operate?

13. Who succeeded Seth Adams as master of *Wagon Train*?

14. What was Lucas McCain better known as?

15. Who played Bronco Layne?

16. In *Bonanza*, what was Eric Cartwright's nickname?

Answers to page 314

DRAMAS 8: **1.** Ruth-Anne Miller **2.** Barry White **3.** Emergency Room **4.** Pauline Collins **5.** 'The Eel' **6.** Felix Cramer **7.** Ramona **8.** *The Crow Road* **9.** *Rumpole of the Bailey* **10.** Ellyn Warren **11.** Natasha Little **12.** 'Hodge' **13.** Julia Sawalha **14.** *Our Friends in the North* **15.** Anne Boleyn **16.** Nampara

Locations 3

Answers on page 315

1. Which drama series is set in the White House?
2. In which American state was *Peyton Place*?
3. Which English city was the setting for *Spender*?
4. What was the name of the fictional village in *Eldorado*?
5. Which city had a *Waterfront Beat*?
6. In which London suburb did *Citizen Smith* live?
7. In which town do *The Simpsons* reside?
8. In which London suburb was the original *Big Brother* house?
9. Which Seventies police series was set in the fictitious Midlands town of Broadstone?
10. *HMS Hero* was the setting for which drama series?
11. In which Surrey town did *Terry and June* live?
12. *The Brothers McGregor* were based in which city?
13. Which fictional Lancashire town was the setting for *Brass*?
14. In which country did *The District Nurse* work?
15. Which city is the setting for *Cold Feet*?
16. Which soap is set in King's Oak?

Answers to page 315

CHILDREN'S TV 4: **1.** Suzanne Ross **2.** The Noo-noo **3.** Ed Stewart **4.** Sally James **5.** Mars **6.** Serge Danot **7.** *Trumpton* **8.** Sam **9.** When they are sad or frightened **10.** Baron Greenback **11.** Lynda Day **12.** Windy Miller **13.** Rabbit **14.** Orange **15.** Ted McKeever and Jim Buckley **16.** Yoo-hoo

Dramas 8

Answers on page 312

1. Which aged storekeeper dispensed psychological insight with each purchase in *Northern Exposure*?
2. Who is John Cage's favourite singer in *Ally McBeal*?
3. What does *ER* stand for?
4. Who played the title role in *Ambassador*?
5. What is slippery legal adviser Alan Birch's nickname in *Chicago Hope*?
6. Which lothario did Trevor Eve play in *A Sense of Guilt*?
7. What is the name of David and Karen's Spanish maid in *Cold Feet*?
8. Which Iain Banks novel was dramatised by the BBC in 1996?
9. Who delighted in calling judges 'Old darling'?
10. In *thirtysomething*, who was Hope's best friend?
11. Who played Rachel in *This Life*?
12. What was Dave Gadd more commonly known as in *Preston Front*?
13. Which *Absolutely Fabulous* actress played Lydia Bennet in the 1995 adaptation of *Pride and Prejudice*?
14. Tosker and Geordie were characters in which 1996 series?
15. In *The Six Wives of Henry VIII*, which of the king's spouses was played by Dorothy Tutin?
16. What was the name of Ross Poldark's home?

Answers to page 312

WESTERNS 2: **1.** Steve McQueen **2.** Paul Brinegar **3.** *Laramie* **4.** *The Virginian* **5.** Fess Parker **6.** *A Man Called Shenandoah* **7.** Ben Calhoun **8.** David Carradine **9.** The Cannons **10.** Master Po **11.** *Little House on the Prairie* **12.** *Paradise* **13.** Chris Hale **14.** *The Rifleman* **15.** Ty Hardin **16.** 'Hoss'

Children's TV 4

Answers on page 313

1. Which *Grange Hill* pupil was played by Susan Tully?
2. What is the name of the *Teletubbies*' vacuum-cleaner?
3. Who followed Michael Aspel as presenter of *Crackerjack*?
4. Who conducted 'almost legendary' pop interviews on *Tiswas*?
5. Where do Biker Mice come from?
6. Who created *The Magic Roundabout*?
7. Which town clock always told the time 'never too quickly, never too slowly'?
8. Which fireman has his own series?
9. When do *Clangers*' ears droop?
10. Who was *Dangermouse*'s arch enemy?
11. Who was editor of the *Junior Gazette* in *Press Gang*?
12. Who rode a penny-farthing bicycle around *Camberwick Green*?
13. What breed of animal is Grabbit?
14. What colour is Jake in *Tweenies*?
15. Who were the two central characters in *Ripcord*?
16. What was the name of the cuckoo on *Billy Bean and His Funny Machine*?

Answers to page 313

LOCATIONS 3: **1.** *The West Wing* **2.** New England **3.** Newcastle-upon-Tyne **4.** Los Barcos **5.** Liverpool **6.** Tooting **7.** Springfield **8.** Bow **9.** *Hunter's Walk* **10.** *Warship* **11.** Purley **12.** Liverpool **13.** Utterley **14.** Wales **15.** Manchester **16.** *Crossroads*

News 2

Answers on page 318

1. Which newsreader presents *Police, Camera, Action*?
2. Which series looked at events in the news 25 years ago?
3. Who was the first BBC television newsreader?
4. Which news programme caused a furore when it moved to a new time of 11 o'clock?
5. Which George is a BBC newsreader?
6. Which *Newsnight* interrogator pressed the then Home Secretary Michael Howard 14 times for an answer to the same question?
7. Helen Rollason, Juliet Morris and Krishnan Guru-Murthy all presented which news programme?
8. What was Nan Winton's claim to fame?
9. Who retired as chairman of *Question Time* in 1989?
10. And who took his place?
11. Which BBC newsreader used to be a Liverpool bus conductor?
12. Which ITN newsreader has written biographies of West Indian Test cricketers Clive Lloyd and Viv Richards?
13. Which presenter closed each programme with the words: 'The next *Tonight* will be tomorrow night'?
14. What do Martyn Lewis, Anna Ford and Julia Somerville have in common?
15. Which news programme was born in 1967?
16. Which Katie reads the ITN news?

Answers to page 318

SOAPS 7: **1.** In his car **2.** Ian McShane **3.** Alistair Matthews **4.** Paul and Annabelle Collins **5.** Doctor **6.** Tom Hopwood **7.** Alvin Stardust **8.** Daphne Clarke **9.** A wartime bomb **10.** Clive James **11.** Caress **12.** Arnold Tripp **13.** Roy's Rolls **14.** Mary Smith **15.** York **16.** Harry Hewitt

Comedy 9

Answers on page 319

1. Who is Denise Royle's chubby best friend?
2. For whom did Angela Thorne's Harriet Emily Farrington work?
3. On which soccer boss was *The Fast Show*'s Ron Manager based?
4. Which trio were *Filthy, Rich and Catflap*?
5. Which comedy great was part of a double act with Reg Varney early in his career?
6. What was Lucien obsessed with in *The Liver Birds*?
7. Which silent buffoon made his debut in 1990?
8. Who wrote *Some Mothers Do 'Ave 'Em*?
9. What was the name of the family in *Third Rock From The Sun*?
10. Which sex-mad Roman did Barbara Windsor play in *Up Pompeii!*?
11. Who plays Nick in *Beast*?
12. Dylan Moran and Bill Bailey star in which dark sitcom?
13. Which of *The Army Game* soldiers was an inveterate knitter?
14. Who adopted the alter ego of Martin Welbourne?
15. *Going Straight* was the sequel to which classic sitcom?
16. Who married Rodney in *Only Fools and Horses*?

Answers to page 319

WHICH YEAR IN TV? 5: **1.** 1983 **2.** 1984 **3.** 1974 **4.** 1982 **5.** 1992 **6.** 1994 **7.** 1984 **8.** 1962 **9.** 1985 **10.** 1959 **11.** 1976 **12.** 1998 **13.** 1995 **14.** 1985 **15.** 1972 **16.** 1990

Soaps 7

Answers on page 316

1. Where did Tom Fletcher suffer a fatal heart attack in *Home and Away*?

2. Which English actor played Don Lockwood in *Dallas*?

3. Which Walford evangelist cast a spell over Sarah Hills?

4. Who were the first occupants of 8 Brookside Close?

5. What was Bernard McAllister's occupation in *Emmerdale*?

6. Who asked Hilda Ogden to marry him in 1987?

7. Which Seventies glam-rock star played a pub landlord in *Hollyoaks*?

8. Which former Ramsay Street resident used to be a stripper?

9. What exploded beneath the Crossroads Motel in 1967?

10. Which chat show host had a walk-on part as a postman in *Neighbours*?

11. In *Dynasty*, who tried to publish a spiteful book about Alexis entitled *Sister Dearest*?

12. Who was editor of the *Angleton Advertiser* in *The Newcomers*?

13. What is the name of Roy Cropper's café in *Coronation Street*?

14. Which punk was mum to Annie in *EastEnders*?

15. In which city did *Brookside*'s Damon Grant die?

16. Which *Coronation Street* resident had a wife called Concepta?

Answers to page 316

NEWS 2: **1.** Alastair Stewart **2.** *All Our Yesterdays* **3.** Richard Baker **4.** *News at Ten* **5.** Alagiah **6.** Jeremy Paxman **7.** *Newsround* **8.** She was the first woman BBC newsreader **9.** Sir Robin Day **10.** Peter Sissons **11.** Peter Sissons **12.** Trevor McDonald **13.** Cliff Michelmore **14.** They have all read the news for both the BBC and ITN **15.** *News at Ten* **16.** Derham

Which Year in TV? 5

Answers on page 317

In which year were the following programmes first shown on British television:

1. *St Elsewhere*
2. *Surprise, Surprise*
3. *It Ain't Half Hot, Mum*
4. *The Young Ones*
5. *A Touch of Frost*
6. *The X Files*
7. *The Bill*
8. *Animal Magic*
9. *The Cosby Show*
10. *Juke Box Jury*
11. *The Muppet Show*
12. *Playing the Field*
13. *Hollyoaks*
14. *Miami Vice*
15. *Record Breakers*
16. *Star Trek: The Next Generation*

Answers to page 317

COMEDY 9: **1.** Cheryl **2.** The Foreign Office **3.** Alec Stock **4.** Nigel Planer, Rik Mayall and Adrian Edmondson **5.** Benny Hill **6.** His rabbits **7.** *Mr Bean* **8.** Raymond Allen **9.** Solomon **10.** Nymphia **11.** Alexander Armstrong **12.** *Black Books* **13.** Pte Hatchett **14.** Reggie Perrin **15.** *Porridge* **16.** Cassandra

Catchphrases 3

Answers on page 322

1. Who referred to 'a nice little earner'?
2. Which pint-sized comedian's catchphrase was 'Hello, my darlings'?
3. Who said: 'I wanna tell you a story'?
4. Whose show ended each week with the words: 'Bye bye everybody, bye bye'?
5. Which law enforcers used to tell villains: 'Shut it!'?
6. Which wellie-wearing Irish comic promises: 'And there's more'?
7. Which character in *The Army Game* would depart by saying: 'I'll be leaving you now, sah'?
8. Which *'Allo 'Allo* character warned: 'Leesten very carefully, I will say zis only wernce'?
9. Which of *The Comedians* boasted: 'I'm too good for this place'?
10. Who 'wouldn't let it lie'?
11. On which show would you hear the catchphrase 'Suits you, sir!'?
12. Which Steve Coogan creation uses the descriptive phrase 'Bag o' shite'?
13. Who referred to his wife as 'She who must be obeyed'?
14. Which game show host praised contestants with the words: 'Didn't he do well'?
15. Who in *Deputy Dawg* used to lament: 'Can't see too well above ground'?
16. Which detective would invariably add: 'Ah, just one more thing'?

Answers to page 322

TV POT LUCK 8: **1.** Quincy **2.** Russell Spam **3.** Massachusetts **4.** Jeremy Clarkson **5.** Mr Roarke **6.** *Lou Grant* **7.** *The Curious Gardeners* **8.** Julian Clary and Phill Jupitus **9.** Ray Mears **10.** *Changing Rooms* **11.** Barbara Dickson **12.** Dee Tate **13.** 1997 **14.** Alan Davies **15.** *The Travel Show* **16.** Neil Morrissey

Cop Shows 6

Answers on page 323

1. The troublesome Skeetsmore estate features in which 1990s police series?
2. Who used to refer to his superior officer as 'Hornrimmed Harry'?
3. Which *NYPD Blue* cop was shot while in the company of a prostitute?
4. Lew Erskine was the leader of which team of crime-fighters?
5. And who abandoned *77 Sunset Strip* to play him?
6. Which priestly detective was created by Ralph McInerny?
7. On whom did Agnes Dipesto have a crush in *Moonlighting*?
8. Which future Prime Minister played a bent copper in *Dixon of Dock Green*?
9. Who played a pair of cocky Australian villains in two stories of *The Sweeney*?
10. Who was Eddie Shoestring's boss at Radio West?
11. Who turned down the role of *Columbo* because it would have kept him off the golf course?
12. Which Olympic decathlon champion starred in *CHiPS*?
13. What was the name of Martin Shaw's character in *The Chief*?
14. What was the title of the final *Inspector Morse* story?
15. Which cop turned DJ was known as the 'Nighthawk'?
16. Which Scottish songstress played rock star Caitlin Davies in *Miami Vice*?

Answers to page 323

BROOKSIDE 1: **1.** Edna **2.** Joe Halsall **3.** Tommy McArdle **4.** Marianne Dwyer **5.** Loyd Grossman and Lily Savage **6.** No. 10 **7.** Emma Reid **8.** Harper **9.** Jackie Corkhill **10.** Christopher Duncan **11.** The Chois **12.** He committed suicide in a fume-filled car **13.** Robert Beck **14.** Sinbad **15.** The Scotty Dogs **16.** Dick Ronson

TV Pot Luck 8

Answers on page 320

1. What was *Mr Magoo*'s first name?
2. Who was 'Twiggy' Rathbone's lookalike in *Hot Metal*?
3. Which American state is the setting for *Dawson's Creek*?
4. Which motoring presenter is a cousin of TV doctor Mark Porter?
5. Who owned *Fantasy Island*?
6. Which newspaper series featured a photographer nicknamed 'Animal'?
7. What were horticulturists Gordon Taylor and Guy Cooper otherwise known as in 2001?
8. Who are the team captains on *It's Only TV...But I Like It*?
9. Who goes in for *Extreme Survival*?
10. Anna Ryder Richardson, Linda Barker and Graham Wynne are designers on which show?
11. Which female singer appeared in *Band of Gold*?
12. Who was Elly Chandler's reluctant partner in *Chandler and Co*?
13. When did Channel 5 begin broadcasting?
14. Which comedian/actor starred as Russel Boyd in *A Many Splintered Thing*?
15. Fi Glover and Simon Calder were reporters on which holiday programme?
16. Who played window-cleaner Sammy the Shammy on *Noel's House Party*?

Answers to page 320

CATCHPHRASES 3: **1.** Arthur Daley **2.** Charlie Drake **3.** Max Bygraves **4.** Sooty **5.** *The Sweeney* **6.** Jimmy Cricket **7.** Sgt Claude Snudge **8.** Michelle of the Resistance **9.** Ken Goodwin **10.** Reeves and Mortimer **11.** *The Fast Show* **12.** Paul Calf **13.** *Rumpole of the Bailey* **14.** Bruce Forsyth **15.** Vince Van Gopher **16.** *Columbo*

Brookside 1

Answers on page 321

1. What was the name of Harry Cross's wife?
2. Which tough little lady opened La Luz in partnership with Barry Grant?
3. Which local gangster wore a camel coat and bred budgies?
4. Who was Mick Johnson about to marry when he was wrongly accused of armed robbery?
5. Which two celebrities were hired to open Grants restaurant?
6. At which house in the Close did Gavin Taylor, Trevor Jordache and Little Jimmy Corkhill all die?
7. Which policewoman asked Rod Corkhill to accompany her to the bedroom at Tommo's party?
8. What was Sue Sullivan's maiden name?
9. Who is Val Walker's sister?
10. Who was the gay boyfriend of Gordon Collins?
11. Which Oriental family moved into 7 Brookside Close in 1989?
12. How did cult leader Simon Howe die?
13. Who played Peter Harrison before moving to *Emmerdale*?
14. Who once lived in a garden shed on the Close?
15. Which band did Frank Rogers used to be in?
16. Who was Ron Dixon's mysterious double?

Answers to page 321

COP SHOWS 6: **1.** *The Cops* **2.** Jack Frost **3.** Andy Sipowicz **4.** *The F.B.I.* **5.** Efrem Zimbalist Jnr **6.** Father Dowling **7.** Herbert Viola **8.** Paul Eddington **9.** Patrick Mower and George Layton **10.** Don Satchley **11.** Bing Crosby **12.** Bruce Jenner **13.** Alan Cade **14.** The Remorseful Day **15.** Jack Killian **16.** Sheena Easton

Bruce Springsteen 1

Answers on page 326

1. Which 1975 track did not make it into the UK singles charts until 1987?
2. On which Springsteen release did Howard Kaylan and Mark Volman from The Turtles sing backing vocals?
3. Which film track gave Springsteen a UK number two in 1994?
4. What is the name of Springsteen's backing band?
5. With which band did Springsteen play as a teenager?
6. What was the title of Springsteen's debut album?
7. Which Springsteen song was covered by Manfred Mann's Earth Band in 1977?
8. From which album was 'Hungry Heart' taken?
9. In which year was the album 'Born In The USA' released?
10. Which Edwin Starr hit did Springsteen cover in 1986?
11. Which was Springsteen's first UK top ten single?
12. What is Springsteen's nickname?
13. From which film was the 1997 single 'Secret Garden' taken?
14. Which of his backing singers did Springsteen marry in 1991?
15. In which year was 'Human Touch' released?
16. Which track formed a double A-side with 'Born In The USA'?

Answers to page 326

INDIE 2: **1.** Oasis **2.** Smashing Pumpkins **3.** 'The Man Who' **4.** 'Say What You Want' **5.** Dodgy **6.** Super Furry Animals **7.** 'Strangeways, Here We Come' **8.** Cast **9.** The Bluetones **10.** 'Different Class' **11.** Counting Crows **12.** Gin Blossoms **13.** Mark and Scott Morriss **14.** Babybird **15.** 'There's No Other Way' **16.** Manic Street Preachers

Chart Toppers 5

Answers on page 327

1. Which American singer enjoyed a UK number one in 1974 with a song of praise to his wife?
2. Which 1977 chart topper from a musical was originally titled 'It's Only Your Lover Returning'?
3. Which act had UK number ones in 1989 with 'Swing The Mood', 'That's What I Like' and 'Let's Party'?
4. What was the title of Stiltskin's UK number one of 1994?
5. For which other artist, besides Mungo Jerry, did Ray Dorset write a UK number one?
6. And what was the title of the song?
7. Which 1980 chart topper, written by an ex-teacher, told of the secret love between a teacher and a pupil?
8. Which Eighties number one was taken from the 1935 musical *Jubilee*?
9. And which former reserve goalkeeper for Real Madrid had the hit with it in 1981?
10. 'The Only Way Is Up' was a 1988 number one for which artist?
11. Who had an instrumental number one with 'Wonderful Land' in 1962?
12. How many UK number one singles have The Rolling Stones had?
13. Which much-maligned singer reached number one with 'I Pretend' in 1968?
14. What was the best-selling UK single of 1968?
15. Whose one and only number one was 'The One And Only'?
16. And who wrote 'The One And Only'?

Answers to page 327

MUSIC POT LUCK 10: **1.** The Pogues (*Pogue Mo Chone*) **2.** Ray Davies **3.** John Lennon **4.** 99 **5.** Amarillo **6.** Stevie Wonder **7.** 'Get Down Shep' **8.** The Sex Pistols **9.** 'Raspberry Beret' **10.** Sky Saxon **11.** Mariah Carey **12.** Procol Harum **13.** Transit Authority **14.** 'California Dreamin'' **15.** Kajagoogoo **16.** Van McCoy

Indie 2

Answers on page 324

1. Which band had a guitarist nicknamed 'Bonehead'?
2. Singer Billy Corgan is associated with which band?
3. What was the title of Travis's best-selling album of 1999?
4. In 1997, which track gave Texas their first UK top ten single for eight years?
5. Nigel Clarke was the singer with which band?
6. Whose 1997 album was titled 'Radiator'?
7. Which Smiths album title name-checked a prison?
8. Who had hits with 'Alright', 'Walkaway' and 'Flying'?
9. Ed Chesters is drummer with which band?
10. From which album was Pulp's 'Common People' taken?
11. Which California-based band was fronted by Adam Duritz?
12. For which US band was Doug Hopkins, who shot himself dead in 1993, the principal songwriter?
13. Which brothers make up one half of The Bluetones?
14. Which band insisted 'You're Gorgeous' in 1996?
15. Which was Blur's first top ten UK single?
16. Who released a 1994 album called 'The Holy Bible'?

Answers to page 324

BRUCE SPRINGSTEEN 1: **1.** 'Born To Run' **2.** 'Hungry Heart' **3.** 'Streets Of Philadelphia' **4.** The E Street Band **5.** The Castiles **6.** 'Greetings From Asbury Park NJ' **7.** 'Blinded By The Light' **8.** 'The River' **9.** 1984 **10.** 'War' **11.** 'Dancing In The Dark' **12.** 'The Boss' **13.** *Jerry Maguire* **14.** Patti Scialfa **15.** 1992 **16.** 'I'm On Fire'

Music Pot Luck 10

Answers on page 325

1. Which band's name is an abbreviation of 'kiss my arse' in Gaelic?
2. Which father of Brit Pop went to the same North London secondary school as Rod Stewart?
3. Thelma Pickles was which rock star's first girlfriend?
4. How old were twin sisters Kin Narita and Gin Kanie when they had a hit single in Japan?
5. Where did Tony Christie want to know the way to in 1971?
6. Who played harmonica on Chaka Khan's 'I Feel For You'?
7. What order did The Barron Knights bark out on behalf of John Noakes?
8. Which punk band starred in the film *The Great Rock 'n' Roll Swindle*?
9. What fruit were Prince and The Revolution wearing on their head in 1985?
10. Which singer with Californian cult band The Seeds used to ask dogs the time and live in a dustbin like his hero Top Cat?
11. Which US diva allegedly said 'I don't do stairs' when asked to climb a small flight to her first-floor suite at BBC's Elstree Studios?
12. Which Sixties group were supposedly named after a friend's pedigree cat?
13. Which two words did Chicago drop from their original name?
14. Which Mamas and The Papas song became a hit again 31 years after its original release when it featured in a TV commercial?
15. Limahl was the lead singer with which Eighties group?
16. Who had a 1975 hit with 'The Hustle'?

Answers to page 325

CHART TOPPERS 5: **1.** John Denver ('Annie's Song') **2.** 'Don't Cry For Me Argentina' **3.** Jive Bunny and The Mastermixers **4.** 'Inside' **5.** Kelly Marie **6.** 'Feels Like I'm In Love' **7.** 'Don't Stand So Close To Me' (The Police, written by Sting) **8.** 'Begin The Beguine' **9.** Julio Iglesias **10.** Yazz **11.** The Shadows **12.** Eight **13.** Des O'Connor **14.** 'Hey Jude' **15.** Chesney Hawkes **16.** Nik Kershaw

Jazz 2

Answers on page 330

1. With what instrument was Erroll Garner associated?
2. What was Eddie Calvert's nickname?
3. Which track from the film *The King and I* gave Kenny Ball and His Jazzmen a number four UK hit in 1962?
4. Which Pittsburgh-born double bass player toured the world with Oscar Peterson from 1951 to 1966?
5. What were Serge Chaloff, Stan Getz, Zoot Sims and Al Cohn collectively known as?
6. What was the original title for 'Stranger On The Shore'?
7. Who had a 1982 hit with 'Cherry Pink And Apple Blossom White'?
8. Which jazz chart topper of 1954 was the first number one hit to be recorded at Abbey Road Studios?
9. What was singer Joe Carroll usually known as?
10. 'Petite Fleur' was a 1959 UK hit for whose jazz band?
11. Who performed the clarinet solo on 'Petite Fleur'?
12. Whose band charted in the UK in 1956 with 'Bad Penny Blues'?
13. What was the name of Acker Bilk's band?
14. Which instrument did Wardell Gray play?
15. What nationality insect gave Herb Alpert a number three hit in 1965?
16. Which group of musicians backed Herb Alpert?

Answers to page 330

NUMBER TWOS 1: **1.** 1965 **2.** 1986 **3.** 1970 **4.** 1970 **5.** 1964 **6.** 1981 **7.** 1970 **8.** 1958 **9.** 1990 **10.** 1993 **11.** 1977 **12.** 1969 **13.** 1962 **14.** 1974 **15.** 1979 **16.** 1983

Elton John 1

Answers on page 331

1. Which was Elton John's first UK chart hit?
2. Which two Beach Boys did backing vocals on 'Don't Let The Sun Go Down On Me'?
3. Which Lennon and McCartney song gave Elton John a 1974 hit?
4. Whose forenames did Reg Dwight borrow for his stage persona?
5. Who sang backing vocals on 'The Bitch Is Back'?
6. Which item of Elton John's stage clothing was checked for drugs when he arrived in Los Angeles in 1972?
7. What did Elton John wear on stage at a Stooges gig in Atlanta in October 1974?
8. What links Elton John and pickled onions?
9. Which song did Elton John perform on *The Muppet Show* with Miss Piggy?
10. On which song did Elton John duet with Kiki Dee in 1993?
11. From which film was 'Circle Of Life' taken?
12. In which year was 'Candle In The Wind' first released?
13. What lifelong ambition did Elton John realise in June 1977?
14. As whom was Elton John dressed when he gatecrashed Rod Stewart's Wembley concert in April 1991?
15. Which Elton John single of 1984 had a strong anti-apartheid message?
16. What honour was bestowed upon Elton John on 7 March 1976?

Answers to page 331

HOME TOWNS 3: **1.** Colchester **2.** Maidstone **3.** Coventry **4.** Haircut 100 **5.** Manchester **6.** Southend **7.** Liverpool **8.** Solihull **9.** Leeds **10.** Newcastle-upon-Tyne **11.** Acton County Grammar School **12.** Hertfordshire **13.** Soft Machine **14.** The Barron Knights **15.** Manic Street Preachers **16.** Londonderry

Number Twos 1

Answers on page 328

In which years did the following tracks reach number two in the UK charts?

1. 'My Generation' (The Who)

2. 'Holding Back The Years' (Simply Red)

3. 'Lola' (The Kinks)

4. 'Let It Be' (The Beatles)

5. 'I'm Gonna Be Strong' (Gene Pitney)

6. 'Invisible Sun' (The Police)

7. 'I Want You Back' (The Jackson Five)

8. 'Tom Hark' (Elias and his Zigzag Flutes)

9. 'Hanky Panky' (Madonna)

10. 'Why Can't I Wake Up With You?' (Take That)

11. 'Boogie Nights' (Heatwave)

12. 'Oh Happy Day' (The Edwin Hawkins Singers)

13. 'Hey! Baby' (Bruce Channel)

14. 'The Cat Crept In' (Mud)

15. 'Crazy Little Thing Called Love' (Queen)

16. 'My Oh My' (Slade)

Answers to page 328

JAZZ 2: **1.** Piano **2.** 'The Man With The Golden Trumpet' **3.** 'March Of The Siamese Children' **4.** Ray Brown **5.** The Four Brothers **6.** 'Jenny' **7.** Modern Romance featuring John Du Prez **8.** 'Oh Mein Papa' (Eddie Calvert) **9.** 'Bebop' **10.** Chris Barber **11.** Monty Sunshine **12.** Humphrey Lyttelton **13.** The Paramount Jazz Band **14.** Tenor saxophone **15.** 'Spanish Flea' **16.** The Tijuana Brass

Home Towns 3

Answers on page 329

1. Which town do Blur come from?
2. Which Kentish town was home to Chicory Tip?
3. Eighties band King hailed from which Midlands city?
4. Which Eighties band, who sang about their Favourite Shirts, came from Beckenham, Kent?
5. Which city did Herman's Hermits come from?
6. The Kursaal Flyers came from which Essex town?
7. Where did The Farm come from?
8. Where was the home town of Sixties band The Applejacks?
9. In which city did Soft Cell meet up?
10. Which city was home to The Animals?
11. Roger Daltrey, Pete Townshend and John Entwistle were all pupils at which school in west London?
12. From which county did Sixties band Unit Four Plus Two come?
13. Which Sixties band, featuring Robert Wyatt and Kevin Ayers, were formed in Canterbury, Kent?
14. Leighton Buzzard is the home town of which comedy group, popular in the Sixties?
15. Which band are arguably the most famous sons of Blackwood in South Wales?
16. Where was The Undertones' home town?

Answers to page 329

ELTON JOHN 1: **1.** 'Your Song' **2.** Carl Wilson and Bruce Johnston **3.** 'Lucy In The Sky With Diamonds' **4.** Saxophonist Elton Dean and R & B singer Long John Baldry **5.** Dusty Springfield **6.** His platform boots with eight-inch lifts **7.** A gorilla suit **8.** In 1975 he was due to marry Linda Woodrow, heiress to the Epicure pickled onion empire **9.** 'Don't Go Breaking My Heart' **10.** 'True Love' **11.** *The Lion King* **12.** 1974 **13.** He became chairman of Watford Football Club **14.** Rod Stewart's new bride, Rachel Hunter **15.** 'Passengers' **16.** He was immortalised in wax at Madame Tussaud's

Reggae 2

Answers on page 334

1. In which year did Bob Marley and The Wailers first release 'No Woman No Cry'?
2. Who had a hit with 'My Boy Lollipop' in 1964?
3. Who led The Maytals from the early Seventies?
4. Whose albums included 'Furnace', 'Flesh of My Skin, Blood Of My Blood' and 'Torch Of Freedom'?
5. What was the name of Desmond Dekker's backing band?
6. Which song did Desmond Dekker take to number two in the UK charts in 1970?
7. Which former member of The Wailers was murdered by burglars at his Jamaican home in 1987?
8. John Taylor and Everton Banner are better known as which reggae duo?
9. How old was Bob Marley when he died?
10. Which brothers were founder members of UB40?
11. Which UB40 hit was written about the unemployment statistics at the time?
12. In which year did Shaggy reach number one in the UK with 'Boombastic'?
13. What was Ken Boothe's follow-up to 'Everything I Own'?
14. Which song, originally recorded by Johnny Osborne in 1969, was a UK top ten hit for UB40 in 1998?
15. From which film was UB40's number one '(I Can't Help) Falling In Love With You' taken?
16. Who had a posthumous hit with 'Buffalo Soldier' in 1983?

Answers to page 334

BUDDY HOLLY 1: **1.** Sonny West **2.** It was mis-spelt on the recording contract **3.** Charles **4.** The Three Tunes **5.** Three **6.** 1958 **7.** Des O'Connor **8.** Cricket Jerry Allison's girlfriend, Peggy Sue Gerron **9.** In his Greenwich Village apartment **10.** 'Peggy Sue Got Married' **11.** 'Rave On' **12.** 'Bo Diddley' **13.** Bob Montgomery **14.** 'Blue Days, Black Nights' **15.** He played only on the downstroke **16.** 3 February 1959

Seventies 3

Answers on page 335

1. Who had the last UK number one single of the Seventies?
2. Who got to number one in 1975 with 'Ms Grace'?
3. Which actress contributed whispers to 'Tonight's The Night' by Rod Stewart?
4. Which 10cc song was written about the experiences of Moody Blue Justin Hayward on a holiday to the Caribbean?
5. What was the lead singer of Fox's Christian name?
6. Who had a 1971 hit with 'My Brother Jake'?
7. Who recorded the album 'I'm A Writer, Not A Fighter'?
8. What were the names of the five Osmonds (before Little Jimmy joined)?
9. Which namesake of a Scottish international footballer of the time was a member of Dave Edmunds's Rockpile?
10. Which song gave Deniece Williams a UK number one in 1977?
11. Which daughter of a TV game show host was a member of Guys 'N' Dolls?
12. Who asked: 'Who Were You With In The Moonlight'?
13. In which year did Slade have their first number one?
14. And what was the title?
15. What did Barry White ask in November 1975?
16. Who released the 1970 album 'Self-Portrait'?

Answers to page 335

OASIS 1: **1.** Burnage **2.** British Gas **3.** The Inspiral Carpets **4.** Alan McGee **5.** Creation **6.** Liam and guitarist Paul Arthurs were involved in a brawl on the ferry from Harwich and returned to Britain immediately **7.** 'Supersonic' **8.** A fan jumped on stage and hit him in the face **9.** Liam **10.** Burt Bacharach **11.** 'Some Might Say' **12.** 'Champagne Supernova' **13.** 1995 **14.** An audience member threw wire-rimmed prescription glasses at him **15.** Tony McCarroll **16.** 'All Around The World'

Buddy Holly 1

Answers on page 332

1. Who originally recorded 'Rave On'?
2. Why was his original name of Holley changed to Holly?
3. What was Buddy Holly's real Christian name?
4. What were The Crickets previously called?
5. How many weeks did 'That'll Be The Day' spend at number one in the UK?
6. In which year did Buddy Holly and The Crickets embark on their only UK tour?
7. Which current chat show host was on the same bill as Holly for that UK tour?
8. After whom was 'Peggy Sue' named?
9. Where did Holly make his last-ever recordings?
10. Which sequel to one of his earlier songs was a posthumous Holly hit in 1959?
11. Which track got to number five in the UK charts in 1958?
12. Which song about an R & B singer was a 1963 hit for Holly?
13. Who was the Bob with whom the teenage Holly played as Buddy & Bob?
14. What was the title of Holly's first single?
15. What was unusual about Holly's guitar-playing?
16. On what date was Holly killed?

Answers to page 332

REGGAE 2: **1.** 1975 **2.** Millie **3.** Toots **4.** Keith Hudson **5.** The Aces **6.** 'You Can Get It If You Really Want' **7.** Peter Tosh **8.** Chaka Demus and Pliers **9.** 36 **10.** Robin and Ali Campbell **11.** 'One In Ten' **12.** 1995 **13.** 'Crying Over You' **14.** 'Come Back Darling' **15.** *Sliver* **16.** Bob Marley

Oasis 1

Answers on page 333

1. In which Manchester suburb did the Gallagher brothers live?
2. For which company did Noel Gallagher work as a storeman?
3. For which band did Noel fail an audition to be lead singer?
4. Which record company boss signed up Oasis in 1993?
5. And what was the name of the record company?
6. Why did the band's planned overseas debut in Amsterdam in February 1994 fail to materialise?
7. What was the title of the band's first single?
8. What happened to Noel at a gig at London's Riverside in August 1994?
9. Who broke his foot in 1994 jumping off the top of a moving tour bus?
10. Half a picture of which songwriter was featured on the cover of the band's debut album 'Definitely Maybe'?
11. What was the first UK number one for Oasis?
12. What is the final track on '(What's The Story) Morning Glory'?
13. In which year were Oasis named Best Newcomer at the Brit Awards?
14. Why did Liam walk off stage at Indianapolis in March 1995?
15. Who did Alan White replace as drummer in 1995?
16. Which Oasis track became, at 9 minutes 38 seconds, the longest single to reach number one in the UK?

Answers to page 333

SEVENTIES 3: **1.** Pink Floyd ('Another Brick In The Wall Part II') **2.** The Tymes **3.** Britt Ekland **4.** 'Dreadlock Holiday' **5.** Noosha **6.** Free **7.** Gilbert O'Sullivan **8.** Alan, Wayne, Merrill, Jay and Donny **9.** Billy Bremner **10.** 'Free' **11.** Julie Forsyth (daughter of Bruce) **12.** Dollar **13.** 1971 **14.** 'Coz I Luv You' **15.** 'What Am I Going To Do With You?' **16.** Bob Dylan

Music Pot Luck 11

Answers on page 338

1. Which female leader of a punk band was jailed in 1977 for obstruction?
2. Which American band took their name from a make of fire engine?
3. Which Salvation Army group had two UK top forty hits in 1964?
4. Who had a 'Constant Craving' in 1993?
5. What was the name of Lulu's backing band on 'Shout'?
6. Which Prince song was a number one for Sinead O'Connor in 1990?
7. Who was the singer with Fine Young Cannibals?
8. Who led The Lovin' Spoonful?
9. What was the title of R & B singer Chuck Willis's last record before his death in 1958?
10. Which 79-year-old bluesman became the oldest artist to get into the UK album charts when 'Don't Look Back' reached number 63 in 1997?
11. Which singer and actress married her manager on 16 March 2002?
12. Which country girl sang about a 'Blanket On The Ground' in 1975?
13. Which TV weatherman was the subject of a 1988 song by A Tribe Of Toffs?
14. What nationality are Ace Of Base?
15. Which British funk band had Leee John as their frontman?
16. Who released the 1974 album 'Diamond Dogs'?

Answers to page 338

MOTOWN 2: **1.** Eddie Kendricks **2.** The Isley Brothers **3.** Dion **4.** Martha and The Vandellas **5.** William **6.** 'Get Ready' **7.** *Mahogany* **8.** 'Make It Happen' **9.** Billy Griffin **10.** Tony Bennett **11.** 'We Can Work It Out' **12.** 'Sir Duke' **13.** 'Chain Reaction' **14.** The Temptations **15.** 'When You're Young And In Love' **16.** The Four Tops

Heavy Metal 3

Answers on page 339

1. Which Def Leppard singer appeared in the soccer movie *When Saturday Comes?*
2. Whose 1987 album was titled 'Slippery When Wet'?
3. Who was lead singer with Deep Purple from 1973 to 1976?
4. Which band did Bruce Dickinson leave to join Iron Maiden?
5. 'Come An' Get It' was the title of which band's 1981 album?
6. Which heavy metal singer was once placed seventh in the British fencing rankings for the men's foil?
7. Which film featured Steppenwolf's 'Born To Be Wild' in its opening sequence?
8. Who wrote 'Born To Be Wild'?
9. What was Iron Maiden's first UK number one album?
10. Who sang about 'Love In An Elevator'?
11. 'November Rain' was a 1992 hit for which band?
12. What was the title of the first UK top ten single for INXS?
13. What is the nickname of Saxon singer Peter Byford?
14. Whose albums included 'Lightning To The Nations' and 'Behold The Beginning'?
15. Which Def Leppard guitarist died in 1988 after consuming a lethal mixture of drugs and alcohol?
16. Which band had a top five album in 1982 with 'The Eagle Has Landed'?

Answers to page 339

NAME CHANGES 5: **1.** Limahl (Chris Hamill) **2.** Soft Machine **3.** Kiki Dee **4.** Steppenwolf **5.** The Miracles **6.** Bo Diddley **7.** Marie MacDonald McLaughlin Lawrie **8.** Bez (The Happy Mondays) **9.** Stevie Wonder **10.** Kelly Marie **11.** David Solberg **12.** Oasis **13.** L.L. Cool J. **14.** Raymond **15.** Cilla Black **16.** The Elgins

Motown 2

Answers on page 336

1. Who took lead vocals on The Temptations' 'Just My Imagination'?
2. Who had a 1969 hit with 'Behind A Painted Smile'?
3. Who originally recorded 'Abraham, Martin And John', a 1970 hit for Marvin Gaye?
4. Who reached number 21 in the UK charts in 1967 with 'Jimmy Mack'?
5. What is Smokey Robinson's real Christian name?
6. What was The Temptations' first UK top ten hit?
7. 'Do You Know Where You're Going To' by Diana Ross was the theme from which film?
8. From which album was Smokey Robinson and The Miracles' 'Tears Of A Clown' taken?
9. Who replaced Smokey Robinson as lead singer with The Miracles in 1972?
10. Who recorded the original version of 'For Once In My Life', which Stevie Wonder released in 1968?
11. Which Beatles track did Stevie Wonder record as a single in 1971?
12. Which Stevie Wonder single was a tribute to Duke Ellington?
13. Which 1986 song gave Diana Ross her first UK number one single for 15 years?
14. Who had a 1970 hit with 'Ball Of Confusion'?
15. What was the title of The Marvelettes only UK hit?
16. Levi Stubbs was the lead singer with which Motown group?

Answers to page 336

MUSIC POT LUCK 11: **1.** Siouxsie **2.** REO Speedwagon **3.** The Joy Strings **4.** k.d. lang **5.** The Luvvers **6.** 'Nothing Compares 2 U' **7.** Roland Gift **8.** John Sebastian **9.** 'What Am I Living For?' **10.** John Lee Hooker **11.** Liza Minnelli **12.** Billie Jo Spears **13.** 'John Kettley (Is A Weatherman)' **14.** Swedish **15.** Imagination **16.** David Bowie

Name Changes 4

Answers on page 337

1. Which frontman of an Eighties band was an anagram of his true surname?
2. Which jazz-rock band used to be known as The Bishops Of Canterbury?
3. Which collaborator with Elton John changed her name from Pauline Matthews?
4. Which heavy metal band used to be called The Sparrows?
5. Which Motown group were previously known as The Matadors?
6. Which R & B star was born Ellas Bates?
7. What is Lulu's real name?
8. Which manic Manchester dancer is really called Mark Berry?
9. Which Motown artist changed his name from Steveland Judkins to something more showbiz?
10. Under what name did Jacqueline McKinnon have a number one disco single?
11. What is David Soul's full name?
12. Which band were previously known as Rain?
13. Which rap artist was born James Todd Smith?
14. What is Gilbert O'Sullivan's real Christian name?
15. Who changed her name from Priscilla White?
16. What were The Temptations formerly known as?

Answers to page 337

HEAVY METAL 3: **1.** Joe Elliott **2.** Bon Jovi **3.** David Coverdale **4.** Samson **5.** Whitesnake **6.** Bruce Dickinson **7.** *Easy Rider* **8.** Dennis Edmonton/Mars Bonfire **9.** 'The Number Of The Beast' **10.** Aerosmith **11.** Guns N' Roses **12.** 'Need You Tonight' **13.** 'Biff' **14.** Diamond Head **15.** Steve Clark **16.** Saxon

Fifties 2

Answers on page 342

1. Which singer had the first-ever UK number one?
2. And what was the title of the song?
3. What was Winifred Atwell's profession before taking up the piano?
4. Which emotional Fifties singer was nicknamed 'The Prince of Wails'?
5. Which Jerry Lee Lewis number one of 1958 was written by Otis Blackwell and Jack Hammer?
6. Which group backed Dickie Valentine on his 1954 chart topper 'The Finger Of Suspicion'?
7. Which Tommy Steele hit was also the theme song to his TV show?
8. Which single taken from the film *Tommy the Toreador* was a 1959 hit for Tommy Steele?
9. Which rock 'n' roller was convicted of transporting a minor across a state line for immoral purposes?
10. Which British female singer had a 1956 UK number one with 'Lay Down Your Arms'?
11. How many UK top ten hits did Ruby Murray have in 1955?
12. How old was Ruby Murray when she had her only number one hit?
13. And what was its title?
14. Which 1955 number one was the last UK chart topper before 'Je T'Aime...Moi Non Plus' to have a foreign title?
15. Which 1954 hit for Rosemary Clooney told the true story of how the body of a mountain man was discovered by hunters in a ramshackle building?
16. Which 1955 number one came from the Jane Russell film *Underwater*?

Answers to page 342

FILM TRACKS 3: **1.** *Aida* **2.** *Rupert and the Frog Song* **3.** 'When The Going Gets Tough, The Tough Get Going' **4.** *Who's That Girl* **5.** *A Countess From Hong Kong* **6.** Charlie Chaplin **7.** 'I'll Remember' **8.** *Shanghai Surprise* **9.** *Summer Holiday* **10.** 'On The Beach' **11.** Shirley Bassey **12.** *Girls! Girls! Girls!* **13.** 'Wooden Heart' **14.** *Buster* **15.** 'Separate Lives' **16.** *The Jazz Singer*

Lyrics 3

Answers on page 343

From which songs are the following lyrics taken?

1. 'Don't underestimate me, boy, I'll make you sorry you were born'
2. 'I want to wake up in a city that doesn't sleep'
3. 'You fooled me with your kisses, you cheated and you schemed'
4. 'You give me one good reason to leave me, I'll give you ten good reasons to stay'
5. 'Once bitten and twice shy, I keep my distance but you still catch my eye'
6. 'We're a thousand miles apart and you know I love you'
7. 'We can try to understand the New York Times' effect on man'
8. 'Mirrors on the ceiling, the pink champagne on ice'
9. 'I know the moment isn't right to hold my emotions inside'
10. 'And don't you make me beg for love, give a sign 'cause I need to know'
11. 'If you want my future forget my past'
12. 'I should've known from the start before you got in my heart'
13. 'Even when the sun is shining I can't avoid the lightning'
14. 'Where did you go when things went wrong for you'
15. 'Acting upon reliable information, a federal deputation laid a deadly ambush'
16. 'I think of the days when the sun used to set on my empty heart, all alone in my bed'

Answers to page 343

TAKE THAT 1: **1.** Nigel Martin-Smith **2.** Mark Owen **3.** Gary Barlow **4.** 'Do What U Like' **5.** Howard Donald **6.** Howard Donald **7.** Robbie Williams **8.** Mark Owen **9.** 'Pray' **10.** 'Everything Changes' **11.** Lulu **12.** Mr Blobby **13.** 'Pray' **14.** 'Back For Good' **15.** 'How Deep Is Your Love' **16.** 1996

Film Tracks 3

Answers on page 340

1. Which Disney film featured Elton John's 'Written In The Stars'?
2. Which animation film spawned 'We All Stand Together' by Paul McCartney and the Frog Chorus?
3. Which Billy Ocean hit came from the film *The Jewel of the Nile*?
4. Madonna's 1987 hit 'The Look Of Love' was taken from which film?
5. 'This Is My Song', a 1967 number one for Petula Clark, was the theme tune for which film?
6. Which silent comedy film star wrote 'This Is My Song'?
7. Which theme from *With Honours* was a 1994 hit for Madonna?
8. Which film featured Madonna's 'Live To Tell', a number two hit in 1986?
9. From which film did Cliff Richard's 'Bachelor Boy' come?
10. Which Cliff Richard single was taken from *Wonderful Life*?
11. Who had a 1967 hit with 'Big Spender' from the film *Sweet Charity*?
12. Elvis Presley's 'Return To Sender' featured in which movie?
13. Which Elvis number one came from *G.I. Blues*?
14. Phil Collins's version of 'A Groovy Kind Of Love' was used in which film?
15. Which Phil Collins single of 1985 was taken from *White Nights*?
16. Neil Diamond's 'Love On The Rocks' was included in which film?

Answers to page 340

FIFTIES 2: **1.** Al Martino **2.** 'Here In My Heart' **3.** Chemist **4.** Johnnie Ray **5.** 'Great Balls Of Fire' **6.** The Stargazers **7.** 'A Handful Of Songs' **8.** 'Little White Bull' **9.** Chuck Berry **10.** Anne Shelton **11.** Seven **12.** 19 **13.** 'Softly Softly' **14.** 'Mambo Italiano' **15.** 'This Ole House' **16.** 'Cherry Pink And Apple Blossom White'

Take That 1

Answers on page 341

1. Who was Take That's manager?
2. Which member of Take That used to work as a bank clerk?
3. Which member of Take That had been seen as a teenager playing the organ on Ken Dodd's TV show?
4. What was the band's debut single?
5. Who was the oldest member of Take That?
6. Which of the five worked as a car mechanic?
7. Who was the youngest in Take That?
8. Who was voted Most Fanciable Male at the 1992 Smash Hits Readers Poll Party Awards?
9. What was Take That's first UK number one single?
10. Which 1994 chart topper was also the title of their second album?
11. Who was guest vocalist on 'Relight My Fire'?
12. Who knocked 'Babe' off the top of the UK singles chart?
13. Which composition was voted Best Contemporary Song at the 1994 Ivor Novello Awards?
14. Which 1995 single sold over 300,000 copies in its first week – the highest first-week tally in ten years?
15. Which cover of a Bee Gees song became the group's eighth single to go straight in to the UK charts at number one?
16. In which year did Take That split up?

Answers to page 341

LYRICS 3: **1.** 'Don't Call Me Baby' (Madison Avenue) **2.** 'New York, New York' (Frank Sinatra) **3.** '(You're The) Devil In Disguise' (Elvis Presley) **4.** 'Too Many Broken Hearts' (Jason Donovan) **5.** 'Last Christmas' (Wham!) **6.** 'Everything Changes' (Take That) **7.** 'Stayin' Alive (The Bee Gees) **8.** 'Hotel California' (The Eagles) **9.** 'Leave A Tender Moment Alone' (Billy Joel) **10.** 'Heart And Soul' (T'Pau) **11.** 'Wannabe' (Spice Girls) **12.** 'Quit Playing Games (With My Heart)' (Backstreet Boys) **13.** 'Why Does It Always Rain On Me?' (Travis) **14.** 'Slight Return' (The Bluetones) **15.** 'The Ballad Of Bonnie And Clyde (Georgie Fame) **16.** 'Waiting For Tonight' (Jennifer Lopez)

Football League 5

Answers on page 346

1. Who beat Bolton Wanderers in the 1999 First Division play-off final?
2. For which club did John Trollope make a record 770 League appearances?
3. Which club plunged from the First to the Fourth Division in successive seasons between 1980 and 1984?
4. Who won 32 out of their 46 games in Division Four in 1975–6?
5. Which club joined the Football League in 1978?
6. And who did they replace?
7. Which former Crystal Palace striker returned to Selhurst Park as a Wimbledon player in July 2001?
8. Which team lost their first 12 matches in Division One in 1930–1?
9. What is the name of Rushden & Diamonds' ground?
10. Which Third Division (North) club won 18 out of their 21 away games in 1946–7?
11. Who was manager of Reading at the start of the 2001–2 season?
12. Which club went 73 years without winning at Anfield before breaking the jinx in 1985?
13. Which club had 19 points deducted for financial irregularities in 1968?
14. Which club won a solitary match in 1899–90 and were promptly kicked out of the League?
15. Which club were expelled from the League in 1938, only to return 12 years later?
16. Which club used to be known as Small Heath Alliance?

Answers to page 346

WHOSE HOME? 4: **1.** Sheffield Wednesday **2.** Everton (1884–92) **3.** Charlton Athletic **4.** Billy Bremner **5.** East Fife **6.** Loakes Park **7.** 1973 **8.** Hibernian **9.** 1989 **10.** Austria **11.** Sunderland **12.** Clapton Orient **13.** Boca Juniors **14.** Rochdale **15.** Indonesia **16.** 1995

England 3

Answers on page 347

1. Against which country did Paul Gascoigne win his first cap?
2. Which three teams were in England's group at the 1966 World Cup?
3. Which midfielder of the 1990s scored 27 goals from 62 caps?
4. In which year did Bobby Moore win his first England cap?
5. Who came on as a late substitute for Gary Lineker when England lost to Sweden in the 1992 European Championship?
6. How many England caps did John Barnes win?
7. Against whom did Peter Shilton make his farewell international appearance at the 1990 World Cup?
8. Which Liverpool player made his England debut against Ukraine in 2000?
9. Who were England's first opponents in the reign of Kevin Keegan?
10. Which Leicester City and former Chelsea, Millwall and Tottenham midfielder won his first England cap under Joe Mercer?
11. Who scored his first international goal when England won 3–0 in Luxembourg in a European Championship qualifier in 1998?
12. Which Arsenal winger won his only cap when coming on as a substitute against Saudi Arabia in 1989?
13. In which year did Don Revie walk out on England?
14. Who beat England 1–0 in their opening match at the 1986 World Cup finals?
15. And which African nation held England to a goalless draw in their second match in that tournament?
16. Which Tottenham player won his only England cap when substitute against Iceland in 1982?

Answers to page 347

ON THE SPOT 2: **1.** 1974 **2.** 4–2 **3.** Roy Brown **4.** Graham Roberts **5.** 44 **6.** Ally McCoist **7.** Aston Villa **8.** Nine **9.** Manchester City **10.** Jan Molby **11.** Nigel Winterburn **12.** Andy Dibble **13.** Billy Smith **14.** Italy **15.** David Platt **16.** David Batty

Whose Home? 4

Answers on page 344

1. Which English League club used to play at Olive Grove?

2. Besides Liverpool, which other club has had Anfield as its home ground?

3. Which current Premiership club did not install floodlights until 1961?

4. Which Doncaster Rovers manager lopped eight yards off the length of the pitch in an effort to improve the club's fortunes?

5. Which Scottish League club is based in Methil?

6. Where did Wycombe Wanderers play for 89 years?

7. In which year did Yorkshire Cricket Club last play at Sheffield's Bramall Lane ground?

8. Who were the first Scottish club to fit undersoil heating?

9. In which year did St Johnstone move to McDiarmid Park?

10. Which country's national stadium is the Ernst Happel Stadion?

11. Which Premiership club used to play at Horatio Street?

12. Which club played two Third Division (South) matches at Wembley Stadium in 1930–1?

13. Which Argentine club plays at The Chocolate Box?

14. Who plays at Spotland?

15. In which country is the Senayan Stadium?

16. When did Middlesbrough move to the Riverside Stadium?

Answers to page 344

FOOTBALL LEAGUE 5: **1.** Watford **2.** Swindon Town **3.** Bristol City **4.** Lincoln City **5.** Wigan Athletic **6.** Southport **7.** Neil Shipperley **8.** Manchester United **9.** Nene Park **10.** Doncaster Rovers **11.** Alan Pardew **12.** Tottenham Hotspur **13.** Peterborough United **14.** Loughborough Town **15.** Gillingham **16.** Birmingham City

On the Spot 2

Answers on page 345

1. At the end of which year's Charity Shield did Wembley stage its first penalty shoot-out?
2. By what score did England beat Spain in the quarter-final shoot-out at Euro 96?
3. Which Notts County goalkeeper saved six successive penalties in 1972–3?
4. Who converted 12 penalties as Chelsea lifted the Second Division title in 1988–9?
5. How many penalties did it take to settle a shoot-out between Argentinos Juniors and Racing Club in 1988?
6. Which once prolific striker scored his only goal for Kilmarnock in 1999–2000 from the penalty spot?
7. Charlie Wallace missed a penalty for which club in the 1913 FA Cup final?
8. How many penalties did Portsmouth miss in 1982–3?
9. Which club missed three penalties in a First Division game against Newcastle in 1912?
10. Whose only hat-trick for Liverpool came from the spot in 1986?
11. Who missed a penalty for Arsenal in the 1988 Littlewoods Cup final?
12. And who saved it?
13. Whose penalty won the FA Cup for Huddersfield Town in 1922?
14. Which country have been eliminated from three successive World Cups on penalties?
15. Which England export missed a penalty on his debut in Italy?
16. Whose penalty miss put England out of the 1998 World Cup?

Answers to page 345

ENGLAND 3: **1.** Denmark **2.** Uruguay, Mexico and France **3.** David Platt **4.** 1962 **5.** Alan Smith **6.** 79 **7.** Italy **8.** Steven Gerrard **9.** Poland **10.** Keith Weller **11.** Gareth Southgate **12.** Brian Marwood **13.** 1977 **14.** Portugal **15.** Morocco **16.** Steve Perryman

Premiership 4

Answers on page 350

1. Which midfielder moved from West Ham to Chelsea in summer 2001?
2. Which Scottish international defender was transferred from Blackburn to Rangers for £4 million in August 1998?
3. Which team won the Premiership Fair Play Award for 1998–9?
4. Which young England defender scored his first goal for Arsenal in September 2000?
5. Which Newcastle player was the leading Premiership scorer in 1993–4?
6. Who was Leeds United's leading scorer in 2000–1?
7. Since which year have Southampton been members of the top division?
8. Which club went 12 games unbeaten at the start of 1995–6?
9. Which Liverpool player was fined £1,000 for hitching his shorts to spectators at Leicester on Boxing Day 1994?
10. Who moved from Elland Road to Old Trafford for £1.2 million in November 1992?
11. Which player was the leading marksman in the first season of the Premiership, 1992–3?
12. Who finished bottom of the Premiership in 1994–5?
13. Where did Leicester City gain their only away win in 1994–5?
14. Which club won the Best Behaved Supporters Award for 1998–9?
15. Who top scored for Arsenal in 1999–2000?
16. Who were the first team to defeat Manchester United in the 1999–2000 Premiership season?

Answers to page 350

CELTIC 1: **1.** John Thomson **2.** Billy McNeill **3.** Tommy Burns **4.** Airdrie **5.** 'Lisbon Lions' **6.** Tommy Gemmell **7.** Henrik Larsson **8.** Bayer Leverkusen **9.** Paradise **10.** Steve Chalmers **11.** Keadue Rovers **12.** Martin Hayes **13.** 'Jacki' Dziekanowski **14.** Danny McGrain **15.** Craig Burley **16.** 1956–7

Oddballs 6

Answers on page 351

1. Which new Arsenal manager saw his team go unbeaten for 17 League matches at the start of season 1947–8?
2. In which year was the FA Cup stolen from a Birmingham shop window?
3. Who scored a hat-trick in the November 1994 Manchester derby?
4. Which team entertained Vale of Leven in Scotland's first floodlit friendly?
5. Which English League club were formerly known as Christ Church?
6. Which Middle Eastern nation made their first appearance at the World Cup finals in 1982?
7. Which team used to play at Trent Bridge?
8. Which former TV commentator turned out for Stockport County Reserves after going to cover the match for the local paper?
9. Which sports commentator is a director of Wycombe Wanderers?
10. Which comedian was a centre-half for Liverpool 'A' team?
11. In which year was a Football League game televised live for the first time?
12. And which two teams were involved?
13. Which club has a fanzine called *The Memoirs of Seth Bottomley*?
14. Which club side were the best-selling Subbuteo team for 1991?
15. Who does athletics commentator Steve Cram support?
16. Which infamous match took place at Belo Horizonte in 1950?

Answers to page 351

GOALKEEPERS 4: **1.** Milija Aleksic **2.** David James **3.** Massimo Taibi **4.** Reggina **5.** Crystal Palace **6.** Gordon Banks **7.** Steve Ogrizovic **8.** Jim Stannard **9.** Northern Ireland **10.** Vitesse Arnhem **11.** Sepp Maier **12.** Chesterfield **13.** Reading **14.** Harry Gregg **15.** Steve Ogrizovic **16.** Sasa Ilic

Celtic 1

Answers on page 348

1. Which goalkeeper died in 1931 after fracturing his skull in a collision during an Old Firm game?
2. Who made 486 League appearances for Celtic between 1957 and 1975?
3. Who succeeded Lou Macari as Celtic manager?
4. Who did Celtic beat in the 1995 Scottish FA Cup final?
5. What nickname was given to the European Cup winning team of 1967?
6. Who scored Celtic's first goal on that momentous afternoon?
7. Who was Celtic's top scorer in 1998–9?
8. From which German club did Celtic sign Andreas Thom in 1995?
9. What is the nickname for Celtic's ground?
10. Which European Cup hero was Celtic's leading scorer in 1966–7?
11. From which Irish club did Celtic sign Pat Bonner?
12. Which forward moved from Arsenal to Celtic in 1990?
13. Which Pole was Celtic's top scorer in 1989–90?
14. Which Celtic full-back was the Scottish Football Writers' Player of the Year for 1977?
15. Who switched from Chelsea to Celtic for £2.5 million in July 1997?
16. In which season did Celtic reach the Scottish League Cup final for the first time?

Answers to page 348

PREMIERSHIP 4: **1.** Frank Lampard **2.** Colin Hendry **3.** Manchester United **4.** Ashley Cole **5.** Andy Cole **6.** Mark Viduka **7.** 1978 **8.** Nottingham Forest **9.** Robbie Fowler **10.** Eric Cantona **11.** Teddy Sheringham **12.** Ipswich Town **13.** Manchester City **14.** Wimbledon **15.** Thierry Henry **16.** Chelsea

Goalkeepers 4

Answers on page 349

1. Who was in goal for Tottenham in the 1981 FA Cup final?
2. Which goalkeeper moved from Aston Villa to West Ham in July 2001?
3. Which accident-prone Sicilian goalkeeper joined Manchester United for £4.5 million in 1999?
4. To which Italian club was he loaned out before the end of the season?
5. From which club did Stockport County sign 6ft 5in Carlo Nash?
6. Which England keeper made his international debut against Scotland in 1963?
7. Which Coventry City goalkeeper scored with a long clearance against Sheffield Wednesday in 1986?
8. Which Gillingham keeper kept 29 clean sheets in 1995–6?
9. Roy Carroll plays international football for which country?
10. From which Dutch club did Liverpool sign Sander Westerveld?
11. Who was in goal for West Germany in the 1974 World Cup final?
12. Mark Leonard kept a clean sheet in eight consecutive Third Division away games in 1994. For which club was he playing?
13. With which League club did Shaka Hislop start his career?
14. Which goalkeeper survived the Munich air crash but was then dropped by Northern Ireland for refusing to fly to Spain for an international?
15. Which goalkeeper and Minor Counties cricketer once clean bowled Viv Richards in a Nat-West Trophy match?
16. Which Australian-born goalkeeper did Charlton Athletic recruit from Dr Martens League team St Leonards Stamcroft?

Answers to page 349

ODDBALLS 6: **1.** Tom Whittaker **2.** 1895 **3.** Andrei Kanchelskis **4.** Third Lanark **5.** Bolton Wanderers **6.** Kuwait **7.** Notts County **8.** David Coleman **9.** Alan Parry **10.** Stan Boardman **11.** 1960 **12.** Blackpool and Bolton Wanderers **13.** Port Vale **14.** Liverpool **15.** Sunderland **16.** USA 1 England 0

Scottish Scene 5

Answers on page 354

1. Benny Rooney, Tommy McLean and Allan McGraw have all managed which Scottish club?
2. Who plays at Somerset Park?
3. From which Scottish club did Chelsea sign Charlie Cooke?
4. Who won the Scottish League Cup three times in the first eight years of the competition?
5. Which Dundee United player appeared in a record 76 European matches?
6. For which club did Jim Fallon make 620 League appearances between 1968 and 1986?
7. Which Scottish League club used to play at Nursery Park?
8. Which Hibernian midfielder was Scotland's Young Player of the Year for 1987–8?
9. Which club are nicknamed 'The Borderers'?
10. Who finished Premier Division runners-up to Rangers for three successive years between 1989 and 1991?
11. Which club won their first-ever promotion since joining the League in 1955 when they topped the Second Division in 1994?
12. Which Scottish club sold Martin Buchan to Manchester United?
13. In which year did St Mirren win the Scottish FA Cup for the first time?
14. Which club suffered three 10–0 defeats in 1937–8?
15. In which year did Berwick Rangers join the Scottish League?
16. Who moved from Bordeaux to Dunfermline for £540,000 in 1989?

Answers to page 354

TRANSFER TRAIL 5: **1.** Rivaldo **2.** Joe Jordan **3.** Anderlecht **4.** Cobh Ramblers **5.** Anders Limpar **6.** Lazio **7.** Manchester City **8.** Billy Bonds **9.** Clarence Seedorf **10.** Ian Ferguson **11.** Keith Weller **12.** David Johnson **13.** Besiktas **14.** Tommy Johnson **15.** AC Milan **16.** David Platt

Early Baths 2

Answers on page 355

1. Which Leeds and England player was sent off in a 1977 friendly against Argentina?
2. Which Scottish club had four players sent off in a match at Airdrie in 1994?
3. Yugoslav Olympic star Boris Stankovic was the first player to be sent off in which stadium?
4. For which West Country club was substitute Ben Rowe sent off in 1990 while still sitting in the dug-out?
5. Who was sent off for the first time in his career in his 971st League game?
6. Which two England internationals started brawling on the way to the tunnel after being sent off in a 1974 League match?
7. Which volatile Frenchman was sent off twice in three days during 2000–1?
8. Which Arsenal youngster was sent off just 33 seconds after making his debut as a substitute in a 1997 League Cup tie?
9. Which two Charlton players were sent off for fighting each other in 1979?
10. Which St Mirren captain was sent off three times in the same match?
11. Which Chelsea hard man was booked three seconds after kick-off in a 1992 FA Cup tie against his former club?
12. Who had a player sent off in each of their Euro 2000 group matches?
13. Against whom did Portsmouth have three men sent off in 1986?
14. Which three Anglos were sent off for Rangers in a 1991 Scottish FA Cup tie with Celtic?
15. On which ground was David Beckham sent off against Argentina in 1998?
16. Which Welsh international was sent off against Georgia in 1995?

Answers to page 355

WORLD CUP 3: **1.** Portugal **2.** Aime Jacquet **3.** New Zealand **4.** He refused to have his hair cut **5.** Israel **6.** Sandor Kocsis **7.** 11 **8.** Greece, Nigeria and Saudi Arabia **9.** Africa **10.** Two **11.** Argentina **12.** Turkey **13.** Norway and Holland **14.** Montevideo **15.** Stefan Effenberg **16.** Holland

Transfer Trail 5

Answers on page 352

1. Which Brazilian star moved from Deportivo La Coruña to Barcelona for £12.5 million in August 1997?
2. Which fearsome Scottish international striker was transferred from Elland Road to Old Trafford in November 1977 for £350,000?
3. From which Belgian club did Newcastle sign Philippe Albert?
4. With which Irish club did Roy Keane begin his career?
5. Which Swede joined Arsenal from Cremonese in July 1990 for £1 million?
6. From which Italian club did Manchester United sign Juan Sebastian Veron?
7. For which club did Ashley Ward make a solitary appearance before being loaned out to Wrexham?
8. Which West Ham stalwart joined the club from Charlton in 1967?
9. Which Dutch midfielder moved from Ajax to Sampdoria for £4.5 million in July 1995?
10. Who did Rangers sign from St Mirren for £850,000 in 1988?
11. Which future England international joined Millwall from Tottenham for £18,000 in 1967?
12. Which striker moved from Ipswich to Nottingham Forest for £3 million in 2001?
13. From which Turkish club did Manchester United sign Ronny Johnsen?
14. Which striker joined Celtic from Aston Villa for £2.3 million in 1997?
15. From which Italian club did Arsenal sign Patrick Vieira?
16. Which Englishman scored just three goals in 16 League games for Juventus after joining them for £6.5 million in 1992?

Answers to page 352

SCOTTISH SCENE 5: **1.** Greenock Morton **2.** Ayr United **3.** Dundee **4.** East Fife **5.** David Narey **6.** Clydebank **7.** Brechin City **8.** John Collins **9.** Berwick Rangers **10.** Aberdeen **11.** Stranraer **12.** Aberdeen **13.** 1926 **14.** Brechin City **15.** 1955 **16.** Istvan Kozma

World Cup 3

Answers on page 353

1. Which nation finished third in the 1966 World Cup?
2. Who managed the victorious French World Cup team of 1998?
3. Which Antipodean country made their only appearance in the World Cup finals in 1982?
4. Why was Argentine midfielder Redondo omitted from their 1998 squad?
5. Which team did Egypt, Turkey, Sudan and Indonesia refuse to play in the qualifying tournament for the 1958 World Cup?
6. Who was leading scorer at the 1954 World Cup finals?
7. And how many goals did he get?
8. Which three countries were first-time qualifiers for the 1994 World Cup finals?
9. Which continent had three representatives at the 1994 World Cup finals for the first time?
10. How many times have the Republic of Ireland reached the final stages?
11. Which country were the first to have a player sent off in a World Cup final?
12. Against whom did England notch up an 8–0 away win in a qualifier for the 1986 World Cup?
13. Which two countries finished ahead of England to deny them qualification for the 1994 World Cup finals?
14. In which city were all matches played in the 1930 World Cup finals?
15. Which German was sent home from the 1994 finals for gesturing at his country's fans?
16. Against whom was Scotland's sole victory at the 1978 finals?

Answers to page 353

EARLY BATHS 2: **1.** Trevor Cherry **2.** Stranraer **3.** Wembley **4.** Exeter City **5.** Peter Shilton **6.** Norman Hunter and Francis Lee **7.** Patrick Vieira **8.** Jason Crowe **9.** Derek Hales and Mike Flanagan **10.** Billy Abercrombie **11.** Vinnie Jones (against Sheffield United) **12.** Yugoslavia **13.** Sheffield United **14.** Terry Hurlock, Mark Walters and Mark Hateley **15.** St Etienne **16.** Vinnie Jones

Managers 6

Answers on page 358

1. Who was voted Manager of the Year in 1975 and 1981?
2. How many times was Malcolm Allison named Manager of the Year?
3. Who coached the 1998 Australian World Cup squad which failed to reach the finals?
4. Which Scottish League club did Ally MacLeod manage in two separate spells?
5. Which former Liverpool star took over as boss at Southend in 1995?
6. Who took Darlington back into the Football League in 1990?
7. What nationality is Dick Advocaat?
8. Which former Republic of Ireland chief became manager of Huddersfield Town in 1988?
9. Who succeeded Jack Charlton as manager of Sheffield Wednesday?
10. Don Mackay, Archie Knox and Simon Stainrod have all managed which Scottish club?
11. Who was appointed Republic of Ireland manager in 1996?
12. Who managed Wolves from 1968 to 1976 and returned briefly in 1985?
13. Who was in charge of Swansea City for just seven days in 1996?
14. Which Manchester City manager was sacked 12 days into the 1996–7 season?
15. Who replaced Olle Nordin as Swedish national coach?
16. Who was hounded out of Southampton in 1994?

Answers to page 358

EVERTON 1: **1.** Kevin Campbell **2.** Manchester City **3.** Colin Harvey **4.** Club Brugge **5.** St Domingo FC **6.** Martin Dobson **7.** Joe Royle **8.** 1953–4 **9.** Leicester City **10.** 349 **11.** 1927–8 **12.** William Ralph Dean **13.** Two **14.** Mike Trebilcock **15.** Pat Van den Hauwe **16.** Strasbourg

The World Game 7

Answers on page 359

1. From which country do Stationery Stores, beaten finalists in the 1981 African Cup-Winners' Cup, come from?
2. What nationality is goalkeeper Michel Preud'Homme?
3. Which club plays at the Estadio da Luz?
4. Which Brazilian goalkeeper played in the 1994 and 1998 World Cup finals?
5. For which Turkish team did Gheorghe Hagi play in 1998–9?
6. Which part-timers reached the French Cup final in 2000?
7. Who was replaced as coach of France in 1993?
8. What is Ronaldo's full name?
9. What nationality is Diego Simeone?
10. Which two Uruguayan forwards lined up for Juventus in 1998–9?
11. Which South African team won the African Cup-Winners' Cup in 1995?
12. Which South American team won the World Club Championship in 2000?
13. In which South American country do Mineros de Guyana play?
14. Who did Bobby Robson succeed as manager of Barcelona?
15. Who won the Spanish League in 2000?
16. What nationality is Alen Boksic?

Answers to page 359

TOTTENHAM HOTSPUR 1: **1.** Teddy Sheringham **2.** 1961 **3.** Wolverhampton Wanderers **4.** Colin Lee **5.** Mike England **6.** Gary Lineker **7.** Marseille **8.** Russian **9.** Port Vale **10.** Cagliari **11.** Bolton Wanderers and Southampton **12.** Gary Mabbutt **13.** Terry Neill **14.** Crewe Alexandra **15.** Mauricio Taricco **16.** Borussia Dortmund

Everton 1

Answers on page 356

1. Who was Everton's top scorer in 1998–9?

2. Who did Everton beat in the 1933 FA Cup final?

3. Whose managerial reign was sandwiched between Howard Kendall's two stints?

4. From which club did Everton sign Daniel Amokachi?

5. What was Everton's original name?

6. Which stylish midfielder joined Everton from Burnley in 1974 for £300,000?

7. Which centre-forward made his debut as a 16-year-old against Blackpool in 1966?

8. What was Everton's last season in Division Two?

9. To whom did they finish runners-up that season?

10. How many League goals did 'Dixie' Dean score for Everton?

11. In which season did Dean score a record 60 League goals?

12. And what was Dean's full name?

13. To how many FA Cup finals did Harry Catterick take Everton as manager?

14. Which Cornishman scored twice for Everton in the 1966 FA Cup final?

15. Which Belgian-born defender left Everton for Tottenham in August 1989?

16. From which French club did Everton sign Olivier Dacourt?

Answers to page 356

MANAGERS 6: **1.** Ron Saunders **2.** None **3.** Terry Venables **4.** Ayr United **5.** Ronnie Whelan **6.** Brian Little **7.** Dutch **8.** Eoin Hand **9.** Howard Wilkinson **10.** Dundee **11.** Mick McCarthy **12.** Bill McGarry **13.** Kevin Cullis **14.** Alan Ball **15.** Tommy Svensson **16.** Ian Branfoot

Tottenham Hotspur 1

Answers on page 357

1. Which England striker rejoined Tottenham in the summer of 2001?

2. When did Spurs last win the League title?

3. Who did Spurs beat in the 1921 FA Cup final?

4. Who scored four times when Spurs hammered Bristol Rovers 9–0 in a Second Division match in 1977?

5. Who moved from Blackburn to Tottenham for £95,000 in 1966 – a record fee for a centre-half?

6. Who was Tottenham's leading scorer in 1990–1?

7. To which French club was Chris Waddle transferred?

8. What nationality is Sergei Rebrov?

9. Which Third Division team knocked Spurs out of the FA Cup in 1988?

10. From which Italian club did Spurs sign Ramon Vega?

11. Which two teams were promoted with Tottenham from Division Two in 1977–8?

12. Which Spurs player put through his own goal in the 1987 FA Cup final?

13. Which former Arsenal player succeeded Bill Nicholson as Spurs boss?

14. Who did Spurs beat 13–2 in a 1960 FA Cup tie?

15. Which Argentinian joined Spurs from Ipswich in 1998–9?

16. From which German club did Steffen Freund join Tottenham?

Answers to page 357

THE WORLD GAME 7: **1.** Nigeria **2.** Belgian **3.** Benfica **4.** Claudio Taffarel **5.** Galatasaray **6.** Calais **7.** Gerard Houllier **8.** Ronaldo Luiz Nazario Da Lima **9.** Argentinian **10.** Daniel Fonseca and Marcelo Zalayeta **11.** Orlando Pirates **12.** Corinthians **13.** Venezuela **14.** Johan Cruyff **15.** Deportivo La Coruña **16.** Croatian

Whose Home? 5

Answers on page 362

1. What is the name of Juventus's stadium?
2. Which Scottish team plays at Central Park?
3. Who plays at Ali Sami Yen Stadium?
4. Where was Reading's home from 1896 to 1998?
5. Which English League club plays at Home Park?
6. Which club used to play at Eastville?
7. Which German team plays at Fritz-Walter Stadion?
8. Which national team's home ground is the Camille Champum Stadium?
9. Who plays at Blundell Park?
10. In which city did England play their 1990 World Cup semi-final against West Germany?
11. Which Dutch team plays at the Philips-stadion?
12. The Arnold Schwarzenegger Stadion is home to which Austrian club?
13. Which Scottish club plays at Shielfield Park?
14. Which Spanish club plays at San Mames Stadium?
15. Which English League club used to play at John Harper's Field?
16. Which Scottish club were the first in Britain to introduce dug-outs?

Answers to page 362

NON-LEAGUE 3: **1.** Bedlington Terriers **2.** Kettering Town **3.** Stevenage Borough **4.** Peterborough United **5.** 'The Lillywhites' **6.** Belle Vue **7.** Burton Albion **8.** Altrincham and Enfield **9.** Tim Buzaglo **10.** Wycombe Wanderers **11.** Northwich Victoria **12.** Fulham **13.** 'The Pitmen' **14.** Nuneaton Borough **15.** Jan Molby **16.** Woking

Which Year in Football? 5

Answers on page 363

1. In which year did Burnley last reach the FA Cup final?
2. When did Oxford United join the Football League?
3. When did Alan Shearer make his League debut?
4. When did Wolves last win the League Championship?
5. When was the World Cup held in the United States?
6. In which year did Celtic's record run of 62 unbeaten matches in the Scottish League come to an end?
7. In which year did Honduras make their first appearance at the World Cup finals?
8. When did Gary and Phil Neville first appear together for Manchester United in an FA Cup final?
9. In which year did New Brighton leave the Football League?
10. When did Kenny Dalglish quit as manager of Liverpool?
11. When were Southampton beaten finalists in the Football League Cup?
12. When did Kilmarnock last win the Scottish FA Cup?
13. When was George Best named Footballer of the Year?
14. In which year did Gillingham play in Division One for the first time in their history?
15. When did Ipswich Town win the Texaco Cup?
16. When did Manchester City move to Maine Road?

Answers to page 363

LEAGUE CUP 2: **1.** Kasey Keller **2.** Garry Birtles **3.** Andy Gray **4.** Norwich City **5.** Sunderland **6.** 1967 **7.** Rotherham United **8.** Luton Town **9.** Brian Stein **10.** Chester **11.** Terry Cooper **12.** 1969–70 **13.** Arsenal, Sheffield Wednesday, Tottenham Hotspur, West Bromwich Albion and Wolverhampton Wanderers **14.** Arsenal **15.** John Sheridan **16.** Steve Morrow

Non-League 3

Answers on page 360

1. Which dogged north-east team knocked Colchester out of the FA Cup in 1998–9?
2. Who were runners-up in the Conference to Cheltenham Town in 1999 but were relegated two years later?
3. Who were the last Conference winners not to be promoted to the Football League?
4. Which Midland League team won at Ipswich in the FA Cup just two years before the East Anglian side swept to the League Championship?
5. What is Telford United's nickname?
6. Where do Doncaster Rovers play?
7. Which non-League side was managed by Nigel Clough in 2001–2?
8. Which two teams have won the Conference twice without being promoted to the Football League?
9. Who scored a hat-trick for Woking when they won 4–2 at West Bromwich Albion in the third round of the FA Cup in 1991?
10. Which current League side won the FA Trophy in 1991 and 1993?
11. The Drill Field is the home of which club?
12. Which current Premiership team were knocked out of the FA Cup by Yeovil in 1993–4?
13. What is the nickname of Hednesford Town?
14. Which team won the Dr Martens League Premier Division in 1998–9?
15. Which manager guided Kidderminster Harriers into the Football League?
16. Which Conference team plays at Kingfield?

Answers to page 360

WHOSE HOME? 5: **1.** Stadio delle Alpi **2.** Cowdenbeath **3.** Galatasaray **4.** Elm Park **5.** Plymouth Argyle **6.** Bristol Rovers **7.** Kaiserslautern **8.** Lebanon **9.** Grimsby Town **10.** Turin **11.** PSV Eindhoven **12.** Sturm Graz **13.** Berwick Rangers **14.** Athletic Bilbao **15.** Wolverhampton Wanderers **16.** Aberdeen

League Cup 2

Answers on page 361

1. Which American kept goal for Leicester City in the 1999 Worthington Cup final?
2. Who was Nottingham Forest's two-goal hero in the 1979 League Cup final?
3. Which Scot's goal won the League Cup for Wolves in 1980?
4. Who won the League Cup in 1985 by virtue of an own goal?
5. And who were the beaten finalists?
6. In which year was the League Cup final first staged at Wembley?
7. Who lost a two-goal lead from the first leg of the 1961 League Cup final to go down 3–2 on aggregate?
8. Who beat Arsenal in the 1988 Littlewoods Cup final?
9. And whose two goals clinched the victory?
10. Which Fourth Division club reached the semi-finals in 1974–5?
11. Who scored Leeds United's winner against Arsenal in the 1968 final?
12. Which was the first year that all 92 League clubs took part in the competition?
13. Which five clubs boycotted the first League Cup?
14. Which club did not enter the League Cup until 1966–7?
15. Who scored Sheffield Wednesday's winner against Manchester United in the 1991 final?
16. Which Arsenal match-winner was injured after the final when captain Tony Adams dropped him during the celebrations?

Answers to page 361

WHICH YEAR IN FOOTBALL? 5: **1.** 1962 **2.** 1962 **3.** 1988 **4.** 1959 **5.** 1994 **6.** 1917 **7.** 1982 **8.** 1996 **9.** 1951 **10.** 1991 **11.** 1979 **12.** 1997 **13.** 1968 **14.** 2000 **15.** 1973 **16.** 1923

General Knowledge 81

Answers on page 366

1. What colours feature on the national flag of El Salvador?

2. What was introduced to Britain on 15 February 1971?

3. What did Norway's Johann Vaaler invent in 1900?

4. In which year did Shergar win The Derby?

5. The clarinet belongs to which group of musical instruments?

6. Which 17th-century judge conducted the 'bloody assizes'?

7. Brian Connolly was the singer with which Seventies band?

8. What colour does jaundice make the skin?

9. The Battle of Inkerman took place during which war?

10. Who played *Elizabeth R* on TV?

11. What nationality was Henry the Navigator?

12. Who was Lenny the Lion's human partner?

13. Which is the only creature where the male becomes pregnant?

14. Which is the only domestic animal not mentioned in the Bible?

15. Which future Hollywood tough-guy had to wear his sister's hand-me-down dresses to school because his family were so poor?

16. Which Cherokee Indian had a UK number one hit in 1958?

Answers to page 366

GENERAL KNOWLEDGE 83: **1.** Justin Henry **2.** Hungarian **3.** Nick Heidfeld **4.** Coniston Water **5.** Clint Eastwood **6.** Leonid Brezhnev **7.** Buzz Aldrin **8.** Duke of Buckingham **9.** Samuel Taylor Coleridge **10.** Marmalade **11.** Chimpanzee **12.** Charles Edward Stuart **13.** Red deer **14.** Southern **15.** Hovis **16.** Northamptonshire

General Knowledge 82

Answers on page 367

1. Who became President of France following the resignation of Charles de Gaulle?
2. Which two artists had UK number ones with 'Everything I Own'?
3. Of whom did Fanny Brice say: 'Wet she's a star. Dry, she ain't'?
4. Which American singer was once ranked joint 85th in the world for the high jump?
5. What was the name of golfer Peter Alliss's father who played in three Ryder Cups for Britain?
6. Ponce is an industrial port in which country?
7. Peace, Just Joey and Whisky Mac are all varieties of what?
8. Michael Savage was Prime Minister of which country from 1935–40?
9. Which BBC newsreader sat on a protesting lesbian during a 1988 invasion of the *Six O'Clock News* studio?
10. What was the name of the mistress who caused Cecil Parkinson's downfall?
11. In which decade was the first series of *The House of Eliott* set?
12. Which channel separates Sicily from Italy?
13. Which actress spent a month in a Rome prison in 1982 over income tax irregularities?
14. Which is the only bird with nostrils at the tip of its beak?
15. Which poet wrote *The Song of Hiawatha*?
16. Which phrase means 'it does not follow' in Latin?

Answers to page 367

GENERAL KNOWLEDGE 84: **1.** *It'll Be Alright on the Night* **2.** 1920s **3.** Egypt **4.** A freshwater fish **5.** Sir Alec Douglas-Home **6.** Cheshire **7.** Green **8.** Worcestershire **9.** Huron **10.** Charles Darwin **11.** 18th **12.** Barry **13.** Norway **14.** Colin Blunstone **15.** Francis Ford Coppola **16.** Germany

General Knowledge 83

Answers on page 364

1. Which former child star was working as a painter and decorator ten years after being nominated for an Oscar for his role in *Kramer vs Kramer*?
2. What nationality was Laszlo Biro, inventor of the ball-point pen?
3. Which German driver raced for Sauber in the 2001 Formula One World Championship?
4. On which lake was Donald Campbell killed in *Bluebird* while attempting to break the World Water Speed Record?
5. Who played Rowdy Yates in the TV Western *Rawhide* before moving on to Hollywood stardom?
6. Who was President of the Soviet Union from 1977–82?
7. Who was the second person to set foot on the Moon?
8. What was the full title of George Villiers, a favourite of James I?
9. Which poet wrote *Kubla Khan* and *The Ancient Mariner*?
10. Which Sixties band used to be called Dean Ford and the Gaylords?
11. Which primate has the Latin name *Pan troglodytes*?
12. What was Bonnie Prince Charlie's full name?
13. What is the largest wild mammal native to Britain?
14. In which hemisphere is the Tropic of Capricorn?
15. Which trade name is derived from the Latin *hominis vis*, meaning 'strength of man'?
16. In which English county is Sir Thomas Tresham's Triangular Lodge?

Answers to page 364

GENERAL KNOWLEDGE 81: **1.** Sky blue and white **2.** Decimalisation **3.** Paper clip **4.** 1981 **5.** Woodwind **6.** Judge Jeffreys **7.** Sweet **8.** Yellow **9.** Crimean War **10.** Glenda Jackson **11.** Portuguese **12.** Terry Hall **13.** Seahorse **14.** Cat **15.** Charles Bronson **16.** Marvin Rainwater

General Knowledge 84

Answers on page 365

1. Which TV programme celebrated only its 13th edition in 2001 even though it began in 1977?
2. In which decade did the Charleston become a popular dance?
3. Fuad I became King of which country from 1922?
4. What is a grayling?
5. Which former British Prime Minister once played first-class cricket for Middlesex?
6. In which English county is Jodrell Bank?
7. What colour was Roobarb the dog in *Roobarb and Custard*?
8. Which county cricket club have their headquarters at New Road?
9. Which is the second largest of the Great Lakes of North America?
10. Who published *On the Origin of Species* in 1859?
11. In which century did Samuel Pepys die?
12. Which boy's name means 'javelin'?
13. Which country stages an annual Grandmothers' Festival at Bodo in July?
14. Which singer didn't believe in miracles in 1972?
15. Who directed *The Godfather*?
16. Which country's football teams play in the Bundesliga?

Answers to page 365

GENERAL KNOWLEDGE 82: **1.** Georges Pompidou **2.** Ken Boothe and Boy George **3.** Esther Williams **4.** Johnny Mathis **5.** Percy Alliss **6.** Puerto Rico **7.** Rose **8.** New Zealand **9.** Nicholas Witchell **10.** Sarah Keays **11.** 1920s **12.** Strait of Messina **13.** Sophia Loren **14.** Kiwi **15.** Henry Wadsworth Longfellow **16.** *Non sequitur*

General Knowledge 85

Answers on page 370

1. The first pair of what brand of boots were made from tyres?
2. What is the capital of Chile?
3. Which insect can spend over a year in its larval stage yet only lives for a day as an adult?
4. How many species of bat are there approximately – 500, 800, 1000?
5. Where on the human body is the femur?
6. The Bessemer process was the first economical method of making which product?
7. Which card game originated in 1925 on a steamer travelling from Los Angeles to Havana?
8. In which country is the town of Coober Pedy?
9. In which county is Blenheim Palace?
10. Which city will stage the 2006 Commonwealth Games?
11. In which year was the breathalyser first introduced to the UK?
12. Which TV show was first broadcast on New Year's Day 1964 from a converted Manchester church?
13. Tony Hadley was the lead singer with which Eighties band?
14. Who was found dead in the opening episode of *EastEnders*?
15. What nationality was the Renaissance scholar Erasmus?
16. Who broke Pete Sampras's run of Wimbledon tennis victories by winning the 1996 men's singles title?

Answers to page 370

GENERAL KNOWLEDGE 87: **1.** Giacomo Agostini **2.** Carmen Miranda **3.** Herring **4.** Eric Morecambe **5.** Yellow **6.** 17th **7.** Augusta **8.** Sir Christopher Wren **9.** Harriet Beecher Stowe **10.** Anita Ward **11.** Pt **12.** Benton Fraser (*Due South*): dog Diefenbaker **13.** Escalator **14.** John Lennon **15.** Honduras **16.** The Jockey Club

General Knowledge 86

Answers on page 371

1. Which astronaut's mother's maiden name was Moon?
2. Which country has a town called A?
3. In the TV series, which *Batman* villain was played by Cesar Romero?
4. For which county cricket team did David Gower play from 1975–89?
5. Who was the god of wine in Roman mythology?
6. How many players are there in a women's lacrosse team?
7. Who composed 'The Entertainer', used as the theme tune for the film *The Sting*?
8. What is a joule?
9. Who won the Men's World Squash Championships six times in the 1980s?
10. Which battle took place south of Calais on 25 October 1415?
11. Where is the administrative centre of Cornwall?
12. What does the CIA stand for?
13. Who was the baker in *Camberwick Green*?
14. Which Hollywood actress was born Shirley Schrift before borrowing part of her new name from a poet?
15. What is a dhole?
16. In which American state is Las Vegas?

Answers to page 371

GENERAL KNOWLEDGE 88: **1.** 1955 **2.** T'Pau **3.** Essex **4.** Wear **5.** Kingcup **6.** Kent **7.** Sir Robert Walpole **8.** Three **9.** The Peninsular War **10.** Henry VII **11.** Bob Beamon **12.** Tom Watson **13.** Scotland **14.** California **15.** Mount McKinley **16.** Stockholm

General Knowledge 87

Answers on page 368

1. Which Italian motorcyclist won a record 122 Grands Prix and 15 world titles?
2. Which Hollywood actress was nicknamed 'The Brazilian Bombshell'?
3. Which is the world's most widely-eaten fish?
4. In 1995 a carving of John Smith was removed from Labour Party HQ when passers-by mistook it for a statue of which comedian?
5. What colour are the flowers of agrimony?
6. In which century did the Baroque style dominate European art?
7. What is the state capital of Maine?
8. Which architect designed the Royal Greenwich Observatory?
9. Which American novelist wrote *Uncle Tom's Cabin*?
10. Whose only UK hit was the 1979 number one 'Ring My Bell'?
11. What is the chemical symbol for platinum?
12. Which TV cop's dog was named after a former Canadian Prime Minister?
13. What did Jesse W. Reno invent in 1892?
14. Which Beatle sang backing vocals on David Bowie's 'Fame'?
15. Tegucigalpa is the capital of which Central American country?
16. What is the governing body of English horse racing?

Answers to page 368

GENERAL KNOWLEDGE 85: **1.** Doc Martens **2.** Santiago **3.** Mayfly **4.** 1000 **5.** The thigh **6.** Steel **7.** Contract bridge **8.** Australia **9.** Oxfordshire **10.** Melbourne **11.** 1967 **12.** *Top of the Pops* **13.** Spandau Ballet **14.** Reg Cox **15.** Dutch **16.** Richard Krajicek

General Knowledge 88

Answers on page 369

1. In which year did ITV start?
2. Which Eighties band took their name from Mr Spock's Vulcan friend in *Star Trek*?
3. For which county did former England cricket captain Graham Gooch play?
4. On which river does Durham stand?
5. What is another name for the marsh marigold?
6. In which county is Leeds Castle?
7. Who was the first British Prime Minister?
8. How many hearts does an octopus have?
9. Salamanca and Vittoria were battles in which war?
10. Who was the first Tudor King of England?
11. Who won the long jump at the 1968 Mexico Olympics?
12. Which golfer won his fifth British Open in 1983?
13. Who was defeated at the Battle of Pinkie?
14. In which American state is the San Andreas fault?
15. Which is the highest mountain in North America?
16. In which city were the 1912 Olympic Games staged?

Answers to page 369

GENERAL KNOWLEDGE 86: **1.** Buzz Aldrin **2.** Norway **3.** The Joker **4.** Leicestershire **5.** Bacchus **6.** 12 **7.** Scott Joplin **8.** A unit of work or energy **9.** Jahangir Khan **10.** Agincourt **11.** Truro **12.** Central Intelligence Agency **13.** Mickey Murphy **14.** Shelley Winters **15.** An Asian wild dog **16.** Nevada

General Knowledge 89

Answers on page 374

1. Who wrote *The Glass Menagerie*?
2. Which Hollywood beauty used to work as a weather-girl on *Sun Up*, a San Diego breakfast show?
3. What nationality is Placido Domingo?
4. In which year did Margaret Thatcher become Prime Minister?
5. Which Scottish football team play in Kirkcaldy?
6. Which band were Annie Lennox and Dave Stewart in before The Eurythmics?
7. Which actress won an Oscar for her role in *The Accused*?
8. Which country is also known as the Friendly Islands?
9. The Tonton Macoutes were sinister death squads operating on which island?
10. What is a tog?
11. On which continent is Lake Titicaca?
12. Who lost the Conservative Party leadership contest in 2001?
13. Who was the first British driver to become Formula One World Champion?
14. Which American band's albums include 'More Songs About Buildings And Food' and 'Little Creatures'?
15. In which county is Bosworth Field where Richard III met his death?
16. What is a takahe?

Answers to page 374

GENERAL KNOWLEDGE 91: **1.** Westland **2.** The Wombles **3.** Winnipeg **4.** French **5.** Gregor Mendel **6.** Lynne Perrie **7.** A flock of starlings landed on the minute hand **8.** Laos **9.** 'Rufus' **10.** Tarrant **11.** Bering Strait **12.** Laa-Laa **13.** Five **14.** German **15.** Alderney **16.** Dachshund

General Knowledge 90

Answers on page 375

1. Which club are the only founder members of the Football League still in existence never to have won the FA Cup?
2. What is the world's only poisonous bird?
3. Which country has a brand of soft drink called Pshitt?
4. What is the Welsh for Wales?
5. Of which trade union organisation was Lech Walesa the leader?
6. Stromboli was a villain in which Disney film?
7. Whose autobiography was entitled *Memoirs of an Unfit Mother*?
8. Who won Best Actor Oscars in both 1993 and 1994?
9. What was invented by the mother of Monkee Michael Nesmith?
10. What links Jim Reeves, Eddie Cochran and Laurel and Hardy?
11. Who was principal conductor of the London Symphony Orchestra 1968–79?
12. What was April Dancer otherwise known as?
13. What is the world's largest rodent?
14. What is a pochard?
15. On which river does Preston stand?
16. Furze is another name for which bush?

Answers to page 375

GENERAL KNOWLEDGE 92: **1.** Kiefer Sutherland **2.** Seven **3.** The Netherlands **4.** Juan Carlos **5.** Latvia **6.** A desert fox **7.** San Francisco **8.** Edmund Ironside **9.** Doctors **10.** Terence **11.** Southend United **12.** 'Sharon' **13.** Natalie Wood **14.** Pelham Grenville **15.** Venezuela **16.** A Vietnamese musical instrument

General Knowledge 91

Answers on page 372

1. Over which helicopter company's future did Cabinet ministers Michael Heseltine and Leon Brittan resign in 1986?

2. Who were the most successful chart act of 1974?

3. What is the capital of the Canadian province of Manitoba?

4. What is the official language of Togo?

5. Which scientist is known as the 'father of genetics'?

6. Which former *Coronation Street* actress appeared on the same bill as both The Beatles and The Rolling Stones in her days as a club singer?

7. What put Big Ben back by five minutes in 1945?

8. The New Kip is the currency in which country?

9. What was the nickname of King William II of England?

10. What was the fictional setting of *Howard's Way*?

11. What is the name of the strait between Alaska and Siberia?

12. Which of the *Teletubbies* is yellow?

13. How many times did Bjorn Borg win the men's singles title at Wimbledon?

14. What nationality was the inventor of the Bunsen burner?

15. What is the third largest of the Channel Islands?

16. What dog's name means 'badger-hound'?

Answers to page 372

GENERAL KNOWLEDGE 89: **1.** Tennessee Williams **2.** Raquel Welch **3.** Spanish **4.** 1979 **5.** Raith Rovers **6.** The Tourists **7.** Jodie Foster **8.** Tonga **9.** Haiti **10.** A unit of measure of thermal insulation **11.** South America **12.** Kenneth Clarke **13.** Mike Hawthorn **14.** Talking Heads **15.** Leicestershire **16.** A flightless bird from New Zealand

General Knowledge 92

Answers on page 373

1. Which American actor starred in the 2002 TV series *24*?
2. How many players are there in a netball team?
3. Enschede is a town in which country?
4. Who became King of Spain in 1975?
5. Riga is the capital of which country?
6. What kind of animal is a fennec?
7. Where did The Flowerpot Men suggest going in their 1967 hit?
8. Which English King was murdered while sitting on the toilet?
9. What profession did Harry Hill and Anton Chekhov once share?
10. What was Steve McQueen's first name?
11. Which Football League club plays at Roots Hall?
12. What is Rod Stewart's nickname for Elton John?
13. Which Hollywood actress, who had a morbid fear of water, drowned in 1981?
14. What did the initials 'P.G.' in P.G. Wodehouse stand for?
15. In which country are the Angel Falls?
16. What is a torong?

Answers to page 373

GENERAL KNOWLEDGE 90: **1.** Stoke City **2.** The pitohui **3.** France **4.** Cymru **5.** Solidarity **6.** *Pinocchio* **7.** Anne Robinson **8.** Tom Hanks **9.** Correction fluid **10.** In each case, their biggest hit was achieved posthumously **11.** André Previn **12.** *The Girl From UNCLE* **13.** Capybara **14.** A type of duck **15.** Ribble **16.** Gorse

General Knowledge 93

Answers on page 378

1. Which international singing star failed the audition for *Opportunity Knocks*?
2. Which sporting contest is named after an English seed merchant?
3. What is the name of Jim Royle's wife in *The Royle Family*?
4. What animals did Dian Fossey study in Rwanda from 1975?
5. In which county are the Quantock hills?
6. Which British jockey won the Epsom Derby six times between 1915 and 1925?
7. Forget-me-nots belong to which genus?
8. In which year did the Russian Revolution take place?
9. What nationality was the poet Robert Frost?
10. Which young singer confessed in 1972 that he had no idea where Liverpool was?
11. Which country consumes more Coca-Cola per head than any other?
12. What was Chad capital Ndjamena formerly known as?
13. Which two South American countries fought the Chaco War in the 1930s?
14. Brass is an alloy of which two metals?
15. Which is the smallest state in the USA?
16. 'Charisma', 'Bayleaf' and 'Vaseline' were all characters in which TV series?

Answers to page 378

GENERAL KNOWLEDGE 95: **1.** The Supremes **2.** Double vision **3.** Eurydice **4.** Kookaburra **5.** Green, white and red **6.** Laurie Lee **7.** Leicestershire **8.** Carole Lombard **9.** Ghosts **10.** 39 **11.** Vatican City **12.** Kampala **13.** Sixpence **14.** Mrs Bridges **15.** London Bridge **16.** 20

General Knowledge 94

Answers on page 379

1. Who was the female star of the 1946 film *It's a Wonderful Life*?
2. What was the name of the dog in *The Herbs*?
3. Who penned *Elegy Written in a Country Churchyard*?
4. Which English King was known as the 'Sailor King'?
5. In which Northern Ireland county is the town of Enniskillen?
6. Who broke Jackie Stewart's record of 27 Formula One Grand Prix wins?
7. Who starred in *On the Waterfront* and *In the Heat of the Night*?
8. Where did Fiddler's Dram go for a day trip in 1979?
9. Which American President was cruelly nicknamed 'The Illinois Baboon' on account of his appearance?
10. Which golfer missed a three-foot putt to win the 1970 British Open and then lost the play-off to fellow countryman Jack Nicklaus?
11. In which US state is the port of Charleston?
12. What is the chemical symbol for potassium?
13. Which baseball player was nicknamed 'The Georgia Peach'?
14. What was the Christian name of the German motor manufacturer Daimler?
15. What is the southernmost point of the English mainland?
16. In which century was the okapi first discovered?

Answers to page 379

GENERAL KNOWLEDGE 96: **1.** The Millennium Bridge **2.** Isobars **3.** Cambridgeshire **4.** Todd Woodbridge and Mark Woodforde **5.** John Huston **6.** Vera Palmer **7.** Praying mantis **8.** Acer **9.** Second World War **10.** Buenos Aires **11.** The Compact Pussycat **12.** Lon Chaney Snr **13.** Don McLean **14.** Nine **15.** Belize **16.** 1990

General Knowledge 95

Answers on page 376

1. Who were the first female group to top the UK singles charts?
2. What is diplopia?
3. In Greek mythology, who was the wife of Orpheus?
4. Which bird is also known as the laughing jackass?
5. What colours are the three horizontal stripes on the national flag of Kuwait?
6. Who wrote *Cider with Rosie*?
7. Which county cricket club's Norwich Union League team are known as the Foxes?
8. Which American comedy actress changed her name from Jane Alice Peters?
9. What is phasmophobia a fear of?
10. How many books are there in the Old Testament?
11. Which is the smallest state in the world?
12. What is the capital of Uganda?
13. Which unit of currency was finally phased out in 1980?
14. What was the name of the cook in *Upstairs, Downstairs*?
15. Which landmark was dismantled and taken to Arizona in 1968?
16. For how many years did Rip Van Winkle sleep?

Answers to page 376

GENERAL KNOWLEDGE 93: **1.** Engelbert Humperdinck **2.** Ryder Cup **3.** Barbara **4.** Gorillas **5.** Somerset **6.** Steve Donoghue **7.** Myosotis **8.** 1917 **9.** American **10.** Little Jimmy Osmond **11.** Iceland **12.** Fort Lamy **13.** Bolivia and Paraguay **14.** Copper and zinc **15.** District of Columbia **16.** *London's Burning*

General Knowledge 96

Answers on page 377

1. Which walkway opened and closed within two days in the summer of 2000?
2. What is the name of the lines drawn on weather maps linking places with the same atmospheric pressure?
3. In which county is the Isle Of Ely?
4. Which tennis pairing were known as the 'Woodies'?
5. Who directed *The Maltese Falcon* and *The African Queen*?
6. What was Jayne Mansfield's real name?
7. The female of which insect frequently bites off the head of the male during reproduction?
8. To which genus does the maple tree belong?
9. The Battle of Anzio took place during which war?
10. Which capital city's name means 'good winds'?
11. What vehicle did Penelope Pitstop drive in *Wacky Races*?
12. Which actor was known as 'The Man of a Thousand Faces'?
13. Who was the subject of Roberta Flack's 'Killing Me Softly With His Song'?
14. How many innings are there in a game of baseball?
15. Which country used to be known as British Honduras?
16. In which year did Adamski have a UK number one with 'Killer'?

Answers to page 377

GENERAL KNOWLEDGE 94: **1.** Donna Reed **2.** Dill **3.** Thomas Gray **4.** William IV **5.** Fermanagh **6.** Alain Prost **7.** Rod Steiger **8.** Bangor **9.** Abraham Lincoln **10.** Doug Sanders **11.** South Carolina **12.** K **13.** Ty Cobb **14.** Gottlieb **15.** The Lizard **16.** 20th

General Knowledge 97

Answers on page 382

1. Which footballer was known as 'Duncan Disorderly' north of the border because of his poor disciplinary record?
2. Which squat Cockney actor used to work as a fire-eater in a circus?
3. Which playwright penned *Absent Friends* and *Way Upstream*?
4. Which mode of transport was invented by Christopher Cockerell?
5. On which islands are the Old Man of Hoy?
6. Which girl's name means 'female sheep' in Hebrew?
7. What is the state capital of South Australia?
8. What was the name of Billy J. Kramer's backing group?
9. What is a shaggy ink cap?
10. Which corrupt architect was jailed for seven years in 1974?
11. Which volcano erupted in AD79, resulting in the destruction of the city of Pompeii?
12. Who launched Skytrain?
13. What event shook the music world on 16 August 1977?
14. Who became Soviet leader in 1985?
15. In which country is Lake Garda?
16. About whom was Stewart Granger talking in 1984 when he said: 'She's common, she can't act – yet she's the hottest female property around these days'?

Answers to page 382

GENERAL KNOWLEDGE 99: **1.** Iceland **2.** Umberto II **3.** Blue-ringed octopus **4.** Dani Behr **5.** Gary Lineker **6.** Eltham, South-East London **7.** Colorado River **8.** Ruth Rendell **9.** Switzerland **10.** She was the first UK entrant in the Eurovision Song Contest **11.** Mike Love **12.** Lake District **13.** Marcia Falkender **14.** Coelacanth **15.** Bay of Pigs **16.** Germany

General Knowledge 98

Answers on page 383

1. Which American band used to be known as The Stilettos?
2. Which was the first garden city in Britain?
3. Who were the Gang of Four who left the Labour Party in 1981 to form the SDP?
4. What instrument did George Formby play?
5. Who played 'Popeye' Doyle in *The French Connection*?
6. In which country is the Indre river?
7. Who designed the Mini car?
8. Who was known as the 'Sun King'?
9. Helena is the capital of which American state?
10. What is an oxlip?
11. Which Scottish King was killed when one of his own cannon exploded?
12. What was the nickname of Howard Hughes's giant flying-boat which flew only once?
13. Which horse won the 1999 Epsom Derby?
14. Animal was the drummer with which band on *The Muppet Show*?
15. The Plough is part of which constellation?
16. Who wrote *Of Mice and Men*?

Answers to page 383

GENERAL KNOWLEDGE 100: **1.** Slade **2.** 100 **3.** Crete **4.** Juan Pablo **5.** *Kind Hearts and Coronets* **6.** Alexandros I **7.** Tchaikovsky **8.** Charles Lindbergh **9.** Lord Haw Haw **10.** Romania **11.** Mrs Corazon Aquino **12.** One **13.** Digitalis **14.** Brechin City **15.** Poseidon **16.** Frank Lloyd Wright

General Knowledge 99

Answers on page 380

1. Which country boasts the oldest parliament in the world?
2. Who was the last King of Italy?
3. What is the only octopus known to have killed humans?
4. Which TV presenter started her career as one third of the group Faith, Hope and Charity?
5. Which former England international footballer once appeared on a national stamp of Gambia?
6. Where was Bob Hope born?
7. Across which river was the Hoover Dam built?
8. Which novelist created the detective Reg Wexford?
9. In which country is the Sauber Formula One motor racing team based?
10. What is Patricia Bredin's role in the history of music?
11. Which Beach Boy has been married nine times (at the latest count)?
12. Where is Wast Water?
13. Which woman was secretary to Harold Wilson from 1956?
14. Which species of fish was believed to be extinct until one was caught off Madagascar in 1938?
15. Which Cuban bay was the site of an unsuccessful invasion by US forces in 1961?
16. In which country is Bayreuth?

Answers to page 380

GENERAL KNOWLEDGE 97: **1.** Duncan Ferguson **2.** Bob Hoskins **3.** Sir Alan Ayckbourn **4.** Hovercraft **5.** The Orkneys **6.** Rachel **7.** Adelaide **8.** The Dakotas **9.** Fungus **10.** John Poulson **11.** Mt Vesuvius **12.** Freddie Laker **13.** The death of Elvis Presley **14.** Mikhail Gorbachev **15.** Italy **16.** Joan Collins

General Knowledge 100

Answers on page 381

1. In which fictitious prison was *Porridge* set?
2. In Bulgarian currency, how many stotinki are there in a lev?
3. Heraklion and Canea are the major cities on which island?
4. What are the first names of the racing driver Montoya?
5. In which 1949 film did Alec Guinness play eight different roles?
6. Which King of Greece died in 1920 from blood poisoning after being bitten by his pet monkey?
7. Who composed the opera *Eugene Onegin*?
8. Who completed the first solo flight across the Atlantic?
9. Which Second World War traitor was born William Joyce?
10. Which was the only Eastern bloc country to take part in the 1984 Los Angeles Olympics?
11. Which widow toppled Ferdinand Marcos from power in the Philippines in 1986?
12. How many humps does a dromedary have?
13. To which genus do foxgloves belong?
14. Which Scottish League team plays at Glebe Park?
15. Who was the Greek god of the sea?
16. Which architect was immortalised on Simon and Garfunkel's *Bridge Over Troubled Water* album?

Answers to page 381

GENERAL KNOWLEDGE 98: **1.** Blondie **2.** Letchworth **3.** Roy Jenkins, David Owen, Shirley Williams and William Rodgers **4.** Ukelele **5.** Gene Hackman **6.** France **7.** Alec Issigonis **8.** Louis XIV **9.** Montana **10.** A plant, related to the cowslip **11.** James II **12.** *Spruce Goose* **13.** Oath **14.** Dr Teeth and the Electric Mayhem **15.** Ursa Major **16.** John Steinbeck

TV Music 3

Answers on page 386

1. Which punk group steadfastly refused to appear on *Top of the Pops*?
2. Which karaoke contest was presided over by Suggs?
3. What is the name of Channel 5's chart show?
4. Which singing family travelled around in an old school bus?
5. Ian Whitcomb and Richard Williams were the original hosts of which music series?
6. Which show axed dance troupes in 1983?
7. Which Saturday evening pop show was introduced by Mike Mansfield?
8. Which comedy trio performed 'Funky Gibbon' on *Top of the Pops*?
9. Which Fifties' show which launched the career of Cliff Richard was briefly revived in 1979?
10. On which night of the week did *The Tube* go out?
11. What was the original theme song of *Ready, Steady, Go!*?
12. And which group recorded it?
13. Katie Puckrik, Dani Behr and Huffty were presenters on which late night music show?
14. Who were the final three contestants in 2002's *Pop Idol*?
15. Which boxer was one of the presenters of *Six-Five Special*?
16. Who is the voice of *TOTP2*?

Answers to page 386

COMEDY 10: **1.** *Radio Active* **2.** Tim Taylor **3.** *Green Acres* **4.** Edward and Tubbs **5.** 'Bulldog' **6.** Norman Gunston **7.** Ben Elton **8.** Arthur Ewing **9.** Ross **10.** For an incident involving some nuns **11.** Carol **12.** Chanel 9 **13.** 'Scorchio!' **14.** *End of Part One* **15.** *The Dustbinmen* **16.** Gwen Taylor

Sci Fi 3

Answers on page 387

1. Which organisation built the space station *Babylon 5*?
2. In which century is *Star Trek: Deep Space Nine* set?
3. Who thawed out 64 years after being trapped in a block of ice?
4. Whose space travels began after she met Zaphod Beeblebrox at a party in Islington?
5. Which was the third story in the *Quatermass* series?
6. In *Blake's 7*, who was Supreme Commander of the Federation's space forces?
7. Sarah Michelle Gellar plays which teen heroine?
8. What does the T stand for in Capt. James T. Kirk?
9. Who was Supreme Councillor Fulvia's assistant in *Star Maidens*?
10. What is Lady Penelope's surname?
11. Who played Rimmer in *Red Dwarf*?
12. What was the name of the hapless Titan spy in *Stingray*?
13. Who is the sidekick of *Xena: Warrior Princess*?
14. Who was the chief enemy of the *Supercar* team?
15. Deep Throat and Cigarette-Smoking Man are villains in which series?
16. In which country was *Xena: Warrior Princess* originally filmed?

Answers to page 387

DRAMAS 9: **1.** 1930s **2.** Yvette **3.** *Real Women* **4.** Peter Egan **5.** *The Monocled Mutineer* **6.** *Market in Honey Lane* **7.** *Karaoke* and *Cold Lazarus* **8.** Michael Landon **9.** 'Charisma' **10.** Dr Erica Matthews **11.** Frank Stubbs **12.** Kira **13.** Rosie Rowell **14.** *Forever Green* **15.** John Galsworthy **16.** Queens Park Rangers

Comedy 10

Answers on page 384

1. Which radio show begat *KYTV*?
2. In *Home Improvement*, who presented a cable TV series called *Tool Time*?
3. Where did Eddie Albert move to in a 1960s US sitcom?
4. Who are the sinister shopkeepers of Royston Vasey?
5. What is Bob Briscoe's nickname in *Frasier*?
6. Who was Australian comedian Garry McDonald's alter ego?
7. Who wrote *The Thin Blue Line*?
8. Who had his own troupe of Musical Mice on *Monty Python's Flying Circus*?
9. Which of the *Friends* worked in a museum?
10. Why was Father Dougal exiled to Craggy Island?
11. What is the name of Alan Partridge's estranged wife?
12. Which was the Spanish TV station featured on *The Fast Show*?
13. And what did its weathergirl say at the end of each forecast?
14. Which ITV series featured Vera and Norman Straightman?
15. Heavy Breathing and Smellie Ibbotson appeared in which hit sitcom?
16. Who played Amy Pearce in *Duty Free*?

Answers to page 384

TV MUSIC 3: **1.** The Clash **2.** *Night Fever* **3.** *The Pepsi Chart* **4.** *The Partridge Family* **5.** *The Old Grey Whistle Test* **6.** *Top of the Pops* **7.** *Supersonic* **8.** The Goodies **9.** *Oh Boy!* **10.** Friday **11.** '5-4-3-2-1' **12.** Manfred Mann **13.** *The Word* **14.** Will Young, Gareth Gates and Darius Danesh **15.** Freddie Mills **16.** Steve Wright

Dramas 9

Answers on page 385

1. In which decade was *South Riding* set?
2. What was Lisa Colbert's codename in *Secret Army*?
3. What were Pauline Quirke, Michelle Collins, Gwyneth Strong, Frances Barber and Lesley Manville in 1998?
4. Who played the title role in *Prince Regent*?
5. What was Percy Toplis better known as?
6. Billy Bush was a stall-holder in which Sixties drama series?
7. What were Dennis Potter's final two linked works?
8. Who starred in *Highway to Heaven*?
9. What was Leslie Appleby's nickname in *London's Burning*?
10. In *Peak Practice*, who jilted Dr Andrew Attwood at the altar?
11. Which promoter was played by Timothy Spall in a 1993 comedy/drama?
12. What was the name of Warren's cousin in *This Life*?
13. Who played Donna Tucker in *Soldier, Soldier*?
14. Which eco-friendly series saw the Boult family move from London to the country?
15. *The Forsyte Saga* was based on whose novels?
16. What was Reg Toomer's favourite football team in *The Boys From the Bush*?

Answers to page 385

SCI FI 3: **1.** The Earth Alliance **2.** The 24th **3.** Adam Adamant **4.** Trillian **5.** *Quatermass and the Pit* **6.** Servalan **7.** *Buffy the Vampire Slayer* **8.** Tiberius **9.** Octavia **10.** Creighton-Ward **11.** Chris Barrie **12.** Agent X20 **13.** Gabrielle **14.** Masterspy **15.** *The X Files* **16.** New Zealand

Soaps 8

Answers on page 390

1. Who was Irene Hills's toy boy in *EastEnders*?

2. Who did Ken Barlow and Albert Tatlock appear as on the Street's Jubilee Day float to celebrate 'Britain Through the Ages'?

3. Who played Bazz in *Hollyoaks* and café owner Tom in the new *Crossroads*?

4. What was the name of Pippa's second husband in *Home and Away*?

5. In *Emmerdale*, which young bride was killed in a car crash following a party at Home Farm?

6. Which *Dynasty* bitch was convicted of murdering Mark Jennings?

7. Which nanny of the Farnhams ran off with a priest in *Brookside*?

8. Who did Mark Little play in *Neighbours*?

9. Who was Brentwich's first manager in *United!*?

10. Who ran the local English-language newspaper in *Eldorado*?

11. *Call Oxbridge 2000* was a spin-off from which British soap?

12. Which was the first twice-weekly BBC serial to be recorded in colour?

13. Who shot Bobby Ewing in *Dallas*?

14. How did Allison MacKenzie leave *Peyton Place*?

15. Who married Miles Colby while suffering from amnesia?

16. In *Crossroads*, who married Glenda Brownlow?

Answers to page 390

QUIZ AND GAME SHOWS 5: **1.** Ulrika Jonsson **2.** Roy Walker **3.** *Wheel of Fortune* **4.** *Mastermind* **5.** *3-2-1* **6.** Norman Vaughan **7.** Jim Davidson **8.** Isla St Clair **9.** Bob Danvers-Walker **10.** Krishnan Guru-Murthy **11.** *Countdown* **12.** *The $64,000 Question* **13.** *Blankety Blank* **14.** *The Golden Shot* **15.** They were the first couple to marry after meeting on *Blind Date* **16.** Reeves and Mortimer

Sport 3

Answers on page 391

1. Which former New Zealand Test player is a Channel 4 cricket commentator?
2. When did Barry Davies join the BBC?
3. Arsenal met Nottingham Forest in the very first edition of which programme?
4. Who was the host of *Sportsmasters*?
5. Who is the BBC horse racing team's man in the betting ring?
6. Which Peter commentates on *Football Italia*?
7. Nigel Starmer-Smith is a commentator on which sport?
8. Which comedian is a regular on Gary Lineker's team in *They Think It's All Over*?
9. Who took over from Dan Maskell as the BBC's senior tennis commentator?
10. Which American ace voiced his opinions in the commentary box at Wimbledon 2001?
11. Which former Liverpool and Sunderland player contributes to *On the Ball*?
12. Which member of the Royal Family appeared on the 200th edition of *A Question of Sport*?
13. Who was BBC Sports Personality of the Year for 2000?
14. Which former World Champion used to be Murray Walker's co-commentator for the BBC's Grand Prix coverage?
15. Dorian Williams was for many years the BBC voice of which sport?
16. Who was the first female presenter of *Grandstand*?

Answers to page 391

LOCATIONS 4: **1.** *City Central* **2.** Bradford **3.** *Peak Practice* **4.** *Casey Jones* **5.** Belgium **6.** *This Life* **7.** Belvedere **8.** *Dawson's Creek* **9.** Chicago **10.** *Dangerfield* **11.** Bel-Air **12.** California **13.** Birmingham **14.** St Swithin's **15.** Colorado Springs **16.** Scott Furlong

Quiz & Game Shows 5

Answers on page 388

1. Who presents *Dog Eat Dog*?
2. Who did Nick Weir succeed as host of *Catchphrase* in 2000?
3. Carol Smillie was a hostess on which game show?
4. Which highbrow quiz was axed in 1997 after running for 25 years?
5. Which game show was based on the Spanish programme *Uno, Dos, Tres*?
6. Which comedian was the co-creator of *Bullseye*?
7. Who hosted *Big Break*?
8. Who was Larry Grayson's Scottish assistant on *The Generation Game*?
9. Who announced the prizes on the original version of *Take Your Pick*?
10. Who hosts *Number 1*?
11. Which long-running word game was created by Armand Jammot?
12. Which popular Fifties quiz was revived in 1990 with Bob Monkhouse as host?
13. Which BBC game show switched to ITV in 2001?
14. On which show did contestants say: 'Up a bit, down a bit, left a bit, fire'?
15. What is Sue Middleton and Alex Tatham's claim to fame?
16. Which comedians presented *Families at War*?

Answers to page 388

SOAPS 8: **1.** Troy Harvey **2.** Sir Edmund Hillary and Sherpa Tensing **3.** Toby Sawyer **4.** Michael Ross **5.** Linda Fowler **6.** Alexis **7.** Margaret Clemence **8.** Joe Mangel **9.** Gerry Barford **10.** Gwen Lockhead **11.** *Emergency – Ward 10* **12.** *The Doctors* **13.** Katherine Wentworth **14.** She vanished on a foggy night **15.** Fallon **16.** Kevin Banks

Locations 4

Answers on page 389

1. Which police series has its station in Christmas Street?
2. Which northern city was the setting for *Band of Gold* and *Gold*?
3. Which medical series has a surgery called 'The Beeches'?
4. Which Fifties hero was an engineer for the Illinois Central Railroad?
5. In which country was *Secret Army* set?
6. Benjamin Street, Southwark, was the address of the house in which Nineties' drama?
7. What was the name of *The Colbys*' estate?
8. Capeside is the setting for which teenage drama?
9. In which American city is *ER* set?
10. Which BBC series was about a Warwickshire police surgeon?
11. Where was Jonathan and Jennifer's mansion in *Hart to Hart*?
12. In which American state was *Falcon Crest* set?
13. *Empire Road* was supposedly a thoroughfare in which city?
14. What was the name of the hospital in *Doctor in the House*?
15. From which town did *Dr Quinn: Medicine Woman* operate?
16. What was the aircraft factory called in *The Plane Makers*?

Answers to page 389

SPORT 3: **1.** Ian Smith **2.** 1969 **3.** *Quiz Ball* **4.** Dickie Davies **5.** Angus Loughran **6.** Peter Brackley **7.** Rugby Union **8.** Rory McGrath **9.** John Barrett **10.** John McEnroe **11.** Barry Venison **12.** Princess Anne **13.** Steve Redgrave **14.** James Hunt **15.** Showjumping **16.** Helen Rollason

Children's TV 5

Answers on page 394

1. *Count Duckula* was a spin-off from which series?
2. Who owned *Bagpuss*?
3. Who had an Eskimo bride called Nooka?
4. Which athlete took over *Record Breakers* in 1998?
5. What was the nickname of *Grange Hill* pupil Samuel McGuire?
6. Who had a magic bicycle on *The Magic Roundabout*?
7. What kind of creature was Yakky Doodle?
8. Which cartoon scientist invented a means of travelling back through time?
9. Which squid was janitor of a sea aquarium?
10. Who was the Rastafarian in *Maid Marian and Her Merry Men*?
11. Who narrated *Mr Benn*?
12. What colour string pudding did *Clangers* eat?
13. What was the name of the star locomotive on the *Chigley* steam railway?
14. Who did Ant McPartlin and Declan Donnelly play in *Byker Grove*?
15. Which series was known in its native France as *La Maison de Tu Tu*?
16. Who was the first male *Blue Peter* presenter?

Answers to page 394

COMEDY 11: **1.** Samantha Janus **2.** Smeeta Smitten **3.** Joan Collins **4.** New York, Paris, Peckham **5.** Terence Brady **6.** Diana Dors **7.** The Crabtrees **8.** Judi Dench and Michael Williams **9.** Ruby **10.** 86 **11.** Hardware **12.** Billy and Johnny **13.** Michael Robbins **14.** The Old Gits **15.** *Married...with Children* **16.** John Alderton and Hannah Gordon

Corrie 2

Answers on page 395

1. What was Geoffrey Nugent's nickname?
2. Who bought 9 Coronation Street for £1,000 in 1968?
3. Who played Prince Charming in the Rovers Amateur Dramatic Society's 1975 production of *Cinderella*?
4. In 1982, who went into partnership in a garage with Ron Sykes?
5. Who was Wayne Hayes' wicked stepfather?
6. Which Street regular was mugged in 1982?
7. Of which supermarket was Reg Holdsworth the manager?
8. What was the name of Alma Baldwin's first husband?
9. Who played Jim McDonald?
10. Who once wrote a novel entitled *Song of a Scarlet Summer*?
11. Who were the first couple to move into the newly-built 6 Coronation Street in 1990?
12. What was the maiden name of Raquel Watts?
13. Which schoolgirl fell for Patrice Podevin on a trip to France?
14. What was the name of Florrie Lindley's wayward husband?
15. Who jilted bride-to-be Lucille Hewitt in 1969?
16. Which businessman once lost all his money in a Spanish land deal?

Answers to page 395
WHICH YEAR IN TV? 6: **1.** 1978 **2.** 1994 **3.** 1975 **4.** 1995 **5.** 1950 **6.** 1960 **7.** 1981 **8.** 1977 **9.** 1993 **10.** 1983 **11.** 1957 **12.** 1955 **13.** 1969 **14.** 1993 **15.** 1975 **16.** 1991

Comedy 11

Answers on page 392

1. Who played Miss Titley in the pilot episode of *The Grimleys*?
2. What is the name of the showbiz gossip columnist in *Goodness Gracious Me*?
3. As whose Fan Club did Julian Clary used to bill himself?
4. Which three destinations were emblazoned on Del Boy's three-wheeler?
5. Who took over from Dinsdale Landen as Barty Wade in *Pig in the Middle*?
6. Which sex symbol-turned-character actress played the Queenie in *Queenie's Castle*?
7. Which family discovered that there was *No Place Like Home*?
8. Which husband-and-wife team starred in *A Fine Romance*?
9. What was the name of the Parkinsons' coarse house cleaner in *Butterflies*?
10. What number agent was *Get Smart*'s Maxwell Smart?
11. What type of store did Howard Cunningham own in *Happy Days*?
12. Which two children's presenters were created by Hale and Pace?
13. Who played Arthur in *On the Buses*?
14. What were the two filthy OAPs on *Harry Enfield's Television Programme* known as?
15. What was Al Bundy's status in life?
16. Who played George and Suzy Bassett in *My Wife Next Door*?

Answers to page 392

CHILDREN'S TV 5: **1.** *Dangermouse* **2.** Emily **3.** *Noggin the Nog* **4.** Linford Christie **5.** 'Zammo' **6.** Mr MacHenry **7.** A duck **8.** *Hector Heathcote* **9.** *Squiddly Diddly* **10.** Barrington **11.** Ray Brooks **12.** Blue **13.** Bessie **14.** PJ and Duncan **15.** *Hector's House* **16.** Christopher Trace

Which Year in TV? 6

Answers on page 393

In which year were the following programmes first shown in the UK?

1. *The South Bank Show*

2. *Men Behaving Badly*

3. *Fawlty Towers*

4. *Father Ted*

5. *Andy Pandy*

6. *Here's Harry*

7. *Hi-De-Hi!*

8. *The Krypton Factor*

9. *Sharpe*

10. *Taggart*

11. *Emergency – Ward 10*

12. *Sunday Night at the London Palladium*

13. *Star Trek*

14. *Seinfeld*

15. *The Good Life*

16. *The Brittas Empire*

Answers to page 393

CORRIE 2: **1.** 'Spider' **2.** Len Fairclough **3.** Bet Lynch **4.** Brian Tilsley **5.** Alex Swinton **6.** Betty Turpin **7.** Bettabuys **8.** Jim Sedgewick **9.** Charles Lawson **10.** Mavis Wilton **11.** Des and Steph Barnes **12.** Wolstenhulme **13.** Jenny Bradley **14.** Norman **15.** Gordon Clegg **16.** Mike Baldwin

Dramas 10

Answers on page 398

1. Which member of the Bellamy household in *Upstairs, Downstairs* went down with the *Titanic*?
2. What was the title of the 1982 sequel to *Take Three Girls*?
3. Who played Tiberius in *I, Claudius*?
4. What is John Cage's nickname in *Ally McBeal*?
5. Which US series features cynical lawyer Miranda Hobbes?
6. Who was the newly-installed leader of Liverpool City Council in *GBH*?
7. What relation was Jolyon Forsyte to Soames?
8. What was stunt man Colt Seavers better known as?
9. Who was the demanding dance teacher in *Fame*?
10. Who created *Playing the Field*?
11. Who played Mike Nicholls in *Harbour Lights*?
12. In which fictional resort did Sarah Preston run the Royal Suffolk Hotel?
13. Which American actor starred in *Colditz*?
14. Jack Ford was the hero of which BBC period drama?
15. What pet did vet Calum Buchanan keep in *All Creatures Great and Small*?
16. Megan Roach, Ewart Plimmer and Kuba Trzcinski were early characters in which series?

Answers to page 398

CHAT SHOWS 1: **1.** Gloria Hunniford **2.** Billy Connolly **3.** Graham Norton **4.** Ricki Lake **5.** Cincinnati **6.** Clive Anderson **7.** *Eldorado* **8.** Gilbert Harding **9.** Peter Ustinov **10.** Prince Philip **11.** Frank Skinner **12.** Patrick Kielty **13.** Phil Donahue **14.** Vanessa Feltz **15.** Vanessa Feltz **16.** Paula Yates

TV Pot Luck 9

Answers on page 399

1. Which Scottish presenter joined *Good Morning Britain* in 1988 before moving on to *GMTV*?
2. Who was the Turner in *Turner Round the World*?
3. Which TV presenter and radio DJ once worked as a paddling pool attendant?
4. Who wrote *The Lakes*?
5. Which adventure series was narrated by Mad Jack?
6. Which comedian stages *Phoenix Nights*?
7. Who plays Alison in *At Home with the Braithwaites*?
8. What nationality is Ulrika Jonsson?
9. Which Saturday evening show featured visits from the Hit Squad?
10. Who demonstrated pub tricks on *TFI Friday*?
11. Who was Cilla Black's co-presenter for the first series of *Surprise, Surprise*?
12. Which TV character was bought for 7s 6d in 1948 and sold for £1.4 million in 1996?
13. Who hosted the Miss World contest in 2000?
14. Which series combined the diverse talents of Kenny Everett, Jonathan Routh and Germaine Greer?
15. Which stunning actress was born Louise Perkins?
16. Which former Pontin's Blue Coat had his own *Experience* on TV?

Answers to page 399

COP SHOWS 7: **1.** Ross Kemp **2.** *A Mind to Kill* **3.** Isobel De Pauli **4.** Helen Mirren **5.** *Prime Suspect* **6.** Mary **7.** *The Professionals* **8.** Bobby Simone **9.** *The Chinese Detective* **10.** Tim Pigott-Smith **11.** Robin Tataglia **12.** Jim Bergerac **13.** Christine Cagney **14.** Mike Dashwood **15.** Inspector Mole **16.** *The Third Man*

Chat Shows 1

Answers on page 396

1. Who holds *Open House* on Channel 5?
2. Which *Parkinson* guest warned Rod Hull and Emu: 'I'll break your neck and his bloody arm'?
3. Which Channel 4 chat show host is *So...*?
4. Which Ricki has her own talk show?
5. Of which American city was Jerry Springer once the mayor?
6. Which chat show host is *All Talk*?
7. To make way for which ill-fated soap was *Wogan* axed in 1992?
8. Which gruff quiz show panellist broke down in tears on *Face to Face*?
9. Who was the most frequent guest on *Parkinson* in the 1970s?
10. Who accused Terry Wogan of reading other people's questions off cards?
11. Which chat show host was born Chris Collins?
12. Which comedian did a series of live late-night chat shows from Belfast in 2001?
13. Which silver-haired American had his own daytime talk show on ITV?
14. Who was left with egg on her face after boasting: 'We're going to trash *Trisha*'?
15. Which former talk show host was voted off early on *Celebrity Big Brother*?
16. Who was the first to conduct interviews on the bed for *The Big Breakfast*?

Answers to page 396

DRAMAS 10: **1.** Lady Marjorie **2.** *Take Three Women* **3.** George Baker **4.** 'The Biscuit' **5.** *Sex and the City* **6.** Michael Murray **7.** Cousin **8.** *The Fall Guy* **9.** Lydia Grant **10.** Kay Mellor **11.** Nick Berry **12.** *Westbeach* **13.** Robert Wagner **14.** *When the Boat Comes In* **15.** A badger **16.** *Casualty*

Cop Shows 7

Answers on page 397

1. Which former *EastEnder* played a drag queen in an episode of *City Central*?
2. Noel Bain is the central character in which police series?
3. Who did Sam Janus play in *Liverpool One*?
4. Whose portrayal of a TV cop won her the BAFTA Best Actress award for three successive years in the 1990s?
5. And in which police series did she star?
6. What was the name of George Dixon's daughter?
7. Which Seventies series was parodied by the Comic Strip production *The Bullshitters*?
8. Which *NYPD Blue* cop died of a heart attack?
9. What was Johnny Ho better known as?
10. Who played Chief Constable John Stafford in *The Chief*?
11. Which fellow officer married Mick Belker in *Hill Street Blues*?
12. Who worked for the Bureau des Etrangers?
13. Which member of *Cagney and Lacey* had a drink problem?
14. Which officer in *The Bill* was played by Jon Iles?
15. Who was *Cluff*'s superior officer?
16. Which series starred Michael Rennie as Harry Lime?

Answers to page 397

TV POT LUCK 9: **1.** Lorraine Kelly **2.** Anthea Turner **3.** Simon Mayo **4.** Jimmy McGovern **5.** *The Life and Times of Grizzly Adams* **6.** Peter Kay **7.** Amanda Redman **8.** Swedish **9.** *The Late, Late Breakfast Show* **10.** Will Macdonald **11.** Christopher Biggins **12.** Sooty **13.** Jerry Springer **14.** *Nice Time* **15.** Louise Lombard **16.** Shane Richie

Soaps 9

Answers on page 402

1. How many different actresses played Lucy Robinson in *Neighbours*?
2. What was 'Biff' Fowler's real name in *Emmerdale*?
3. Which Queen Vic barmaid was a former prostitute?
4. Who was Ollie Simpson's neurotic wife in *Brookside*?
5. Which *Coronation Street* resident sprang a 'This Is Your Life' on Annie Walker in 1963?
6. With whom did Miss Ellie leave for Europe in *Dallas*?
7. Which short-lived daytime soap of the 1980s was set in a Community Advice office?
8. Which *EastEnders* actress used to play Joyce Harker in *The Newcomers*?
9. In which Sixties soap did Ronnie Allen play a football manager?
10. Who in Summer Bay married ex-soldier Ben Lucini in 1990?
11. Who played Will Cairns in *Emmerdale* and Mike Baldwin's son Mark in *Coronation Street*?
12. Who married Rita Jacks in *Peyton Place*?
13. In *Coronation Street*, what was Hayley Cropper's maiden name?
14. Which pub did Greg Andersen run in *Hollyoaks*?
15. Who married his secretary, Sally, in *Compact*?
16. What was the name of Tiffany Mitchell's daughter in *EastEnders*?

Answers to page 402

TV POT LUCK 10: **1.** A chef **2.** *Gladiators* **3.** Jack Hargreaves **4.** Maggie Philbin **5.** *Location, Location, Location* **6.** *New Faces* **7.** Lee **8.** Neil Morrissey **9.** *Aquarius* **10.** Gloria Hunniford **11.** Leonard Sachs **12.** Michael Fish **13.** *Antiques Inspectors* **14.** Ali G **15.** Big Tim Champion **16.** McDonald Hobley

Comedy 12

Answers on page 403

1. Which show featured a TV cop called Monkfish?
2. Which classic sitcom stemmed from a *Comedy Playhouse* production, *The Offer*?
3. The Man With a Stick was a regular on which show?
4. Who re-performed a selection of Galton and Simpson scripts in 1996?
5. Which comedian made his TV debut on the 1948 BBC talent show *New to You*?
6. Bill and Barbie Reynolds were the black couple in which politically-incorrect Seventies sitcom?
7. What was the name of Hyacinth Bucket's long-suffering husband?
8. Who is Phoebe's twin sister in *Friends*?
9. From which city does *Frasier*'s Daphne Moon hail?
10. Which charity night was first staged on BBC in 1988?
11. What was the title of Rory Bremner's first starring series?
12. *Benson* was a spin-off from which series?
13. What was the setting for *Only When I Laugh*?
14. Who urged her elderly audience: 'Let's have a heated debate'?
15. Who had a butler called Badger?
16. On which US comedy series did Edina and Patsy from *Absolutely Fabulous* make guest appearances?

Answers to page 403

TV CHEFS 2: **1.** Emma Forbes **2.** Simon Bates and Gillian Miles **3.** Keith Floyd **4.** Fanny and Johnnie Cradock **5.** 1990 **6.** Jennifer Paterson and Clarissa Dickson Wright **7.** Motorcycle and sidecar **8.** *Friends For Dinner* **9.** Gary Rhodes **10.** Delia Smith **11.** Antony Worrall Thompson **12.** Henry Kelly **13.** Philip Harben **14.** Rick Stein **15.** Nick Nairn **16.** Antony Worrall Thompson

TV Pot Luck 10

Answers on page 400

1. In the Channel 4 series *Faking It*, Ed Devlin had to convince a panel of experts that he was what?
2. Lightning, Warrior and Trojan all appeared on which show?
3. Who demonstrated rural crafts in *Out of Town*?
4. Which former *Tomorrow's World* presenter used to be married to Keith Chegwin?
5. What is the key factor to buying a house according to Kirstie Allsopp and Phil Spencer?
6. Les Dennis, Victoria Wood and Jim Davidson are all graduates of which TV talent show?
7. What is Miss Piggy's surname?
8. Who played bus driver Will Green in *Happy Birthday Shakespeare*?
9. Which arts programme was the predecessor of *The South Bank Show*?
10. Who presented *We Love TV*?
11. Who was the wordy chairman of *The Good Old Days*?
12. Which current BBC weatherman made his debut back in 1974?
13. What was the title of Jill Dando's last series?
14. Who is Sacha Baron Cohen's alter ego?
15. Who adopted Corky in *Circus Boy*?
16. Who presented the BBC magazine series *Kaleidoscope*?

Answers to page 400

SOAPS 9: **1.** Three – Kylie Flinker, Sasha Close and Melissa Bell **2.** Brian **3.** Nina Harris **4.** Bel **5.** Dennis Tanner **6.** Clayton Farlow **7.** *Miracles Take Longer* **8.** Wendy Richard **9.** *United!* **10.** Carly Morris **11.** Paul Fox **12.** Norman Harrington **13.** Patterson **14.** The Dog and Pond **15.** Ian Harmon **16.** Courtney

TV Chefs 2

Answers on page 401

1. Which all-round presenter made her TV debut in the cookery slot on *Going Live!*?
2. Who were the original hosts of *Food and Drink*?
3. Which garrulous TV chef was *Far Flung*?
4. Which Fifties TV cooks wrote the 'Bon Viveur' column in the *Daily Telegraph*?
5. In which year did *Masterchef* begin?
6. Who were television's *Two Fat Ladies*?
7. What was their usual mode of transport?
8. In which series does a leading chef assist with a dinner party?
9. Which chef introduced his *New British Classics*?
10. Which TV cook's first programme was *Family Fare* in 1973?
11. Who succeeded Michael Barry as head chef on *Food and Drink*?
12. Apart from Chris Kelly, which other Kelly has presented *Food and Drink*?
13. Who presented *What's Cooking* and *The Tools of Cookery*?
14. Who went on a *Seafood Odyssey*?
15. Which Nick is a TV chef?
16. Which TV chef is known to his friends as 'Woz'?

Answers to page 401

COMEDY 12: **1.** *The Fast Show* **2.** *Steptoe and Son* **3.** *Vic Reeves' Big Night Out* **4.** Paul Merton **5.** Bob Monkhouse **6.** *Love Thy Neighbour* **7.** Richard **8.** Ursula **9.** Manchester **10.** *Comic Relief* **11.** *Now – Something Else* **12.** *Soap* **13.** A hospital **14.** Mrs Merton **15.** Lord Rustless **16.** *Roseanne*

Indie 3

Answers on page 406

1. Who found their way to 'Hope Street' in 1995?
2. Which was the first Lightning Seeds single to make the UK top twenty?
3. Which lead singer with The Verve has been concentrating on a solo career?
4. Which impersonator appeared on the Manic Street Preachers' album 'Everything Must Go'?
5. Who did Jarvis Cocker walk home from school in 'Disco 2000'?
6. What was the title of The Smiths' first album?
7. Which actor did the narration on the Blur single 'Parklife'?
8. Which characters from *The X Files* gave Catatonia their first chart success?
9. Who had a hit with 'Trouble' in 2000?
10. Who asked: 'Why Does It Always Rain On Me'?
11. 'Supersonic' was which band's first UK hit?
12. Which band were named Best Newcomers at the 1995 Brit Awards?
13. Which band released the album 'Jollification'?
14. Which singer released an album of collaborations entitled 'Mali Music' in 2002?
15. Danny Goffey, Gary Coombes and Mickey Quinn were the original members of which band?
16. Which Manic Street Preachers' single was dedicated to a photographer friend of the band who had committed suicide?

Answers to page 406

GARAGE 1: **1.** Romina Johnson **2.** DJ Luck and MC Neat **3.** Truesteppers **4.** Misteeq **5.** Ashley Walters **6.** Melanie Blatt **7.** Craig David **8.** Bomfunk MCs **9.** 'Woman Trouble' **10.** Donell Jones and Brian Harvey **11.** Finland **12.** 'Fill Me In' **13.** DJ Luck and MC Neat **14.** Oxide and Neutrino **15.** Break dancing **16.** 'Lickin' On Both Sides'

Eurovision 2

Answers on page 407

1. Which country's 1960 entry, 'Voi-Voi', was an arrangement of a traditional Lapp reindeer-herding call?
2. Which country boycotted the 1981 contest, saying that it was too old-fashioned?
3. Which country blacked out Israel's victorious 1978 entry?
4. Who was 'A Man Without Love' for the UK in the 1966 contest?
5. Which country called their 1977 entry 'Boom Boom Boomerang' in protest at inane Eurovision song titles?
6. Which blonde actress came tenth for the UK in 1991?
7. In which year did the UK win the Eurovision for the first time?
8. Who won for Monaco in 1971 with 'Un Banc, Un Arbre, Une Rue'?
9. Which country gained their first win in the contest in 2001?
10. Which transsexual won for Israel in 1998?
11. Where did Lynsey De Paul and Mike Moran finish with 'Rock Bottom' in 1977?
12. Which nation achieved an unprecedented hat-trick of wins between 1992 and 1994?
13. In 1973, which country became the first to retain the Eurovision crown?
14. What was the UK entry when Abba won in 1974?
15. Which country's 1985 entrant was Vikki, followed two years later by Rikki?
16. In 1987, which country's group were referred to by BBC presenter Ray Moore as 'an ugly crowd', thereby sparking a diplomatic row?

Answers to page 407

DISCO 1: **1.** 'How Deep Is Your Love' **2.** Donna Summer **3.** Baccara **4.** 'Night Fever' **5.** 'Stayin' Alive' **6.** John Travolta and Olivia Newton-John **7.** Disco Tex **8.** 'Love To Love You Baby' **9.** Biddu **10.** 'I Love To Love (But My Baby Loves To Dance)' **11.** Baccara **12.** 'I Feel Love' **13.** 'Down Deep Inside' **14.** Seven **15.** 'Sorry I'm A Lady' **16.** The Electric Dolls

Garage 1

Answers on page 404

1. Who featured on Artful Dodger's single 'Movin' Too Fast'?
2. Who had a hit with 'A Little Bit Of Luck'?
3. Dane Bowers sang with which Garage band?
4. Which group released 'All I Want'?
5. Which member of So Solid Crew was sent to prison for 18 months in March 2002?
6. Which member of All Saints sang on Artful Dodger's 2001 single 'TwentyFourSeven'?
7. Who had hits with '7 Days' and 'Walking Away'?
8. Which band had a hit with 'Freestyler'?
9. Robbie Craig and Craig David sang on which Artful Dodger single?
10. Which two male artists sang on 'True Step Tonight'?
11. Bomfunk MCs are from which country?
12. What was Craig David's first solo single?
13. Who released 'Piano Loco'?
14. Who sampled the *Casualty* theme tune in one of their singles?
15. What type of dancing do Bomfunk MCs feature in their performances?
16. What was the title of Misteeq's first album?

Answers to page 404

INDIE 3: **1.** The Levellers **2.** 'Pure' **3.** Richard Ashcroft **4.** 'Elvis Impersonator' **5.** Deborah **6.** 'The Smiths' **7.** Phil Daniels **8.** 'Mulder And Scully' **9.** Coldplay **10.** Travis **11.** Oasis **12.** Oasis **13.** The Lightning Seeds **14.** Damon Albarn **15.** Supergrass **16.** 'Kevin Carter'

Disco 1

Answers on page 405

1. Which was the first Bee Gees single to be released from *Saturday Night Fever*?
2. Which disco queen was born LaDonna Andrea Gaines?
3. Maria Mendiola and Mayte Mateus were better known as which duo?
4. Which disco record did The Bee Gees take to number one in April 1978?
5. Which Bee Gees hit did N-Trance take into the charts 17 years later?
6. Which Seventies duo's first two singles reached number one in the UK?
7. Who sang with The Sex-O-Lettes?
8. Which Donna Summer hit was inspired by a re-issue of 'Je T'Aime…Moi Non Plus'?
9. Which Indian producer worked with Tina Charles?
10. Which song did Tina Charles take to number one in 1976?
11. Who became the first Spanish act to hit number one in the UK?
12. Which Donna Summer record was at number one when Elvis Presley died?
13. Which Donna Summer hit was taken from the film *The Deep*?
14. How many Bee Gees songs were on the 'Saturday Night Fever' album?
15. What was Baccara's follow-up to 'Yes, Sir, I Can Boogie'?
16. Who originally recorded 'Dr Love', a disco hit for Tina Charles in 1976?

Answers to page 405

EUROVISION 2: **1.** Norway **2.** Italy **3.** Jordan **4.** Kenneth McKellar **5.** Austria **6.** Samantha Janus **7.** 1967 **8.** Severine **9.** Estonia **10.** Dana International **11.** Second **12.** Ireland **13.** Luxembourg **14.** 'Long Live Love' (Olivia Newton-John) **15.** United Kingdom **16.** Turkey

One-Hit Wonders 4

Answers on page 410

1. Whose only UK hit was the 1975 single 'Eighteen With A Bullet'?
2. In 1957, which song gave The Southlanders their only UK top twenty hit?
3. Which 1968 song gave The Paper Dolls their only chart success?
4. Which Sixties namesakes of a Nineties heavy rock band had their only hit with 'Rainbow Chaser' in 1968?
5. Which song from *Paint Your Wagon* gave actor Lee Marvin an unexpected number one?
6. Who insisted: 'I'm Gonna Run Away From You' in 1971?
7. Which two disc jockeys parodied 'Convoy' as Laurie Lingo and The Dipsticks in 1976?
8. Whose only chart success was with the 1960 Eurovision Song Contest entry 'Looking High, High, High'?
9. Who was 'Swinging On A Star' in 1963?
10. Which forerunners of 10cc got to number two with 'Neanderthal Man' in 1970?
11. Who sang about 'Johnny Reggae' in 1971?
12. Who begged: 'Gimme Dat Ding' in 1970?
13. With which song did The Fantastics chart in 1971?
14. Who covered The Honeycombs' 'Have I The Right' in 1977?
15. Whose only chart action was with 'Mr Bass Man' in 1963?
16. Who reached number 14 in the UK charts with 'That's Nice' in 1966?

Answers to page 410

CHART TOPPERS 6: **1.** 1966 **2.** 1974 **3.** 1984 **4.** 1986 **5.** 1957 **6.** 1998 **7.** 1995 **8.** 1977 **9.** 1966 **10.** 1972 **11.** 1980 **12.** 1984 **13.** 1993 **14.** 1959 **15.** 1967 **16.** 1964

Lyrics 4

Answers on page 411

From which songs are the following lyrics taken?

1. 'Once upon a time I was falling in love, now I'm only falling apart'
2. 'I'm on the hunt down after you'
3. 'When they said you was high-classed, well that was just a lie'
4. 'How many heartaches must I stand before I find the love to let me live again'
5. 'Her eyes were making silent demands as her hair came undone in my hands'
6. 'Bittersweet memories, that is all I'm taking with me'
7. 'Every night I'm lying in bed holding you close in my dreams'
8. 'Some people live with the fear of a touch and the anger of having been a fool'
9. ''Cause the boy with the cold hard cash is always Mr Right'
10. 'Maybe I will never be all the things that I want to be'
11. 'But he's a liar and I'm not sure about you'
12. 'The young dreams should be dreamed together'
13. 'The Sweeney's doing ninety cos they've got the word to go and get a gang of villains in a shed up at Heathrow'
14. 'All the leaves are brown and the sky is grey'
15. 'Every morning I would see her waiting at the stop, sometimes she'd shop and she would show me what she'd bought'
16. 'Some girls like to run around, like to handle everything they see'

Answers to page 411

ROBBIE WILLIAMS 1: **1.** 'Freedom' **2.** 'Life Thru A Lens' **3.** Guy Chambers **4.** Tom Jones **5.** 1997 **6.** 'Life Thru A Lens' **7.** Barry Davies **8.** 'Millennium' **9.** 'No Regrets' **10.** 'I've Been Expecting You' **11.** Liam Gallagher **12.** Double-glazing **13.** Nicole Kidman **14.** 'Back For Good' **15.** 3 **16.** Port Vale

Chart Toppers 6

Answers on page 408

In which years did the following tracks reach number one in the UK charts?

1. 'Pretty Flamingo' (Manfred Mann)
2. 'Jealous Mind' (Alvin Stardust)
3. 'Freedom' (Wham!)
4. 'Papa Don't Preach' (Madonna)
5. 'Diana' (Paul Anka)
6. 'Millennium' (Robbie Williams)
7. 'Back For Good' (Take That)
8. 'So You Win Again' (Hot Chocolate)
9. 'Strangers In The Night' (Frank Sinatra)
10. 'School's Out' (Alice Cooper)
11. 'Crying' (Don McLean)
12. 'The Reflex' (Duran Duran)
13. 'No Limit' (2 Unlimited)
14. 'Dream Lover' (Bobby Darin)
15. 'A Whiter Shade Of Pale' (Procul Harum)
16. 'The House Of The Rising Sun' (The Animals)

Answers to page 408

ONE-HIT WONDERS 4: **1.** Pete Wingfield **2.** 'Alone' **3.** 'Something Here In My Heart (Keeps A Tellin' Me No)' **4.** Nirvana **5.** 'Wand'rin' Star' **6.** Tami Lynn **7.** Paul Burnett and Dave Lee Travis **8.** Bryan Johnson **9.** Big Dee Irwin **10.** Hotlegs **11.** The Piglets **12.** Pipkins **13.** 'Something Old, Something New' **14.** The Dead End Kids **15.** Johnny Cymbal **16.** Neil Christian

Robbie Williams 1

Answers on page 409

1. Which cover of a George Michael song gave Robbie Williams his first solo hit?
2. What was the autobiographical title of his first solo album?
3. Who is Robbie's usual co-writer?
4. With whom did Robbie duet at the 1998 Brit Awards?
5. In which year was 'Angels' released?
6. From which album was 'Angels' taken?
7. Which sports commentator spoke on the video for 'She's The One'?
8. Which single sampled the theme from the James Bond movie *You Only Live Twice*?
9. Neil Tennant and Neil Hannon did guest vocals on which single?
10. Which was Robbie's number one album of 1998?
11. Which rival band member has Robbie publicly challenged to a fight?
12. What did Robbie used to sell for a living before joining Take That?
13. With whom did Robbie Williams duet on the single 'Somethin' Stupid'?
14. What was Robbie's last single with Take That?
15. What was the highest UK chart position of 'Let Me Entertain You'?
16. Which football team does Robbie support?

Answers to page 409

LYRICS 4: **1.** 'Total Eclipse Of The Heart' (Bonnie Tyler) **2.** 'Hungry Like The Wolf' (Duran Duran) **3.** 'Hound Dog' (Elvis Presley) **4.** 'You Can't Hurry Love' (The Supremes) **5.** 'Oh Yeah' (Ash) **6.** 'I Will Always Love You' (Whitney Houston) **7.** 'The Best Of My Love' (The Eagles) **8.** 'An Innocent Man' (Billy Joel) **9.** 'Material Girl' (Madonna) **10.** 'Live Forever' (Oasis) **11.** 'There's A Guy Works Down The Chip Shop Swears He's Elvis' (Kirsty MacColl) **12.** 'The Young Ones' (Cliff Richard) **13.** 'Cool For Cats' (Squeeze) **14.** 'California Dreamin' (Mamas and The Papas) **15.** 'Bus Stop' (The Hollies) **16.** 'She'd Rather Be With Me' (The Turtles)

Cover Versions 3

Answers on page 414

1. Who had a 1979 hit with K.W.S.'s 1992 chart topper 'Please Don't Go'?
2. Which Congregation hit did Paul Young cover in 1990?
3. Which song, previously a hit for Bobby Day in 1958 and Michael Jackson in 1972, was covered by Lolly in 1999?
4. Who recorded the original version of The Commitments' 'Mustang Sally'?
5. Which *EastEnders* re-hashed a Chris Montez hit in 1999?
6. Who had a 1983 hit with a version of Ricky Nelson's 'It's Late'?
7. Who originally recorded 'Freak Me', a 1998 number one for Another Level?
8. Which David Bowie hit did Glamma Kid cover in 1998?
9. Which Kinks song was covered by Kirsty MacColl in 1989?
10. Which Mamas and The Papas song did Bitty McLean take to number six in the UK charts in 1994?
11. Which song links The Ronettes, Dave Edmunds and The Ramones?
12. Which song, a hit for both David Whitfield and Frankie Laine in 1953, also proved successful for Barbara Dickson in 1976?
13. Which Nilsson hit was covered by The Beautiful South?
14. Before The Rolling Stones, who had a hit in the Sixties with 'Harlem Shuffle'?
15. Which sentiment was shared by Stephen Stills in 1971 and Luther Vandross in 1994?
16. Who originally had a UK hit with 'Red Red Wine', a 1983 number one for UB40?

Answers to page 414

NINETIES 3: **1.** Martine McCutcheon **2.** 'Talk On Corners' (The Corrs) **3.** The Beautiful South **4.** 'Say What You Want' **5.** Sharleen Spiteri **6.** Shirley Manson (Garbage) **7.** 'I Believe I Can Fly' **8.** 'Ice Ice Baby' **9.** Run-DMC vs. Jason Nevins **10.** Erasure **11.** 'Australia' **12.** Crystal Waters **13.** 'Sunchyme' **14.** 'A Red Letter Day' **15.** 'Cotton Eye Joe' **16.** Tina Turner

Music Pot Luck 12

Answers on page 415

1. Which eccentric singer from Jethro Tull was often witnessed wandering around Luton with a lampshade on his head?
2. Which airport did Cats U.K. sing about in 1979?
3. And which Hampshire city was the subject of a Mike Oldfield instrumental?
4. Which band chose their name from an old newspaper story about Frankie Vaughan moving into films?
5. Which American singer, who had a UK number one in 1976, was once ranked joint 85th in the world for the high jump?
6. Which actor is generally thought to be the subject of Carly Simon's 'You're So Vain'?
7. Which folk singer once gave the kiss of life to a sheep?
8. Which district of London did Suggs sing about in 1995?
9. What was the name of Wayne Fontana's backing group?
10. Who originally recorded Madness's 'One Step Beyond…'?
11. Who was the leader of The Bonzo Dog Doo-Dah Band?
12. What happened while Calgary's KFSM radio station played Carole King's 'I Feel The Earth Move' in 1971?
13. Which female artist helped out with the vocals on Peter Gabriel's 'Games Without Frontiers'?
14. Who recorded the album 'Oxygene'?
15. What is Dave Dee's surname?
16. Which enigmatic frontman of the Eighties started his career as a music reviewer with *Record Mirror*?

Answers to page 415

NEW ROMANTICS 1: **1.** Bow Wow Wow **2.** Adam and The Ants **3.** Reformation **4.** David Sylvian **5.** 'Planet Earth' **6.** John Foxx **7.** 'No Regrets' **8.** Steve Strange **9.** 'Rio' **10.** 'Is There Something I Should Know' **11.** Tony Hadley **12.** Martin Kemp **13.** Modern Romance **14.** 'Goody Two Shoes' **15.** 'Fade To Grey' **16.** 1983

Nineties 3

Answers on page 412

1. Which ex-*EastEnder* enjoyed a 'Perfect Moment' in 1999?
2. Which was the biggest-selling UK album of 1998?
3. Whose 1998 album was titled 'Quench'?
4. What was Texas's first UK top ten hit of the 1990s?
5. Who is the lead singer with Texas?
6. Which Scottish singer with a band used to work in Miss Selfridge before joining Goodbye Mr Mackenzie and then Angelfish?
7. What was R. Kelly's first UK number one?
8. Which 1990 chart topper sampled Queen and David Bowie's 'Under Pressure'?
9. Who had a number one with 'It's Like That' in 1998?
10. Who had a 1994 album called 'I Say I Say I Say'?
11. Which continent did Manic Street Preachers sing about in 1996?
12. Which singer had a hit with 'Gypsy Woman' in the early 1990s?
13. Which Dario G single sampled Dream Academy's 'Life In A Northern Town'?
14. Which Pet Shop Boys hit of 1997 features the Choral Academy of Moscow?
15. Bob Wills and his Texas Playboys recorded the original version of which 1994 line-dancing number one?
16. Who did Rod Stewart join in a 1990 duet for 'It Takes Two'?

Answers to page 412

COVER VERSIONS 3: **1.** KC and the Sunshine Band **2.** 'Softly Whispering I Love You' **3.** 'Rockin' Robin' **4.** Wilson Pickett **5.** Barbara Windsor and Mike Reid **6.** Shakin' Stevens **7.** Silk **8.** 'Fashion' **9.** 'Days' **10.** 'Dedicated To The One I Love' **11.** 'Baby I Love You' **12.** 'Answer Me' **13.** 'Everybody's Talkin'' **14.** Bob and Earl **15.** 'Love The One You're With' **16.** Jimmy James and The Vagabonds

New Romantics 1

Answers on page 413

1. Which act did Malcolm McLaren form from Adam Ant's original backing group?
2. Which band's debut album was titled 'Dirk Wears White Sox'?
3. On which music label did Spandau Ballet record until 1988?
4. Who was the lead singer of Japan?
5. What was the title of Duran Duran's first single?
6. Who did Midge Ure replace as singer with Ultravox?
7. Which Walker Brothers' hit did Midge Ure cover in 1982?
8. Who fronted Visage?
9. From which Duran Duran album was 'Hungry Like The Wolf' taken?
10. Which Duran Duran single went straight into the UK charts at number one in March 1983?
11. Which member of Spandau Ballet once featured in a photo-love story in *My Guy* magazine?
12. Which member of Spandau Ballet had been a promising footballer and had trained with Arsenal in 1975?
13. 'Everybody Salsa' was the first UK hit for which band?
14. Which song gave Adam Ant his first solo number one?
15. Which was Visage's biggest-selling single in the UK?
16. In which year did Spandau Ballet release the album 'True'?

Answers to page 413

MUSIC POT LUCK 12: **1.** Ian Anderson **2.** 'Luton Airport' **3.** Portsmouth **4.** Frankie Goes To Hollywood **5.** Johnny Mathis **6.** Warren Beatty **7.** Roy Harper **8.** 'Camden Town' **9.** The Mindbenders **10.** Prince Buster and The All-Stars **11.** Viv Stanshall **12.** The studio collapsed **13.** Kate Bush **14.** Jean-Michel Jarre **15.** Harman **16.** Morrissey

Name Changes 6

Answers on page 418

1. Which rap pioneer changed his name from Joseph Saddler?
2. Which New Romantics were previously known as The Makers?
3. Stanley Kirk Burrell is the real name of which rap artist?
4. Which colourful American band used to be known as Wicked Lester?
5. Which Sixties duo were originally known as The Paramours?
6. The Zips, The Innocents and Fire of London were previous names of which band that had a powerful hit about a European city in 1981?
7. Which rap performer changed his name from Rexton Fernando Gordon?
8. Which frontman of an Eighties band was formerly known as Steve Harrington?
9. What was Ricky Nelson's real Christian name?
10. Which Seventies band were previously known as The Shakedown Sound and Silence before taking their new name from a 1967 novel by Willard Manus?
11. Which US singer of the Sixties was born Thomas Gregory Jackson?
12. Who changed his name from Richard Starkey?
13. Which band used to be known as Café Racers before finding a name which reflected their financial plight?
14. Which singer/songwriter was born Henry John Deutschendorf?
15. Which American singer of the Fifties and Sixties changed his name from Walden Robert Cassotto?
16. Whose full name is Robert Thomas Velline?

Answers to page 418

CLASSICAL GAS 2: **1.** Hungarian **2.** Mendelssohn **3.** Saint-Saëns **4.** Richard Wagner **5.** Ten **6.** 31 **7.** *The Golden Cockerel* **8.** Polish **9.** Six **10.** Elgar **11.** *Almira* **12.** Handel **13.** Haydn **14.** Mozart **15.** Debussy **16.** Stravinsky

Cliff Richard 1

Answers on page 419

1. Who wrote 'Living Doll'?

2. What was the name of the teenage rock star Cliff played in *Expresso Bongo*?

3. Which of Cliff's number ones was co-written by the son of a comedian?

4. Who did Cliff join on stage at Earls Court in June 1966?

5. With which song did Cliff come third in the 1973 Eurovision Song Contest?

6. In which year did Cliff sing at Wimbledon during a break for rain at the tennis?

7. Who originally recorded 'I'm Lookin' Out The Window'?

8. From which film was 'On The Beach' taken?

9. Which 1960 number one was chosen by members of Cliff's fan club to be his next single?

10. Which 1979 hit provided Cliff with his first UK number one in over a decade?

11. Who didn't live here any more in 1980?

12. Which 1976 hit was originally recorded by a *Crackerjack* presenter?

13. Which of Cliff's hits was written by Compo from *Last of the Summer Wine*?

14. In which year did Cliff release the album 'I'm Nearly Famous'?

15. In which Shakespeare play did Cliff perform with old schoolfriends in 1974?

16. Which 1964 release had been a US hit for Johnny Mathis in 1957?

Answers to page 419

RAP 1: **1.** 2Pac **2.** Outkast **3.** Eminem **4.** Dr Dre **5.** Dirty Dozen **6.** Jay-Z **7.** Marshall Mathers **8.** Bloodhound Gang **9.** Lil' Kim and Missy Elliott **10.** Missy Elliott **11.** Shaggy **12.** Five **13.** Puff Daddy **14.** Lil' Bow Wow **15.** Eminem **16.** Nelly

Classical Gas 2

Answers on page 416

1. What nationality was Liszt?
2. Who composed *Fingal's Cave*?
3. Which French composer wrote *Carnival Of The Animals*?
4. Whose operatic works included *Tannhäuser*, *Lohengrin* and *Tristan and Isolde*?
5. How many symphonies did Schubert compose?
6. How old was Schubert when he died?
7. Which Rimsky-Korsakov opera, written in 1907, was banned until 1909 because it was considered too satirical?
8. What nationality was Chopin?
9. How many Brandenburg Concertos are there?
10. Who composed *Pomp and Circumstance*?
11. What was the title of Handel's first opera?
12. Which German-born composer moved to England and became a British subject in 1726?
13. Who composed the 'Emperor's Hymn', adopted as the Austrian, and later the German, national anthem?
14. Who composed *The Magic Flute*?
15. Which composer was born in the small French town of Saint-Germain-en-Laye in 1862?
16. Which Russian composer became an American citizen in 1945?

Answers to page 416

NAME CHANGES 6: **1.** Grandmaster Flash **2.** Spandau Ballet **3.** M.C. Hammer **4.** Kiss **5.** The Righteous Brothers **6.** Ultravox **7.** Shabba Ranks **8.** Steve Strange **9.** Eric **10.** Mott The Hoople **11.** Tommy James **12.** Ringo Starr **13.** Dire Straits **14.** John Denver **15.** Bobby Darin **16.** Bobby Vee

Rap 1

Answers on page 417

1. Which rap artist released the single 'Changes'?
2. Who had to say sorry to Ms Jackson?
3. Who is also known as the Real Slim Shady?
4. Who released 'The Next Episode'?
5. What does D12 stand for?
6. Who sampled parts from the film *Oliver* in one of his singles?
7. What is Eminem's real name?
8. Who had a single titled 'The Bad Touch'?
9. Which female rap artists sang on 'Lady Marmalade' in 2001?
10. Who had a thing about 'Hot Boys'?
11. 'Angel' and 'It Wasn't Me' were singles by which rap artist?
12. How many members are there in Bloodhound Gang?
13. Which American rapper used to date Jennifer Lopez?
14. Who claims to be 'all that and a bag of chips'?
15. Who was the main singer with D12 on the 2001 single 'Purple Hills'?
16. Whose singles have included 'Country Grammar' and 'E.1'?

Answers to page 417

CLIFF RICHARD 1: **1.** Lionel Bart **2.** Bongo Herbert **3.** 'Please Don't Tease' (written by Bruce Welch and Pete Chester, son of Charlie Chester) **4.** Billy Graham **5.** 'Power To All Our Friends' **6.** 1996 **7.** Peggy Lee **8.** *Wonderful Life* **9.** 'Please Don't Tease' **10.** 'We Don't Talk Anymore' **11.** 'Carrie' **12.** 'Devil Woman' (originally recorded by Kristine aka Christine Holmes) **13.** 'Marianne' (written by Bill Owen) **14.** 1976 **15.** *A Midsummer Night's Dream* (he played Bottom) **16.** 'The Twelfth Of Never'

Fifties 3

Answers on page 422

1. Who had a UK number one in 1958 with 'It's All In The Game'?
2. Which pianist started life as Trevor Stanford?
3. Which husband and wife team wrote 'Bye Bye Love'?
4. Which laid-back singer had hits with 'Catch A Falling Star' and 'Magic Moments'?
5. Which 1957 Everly Brothers' song was banned from airplay in Boston, Massachusetts, because its lyrics were deemed mildly suggestive?
6. Who was 'Putting On The Style' in 1957?
7. Dick James, Gary Miller and Frankie Vaughan all covered which US hit for Joe Valino?
8. What was the name of Frankie Lymon's backing group?
9. Who sang about her 'Dreamboat' in 1955?
10. Which singing sisters backed Frankie Vaughan on 'Come Softly To Me'?
11. The theme from which American B-film provided Jimmy Young with a UK number one in 1955?
12. Which title, reminiscent of a casino game, gave Russ Conway a UK chart topper in 1959?
13. Who transformed himself from an Isle of Wight milkman named Terence Perkins into a Sixties singing heart-throb?
14. Such diverse talents as Bobby Darin and Charlie Drake both had 1958 hits with which song?
15. Who reached number one in 1958 with 'Hoots Mon'?
16. What was the original title of Buddy Holly's 'Peggy Sue'?

Answers to page 422

FILM TRACKS 4: **1.** 'The Time Has Come' **2.** 'Pinball Wizard' **3.** 'On Our Own' **4.** 'Gotham City' **5.** Two – 'Goldfinger' and 'Diamonds Are Forever' **6.** *Terminator 2 Judgement Day* **7.** *The Three Musketeers* ('All For Love') **8.** Tina Turner **9.** *War of the Worlds* **10.** *Grease* **11.** Moby **12.** The B-52s **13.** 'Don't Cry For Me Argentina' **14.** *Austin Powers – The Spy Who Shagged Me* **15.** Gladys Knight **16.** Diana Ross and Lionel Richie

Queen 1

Answers on page 423

1. Who did Queen support on their 1973 UK tour?
2. What were Freddie Mercury, Brian May and Roger Taylor still calling themselves in the summer of 1973?
3. What was Queen's first US hit single?
4. Which Queen single was taken from the film *Highlander*?
5. What was the title of Queen's number one album of 1975?
6. Constant airplay from which Capital Radio DJ helped force EMI to release the six-minute 'Bohemian Rhapsody' as a single?
7. With which song did 'Bohemian Rhapsody' tie as Best British Pop Single (1952–77) at the British Record Industry Britannia Awards in 1977?
8. In which year did Freddie Mercury die?
9. How many weeks did 'Bohemian Rhapsody' spend at the top of the UK charts in 1975?
10. Which single did Freddie Mercury write while he was taking a bath in Munich's Hilton Hotel?
11. In what subject did John Deacon graduate with first-class honours?
12. Which single prevented 'Radio Ga Ga' from being a UK number one?
13. Who said of Freddie Mercury's performance at Live Aid: 'It was the perfect stage for Freddie. He could ponce about in front of the whole world'?
14. In which year was the album 'A Kind Of Magic' released?
15. Which 1976 single reached number two in the UK charts?
16. Which Queen single was the soundtrack of a futuristic 1980 movie?

Answers to page 423

SEVENTIES 4: **1.** The Stranglers **2.** Pickettywitch **3.** R. Dean Taylor **4.** Focus **5.** The Pretenders **6.** Sweet **7.** The Chi-Lites **8.** Carole King **9.** Lulu **10.** David Cassidy **11.** Status Quo **12.** Leo Sayer **13.** The Nolans **14.** The Tams **15.** 10cc **16.** Elvis Presley

Film Tracks 4

Answers on page 420

1. Which Adam Faith single of 1961 was taken from the film *What a Whopper!*?
2. Which track from *Tommy* was a hit for both The Who and Elton John?
3. Which Bobby Brown hit of 1999 featured in *Ghostbusters II*?
4. Which R. Kelly hit came from the film *Batman and Robin*?
5. How many Bond movie themes has Shirley Bassey sung?
6. From which film was the Guns N' Roses single 'You Could Be Mine' taken?
7. Bryan Adams, Rod Stewart and Sting combined for the theme song from which 1994 film?
8. Who had a 1985 top three hit with 'We Don't Need Another Hero' from *Thunderdome*?
9. Justin Hayward's hit 'Forever Autumn' came from which film?
10. Which film featured 'Summer Nights'?
11. Who had a hit in 1997 with his own version of the theme from the Bond film *Tomorrow Never Dies*?
12. Who had a 1994 hit with the theme song from *The Flintstones*?
13. Which UK top ten hit of 1996 for Madonna was taken from the film *Evita*?
14. Madonna's 'Beautiful Stranger' featured in which Mike Myers movie?
15. Which former Motown artist had a 1989 hit with the theme from the Bond movie *Licence To Kill*?
16. Which duo had a 1981 hit with 'Endless Love' from the film of the same name?

Answers to page 420

FIFTIES 3: **1.** Tommy Edwards **2.** Russ Conway **3.** Boudleaux and Felice Bryant **4.** Perry Como **5.** 'Wake Up Little Susie' **6.** Lonnie Donegan **7.** 'Garden Of Eden' **8.** The Teenagers **9.** Alma Cogan **10.** The Kaye Sisters **11.** *Unchained* ('Unchained Melody') **12.** 'Roulette' **13.** Craig Douglas **14.** 'Splish Splash' **15.** Lord Rockingham's XI **16.** 'Cindy-Lou'

Seventies 4

Answers on page 421

Which artists had UK hits with the following tracks in the Seventies?

1. 'Something Better Change'
2. 'That Same Old Feeling'
3. 'There's A Ghost In My House'
4. 'Sylvia'
5. 'Kid'
6. 'Co-Co'
7. 'Homely Girl'
8. 'It's Too Late'
9. 'The Man Who Sold The World'
10. 'The Puppy Song'
11. 'Rockin' All Over The World'
12. 'You Make Me Feel Like Dancing'
13. 'I'm In The Mood For Dancing'
14. 'Hey Girl Don't Bother Me'
15. 'Good Morning Judge'
16. 'Burning Love'

Answers to page 421

QUEEN 1: **1.** Mott The Hoople **2.** Larry Lurex **3.** 'Killer Queen' **4.** 'A Kind Of Magic' **5.** 'A Night At The Opera' **6.** Kenny Everett **7.** 'A Whiter Shade Of Pale' **8.** 1991 **9.** Nine **10.** 'Crazy Little Thing Called Love' **11.** Electronics **12.** 'Relax' **13.** Bob Geldof **14.** 1986 **15.** 'Somebody To Love' **16.** 'Flash' (*Flash Gordon*)

Manchester United 1

Answers on page 426

1. Who was Manchester United's top scorer in 1999–2000?
2. For which Spanish club did Mark Hughes play?
3. Which United player made his League debut at the age of 16 in 1950?
4. Who joined United from Celtic for £56,000 in 1963?
5. Who brought United's first European Cup campaign to an end at the semi-final stage in 1957?
6. And on which ground did United play the home leg of that tie?
7. What was Peter Schmeichel's first club?
8. Who strolled from Highbury to Old Trafford for £120,000 in October 1972?
9. Who kept goal for United in the 1948 FA Cup final?
10. Which player joined United for a club record £18,000 from Bradford Park Avenue in 1949?
11. Which left-winger of the 1970s played for Southall and Millwall before moving to United?
12. Which Hungarian club beat United in the quarter-finals of the UEFA Cup in 1985?
13. In United's treble season of 1998–9 (League, FA Cup and European Champions' League), who knocked them out of the League Cup?
14. Who was United's leading marksmen in their Second Division season of 1974–5?
15. In which year did Tommy Docherty become United manager?
16. How many League appearances did Bobby Charlton make for United?

Answers to page 426

EUROPEAN CUPS 4: **1.** Lens **2.** Paris **3.** Real Madrid **4.** Ajax **5.** Celta Vigo **6.** Fabio Capello **7.** 1992 **8.** Antwerp **9.** Mario Basler **10.** 83 **11.** Munich 1860 **12.** Bobby Moncur **13.** 1960 **14.** Eintracht Frankfurt **15.** AC Milan **16.** 1985

FA Cup 5

Answers on page 427

1. Who scored for both sides within a minute in the 1946 FA Cup final?
2. Which Midland League team held Spurs to a goalless draw at White Hart Lane in the first round of the 1922–3 competition?
3. By what score did Spurs win the replay?
4. Who kept goal for Watford in the 1984 final?
5. Which Queens Park Rangers defender was the first Jamaican-born player to appear in an FA Cup final?
6. Which manager led Newcastle United to six FA Cup finals?
7. Who scored a hat-trick for Notts County in the 1894 Cup final?
8. Which goalkeeper won a Cup-winners' medal with Manchester United yet played just two League matches for the club?
9. Who played against Liverpool in the 1971 final and for them in the 1977 final?
10. Which future England manager was a member of the Spurs team humbled by York City in the FA Cup in 1955?
11. And which future England manager was a member of the Chelsea team which went down 2–1 at home to Crewe Alexandra in a 1961 tie?
12. Which Argentinian grabbed the winner for Spurs in the 1981 final?
13. Who was manager of Brighton when they crashed 4–0 at home to Isthmian Leaguers Walton & Hersham in 1973?
14. In which year's final did the ball burst for the first time?
15. And when did it burst for the second time?
16. And which club was involved in both finals?

Answers to page 427

FOOTBALL LEAGUE 6: **1.** West Bromwich Albion **2.** Tottenham Hotspur **3.** Liverpool **4.** Hereford United **5.** Leyton Orient **6.** Carlisle United **7.** Chelsea and Luton **8.** Millwall **9.** Chelsea **10.** Oldham Athletic **11.** Stoke **12.** David Hopkin **13.** Graham Taylor **14.** Wigan Athletic **15.** Geoff Horsfield **16.** Three

European Cups 4

Answers on page 424

Answers on page 424

1. Which French club embarked on their first Champions' League campaign in 1998–9?
2. In which city did Liverpool lift the European Cup in 1981?
3. And which Spanish team did they beat in the final?
4. Who notched a hat-trick of European Cup successes between 1971 and 1973?
5. Which Spanish team knocked Liverpool out of the 1998–9 UEFA Cup?
6. Who was coach of AC Milan when they defeated Barcelona in the 1994 European Champions' League final?
7. When was the Champions' League introduced?
8. Which Belgian team lost to Parma in the final of the 1993 European Cup-Winners' Cup?
9. Who scored Bayern Munich's goal in the 1999 Champions' League final against Manchester United?
10. For how many minutes were Bayern ahead in that match?
11. Who were the first German team to reach the final of the European Cup-Winners' Cup?
12. Who captained Newcastle to Fairs Cup glory in 1969?
13. When was the only year that Rangers reached the semi-finals of the European Cup?
14. Who knocked them out of the competition?
15. Which team reached the Champions' League final in 1993, 1994 and 1995?
16. When did Juventus win the European Cup for the first time?

Answers to page 424

MANCHESTER UNITED 1: **1.** Dwight Yorke **2.** Barcelona **3.** Jeff Whitefoot **4.** Pat Crerand **5.** Real Madrid **6.** Maine Road **7.** Hvidovre **8.** George Graham **9.** Jack Crompton **10.** Johnny Downie **11.** Gordon Hill **12.** Videoton **13.** Tottenham Hotspur **14.** Stuart Pearson **15.** 1972 **16.** 606

Football League 6

Answers on page 425

1. Which club won their only League Championship in 1919–20?

2. Based on final League positions, which was the most successful club in the 1960s?

3. And which was the most successful of the 1970s?

4. In 1973, which club gained promotion from the Fourth Division in their first season in the League?

5. Which Third Division club lost play-off finals in 1999 and 2001?

6. In 1974–5, which club played in the top division for the only time?

7. With whom were they relegated at the end of that season?

8. In 1988, which London club reached Division One for the first time in their 103-year history?

9. Five players from which London club left the pitch before the end of a match at Blackpool in 1931 because they were cold?

10. Which Lancashire club used to play at Sheepfoot Lane?

11. For whom did Eric Skeels make 506 League appearances from 1958 to 1976?

12. Whose goal ten seconds from the end of the 1996–7 First Division play-off final earned Crystal Palace promotion at the expense of Sheffield United?

13. Which future Watford manager played at left-back for Grimsby in a 7–1 defeat at Vicarage Road in 1967?

14. In 1999, who sacked their manager a month after winning a Wembley trophy?

15. Who was Fulham's top scorer in 1998–9?

16. How many First Division games did Stoke City win in 1984–5?

Answers to page 425

FA CUP 5: **1.** Bert Turner (Charlton Athletic) **2.** Worksop Town **3.** 9–0 **4.** Steve Sherwood **5.** Bob Hazell **6.** Frank Watt **7.** Jimmy Logan **8.** Les Sealey **9.** Ray Kennedy **10.** Alf Ramsey **11.** Terry Venables **12.** Ricky Villa **13.** Brian Clough **14.** 1946 **15.** 1947 **16.** Charlton Athletic

Sharpshooters 4

Answers on page 430

1. Who scored 59 League goals in 37 games for Middlesbrough in 1926–7?
2. What nationality is Martin Pringle?
3. Which Manchester United forward scored 16 England goals in 19 appearances during the 1950s?
4. From which Norwegian club did Chelsea sign Tore Andre Flo?
5. Which Bournemouth striker scored against three different Rotherham goalkeepers in a Third Division match at Millmoor in 1972?
6. Which Arsenal player scored on 12 successive first-team appearances in 1994?
7. Which future TV personality scored a hat-trick in two and a half minutes playing for Motherwell at Hibernian in 1959?
8. What nationality is Bayern Munich's Giovane Elber?
9. Which Tottenham player was the League's leading marksman for 1986–7?
10. How many Stirling Albion players scored when they hammered Selkirk 20–0 in a 1984 Scottish FA Cup tie?
11. Which Colombian striker joined Middlesbrough from Deportivo Cali?
12. Who was Millwall's top scorer in 2000–1?
13. For which English club did Gordon Turner score 243 League goals from 1949–64?
14. Which Celtic player topped the Scottish Premier Division scoring charts in 1982–3?
15. Who was Arsenal's top scorer when they won the double in 1970–1?
16. What was Andy Payton's first League club?

Answers to page 430

TRANSFER TRAIL 6: **1.** Alan Mullery **2.** Real Madrid **3.** Salernitana **4.** Lee Bowyer **5.** Manchester United **6.** Barnsley **7.** Peterborough United **8.** Thierry Henry **9.** Middlesbrough **10.** Alan Hudson **11.** Chris Waddle **12.** Coventry City **13.** Tottenham Hotspur **14.** Alfie Conn **15.** Lee Peacock **16.** St Johnstone

Republic of Ireland 2

Answers on page 431

1. Who were Eire's first international opponents in 1924?
2. In which city was that game played?
3. As a player with which club did Shay Given win his first cap?
4. When did Jack Charlton take over as Republic manager?
5. When did Mark Lawrenson win his first international cap?
6. And with which club was he a player at the time?
7. How many times did the Republic lose to England during Jack Charlton's reign?
8. Who scored twice against Malta in 1989 to secure their place in the World Cup finals?
9. Who was Jack Charlton's assistant at the 1994 World Cup?
10. To whom did the Republic lose in Group E at the 1994 World Cup finals?
11. Against which country did Frank Stapleton score in 1990 to set a new goalscoring record for the Republic?
12. Which nation won a decider in Paris to deny the Republic a place in the 1966 World Cup finals?
13. Who did the Republic defeat 3–0 in a World Cup qualifier in October 1989?
14. How many Irish caps did Mick McCarthy win as a player?
15. Which midfielder made his Republic debut against France in 1989 while a player with Norwich City?
16. Who was the first black player to win a cap for the Republic?

Answers to page 431

SCOTTISH SCENE 6: **1.** Rangers **2.** Stirling **3.** Edinburgh City **4.** Vale of Leven **5.** Aberdeen **6.** St Johnstone **7.** Forfar Athletic **8.** Raith Rovers **9.** Heart of Midlothian **10.** Clydebank **11.** Montrose **12.** Dundee Hibernian **13.** Armadale and Bo'ness **14.** Motherwell **15.** Arbroath **16.** Cowdenbeath

Transfer Trail 6

Answers on page 428

1. Which future England international moved from Fulham to Tottenham for £72,500 in March 1964?
2. From whom did Inter Milan sign Christian Panucci for £9 million in 1999?
3. From which Italian club did Liverpool sign Rigobert Song?
4. Who moved from Charlton to Leeds for £2.6 million in 1996?
5. Which club did Bournemouth striker Ted MacDougall join in 1972?
6. From which Yorkshire club did Manchester United sign Tommy Taylor in 1953?
7. With which club did David Seaman make his League debut?
8. Which current Gunner switched from Monaco to Juventus for £11 million in 1999?
9. From which club did Tottenham sign Cyril Knowles of 'Nice One Cyril' fame?
10. Which Chelsea midfielder moved to Stoke for £240,000 in 1974?
11. Who left Tottenham for Marseille in 1989?
12. Which Premiership club was John Hartson unable to save from relegation after joining them in spring 2001?
13. Who paid Newcastle £4.2 million for Ruel Fox in 1995?
14. Which floppy-haired Rangers forward did Spurs sign for £150,000 in July 1974?
15. Which striker did Bristol City recruit from Manchester City for £600,000 in 2000?
16. Which Scottish club bought Billy Dodds from Dundee in 1994?

Answers to page 428

SHARPSHOOTERS 4: **1.** George Camsell **2.** Swedish **3.** Tommy Taylor **4.** Brann Bergen **5.** Brian Clark **6.** Ian Wright **7.** Ian St John **8.** Brazilian **9.** Clive Allen **10.** Nine **11.** Hamilton Ricard **12.** Neil Harris **13.** Luton Town **14.** Charlie Nicholas **15.** Ray Kennedy **6.** Hull City

Scottish Scene 6

Answers on page 429

1. Which club won all six competitions they entered in 1929–30?
2. King's Park used to play in which Scottish city?
3. Which now defunct club conceded 146 Second Division goals in 1931–2?
4. Which club failed to win any of their 22 League games in 1891–2?
5. Which was the last club outside Glasgow to win the Scottish League title?
6. Who finished third in the Premier Division in 1998–9?
7. Who emerged victorious in just one out of 38 Second Division matches in 1974–5?
8. And which was the team they beat?
9. Which Scottish club's full name was inspired by a famous old Edinburgh dance club?
10. Which team merged with East Stirlingshire for a year in 1964–5?
11. Which League club once bought a second-hand stand from the local Highland Games?
12. What were Dundee United previously known as?
13. Which two clubs were expelled from the Scottish League in 1932 for failing to meet gate money guarantees to their opponents?
14. Who were runners-up to Rangers in 1994–5?
15. Which club sold Paul Tosh to Dundee for £120,000 in 1993?
16. Which club are fondly known by their fans as 'The Blue Brazil'?

Answers to page 429

REPUBLIC OF IRELAND 2: **1.** Bulgaria **2.** Paris **3.** Blackburn Rovers **4.** 1986 **5.** 1977 **6.** Preston North End **7.** None **8.** John Aldridge **9.** Maurice Setters **10.** Mexico **11.** Malta **12.** Spain **13.** Northern Ireland **14.** 57 **15.** Andy Townsend **16.** Chris Hughton

Premiership 5

Answers on page 434

1. For how many seasons did Bradford City stay in the Premiership?
2. In January 1999, which former England midfielder became Ron Atkinson's first signing as manager of Nottingham Forest?
3. Who were the only visiting team to win a League match at Old Trafford in 1994–5?
4. Which team attracted a gate of under 5,000 for a Premiership fixture with Coventry in 1993–4?
5. Who was Leeds United's leading Premiership scorer in 1992–3?
6. Which recovering alcoholic complained about a gambling and drinking culture at Middlesbrough before moving to Aston Villa?
7. Which forward moved from Everton to Liverpool in the summer of 2000?
8. Which Premiership star is married to pop star Louise?
9. What is the name of Gary and Phil Neville's father?
10. Two clubs from which region of England were relegated from the Premiership in 1996–7?
11. When did Sunderland move to the Stadium of Light?
12. In which year did Carling take over sponsorship of the Premiership?
13. From whom did Charlton sign Jonatan Johansson in the summer of 2000?
14. From which ground was Joe Kinnear rushed to hospital following a heart attack in March 1999?
15. Which Moroccan joined Southampton from St Etienne?
16. Who went 16 months without an away win in the Premiership between 1999 and 2000?

Answers to page 434

LEEDS UNITED 1: **1.** Tony Currie **2.** 1998 **3.** Peter Lorimer **4.** Lee Sharpe **5.** 1963–4 **6.** 1982 **7.** Newcastle United **8.** 1950 **9.** Liverpool **10.** Birmingham City **11.** Mick Jones **12.** David Harvey **13.** Huddersfield Town **14.** Rangers **15.** Charlton Athletic **16.** Lucas Radebe

The World Game 8

Answers on page 435

1. Which coach led Italy at Euro 96?

2. Which German was European Footballer of the Year in 1980 and 1981?

3. Who resigned as German national coach in September 1998?

4. Which country transferred 53 players to Europe in the summer of 1998?

5. Which two East German teams joined the Bundesliga First Division in 1990?

6. Which Croatian scored 24 goals to help Real Madrid to the Spanish League title in 1997?

7. Who succeeded Javier Clemente as coach of Spain?

8. Which Scot was manager of Dutch club NEC Nijmegen in 1998–9?

9. In which South American country do Flamengo play?

10. With which Dutch team did Johan Cruyff end his playing career?

11. River Plate, Velez Sarsfield and Union Santa Fe are all clubs from which country?

12. Which Fiorentina player topped the Italian scoring charts in 1994–5?

13. Which Swedish club did Roy Hodgson manage from 1976 to 1980?

14. Which Frenchman was European Footballer of the Year for 1998?

15. Which country went unbeaten in 37 internationals from 1993 to 1996?

16. Who brought their run to an end?

Answers to page 435

WHICH YEAR IN FOOTBALL? 6: **1.** 1958 **2.** 1974 **3.** 1994 **4.** 1996 **5.** 1981 **6.** 1991 **7.** 1921 **8.** 1930 **9.** 1995 **10.** 1979 **11.** 1967 **12.** 1978 **13.** 1895 **14.** 1920 **15.** 1976 **16.** 1959

Leeds United 1

Answers on page 432

1. Which midfield maestro did Leeds sign from Sheffield United for £240,000 in July 1976?
2. In which year did David O'Leary take over as manager?
3. Which Scottish hotshot scored a record 168 League goals for Leeds?
4. Which Leeds player became David Platt's first recruit at Sampdoria in January 1999?
5. In which season did Leeds first play in all white?
6. When were Leeds last relegated from the top division?
7. Who did Leeds defeat on the final day of the 1961–2 season to avoid being relegated to Division Three?
8. When did Leeds reach the last eight of the FA Cup for the first time?
9. Who were runners-up when Leeds won the League Championship in 1969?
10. Which Second Division side did Leeds beat in the semi-finals of the FA Cup in 1971–2?
11. Who scored Leeds' goal in their replay defeat to Chelsea in the 1970 FA Cup final?
12. And who kept goal for Leeds in that match?
13. From which Yorkshire club did Leeds sign Trevor Cherry?
14. Which fellow British team knocked Leeds out of the European Cup in 1992–3?
15. Which team denied Leeds promotion to Division One in a 1987 play-off?
16. Who moved to Elland Road from South African club Kaiser Chiefs?

Answers to page 432

PREMIERSHIP 5: **1.** Two **2.** Carlton Palmer **3.** Nottingham Forest **4.** Wimbledon **5.** Lee Chapman **6.** Paul Merson **7.** Nick Barmby **8.** Jamie Redknapp **9.** Neville Neville **10.** North-east (Sunderland and Middlesbrough) **11.** 1997 **12.** 1993 **13.** Rangers **14.** Hillsborough **15.** Hassan Kachloul **16.** Coventry City

Which Year in Football? 5

Answers on page 433

1. When was the Munich air crash?
2. When was League football first played on a Sunday in England?
3. When was Terry Venables appointed England coach?
4. In which year did Bob Paisley die?
5. When was the centenary FA Cup final?
6. When did Barnet join the Football League?
7. In which year did Burnley win their first League Championship?
8. When did Montrose first join the Scottish League?
9. When did the European Court of Justice uphold the Bosman ruling?
10. When was Kevin Keegan European Footballer of the Year?
11. When was Alf Ramsey knighted?
12. When did Leyton Orient reach the FA Cup semi-finals for the only time in their history?
13. In which year were West Ham United formed?
14. In which year were Albion Rovers beaten finalists in the Scottish FA Cup?
15. When did Luther Blissett make his Watford debut?
16. In which year did Bill Shankly become Liverpool manager?

Answers to page 433

THE WORLD GAME 8: **1.** Arrigo Sacchi **2.** Karl Heinz Rummenigge **3.** Berti Vogts **4.** Argentina **5.** Dynamo Dresden and Hansa Rostock **6.** Davor Suker **7.** Jose Antonio Camacho **8.** Jim Calderwood **9.** Brazil **10.** Feyenoord **11.** Argentina **12.** Gabriel Batistuta **13.** Halmstad **14.** Zinedine Zidane **15.** Brazil **16.** Mexico

Oddballs 7

Answers on page 438

1. With which League club did comedian Bradley Walsh play as a full-back?
2. Who in 1959 became the second foreign team to beat England at Wembley?
3. Which team gained revenge on Manchester United in 2001 by knocking them out of the European Champions' League?
4. What nationality is Lilian Thuram?
5. Which Forfar manager resigned in 1980 after five days in charge before even seeing his side play?
6. What was the nickname of Aston Villa forward Waring?
7. Which Cup winner as a player with Coventry took over as Hartlepool manager in 1995?
8. In which year did Wimbledon turn professional?
9. Which three brothers played together for Southampton in 1988–9?
10. Which former Barnet man was Wycombe Wanderers' top scorer in 1999–2000?
11. What nationality was the manager who succeeded Gary Megson at Stoke?
12. Which former Walsall captain returned to the town in 1997 as a vicar?
13. Which Liverpool striker picked up a knee injury while stretching to pick up the remote control for the TV?
14. Which Welsh club beat Real Madrid 3–0 in 1927 during a pre-season tour of Spain?
15. Which cash-strapped First Division club tried to save money in 1999 by cancelling their weekly order of new jockstraps?
16. Which Yorkshire club only added the name of their city in 1929?

Answers to page 438

NICKNAMES 2: **1.** Alloa Athletic **2.** Queen's Park **3.** Mark Hughes **4.** Torquay United **5.** 'The Vulture' **6.** Hull City **7.** Bryan Robson **8.** Darren Anderton **9.** 'The Red Imps' **10.** St Mirren **11.** Kevin Keegan **12.** Sunderland **13.** Southport **14.** York City **15.** Celtic **16.** Stuart Pearce

Goalkeepers 5

Answers on page 439

1. Who was in goal for Everton in the 1986 FA Cup final?
2. In which country was Pegguy Arphexad born?
3. In 1999, which keeper made his international debut for Wales at the age of 31?
4. Which former Welsh international keeper was on Torquay United's books in 1999?
5. Which Forfar Athletic goalkeeper moved to Notts County in summer 2001?
6. Who was in goal for France in the 1998 World Cup final?
7. Who is Scotland's most capped goalkeeper?
8. Which Italian keeper achieved a 1,142-minute shut-out in international matches between September 1972 and June 1974?
9. Which goalkeeper came upfield to head a last-minute equaliser in a 1995 UEFA Cup tie with Rotor Volgograd?
10. Which Manchester City keeper won nine England caps from 1978 to 1982?
11. Where was Peter Shilton born?
12. What was Gordon Banks's nickname?
13. Which international goalkeeper moved from Millwall to Leicester City in 1996?
14. What was David James's first League club?
15. Which goalkeeper was ever present for Rotherham United in 1998–9?
16. What nationality is Raimond Van der Gouw?

Answers to page 439

MANAGERS 7: **1.** Vassilis Danill **2.** Rochdale **3.** Notts County **4.** Phil Taylor **5.** Torino **6.** Attilio Lombardo **7.** Ken Shellito **8.** Frank Burrows **9.** Ayr United **10.** George Graham **11.** Alex Totten **12.** Gigi Simoni **13.** Ron Atkinson **14.** Switzerland **15.** Terry Yorath **16.** Steve Coppell

Nicknames 2

Answers on page 436

1. Which Scottish club are known as 'The Wasps'?

2. Which Scottish club are nicknamed 'The Spiders'?

3. Which international manager is nicknamed 'Sparky' as a player?

4. Which team are known as 'The Gulls'?

5. What was the nickname of Emilio Butragueno?

6. Which English club are nicknamed 'The Tigers'?

7. Which England skipper was christened 'Captain Marvel'?

8. Which injury-prone Tottenham player is cruelly nicknamed 'Sicknote'?

9. What is Lincoln City's nickname?

10. Which Scottish club are 'The Buddies'?

11. Which Englishman did the Germans name 'Mighty Mouse'?

12. Which team are called 'The Black Cats'?

13. Which Conference team are called 'The Sandgrounders'?

14. Which English club are nicknamed 'The Minstermen'?

15. Which Scottish club are known as 'The Bhoys'?

16. Which former England defender rejoices in the nickname of 'Psycho'?

Answers to page 436

ODDBALLS 7: **1.** Brentford **2.** Sweden **3.** Bayern Munich **4.** French **5.** Steve Murray **6.** 'Pongo' **7.** Keith Houchen **8.** 1964 **9.** Danny, Ray and Rod Wallace **10.** Sean Devine **11.** Icelandic **12.** Peter Hart **13.** Robbie Fowler **14.** Swansea **15.** Portsmouth **16.** Sheffield Wednesday (until then they had been known as The Wednesday)

Managers 7

Answers on page 437

1. Who took over as coach of Greek club Panathinaikos in 1997?
2. Which League club did Harry Catterick manage from 1953 to 1958?
3. Jimmy Sirrel had three spells as manager of which club?
4. Who preceded Bill Shankly as manager of Liverpool?
5. Which Italian club did Graeme Souness manage?
6. Which Italian star became manager of Crystal Palace in 1998 despite not speaking a word of English?
7. Who took over as Chelsea boss in 1977?
8. Who returned as Cardiff City boss in 1998?
9. With which Scottish club did George Burley start out his managerial career?
10. Who was named Manager of the Year in 1989 and 1991?
11. Which St Johnstone boss was voted Scottish Manager of the Year for 1991?
12. Who took over as Inter Milan coach in 1997?
13. Which manager has had two spells with both Sheffield Wednesday and West Bromwich Albion?
14. Which national team did Roy Hodgson coach?
15. Which former Welsh manager went on to coach the Lebanon?
16. Which manager spent just 32 days at Manchester City in 1996?

Answers to page 437

GOALKEEPERS 5: **1.** Bobby Mimms **2.** Guadeloupe **3.** Roger Freestone **4.** Neville Southall **5.** Stuart Garden **6.** Fabien Barthez **7.** Jim Leighton **8.** Dino Zoff **9.** Peter Schmeichel **10.** Joe Corrigan **11.** Leicester **12.** 'Fernandel' **13.** Kasey Keller **14.** Watford **15.** Mike Pollitt **16.** Dutch

Aberdeen 1

Answers on page 442

1. Who succeeded Alex Ferguson as Aberdeen manager?
2. When did Aberdeen win their first Scottish League title?
3. How many Scottish League Championships have Aberdeen won?
4. Who did the Dons defeat in the 1947 Scottish FA Cup final?
5. What was unusual about Aberdeen's hat-trick of Scottish FA Cup wins between 1982 and 1984?
6. Who did Aberdeen beat in the 1983 final?
7. And who scored the only goal of the game?
8. Who was Aberdeen's top scorer in 1988–9 and 1989–90?
9. In which city did Aberdeen lift the European Cup-Winners' Cup?
10. What was Aberdeen's original nickname?
11. Who was Aberdeen's leading scorer in 1998–9?
12. Who scored Aberdeen's winner in the 1984 Scottish FA Cup final?
13. Who did Aberdeen beat 3–1 in the 1970 Scottish FA Cup final?
14. In which season did Aberdeen make their debut in Europe?
15. Who knocked Aberdeen out of the 1984 European Cup-Winners' Cup at the semi-final stage?
16. Who moved from Aberdeen to Tottenham for £830,000 in May 1980?

Answers to page 442

WHOSE HOME? 6: **1.** Alloa Athletic **2.** Tranmere Rovers **3.** Amsterdam **4.** Bristol City **5.** Rotherham United **6.** 1955 **7.** Lens **8.** Cairo **9.** Carrow Road **10.** Arsenal **11.** Southampton **12.** Brockville **13.** Luzniki Stadium **14.** Preston North End **15.** Panathinaikos **16.** Hull City

World Cup 4

Answers on page 443

1. Which country topped Wales's qualifying group for the 1994 World Cup?
2. Who finished third in the 1986 World Cup?
3. Whose penalty won the 1990 World Cup for West Germany?
4. In which year did Colombia first qualify for the World Cup finals?
5. Against whom did Kuwait obtain their solitary point in World Cup finals?
6. Who was the captain of Mexico's team at the 1986 World Cup finals?
7. Who scored the opening goal at the 1994 finals?
8. Which Scot put through his own goal against Brazil in the 1998 finals?
9. Whose only goal for Scotland was against Brazil in the 1982 finals?
10. When did South Africa reach the final stages for the first time?
11. And who were their first opponents in those finals?
12. Against whom did Andres Escobar put through his own goal in the 1994 finals?
13. Which world star failed a drug test following the match with Nigeria at the 1994 finals?
14. Whose dramatic late goal against Belgium put England into the last eight of the 1990 World Cup?
15. Which country's 1998 World Cup qualifier with Morocco was abandoned following a pitch invasion?
16. How many penalties did Italy miss in the shoot-out at the 1994 final?

Answers to page 443

SCOTTISH SCENE 7: **1.** Albion Rovers **2.** Jimmy Johnstone **3.** 1959 **4.** 62 **5.** Costa Rica **6.** Genoa **7.** John Wark **8.** 12 **9.** Wales **10.** Anfield **11.** 1974 **12.** Don Masson **13.** Cordoba **14.** Andy Roxburgh **15.** 1972 **16.** Austria

Whose Home? 6

Answers on page 440

1. Which Scottish club play at Recreation Park?
2. Which English League team used to play at Steeles Field?
3. In which city do Ajax play?
4. Who plays at Ashton Gate?
5. Which Yorkshire club used to play at the Red House Ground before moving to their present home?
6. In which year was Roots Hall built?
7. Which French club plays at the Stade Felix-Bollaert?
8. In which city is the Nasser Stadium?
9. What is the name of Norwich City's home ground?
10. Which of the current Premiership clubs were the first to install floodlights at their ground?
11. And who were the second?
12. Where do Falkirk play?
13. What is the name of Moscow Spartak's home ground?
14. Who plays at Deepdale?
15. Who plays at the Spiros Louis Stadium?
16. Who used to play at the Boulevard Ground?

Answers to page 440

ABERDEEN 1: **1.** Ian Porterfield **2.** 1955 **3.** Four **4.** Hibernian **5.** They all went to extra time **6.** Rangers **7.** Eric Black **8.** Charlie Nicholas **9.** Gothenburg **10.** 'The Wasps' **11.** Eoin Jess **12.** Mark McGhee **13.** Celtic **14.** 1967–8 **15.** FC Porto **16.** Steve Archibald

Scottish Scene 7

Answers on page 441

1. Jock White is the only player from which club to have won a full Scotland cap?
2. Which Scottish international winger was involved in the infamous Largs boating incident?
3. When did Scotland last beat West Germany?
4. How many caps did Danny McGrain win?
5. Who did Scotland lose to in their opening match at the 1990 World Cup finals?
6. In which city did that game take place?
7. Which Ipswich Town midfielder won the first of his 29 caps in 1979?
8. How many goals did Alan Gilzean score for Scotland?
9. Who did Scotland beat in October 1977 to qualify for the 1978 World Cup finals?
10. On which ground was that game played?
11. When did Scotland last avoid defeat against Brazil?
12. Which midfield general won 17 caps with Queens Park Rangers and Derby from 1976 to 1978?
13. At which venue did Scotland play their first two matches at the 1978 World Cup finals?
14. Who became Scotland coach in 1986?
15. When did Asa Hartford win his first cap?
16. A 1963 Hampden Park friendly against which country was abandoned to prevent further injury after two visitors had been sent off and one carried off?

Answers to page 441

WORLD CUP 4: **1.** Romania **2.** France **3.** Andreas Brehme **4.** 1962 **5.** Czechoslovakia **6.** Hugo Sanchez **7.** Jürgen Klinsmann **8.** Tom Boyd **9.** David Narey **10.** 1998 **11.** France **12.** United States **13.** Diego Maradona **14.** David Platt **15.** Gabon **16.** Three

General Knowledge 101

Answers on page 446

1. Who starred opposite Trevor Howard in *Brief Encounter*?
2. What are hertz?
3. Which musical instrument takes its name from its almond-shaped body?
4. Who took over as manager of Middlesbrough FC in summer 2001?
5. Which statesman was released from jail in 1990, ending 27 years of imprisonment?
6. Which is the only seaport in Alabama?
7. Whereabouts on the human body is the mandible?
8. About which American river did Pussycat sing in 1976?
9. Which racing driver was killed in a plane crash on a Hertfordshire golf course in 1975?
10. Which London football club used to be called Dial Square?
11. Who was Baroness Orczy's most famous literary creation?
12. How old was Mary Shelley when she wrote *Frankenstein*?
13. As whom was Haitian dictator François Duvalier better known?
14. In which year were the Olympic Games first held in London?
15. What was the name of Tintin's dog?
16. Which novelist was born in Eastwood, Nottinghamshire?

Answers to page 446

GENERAL KNOWLEDGE 103: **1.** Nicolas Cage **2.** Ian Botham and Bob Willis **3.** Black Sea **4.** A plant **5.** Donald Budge **6.** Carat **7.** Travellers' cheques **8.** Grimsby Town **9.** Beachy Head **10.** Echo **11.** Black Death **12.** Elizabeth Hurley **13.** A West African tribe **14.** Frequency modulation **15.** Flute **16.** 1970

General Knowledge 102

Answers on page 447

1. A dab is a member of which family of fish?
2. The sloe is the fruit of which shrub?
3. What does R.E.M. stand for?
4. Koper is the chief port of which country?
5. Which United Kingdom singer was involved in a four-way tie for first place at the 1969 Eurovision Song Contest?
6. Which short-lived TV soap of 1992 was set in Spain?
7. Which political party did Jimmy Carter represent in the White House?
8. Which three disciplines make up a triathlon?
9. What did the Greek army leave outside the gates of the city during the siege of Troy?
10. What is the name of the channel between mainland England and the Isle of Wight?
11. What is a dirk?
12. Which guitarist released 'Layla' under the name Derek and the Dominos?
13. According to Shakespeare's *Richard III*, who was drowned in a butt of Malmsey wine?
14. What was the former name of Ethiopia?
15. Which American novelist wrote *The Great Gatsby*?
16. On which continent is the Limpopo river?

Answers to page 447

GENERAL KNOWLEDGE 104: **1.** Julia Roberts (Benjamin Bratt) **2.** Bugle **3.** Romania **4.** A bird **5.** Paris **6.** 'Into The Groove' **7.** Julia Louis-Dreyfus **8.** Meg Mathews **9.** St Albans **10.** Gloucester **11.** Sculpture **12.** A minim **13.** Australian **14.** 1984 **15.** The Milky Bar Kid **16.** France

General Knowledge 103

Answers on page 444

1. Which actor started life as Nicholas Coppola but changed it to distance himself from his uncle, director Francis Ford Coppola?
2. Which two cricketers were the heroes of the 1981 Headingley Test where England recovered from a seemingly impossible position to defeat Australia?
3. Burgas and Varna are ports on which sea?
4. What is a bugloss?
5. Who was the first tennis player to perform the Grand Slam?
6. What is the unit for measuring purity in gold?
7. What 1870s innovations from Thomas Cook were originally called 'circular notes'?
8. Which Football League club plays at Blundell Park?
9. What is the highest headland on the south coast of England?
10. In Greek mythology, who was the nymph who pined away after being rejected by Narcissus until only her voice remained?
11. What killed about 30 per cent of the population of England in 1348–9?
12. Who gave birth to a baby boy – Damian Charles – in April 2002?
13. Who are the Fang?
14. In physics, what is FM short for?
15. Which musical instrument does James Galway play?
16. In which year did Jimi Hendrix die?

Answers to page 444

GENERAL KNOWLEDGE 101: **1.** Celia Johnson **2.** Units of frequency **3.** Mandolin **4.** Steve McClaren **5.** Nelson Mandela **6.** Mobile **7.** Jaw **8.** 'Mississippi' **9.** Graham Hill **10.** Arsenal **11.** *The Scarlet Pimpernel* **12.** 19 **13.** Papa Doc **14.** 1908 **15.** Snowy **16.** D.H. Lawrence

General Knowledge 104

Answers on page 445

1. Which actress split up from a Bratt in 2001?
2. What blue flower is also the name of a brass musical instrument?
3. Bucharest is the capital of which European country?
4. What is a dotterel?
5. In which city is the Elysée Palace?
6. What was Madonna's first UK number one single?
7. Who played Elaine Benes in *Seinfeld*?
8. Who was the subject of the Oasis hit *Wonderwall*?
9. Which English city was the Roman Verulamium?
10. Where did Dr Foster go in a shower of rain?
11. In what branch of the arts was Donatello versed?
12. In music, what is half of a semibreve?
13. What nationality is the athlete Cathy Freeman?
14. In which year was Prince Harry born?
15. What was 11-year-old Terry Brooks the first in a long line of in the world of TV commercials?
16. In which country is the River Gers?

Answers to page 445

GENERAL KNOWLEDGE 102: **1.** Flounder **2.** Blackthorn **3.** Rapid Eye Movement **4.** Slovenia **5.** Lulu **6.** *Eldorado* **7.** Democrat **8.** Swimming, cycling and running **9.** Large wooden horse **10.** The Solent **11.** A dagger **12.** Eric Clapton **13.** Duke of Clarence **14.** Abyssinia **15.** F. Scott Fitzgerald **16.** Africa

General Knowledge 105

Answers on page 450

1. In which US sitcom is a dog played by a Moose?
2. Who tripped over Zola Budd's heel at the 1984 Los Angeles Olympics?
3. Who invited us to do the 'Funky Gibbon'?
4. Where would you find the Giant's Causeway?
5. Who preceded Harold II as King of England?
6. On the shore of which lake is the Ugandan town of Entebbe?
7. What is a niblick?
8. How many players are there on each side in a game of Australian Rules football?
9. Which two American states border Chesapeake Bay?
10. Andy Partridge was the singer with which Eighties band?
11. Which star of *The Odd Couple* died in 2000?
12. What are missing from dalmatians when they are born?
13. On which river does Damascus stand?
14. Which football club won the French League title in 2000–1?
15. Where would you find the Sea of Tranquility?
16. Jim Bolger was Prime Minister of which country from 1990–7?

Answers to page 450

GENERAL KNOWLEDGE 107: **1.** 24 **2.** Lombardy **3.** Aidan O'Brien **4.** Inverness-shire **5.** Butlin's Redcoats **6.** Ringo Starr **7.** Radio West **8.** Fred Perry **9.** Armadillo **10.** Navy, Army and Air Force Institutes **11.** Omnivore **12.** Yellow **13.** Dublin **14.** Weedkiller **15.** Parker and Barrow **16.** Lester Piggott

General Knowledge 106

Answers on 451

1. Who was famously called up for American military service in 1958?
2. Who were beaten in the Battle of Dettingen in 1743?
3. Puck and Bottom appear in which Shakespeare play?
4. What is a devil's coach horse?
5. What are dried in oast-houses?
6. Which element was the atomic number 1?
7. What can be a blue-flowered trailing plant or a marine snail?
8. For which home international country did Gavin Hastings play rugby union?
9. Geoffrey of Anjou's habit of wearing a sprig of broom in his hat gave the name to which English royal house?
10. As whom is cleric Geraldine Granger better known?
11. What is the highest adult male voice?
12. In which year did Take That have a UK number one single with 'Pray'?
13. The tugrik is the unit of currency in which country?
14. Which three countries border Paraguay?
15. Who wrote *Madame Bovary*?
16. Who invented the C5?

Answers to page 451

GENERAL KNOWLEDGE 108: **1.** 86 degrees **2.** Lawnmower **3.** Fides **4.** Edinburgh **5.** She was the world's first test-tube baby **6.** *Grange Hill* **7.** Laurent Blanc **8.** A bat **9.** Lake Superior **10.** *Crossroads* **11.** The Stranglers **12.** The Gulf Stream **13.** Triple jump **14.** Jason and the Argonauts **15.** San Francisco **16.** Nurse

General Knowledge 107

Answers on page 448

1. How many sheets of writing-paper are there in a quire?
2. In which Italian region is Lake Como?
3. Which Irish racehorse trainer has stables at Ballydoyle?
4. In which county was the Battle of Culloden fought?
5. What did Sir Cliff Richard, William G. Stewart and Michael Barrymore all start out as?
6. Which Beatle directed the 1972 film *Born To Boogie*?
7. For which radio station did Eddie Shoestring work?
8. Who was the last British tennis player to win the men's singles at Wimbledon?
9. What creature can be fairy or three-banded?
10. What did NAAFI stand for?
11. What is the term for an animal that feeds on both vegetation and meat?
12. What colour is sulphur?
13. Near which city is the port of Dun Laoghaire?
14. What is paraquat?
15. What were the surnames of Bonnie and Clyde?
16. Which jockey was known as the 'long fellow'?

Answers to page 448

GENERAL KNOWLEDGE 105: **1.** *Frasier* (Eddie the dog's real name is Moose) **2.** Mary Decker **3.** The Goodies **4.** On the north coast of Antrim, Northern Ireland **5.** Edward the Confessor **6.** Lake Victoria **7.** A golf club **8.** 18 **9.** Maryland and Virginia **10.** XTC **11.** Walter Matthau **12.** Spots **13.** Barada **14.** Nantes **15.** On the Moon **16.** New Zealand

General Knowledge 108

Answers on page 449

1. What is 30 degrees Centigrade in Fahrenheit?
2. What gardening aid did James Edward Ransome invent in 1902?
3. Who was the Roman god of honesty?
4. Which city is served by Turnhouse Airport?
5. What is Louise Brown's claim to fame?
6. Gripper Stebson was the school bully of which establishment?
7. Which French World Cup winner signed for Manchester United to replace Jaap Stam?
8. What is a flying fox?
9. Which is the northernmost of the Great Lakes?
10. Which former motel was rebuilt as a four-star hotel in 2001?
11. Jean-Jacques Burnel was bass guitarist with which punk band?
12. What flows from the Gulf of Mexico to keep Britain warm?
13. In which athletics event does Jonathan Edwards compete?
14. According to Greek mythology, who stole the Golden Fleece?
15. In which city is the Golden Gate bridge?
16. What was Dorothy's job in *Men Behaving Badly*?

Answers to page 449

GENERAL KNOWLEDGE 106: **1.** Elvis Presley **2.** The French **3.** *A Midsummer Night's Dream* **4.** A beetle **5.** Hops **6.** Hydrogen **7.** Periwinkle **8.** Scotland **9.** Plantagenet (from the Latin *planta genista*) **10.** *The Vicar of Dibley* **11.** Alto **12.** 1993 **13.** Mongolia **14.** Bolivia, Brazil and Argentina **15.** Gustave Flaubert **16.** Sir Clive Sinclair

General Knowledge 109

Answers on page 454

1. What musical instrument did Benny Goodman play?
2. Which Football League club are nicknamed the 'Quakers'?
3. In which *Carry On* film did Sid James play The Rumpo Kid?
4. Which singer was found hanging in a Sydney hotel room in 1997?
5. Which King of Norway died after slipping on the soap in his bath and banging his head on one of the taps?
6. From which country does the kiwi fruit originate?
7. Which shipping forecast area covers the coastline from Scarborough to Great Yarmouth?
8. Which planet was first located in 1846?
9. Who lived on Festive Road and made daily visits to a local fancy-dress shop?
10. In which city is Temple Meads railway station?
11. Which type of water lathers easily with soap – soft or hard?
12. Who released the 1995 album 'Crazysexycool'?
13. In which sport do teams compete for the Super Bowl?
14. TB is an abbreviation for which disease?
15. From which country does the singer Dame Kiri Te Kanawa come?
16. What is the longest river in Scotland?

Answers to 454

GENERAL KNOWLEDGE 111: **1.** His mask **2.** Galley **3.** Yoko Ono **4.** Stammers **5.** Halle Berry **6.** Geoffrey Chaucer **7.** Cobalt **8.** Clwyd **9.** Foyle **10.** Wheel-clamping **11.** Shane Lynch **12.** Finnish **13.** Jack London **14.** Habeas corpus **15.** Dustin Hoffman **16.** J. Edgar Hoover

General Knowledge 110

Answers on page 455

1. In which year was the Wall Street crash?
2. Where do the England rugby union team play home matches?
3. In which county is Melton Mowbray?
4. What method of weaponry was first used at the Battle of the Somme in 1916?
5. Which of the Lipari Islands has an active volcano?
6. Who starred in *Patriot Games* and *The Fugitive*?
7. What is the name of Michael Schumacher's younger brother who is also a Formula One driver?
8. Who was US Vice-President from 1989–93?
9. To what did Isaac Pitman lend his name?
10. Which girl group backed Martha Reeves?
11. In which American state is the industrial city of Pittsburgh?
12. From 1899, who painted a series of water lilies in the garden of his house at Giverny, Normandy?
13. Which brother of Martha was raised by Jesus from the dead?
14. Which English horse race starts in Cambridgeshire and ends in Suffolk?
15. Which Western hero was 'king of the wild frontier'?
16. How many pints are there in a quart?

Answers to page 455

GENERAL KNOWLEDGE 112: **1.** Manic Street Preachers **2.** Princess Anne (to Capt. Mark Phillips) **3.** Norman Scott **4.** Umbrella **5.** Exeter **6.** 'The Terrible' **7.** Machu Picchu **8.** Enron Corp. **9.** Zither **10.** Leeds **11.** William McGonagall **12.** Molotov cocktail **13.** *Endurance* **14.** Somalia **15.** Eden and Esk **16.** Quasi-Autonomous Non-Governmental Organisation

General Knowledge 111

Answers on page 452

1. What did the Lone Ranger never remove in public?
2. What is the name for a ship's kitchen?
3. Of whom did Joan Rivers once say: 'If I found her floating in my pool, I'd punish my dog'?
4. What did Bruce Willis, Harvey Keitel and Sir Winston Churchill all have to overcome?
5. Who won the best actress Oscar in 2002 for her performance in *Monster's Ball*?
6. Who wrote *The Canterbury Tales*?
7. What chemical element has the symbol Co?
8. Colwyn Bay is situated in which county of North Wales?
9. On which river does Londonderry stand?
10. What new experiment brought misery to London motorists in 1983?
11. Which former member of Boyzone has two sisters in B*Witched?
12. What nationality was the composer Sibelius?
13. Who wrote the novels *Call of the Wild* and *White Fang*?
14. Which legal term means 'you may have the body' in Latin?
15. Who won Academy Awards for his performances in *Kramer vs Kramer* and *Rain Man*?
16. Who became director of the FBI in 1924?

Answers to page 452

GENERAL KNOWLEDGE 109: **1.** Clarinet **2.** Darlington **3.** *Carry On Cowboy* **4.** Michael Hutchence **5.** Haakon VII **6.** China **7.** Humber **8.** Neptune **9.** *Mr Benn* **10.** Bristol **11.** Soft **12.** TLC **13.** American Football **14.** Tuberculosis **15.** New Zealand **16.** Tay

General Knowledge 112

Answers on page 453

1. James Dean Bradfield is the lead singer with which band?
2. Which member of the royal family was married on 14 November 1973?
3. Who was former Liberal leader Jeremy Thorpe accused of conspiring to murder?
4. In Dickensian London, what was a gamp?
5. St David's railway station serves which west country city?
6. What was the nickname of Russian ruler Ivan IV?
7. Which lost city of the Incas was rediscovered in the Peruvian Andes by Hiram Bingham in 1911?
8. Which giant US company went bankrupt in 2002?
9. What musical instrument did Shirley Abicair play?
10. Headingley cricket ground is located in which city?
11. Which 19th-century Scottish poet was renowned for his appalling verse?
12. What kind of cocktail was popular with Resistance groups during the Second World War?
13. What was the name of the ship abandoned by Ernest Shackleton during his 1914–16 Antarctic expedition?
14. Mogadishu is the capital of which African nation?
15. The estuaries of which two rivers form the Solway Firth?
16. For what is quango an acronym?

Answers to page 453

GENERAL KNOWLEDGE 110: **1.** 1929 **2.** Twickenham **3.** Leicestershire **4.** Tank **5.** Stromboli **6.** Harrison Ford **7.** Ralf **8.** Dan Quayle **9.** A form of shorthand **10.** The Vandellas **11.** Pennsylvania **12.** Claude Monet **13.** Lazarus **14.** The Cesarewitch **15.** Davy Crockett **16.** Two

General Knowledge 113

Answers on page 458

1. What was Richard Burton's last film?

2. Which poet wrote *A Shropshire Lad*?

3. What is the state capital of Queensland?

4. At what time of year does Detective Chief Inspector Barnaby investigate cases of foul play?

5. What is an oleander?

6. What is the Christian name of the fashion designer Oldfield?

7. Which singer was the subject of Don McLean's 'American Pie'?

8. Scar was the villain in which Disney film?

9. In which year was the Gulf War?

10. With which musical instrument was Duke Ellington associated?

11. Who scored Germany's golden goal winner in the final of Euro 96?

12. Which nuclear power station changed its name to Sellafield in 1971?

13. Which town in Kent got its name from its septet of fine trees?

14. Who did the Princess of Wales come to know as 'Squidgy'?

15. With which country was Greece at war between 499 and 449BC?

16. Which two teams kicked off the 2002 World Cup Finals?

Answers to page 458

GENERAL KNOWLEDGE 115: **1.** The first floodlit match **2.** Bournemouth Gynaecologists **3.** The eye **4.** Cecil B. de Mille **5.** Denmark **6.** Lesotho **7.** Batman **8.** Adam Ant **9.** Barbary lion **10.** Each represented England at both cricket and soccer **11.** Squirrel **12.** Tom Selleck **13.** Christy Brown **14.** The *Mary Rose* **15.** York Minster **16.** The aerosol

General Knowledge 114

Answers on page 459

1. In which county of England is Fountains Abbey?
2. What is Jodie Foster's real first name?
3. What does NASA stand for?
4. What was the name of Scooby-Doo's pup nephew?
5. Who won the 2001 FA Cup Final?
6. What is a narwhal?
7. What do Scotsmen like to toss at the Highland Games?
8. As whom was Martha Jane Burke better known in 19th-century South Dakota?
9. Who created the private detective Philip Marlowe?
10. Which animals are vulnerable to the disease myxomatosis?
11. On whose head couldn't you see the join?
12. Who was the Roman goddess of love?
13. What do 'Stairway To Heaven' and 'Bohemian Rhapsody' have in common?
14. On what racecourse is the 1,000 Guineas run?
15. Who composed the opera *Porgy and Bess*?
16. What is the official language of Belize?

Answers to page 459

GENERAL KNOWLEDGE 116: **1.** Forearm **2.** Channel Islands **3.** Joseph Conrad **4.** The Beach Boys **5.** Virginia Wade **6.** Germany, Austria and Switzerland **7.** *Hamish Macbeth* **8.** Jansher Khan **9.** It is the world's only vegetarian bird of prey **10.** Japan **11.** Britain **12.** Badminton **13.** East Sussex **14.** Cameroon **15.** Maurice Chevalier **16.** Revelation

General Knowledge 115

Answers on page 456

1. What football landmark took place at Bramall Lane, Sheffield, in 1878?
2. Who ran rings around the Watford Long John Silver Impersonators in a football match on *Monty Python's Flying Circus*?
3. Conjunctivitis affects which part of the body?
4. Who directed *King of Kings* and *The Ten Commandments*?
5. The Skagerrak is the strip of water on the north side of which country?
6. Which African country was formerly known as Basutoland?
7. Which comic-strip hero was created by Bob Kane?
8. Who changed his name from Stuart Goddard to become 'Prince Charming'?
9. The last specimen of which breed of lion was killed in the Great Atlas Mountains in 1922?
10. What links C.B. Fry, Arthur Milton and Willie Watson?
11. What animal lives in a drey?
12. Who starred as *Magnum PI*?
13. Which Irish novelist could only type with the toes of one foot?
14. What was sunk in 1545 and took 437 years to re-surface?
15. A bolt of lightning devastated which cathedral in 1984?
16. What did Norway's Erik Rotheim invent in 1926?

Answers to page 456

GENERAL KNOWLEDGE 113: **1.** *1984* **2.** A.E. Housman **3.** Brisbane **4.** *Midsomer (Murders)* **5.** An evergreen shrub **6.** Bruce **7.** Buddy Holly **8.** *The Lion King* **9.** 1991 **10.** Piano **11.** Oliver Bierhoff **12.** Windscale **13.** Sevenoaks **14.** James Hewitt **15.** Persia **16.** France and Senegal

General Knowledge 116

Answers on page 457

1. Where in the human body is the ulna?
2. Brechou, Jethou and Lihou can be found in which group of islands?
3. Which Ukraine-born novelist wrote *Lord Jim*?
4. Which Sixties group used to be called Carl and the Passions?
5. Who won the Wimbledon ladies' singles title in the Queen's Silver Jubilee year?
6. Which three countries border Lake Constance ?
7. Which TV policeman owned a dog called Wee Jock?
8. Who won the Men's World Squash Championships seven years out of eight between 1989 and 1996?
9. What is unique about the palm nut vulture of West Africa?
10. In which country were Venetian blinds invented?
11. Which is the only country in the world that doesn't have its name on its postage stamps?
12. At which sport did Gillian Gilks represent England?
13. In which county is Herstmonceux Castle?
14. Douala is the chief port of which African country?
15. Which French singer said 'thank 'eavens for leetle girls'?
16. Which is the last book of the New Testament?

Answers to page 457

GENERAL KNOWLEDGE 114: **1.** North Yorkshire **2.** Alicia **3.** National Aeronautics and Space Administration **4.** Scrappy-Doo **5.** Liverpool **6.** A small whale **7.** Caber **8.** Calamity Jane **9.** Raymond Chandler **10.** Rabbits **11.** Ernie Wise **12.** Venus **13.** Both have been covered by Rolf Harris **14.** Newmarket **15.** George Gershwin **16.** English

General Knowledge 117

Answers on page 462

1. 'Goat's Head Soup' was a 1973 album by which band?
2. What is clubroot?
3. In which century was Don Juan supposed to have lived?
4. Who resigned as manager of the England football team in 2000?
5. Which former England cricket captain shares a name with a Welsh peninsula?
6. What is the state capital of Florida?
7. Who was the first woman to fly solo from England to Australia?
8. Which Hollywood actress was born Natasha Gurdin?
9. What did America's Lucien B. Smith invent in 1867?
10. RA is the international vehicle index mark for which country?
11. Translated literally, which phrase means 'blow of mercy' in French?
12. Who completed the first British cicumnavigation of the globe?
13. Who was in charge of the *Trumpton* fire brigade?
14. What do the D'Oyly Carte Company produce?
15. Which line of hills stretches from Bristol to Chipping Camden?
16. The cougar is another name for which North American cat?

Answers to page 462

GENERAL KNOWLEDGE 119: **1.** Will Hay **2.** Persian Gulf **3.** Gustav Holst **4.** Vera Lynn **5.** Lincolnshire **6.** Emma Bunton **7.** Willow **8.** Sam **9.** The fake Hitler diaries **10.** Mike Gatting **11.** Barcelona **12.** Arthur Ashe **13.** 1975 **14.** 70mph **15.** Saturn **16.** Siam

General Knowledge 118

Answers on page 463

1. Which British Prime Minister became the first Earl of Avon?

2. How many points is a touchdown worth in American football?

3. To which group of musical instruments does the glockenspiel belong?

4. What number is used to classify book titles?

5. What variety of lettuce takes its name from a Greek island?

6. Which singer could only be filmed from the waist up on *The Ed Sullivan Show* because his act was considered so overtly sexual?

7. Which city did the very first Cook's overseas tour visit in 1855?

8. In which country is the Cleve-Garth waterfall?

9. A young Jeffrey Archer was once employed doing which job on the sands at Weston-super-Mare?

10. Odontophobia is a fear of what?

11. To which century does the umbrella date back?

12. What was the Fonz's Christian name?

13. Which Football League club plays at Plainmoor?

14. Which group backed Gary Puckett?

15. Chris Norman was the lead singer with which Seventies band?

16. Den Haag is the Dutch form of which town in the Netherlands?

Answers to page 463

GENERAL KNOWLEDGE 120: **1.** Cribbage **2.** Benazir Bhutto **3.** Jack Dempsey **4.** India **5.** Red Sea **6.** Indian Ocean **7.** Stevie Wonder **8.** Tomato **9.** Princess Beatrice **10.** Margot Fonteyn **11.** The Japanese art of flower arrangement **12.** Ben Johnson **13.** Gary Kasparov **14.** She shot J.R. Ewing in *Dallas* **15.** George IV **16.** Nanette Newman

General Knowledge 119

Answers on page 460

1. Which comedy actor starred in *Oh Mr Porter* and *Ask a Policeman*?
2. In which stretch of water is Kharg Island?
3. Who composed 'The Planets' suite?
4. Who was known as the 'forces sweetheart' during the Second World War?
5. In which English county is Burghley House?
6. Which Spice Girl once played a teenage mugger in *EastEnders*?
7. From which wood are cricket bats traditionally made?
8. Which Uncle is the nickname for the US government?
9. What fooled the *Sunday Times* and historian Hugh Trevor-Roper in 1983?
10. A kiss-and-tell barmaid brought about the downfall of which England cricket captain?
11. From which city did Manuel come in *Fawlty Towers*?
12. Who was the first black men's singles champion at Wimbledon?
13. In which year did 'Bohemian Rhapsody' first reach number one?
14. What speed limit was introduced on British roads in 1965?
15. Titan is the largest moon of which planet?
16. What was Thailand formerly known as?

Answers to page 460

GENERAL KNOWLEDGE 117: **1.** The Rolling Stones **2.** A disease affecting cabbages and turnips **3.** 14th **4.** Kevin Keegan **5.** Gower **6.** Tallahassee **7.** Amy Johnson **8.** Natalie Wood **9.** Barbed wire **10.** Argentina **11.** Coup de grâce **12.** Sir Francis Drake **13.** Captain Flack **14.** Operas **15.** Cotswolds **16.** Puma

General Knowledge 120

Answers on page 461

1. Which card game was invented in the 17th century by English poet John Suckling?
2. Who was the first woman Prime Minister of Pakistan?
3. Which boxer was nicknamed 'the Manassa Mauler'?
4. In which country was fingerprinting first used to identify crime suspects?
5. Which sea separates Egypt and Sudan from Saudi Arabia?
6. In which ocean are the Maldives?
7. Who was the Ebony to Paul McCartney's Ivory?
8. Which popular salad ingredient was thought to be poisonous until 1830?
9. Which is the first female in the line of succession to the British monarchy?
10. Which ballet dancer changed her name from Margaret Hookham?
11. What is ikebana?
12. Who was stripped of his 100 metres gold medal at the 1988 Olympics after testing positive for drugs?
13. In 1985, which 22-year-old Russian became the youngest chess player to win the world title?
14. What crime did Kristin Shepard commit in 1980?
15. Which English King had a secret wife named Mrs Fitzherbert?
16. Which compulsive dish-washer is Emma Forbes's mother?

Answers to page 461

GENERAL KNOWLEDGE 118: **1.** Anthony Eden **2.** Six **3.** Percussion **4.** ISBN **5.** Cos **6.** Elvis Presley **7.** Paris **8.** New Zealand **9.** Deckchair attendant **10.** Teeth **11.** Second century BC **12.** Arthur **13.** Torquay United **14.** The Union Gap **15.** Smokie **16.** The Hague

Soaps 10

Answers on page 466

1. Who was Chase Gioberti's wife in *Falcon Crest*?
2. Which Walford resident fell for toy boy Troy?
3. Who shot *Crossroads'* David Hunter?
4. Which family in Ramsay Street had a son called Brad and a daughter named Cody?
5. Which *Brookside* siren was pushed down the stairs by her twice ex-husband?
6. In *Home and Away*, who was jilted at the altar by Roo?
7. Who was *Coronation Street*'s eco-warrior?
8. Which *Dallas* beauty spent weeks in bandages after being mown down by a truck?
9. Which husband of Meg Richardson tried to poison her in *Crossroads*?
10. Which star of *Straw Dogs* joined the cast of *EastEnders* in 2001?
11. What is the name of Diane Murray's mother in *Brookside*?
12. Who in *Family Affairs* has a daughter in jail for murder?
13. Which actress used to play Mrs Eckersley in *Emmerdale* before becoming a regular in *EastEnders*?
14. Which movie star got his big break as Rodney Harrington in *Peyton Place*?
15. What was the name of Michelle Fowler's daughter in *EastEnders*?
16. In *Brookside*, why did Jimmy Corkhill split up from wife Jackie?

Answers to page 466

COMEDY 13: **1.** Jennifer Aniston **2.** Charlie Drake **3.** Howard and Hilda **4.** Fulham **5.** Ronnie Barker **6.** *The Fall and Rise of Reginald Perrin* **7.** Jim Backus **8.** Shoe-shine Johnny **9.** Kenny **10.** Swiss Toni **11.** Documentary film-maker **12.** Jools Holland and Rowland Rivron **13.** Gil Chesterton **14.** 16th **15.** Dirk McQuickly **16.** *Surgical Spirit*

TV Pot Luck 11

Answers on page 467

1. Which Kate presents *Watchdog Healthcheck*?
2. Who cycles around the country in search of *Local Heroes*?
3. Which ubiquitous TV personality promises *Better Homes*?
4. Who led her *Garden Army* in 2001?
5. Which comedian won *Celebrity Big Brother in 2001*?
6. Who asks: *So You Think You're a Good Driver?*
7. Who gardened at Barnsdale?
8. What title did Sir John Harvey-Jones adopt for television?
9. Which BBC2 series takes company bosses down to workforce level for a week?
10. Which TV presenter once swallowed a fly during a live broadcast?
11. Who is Channel 5's no-nonsense *House Doctor*?
12. What is the name of the clown in *The Simpsons*?
13. Which refugee from *Red Dwarf* introduces *Robot Wars*?
14. Who wrote *The Lakes*?
15. Which professor investigated baby behaviour in *Child of Our Time*?
16. What type of programmes does Tiff Needell present?

Answers to page 467

BROOKSIDE 2: **1.** His daughter Kylie **2.** Mo McGee **3.** Jacqui Dixon **4.** Angela Lambert **5.** Madge Richmond **6.** Barbara **7.** Adele Murray **8.** Leo Johnson **9.** Lance Powell **10.** Carmel **11.** Paul Collins **12.** Peter Montague **13.** Leanne Powell **14.** David Crosbie **15.** Nursing **16.** A night-club

Comedy 13

Answers on page 464

1. Which *Friends* actress had Telly Savalas as a godfather?
2. Which pint-sized comedian asked in 1967: *Who Is Sylvia*?
3. Which claustrophobically married couple wore identical clothes in *Ever Decreasing Circles*?
4. Which football team did Wolfie Smith support?
5. Who wrote *Clarence* under the pseudonym of Bob Ferris?
6. *Fairly Secret Army* was a spin-off from which series?
7. Who played Judge Bradley Stevens in *I Married Joan*?
8. What was the name of Frank Drebin's informant in *Police Squad*?
9. Who is killed in every episode of *South Park*?
10. Which *Fast Show* character compared everything to 'making love to a beautiful woman'?
11. What did Michael Adams do for a living in *Loved By You*?
12. Who were *The Groovy Fellers*?
13. Who is the camp restaurant critic in *Frasier*?
14. In which century was *Blackadder II* set?
15. Which member of *The Rutles* was a parody of Paul McCartney?
16. Which medical sitcom starred Nichola McAuliffe as Sheila Sabatini?

Answers to page 464

SOAPS 10: **1.** Maggie **2.** Irene Raymond **3.** His wife, Rosemary **4.** The Willis family **5.** Susannah Morrisey **6.** Frank Morgan **7.** Spider Nugent **8.** Pam Ewing **9.** Malcolm Ryder **10.** Susan George **11.** Brigid **12.** Sadie Hargreaves **13.** Pam St Clement **14.** Ryan O'Neal **15.** Vicki **16.** He thought she'd had a lesbian affair

Brookside 2

Answers on page 465

1. Inside whose teddy bear did Gary Stanlow hide a bag of heroin?
2. What was the name of Rosie Banks's larger-than-life sister?
3. Who ditched an aristocrat at the altar and fell for a psycho instead?
4. Who was the first occupant of the hair salon on Brookside Parade?
5. Which gold-digger set out to dupe Harry Cross?
6. Which member of the Harrison family was deputy head at Brookside Comprehensive?
7. Which teenager had an abortion in 2001?
8. Who was the father?
9. Which *Brookside* character is played by Mickey Poppins?
10. What is the name of Tim O'Leary's mother?
11. Who owned a dog called Lucky that was run over on the Close?
12. Which geography teacher had a fling with Tracy Corkhill?
13. Who once tried to blind Jacqui Dixon?
14. Who left the Close to live with Molly Marchbank?
15. What was Kirsty Brown's chosen career?
16. What was La Luz?

Answers to page 465

TV POT LUCK 11: **1.** Kate Sanderson **2.** Adam Hart-Davis **3.** Carol Vorderman **4.** Charlie Dimmock **5.** Jack Dee **6.** Nick Ross **7.** Geoff Hamilton **8.** *Trouble Shooter* **9.** *Back to the Floor* **10.** Patrick Moore **11.** Ann Maurice **12.** Krusty **13.** Craig Charles **14.** Jimmy McGovern **15.** Robert Winston **16.** Motoring

Children's TV 6

Answers on page 470

1. Who is the friendly ghost?
2. Which whistling characters live on a blue moon?
3. What kind of creature is *Barney*?
4. Who narrates *Funnybones*?
5. Where does Puppyduck hang out?
6. Who was *Arthur of the Britons*' chief rival?
7. Which member of *The Banana Splits* had a pet flea called Fletcher?
8. Which *Cold Feet* actor narrates the new adventures of *The Flowerpot Men*?
9. Which comedy double act steered a *Crazy Bus* in the Seventies?
10. Which Womble is also the name of a city in New Zealand?
11. Who lived in *Ivor the Engine*'s boiler?
12. Which *Blue Peter* puppy replaced Patch?
13. From which country did *Cristobal and Company* originate?
14. Who played one of Billy Bunter's chums before starring in *Blow Up*?
15. Which singer was in *Jumbleland*?
16. Who started to Fix It in 1975?

Answers to page 470

COP SHOWS 8: **1.** Jennifer **2.** John Hurt **3.** Joe Friday **4.** Annabelle Hurst **5.** Hale and Pace **6.** Lorcan Cranitch **7.** Caroline Quentin **8.** Suzanne Anderson *(Police Woman)* **9.** *Moonlighting* **10.** *Miami Vice* **11.** Plane crash **12.** Zeus and Apollo **13.** Edmond O'Brien **14.** Charles **15.** C15 **16.** Ian Ogilvy

Locations 5

Answers on page 471

1. Which hapless soldiers were based at Fort Courage?
2. Which Sixties children's character lived in Stray Town?
3. In which town was the showroom of *Morris Minor's Marvellous Motors*?
4. In which South Carolina town was *American Gothic* set?
5. Who lived on Berrydown Farm?
6. In which city is *Hollyoaks* set?
7. Which Polish-American TV detective lived in the exclusive Beacon Hill area of Boston?
8. Which 2001 sitcom is set on an industrial estate in Slough?
9. Where do *The Royle Family* live?
10. Skipdale is one of the nearest towns to which village?
11. Who was Jersey's most famous police officer?
12. In which city was *Boys From the Blackstuff* set?
13. Who lived at 33 Lobelia Avenue, Tooting?
14. Who came from the planet Ork?
15. Which Jasmine is a notorious estate on *The Bill*?
16. In which road did Eddie and Joan Booth live in *Love Thy Neighbour*?

Answers to page 471

TV POT LUCK 12: **1.** Monty Don **2.** *Up Rising* **3.** The Car **4.** Russell Grant **5.** *You Only Live Once* **6.** *Tonight* **7.** Macdonald Hastings **8.** Richard Madeley **9.** *Bargain Hunt* **10.** *The South Bank Show* **11.** Magenta De Vine **12.** Simon Callow **13.** Liza Tarbuck **14.** Holland **15.** The moon **16.** Patricia Routledge

Cop Shows 8

Answers on page 468

1. What was the name of Jonathan Hart's wife in *Hart to Hart*?

2. Which film star played an escaped prisoner in an episode of the Sixties police series *Gideon's Way*?

3. Ben Romero was the partner of which American cop?

4. Who was the computer expert of *Department S*?

5. Which comedy double act had a best-forgotten run as *Dalziel and Pascoe*?

6. Who is the male lead in *McCready and Daughter*?

7. Which comedy actress stars in *Jonathan Creek*?

8. Which female police sergeant was known as 'Pepper'?

9. Which quirky U.S. detective series featured an episode written in iambic pentameters?

10. Little Richard, Iggy Pop and Frank Zappa all made guest appearances in which hip Eighties cop show?

11. How was Sally McMillan killed off in *McMillan and Wife*?

12. Which pair of Dobermans frequently threatened to take lumps out of Thomas Magnum?

13. Who played *Johnny Midnight*?

14. What was *Wycliffe*'s first name?

15. For which organisation did Bodie and Doyle work in *The Professionals*?

16. Who played Simon Templar in *The Return of the Saint*?

Answers to page 468

CHILDREN'S TV 6: **1.** *Casper* **2.** *Clangers* **3.** A purple dinosaur **4.** Griff Rhys Jones **5.** *Mopatop's Show* **6.** Mark of Cornwall **7.** Drooper **8.** John Thomson **9.** Hope and Keen **10.** Wellington **11.** Idris the dragon **12.** Shep **13.** France **14.** David Hemmings **15.** Anita Harris **16.** Jimmy Savile

TV Pot Luck 12

Answers on page 469

1. Who presents Channel 4's *Real Gardens*?
2. Which rural comedy starred Nicola Pagett, Anton Rodgers and Michelle Collins?
3. According to Quentin Willson, what's the Star?
4. Which astrologer sends short postcards on Channel 5?
5. In which series does Nick Hancock quiz celebrities about their lives and careers?
6. On which magazine programme did Alan Whicker originally make his name?
7. Who presented *Call the Gun Expert*?
8. Who often finds himself at the *Eye of the Storm*?
9. In which BBC daytime show does antiques dealer David Dickinson test two teams of collectors?
10. Which ITV arts programme began in 1978?
11. Which exotically-named presenter took viewers on a *Rough Guide to Europe*?
12. Who played Tom Chance in *Chance in a Million*?
13. Which comedian's daughter presented *The Big Breakfast*?
14. In which country was *Van Der Valk* set?
15. Where did Wallace and Gromit go for *A Grand Day Out*?
16. Who played amateur sleuth Hetty Wainthropp?

Answers to page 469

LOCATIONS 5: **1.** *F Troop* **2.** Twizzle **3.** Normalton **4.** Trinity **5.** *Pingwings* **6.** Chester **7.** *Banacek* **8.** *The Office* **9.** Manchester **10.** *Emmerdale* **11.** *Bergerac* **12.** Liverpool **13.** *Hugh and I* **14.** Mork (in *Mork and Mindy*) **15.** Jasmine Allen **16.** Maple Terrace

Quiz & Game Shows 6

Answers on page 474

1. Who presents *The Other Half*?

2. Who urges *Don't Try This at Home*?

3. Who were the original hosts of *Friends Like These*?

4. Which newsreader ensured the rules were obeyed on *Survivor*?

5. Who demonstrates trick shots on *Big Break*?

6. Who announced the prizes on *Sale of the Century*?

7. Which 'dodgy' comedian presented *The Golden Shot*?

8. Which daytime quiz based on famous quotes was presented by Vanessa Feltz?

9. On which panel show are Alan Coren and Sandi Toksvig the team captains?

10. The finale of which game show is the 'Showcase Showdown'?

11. Paul Daniels and Bob Monkhouse have both hosted which show?

12. On which show would you find 'Dictionary Corner'?

13. How many contestants are there at the start of William G. Stewart's Channel 4 quiz?

14. *Number One* is a quiz on which channel?

15. Which implement was in the care of Alec Dane on *Take Your Pick*?

16. Audrey Graham sang on which ITV game show of the 1970s?

Answers to page 474

COMEDY 14: **1.** Rhona Cameron **2.** *Pay and Display* **3.** *Full House* **4.** Mr Leeman **5.** Arnold's Drive-In **6.** Benny Hill **7.** Paul Whitehouse and Kathy Burke **8.** Piers Fletcher-Dervish **9.** *Operation Good Guys* **10.** Dennis Moore **11.** Karl Howman **12.** *The Mary Whitehouse Experience* **13.** Father Mulcahy **14.** The Fourmiles **15.** Sir Humphrey Appleby **16.** Audrey fforbes-Hamilton

Corrie 3

Answers on page 475

1. Which baby was kidnapped outside Gamma Garments in 1962?
2. What was Sally Webster's maiden name?
3. Where did Martin Platt take Sally Webster and their kids on a camping holiday?
4. In which year did Deirdre and Ken marry?
5. What was Hayley known as before the sex change?
6. Derek Wilton and Norris Cole were both married to which captain of industry?
7. Who plays Sarah Platt?
8. How many times has Mike Baldwin been married?
9. Which unlikely rebel was once jailed for taking part in an anti-Vietnam war demo?
10. At which sport did Duggie Ferguson excel?
11. What was his nickname?
12. Which Street resident is a keen astronomer?
13. Who rescued Bet Lynch from a fire at the Rovers?
14. Who was fooled by a fake airline pilot?
15. In 1967, who became coach to the Weatherfield Hotspurs women's football team?
16. Which shady character was played by Kenneth Cope?

Answers to page 475

DRAMAS 11: **1.** *Man at the Top* **2.** *The Misfit* **3.** Michelle Collins **4.** Barbara Gray **5.** *Private Schulz* **6.** *Border Café* **7.** Ferdy **8.** Channel 4 and E4 **9.** Richard Griffiths **10.** Frank and Danny Kane **11.** Nancy Mitford **12.** Sarah Lancashire **13.** Richard **14.** 18th **15.** *Quiller* **16.** James Bolam

Comedy 14

Answers on page 472

1. Which Scottish comedienne was the *Rhona* in the series of the same title?
2. Which ITV sitcom of 2000 was set in a multi-storey car park?
3. Which Eighties sitcom had the Hatfields and the McCoys all living under one roof?
4. Which guest did Basil Fawlty find dead in bed?
5. At which hamburger restaurant did the gang hang out in *Happy Days*?
6. Who was named Personality of the Year at the *Daily Mail* Television Awards for 1954–5?
7. Who were Harry Enfield's two Chums?
8. Who was Alan B'Stard's whipping boy in *The New Statesman*?
9. Which spoof docusoap follows an undercover police squad?
10. Which *Monty Python* character demanded: 'Your lupins or your life!'?
11. Who played *Mulberry*?
12. Steve Punt, Hugh Dennis, Rob Newman and David Baddiel teamed up for which TV experience?
13. Who was *M*A*S*H*'s gentle man of the cloth?
14. In *George and Mildred*, which family lived next door to the Ropers?
15. Who was Jim Hacker's Permanent Secretary?
16. Whose butler was called Brabinger?

Answers to page 472

QUIZ AND GAME SHOWS 6: **1.** Dale Winton **2.** Davina McCall **3.** Ant and Dec **4.** Mark Austin **5.** John Virgo **6.** John Benson **7.** Norman Vaughan **8.** *Quotation Marks* **9.** *Call My Bluff* **10.** *The Price Is Right* **11.** *Wipeout* **12.** *Countdown* **13.** 15 (*Fifteen to One*) **14.** Channel 4 **15.** The gong **16.** *The Sky's The Limit*

Dramas 11

Answers on page 473

1. Which series starred Kenneth Haigh as Joe Lampton?

2. What was Basil Allenby-Johnson when he returned to England from Malaya?

3. Which ex-*EastEnder* committed *Daylight Robbery*?

4. What was the name of Wendy Craig's *Nanny*?

5. Which German soldier, played by Michael Elphick, tried to flood Britain with forged banknotes?

6. In which series did Elizabeth Carling play a rock star who bought her boyfriend a diner?

7. Who was the gay despatch rider in *This Life*?

8. Which channels screen *Ally McBeal*?

9. Which weighty actor played Henry Jay in *Bird of Prey*?

10. Which brothers ran *The Paradise Club*?

11. Whose novels inspired the 2001 adaptation of *Love in a Cold Climate*?

12. Who played John Thaw's girlfriend in *The Glass*?

13. What was the first name of *Boyd QC*?

14. In which century was *Poldark* set?

15. Which secret government agent, played by Michael Jayston, worked for 'the Bureau'?

16. Which Likely Lad starred in *The Beiderbecke Affair*?

Answers to page 473

CORRIE 3: **1.** Christopher Hewitt **2.** Seddon **3.** Peak District **4.** 1981 **5.** Harold **6.** Angela **7.** Tina O'Brien **8.** Three **9.** Ken Barlow **10.** Rugby League **11.** 'Crusher' **12.** Curly Watts **13.** Kevin Webster **14.** Deirdre Rachid **15.** David Barlow **16.** Jed Stone

Children's TV 7

Answers on page 478

Which children's TV shows featured the following characters?

1. Big Tim Champion
2. Doughnut
3. Captain Fantastic
4. Dipsy
5. Mr Quelch
6. Gurth
7. Musky
8. The Ant Hill Mob
9. Morton Frog
10. Mr Rusty
11. Marina
12. Hartley Hare
13. Cut Throat Jake
14. Constable Knapweed
15. Mrs Scrubbitt
16. Orinoco

Answers to page 478

SCI FI 4: **1.** Marvin **2.** Holly **3.** Kyrano **4.** Tin-Tin **5.** Sarek **6.** Lucy Lawless **7.** Colonel Raeburn **8.** Peter Davison **9.** Weaponry **10.** The Face **11.** *The Andromeda Breakthrough* **12.** Jellybabies **13.** Captain Roke **14.** *Moonbase 3* **15.** Judy, Penny and Will **16.** B'Elanna Torres

Soaps 11

Answers on page 479

1. Which *Coronation Street* character discovered on his wedding day that his bride had been having an affair with his son?
2. Who was the only person killed in the *Crossroads* fire of 1981?
3. What surname did Andy and Disa share in *EastEnders*?
4. Which handsome *Peyton Place* medic was played by Ed Nelson?
5. Which former *Neighbours* actor played Shane Cochran in *Brookside*?
6. Which beauty title did *Dallas*'s Sue Ellen once hold?
7. What was the name of the Eighties soap set in a South Wales village?
8. Al Corley and Jack Coleman both played which *Dynasty* character?
9. Who lovingly restored a vintage motorbike in *Emmerdale*?
10. Who was fostered in *Home and Away* after his parents were killed in a fire?
11. What is the name of Cat Matthews' son in *Family Affairs*?
12. Which Weatherfield citizen ended up in court after giving Emily Nugent driving lessons?
13. Which *Brookside* character committed suicide in prison after being wrongly convicted of the murders of Sue and Danny Sullivan?
14. Who in *Crossroads* died of a heart attack after cheating Dick Jarvis out of their car-hire partnership?
15. In *EastEnders*, which Fowler emigrated to America?
16. Who plays Jack Sugden in *Emmerdale*?

Answers to page 479

TV POT LUCK 13: **1.** *Big Brother* **2.** Rachel de Thame **3.** BBC2 **4.** 80 Raves **5.** *Smack the Pony* **6.** Antoine de Caunes **7.** Buffy **8.** Grandpa **9.** *Spitting Image* **10.** Judy Finnegan **11.** Peter Snow **12.** Kathleen Harrison **13.** Dick Emery **14.** Harold Wilson **15.** Tony Hatch **16.** Robert Winston

Sci Fi 4

Answers on page 476

1. In *The Hitch-Hiker's Guide to the Galaxy*, which android was designed with GPP – Genuine People Personality?
2. Which *Red Dwarf* character's first love was a Sinclair ZX81?
3. Who was the Tracys' faithful family retainer in *Thunderbirds*?
4. And what was his daughter's name?
5. What was the name of Mr Spock's father?
6. Who plays *Xena: Warrior Princess*?
7. In *Space Patrol*, who had a blonde Venusian secretary called Marla?
8. Which *Doctor Who* teamed up with a young alien named Turlough?
9. In what field was Dayna Mellanby able to assist *Blake's 7*?
10. Who was Adam Adamant's arch enemy?
11. What was the title of the sequel to *A For Andromeda*?
12. Which were the favourite sweets of Tom Baker's *Doctor Who*?
13. Who was the commander of the galactic patrol ship *Phoenix Five*?
14. Which 1970s sci-fi series starred Donald Houston as David Caulder?
15. What were the names of the three Robinson children who were *Lost in Space*?
16. Which member of the *Star Trek: Voyager* crew was half-Klingon?

Answers to page 476

CHILDREN'S TV 7: **1.** *Circus Boy* **2.** *The Double Deckers* **3.** *Do Not Adjust Your Set* **4.** *Teletubbies* **5.** *Billy Bunter of Greyfriars School* **6** *Ivanhoe* **7.** *Deputy Dawg* **8.** *Wacky Races* **9.** *Pinky and Perky* **10.** *The Magic Roundabout* **11.** *Stingray* **12.** *Pipkins* **13.** *Captain Pugwash* **14.** *The Herbs* **15.** *The Woodentops* **16.** *The Wombles*

TV Pot Luck 13

Answers on page 477

1. Which series made a star of 'Nasty' Nick?
2. Which former model is a member of the *Gardeners' World* team?
3. Which channel screened *Meetings With Remarkable Trees*?
4. What did Channel 4 film six young Britons travelling around the world in?
5. Which sketch show combines the talents of Fiona Allen, Doon MacKichan and Sally Phillips?
6. Who presents *Eurotrash*?
7. What is the name of BBC2's Vampire Slayer?
8. Which of *The Munsters* could change into a bat?
9. Peter Fluck and Roger Law were the driving forces of which satirical series?
10. Who boobed when her dress came adrift at the 2000 National Television Awards?
11. Which king of the swingometer presents *Tomorrow's World*?
12. Who turned down the title role in *Edna the Inebriate Woman*?
13. Lampwick, Mandy and College were characters created by which comedian?
14. Which ex-Premier had his own series, *A Prime Minister on Prime Ministers*?
15. Which *New Faces* panellist gave comedian Harry Dickman 'two points for his nerve'?
16. Who presented *The Human Body*?

Answers to page 477

SOAPS 11: **1.** Mike Baldwin **2.** Sam Hurst **3.** O'Brien **4.** Dr Michael Rossi **5.** Richard Norton **6.** Miss Texas **7.** *Taff Acre* **8.** Steven Carrington **9.** Alan Turner **10.** Steven Matheson **11.** Davey **12.** Leonard Swindley **13.** Graeme Curtis **14.** Victor Amos **15.** Michelle **16.** Clive Hornby

Which Year in TV? 7

Answers on page 482

In which year did the following programmes begin in the UK?

1. *Red Dwarf*
2. *The Fast Show*
3. *Top Gear*
4. *Sykes*
5. *Wagon Train*
6. *Bergerac*
7. *Between the Lines*
8. *EastEnders*
9. *Upstairs, Downstairs*
10. *Magpie*
11. *Drop The Dead Donkey*
12. *Elizabeth R*
13. *This Is Your Life*
14. *Frasier*
15. *Blake's 7*
16. *Have I Got News For You?*

Answers to page 482

EASTENDERS 3: **1.** Sheila Hancock **2.** Sarah **3.** Diane Butcher **4.** Joe Wicks **5.** Dr Fred Fonseca **6.** Christine Hewitt **7.** Nick Cotton **8.** Duncan Boyd **9.** Magda Czaikowski **10.** Susan **11.** Mary Flaherty **12.** Della Alexander and Binnie Roberts **13.** Richard Cole **14.** Clyde **15.** Phil Mitchell **16.** James Willmott-Brown

Comedy 15

Answers on page 483

1. As played by Brian Murphy, what did Lester Small do for a living?
2. *How Do You View?* was a 1949 showcase for which gap-toothed comic?
3. Paul and Barry Elliot are better known as which comedy double act?
4. Which American played Bill Hooper in *Nobody's Perfect*?
5. Who lent their initials to Channel 4's *S and M*?
6. Who was *Waiting for God* as Diana Trent?
7. Which laconic comedian had his own *Happy Hour* in 2001?
8. Who wrote *The Savages*?
9. Which Seventies show launched the careers of Jim Bowen, Bernard Manning and Ken Goodwin?
10. Which series had its origins in a stage play entitled *The Banana Box*?
11. Who told *Staggering Stories*?
12. Which two Browns were regulars on *Who Do You Do*?
13. Which former model starred opposite John Standing in *The Other 'Arf*?
14. Who blacked up to play Rangi Ram in *It Ain't Half Hot Mum*?
15. *In Sickness and In Health* was the sequel to which controversial sitcom?
16. Who was Audrey fforbes-Hamilton's best friend?

Answers to page 483

CHAT SHOWS 2: **1.** The Bee Gees **2.** Ian Wright **3.** Michael Parkinson **4.** Goddard **5.** Richard Madeley and Judy Finnigan **6.** Chris Evans **7.** Russell Harty **8.** Mrs Merton **9.** Madge Allsop **10.** John Freeman **11.** Robert Kilroy-Silk **12.** David Frost **13.** Clive Anderson **14.** Margaret Thatcher **15.** Terry Wogan **16.** Emu

EastEnders 3

Answers on page 480

1. Who played Steve Owen's mum?
2. What was the name of Tony Hills' God-fearing sister?
3. Who ran off to France after receiving a marriage proposal from Mark Fowler?
4. Who went mad and wrapped all his furniture in kitchen foil?
5. Who 'came out' on a wild weekend in Brighton?
6. With whom did Arthur Fowler have an affair?
7. Who killed Eddie Royle?
8. Which curate became engaged to Sharon Watts?
9. Which half-Polish caterer for the Queen Vic had a fling with Dennis Watts?
10. What was the name of Michael Rose's wife?
11. Which arrival from Ireland was played by Melanie Clark Pullen?
12. Who were *EastEnders'* first lesbian couple?
13. Which market inspector was known as 'Tricky Dicky'?
14. Which member of the Tavernier family was a keen boxer?
15. Who entered into a marriage of convenience with Romanian refugee Nadia Berovac?
16. Who owned the Dagmar wine bar and raped Kathy Beale?

Answers to page 480

WHICH YEAR IN TV? 7: **1.** 1988 **2.** 1994 **3.** 1978 **4.** 1960 **5.** 1958 **6.** 1981 **7.** 1992 **8.** 1985 **9.** 1971 **10.** 1968 **11.** 1990 **12.** 1971 **13.** 1955 **14.** 1994 **15.** 1978 **16.** 1990

Chat Shows 2

Answers on page 481

1. Which band walked out on Clive Anderson?
2. Which former England footballer had his own chat show?
3. Which chat show host made a television comeback in the late 1990s?
4. What is *Trisha*'s surname?
5. Which daytime husband-and-wife team had O.J. Simpson as guest on their first evening show?
6. Who hosted *TFI Friday*?
7. Which chat show host was assaulted by singer Grace Jones for ignoring her?
8. Who cheekily said to Debbie McGee: 'What did you first see in the short, balding millionaire Paul Daniels?'
9. What is the name of Dame Edna Everage's silent friend?
10. Who conducted *Face to Face* interviews from 1959?
11. Which former MP has a morning talk show on BBC1?
12. With whom do politicians take Sunday breakfast on BBC1?
13. Who asked Jeffrey Archer: 'Is there no beginning to your talents?'
14. Which workaholic told Michael Aspel on *Aspel and Company*: 'I'm always on the job'?
15. Who fell over on the first edition of his new live chat show in 1985?
16. Which bird famously wrestled Michael Parkinson to the floor?

Answers to page 481

COMEDY 15: **1.** Driving instructor **2.** Terry-Thomas **3.** The Chuckle Brothers **4.** Elaine Stritch **5.** Tony Slattery and Mike McShane **6.** Stephanie Cole **7.** Jack Dee **8.** Simon Nye **9.** *The Comedians* **10.** *Rising Damp* **11.** Ferdinand De Bargos **12.** Faith Brown and Janet Brown **13.** Lorraine Chase **14.** Michael Bates **15.** *Till Death Us Do Part* **16.** Marjory Frobisher

Music Pot Luck 13

Answers on page 486

1. What was George Martin's first UK number one as a producer?
2. Which track won Best British Single at the 1992 Brits – 17 years after its original release?
3. What working words did Paul McCartney use in place of 'yesterday' while composing the lyrics for his song?
4. Which Puff Daddy chart topper sampled The Police's 'Every Breath You Take'?
5. 'Unchained Melody' and 'I Believe' gave which act their first two number ones in 1995?
6. Which Radio 1 DJ refused to play 'Relax' by Frankie Goes To Hollywood?
7. From where was Gene Pitney only 24 hours in 1963?
8. Which international superstar sang supporting vocals on Rockwell's 'Somebody's Watching You'?
9. In which year was Glenn Miller killed in a plane crash?
10. Who recorded the theme song from *Postman Pat*?
11. At 44 letters, which Rolling Stones single has the longest title?
12. Which Sixties group starred in the film *Catch Us If You Can*?
13. Which fruit did Roger Miller sing about in 1968?
14. What was America's answer to Band Aid?
15. Which drummer specialised in dumping Rolls-Royces in swimming pools?
16. How did Lena Gilbert Ford, lyricist of the song 'Keep The Home Fires Burning', meet her death?

Answers to page 486

BRITNEY SPEARS 1: **1.** 'I Will Still Love You' **2.** '(You Drive Me) Crazy' **3.** Sweden **4.** 'Don't Let Me Be The Last To Know' **5.** '...Baby One More Time' **6.** The Mickey Mouse Club **7.** Louisiana **8.** 'Dear Diary' **9.** 'Time Out With Britney Spears' **10.** *Dawson's Creek* **11.** Skechers **12.** Bryan **13.** 'Oops!...I Did It Again' **14.** 'Lucky' **15.** *Sabrina the Teenage Witch* **16.** '...Baby One More Time'

New Wave 1

Answers on page 487

1. Which forerunners of Crowded House had a hit with 'I Got You'?
2. Who eulogised about 'My Sharona'?
3. Who was the singer with Teardrop Explodes?
4. Who were 'Making Plans For Nigel'?
5. What was Cheap Trick's biggest-selling single in the UK?
6. Who wrote The Pretenders' 'I Go To Sleep'?
7. In 1989, which committed vegetarian claimed that she once fire-bombed McDonald's?
8. Which New Wave band took their name from the last Velvet Underground album?
9. Which band was formed by Stuart Adamson in 1981?
10. Which member of The Police released 'Don't Care' under the name of Klark Kent?
11. Which song gave XTC their highest UK chart position?
12. According to Elvis Costello, for which flowers was it a good year in 1981?
13. Which 1984 single gave The Cars their first UK top ten success for six years?
14. Which single kept Squeeze's 'Up The Junction' from the UK number one spot in 1979?
15. Which track, rejected by Roxy Music, gave Simple Minds their first UK top ten hit?
16. What was the name of Elvis Costello's backing band?

Answers to page 487

MERSEYBEAT 2: **1.** The Searchers **2.** 'Sweets For My Sweet' **3.** *Carousel* **4.** The Fourmost **5.** Elkie Brooks **6.** The Mojos **7.** 'You're My World' (Il Mio Mondo) **8.** 'Wishin' And Hopin'' **9.** The Pete Best Four **10.** The Big Three **11.** 'Hippy Hippy Shake' **12.** 'Needles And Pins' **13.** 'What Have They Done To The Rain' **14.** The Merseys **15.** 'Sorrow' **16.** 'Ferry Across The Mersey'

Britney Spears 1

Answers on page 484

1. Which track on Britney's debut album was a duet with Don Philip?
2. What was the title of Britney's third single?
3. In which country was 'Oops!...I Did It Again' recorded?
4. Which song off the second album was co-written by Shania Twain?
5. What was the title of Britney's first album?
6. What was the name of the club which Britney attended with Christina Aguilera and Justin Timberlake?
7. In which American state was Britney born?
8. Which track from her second album did Britney help to write?
9. What was the title of Britney's debut home video?
10. In which Channel 4 teen drama has Britney appeared?
11. What make of trainers has Britney modelled?
12. What is the name of Britney's older brother?
13. What was the title of Britney's second album?
14. Which track from that album was the story of a girl who is a superstar?
15. In which TV series did Britney appear with Melissa Joan Hart?
16. Which Britney release was the best-selling UK single for 1999?

Answers to page 484

MUSIC POT LUCK 13: **1.** 'You're Driving Me Crazy' by The Temperance Seven **2.** 'Bohemian Rhapsody' **3.** Scrambled eggs **4.** 'I'll Be Missing You' **5.** Robson and Jerome **6.** Mike Read **7.** Tulsa **8.** Michael Jackson **9.** 1944 **10.** Ken Barrie **11.** 'Have You Seen Your Mother Baby, Standing In The Shadow' **12.** The Dave Clark Five **13.** 'Little Green Apples' **14.** USA For Africa **15.** Keith Moon **16.** In a fire at her home

Merseybeat 2

Answers on page 485

1. Which Merseybeat group toppled Elvis's 'Devil In Disguise' from the top of the UK charts in 1963?
2. And what was the title of the song?
3. From which musical was 'You'll Never Walk Alone' taken?
4. Brian O'Hara, Mike Millward, Billy Hatton and Dave Lovelady formed which Merseybeat group?
5. Which singer is the sister of former Billy J. Kramer and The Dakotas' drummer Tony Mansfield?
6. Which band had a 1964 hit with 'Everything's Alright'?
7. Which Cilla Black number one of 1964 was adapted from an Italian tune?
8. Which Bacharach and David song gave The Merseybeats chart success in 1964?
9. Which group did Pete Best form on being ousted from The Beatles?
10. Brian Griffiths, John Gustafson and John Hutchinson comprised which Merseybeat group?
11. Which song was the first top five hit for The Swinging Blue Jeans?
12. Which Searchers hit was co-written by Sonny Bono?
13. And which Searchers single was an anti-nuclear protest song originally recorded by Malvina Reynolds?
14. Which duo did Tony Crane and Billy Kinsley form following the demise of The Merseybeats?
15. And what was their only hit under their new name?
16. Which film title track was a hit for Gerry and The Pacemakers in 1964?

Answers to page 485

NEW WAVE 1: **1.** Split Enz **2.** The Knack **3.** Julian Cope **4.** XTC **5.** 'I Want You To Want Me' **6.** Ray Davies **7.** Chrissie Hynde **8.** Squeeze **9.** Big Country **10.** Stewart Copeland **11.** 'Senses Working Overtime' (10) **12.** Roses **13.** 'Drive' **14.** 'Are "Friends" Electric' (Tubeway Army) **15.** 'Don't You (Forget About Me)' **16.** The Attractions

Albums 4

Answers on page 490

1. What was the title of the Red Hot Chili Peppers' number two UK album of 1995?
2. Which Four Seasons album featured 'December 63 (Oh What A Night)'?
3. Who released the album 'Honky Chateau'?
4. 'Venus And Mars' was a number one album for which band?
5. Whose 1979 big-selling album was titled 'Discovery'?
6. What was the title of Roxy Music's number one UK album of 1982?
7. Whose 1985 album was called 'Alf'?
8. Which Lionel Richie offering was the best-selling UK album of 1984?
9. 'Seven And The Ragged Tiger' was a 1983 chart-topping album for which band?
10. Which Eagles album ends with 'The Last Resort'?
11. For the recording of which album did Crowded House spend much of the time naked, apparently in order to create the right atmosphere?
12. Which Rolling Stones album cover was a plain white sleeve depicting an invitation?
13. Whose second album was titled 'In Gorbachev We Trust'?
14. 'Let's Go Crazy' was a track from which Prince album?
15. On which album's sleeve notes did Michael Jackson thank Cary Grant and Marlon Brando?
16. Which Michael Jackson album of 1982 reached number one in every western country?

Answers to page 490

NUMBER TWOS 2: **1.** 'All Right Now' **2.** 'American Pie' **3.** Marillion **4.** The Osmonds **5.** 'Heartbreak Hotel' **6.** Manfred Mann **7.** Billy Fury **8.** Stan ('My Friend Stan') **9.** 'Knock Three Times' by Dawn **10.** Neil Reid **11.** The Moody Blues **12.** King **13.** Herman's Hermits **14.** Deep Purple **15.** Blondie **16.** 'I Believe'

Boy Bands 2

Answers on page 491

1. How did New Kids On The Block's Danny Wood injure himself on stage at Manchester in 1990?
2. How many members are there in Point Break?
3. Which Channel 4 programme traced the formation of O-Town?
4. Lance, Justin and JC are members of which group?
5. What does LFO stand for?
6. Which boy band released the album 'Invincible'?
7. What nationality is Christian from a1?
8. Which group released 'You Needed Me' in 1999?
9. Which boy band are named after a branch of the London Underground?
10. Which country do The Moffatts come from?
11. 'If Only' was a single from which pop threesome?
12. Which member of Another Level once dated the model Jordan?
13. What was East 17's only UK number one?
14. Which items of New Kids On The Block merchandise were unveiled in February 1990?
15. Which boy band had their first UK top ten hit with 'Crazy For You' in 1994?
16. Which two boy bands had hits with 'Love Me For A Reason' 20 years apart?

Answers to page 491

COUNTRY AND WESTERN 3: **1.** Loretta Lynn **2.** Tammy Wynette ('D.I.V.O.R.C.E.') **3.** Lyle Lovett **4.** *Even Cowgirls Get The Blues* **5.** Garth Brooks **6.** Johnny Cash **7.** Mary-Chapin Carpenter **8.** Billy Ray Cyrus **9.** Suzy Bogguss **10.** Crystal Gayle **11.** 'Lefty' **12.** Waylon Jennings **13.** Seven **14.** Johnny Cash **15.** Homer and Jethro **16.** Emmylou Harris

Number Twos 2

Answers on page 488

1. Which classic Free track reached number two in the UK charts in 1970?
2. Which Don McLean song, subsequently covered by Madonna, got to number two in 1972?
3. Who reached number two in 1985 with 'Kayleigh'?
4. Whose 'Crazy Horses' missed out on the top spot in 1972?
5. Which 1956 single from Elvis rose to number two in the UK charts?
6. Who got to number two in 1966 with 'Semi-Detached Suburban Mr James'?
7. Which male singer took 'Jealousy' to number two in 1961?
8. Which friend of Slade's only made it to number two in 1973?
9. Which middle-of-the-road single kept the Stones' 'Brown Sugar' off the top spot?
10. Which youthful *Opportunity Knocks* winner got to number two with 'Mother Of Mine' in 1972?
11. Which band made number two with 'Question' in 1970?
12. Which band fell one short of the top with 'Love & Pride' in 1985?
13. Who reached number two with 'My Sentimental Friend' in 1969?
14. Which heavy metal band rose to second spot with 'Black Night' in 1970?
15. Which American band were 'Dreaming' of the number one spot in 1979, only to narrowly miss out?
16. Which Bachelors song only reached number two in 1964 before Robson and Jerome went one better 31 years later?

Answers to page 488

ALBUMS 4: **1.** 'One Hot Minute' **2.** 'Who Loves You' **3.** Elton John **4.** Wings **5.** Electric Light Orchestra **6.** 'Avalon' **7.** Alison Moyet **8.** 'Can't Slow Down' **9.** Duran Duran **10.** 'Hotel California' **11.** 'Together Alone' **12.** 'Beggars Banquet' **13.** Shamen **14.** 'Purple Rain' **15.** 'Bad' **16.** 'Thriller'

Country and Western 3

Answers on page 489

1. Who teamed up with Tammy Wynette and Dolly Parton for the 1993 'Honky Tonk Angels' album?
2. Who spelt out her marital problems in a 1975 hit?
3. Whose 1996 album was called 'The Road To Ensenada'?
4. From which film was k.d. lang's 'Just Keep Me Moving' taken?
5. What is the name of country singer Colleen Carroll's famous son?
6. Who recorded an album at San Quentin Prison in 1969?
7. Whose debut album in 1987 was titled 'Hometown Girl'?
8. Which Kentucky-born country singer worked as a car salesman before making his 1992 breakthrough album 'Some Gave All'?
9. Who duetted with Lee Greenwood on the US country hit 'Hopelessly Yours' and was named Most Promising Artist at the 1992 Country Music Awards?
10. Which country artist had mainstream hits in the Seventies with 'Don't It Make My Brown Eyes Blue' and 'Talking In Your Sleep'?
11. What was William Orville Frizzell's nickname?
12. Whose albums have included 'Dreaming My Dreams', 'Will The Wolf Survive?' and 'Highwayman'?
13. How old was Willie Nelson when he wrote his first 'cheating-heart-style' song?
14. Who had a hit with 'Ring Of Fire' in 1963?
15. As which duo were Henry Haynes and Kenneth Burns better known?
16. 'Roses In The Snow' was which artist's fourth US top forty album?

Answers to page 489

BOY BANDS 2: **1.** He damaged his ankle after tripping over a stuffed toy thrown on stage by a fan **2.** Three **3.** *Making the Band* **4.** N Sync **5.** Lyte Funkie Ones **6.** Five **7.** Norwegian **8.** Boyzone **9.** Northern Line **10.** Canada **11.** Hanson **12.** Dane Bowers **13.** Stay Another Day **14.** Dolls **15.** Let Loose **16.** The Osmonds and Boyzone

Eighties 3

Answers on page 494

1. Which American singer had hits with 'Time After Time' and 'True Colors'?
2. Under what name did John Mellencamp used to record?
3. Colin Hay was the vocalist with which Australian band?
4. At which club did Wham! hang out in 1983?
5. Peter Cox and Richard Drummie made up which band?
6. What did Bros want to know in 1988?
7. Who was employed as a tape operator with Stock, Aitken and Waterman before being launched on a singing career?
8. Who had a number two hit with 'Sign Your Name' in 1988?
9. Who took over as singer with Haircut 100 following Nick Heyward's departure?
10. Which band did Norman Cook join in 1985?
11. Who had a 1987 album called 'Dancing With Strangers'?
12. Which artist's full name is Helen Folasade Adu?
13. Joanne Catherall and Susanne Sulley were singers/dancers with which band?
14. Which girl duo had a 1987 hit with 'Heartache'?
15. Which member of The Housemartins left the band to open a vegetarian restaurant?
16. Who was the head of Factory Records?

Answers to page 494

LYRICS 5: **1.** 'The Reflex' (Duran Duran) **2.** 'We Don't Talk Anymore' (Cliff Richard) **3.** 'My Way' (Frank Sinatra) **4.** 'Music To Watch Girls By' (Andy Williams) **5.** 'I Should Be So Lucky' (Kylie Minogue) **6.** 'A Million Love Songs' (Take That) **7.** 'All That She Wants' (Ace Of Base) **8.** 'I Heard It Through The Grapevine' (Marvin Gaye) **9.** 'Reach Out I'll Be There' (The Four Tops) **10.** 'Grease' (Frankie Valli) **11.** 'Will You Love Me Tomorrow?' (The Shirelles) **12.** 'Man On The Moon' (R.E.M.) **13.** 'How Do I Live?' (LeAnn Rimes) **14.** 'Making Your Mind Up' (Bucks Fizz) **15.** 'The Boxer' (Simon and Garfunkel) **16.** 'Romeo And Juliet' (Dire Straits)

R.E.M. 1

Answers on page 495

1. What subjects did Michael Stipe study at the University of Georgia in Athens?
2. Which band member used to work in an Athens record store, learning guitar licks between serving customers?
3. Which member of R.E.M. was cleared of an alleged air rage offence in a UK court in April 2002?
4. Which British band did R.E.M. support on a short US tour in 1983?
5. Which R.E.M. single was a tribute to comedian Andy Kaufman?
6. Who contributed backing vocals on 'Shiny Happy People'?
7. Which was R.E.M.'s first number one album in the UK?
8. The title of which album was taken from a sign at Weaver D's soul food diner in Athens?
9. Why did R.E.M. cancel part of their 1995 European tour?
10. Who sang backing vocals on 'E-Bow The Letter?'
11. In which year did 'Losing My Religion' reach number 19 in the UK charts?
12. As a youngster, what nickname was Michael Stipe given by his father?
13. Who joined the band on stage during their 1984 US tour to sing 'So You Want To Be A Rock 'n' Roll Star'?
14. Which tennis player took over on drums for an encore of 'Wichita Lineman' during R.E.M.'s 1995 tour of Australia?
15. What was the title of R.E.M.'s first full-length album?
16. On which album did 'The One I Love' appear?

Answers to page 495

GIRL BANDS 2: **1.** The Crystals (Crystal Bates) **2.** Gerry Goffin and Carole King **3.** 'Someday' **4.** 1979 **5.** The Chiffons **6.** 'Never Ever' **7.** Veronica and Estelle Bennett **8.** Smokey Robinson **9.** The Bangles (Michael Steele) **10.** Siobhan Fahey **11.** 'Da Doo Ron Ron' **12.** 'Remember (Walkin' In The Sand)' **13.** The youngest, Mary Weiss, stayed on at school **14.** 'Nathan Jones' **15.** Misteeq **16.** Victoria Beckham

Lyrics 5

Answers on page 492

From which songs are the following lyrics taken?

1. 'I tell you somebody's fooling around with my chances on the dangerline'
2. 'But I ain't losing sleep and I ain't counting sheep'
3. 'I did what I had to do and saw it through without exemption'
4. 'Eyes watch girls walk with tender loving care'
5. 'My heart is close to breaking and I can't go on faking the fantasy that you'll be mine'
6. 'A million words just trying to make the love song of the year'
7. 'So if you are in sight and the day is right, she's the hunter, you're the fox'
8. 'I bet you're wondering how I knew 'bout your plans to make me blue'
9. 'And your life is filled with confusion, and happiness is just an illusion'
10. 'It's got groove, it's got meaning'
11. 'Is this a lasting treasure or just a moment's pleasure'
12. 'If you believe there's nothing up my sleeve, then nothing is cool'
13. 'If you ever leave, baby, you would take away everything good in my life'
14. 'Don't let your indecision take you from behind'
15. 'I am just a poor boy though my story's seldom told, I have squandered my resistance for a pocketful of mumbles, such are promises'
16. 'I can't do the talk like they talk on TV and I can't do a love song like the way it's meant to be'

Answers to page 492

EIGHTIES 3: **1.** Cyndi Lauper **2.** John Cougar **3.** Men At Work **4.** Club Tropicana **5.** Go West **6.** 'When Will I Be Famous?' **7.** Rick Astley **8.** Terence Trent D'Arby **9.** Mark Fox **10.** The Housemartins **11.** Chris Rea **12.** Sade **13.** Human League **14.** Pepsi and Shirlie **15.** Ted Key **16.** Tony Wilson

Girl Bands 2

Answers on page 493

1. The daughter of songwriter Leroy Bates gave which Sixties girl group their name?
2. Who wrote The Shirelles' 'Will You Love Me Tomorrow'?
3. Which Eternal single came from the film *The Hunchback of Notre Dame*?
4. In which year were The Nolans In The Mood For Dancing?
5. Which girl group comprised Judy Craig, Barbara Lee, Patricia Bennett and Sylvia Peterson?
6. What was All Saints' first UK number one?
7. Which two sisters were the cornerstone of The Ronettes?
8. Who wrote and produced 'Floy Joy' for The Supremes?
9. Which all-girl band had a bass guitarist called Michael?
10. Who left Bananarama in 1988?
11. Which Crystals hit of 1963 is generally regarded as the first true example of the Phil Spector sound?
12. What was The Shangri-Las first US hit?
13. Why were the four-piece Shangri-Las a three-piece on their first promotional tour to Britain?
14. Which Supremes song did Bananarama cover in 1988?
15. Which girl band released the single 'B With Me' in 2002?
16. Which former Spice Girl announced her second pregnancy in February 2002?

Answers to page 493

R.E.M. 1: **1.** Painting and photography **2.** Peter Buck **3.** Peter Buck **4.** The Police **5.** 'Man On The Moon' **6.** Kate Pierson of The B-52s **7.** 'Out Of Time' **8.** 'Automatic For The People' **9.** Drummer Bill Berry was taken ill **10.** Patti Smith **11.** 1991 **12.** 'Mr Mouse' **13.** Roger McGuinn **14.** Jim Courier **15.** 'Murmur' **16.** 'Document'

Sixties 4

Answers on page 498

Which acts had UK hits in the Sixties with the following tracks?

1. 'Step Inside Love'
2. 'Midnight In Moscow'
3. 'Lovin' Things'
4. 'Google Eye'
5. 'A Groovy Kind Of Love'
6. 'Halfway To Paradise'
7. 'Tell Me When'
8. 'The Ballad Of Bonnie And Clyde'
9. 'Blue Bayou'
10. 'But I Do'
11. 'Creeque Alley'
12. 'A Lover's Concerto'
13. 'Mama'
14. 'Silhouettes'
15. 'She Wears My Ring'
16. 'The Boat That I Row'

Answers to page 498

NAME CHANGES 7: **1.** Simple Minds **2.** Elkie Brooks **3.** Tab Hunter **4.** Norman **5.** Sid Vicious **6.** Gerard **7.** Queen **8.** Gram Parsons **9.** Gary Webb **10.** Nirvana **11.** New Kids On The Block **12.** Denny Laine **13.** The Moody Blues **14.** Manfred Mann **15.** Little Richard **16.** Human League

Music Pot Luck 14

Answers on page 499

1. What job did the teenage Sting get before going to Warwick University?
2. What did Neil Diamond train to be before taking up a career in music?
3. Producer Phil Spector once held a gun to which singer's head in the studio to get the performance he wanted?
4. Who was the subject of The Beatles' 'Baby You're A Rich Man'?
5. Which London Underground station did The New Vaudeville Band sing about in 1967?
6. Which band took their name from the robot who appeared in the *Beano* comic, adding an 'h' because they thought it wouldn't be sounded in their native Ireland?
7. Which punk rocker was charged with murdering his girlfriend Nancy Spungen in 1978?
8. What was the first posthumous UK number one single?
9. Which are the only US group to have had UK number one singles in the Seventies, Eighties and Nineties?
10. Which knight sang backing vocals on Scaffold's 'Lily The Pink'?
11. What was the name of Joe Brown's backing group?
12. With whom did Tom Jones duet in 1999 on 'Baby It's Cold Outside'?
13. What was Imagination's first UK chart success?
14. Who sang on Electronic's 1989 hit 'Getting Away With It'?
15. Which Tony Christie hit was the theme from the TV series *The Protectors*?
16. What role did 'Flowers In The Rain' by The Move play in radio music history?

Answers to page 499

FOLK 2: **1.** Paul McCartney **2.** 'Gaudete' **3.** 'Meet Me On The Corner' **4.** The Dirt Band **5.** Buddy Holly **6.** The Springfields **7.** Jim Dale **8.** 'If You Gotta Go, Go Now' **9.** The Poppy Family **10.** Judith Durham **11.** Loudon Wainwright III **12.** Richard and Linda Thompson **13.** Jack The Lad **14.** Joan Baez **15.** Julie Felix **16.** *Holiday*

Name Changes 7

Answers on page 496

1. Which band changed their name from Johnny and The Self-Abusers?

2. What did Elaine Bookbinder change her name to?

3. Which US singer of the Fifties was born Arthur Kelm?

4. What was Hurricane Smith's real Christian name?

5. What did punk John Ritchie choose as a stage name?

6. What is Leo Sayer's true Christian name?

7. Which internationally famous group used to be known as Smile before opting for something more regal?

8. Which late country rocker was born Cecil Connor III?

9. What is Gary Numan's real name?

10. Which heavy metal band were previously known as Ed Ted and Fred?

11. Which US boy band changed their name from Nynuk?

12. Which former member of The Moody Blues and Wings was born Brian Hines?

13. Which band used to be called The MB Five in deference to Birmingham brewers Mitchell & Butler?

14. Which Sixties keyboard player, who lent his name to the band, was really called Manfred Lubowitz?

15. As what was Richard Wayne Penniman better known?

16. Which Eighties band from Sheffield used to be called The Future?

Answers to page 496

SIXTIES 4: **1.** Cilla Black **2.** Kenny Ball and his Jazzmen **3.** Marmalade **4.** The Nashville Teens **5.** The Mindbenders **6.** Billy Fury **7.** The Applejacks **8.** Georgie Fame **9.** Roy Orbison **10.** Clarence 'Frogman' Henry **11.** The Mamas and The Papas **12.** The Toys **13.** Dave Berry **14.** Herman's Hermits **15.** Solomon King **16.** Lulu

Folk 2

Answers on page 497

1. Which Beatle sang backing vocals on Donovan's 'Mellow Yellow'?
2. Which Latin title was a 1973 hit for Steeleye Span?
3. What was Lindisfarne's first UK hit?
4. Which band dropped the 'Nitty Gritty' in 1976?
5. Which dead singer was the principal subject of Don McLean's 'American Pie'?
6. Which folk band had a 1962 hit with 'Island Of Dreams'?
7. Which *Carry On* star co-wrote 'Georgy Girl' for The Seekers?
8. Which cover of a Manfred Mann song gave Fairport Convention their only mainstream UK chart success?
9. Which band, led by Terry Jacks, had a 1970 hit with 'Which Way You Goin' Billy'?
10. Who was the lead singer with The Seekers?
11. Who had a hit with 'Dead Skunk'?
12. Which husband and wife duo released the Seventies albums 'Hokey Pokey' and 'Sunnyvista'?
13. Simon Cowe, Ray Laidlaw and Rod Clements left Lindisfarne in 1973 to form which group?
14. Who had a 1971 hit with 'The Night They Drove Old Dixie Down'?
15. Which toothy singer, famous for her appearances on TV's *The Frost Report*, enjoyed a 1970 hit with a cover of Simon and Garfunkel's 'El Condor Pasa'?
16. Gordon Giltrap's 'Heartsong' was used as the theme to which TV series in the Eighties?

Answers to page 497

MUSIC POT LUCK 14: **1.** Bus conductor **2.** Doctor **3.** Leonard Cohen **4.** Brian Epstein **5.** Finchley Central **6.** Thin Lizzy (Tin Lizzie) **7.** Sid Vicious **8.** 'It Doesn't Matter Anymore' (Buddy Holly) **9.** Blondie **10.** Tim Rice **11.** The Bruvvers **12.** Cerys Matthews **13.** 'Body Talk' **14.** Neil Tennant (Pet Shop Boys) **15.** 'Avenues And Alleyways' **16.** It was the first record to be played on Radio 1

Michael Jackson 1

Answers on page 502

1. With whom did Michael Jackson duet on the 1982 single 'The Girl Is Mine'?
2. Who recorded the original version of Jackson's 1972 hit 'Ain't No Sunshine'?
3. How old was Jackson when he had his first solo hit?
4. And what was the title of the song?
5. Which style of dancing did Jackson perfect in the Eighties?
6. Which heavy metal guitarist played for free on 'Beat It'?
7. Which single could have been – but wasn't – written about a tennis player?
8. Which Michael Jackson UK number one was written and produced by R. Kelly?
9. What was Jackson's first UK solo number one?
10. Which Michael Jackson single featured Slash from Guns N' Roses on guitar?
11. Which horror-movie star provided a ghostly rap on the title track of 'Thriller'?
12. What was Jackson doing when his hair caught fire in 1984?
13. Who said that Jackson was 'an inspiration to all of us' in a 1984 congratulatory telegram?
14. In which year was the album 'Bad' released?
15. Which member of Jackson's entourage was refused admission to the UK in 1988?
16. Who marched on stage and interrupted Jackson's performance of 'Earth Song' at the 1996 Brit Awards?

Answers to page 502

SOLO ARTISTS 3: **1.** 'You Can't Hurry Love' **2.** Barry Gibb **3.** 'Joanna' **4.** Sandie Shaw **5.** Richard Marx **6.** The Sutherland Brothers **7.** 'Oh Julie' **8.** Argentina **9.** Cliff Richard ('Honky Tonk Angels') **10.** Hurricane Smith **11.** Michael Bolton **12.** Whistling **13.** 'I Was Kaiser Bill's Batman' **14.** Joan Osborne **15.** Kenneth McKellar **16.** Jose Feliciano

Nineties 4

Answers on page 503

1. Which 1992 track allegedly recounting the joys of Ecstasy reached number one in the UK during Drug Awareness Week?
2. Felix Buxton and Simon Ratcliffe make up which duo?
3. To which TV presenter is Toploader guitarist Dan Hipgrave married?
4. Who reached the top of the charts in 1992 with 'Sleeping Satellite'?
5. Who released the album 'Diva' in 1993?
6. Who duetted with Mariah Carey on 'Endless Love'?
7. Which boy band took a cover of a Dr Hook hit to the top of the UK charts in 1999?
8. And what was the title of the song?
9. Sarah Cracknell is the singer with which band?
10. Who were 'Missing' in 1995?
11. Which animated family had a number one single in 1991?
12. Who had a 1996 UK number one single with 'I Feel You'?
13. Who was the female singer with The Fugees before going solo?
14. Which star of the TV docusoap *The Cruise* had a number one album in 1998?
15. Which band went 'Dizzy' with Vic Reeves in 1991?
16. Which Super Furry Animals hit incorporated the names of Einstein's parents?

Answers to page 503

COVER VERSIONS 4: **1.** 'Words' **2.** 'Something' **3.** 'She' **4.** 'Happy Together' **5.** 'Go West' **6.** 'Sorrow' **7.** The Delfonics **8.** 'The Air That I Breathe' **9.** The Stranglers **10.** Denise Welch **11.** Argent **12.** 'Going Underground' **13.** 'Love Letters' **14.** 'Love Me Tender' **15.** 'Looking Thru The Eyes Of Love' **16.** Itchycoo Park

Solo Artists 3

Answers on page 500

1. Which Supremes cover gave Phil Collins his first UK number one as a solo artist?
2. Who sang backing vocals on Dionne Warwick's 1982 hit 'Heartbreaker'?
3. Tony Hatch and Jackie Trent originally recorded which Scott Walker hit from 1968?
4. Which Sixties singer made a comeback with The Smiths in 1984?
5. Which American singer's biggest hit was 'Right Here Waiting' in 1989?
6. Who recorded the original version of Rod Stewart's number one 'Sailing'?
7. What was the title of Shakin' Stevens' third UK number one?
8. In which country was Chris De Burgh born?
9. Which artist demanded that his record company withdraw his new single after discovering that it was about prostitutes?
10. Who had Seventies hits with 'Don't Let It Die' and 'Oh Babe, What Would You Say'?
11. Who asked: 'How Am I Supposed To Live Without You' in 1990?
12. In which field of musical performance did Jack Smith excel in 1967?
13. And what was the title of his surprise hit?
14. Which American female singer's 1996 album was titled 'Relish'?
15. Which Scotsman sang Handel on a 1960 EP?
16. Which solo artist had a 1968 hit with 'Light My Fire'?

Answers to page 500

MICHAEL JACKSON 1: **1.** Paul McCartney **2.** Bill Withers **3.** 13 **4.** 'Got To Be There' **5.** Moonwalking **6.** Eddie Van Halen **7.** 'Billie Jean' **8.** 'You Are Not Alone' **9.** 'One Day In Your Life' **10.** 'Black Or White' **11.** Vincent Price **12.** Filming a Pepsi commercial **13.** President Reagan **14.** 1987 **15.** His chimp, Bubbles **16.** Jarvis Cocker

Cover Versions 4

Answers on page 501

1. Which Bee Gees song has been covered successfully by Rita Coolidge and Boyzone?
2. Which song was a hit for both The Beatles and Shirley Bassey within the space of eight months?
3. Which ballad was a hit for Charles Aznavour in 1974 and Elvis Costello in 1999?
4. What were The Turtles in 1967 and Jason Donovan in 1991?
5. Which Village People song did The Pet Shop Boys cover in 1993?
6. Which song links The Merseys and David Bowie?
7. Who originally had a hit with The Fugees' 1996 smash 'Ready Or Not'?
8. Which Hollies single was covered by Simply Red in 1998?
9. Who covered The Kinks' 'All Day And All Of The Night' in 1988?
10. Which former *Coronation Street* actress reached number 23 in the UK charts in 1995 with her version of Julie London's 1957 hit 'Cry Me A River'?
11. Which band originally had a hit with 'God Gave Rock And Roll To You', a 1992 success for Kiss?
12. Which Jam number one also charted for Buffalo Tom in 1999?
13. Which song has been a UK top ten hit for Ketty Lester, Elvis Presley and Alison Moyet?
14. Which song was a hit for both Elvis Presley and Roland Rat?
15. Which song links Gene Pitney and The Partridge Family?
16. Which Small Faces park was revisited by M People in 1995?

Answers to page 501

NINETIES 4: **1.** 'Ebenezer Goode' (Shamen) **2.** Basement Jaxx **3.** Gail Porter **4.** Tasmin Archer **5.** Annie Lennox **6.** Luther Vandross **7.** 911 **8.** 'A Little Bit More' **9.** Saint Etienne **10.** Everything But The Girl **11.** The Simpsons ('Do The Bartman') **12.** Peter Andre **13.** Lauryn Hill **14.** Jane McDonald **15.** The Wonder Stuff **16.** 'Hermann Loves Pauline'

Premiership 6

Answers on page 506

1. Which club finished runner-up to Manchester United in the first FA Premier League season in 1992–3?

2. Which current Premiership club was founded in 1881 as Stanley?

3. Which Arsenal manager brought Dennis Bergkamp to Highbury?

4. By the start of season 2001–2, which are the only two clubs other than Manchester United to have won the Premiership?

5. What did the three clubs relegated from the Premiership at the end of season 2000–1 have in common?

6. Which current Premiership club sold Alan Shearer to Blackburn in 1992?

7. Which two clubs relegated from the Premiership in 1994 now play in Division Two of the Football League?

8. For whom did Chelsea pay Blackburn Rovers £10 million in July 1999?

9. Who were relegated from the Premiership in 1994 following a last-minute defeat at Stamford Bridge?

10. And who secured their safety in the same season by coming back from 2–0 down to defeat Wimbledon 3–2 on the final day?

11. Which club currently has the longest unbroken run as members of the top division of English football?

12. Which club enjoyed just one season in the Premier League in 1997–8?

13. Which mishap linked Derby v Wimbledon (14 Aug 1997), West Ham v Crystal Palace (3 Nov 1997) and Wimbledon v Arsenal (22 Dec 1997)?

14. Who appeared to simulate snorting cocaine by rubbing his nose along the six-yard line during the 1999 Merseyside derby?

15. Which current Premiership club had never sacked a manager until 1990?

16. Who lost 8–1 at home to Manchester United in February 1999?

Answers to page 506

FOOTBALL LEAGUE 7: **1.** Millwall **2.** Sheffield United **3.** Cardiff City **4.** Northampton Town **5.** Mansfield Town **6.** Scunthorpe United **7.** Cyril (the Swan) **8.** Barrow **9.** Martin Phillips **10.** Gillingham **11.** Chic Brodie **12.** Sincil Bank **13.** Hull City **14.** John Aldridge **15.** Port Vale **16.** Aldershot

FA Cup 6

Answers on page 507

1. Which club's players allegedly took a monkey gland potion before losing to Portsmouth in the 1939 FA Cup final?
2. Which team scored 19 goals in the opening two rounds of the 1968–9 competition?
3. Which brothers played for Manchester United in the 1977 Cup final?
4. Which club lost both the 1998 and 1999 finals?
5. Which two clubs were drawn together for three successive years in the third round between 1956 and 1958?
6. Where was the 2001 FA Cup final played?
7. Who played on in goal for Manchester City in the 1956 final despite sustaining a broken neck?
8. Which non-League side beat Coventry City in a third-round tie in 1989?
9. Which TV presenter suffered FA Cup humiliation at the hands of Harlow Town in 1980?
10. Whose own goal won the Cup for Spurs in 1991?
11. Which Second Division team reached the semi-finals of the Cup in 2001?
12. What nationality were the Robledo brothers who played for Newcastle in the 1952 final?
13. In which year was the first Wembley final?
14. For which club did John Barnes make his first Cup final appearance?
15. Which Bobby won the Cup for Southampton?
16. For whom did Ted MacDougall score nine goals against Margate in 1971?

Answers to page 507

WHOSE HOME? 7: **1.** Stockport County **2.** Torquay United **3.** Charlton Athletic **4.** Chester City **5.** Crewe Alexandra **6.** Forfar Athletic **7.** Chesterfield **8.** Colchester United **9.** Aberdeen **10.** Oldham Athletic **11.** Derby County **12.** Carlisle United **13.** Bolton Wanderers **14.** Stirling Albion **15.** Grimsby Town **16.** The Shay

Football League 7

Answers on page 504

1. Who won the Second Division title in 2000–1?
2. Which club is nicknamed 'The Blades'?
3. Who paid Stoke City £1 million for midfielder Graham Kavanagh in the summer of 2001?
4. Which club went from the Fourth to the First Division and back again during the 1960s?
5. Which team failed to score in any of their first nine home games in Division Three in 1971–2?
6. From which club did Liverpool sign Kevin Keegan?
7. What is the name of Swansea City's controversial mascot?
8. Which club was voted out of the Football League in 1972?
9. Which winger did Manchester City buy from Exeter for £500,000 in 1995?
10. Which club used to be known as New Brompton?
11. Which former Brentford goalkeeper had to retire from playing after being attacked by a dog during a match at Colchester?
12. What is the name of Lincoln City's ground?
13. For which club did Chris Chilton, Ken Wagstaff, Ken Houghton and Ian Butler form a formidable strike force in the 1960s?
14. Who resigned as manager of Tranmere Rovers in 2001?
15. When Division Four was introduced in 1958–9, who were its first champions?
16. Which club, no longer members of the Football League, defeated Wolves in the Third Division promotion play-offs in 1986–7?

Answers to page 504

PREMIERSHIP 6: **1.** Aston Villa **2.** Newcastle United **3.** Bruce Rioch **4.** Blackburn Rovers and Arsenal **5.** They were all named City – Coventry, Manchester and Bradford **6.** Southampton **7.** Oldham Athletic and Swindon Town **8.** Chris Sutton **9.** Sheffield United **10.** Everton **11.** Arsenal **12.** Barnsley **13.** Floodlight failures **14.** Robbie Fowler **15.** Ipswich Town **16.** Nottingham Forest

Whose Home? 7

Answers on page 505

1. Who plays at Edgeley Park?
2. Whose home ground is Plainmoor?
3. Which club shared Upton Park with West Ham in the early 1990s?
4. Which former League club plays at the Deva Stadium?
5. Gresty Road is the home of which club?
6. Which Scottish team plays at Station Park?
7. Who plays at Saltergate?
8. Layer Road is home to which club?
9. Whose home ground is Pittodrie?
10. Who plays at Boundary Park?
11. Which club moved from the Baseball Ground to Pride Park?
12. Brunton Park is home to which club?
13. Who plays at the Reebok Stadium?
14. Which Scottish club used to play at Anfield?
15. Which club plays its home games in Cleethorpes?
16. What is the name of Halifax Town's ground?

Answers to page 505

FA CUP 6: **1.** Wolverhampton Wanderers **2.** Southend United **3.** Brian and Jimmy Greenhoff **4.** Newcastle United **5.** Cardiff City and Leeds United **6.** The Millennium Stadium, Cardiff **7.** Bert Trautmann **8.** Sutton United **9.** Gary Lineker with Leicester City **10.** Des Walker (Nottingham Forest) **11.** Wycombe Wanderers **12.** Chilean **13.** 1923 **14.** Watford **15.** Stokes **16.** Bournemouth

Oddballs 8

Answers on page 510

1. In which Italian city do Lazio play?
2. Which club does Des Lynam support?
3. In which year was the back-pass rule introduced?
4. In 1972, which English club became the first winners of the UEFA Cup?
5. Which manager took Rushden & Diamonds into the Football League?
6. Which goalkeeper gave away two penalties on his England debut in June 2000?
7. Which player was nicknamed 'The Giraffe'?
8. In which year was *Match of the Day* first shown?
9. Which player scored 397 League goals for Celtic between 1922 and 1938?
10. Which London club's home address is Braemar Road?
11. Which Football League club used to be known as Headington United?
12. Halmstad, Norrköing, and Helsingborg have all won the League Championship in which country?
13. Which British League ground is nearest to the sea?
14. Which former Arsenal winger's England international career lasted just nine minutes?
15. Who was voted Footballer of the Year in 1999?
16. Who became the first player from Guinea to play in the Premiership?

Answers to page 510

MANAGERS 8: **1.** Dario Gradi (Crewe Alexandra) **2.** Ray Harford (Luton Town) **3.** Queens Park Rangers **4.** East Stirlingshire **5.** Ted Drake **6.** Terry Venables **7.** Frank Clark **8.** Derek Dooley **9.** Southampton **10.** Christian Gross **11.** Burnley **12.** 15 **13.** Ruud Gullit (Chelsea) **14.** Steve Gritt **15.** Preston North End **16.** Harry Redknapp

World Cup 5

Answers on page 511

1. Which country won the first World Cup?
2. Who became the first player to score for two different countries in the World Cup when he netted for Croatia against Jamaica in the 1998 finals?
3. Which English referee awarded a first-minute penalty for Holland in the 1974 World Cup final with West Germany?
4. For which country did Grzegorz Lato play?
5. Who won the 1998 World Cup?
6. Against whom were Portugal 3–0 down after 22 minutes in 1966 before storming back to win 5–3?
7. Who scored two goals for Argentina in the 1978 final?
8. In 1998, who had the honour of scoring Jamaica's first goal in the World Cup finals?
9. What was the name of the dog that found the stolen World Cup in 1966?
10. Which 1994 World Cup winner went on to play for Middlesbrough?
11. Who scored the Republic of Ireland's first goal in the 1994 World Cup finals?
12. Who did Brazil beat in the 1958 World Cup final?
13. In which country were the 1962 finals staged?
14. Which is the only country to have appeared in the final stages of every World Cup?
15. Who knocked England out of the 1986 World Cup?
16. Which was the only year when England, Scotland, Northern Ireland and Wales all qualified for the final stages of the World Cup?

Answers to page 511

ENGLAND 4: **1.** 48 **2.** Scotland **3.** AC Milan **4.** Peter Shilton **5.** 125 **6.** Gary Stevens (one played for Spurs, the other for Everton) **7.** Alan Shearer **8.** Derby County and Middlesbrough **9.** Billy Wright **10.** Portugal **11.** Wealdstone **12.** Steve Bull (Wolverhampton Wanderers) **13.** Neil Webb **14.** Paul Scholes **15.** 90 **16.** Paul Mariner

Managers 8

Answers on page 508

1. At the start of the 2001–2 season, which English League manager had the longest current reign with the same club?

2. Which manager was sacked in 1989 partly for 'not smiling enough'?

3. Alec Stock, Gordon Jago and Dave Sexton were all managers of which club?

4. At which Scottish club did Sir Alex Ferguson cut his managerial teeth?

5. Which manager steered Chelsea to their only League title in 1955?

6. Which former England boss helped out Bryan Robson at Middlesbrough in 2000–1?

7. Who succeeded Brian Clough as manager of Nottingham Forest?

8. Which Sheffield Wednesday goalscoring legend was sacked as the club's manager on Christmas Eve 1973?

9. Which club did Ted Bates manage from 1955 to 1973?

10. Who preceded George Graham in charge of Tottenham?

11. At which Lancashire club did Chris Waddle have a brief spell as manager from 1997?

12. For how many years was Bill Shankly manager of Liverpool?

13. Which London club manager said of the British press in 1997: 'They make from a little mosquito a big elephant'?

14. Who was Alan Curbishley's managerial partner at Charlton from 1991 to 1995?

15. Bobby Charlton managed which club from 1973 to 1975?

16. Who surprisingly resigned as West Ham manager in 2001?

Answers to page 508

ODDBALLS 8: **1.** Rome **2.** Brighton & Hove Albion **3.** 1992 **4.** Tottenham Hotspur **5.** Brian Talbot **6.** Richard Wright **7.** Jack Charlton **8.** 1964 **9.** Jimmy McGrory **10.** Brentford **11.** Oxford United **12.** Sweden **13.** Gayfield (Arbroath) **14.** Brian Marwood **15.** David Ginola **16.** Titi Camara

England 4

Answers on page 509

1. How many goals did Gary Lineker score for England?
2. Who were the first nation to defeat England after their 1966 World Cup triumph?
3. For which Italian club was Mark Hateley playing when selected for England in 1985?
4. Who holds the record for the most number of England caps?
5. And how many did he win?
6. At the 1986 World Cup finals, England fielded two players with the same name. What was it?
7. Who captained England at Euro 2000?
8. Steve Bloomer won 23 England caps between 1895 and 1907. For which two clubs did he play in that time?
9. Which former England captain married one of the Beverley Sisters?
10. Against which country did Trevor Brooking win his first England cap?
11. With which non-League side did Stuart Pearce play before his transfer to Coventry City?
12. Who was the last Third Division player to be capped by England?
13. Who became the 1,000th player to be selected for England, in September 1987?
14. Who scored a hat-trick against Poland in a 1999 European Championship qualifier at Wembley?
15. How many England caps did Bryan Robson win?
16. Who scored in six consecutive England appearances from 1981 to 1982?

Answers to page 509

WORLD CUP 5: **1.** Uruguay **2.** Robert Prosinecki (he had scored for Yugoslavia in 1990) **3.** Jack Taylor **4.** Poland **5.** France **6.** North Korea **7.** Mario Kempes **8.** Robbie Earle **9.** Pickles **10.** Branco **11.** Ray Houghton **12.** Sweden **13.** Chile **14.** Brazil **15.** Argentina **16.** 1958

Transfer Trail 7

Answers on page 514

1. From which Dutch club did Manchester United sign Jaap Stam?
2. Who moved from White Hart Lane to Highbury in the summer of 2001?
3. Who did Aston Villa sign from Liverpool for £7 million in May 1997?
4. Alf Common was the first £1,000 transfer, back in 1905. Who signed him?
5. Who left Aston Villa for Everton in 1998, less than a week after joining the Midlands club from West Ham?
6. Who joined Newcastle from Parma for £6.7 million in February 1996?
7. Which Bristol Rovers forward did Reading sign for a bargain £250,000 in August 2000?
8. For whom did Rochdale pay Stoke a club record fee of £150,000 in 2000–1?
9. Which Scottish club signed Eyal Berkovic from West Ham?
10. Who was Britain's first million-pound goalkeeper?
11. For which player did Carlisle United receive their record fee?
12. Which Footballer of the Year was once loaned out to Aldershot?
13. Which Scottish club sold Steve Nicol to Liverpool?
14. From which Italian club did Benito Carbone join Sheffield Wednesday?
15. Who joined Manchester City from Portsmouth for £3.5 million in July 1997?
16. Which former Republic of Ireland international was once sold for a set of tracksuits?

Answers to page 514

EUROPEAN CUPS 5: **1.** Juventus **2.** Celtic **3.** Inter Milan **4.** Fiorentina **5.** Nottingham Forest **6.** Peter Withe **7.** Dundee United **8.** Real Madrid **9.** Gothenburg **10.** John Hewitt **11.** Luxembourg **12.** Nigel Spink **13.** Jimmy Rimmer **14.** Marseille **15.** Bayern Munich **16.** Birmingham City

Oddballs 9

Answers on page 515

1. Which English League club used to play at Whittles Whippet Ground?
2. What was the title of the 1970 England World Cup Squad's song?
3. Which former England international used to work in a sausage-making factory?
4. Which Scottish club does TV presenter John Leslie support?
5. Who was the manager of Walsall at the start of 2001–2?
6. In which year were crossbars first introduced?
7. Which English League ground used to be known as the Celery Trenches?
8. With which club was Des O'Connor a promising winger?
9. Who plays at Whaddon Road?
10. Who managed Arsenal from 1966 to 1976?
11. Which club used to be known as Thames Ironworks?
12. From which club did Manchester United sign Denis Irwin?
13. What was the name of the Futcher twins?
14. Which former Liverpool star became manager of Oxford United in summer 2001?
15. Jack Brownsword set a League appearance record for which club?
16. Who have been at their ground longer than any other Football League club?

Answers to page 515

SHARPSHOOTERS 5: **1.** Terry Bly (Peterborough United) **2.** Pierre van Hooijdonk (Nottingham Forest) **3.** Malcolm Macdonald **4.** 1997 **5.** Cambridge City **6.** Mick Quinn **7.** Jermaine Defoe **8.** Bristol City **9.** AC Milan **10.** Dixie Dean **11.** Dion Dublin **12.** Chester **13.** Morocco **14.** Gordon Durie **15.** Gary Lineker **16.** Newport County

European Cups 5

Answers on page 512

1. Who did Manchester United beat in the semi-finals of the 1999 Champions' League?
2. Who were the first British team to win the European Cup?
3. And who did they beat in the final?
4. Which Italian club were the first winners of the European Cup-Winners' Cup?
5. Which English club won the European Cup in both 1979 and 1980?
6. Who scored Aston Villa's goal in their 1982 European Cup final victory over Bayern Munich?
7. Which Scottish club reached the 1987 UEFA Cup final?
8. Who won the Champions' League in 2000?
9. In which city did Aberdeen win the 1983 European Cup-Winners' Cup?
10. And who scored their winning goal?
11. From which country were Jeunesse Hautcharage beaten 21–0 on aggregate by Chelsea in the 1971 European Cup-Winners' Cup?
12. Who was playing only his second senior game when coming on to keep goal for Aston Villa in the 1982 European Cup final?
13. And who did he replace?
14. Who are the only French team to have won the European Cup?
15. Which club recorded a hat-trick of European Cup wins between 1974 and 1976?
16. Which English club was beaten in the finals of both the 1960 and 1961 Inter-Cities Fairs Cup?

Answers to page 512

TRANSFER TRAIL 7: **1.** PSV Eindhoven **2.** Sol Campbell **3.** Stan Collymore **4.** Middlesbrough **5.** David Unsworth **6.** Faustino Asprilla **7.** Jamie Cureton **8.** Paul Connor **9.** Celtic **10.** Nigel Martyn **11.** Matt Jansen (£1.5 million to Crystal Palace) **12.** Teddy Sheringham **13.** Ayr United **14.** Inter Milan **15.** Lee Bradbury **16.** Tony Cascarino (Crockenhill to Gillingham)

Sharpshooters 5

Answers on page 513

1. Who was the last player to score over 50 League goals in an English season?

2. Which Dutch player topped the English League scoring charts in 1997–8?

3. Who scored all five goals for England against Cyprus in 1975?

4. In what year did Michael Owen make his Liverpool debut?

5. From which non-League club did Millwall sign Neil Harris?

6. Which Newcastle striker was the League's top scorer in 1989–90?

7. Which Bournemouth player on loan from West Ham equalled the record for consecutive scoring in 2001?

8. John Atyeo scored 315 League goals between 1951 and 1966. For which club did he play?

9. For which Italian club did Jimmy Greaves play?

10. Who is Everton's record goalscorer?

11. Which striker did Cambridge United sell to Manchester United for £1 million in 1992?

12. What was Ian Rush's first League club?

13. In which country was former French international Just Fontaine born?

14. Who scored a hat-trick for Rangers when they beat Hearts 5–1 in the 1996 Scottish FA Cup final?

15. Which Everton striker bagged 30 League goals in the 1985–6 season?

16. With which Welsh club did John Aldridge make his League debut?

Answers to page 513

ODDBALLS 9: **1.** Leyton Orient **2.** 'Back Home' **3.** Chris Waddle **4.** Hibernian **5.** Ray Graydon **6.** 1875 **7.** Abbey Stadium (Cambridge United) **8.** Northampton Town **9.** Cheltenham Town **10.** Bertie Mee **11.** West Ham United **12.** Oldham Athletic **13.** Paul and Ron **14.** Mark Wright **15.** Scunthorpe United **16.** Chesterfield (since 1866)

Nicknames 3

Answers on page 518

1. Which club are known as 'The Pilgrims'?
2. Which Scottish club are nicknamed 'The Gable Endies'?
3. Who are 'The Shakers'?
4. Which club are called 'The Pirates'?
5. What is the nickname of Bolton Wanderers?
6. Who in Scotland are 'The Bully Wee'?
7. Which club are known as 'The Cobblers'?
8. Who are 'The Posh'?
9. Who are known as 'The Cottagers'?
10. Which Scottish club are 'The Jam Tarts'?
11. What is Reading's nickname?
12. Who are 'The Shrimpers'?
13. What is Falkirk's nickname?
14. Which club is nicknamed 'The Rams'?
15. Which club used to be 'The Pensioners' but are now just called 'The Blues'?
16. Who are 'The Stags'?

Answers to page 518

SCOTTISH SCENE 8: **1.** Rangers **2.** Hamilton Academicals **3.** Partick Thistle **4.** Dundee **5.** Queen's Park and Stirling Albion **6.** Queen of the South **7.** Brechin City (Glebe Park) **8.** Ross County and Inverness Caledonian Thistle **9.** Joe Harper **10.** East Fife **11.** Motherwell **12.** Forfar Athletic **13.** Dunfermline Athletic **14.** Swedish **15.** Dundee United **16.** Graeme Souness

Manchester United 2

Answers on page 519

1. In which city did United clinch their unique treble in 1999 by winning the European Champions' League?
2. Who scored the goal that sent United down to Division Two in 1974?
3. What was United's original name?
4. Who kept goal in United's 1991 European Cup-Winners' Cup victory?
5. From which club did United sign Peter Schmeichel?
6. Against whom was United's record League win recorded?
7. Who succeeded Sir Matt Busby as manager in 1971?
8. Who knocked United out of the FA Cup in January 1984?
9. In which year did United first become League champions?
10. Who joined United from Slavia Prague in 1996?
11. Who finished runners-up to United in the League in both 1996 and 1997?
12. When United were promoted back to the top flight in 1975, which two teams joined them?
13. What was Andy Cole's first League club?
14. Who knocked United out of the Champions' League in 1999–2000?
15. From which club did United sign Albert Quixall?
16. In which year did Alex Ferguson become United manager?

Answers to page 519

FOOTBALL LEAGUE 8: **1.** Scarborough **2.** Brentford **3.** Huddersfield Town **4.** Luton Town **5.** Cambridge United **6.** Macclesfield Town **7.** Blackpool **8.** Watford **9.** Oxford United **10.** 1977 **11.** Port Vale **12.** Darren Ward **13.** Southport **14.** Brunton Park (Carlisle United) **15.** Cardiff City **16.** Wigan Athletic

Scottish Scene 8

Answers on page 516

1. Celebrity chef Gordon Ramsay was a defender on the books of which Scottish club?
2. Which club had 15 points deducted from their total in 2000–1 for refusing to fulfil a fixture?
3. Which club shocked Celtic 4–1 in the 1972 Scottish League Cup final?
4. Who won the Scottish FA Cup for the only time in their history in 1910?
5. Which two clubs were relegated from the Scottish Second Division at the end of season 2001–2?
6. Which Scottish club is based in Dumfries?
7. Whose ground has a hedge growing along one side?
8. Which two clubs joined the Scottish League in 1994?
9. Who scored a hat-trick for Hibernian in the 1975 Scottish League Cup final but still ended up on the losing side?
10. Who are the only Second Division club to have won the Scottish FA Cup?
11. For which club did Bobby Ferrier make 626 League appearances between 1918 and 1937?
12. In 1995, who were the first winners of the Scottish Third Division title?
13. Who plays at East End Park?
14. What nationality is Celtic striker Henrik Larsson?
15. Jim McLean was the long-serving manager of which club?
16. Which manager left Ibrox for Anfield in 1991?

Answers to page 516

NICKNAMES 3: **1.** Plymouth Argyle **2.** Montrose **3.** Bury **4.** Bristol Rovers **5.** The Trotters **6.** Clyde **7.** Northampton Town **8.** Peterborough United **9.** Fulham **10.** Hearts **11.** The Royals **12.** Southend United **13.** The Bairns **14.** Derby County **15.** Chelsea **16.** Mansfield Town

Football League 8

Answers on page 517

1. Which club was promoted from the Conference to replace Lincoln City in 1986–7?
2. From which club did Birmingham City sign full-back Martin Grainger?
3. Bill Shankly, Malcolm Macdonald and Steve Bruce all managed which club?
4. For which club did Joe Payne score ten goals in a 12–0 thrashing of Bristol Rovers in 1936?
5. Who went 31 matches without a win in Division Two in 1983–4?
6. Radio commentator Alan Green supports which Third Division club?
7. Bob Hatton was the leading Second Division scorer in 1977–8, but his team were still relegated. Who was he playing for?
8. Who did Plymouth Argyle lose to in the semi-finals of the 1984 FA Cup?
9. Which club sold Ray Houghton to Liverpool in 1987?
10. In which year were Mansfield Town promoted to Division Two for the first time?
11. For whom did Roy Sproson make a club record 761 League appearances?
12. Which goalkeeper made the short journey across the Trent from Notts County to Nottingham Forest in the summer of 2001?
13. Which former League club plays at Haig Avenue?
14. On which Third Division ground did sheep used to graze behind one goal?
15. For which club did John Toshack make his League debut?
16. Former Blackburn defender Dave Whelan is the chairman of which club?

Answers to page 517

MANCHESTER UNITED 2: **1.** Barcelona **2.** Denis Law (for Manchester City) **3.** Newton Heath **4.** Les Sealey **5.** Brøndby **6.** Ipswich Town (9-0 in 1995) **7.** Frank O'Farrell **8.** Bournemouth **9.** 1908 **10.** Karel Poborsky **11.** Newcastle United **12.** Aston Villa and Norwich City **13.** Arsenal **14.** Real Madrid **15.** Sheffield Wednesday **16.** 1986

Transfer Trail 8

Answers on page 522

1. Which Italian club paid Lazio £31 million for Christian Vieri in 1999?
2. Allan Clarke joined Leeds United from which club?
3. Which defender moved from Willem II to Liverpool in 1999?
4. From whom did West Bromwich Albion sign striker Jason Roberts for £2 million in summer 2000?
5. Which striker joined Spurs from Rosenborg?
6. Who sold Neil Cox to Aston Villa for £350,000 in 1991?
7. Who was the subject of Britain's first million-pound transfer?
8. Which controversial striker moved from Southend United to Nottingham Forest for £2.2 million in 1993?
9. Which Italian club signed John Charles from Leeds in 1957?
10. Which defender moved from Manchester United to Middlesbrough for £2.5 million in July 1998?
11. Which goalkeeper was transferred from Ajax to Juventus for £6 million in 1999?
12. From whom did Robert Pires join Arsenal?
13. Which German club signed Kevin Keegan in 1977?
14. Whose transfer to Spurs in 1961 was fixed at £99,999 because manager Bill Nicholson didn't want him burdened with the tag of Britain's first £100,000 player?
15. Which forward moved from Millwall to Gillingham in summer 2000?
16. Who signed Jason Euell from Wimbledon in 2001?

Answers to page 522

ODDBALLS 10: **1.** Pat Kruse **2.** Shrewsbury Town **3.** Ryan Giggs **4.** Middlesbrough **5.** 1940s **6.** Stoke City **7.** Oxford United **8.** Milkman **9.** Viv Anderson **10.** Laurie Cunningham **11.** Dundee and Dundee United (200 yards apart) **12.** Manchester United **13.** Real Madrid **14.** John Toshack **15.** David Webb **16.** Portsmouth

The World Game 9

Answers on page 523

1. Which former Luton player quit as boss of Real Oviedo in July 2001?
2. Which club holds the record for the most Turkish Cup wins?
3. Who won the French League in 1998–9?
4. What nationality is Marcelo Salas?
5. Beerschot, Waterschei and Beveren have all won the national cup competition in which country?
6. Which Italian team's fans walked 20 miles to a mountain sanctuary in 1969 to thank the Madonna for saving them from relegation?
7. What nationality are Frank and Ronald de Boer?
8. In which country do Grasshoppers play?
9. Which club were the first winners of South America's Copa Libertadores?
10. Which African country had most of their team wiped out in a plane crash in 1993?
11. Who are the most successful club in Greek footballing history?
12. Which Italian star was nicknamed 'Il Codino Divino' (The Divine Ponytail)?
13. For which Italian club did goalkeeper Dino Zoff make his League debut?
14. Against whom did San Marino win their first point in international competition?
15. Which Dutch club were originally called Wilhelmina?
16. Which two German teams contest the Ruhr derby?

Answers to page 523

FA CUP 7: **1.** Paul Allen **2.** 1894 **3.** Allan Clarke **4.** Alan Ashman **5.** Roy Essandoh **6.** Bobby Gould **7.** Sunderland **8.** Peterborough United **9.** 1953 **10.** Arsenal **11.** John Harkes (Sheffield Wednesday) **12.** Bobby Smith **13.** Tommy Hutchison (Manchester City) **14.** Chorley **15.** 1926 **16.** Millwall

Oddballs 10

Answers on page 520

1. Which Torquay United defender headed past his own goalkeeper after just eight seconds of a Fourth Division game with Cambridge United in 1977?
2. Which club did Arthur Rowley manage between 1958 and 1968?
3. Who once played for England Under-18s in the name of Ryan Wilson?
4. Which club does comedian Bob Mortimer support?
5. In which decade did Derby County first win the FA Cup?
6. Which club provided the action scenes for the 1960s soap *United!*?
7. Brothers Ron and Graham Atkinson played for which club?
8. Before becoming a footballer, what was Pat Jennings's first job?
9. Who was the first black footballer to play for England?
10. And who was the second?
11. Which two British League clubs' grounds are nearest to each other?
12. Who won the FA Youth Cup for the first five years of its existence?
13. Singer Julio Iglesias was reserve team goalkeeper with which club?
14. Who resigned as manager of Wales in 1994 after just one game in charge?
15. In 1971, which Chelsea defender played an entire match against Ipswich in goal because the club's two regular keepers were injured?
16. Who pipped Manchester City for promotion to the First Division in 1927 by five-thousandths of a goal?

Answers to page 520

TRANSFER TRAIL 8: **1.** Inter Milan **2.** Leicester City **3.** Sammy Hyypia **4.** Bristol Rovers **5.** Steffen Iversen **6.** Scunthorpe United **7.** Trevor Francis **8.** Stan Collymore **9.** Juventus **10.** Gary Pallister **11.** Edwin Van der Sar **12.** Marseille **13.** Hamburg **14.** Jimmy Greaves **15.** Paul Shaw **16.** Charlton Athletic

FA Cup 7

Answers on page 521

1. Which West Ham midfielder became the youngest player to appear in an FA Cup final when he took the field against Arsenal in 1980?
2. When did Notts County win the FA Cup for the only time?
3. Who scored Leeds United's winning goal against Arsenal in the 1972 FA Cup final?
4. Who was manager of West Bromwich Albion when they reached the 1968 Cup final?
5. Whose goal for Wycombe Wanderers knocked Leicester City out of the 2000–1 FA Cup?
6. Who headed a goal for West Ham in a third-round tie at Southampton in 1975 despite having a broken leg?
7. Who did Liverpool beat in the 1992 Cup final?
8. Whose 9–1 win over Kingstonian in 1992 was expunged because the Kingstonian keeper had been hit on the head with a coin?
9. In which year was the 'Matthews Final'?
10. Who defeated Sheffield United 1–0 in the 1936 FA Cup final?
11. Who was the first American player to appear in an FA Cup final?
12. Which Spurs player scored in successive finals, in 1961 and 1962?
13. Who scored at both ends in the 1981 Cup final?
14. Which Northern Premier League outfit knocked Wolves out of the Cup in 1986?
15. When did Swansea City first reach the semi-finals of the FA Cup?
16. Who knocked Chelsea out of the FA Cup in 1914, 1937, 1985 and 1995?

Answers to page 521

THE WORLD GAME 9: **1.** Raddy Antic **2.** Galatasaray **3.** Bordeaux **4.** Chilean **5.** Belgium **6.** Sampdoria **7.** Dutch **8.** Switzerland **9.** Peñarol **10.** Zambia **11.** Olympiakos **12.** Roberto Baggio **13.** Udinese **14.** Turkey **15.** Feyenoord **16.** Borussia Dortmund and Schalke 04

General Knowledge 121

Answers on page 526

1. Which TV detective kept a pet alligator named Elvis?
2. What can be a colour or a loud cry in pursuit of a criminal?
3. In which county is Aylesbury?
4. Who was the only English monarch to be a member of the House of Saxe-Coburg?
5. What was the Christian name of the British sculptor Moore?
6. Which actor won a posthumous BAFTA award in 2002 for his role in the ITV drama, *Buried Treasure*?
7. Which grand old soldier had 10,000 men?
8. On which island is Mount Etna?
9. What is the capital of the Falkland Islands?
10. Which Australian golfer is nicknamed the 'Great White Shark'?
11. Which Dutch artist once taught languages and maths at a school in Ramsgate?
12. Cornish Yarg cheese is traditionally served coated in what?
13. In which national park did Yogi Bear live?
14. Which football club won the Danish League title in 2001?
15. Of what musical instrument are you afraid if you suffer from aulophobia?
16. Who played the second *Doctor Who*?

Answers to page 526

GENERAL KNOWLEDGE 123: **1.** Walk on dry land **2.** 1942 **3.** Noah **4.** Tony Christie **5.** Neil **6.** Wrexham (v Arsenal) **7.** Herman and Lily Munster **8.** Joe Louis **9.** Manuel Noriega **10.** Around the north of Canada **11.** George V **12.** Luton **13.** Six **14.** Stephen Sondheim **15.** Jimmy Somerville **16.** Surrey

General Knowledge 122

Answers on page 527

1. Which former Radio 1 disc jockey was named Pipe Smoker of the Year in 1982?
2. What did George Burns, Irving Berlin and Hal Roach have in common?
3. Which English comedian was awarded the freedom of the capital city of Albania?
4. Who shot Phil Mitchell in *EastEnders* in 2001?
5. If something is cerebral, to what part of the body does it pertain?
6. Who was the singer with Frankie Goes to Hollywood?
7. What is unusual about the populations of Australia, Mongolia and New Zealand?
8. Which footballer was known as 'The Black Panther'?
9. What was the biggest-selling toy of 1957?
10. In which country was the artist Chagall born?
11. Who traditionally lives at 11 Downing Street?
12. Which actress won a 1972 Academy Award for Best Actress for *Cabaret*?
13. Who was Gary's first flatmate in *Men Behaving Badly*?
14. Where is the volcano Olympus Mons?
15. Which Prime Minister's father-in-law used to be a 'randy Scouse git'?
16. Which is the world's second smallest state?

Answers to page 527

GENERAL KNOWLEDGE 124: **1.** *Midnight Cowboy* **2.** Dingwall **3.** Rabbit **4.** David Vine **5.** Dustin Hoffman and Jon Voight **6.** 'Achy Breaky Heart' **7.** Juan Carlos **8.** Swiss **9.** Hitler **10.** The emperor **11.** Penelope **12.** Blair General **13.** 'A Little Bit More' **14.** Steve Redgrave **15.** St John's **16.** Newt

General Knowledge 123

Answers on page 524

1. What can a mudskipper do that other fish can't?
2. In which year was the Battle of El Alamein?
3. In the Old Testament, who was the father of Shem, Ham and Japheth?
4. Which singer maintained that he did what he did for Maria?
5. Which member of *The Young Ones* had a hit with 'Hole In My Shoe'?
6. In January 1992, who became the first team finishing bottom of the Football League the previous season to knock the reigning champions out of the FA Cup?
7. Who were the first American sitcom couple to be seen regularly sharing a bed on TV?
8. Which boxer was known as 'The Brown Bomber'?
9. Which Panama ruler was arrested in 1989 following an American invasion of the country?
10. Where is the Northwest Passage?
11. Who was the first British monarch from the House of Windsor?
12. Which Bedfordshire town used to be synonymous with hat-making?
13. How many points is the pink ball in snooker worth?
14. Who wrote the lyrics of *West Side Story*?
15. Who was the lead singer with Bronski Beat on 'Smalltown Boy'?
16. Which county cricket club have their headquarters at The Oval?

Answers to page 524

GENERAL KNOWLEDGE 121: **1.** 'Sonny' Crockett (*Miami Vice*) **2.** Hue **3.** Buckinghamshire **4.** Edward VII **5.** Henry **6.** John Thaw **7.** Duke of York **8.** Sicily **9.** Stanley **10.** Greg Norman **11.** Van Gogh **12.** Nettles **13.** Yellowstone **14.** FC Copenhagen **15.** Flute **16.** Patrick Troughton

General Knowledge 124

Answers on page 525

1. John Schlesinger won a 1969 Academy Award for directing which movie?
2. In which town do Scottish football team Ross County play their home matches?
3. Coney is the fur of which animal?
4. Who was the first host of *A Question of Sport*?
5. Who were the two main male actors in *Midnight Cowboy*?
6. What was Billy Ray Cyrus suffering from in 1992?
7. Who became King of Spain in 1975?
8. What nationality was the psychiatrist Carl Jung?
9. The July Conspiracy was an unsuccessful plot to assassinate which dictator?
10. Which is the largest breed of penguin?
11. According to Greek legend, who was the wife of Odysseus?
12. At which hospital did *Dr Kildare* work?
13. Which Dr Hook song did 911 take to number one in the singles charts in 1999?
14. Who was BBC Sports Personality of the Year for 2000?
15. What is the capital of Newfoundland?
16. Crested, smooth and palmate are all types of what?

Answers to page 525

GENERAL KNOWLEDGE 122: **1.** Dave Lee Travis **2.** They all lived to be 100 **3.** Norman Wisdom **4.** Lisa Shaw **5.** Brain **6.** Holly Johnson **7.** There are more sheep than humans **8.** Eusebio **9.** The hula hoop **10.** Russia **11.** Chancellor of the Exchequer **12.** Liza Minnelli **13.** Dermot **14.** Mars **15.** Tony Blair (father-in-law Tony Booth played Liverpudlian Mike in *Till Death Us Do Part*) **16.** Monaco

General Knowledge 125

Answers on page 530

1. What is Muckle Flugga's geographical significance?

2. Who was the winged horse in Greek mythology?

3. Which 20th-century playwright penned *Equus* and *Amadeus*?

4. How many England caps did goalkeeper Peter Shilton win?

5. Which American jockey was nicknamed 'The Shoe'?

6. Which US record producer created the 'wall of sound'?

7. Who longed to become a Yellowcoat in *Hi-De-Hi!* ?

8. In which country is Spitzbergen?

9. Which American paediatrician wrote *The Common Sense Book of Baby and Child Care*?

10. Which singer wanted to 'Fly Away' in 1999?

11. In which century did the Chinese Ming dynasty start?

12. Who was Pope during the Second World War?

13. What is the state capital of New Jersey?

14. What takes place at Cadwell Park and Mallory Park?

15. Which TV sports presenter married a Scottish rugby international in 2001?

16. Which two acts topped the UK singles charts with 'Mary's Boy Child'?

Answers to page 530

GENERAL KNOWLEDGE 127: **1.** Shoulder-blade **2.** The Bangles **3.** *Sense and Sensibility* **4.** Mr Venables **5.** Indiana **6.** Kalahari **7.** Queens Park Rangers **8.** Kabul **9.** Harold Wilson **10.** Austrian **11.** Greece and Turkey **12.** 180 **13.** North America **14.** The Boswells **15.** Blondie **16.** Jose Maria Olazabal

General Knowledge 126

Answers on page 531

1. Which King of England employed a groom whose job it was to wipe the royal bottom?
2. Which former England rugby captain famously split up with Gary Lineker's sister-in-law?
3. Which actress won an Oscar at the age of 80 in 1989 for *Driving Miss Daisy*?
4. Who hosts *They Think It's All Over* ?
5. In which county is Chepstow?
6. How many square yards are there in an acre?
7. What is the fifth book of the New Testament?
8. Which singer's real name is Richard Melville Hall?
9. Who played Jim Rockford in *The Rockford Files*?
10. Septicaemia is the technical term for what?
11. Who won the Formula One World Drivers' Championship in 1988, 1990 and 1991?
12. What is the minimum number of games needed to win a set of tennis?
13. In which London park is the Serpentine?
14. Which is the only Australian state to have borders with five others?
15. The name of which English county is sometimes abbreviated to Salop?
16. What is a sidewinder?

Answers to page 531

GENERAL KNOWLEDGE 128: **1.** *A Beautiful Mind* **2.** *Braveheart* **3.** Tessa Sanderson **4.** *Fawlty Towers* **5.** Benjamin Disraeli **6.** Jane Fonda **7.** 12 **8.** Jethro Tull **9.** Leicester City **10.** Northumberland **11.** Coral Sea **12.** Mussorgsky **13.** All are born-again Christians **14.** 'When Smokey Sings' **15.** Cob **16.** Greg Medavoy

General Knowledge 127

Answers on page 528

1. What part of the human body is the scapula?
2. Which girl band, who spilt up shortly after a 1989 number one, reformed in 2001?
3. Elinor Dashwood was a heroine in which Jane Austen novel?
4. What was the name of the prison governor in *Porridge*?
5. Fort Wayne and Gary are towns in which American state?
6. The Okavango is the only permanent river in which southern African desert?
7. Which club staged the first Football League game on artificial turf?
8. What is the capital of Afghanistan?
9. Which political rival called former British Prime Minister Edward Heath 'a shiver looking for a spine to run up'?
10. What nationality is ex-Formula One World Champion Niki Lauda?
11. Which two countries signed the Treaty of Lausanne in 1923?
12. How many degrees do the hands of a clock pass through to travel from three o'clock to nine o'clock?
13. In which continent is the Okefenokee swamp?
14. What was the name of the family in *Bread* ?
15. Who are the only American group to have had UK number one hits in the Seventies, Eighties and Nineties?
16. Which Spanish golfer's nickname is 'Olly'?

Answers to page 528

GENERAL KNOWLEDGE 125: **1.** It is the most northerly island in the British Isles **2.** Pegasus **3.** Peter Shaffer **4.** 125 **5.** Willie Shoemaker **6.** Phil Spector **7.** Peggy **8.** Norway **9.** Dr Spock **10.** Lenny Kravitz **11.** 14th **12.** Pius XII **13.** Trenton **14.** Motor-cycle racing **15.** Gabby Logan (nee Yorath) **16.** Harry Belafonte and Boney M

General Knowledge 128

Answers on page 529

1. For what film did Ron Howard win his Best Director Oscar in 2002?
2. Which Mel Gibson movie won the 1995 Academy Award for Best Picture?
3. Who was the first British athlete to win an Olympic gold medal in a throwing event?
4. Miss Tibbs and Miss Gatsby were resident guests at which establishment?
5. Which 19th-century British Prime Minister became the Earl of Beaconsfield?
6. Which member of a famous acting family starred in *Cat Ballou* and *Barbarella*?
7. In poetic terms, how many syllables are there in an Alexandrine?
8. With which band did Ian Anderson play the flute and sing?
9. From which club did Liverpool sign footballer Emile Heskey?
10. In which English county is Alnwick?
11. Which is the biggest sea in the world?
12. Who composed 'Pictures From An Exhibition'?
13. What do Cannon and Ball, Samantha Fox and Glenn Hoddle have in common?
14. What was the title of ABC's tribute to Smokey Robinson?
15. What can be a male swan or a bread roll?
16. Who does Gordon Clapp play in *NYPD Blue*?

Answers to page 529

GENERAL KNOWLEDGE 126: **1.** Henry VIII **2.** Will Carling **3.** Jessica Tandy **4.** Nick Hancock **5.** Gwent **6.** 4,840 **7.** The Acts **8.** Moby **9.** James Garner **10.** Blood poisoning **11.** Ayrton Senna **12.** Six **13.** Hyde Park **14.** South Australia **15.** Shropshire **16.** A rattlesnake

General Knowledge 129

Answers on page 534

1. Which is the second largest planet in the solar system?
2. Philip Pirrip is the central character in which Dickens novel?
3. Which four countries share borders with Italy?
4. Which sea separates Vietnam from the Philippines?
5. What nationality is Peter Andre?
6. Which two Davids led the Liberal-SDP alliance of the 1980s?
7. What is the trade name for polytetrafluoroethene?
8. Which Israeli city gives its name to a type of orange?
9. Which football club played at Anfield before Liverpool?
10. Who directed *This Is Spinal Tap* and *When Harry Met Sally* ?
11. In which year was 'Love Me For A Reason' a UK number one for The Osmonds?
12. Who did Billy Wilder say had 'breasts like granite and a brain like Swiss cheese'?
13. Who played the title role in the film *Shirley Valentine*?
14. Which French jockey won the 1998 Epsom Derby on High Rise?
15. What is a whippoorwill?
16. From which Yorkshire port did Captain Cook sail in the *Resolution* on his 1768 voyage to the Pacific?

Answers to page 534

GENERAL KNOWLEDGE 131: **1.** 'My Way' **2.** Richard Hannon **3.** *Jane Eyre* **4.** Yellow no-parking lines **5.** 1982 **6.** One-pound coins **7.** Bear **8.** Cambridge's run of seven wins in a row **9.** The Bee Gees **10.** Kroner **11.** Lifting machinery on a ship **12.** George Eliot **13.** Emily's **14.** Paul Weller **15.** *Women in Love* **16.** Green

General Knowledge 130

Answers on page 535

1. Who wrote *Rebecca*?
2. Which stretch of water separates Edinburgh from Fife?
3. Boavista play their football in which country?
4. As whom was William Simmonite better known in a long-running BBC sitcom?
5. Findus is an abbreviation of the name of which Swedish company?
6. The name of which Central American capital city means 'holy saviour'?
7. In which cathedral was Thomas à Becket murdered?
8. In which ship did Francis Drake sail around the world?
9. Dresden is the capital of which German state?
10. On which race track is the Champion Hurdle run?
11. What is a female rabbit called?
12. Who wrote the stories of *Thomas the Tank Engine*?
13. What is a merganser?
14. Where were The Police walking in 1979?
15. In 1993, which horse won the Grand National that never was?
16. Nancy Wilkinson was the first winner of which TV title in 1972?

Answers to page 535

GENERAL KNOWLEDGE 132: **1.** Farnborough **2.** Lucinda Prior-Palmer **3.** Australian **4.** Audrey fforbes-Hamilton **5.** Samuel Crompton **6.** Rhine **7.** Nutmeggers **8.** Hungary **9.** Will Smith **10.** 1955 **11.** Liberia **12.** Wiltshire **13.** Edward VI **14.** Al Martino **15.** 12 **16.** Duke of Edinburgh

General Knowledge 131

Answers on page 532

1. Which record did Sir David Frost, Geoffrey Boycott and Johnny Speight all choose on *Desert Island Discs*?
2. Which racehorse trainer used to be a drummer with The Troggs?
3. Edward Rochester featured in which Charlotte Brontë novel?
4. What did Slough acquire in 1956 that no other British town had?
5. In which year was Prince William born?
6. What were introduced to the British currency in 1983?
7. What kind of animal was *Gentle Ben*?
8. What sequence was broken by Oxford in the 2000 University Boat Race?
9. Which internationally successful pop brothers were born on the Isle of Man?
10. What is the currency of Denmark?
11. What is a derrick?
12. What was the pen name of author Mary Ann Evans?
13. In whose shop window did *Bagpuss* sit?
14. Whose 1995 album was titled 'Stanley Road'?
15. For which film did Glenda Jackson win an Academy Award for Best Actress in 1970?
16. What colour is emerald?

Answers to page 532

GENERAL KNOWLEDGE 129: **1.** Saturn **2.** *Great Expectations* **3.** France, Switzerland, Austria and Slovenia **4.** South China Sea **5.** British **6.** Steel and Owen **7.** Teflon **8.** Jaffa **9.** Everton **10.** Rob Reiner **11.** 1974 **12.** Marilyn Monroe **13.** Pauline Collins **14.** Olivier Peslier **15.** A bird **16.** Whitby

General Knowledge 132

Answers on page 533

1. Which Hampshire town is famous for its air show?
2. What was the maiden name of British three-day eventer Lucinda Green?
3. What nationality is feminist Germaine Greer?
4. Who did Penelope Keith play in *To The Manor Born*?
5. Whose mule was a key invention during the Industrial Revolution?
6. Which river is straddled by the Bendorf Bridge at Coblenz?
7. What are inhabitants of Connecticut known as?
8. Who were the first non-British football nation to defeat England at Wembley?
9. Who reached number one in 1997 with 'Men In Black'?
10. In which year was James Dean killed in a car crash?
11. Monrovia is the capital of which country?
12. In which county is Stonehenge?
13. Who succeeded Henry VIII as King of England?
14. Who had the first-ever UK number one single?
15. How many countries adopted the Euro in January 2002?
16. What was Edmund's title in the first series of *Blackadder*?

Answers to page 533

GENERAL KNOWLEDGE 130: **1.** Daphne du Maurier **2.** Firth of Forth **3.** Portugal **4.** 'Compo' **5.** Fruit Industries **6.** San Salvador **7.** Canterbury **8.** *Golden Hind* **9.** Saxony **10.** Cheltenham **11.** Doe **12.** Rev W. Awdry **13.** A type of duck **14.** On the moon **15.** Esha Ness **16.** *Mastermind*

General Knowledge 133

Answers on page 538

1. On which TV show did music-hall comedian Arthur Atkinson appear?
2. Which nun won the Nobel Peace Prize in 1979?
3. Which former boxer made a citizen's arrest at Gatwick Airport in August 2001?
4. Which dog is sometimes called a bobtail?
5. Which French composer is best-known for his 'Symphonie Espagnole'?
6. Which space-age hero was created by Kenny Everett?
7. Aboard which ship did Captain Scott sail to the Antarctic in 1901?
8. Who was Othello's wife?
9. How many sides are there to an octagon?
10. What was the title of All Saints' first UK number one single?
11. Gibraltar Point is situated to the south of which east-coast resort?
12. At which sport do Neil Hodgson and John Reynolds compete?
13. Which explorer introduced the potato and tobacco to Europe?
14. What does a phonophobe fear?
15. Who was Britain's first Christian martyr?
16. The resort of Biarritz is on which coast of France?

Answers to page 538

GENERAL KNOWLEDGE 135: **1.** Trevor Brooking **2.** George Harrison **3.** Jimmy 'Schnozzle' Durante **4.** Marcel Marceau **5.** Geri Halliwell **6.** Ankara **7.** A half **8.** William of Orange **9.** Wilmington **10.** *David Copperfield* **11.** On the moon **12.** The March Hare **13.** Jamaica **14.** Pauline **15.** Prince **16.** Gloucestershire

General Knowledge 134

Answers on page 539

1. Which lead singer with university band The Ugly Rumours has gone on to achieve fame in a different field?
2. Which cartoon lion's catchphrase was 'Heavens to Murgatroyd'?
3. What is the term for an over in cricket where no runs are scored?
4. What bodily function can exceed a speed of 200mph?
5. In which country's currency do 100 centavos make a sucre?
6. For which film did Kevin Spacey win an Oscar for Best Actor in 1999?
7. Who wrote *Tess of the D'Urbervilles*?
8. Immortalised by the rhyme, the bridge of Avignon in France crosses which river?
9. Mn is the chemical symbol for which element?
10. As whom is Princess Aurora better known?
11. What is Spencer Perceval's unfortunate claim to fame?
12. Which band frequently supported Bob Dylan?
13. In which English city would you find The Shambles?
14. How long did the Hundred Years War last?
15. Which German composer, whose name was adopted by a 20th-century singer, wrote the fairy opera *Hansel and Gretel*?
16. Which house on the Isle of Wight was one of Queen Victoria's homes?

Answers to page 539

GENERAL KNOWLEDGE 136: **1.** A sperm whale **2.** Mansfield Town **3.** Colon **4.** The Pharos **5.** Austria and Prussia **6.** Ti **7.** Austria and Italy **8.** Brighton **9.** Featherweight **10.** Mark Williams **11.** Cancer **12.** Tinkerbell **13.** Prune **14.** Robert Mitchum **15.** Billie Jean King **16.** Hercule Poirot

General Knowledge 135

Answers on page 536

1. Of which footballer did Brian Clough remark: 'Floats like a butterfly, and stings like one'?
2. Who played guitar under the name of L'Angelo Mysterioso on Cream's 'Badge'?
3. Which vaudeville comedian had his bulbous nose insured for $100,000?
4. Who spoke the only word in Mel Brooks' *Silent Movie*?
5. Which singer pleaded 'Look At Me' in 1999?
6. What is the capital of Turkey?
7. What is the square root of a quarter?
8. Which Dutchman became King of England in 1688?
9. Which port in Delaware was formerly known as Fort Christina?
10. Betsey Trotwood is a character in which Dickens novel?
11. Where is the Marsh of Decay?
12. Who put butter in the Mad Hatter's watch?
13. The film *Cool Runnings* was based on the true story of which country's bobsled team at the 1998 Winter Olympics?
14. What is the name of Adrian Mole's mother?
15. Who wrote Sinead O'Connor's hit 'Nothing Compares 2 U'?
16. Which county won all three one-day cricket titles in 2000?

Answers to page 536

GENERAL KNOWLEDGE 133: **1.** *The Fast Show* **2.** Mother Teresa **3.** Nigel Benn **4.** Old English sheepdog **5.** Edouard Lalo **6.** Captain Kremmen **7.** The *Discovery* **8.** Desdemona **9.** Eight **10.** 'Never Ever' **11.** Skegness **12.** Motorcycle racing **13.** Sir Walter Raleigh **14.** Noise **15.** St Alban **16.** West

General Knowledge 136

Answers on page 537

1. What is a cachalot?
2. Which Football League team plays at Field Mill?
3. What can be part of the large intestine or a punctuation mark?
4. Which lighthouse was one of the Seven Wonders of the World?
5. Which two countries fought the Seven Weeks' War in 1866?
6. What is the chemical symbol for titanium?
7. The Brenner Pass links which two countries?
8. In which English seaside resort are The Lanes?
9. In boxing which is heavier – featherweight or flyweight?
10. Which Welsh snooker player is the namesake of a member of *The Fast Show* team?
11. Which zodiac sign has the symbol of a crab?
12. What was the name of the fairy in *Peter Pan*?
13. What is a dried plum called?
14. Which Hollywood actor served 59 days in a California jail in 1948 for possessing narcotics?
15. Which tennis ace was the subject of Elton John's 'Philadelphia Freedom'?
16. Which literary detective makes great use of his 'little grey cells'?

Answers to page 537

GENERAL KNOWLEDGE 134: **1.** Tony Blair **2.** Snagglepuss **3.** Maiden **4.** A sneeze **5.** Ecuador **6.** *American Beauty* **7.** Thomas Hardy **8.** Rhone **9.** Manganese **10.** Sleeping Beauty **11.** He is the only British Prime Minister to have been assassinated **12.** The Band **13.** York **14.** 116 years **15.** Engelbert Humperdinck **16.** Osborne House

General Knowledge 137

Answers on page 542

1. Who was the first driver to win the Formula One World Championship in his own make of car?
2. At which Irish battle in 1690 was James II defeated by William III?
3. On a compass, which point is directly opposite south south-west?
4. What is the main prey of the monkey-eating eagle?
5. The Tyrrehenian Sea is situated to the west of which country?
6. What Oscar Wilde character possessed a supernatural picture?
7. Who survived 24 years of the old *Crossroads*, but was killed off three months after the return of the new series?
8. Relating to the time of day, what does pm stand for?
9. What is the capital of Tasmania?
10. Eddie Butler and Nigel Starmer-Smith are TV commentators on which sport?
11. Which country resigned from the Commonwealth in 1949?
12. Which entertainer was born Priscilla White?
13. Who became leader of the Labour Party in 1992?
14. When does an ounce have four legs?
15. In what type of bowling did West Indies cricketer Lance Gibbs specialise?
16. Which American Indian chief was killed at Wounded Knee?

Answers to page 542

GENERAL KNOWLEDGE 139: **1.** Rome **2.** Vegetable **3.** Spain **4.** Hong Kong **5.** Montague and Capulet **6.** The eye **7.** Zsa Zsa Gabor **8.** *The Dukes of Hazzard* **9.** Electrical voltage **10.** Its hot springs **11.** The heel **12.** Pepsi-Cola **13.** Lanfranco **14.** 'Rotterdam' **15.** Belgian **16.** Norman Mailer

General Knowledge 138

Answers on page 543

1. Andorra lies between which two countries?
2. What did the Knave of Hearts steal?
3. Formentera is part of which group of islands?
4. As what did Sir John Barbirolli make his name?
5. Which author's real name was Charles Lutwidge Dodgson?
6. Which Michael Cimino film starring Robert DeNiro won the Oscar for Best Picture in 1978?
7. Which Great Dane joined Aston Villa in 2001?
8. Who presents *Big Brother*?
9. The entire population of which country were sentenced to death in their absence by the Spanish Inquisition?
10. What is the name for a female swan?
11. Of which Prime Minister did Malcolm Muggeridge once say: 'He is not only a bore, but he bores for England'?
12. Who was non-playing captain of Europe's triumphant 1985 Ryder Cup golf team?
13. Which 150-1 outsider became World Snooker Champion in 1986?
14. Under which name did Sister Luc-Gabrielle have a surprise 1963 hit?
15. In which century did brown bears become extinct in the UK?
16. Which Victorian murderer was known as 'The Staffordshire Poisoner'?

Answers to page 543

GENERAL KNOWLEDGE 140: **1.** 36 **2.** Semaphore **3.** Chicken **4.** Devon, Bath and NE Somerset, Dorset and Wiltshire **5.** A wading bird **6.** Cairngorms **7.** Colonel Harry Llewellyn **8.** Louisa May Alcott **9.** *Gipsy Moth IV* **10.** Corky **11.** Mud **12.** Sweeney Todd **13.** It was contested by two English teams – Bristol City and Tranmere Rovers **14.** Corona **15.** Wilpur Post **16.** On a trampoline

General Knowledge 139

Answers on page 540

1. Lazio Football Club play their home games in which city?
2. What is a mangelwurzel?
3. Navarre is a mountain region of which country?
4. In which harbour did the *Queen Elizabeth* liner sink in 1972?
5. What were the names of the opposing families in *Romeo and Juliet*?
6. What does an ophthalmologist study?
7. Who said: 'I never hated a man enough to give him his diamonds back'?
8. Luke, Bo and Daisy were cousins in which TV series?
9. What does an oscilloscope measure?
10. What is the New Zealand town of Rotorua renowned for?
11. Where is the human skin least sensitive?
12. What was the first US consumer product to be sold in the Soviet Union?
13. What is jockey Frankie Dettori's full Christian name?
14. Which Dutch port provided The Beautiful South with a 1996 hit?
15. What nationality was the artist Magritte?
16. Which American novelist wrote *The Executioner's Song*?

Answers to page 540

GENERAL KNOWLEDGE 137: **1.** Jack Brabham **2.** Battle of the Boyne **3.** North north-east **4.** Flying lemurs **5.** Italy **6.** Dorian Gray **7.** Jill Richardson/Harvey/Chance **8.** Post meridiem **9.** Hobart **10.** Rugby union **11.** Republic of Ireland **12.** Cilla Black **13.** John Smith **14.** When it's another name for a snow leopard **15.** Off-spin **16.** Sitting Bull

General Knowledge 140

Answers on page 541

1. What do the numbers go up to on a roulette wheel?
2. What is the name for the visual signalling code conducted with flags?
3. If you ordered pollo in an Italian restaurant, what would you be served?
4. Which four counties border Somerset?
5. What is an avocet?
6. In which mountain range is the town of Aviemore?
7. Who rode a clear round on Foxhunter to give Britain an equestrian gold medal at the 1952 Olympics?
8. Who wrote *Little Women*?
9. In which yacht did Sir Francis Chichester sail solo around the world?
10. What was the name of the friendly neighbourhood policeman in *Sykes*?
11. Which band were feeling 'Lonely This Christmas' in 1974?
12. Who was the demon barber of Fleet Street?
13. In football, what was unusual about the 1934 Welsh Cup final?
14. What is the name for the outermost part of the Sun's atmosphere?
15. Who owned the talking horse *Mister Ed*?
16. Where are adolphs, randolphs and rudolphs performed?

Answers to page 541

GENERAL KNOWLEDGE 138: **1.** France and Spain **2.** Tarts **3.** Balearic **4.** Conductor **5.** Lewis Carroll **6.** *The Deer Hunter* **7.** Peter Schmeichel **8.** Davina McCall **9.** The Netherlands **10.** Pen **11.** Anthony Eden **12.** Tony Jacklin **13.** Joe Johnson **14.** The Singing Nun **15.** 11th **16.** William Palmer

TV Pot Luck 14

Answers on page 546

1. Which Icelandic TV presenter wrote *Vikings!*?
2. Who played drama student Tim in *The Biz* before moving to Albert Square?
3. Which annual entertainment extravaganza was first televised in 1960?
4. Pierce Brosnan used to play which TV detective?
5. Penny Junor and Juliet Morris both presented which holiday programme?
6. In what kind of business was the 2002 series *Rescue Me* set?
7. Who conducts *Trigger Happy TV*?
8. What is Gay Search's specialist field?
9. Who finds himself *in the Middle* on BBC2?
10. Which rap artist starred as *The Fresh Prince of Bel Air*?
11. Which Charlotte supported Anne Robinson on *Watchdog*?
12. Which TV presenter was upset after appearing to promote a chocolate bar at her wedding?
13. What once replaced Roy Hattersley on the panel of *Have I Got News For You*?
14. What was Lucy Sullivan doing on her ITV drama series?
15. Who was the executive producer of *Def II*?
16. Which Goon presented and sang on *Highway*?

Answers to page 546

SCI FI 5: **1.** *Lost in Space* **2.** *Stingray* **3.** *Babylon 5* **4.** *Land of the Giants* **5.** *Doomwatch* **6.** *Buck Rogers in the 25th Century* **7.** *Space: 1999* **8.** *Timeslip* **9.** *The X Files* **10.** *Space Patrol* **11.** *Star Trek: The Next Generation* **12.** *Quantum Leap* **13.** *Buffy the Vampire Slayer* **14.** *Man From Atlantis* **15.** *Survivors* **16.** *U.F.O.*

Quiz & Game Shows 7

Answers on page 547

1. Who watches over the Saturday challengers on *Don't Try This at Home*?
2. Which game show features a conveyor belt of prizes?
3. Which musical quiz was hosted by both Lionel Blair and Tom O'Connor?
4. What was the name of ITV's popular charades game?
5. Who played Mrs White in the first series of *Cluedo*?
6. How many people do *Family Fortunes* claim to ask in their surveys?
7. On which show did Bruce Forsyth ask: 'What do points make? Prizes!'?
8. Who hosted *Odd One Out*?
9. Which was the US version of *Celebrity Squares*?
10. Which weather girl kept an eye on the clock in *Treasure Hunt*?
11. Which daily general knowledge quiz began on Channel 4 in 1988?
12. Which cut-throat quiz has the 'walk of shame'?
13. Which game show used to be hailed as 'the quiz of the week'?
14. What is the name of the game show hosted by Ruby Wax?
15. Who hosted *Telly Addicts*?
16. *Gibberish* and *Brainstorm* were hosted by which zany comedian?

Answers to page 547

BROOKSIDE 3: **1.** Ron Dixon **2.** Torquay United **3.** Rome **4.** Peter Phelan **5.** Shelley Bowers **6.** Julia Brogan **7.** Lyn Matthews **8.** James Markham **9.** A mystery virus **10.** Gary and Little George **11.** The Rogers **12.** Rosie Banks **13.** Bev McLoughlin **14.** Russell Grant **15.** Jean **16.** A gas blast

Sci Fi 5

Answers on page 544

In which sci fi series have the following characters appeared?

1. Dr Zachary Smith
2. Commander Sam Shore
3. Catherine Sakai
4. Steve Burton
5. Dr Spencer Quist
6. Col. Wilma Deering
7. Dr Helena Russell
8. Liz Skinner
9. Alex Krycek
10. Capt. Larry Dart
11. Dr Beverly Crusher
12. Al Calavicci
13. Willow Rosenberg
14. Mark Harris
15. Abby Grant
16. Commander Edward Straker

Answers to page 544

TV POT LUCK 14: **1.** Magnus Magnusson **2.** Paul Nicholls **3.** The Royal Variety Performance **4.** *Remington Steele* **5.** *The Travel Show* **6.** A magazine publishing house **7.** Dom Joly **8.** Gardening **9.** *Malcolm* **10.** Will Smith **11.** Charlotte Hudson **12.** Anthea Turner **13.** A tub of lard **14.** *Getting Married* **15.** Janet Street-Porter **16.** Sir Harry Secombe

Brookside 3

Answers on page 545

1. Who built a fence of doors between his house and the Farnhams'?
2. Which football club did Geoff Rogers join?
3. To which city did Bobby and Sheila Grant go in a bid to patch up their marriage?
4. Which hairdresser love rival did Barry Grant dismiss as 'Scissorhands'?
5. With whom did Lindsey Corkhill have a lesbian relationship?
6. Which character did Gladys Ambrose play?
7. Who became Frank Rogers' second wife?
8. Which boyfriend of Caroline Choi swindled her and was killed in a car crash?
9. What swept the Close in 1995, killing three people?
10. What were the names of the Jacksons' two sons?
11. Which family moved into No. 7 in 1987?
12. Who tried to frame her own son for theft to cover up her gambling addiction?
13. Who burnt down Casa Bevron in a fit of pique?
14. Which TV astrologer opened the hospital fete in 1985?
15. What was the name of David Crosbie's wife?
16. What destroyed part of Brookside Parade in 1998?

Answers to page 545

QUIZ AND GAME SHOWS 7: **1.** Kate Thornton **2.** *The Generation Game* **3.** *Name That Tune* **4.** *Give Us a Clue* **5.** June Whitfield **6.** 100 **7.** *Play Your Cards Right* **8.** Paul Daniels **9.** *Hollywood Squares* **10.** Wincey Willis **11.** *Fifteen to One* **12.** *The Weakest Link* **13.** *Sale of the Century* **14.** *The Waiting Game* **15.** Noel Edmonds **16.** Kenny Everett

Dramas 12

Answers on page 550

1. Anthony Valentine played gold smuggler George Webster in which series?
2. Who did Jimmy Smits play in *LA Law*?
3. Who was Egg's girlfriend in *This Life*?
4. Who was diagnosed with ovarian cancer in *thirtysomething*?
5. Lord Brett Sinclair and Danny Wilde made up which team?
6. What was the sequel to *Mogul*?
7. What was the nickname of slippery Roland Cartwright in *London's Burning*?
8. Who wrote *Lipstick On Your Collar*?
9. Who played Nev in *Common as Muck*?
10. Shannen Doherty and Jason Priestley starred in which Teenage drama?
11. What did the car name KITT stand for in *Knight Rider*?
12. Which of the *Auf Wiedersehen, Pet* gang was a boring Brummie electrician?
13. What school subject did Trevor Chaplin teach in *The Beiderbecke Affair*?
14. Who was killed by a shark in the first season of *Baywatch*?
15. What is Maddy Magellan's profession in *Jonathan Creek*?
16. Whose novels were dramatised for *The Pallisers*?

Answers to page 550

CHILDREN'S TV 8: **1.** Raggy Dan **2.** Perky **3.** Gilbert Harding **4.** Doodles **5.** PAT 1 **6.** A fancy-dress shop **7.** *Bagpuss* **8.** Toyah Willcox **9.** Miss Adelaide **10.** Morocco Mole **11.** *Sexton Blake* **12.** Peter Butterworth **13.** The Mystery Machine **14.** 1989 **15.** On the front of his hat **16.** *Andy Pandy*

Comedy 16

Answers on page 551

1. Who is always trying to sell knock-off goods to *The Royle Family*?

2. Amanda Ripley, Jennifer Marsh, Candice Valentine and Shelley Dupont made up which Eighties foursome?

3. Which cop caper starred Michael Robbins as Det. Sgt Sidney Marble?

4. What was the name of the TV station in *Drop the Dead Donkey*?

5. What was *Desmond's* surname?

6. Bob Louis and Dave Briggs were otherwise known as what?

7. Who created *Brothers in Law*?

8. Who was *A Prince Among Men* in 1997?

9. Of which fictitious heavy metal band was Nigel Cochrane a member in *Roll Over Beethoven*?

10. Which *Dad's Army* actor starred in *Romany Jones*?

11. Which musical instrument does Lisa play in *The Simpsons*?

12. What were Lenny Henry, Tracey Ullman and David Copperfield in 1981?

13. Who played the Balowski family in *The Young Ones*?

14. What was Sgt Wilson's Christian name in *Dad's Army*?

15. What does Caroline do for a living in *Caroline in the City*?

16. Which soul musician provides the voice of Chef in *South Park*?

Answers to page 551

COP SHOWS 9: **1.** Henry Crabbe (*Pie in the Sky*) **2.** *Murder Bag* **3.** *Miss Marple* **4.** Captain Hastings **5.** John Nettles **6.** *Inspector Morse* **7.** Roderick **8.** Douglas Wilmer **9.** Cricket **10.** Julie Rogers **11.** Theodore 'TC' Calvin **12.** *Juliet Bravo* **13.** Jessica Fletcher **14.** Kenneth More **15.** *Hill Street Blues* **16.** *Spender*

Children's TV 8

Answers on page 548

1. Who was *Trumpton*'s rag and bone man?
2. Which of *Pinky and Perky* wore a hat?
3. Which *What's My Line* panellist was 'hideously embarrassed' at meeting Sooty?
4. What is the name of the dog in *Tweenies*?
5. What was the registration number of *Postman Pat*'s van?
6. Which shop did *Mr Benn* visit in every episode?
7. Which children's series featured a Marvellous Mechanical Mouse Organ?
8. Who provides the opening narration for *Teletubbies*?
9. Which Womble takes her name from an Australian city?
10. Who was Secret Squirrel's partner?
11. Who drove the Grey Panther?
12. Which future *Carry On* star appeared with Buddy Budgerigar?
13. What was the name of the van in which Scooby-Doo and the gang travelled?
14. In which year did *Byker Grove* begin?
15. Where was Torchy's battery-powered lamp situated?
16. Who was 'waving goodbye, goodbye' at the end of each episode?

Answers to page 548

DRAMAS 12: **1.** *The Knock* **2.** Victor Sifuentes **3.** Milly **4.** Nancy Weston **5.** *The Persuaders* **6.** *The Troubleshooters* **7.** 'Vaseline' **8.** Dennis Potter **9.** Edward Woodward **10.** *Beverly Hills 90210* **11.** Knight Industries Two Thousand **12.** Barry Taylor **13.** Woodwork **14.** Jill Riley **15.** Journalist **16.** Anthony Trollope

Cop Shows 9

Answers on page 549

1. Which detective opened a restaurant on retiring from the police force?
2. In which series did Tom Lockhart make his debut?
3. Which amateur sleuth constantly outwitted DCI Slack?
4. Which associate of Hercule Poirot drove a green Lagonda?
5. Who plays DCI Tom Barnaby in *Midsomer Murders*?
6. Which detective was killed off in 2000 after 13 years' service to the ITV ratings?
7. What is Inspector Alleyn's Christian name?
8. Who played Sherlock Holmes in his 1965 BBC incarnation?
9. Which sport was the passion of *Charters and Caldicott*?
10. Who replaced Tiffany Welles as one of *Charlie's Angels*?
11. Who ran the Island Hoppers helicopter company in *Magnum PI*?
12. Jean Darblay and Kate Longton were the police inspectors in which series?
13. Seth Haslett was which sleuth's family doctor?
14. Who played *Father Brown*?
15. Which series featured a regular informant by the name of Sid the Snitch?
16. Stick was which detective's supergrass?

Answers to page 549

COMEDY 16: **1.** Twiggy **2.** *Girls on Top* **3.** *The Fuzz* **4.** Globelink News **5.** Ambrose **6.** *The Detectives* **7.** Henry Cecil **8.** Chris Barrie **9.** Graf Spee **10.** James Beck **11.** Saxophone **12.** *Three of a Kind* **13.** Alexei Sayle **14.** Arthur **15.** Cartoonist **16.** Isaac Hayes

Soaps 12

Answers on page 554

1. Who had a child named Sky in *Neighbours*?
2. What is the Christian name of ex-Walford medic Dr Legg?
3. Which member of *Coronation Street*'s Tilsley family died in 1984?
4. In which US daytime soap did David Hasselhoff play Snapper Foster?
5. Whose illegitimate daughter was Lisa Walters in *Crossroads*?
6. Which game show host played Steve Murray's boss, Jeff Evans, in *Brookside*?
7. Which movie star's final role was that of Daniel Reece in *Dynasty*?
8. What were the names of the three Cooper children in *The Newcomers*?
9. What was the major industry in *Falcon Crest*?
10. Which chocolate firm sponsors *Coronation Street*?
11. What is Angie Reynolds' job in *Emmerdale*?
12. Which irascible individual runs the local store in Summer Bay?
13. Which Sixties singer played hairdresser Viv Harker in *Albion Market*?
14. Which *Dallas* character met his death in a helicopter crash in South America?
15. Who spotted a UFO from *Coronation Street* in 1984?
16. Which *EastEnders* couple eloped to Gretna Green?

Answers to page 554

LOCATIONS 6: **1.** *Jonathan Creek* **2.** Wallace and Gromit **3.** Villiers Street **4.** Melbourne **5.** *Starr and Company* **6.** California **7.** *Duty Free* **8.** *LA Law* **9.** *Cracker* **10.** *Weavers Green* **11.** *Common as Muck* **12.** Midland General **13.** Hercule Poirot **14.** Surbiton **15.** Provence **16.** *Worzel Gummidge*

Commercials 2

Answers on page 555

1. Which female comedy double act advertise Kingsmill bread?
2. Which vodka ad features a piano-playing dog?
3. Which Brummie comic had a *Commercial Breakdown*?
4. What drink did Lorraine Chase sip at Luton Airport?
5. What was softness a thing called?
6. Terry Brooks was the first lad to play which commercial cowboy?
7. 'Born To Be With You' is the song accompanying which car commercial?
8. What was the name of Katie's husband in the long-running Oxo ads?
9. Which advertising animals made their debuts in 1956?
10. Which car ad promises: 'You can take the car out of the city, but you can't take the city out of the car'?
11. Which was the first commercial to be shown on British television?
12. What do Lambrini girls just want to have?
13. Which coffee saga originated in 1988?
14. What was the name of Maureen Lipman's British Telecom mother?
15. Which action man jumped on to moving trains and swung from helicopters just to deliver a box of chocolates?
16. Which cat food did Arthur promote?

Answers to page 555

CORRIE 4: **1.** Susan Barlow **2.** Judy Mallett **3.** Karen Phillips **4.** The Tilsleys **5.** May Hardman **6.** 1977 **7.** Confectionery **8.** Kevin Webster **9.** Vicky Entwistle **10.** Derek Wilton **11.** Jez Quigley **12.** Reg Holdsworth **13.** No 11 **14.** Wakefield **15.** Don Brennan **16.** Tony

Locations 6

Answers on page 552

1. Which magical sleuth lives in an East Anglian windmill?
2. Which animated characters live at 62 West Wallaby Street?
3. What is the name of the police station in *The Vice*?
4. Which city was the setting for *Prisoner: Cell Block H*?
5. Which Fifties drama series was set in Sullbridge?
6. In which American state was *Knots Landing*?
7. Which sitcom was set at the San Remo Hotel, Marbella?
8. McKenzie, Brackman, Chaney and Kuzak were the legal firm in which US series?
9. The police officers in which series were stationed at Anson Road?
10. Which fictional East Anglian village was the setting for a 1966 soap?
11. Which Nineties drama series about refuse collectors was set in Hepworth?
12. What was the name of the hospital in the ITV afternoon soap of the 1970s?
13. Which TV detective lived at Whitehaven Mansions?
14. In which London suburb was *The Good Life* set?
15. Where did John Thaw and Lindsay Duncan spend a year in 1993?
16. Who stood in Ten Acre Field at Scatterbrook Farm?

Answers to page 552

SOAPS 12: **1.** Kerry Bishop **2.** Harold **3.** Bert **4.** *The Young and the Restless* **5.** Paul Ross **6.** Les Dennis **7.** Rock Hudson **8.** Philip, Maria and Lance **9.** Wine production **10.** Cadbury's **11.** Police officer **12.** Alf Stewart **13.** Helen Shapiro **14.** Jock Ewing **15.** Curly Watts **16.** Sam Mitchell and Ricky Butcher

TV Pot Luck 15

Answers on page 559

1. Which former *Ballykissangel* actress starred in *Hearts and Bones?*
2. Eric McCormack and Debra Messing star as unusual flatmates in which US sitcom?
3. Which former presenter of *Points of View* died in April 2002?
4. Which channel offers *Sex Tips For Girls?*
5. Who presents *DIY SOS?*
6. Which former swimmer fronted *The Big Breakfast?*
7. Which koala bear puppet partnered Rolf Harris in the early 1960s?
8. Which duo undertook *Jobs for the Boys?*
9. Which was the first British series to feature an all-black cast?
10. Which comedy writers had their one major flop with *Roots?*
11. Which controversial royal series was screened in the same year as Princess Margaret's divorce?
12. Which former member of the Bonzo Dog Doo Dah Band produced his *Book of Records* in 1979?
13. Who succeeded Kenneth Robinson as presenter of *Points of View?*
14. Which crime appeal show designed as a filler ran for 28 years?
15. And who presented it?
16. Which former producer of *The Price Is Right* is now a quiz show presenter?

Answers to page 559

DRAMAS 13: **1.** Razor Eddie **2.** *The Scarlet Pimpernel* **3.** Great British Holiday **4.** 1940s **5.** Cousin **6.** Dr Gillespie **7.** Danny Kavanagh **8.** Robert Hardy **9.** Lonely **10.** *The Forsyte Saga* **11.** Patrick McGoohan (*The Prisoner*) **12.** *The Fellows* **13.** *Redcap* **14.** Sgt John Mann **15.** *Preston Front* **16.** Alison Steadman

Comedy 17

Answers on page 556

1. Who devised *It's a Square World*?
2. What was the name of Nellie Boswell's unfaithful husband in *Bread*?
3. Who played Duncan Waring in *Doctor in the House*?
4. What was Bill Maynard's character Fred Moffat known as?
5. Which Page Three girl was created by Brenda Gilhooly?
6. Who was *The Man From Auntie*?
7. Who got his big break on *Do Not Adjust Your Set*?
8. Who played Reggie Perrin's brother-in-law, Jimmy?
9. Which *On the Buses* character went on to star in *Don't Drink the Water*?
10. And which *On the Buses* character joined the revival of *The Rag Trade*?
11. Which sketch show performed 'Nice Video, Shame About the Song'?
12. Who had a friend called Butthead?
13. Which three words begin the title of each *Friends* episode?
14. Who was famed for his impersonation of Harold Macmillan on *That Was The Week That Was?*
15. Which school sitcom was inspired by the film *To Sir With Love*?
16. Who starred as Dr Terrible in *Dr Terrible's House of Horrible*?

Answers to page 556
WHICH YEAR IN TV? 8: **1.** 1956 **2.** 1993 **3.** 1962 **4.** 1990 **5.** 1974 **6.** 1997 **7.** 1971 **8.** 1979 **9.** 1967 **10.** 1976 **11.** 1989 **12.** 1974 **13.** 1959 **14.** 1966 **15.** 1993 **16.** 1990

Dramas 13

Answers on page 557

1. Who was Turtle's muscular sidekick in *Turtle's Progress*?
2. Marius Goring and Richard E. Grant have both played which fearless adventurer on TV?
3. What did *GBH* stand for?
4. In which decade was *Enemy at the Door* set?
5. What relation was Luke to Bo Duke in *The Dukes of Hazzard*?
6. Who was *Dr Kildare*'s mentor?
7. Which poetry-loving tearaway left Liverpool for *The Lakes*?
8. Who played Alec Stewart in *The Troubleshooters*?
9. Which associate of *Callan* 'stank like a skunk' when nervous?
10. Which was the last major BBC drama series to be made in black and white?
11. In 1967, who was besieged in his own home by fans angry at the inconclusive ending to his series?
12. Which series was a spin-off from *The Man In Room 17*?
13. Which was John Thaw's first starring series?
14. And who did he play?
15. In which series did impressionist Alistair McGowan take over from Stephen Tompkinson in the role of 'Spock'?
16. Who played Mrs Bennet in the 1995 adaptation of *Pride and Prejudice*?

Answers to page 557

TV POT LUCK 15: **1.** Dervla Kirwan **2.** *Will and Grace* **3.** Barry Took **4.** Channel 4 **5.** Lowri Turner **6.** Sharron Davies **7.** Coojee Bear **8.** Hale and Pace **9.** *The Fosters* **10.** Laurence Marks and Maurice Gran **11.** *Edward and Mrs Simpson* **12.** Neil Innes **13.** Barry Took **14.** *Police 5* **15.** Shaw Taylor **16.** William G. Stewart

Soaps 13

Answers on page 562

In which soaps have the following characters appeared?

1. Lynn Whiteley
2. Dex Dexter
3. Vera Bennett
4. Cassie Charlton
5. Donna Ludlow
6. Hannah Martin
7. Mark Graison
8. Sam Pearson
9. Joanne Minster
10. Idris Hopkins
11. Nigel Bates
12. Morag Bellingham
13. Dieter Schultz
14. Jenna Wade
15. Linda Cheveski
16. Declan Byrne

Answers to page 562

WESTERNS 3: **1.** Dove **2.** Clint Walker **3.** William Boyd **4.** *The Lone Ranger* **5.** Bodie **6.** *The Cisco Kid* **7.** Roy Rogers **8.** *Annie Oakley* **9.** *Davy Crockett* **10.** The Buntline Special **11.** Jim Newton **12.** Matt Dillon **13.** *Gunsmoke* **14.** Jim Hardie **15.** *Tenderfoot* **16.** Roger Moore

Children's TV 9

Answers on page 563

1. What was Billy Bunter's middle name?
2. In 1976, which programme became the BBC's first Saturday morning entertainment show?
3. What was *Mr Pastry*'s theme tune?
4. What is Spiderman's real name?
5. Which Saturday morning show featured 'The Cage'?
6. Who was the resident chimney sweep of *Camberwick Green*?
7. Which family had a magic bean plant?
8. Mick the Marmaliser and Nigel Ponsonby-Smallpiece were members of which troupe?
9. Which young member of the Royal Family came into the *Blue Peter* studio to meet a lion cub?
10. Jon Miller and Bunty James were panellists on which show?
11. Which Sixties pop star presented *Little Big Time*?
12. What was the name of *Postman Pat*'s wife?
13. Which rag-doll puppets came to life when their bargee friend turned his back?
14. What colour was the Graculus, the strange talking bird in *The Saga of Noggin the Nog*?
15. What did Mrs Cobbit sell in *Trumpton*?
16. Which space-age family had a foodarackacycle?

Answers to page 563

SCI FI 6: **1.** Skinner **2.** 'Bones' **3.** Urko **4.** Vic Perrin **5.** *Fireball XL5* **6.** Humans, Minbari, Centauri, Narn and Vorlons **7.** The Vogons **8.** Colin Baker **9.** Australian **10.** Apollo **11.** Sally Knyvette **12.** *First Born* **13.** Visual Instrument and Sight Organ Replacement **14.** Galasphere 347 **15.** Gil Gerard **16.** The Tanners

Westerns 3

Answers on page 560

1. Which bird was Lonesome in the title of a modern Western?
2. Which Western star walked out of his contract with Warner Brothers, saying he was tired of shooting 'the same old Indian'?
3. Who played *Hopalong Cassidy*?
4. John Reid is the real name of which Western hero?
5. What was *Cheyenne*'s surname?
6. O. Henry created which durable Hispanic hero?
7. Which singing cowboy lived on the Double R Bar Ranch?
8. Which female gunslinger had a younger brother named Tagg?
9. Who was known as the 'King of the Wild Frontier'?
10. What was the name of Wyatt Earp's gun?
11. Who owned the Broken Wheel Ranch in *Fury*?
12. Which Marshal had a deputy named Festus Hagen?
13. And in which long-running Western series did they appear?
14. Which sharpshooter did Dale Robertson play in *Tales of Wells Fargo*?
15. What was Tom Brewster otherwise known as?
16. Which English actor played Beau Maverick?

Answers to page 560

SOAPS 13: **1.** *Emmerdale* **2.** *Dynasty* **3.** *Prisoner: Cell Block H* **4.** *Brookside* **5.** *EastEnders* **6.** *Neighbours* **7.** *Dallas* **8.** *Emmerdale Farm* **9.** *Compact* **10.** *Coronation Street* **11.** *EastEnders* **12.** *Home and Away* **13.** *Eldorado* **14.** *Dallas* **15.** *Coronation Street* **16.** *Family Affairs*

Sci Fi 6

Answers on page 561

1. What was the name of Mulder's chief in *The X Files*?
2. What was Dr Leonard McCoy's nickname in *Star Trek*?
3. What was the name of the evil gorilla leader in *Planet of the Apes*?
4. Who narrated *The Outer Limits*?
5. Which Gerry Anderson series featured Robert the Robot?
6. Which five races are on board *Babylon 5*?
7. In *The Hitch-Hiker's Guide to the Galaxy*, which race of aliens wrote the worst poetry in the Universe?
8. Who became the sixth *Doctor Who* in 1984?
9. In *Captain Scarlet and the Mysterons*, what nationality was Dr Fawn?
10. Who was Adama's son in *Battlestar Galactica*?
11. Who played Jenna Stannis in *Blake's 7* before marrying Joe Sugden in *Emmerdale*?
12. Genetic scientist Edward Forester was the central character of which 1988 series starring Charles Dance?
13. What did Geordi La Forge's VISOR stand for in *Star Trek: The Next Generation*?
14. What was the name of the lead ship in *Space Patrol*?
15. Who played Buck Rogers?
16. With which family did *ALF* live?

Answers to page 561

CHILDREN'S TV 9: **1.** George **2.** *Multi-Coloured Swap Shop* **3.** 'Pop Goes the Weasel' **4.** Peter Parker **5.** *Tiswas* **6.** Roger Varley **7.** *The Pogles* **8.** The Diddymen **9.** Prince Edward **10.** *How!* **11.** Freddie Garrity **12.** Sarah **13.** *Rosie and Jim* **14.** Green **15.** Flowers **16.** *The Jetsons*

Music Pot Luck 15

Answers on page 566

1. Which one-time drummer with The Farm is a scriptwriter for *Brookside*?
2. Which band's albums included 'Pictures At An Exhibition', 'Tarkus' and 'Brain Salad Surgery'?
3. What was the name of Dion's backing group?
4. Jake Hooker, Alan Merrill and Paul Varley made up which Seventies teenybop group that had their own TV series?
5. Which American country singer who enjoyed widespread chart success in the late Sixties used to be backed by a band known as The Western Wranglers?
6. What were the names of the two Bellamy Brothers?
7. Who went to number one in 2002 with a cover of *Unchained Melody*?
8. Which band named themselves after an unpopular gym teacher at their school?
9. Which Beatle was previously paid £2 10s a week as a messenger for British Railways?
10. Gwen Stefani led which chart-topping band of the Nineties?
11. Who was the vocalist with Sad Café before going solo?
12. Which successful American singer/songwriter of the Seventies once worked as a computer specialist at a Los Angeles bank?
13. Which four-piece band lost two of its members to drug deaths in successive years – 1982 and 1983?
14. Which UK Sixties band were previously known as The Ravens?
15. In which year did Roy Orbison die?
16. How many UK number ones has Engelbert Humperdinck had?

Answers to page 566

ABBA 1: **1.** The Hep Stars **2.** 'Ring Ring' **3.** 'S.O.S.' **4.** 'Mamma Mia' **5.** Five **6.** 'Money, Money, Money' (it only reached no. 3) **7.** 'Fernando' **8.** 1978 **9.** 1978 **10.** 'Voulez-Vous' **11.** Because of statements they made on TV supporting Polish Solidarity **12.** 1981 **13.** 'Super Trouper' **14.** It is the only case of a palindromic artist and title **15.** 'Knowing Me, Knowing You' **16.** 'Thank You For The Music'

Albums 5

Answers on page 567

1. Which band released the 1996 album 'Moseley Shoals'?
2. Who had a number one album called 'Very' in 1993?
3. Which 1983 UK number one album was inspired by the teachings of therapist Arthur Janov?
4. Which Michael Jackson album spent 173 weeks in the UK charts?
5. What was the biggest-selling UK album of 1989?
6. Which Irish band released a 1994 album titled 'Everybody Else Is Doing It, So Why Can't We?'
7. Which is the best-selling album of all time in the UK?
8. 'Pet Sounds' was a ground-breaking 1966 album for which American band?
9. What was the eagerly awaited follow-up to Oasis's '(What's The Story) Morning Glory'?
10. Which 1978 album went on to spend 395 weeks in the UK charts?
11. Which Michael Jackson album was the UK best-seller of 1987?
12. Whose number one album was 'Back To Front' in 1992?
13. Which band released 'A Question Of Balance' in 1970?
14. 'Electric Warrior' was a number one album for which band in 1972?
15. Who reckoned 'Blondes Have More Fun' in 1978?
16. Who released the double album 'Tusk' in 1979?

Answers to page 567

COVER VERSIONS 5: **1.** Saragossa Band **2.** 'I Still Believe' **3.** Westlife **4.** 'It Only Takes A Minute' **5.** Randy and The Rainbows **6.** 'I Shot The Sheriff' **7.** 'Indian Love Call' **8.** Mariah Carey **9.** Sunny Dae and The Knights **10.** Undercover **11.** 'Could It Be Magic' **12.** Harold Melvin and The Bluenotes **13.** Fine Young Cannibals **14.** 'Reach Out I'll Be There' **15.** Doris Troy **16.** 'Can't Take My Eyes Off You'

Abba 1

Answers on page 564

1. With which top Swedish band was Benny Andersson the pianist before forming Abba?
2. The year before *Waterloo*, which other Abba composition had failed to be chosen as Sweden's Eurovision Song Contest entry?
3. Which Abba single had previously been recorded by Agnetha on her solo album 'Eleven Women In One Building'?
4. Which Abba song ended the nine-week reign of Queen's 'Bohemian Rhapsody' at the top of the UK singles chart?
5. How many singles did Abba have in Australia's top 30 at one time in 1976?
6. Six out of seven successive Abba singles reached number one in the UK. Which was the one to miss out?
7. Which single had already been recorded by Frida on her album 'Frida Alone'?
8. Which year saw the premier of *Abba – The Movie*?
9. In which year did Benny and Frida marry and Bjorn and Agnetha file for divorce?
10. Which was the first album recorded at Abba's Polar Studios in Stockholm?
11. Why were Abba banned from the Soviet Union in 1982?
12. When did Benny and Frida split up?
13. Which was Abba's last UK number one single?
14. What is unique about 'S.O.S.' by Abba?
15. Which Abba track was the title of a Steve Coogan comedy series?
16. What was Abba's last single before the break-up of the group?

Answers to page 564

MUSIC POT LUCK 15: **1.** Roy Boulter **2.** Emerson, Lake and Palmer **3.** The Belmonts **4.** Arrows **5.** Glen Campbell **6.** Howard and David **7.** Gareth Gates **8.** Lynyrd Skynyrd (Leonard Skinner) **9.** Ringo Starr **10.** No Doubt **11.** Paul Young **12.** Harry Nilsson **13.** The Pretenders **14.** The Kinks **15.** 1988 **16.** Two – 'Release Me' and 'The Last Waltz'

Cover Versions 5

Answers on page 565

1. Who originally recorded 'Agadoo', covered by Black Lace in 1984?
2. Which song links Brenda K. Starr and Mariah Carey?
3. Who covered Billy Joel's 'Uptown Girl' in 2001?
4. One Hundred Ton and A Feather, Tavares and Take That have all recorded which song?
5. Who originally recorded Blondie's 1978 hit 'Denis'?
6. Which Eric Clapton hit did Warren G cover in 1997?
7. Which song was recorded by Slim Whitman, Karl Denver and Ray Stevens in three different decades?
8. Who recently covered 'Against All Odds (Take A Look At Me Now)', a hit for Phil Collins in 1984?
9. Who recorded the original version of 'Rock Around The Clock' in 1952?
10. Who covered Gerry Rafferty's 'Baker Street' in 1992?
11. Donna Summer, Barry Manilow and Take That have all recorded which song?
12. Who originally recorded 'Don't Leave Me This Way', a 1986 hit for The Communards?
13. Who covered Elvis Presley's 'Suspicious Minds' in 1986?
14. Which song links The Four Tops, Gloria Gaynor and Michael Bolton?
15. Who was the first artist to record The Hollies' 'Just One Look'?
16. Frankie Valli, Andy Williams and Boystown Gang have all recorded which song?

Answers to page 565

ALBUMS 5: **1.** Ocean Colour Scene **2.** The Pet Shop Boys **3.** 'The Hurting' (Tears For Fears) **4.** 'Thriller' **5.** 'Ten Good Reasons' (Jason Donovan) **6.** The Cranberries **7.** 'Sgt. Pepper's Lonely Hearts Club Band' **8.** The Beach Boys **9.** 'Be Here Now' **10.** 'Bat Out Of Hell' (Meat Loaf) **11.** 'Bad' **12.** Lionel Richie **13.** The Moody Blues **14.** T. Rex **15.** Rod Stewart **16.** Fleetwood Mac

Singer/Songwriters 2

Answers on page 570

1. How old was Kate Bush when she wrote the lyrics to 'The Man With The Child In His Eyes'?
2. What was the title of Tracy Chapman's biggest-selling single?
3. What was Neil Diamond's first UK hit?
4. Which Neil Diamond song was autobiographical?
5. About whom did Elton John write 'Someone Saved My Life Tonight'?
6. Which singer/songwriter released a single called 'Freeek' in 2002?
7. Which song did Billy Joel write about his first wife and manager, Elizabeth?
8. What is Prince's full name?
9. What was the title of Prince's debut album?
10. Which Neil Sedaka song was banned by several US radio stations?
11. Which Neil Sedaka hit was subsequently covered by The Partridge Family?
12. As what was Stevie Wonder known on his early releases?
13. Who cut his first solo record under the name True Taylor?
14. Who provided falsetto backing on Elton John's 'Nikita'?
15. What was George Michael's second solo UK number one?
16. Who received 461 Valentine's Day cards after indicating that she never received any in the lyrics of her 1975 song 'At Seventeen'?

Answers to page 570

DANCE 2: **1.** Bryan Adams **2.** Fragma **3.** Ibiza **4.** Fatboy Slim **5.** 'Move Your Body' **6.** Des Mitchell **7.** Taka Boom **8.** Germany **9.** 9pm **10.** Alice Deejay **11.** Moloko **12.** Antoine Clamaran **13.** Shout **14.** Gram'ma Funk **15.** Spiller **16.** French

Chart Toppers 7

Answers on page 571

1. Who were the first father and son to have topped the UK charts?
2. Who were the first father and daughter to top the UK charts?
3. Which soul artist was the subject of 'Geno' by Dexy's Midnight Runners?
4. What nationality is Johnny Logan?
5. Which TV theme reached number one in the UK in 1980?
6. Who sang on Adamski's 1990 number one 'Killer'?
7. Who was the first black female artist to reach number one in the UK?
8. Who were the first female duo to top the UK singles chart?
9. Which 1972 number one was a tribute to a 19th-century artist?
10. Who had a number one in 1999 with 'Flat Beat'?
11. What was the best-selling UK single of 1976?
12. Who was the lead singer of Union Gap who had a 1968 number one with 'Young Girl'?
13. Which 1969 chart topper was born Roberta Lee Streeter before taking her stage surname from a film?
14. Which Eurovision Song Contest winner topped the UK charts in 1982?
15. Who had a 1959 number one with 'Here Comes Summer'?
16. Who were the first mother and son to reach number one in the UK?

Answers to page 571

BOB DYLAN 1: **1.** Robert Zimmerman **2.** Dylan Thomas **3.** 1962 **4.** His girlfriend Suze Rotolo **5.** 'The Times They Are A-Changin' **6.** 'Bringing It All Back Home' **7.** Newport Folk Festival **8.** 'Mr Tambourine Man' **9.** 'Like A Rolling Stone' **10.** Manfred Mann **11.** *Pat Garrett and Billy the Kid* **12.** 1991 **13.** Al Kooper **14.** His then wife Sarah Lowndes **15.** The Grateful Dead **16.** 'Tarantula'

Dance 2

Answers on page 568

1. Which male solo artist sang with Chicane on the single 'Don't Give Up'?
2. Which dance group had a number one hit with 'Toca's Miracle'?
3. Where were Vengaboys going to in the title of their 1999 single?
4. Who is Norman Cook better known as?
5. What was Eiffel 65's follow-up to 'Blue'?
6. Who Welcomed You To The Dance?
7. Who featured with Joey Negro on the single 'Must Be The Music'?
8. Which country does the DJ Sash come from?
9. At what time did ATB say they would come in the title of their 1999 single?
10. Who released the single 'Better Off Alone'?
11. Who wanted you to 'Sing It Back'?
12. Who had a single titled 'We Come To Party'?
13. Basement Jaxx wanted everyone to 'Jump 'n''...what?
14. Who did Groove Armada feature in their single 'I See You Baby'?
15. Who had a number one in 2000 with 'Groovejet'?
16. What nationality are Modjo?

Answers to page 568

SINGER/SONGWRITERS 2: **1.** 14 **2.** 'Fast Car' **3.** 'Crackling Rosie' **4.** 'I Am...I Said' **5.** Long John Baldry **6.** George Michael **7.** 'Just The Way You Are' **8.** Prince Rogers Nelson **9.** 'For You' **10.** 'I Go Ape' **11.** 'Breaking Up Is Hard To Do' **12.** Little Stevie Wonder **13.** Paul Simon **14.** George Michael **15.** 'A Different Corner' **16.** Janis Ian

Bob Dylan 1

Answers on page 569

1. What is Bob Dylan's real name?
2. After which poet did he reputedly name himself?
3. In which year did Dylan make his first appearance in the UK?
4. Who was pictured on the cover of his second album, 'The Freewheelin' Bob Dylan'?
5. Which was Dylan's first UK single?
6. Which Dylan album features 'Subterranean Homesick Blues'?
7. At which 1965 festival did folk purists in the audience try to boo Dylan off stage?
8. Which Dylan song was a US number one for The Byrds in 1965?
9. Which six-minute track became Dylan's first million-selling single?
10. Which UK band had a 1966 hit with a cover version of Dylan's 'Just Like A Woman'?
11. In which Sam Peckinpah film did Dylan play an outlaw named Alias?
12. In which year did Dylan receive a Lifetime Achievement Award at the Grammys?
13. Which member of Blood Sweat and Tears played the organ on 'Like A Rolling Stone'?
14. For whom did Dylan write 'Lay Lady Lay'?
15. Which band collaborated with Dylan on the 1989 album 'Dylan And The Dead'?
16. Which Dylan novel was published in 1970?

Answers to page 569

CHART TOPPERS 7: **1.** Ringo Starr (Beatles) and Zak Starkey (who sang with The Crowd on the charity record 'You'll Never Walk Alone' in 1985) **2.** Frank and Nancy Sinatra ('Something Stupid') **3.** Geno Washington **4.** Australian **5.** 'Theme From M*A*S*H (Suicide Is Painless)' **6.** Seal **7.** Winifred Atwell **8.** Baccara **9.** 'Vincent' (Van Gogh) by Don McLean **10.** Mr Oizo **11.** 'Save Your Kisses For Me' **12.** Gary Puckett **13.** Bobbie Gentry **14.** 'A Little Peace' by Nicole **15.** Jerry Keller **16.** Hilda and Rob Woodward of Lieutenant Pigeon

Eighties 4

Answers on page 574

Who had UK hits with the following tracks in the Eighties?

1. 'Driving In My Car'
2. 'The Riddle'
3. 'Sweet Dreams (Are Made Of This)'
4. 'Suburbia'
5. 'Happy Hour'
6. 'The Cutter'
7. 'Da Da Da'
8. 'Ghostdancing'
9. 'Hard Habit To Break'
10. 'Truly'
11. 'Mystify'
12. 'Somewhere In My Heart'
13. 'A View To A Kill'
14. 'Only When You Leave'
15. 'Fields Of Fire (400 Miles)'
16. 'Is That Love?'

Answers to page 574

MUSIC POT LUCK 16: **1.** Cathy Dennis **2.** The Clash **3.** 1970 **4.** Girlschool **5.** Kid Creole and The Coconuts **6.** Dusty Springfield **7.** Olivia Newton-John **8.** They used to ban any song about death **9.** Eric Bazilian **10.** Howard Greenfield **11.** James Taylor **12.** Showaddywaddy **13.** The Dreamers **14.** 'Red Red Wine' **15.** Peter Gabriel **16.** Jimmy Page

Lyrics 6

Answers on page 575

From which songs are the following lyrics taken?

1. 'You gave away the things you loved, and one of them was me'
2. 'Good or bad, like it or not, it's the only one we've got'
3. 'Oh yeah, I'll tell you something, I think you'll understand'
4. 'Since you've been gone I've been lost'
5. 'All I want is a photo in my wallet, a small remembrance of something more solid'
6. 'Street's like a jungle so call the police, following the herd down to Greece'
7. 'We don't talk about love, we only want to get drunk'
8. 'I never thought it would happen with me and a girl from Clapham'
9. 'These are my salad days slowly being eaten away'
10. 'Well, I'm standing on a corner in Winslow, Arizona'
11. 'You've found the secret code I use to wash away my lonely blues'
12. 'My hands are shaky and my knees are weak, I can't seem to stand on my own two feet'
13. 'You got beautiful eyes, you got beautiful thighs, you've got a lot without a doubt'
14. 'She calls out to the man on the street, he can see she's been crying'
15. 'You're my sun, my moon, my guiding star'
16. 'Once I get you up there I'll be holding you so near'

Answers to page 575

GIRL BANDS 3: **1.** Vicki and Debbi Peterson **2.** Siobhan Fahey **3.** Jean Terrell **4.** The Shangri-Las **5.** Martha and The Vandellas **6.** 'Too Much' **7.** Prince **8.** Christopher **9.** 'Venus' **10.** Fun Boy Three **11.** Lois **12.** It was his motorbike that was revved on 'Leader Of The Pack' **13.** The Supremes **14.** 'Walk Like An Egyptian' **15.** 1989 **16.** The Shirelles

Music Pot Luck 16

Answers on page 572

1. Which former singer co-wrote Kylie Minogue's 'Can't Get You Out of My Head'?
2. 'Topper' Headon was drummer with which punk band?
3. In which year was the Glastonbury Festival first held?
4. Enid Williams and Kim McAuliffe founded which all-female heavy metal band?
5. Which band had seven UK hits between 1981 and 1983, including three in the top ten, but never once entered the US top 100?
6. Which Sixties singer had been sacked from her sales job at Bentalls department store in Kingston, Surrey, after blowing all the fuses?
7. Which Australian singer's grandfather won the 1954 Nobel Prize for physics?
8. Why did the BBC ban 'Tell Laura I Love Her', Ricky Valance's 1960 hit?
9. Who wrote Joan Osborne's 1996 hit 'One Of Us'?
10. With which lyricist did Neil Sedaka team up in the early Fifties?
11. To whom was Carly Simon married from 1972 to 1983?
12. Dave Bartram was lead singer with which rock 'n' roll revival band?
13. What was the name of Freddie Garrity's backing band?
14. Which Neil Diamond song did UB40 take to number one in 1983?
15. Who played flute on Cat Stevens's 'Lady D'Arbanville'?
16. Which legendary rock guitarist played on Donovan's 'Sunshine Superman'?

Answers to page 572

EIGHTIES 4: **1.** Madness **2.** Nik Kershaw **3.** The Eurythmics **4.** Pet Shop Boys **5.** The Housemartins **6.** Echo and The Bunnymen **7.** Trio **8.** Simple Minds **9.** Chicago **10.** Lionel Richie **11.** INXS **12.** Aztec Camera **13.** Duran Duran **14.** Spandau Ballet **15.** Big Country **16.** Squeeze

Girl Bands 3

Answers on page 573

1. Which two sisters were members of The Bangles?
2. Which member of Bananarama used to work in the press office at Decca Records?
3. Who replaced Diana Ross in The Supremes?
4. Which Sixties band were composed of two pairs of sisters?
5. Which girl band had a 1965 hit with 'Nowhere To Run'?
6. Which single enabled the Spice Girls to become the first act to have their first six releases reach number one in the UK charts?
7. Who wrote The Bangles' 'Manic Monday'?
8. Under what pseudonym did he write it?
9. Which cover of a Shocking Blue hit from 1970 did Bananarama take to number eight in the UK charts in 1986?
10. With whom did Bananarama team up for the 1982 hit 'It Ain't What You Do, It's The Way That You Do It'?
11. Which sister of Martha Reeves joined the Vandellas in 1968?
12. What important role did Joey Veneri play in the history of The Shangri-Las?
13. Which girl group appeared as nuns in a 1968 episode of the TV series *Tarzan*?
14. Which Bangles hit had previously been rejected by Toni Basil?
15. In which year did The Bangles split up?
16. Shirley Owens, 'Micki' Harris, Doris Coley and Beverly Lee were the original members of which girl group?

Answers to page 573

LYRICS 6: **1.** 'You're So Vain' (Carly Simon) **2.** 'I Won't Let The Sun Go Down On Me' (Nik Kershaw) **3.** 'I Want To Hold Your Hand' (The Beatles) **4.** 'Every Breath You Take' (The Police) **5.** 'Picture This' (Blondie) **6.** 'Girls And Boys' (Blur) **7.** 'A Design For Life' (Manic Street Preachers) **8.** 'Up The Junction' (Squeeze) **9.** 'Gold' (Spandau Ballet) **10.** 'Take It Easy' (The Eagles) **11.** 'Sex Bomb' (Tom Jones) **12.** 'All Shook Up' (Elvis Presley) **13.** 'Rabbit' (Chas and Dave) **14.** 'Another Day In Paradise' (Phil Collins) **15.** 'You're The First, The Last, My Everything' (Barry White) **16.** 'Come Fly With Me' (Frank Sinatra)

Led Zeppelin 1

Answers on page 578

1. Whose remark about a disastrous gig 'going down like a lead zeppelin' resulted in the band acquiring their new name?

2. Which headliners at a 1969 Boston gig refused to take the stage after support act Led Zeppelin had gone down so well?

3. In which year was the 'Led Zeppelin' album released?

4. In which year did Led Zeppelin release their first single in the UK?

5. Which track earned the band their only US gold disc single?

6. Why did the band play a 1970 gig in Copenhagen as The Nobs?

7. 'Stairway To Heaven' first appeared on which album?

8. What is the playing time of 'Stairway To Heaven'?

9. On which island was Robert Plant badly injured in a 1975 car crash?

10. In which year did John Bonham die?

11. Who replaced Bonham when Led Zeppelin reformed in 1988?

12. What was the name of Led Zeppelin's own record label, first used in 1974?

13. Which band did Jimmy Page join in 1960?

14. With which band was Robert Plant performing when Jimmy Page first saw him?

15. The keys to which American city were Led Zeppelin given in April 1970?

16. Which album featured 'Immigrant Song'?

Answers to page 578

FILM TRACKS 5: **1.** 'Blaze Of Glory' **2.** *Bean: The Movie* **3.** Stealers Wheel **4.** 'She' **5.** 'A View To A Kill' **6.** 'Silver Dream Machine' **7.** *Wild Wild West* **8.** Huey Lewis and The News **9.** 'The King Of Wishful Thinking' **10.** *Trainspotting* **11.** *The Graduate* **12.** 'I Still Haven't Found What I'm Looking For' **13.** *Footloose* **14.** 'Raindrops Keep Falling On My Head' **15.** 'It Must Have Been Love' **16.** Barbra Streisand

Novelty Numbers 2

Answers on page 579

1. Who was strongly advised not to look in the lyrics of Ray Stevens's 'The Streak'?
2. Which midget did Ray Stevens take to number two in the UK charts in 1971?
3. Which TV soldiers had a number one with an old Inkspots song in 1975?
4. And what was the title of the song?
5. Which long-deceased comedians had a number two hit in 1975?
6. Which song did the 1970 England World Cup Squad take to number one?
7. Which footballer was the subject of The Cockerel Chorus's 1973 hit?
8. Which star of a TV docusoap covered a Madness hit in 1997?
9. Who had a hit with 'Vindaloo' in 1998?
10. Who were 'Doctorin' The Tardis' in 1988?
11. Which doll did Aqua take to number one for four weeks in 1997?
12. Which Indie band teamed up with Frank Skinner and David Baddiel for 'Three Lions' in 1996?
13. What did Baz Luhrmann say everybody was free to wear in 1999?
14. Which comedian charted in 1962 using his catchphrase in a version of 'Singin' In The Rain'?
15. Which old Traffic number was a hit for one of *The Young Ones* in 1984?
16. Which TV policeman had a number two hit with the theme from his series in 1992?

Answers to page 579

SEVENTIES 5: **1.** C.W. McCall ('Convoy') **2.** 'Love Grows (Where My Rosemary Goes)' by Edison Lighthouse **3.** Chicory Tip **4.** Chas Chandler **5.** David Cassidy **6.** The Bay City Rollers **7.** Curved Air **8.** He often wore a bee-like, black and yellow striped top **9.** The Rolling Stones **10.** Genesis **11.** 'Tie A Yellow Ribbon Round The Old Oak Tree' **12.** Slade **13.** The Rubettes **14.** David Essex **15.** Mott The Hoople **16.** Grace Slick (Jefferson Airplane)

Film Tracks 5

Answers on page 576

1. Which Bon Jovi song was used in the film *Young Guns II*?
2. Which film featured Boyzone's 'Picture Of You'?
3. Who recorded 'Stuck In The Middle With You' which was heard in the Quentin Tarantino film *Reservoir Dogs*?
4. Which Elvis Costello song was used in *Notting Hill*?
5. Which Duran Duran song was the theme to a Bond movie?
6. Which David Essex hit was taken from *Silver Dream Racer*?
7. Which 1999 film featured 'Balaimos' by Enrique Iglesias?
8. Whose recording of 'Power Of Love' was heard in *Back To The Future*?
9. Which Go West song was used in the film *Pretty Woman*?
10. Which film included Iggy Pop's 'Lust For Life'?
11. Simon and Garfunkel's 'Mrs Robinson' was taken from which film?
12. Which U2 hit was used in *Runaway Bride*?
13. Bonnie Tyler's 'Holding Out For A Hero' was taken from which film?
14. Sacha Distel had a hit with which track from *Butch Cassidy and the Sundance Kid*?
15. Which Roxette hit was taken from *Pretty Woman*?
16. Who had a 1977 hit with the theme from *A Star Is Born*?

Answers to page 576

LED ZEPPELIN 1: **1.** Keith Moon **2.** Iron Butterfly **3.** 1969 **4.** 1997 **5.** 'Whole Lotta Love' **6.** Eva von Zeppelin, relative of the airship designer, had threatened to sue if the family name was used in Denmark **7.** 'Led Zeppelin IV' **8.** 8min 1 sec **9.** Rhodes **10.** 1980 **11.** His son Jason **12.** Swan Song **13.** Neil Christian and The Crusaders **14.** Hobbstweedle **15.** Memphis **16.** 'Led Zeppelin III'

Seventies 5

Answers on page 577

1. Which one-hit wonder of 1976 went on to become mayor of Ouray, Colorado?
2. Which 1970 UK number one was recorded by a group of session musicians?
3. Peter Hewson was the singer with which 1972 UK chart toppers?
4. Which Animal managed Slade?
5. Who was featured bare-chested on the cover of *Rolling Stone* in January 1972?
6. Which teenybop group had their own TV series called *Shang-A-Lang*?
7. With which progressive rockers was Stewart Copeland the drummer before forming The Police?
8. How did Gordon Sumner acquire his nickname of 'Sting'?
9. Which band's equipment van was dynamited during a 1972 tour of Canada?
10. Which band recorded the album 'Selling England By The Pound'?
11. Which 1973 hit told the story of an ex-con returning home to his loved one after serving a three-year jail sentence?
12. Which band were pilloried by teachers in the belief that their phonetic spelling of titles set a bad example to children?
13. Who had a 1974 hit with 'Juke Box Jive'?
14. 'Gonna Make You A Star' was the first number one for which artist?
15. Overend Watts, 'Buffin' and Ariel Bender were members of which Seventies band?
16. Which singer with an American band wanted to name her daughter God before settling for China?

Answers to page 577

NOVELTY NUMBERS 2: **1.** Ethel **2.** Bridget **3.** Windsor Davies and Don Estelle **4.** 'Whispering Grass' **5.** Laurel and Hardy **6.** 'Back Home' **7.** Cyril Knowles ('Nice One Cyril') **8.** Maureen Rees ('Driving In My Car') **9.** Fat Les **10.** The Timelords **11.** Barbie **12.** The Lightning Seeds **13.** Sunscreen **14.** Norman Vaughan ('Swinging In The Rain') **15.** 'Hole In My Shoe' (Neil) **16.** Nick Berry ('Heartbeat')

Folk 3

Answers on page 582

1. Which dead-pan Yorkshire folk singer told the story of 'Sister Josephine'?
2. Who was born Janis Fink?
3. Which trio originally comprised Bob Shane, Nick Reynolds and Dave Guard?
4. George, Finbar, Eddie and Paul made up which Irish family band?
5. What was Peter, Paul and Mary's first UK chart success?
6. Who had a lovely time on a 1979 day trip to North Wales?
7. With which song did Steeleye Span have a top five hit in 1975?
8. Whose debut album was 'If You Saw Through My Eyes'?
9. Which dead comedy genius was the subject of Al Stewart's 1977 hit 'Year Of The Cat'?
10. From which country do Runrig hail?
11. Which of The Spinners has an actor son who has appeared in *Soldier, Soldier* and *Brookside*?
12. Which Lancashire group were originally known as The Wednesday Folks?
13. Which band were formed in 1962 in the back of O'Donoghue's bar in Dublin?
14. What nationality were The Bushwackers?
15. Mike Heron, Robin Williamson and Clive Palmer formed which folk band in Glasgow in 1965?
16. Which band had a 1966 UK hit with 'Three Wheels On My Wagon'?

Answers to page 582

MUSIC POT LUCK 17: **1.** 'When Irish Eyes Are Smiling' **2.** Love Affair **3.** 'A Hard Rain's A-Gonna Fall' **4.** 'Gypsies, Tramps And White Trash' **5.** 'Speedy Gonzales' **6.** Keith Richard **7.** 'What's The New Mary Jane' **8.** Bread **9.** Rochdale **10.** 'It's Good News Week' **11.** Tina Turner **12.** Annie Lennox **13.** David Bowie **14.** Eddie Miller **15.** 'Saturday Night Fever' **16.** Marty Wilde

Beach Boys 1

Answers on page 583

1. Which Beach Boys' single put new lyrics to Chuck Berry's 'Sweet Little Sixteen'?
2. Which guest artist played lead guitar on 'Good Vibrations'?
3. Which group originally recorded 'Barbara Ann'?
4. Which B-side of 'I Get Around' had been written for The Ronettes but had been rejected by Phil Spector?
5. Who joined the band as a temporary replacement for Brian Wilson in 1965?
6. Who became a full-time Beach Boy in 1965?
7. Which half of a surfing duo sang backing vocals on 'Barbara Ann'?
8. Which Beach Boys single was a traditional Caribbean tune dating back to 1927?
9. Which song beat 'Good Vibrations' to win a 1967 Grammy Award?
10. Which Beach Boy was acquitted of draft evasion in 1967?
11. In which year was 'Darlin'' released?
12. From which album was 'Cottonfields' taken?
13. What was The Beach Boys' second UK number one single?
14. Who joined The Beach Boys for 'Fun Fun Fun' in 1996?
15. What relation was Mike Love to the Wilson brothers?
16. Who suffered a mental breakdown after '*Pet Sounds*'?

Answers to page 583

ALBUMS 6: **1.** Slade **2.** The Bee Gees **3.** Cher **4.** Squeeze **5.** Paul Simon **6.** Carly Simon **7.** Paul McCartney **8.** Catatonia **9.** The Eagles **10.** Roxy Music **11.** Elton John **12.** Madonna **13.** Neil Young **14.** Mariah Carey **15.** Bread **16.** Billy Joel

Music Pot Luck 17

Answers on page 580

1. Which traditional Irish song was written by George Graff, a German who never set foot in Ireland in his life?
2. Steve Ellis was lead singer with which Sixties band?
3. Which Bob Dylan song gave Bryan Ferry his first solo hit?
4. What was the original title of Cher's hit 'Gypsies, Tramps And Thieves'?
5. Which Pat Boone song was banned in the US for being offensive to Mexicans?
6. Which member of The Rolling Stones was jailed in 1967 for allowing his house to be used for the illegal smoking of cannabis?
7. What would have been the next Beatles single had the band not split?
8. Which band came up with their name after being stuck in traffic behind a Wonder Bread lorry?
9. Where did Mike Harding's Cowboy come from?
10. What was the only hit of Hedgehoppers Anonymous?
11. Which glamorous granny was born Annie Mae Bullock?
12. Which female singer used to work in an Aberdeen fish factory?
13. Bing Crosby and Marc Bolan both died within weeks of recording TV shows with which singer?
14. Who originally recorded the Engelbert Humperdinck number one 'Release Me'?
15. Which was the biggest-selling album of 1978?
16. Which rock 'n' roller wrote the Status Quo hit 'Ice In The Sun'?

Answers to page 580

FOLK 3: **1.** Jake Thackray **2.** Janis Ian **3.** The Kingston Trio **4.** The Fureys **5.** 'Blowing In The Wind' **6.** Fiddler's Dram ('Day Trip To Bangor (Didn't We Have A Lovely Time)') **7.** 'All Around My Hat' **8.** Iain Matthews **9.** Tony Hancock **10.** Scotland **11.** Mick Groves (father of David Groves) **12.** Fivepenny Piece **13.** The Dubliners **14.** Australian **15.** Incredible String Band **16.** The New Christy Minstrels

Albums 6

Answers on page 581

Which artists released the following albums?

1. 'Slayed?' (1973)
2. 'Spirits Having Flown' (1979)
3. 'Love Hurts' (1991)
4. 'East Side Story' (1981)
5. 'Graceland' (1987)
6. 'No Secrets' (1973)
7. 'Flowers In The Dirt' (1989)
8. 'Equally Cursed And Blessed' (1999)
9. 'The Long Run' (1979)
10. 'Manifesto' (1979)
11. 'Don't Shoot Me I'm Only The Piano Player' (1973)
12. 'True Blue' (1986)
13. 'After The Goldrush' (1970)
14. 'Daydream' (1995)
15. 'On The Waters' (1970)
16. 'An Innocent Man' (1983)

Answers to page 581

BEACH BOYS 1: **1.** 'Surfin' USA' **2.** Glen Campbell **3.** The Regents **4.** 'Don't Worry Baby' **5.** Glen Campbell **6.** Bruce Johnston **7.** Dean Torrence of Jan and Dean **8.** 'Sloop John B' **9.** 'Winchester Cathedral' by The New Vaudeville Band **10.** Carl Wilson **11.** 1967 **12.** '20/20' **13.** 'Do It Again' **14.** Status Quo **15.** Cousin **16.** Brian Wilson

Transfer Trail 9

Answers on page 586

1. Which Spanish club did Dalian Atkinson join in August 1990?
2. From which Italian club did Middlesbrough sign Gianluca Festa?
3. Which Dutch international joined Rangers from PSV Eindhoven for £5 million in July 1998?
4. Which striker swapped Benfica for the Riverside Stadium in October 1998?
5. From which club did Spurs sign Cliff Jones in 1958?
6. Which Welsh international winger moved from Burnley to Derby for £310,000 in 1975?
7. With which club did Tommy Mooney make his League debut?
8. Which Brazilian forward joined Newcastle from Palmeiras in 1987?
9. Who joined Manchester United from Nottingham Forest for £1.5 million in June 1989?
10. From which Italian club did Chelsea sign Roberto Di Matteo?
11. Which Italian team did Brazilian star Zico join in July 1983?
12. Which winger switched from Millwall to Liverpool for £800,000 in 1991?
13. Who cost AC Milan £15.7 million in June 1999 when he moved from Dynamo Kiev?
14. From which German club did Leeds sign Tony Yeboah?
15. Which Czech bounced from Old Trafford to Benfica in 1997?
16. Who joined Derby County for £3 million from Crewe Alexandra in May 1999?

Answers to page 586

WEST HAM UNITED 1: **1.** Ronnie Boyce **2.** Geoff Hurst **3.** 1993 **4.** Blackpool **5.** Bobby Ferguson **6.** Trevor Morley **7.** Oldham Athletic **8.** Rio Ferdinand **9.** Graham Paddon **10.** Nottingham Forest **11.** Mervyn Day **12.** Eyal Berkovic **13.** 1981 **14.** Liverpool **15.** Lou Macari **16.** Ray Stewart

League Cup 3

Answers on page 587

1. Who did Tottenham beat in the semi-finals of the 1999 Worthington Cup?
2. Which First Division team reached the final in 2000?
3. To whom did they lose?
4. Which Italian player scored in the 1997 Coca-Cola Cup final?
5. Who scored Manchester City's winning goal against Newcastle in the 1976 League Cup final?
6. Which future England manager converted a penalty in the first leg of the 1965 final?
7. Who was Swindon Town's two-goal hero in the 1969 final?
8. Who scored Swindon's other goal in that final?
9. And who did Swindon defeat in the semi-final that year?
10. Which two London sides did Liverpool defeat on their way to the 1984 final?
11. Who did Liverpool meet in the 1984 final?
12. And whose goal won the trophy for Liverpool after a replay?
13. Which three League Cup winners of the 1980s were denied possible European debuts because of the ban on British clubs following the Heysel tragedy?
14. Who scored Arsenal's two goals in the 1987 final against Liverpool?
15. Who were runners-up in the 1990 competition – their first major final?
16. Who beat them 1–0?

Answers to page 587

FA CUP 8: **1.** Eric Cantona **2.** Brighton & Hove Albion **3.** Denis and Leslie Compton **4.** Cyrille Regis **5.** 1934 **6.** Manchester City **7.** Mickey Thomas **8.** Paul Hendrie **9.** Ben Roberts **10.** Alex Dawson **11.** Norman Whiteside **12.** 1902 **13.** Paul Rideout **14.** Leeds United **15.** Hartlepool United **16.** Wanderers (in 1871–2)

West Ham United 1

Answers on page 584

1. Who scored West Ham's last-minute winner in the 1964 FA Cup final?

2. And who had equalised for the Hammers a minute earlier?

3. When were West Ham last promoted back to the top division?

4. With which club did Trevor Sinclair make his League debut?

5. Which Scottish international goalkeeper joined West Ham from Kilmarnock for a record £65,000 in 1967?

6. Which former Manchester City player was West Ham's top scorer in 1993–4?

7. Which club pipped West Ham for the Second Division title in 1991?

8. Which central defender was once loaned out to Bournemouth before being sold to Leeds for £18 million in 2000–1?

9. Which midfielder moved from Norwich City to West Ham for £170,000 in December 1973?

10. Who beat West Ham 4–0 in the 1991 FA Cup semi-finals?

11. Who kept goal for West Ham in the 1975 FA Cup final?

12. Who did West Ham sell to Celtic for £5.5 million in July 1999?

13. In which year did West Ham last reach the Football League Cup final?

14. And who beat them after a replay?

15. Who managed West Ham from 1989 to 1990?

16. Which Hammers full-back won ten Scotland caps between 1981 and 1987?

Answers to page 584

TRANSFER TRAIL 9: **1.** Real Sociedad **2.** Inter Milan **3.** Arthur Numan **4.** Brian Deane **5.** Swansea **6.** Leighton James **7.** Scarborough **8.** Mirandinha **9.** Neil Webb **10.** Lazio **11.** Udinese **12.** Jimmy Carter **13.** Andrei Shevchenko **14.** Eintracht Frankfurt **15.** Karel Poborsky **16.** Seth Johnson

FA Cup 8

Answers on page 585

1. Who scored two penalties in the 1994 FA Cup final?
2. In 1983, which club lost the FA Cup final and were relegated to Division Two?
3. Which brothers played for Arsenal in the 1950 Cup final?
4. In 1987, who became the first player born in French Guyana to play in an FA Cup final?
5. In which year did Matt Busby earn a Cup winners' medal as a player?
6. And with which team?
7. Which Wrexham Cup hero of 1992 was nicknamed 'The Welsh Tenner' after being convicted for his part in a forged £10 note racket?
8. Who scored Halifax Town's winning goal against Manchester City in 1980?
9. Who was in goal for Middlesbrough in the 1997 FA Cup final?
10. Which member of Manchester United's 1958 Cup final side was just 18?
11. Whose goal for Manchester United in 1983 made him the youngest player ever to score in a Cup final?
12. When was the last time Lincoln City reached the final 16 of the FA Cup?
13. Who scored Everton's winner in the 1995 Cup final?
14. Who finished runners-up in both the Cup and the League in 1965?
15. Which Third Division (North) side were knocked out of the Cup by non-League opposition four times in five seasons between 1925–6 and 1929–30?
16. Which team lifted the FA Cup by winning only two matches?

Answers to page 585

LEAGUE CUP 3: **1.** Wimbledon **2.** Tranmere Rovers **3.** Leicester City **4.** Fabrizio Ravanelli **5.** Dennis Tueart **6.** Terry Venables **7.** Don Rogers **8.** Roger Smart **9.** Burnley **10.** Brentford and Fulham **11.** Everton **12.** Graeme Souness **13.** Norwich City, Oxford United and Luton Town **14.** Charlie Nicholas **15.** Oldham Athletic **16.** Nottingham Forest

Wales 2

Answers on page 590

1. Which team did Wales defeat in a play-off at the 1958 World Cup finals?
2. In 1998, which Wolves player became the youngest to be capped by Wales?
3. Against which country did he play?
4. And whose record did he break?
5. Which balding wing-half won the first of his 39 caps in 1962 while a player with Birmingham City?
6. How many goals did Trevor Ford score for Wales?
7. Which nation knocked Wales out of the 1976 European Championship at the quarter-final stage?
8. In which year did Wales play their first international?
9. Who beat them 4–0 that day?
10. Which city did Wales use as a home venue for the first time in 1896?
11. And who beat them 9–1 on that occasion?
12. Which Wrexham manager won the first of his 66 caps as a player in 1975?
13. Which nation did Wales hold to a goalless draw in Cardiff in a 1989 World Cup qualifier?
14. Which former European Championship winners did Wales defeat on home soil in a 1998 qualifier?
15. Who scored Wales's winner in that match?
16. When did Gary Sprake win his first cap?

Answers to page 590

BLACKBURN ROVERS 1: **1.** 1991 **2.** Leamington Road **3.** Graeme Le Saux **4.** Henning Berg **5.** 1960 **6.** Ronnie Clayton and Bryan Douglas **7.** Scunthorpe United **8.** 1992 **9.** Simon Garner **10.** Malvern **11.** Paul Warhurst **12.** Rochdale **13.** Newcastle United **14.** Ken Furphy **15.** Derek Fazackerley **16.** Kevin Gallacher and Ashley Ward

Football League 9

Answers on page 591

1. Which Third Division club sold Tommy Miller to Ipswich Town in July 2001?
2. Which manager regained Halifax's Football League status in 1998 and was sacked a year later?
3. Which Welsh team left the Football League in 1927?
4. Which club went unbeaten in Division One for 42 matches from November 1977?
5. Who brought the run to an end?
6. Which club won the Fourth Division title and scored a record 134 goals in their first season in the League?
7. In 1914, which English League club provided the opponents for the first-ever Brazilian national team?
8. Which club's most recent League title was the championship of Division Three in 1965–6?
9. Who won their first 11 Division One games in 1960–1?
10. Glenn Roeder became manager of which club in summer 2001?
11. Which League babies won the Third Division title in 1975–6?
12. In May 2001, who beat Barnet in a last-day decider to retain League status?
13. Who won the First Division title in 1912–13 despite taking just two points from their first seven matches?
14. Who was Stoke City's top scorer in 1999–2000 and 2000–1?
15. Which north-eastern club were no longer United from 1968 to 1977?
16. Who are nicknamed 'The Quakers'?

Answers to page 591

WHOSE HOME? 8: **1.** Dumbarton **2.** Ipswich Town **3.** Cowdenbeath **4.** Stenhousemuir **5.** Southend United **6.** Hamilton Academicals **7.** Swindon Town **8.** Raith Rovers **9.** West Bromwich Albion **10.** Albion Rovers **11.** Arsenal **12.** Wigan Athletic **13.** Kilmarnock **14.** Stoke City **15.** Middlesbrough **16.** Coventry City

Blackburn Rovers 1

Answers on page 588

1. In which year did Kenny Dalglish become Blackburn manager?
2. Where did Rovers play for nine years immediately before moving to Ewood Park?
3. Who did Blackburn sell to Chelsea for £5 million in August 1997?
4. And which Norwegian defender did they sell to Manchester United in the same month?
5. When did Blackburn last reach the FA Cup final?
6. Which two England internationals were part of Rovers' line-up that day?
7. From which club did Blackburn sign Mark Atkins?
8. When did Blackburn sign Alan Shearer?
9. Who scored 168 League goals for Rovers between 1978 and 1992?
10. Which public school inspired Blackburn's strip?
11. Who moved from Sheffield Wednesday to Blackburn for £2.7 million in 1993?
12. Who beat Rovers in the semi-finals of the 1961–2 Football League Cup?
13. From which club did Blackburn sign Glen Keeley?
14. Which former Watford boss managed Blackburn from 1971 to 1973?
15. Who made a club record 596 League appearances for Rovers between 1970 and 1986?
16. Which two players top scored with just five League goals in 1998–9?

Answers to page 588

WALES 2: **1.** Hungary **2.** Ryan Green **3.** Malta **4.** Ryan Giggs **5.** Terry Hennessey **6.** 23 **7.** Yugoslavia **8.** 1876 **9.** Scotland **10.** Cardiff **11.** England **12.** Brian Flynn **13.** West Germany **14.** Denmark **15.** Craig Bellamy **16.** 1964

Whose Home? 8

Answers on page 589

1. Which Scottish club used to play at Broadmeadow?
2. Which Premiership team once played at Broom Hill?
3. Colliers Den was once the home of which Scottish team?
4. Who used to play at The Tryst?
5. Who once played at the Kursaal Ground?
6. Which Scottish club were once based at Bent Farm?
7. Which English Second Division side used to play at The Croft?
8. Sands Brae is a former home ground of which Scottish club?
9. Which Midlands club used to have a home ground called Four Acres?
10. Which Scots played at Cowheath Park?
11. Which London Premiership club once played at the Invicta Ground?
12. Which Lancashire club played at Springfield Park until 1999?
13. Which Scottish club used to play at Holm Quarry?
14. Which Midlands club played at the Victoria Ground until 1997?
15. Ayresome Park was the previous home of which club?
16. Which Midlands team once had a home called Dowells Field?

Answers to page 589

FOOTBALL LEAGUE 9: **1.** Hartlepool United **2.** Kieran O'Regan **3.** Aberdare Athletic **4.** Nottingham Forest **5.** Liverpool **6.** Peterborough United **7.** Exeter City **8.** Hull City **9.** Tottenham Hotspur **10.** West Ham United **11.** Hereford United **12.** Torquay United **13.** Sunderland **14.** Peter Thorne **15.** Hartlepool United (they were just Hartlepool for those nine years) **16.** Darlington

Nicknames 4

Answers on page 594

1. Which player was known as 'The Lawman'?
2. Which Italian is 'The White Feather'?
3. Which England international was nicknamed 'Digger'?
4. Which 1960s star was called 'Budgie'?
5. Which goal-poacher was nicknamed 'Sniffer'?
6. Which German striker was known as 'Der Bomber'?
7. Who was 'Crazy Horse'?
8. Which Italian was nicknamed 'The Rumble of Thunder'?
9. Which Welsh international was known as 'The Gentle Giant'?
10. Which Brazilian was nicknamed 'Little Bird'?
11. Which predatory Scottish striker rejoiced in the nickname of 'The Shark'?
12. Which 1960s hard man was known as 'Chopper'?
13. Which German skipper was called 'Der Kaiser'?
14. Which former Spurs and Liverpool defender was nicknamed 'Razor'?
15. Which Scottish international of the 1950s and 1960s was known as 'The Little General'?
16. Which nickname has Paul Ince bestowed upon himself?

Answers to page 594

HEARTS 1: **1.** 1958 **2.** Powderhall **3.** Dave Mackay **4.** Kilmarnock **5.** Four **6.** 1960 **7.** John Robertson **8.** 13 **9.** Rangers **10.** Mike Galloway **11.** Craig Levein **12.** John Colquhoun **13.** Willie Bauld **14.** Motherwell **15.** Dunfermline Athletic **16.** Derek Ferguson

The World Game 10

Answers on page 595

1. For which country does Albert Ferrer play?

2. Which country does Ibrahim Bakayoko represent at international level?

3. Alain Giresse was replaced as coach with which French club in October 1998?

4. Jan Ceulemans won a record number of caps for which country?

5. Which Argentine club won the Copa Libertadores in four successive years between 1972 and 1975?

6. In 1990, Barcelona become the first club from which country to reach the final of the Copa Libertadores?

7. Which club won the Belgian League in 2000–1?

8. Which country's League produced suspicious scores of 134–1 and 88–0 on the final day of the 1978–9 season?

9. Three members of which national team defected to India in 1984?

10. Who became coach of Argentina in 1998?

11. Which Belgian team sacked coach Johan Boskamp in 1998?

12. Which national team were kicked out of England in 1990 after going on an illegal shopping spree at Heathrow Airport?

13. Who was the first Dutch player to be sent off in an international?

14. Which country appointed ex-Brazilian World Cup star Mario Perez as their national coach in 1998?

15. Which team from the United Arab Emirates took part in the 2000 World Club Championship?

16. In which city do Fluminense play?

Answers to page 595

MANAGERS 9: **1.** Alex McLeish **2.** 1963 **3.** Ian Greaves **4.** George Graham **5.** Jack Charlton **6.** Graham Rix **7.** Steaua Bucharest **8.** Bury **9.** Red Star Belgrade **10.** Cesare Maldini **11.** Willie and Alex **12.** Andy Kilner **13.** Bruce Rioch **14.** Arthur Cox **15.** Crewe Alexandra **16.** Graeme Souness

Hearts 1

Answers on page 592

1. When did Hearts first play in Europe?
2. On which ground did Hearts play from 1878 to 1881?
3. Which player did Hearts sell to Tottenham for £30,000 in 1959?
4. Who defeated Hearts 2–0 on the final day of the 1964–5 season to snatch the Scottish League title from the Edinburgh club by a superior goal average of 0.042?
5. How many times have Hearts been crowned Scottish League champions?
6. When did they last win the title?
7. Who scored 214 goals for Hearts between 1983 and 1998?
8. By how many points did Hearts win the League title in 1958?
9. Who finished runners-up that year?
10. Who moved from Hearts to Celtic for £550,000 in June 1989?
11. Which Hearts man was named Scotland Young Player of the Year in both 1985 and 1986?
12. Which Hearts winger moved south to Millwall for £440,000 in 1991?
13. Who scored a hat-trick for Hearts in the 1954–5 Scottish League Cup final?
14. Who did they beat?
15. Who defeated Hearts 3–1 in the 1968 Scottish FA Cup final?
16. Who joined Hearts from Rangers for £750,000 in 1990?

Answers to page 592

NICKNAMES 4: **1.** Denis Law **2.** Fabrizio Ravanelli **3.** John Barnes **4.** Johnny Byrne **5.** Allan Clarke **6.** Gerd Müller **7.** Emlyn Hughes **8.** Luigi Riva **9.** John Charles **10.** Garrincha **11.** Joe Jordan **12.** Ron Harris **13.** Franz Beckenbauer **14.** Neil Ruddock **15.** Bobby Collins **16.** 'The Guv'nor'

Managers 9

Answers on page 593

1. Who was manager of Hibernian at the start of 2001–2?
2. In which year did Helmut Schoen become coach of West Germany?
3. Who was manager of Huddersfield Town from 1968 to 1974?
4. Who got his managerial break at Millwall from 1982 to 1986?
5. Which Middlesbrough boss was named Manager of the Year in 1974?
6. Who succeeded Steve Claridge as manager of Portsmouth in 2001?
7. Emeric Ienei guided which team to European Cup glory in 1986?
8. Sam Ellis, Mike Walsh and Stan Ternent all managed which Lancashire club?
9. Milorad Kosanovic quit as coach with which Yugoslav team in 1998 following a UEFA Cup defeat to Lyon?
10. Which Italian national coach played in AC Milan's 1963 European Cup winning team?
11. Which two Millers sandwiched Roy Aitken as manager of Aberdeen?
12. Who was named manager of Stockport County in July 1999?
13. Which noted disciplinarian had his managerial baptism with Torquay United from 1982 to 1984?
14. Who managed Derby County from 1984 to 1993 before resigning through ill health?
15. Ernie Tagg was manager of which English League club from 1964 to 1971?
16. Which victorious manager caused a riot by placing the Galatasaray club flag in the centre circle following the 1996 Turkish Cup final?

Answers to page 593

THE WORLD GAME 10: **1.** Spain **2.** Ivory Coast **3.** Paris Saint-Germain **4.** Belgium **5.** Independiente **6.** Ecuador **7.** Anderlecht **8.** Yugoslavia **9.** Afghanistan **10.** Marcelo Bielsa **11.** Gent **12.** Albania **13.** Johan Cruyff **14.** El Salvador **15.** Al Nassr **16.** Rio de Janeiro

World Cup 6

Answers on page 598

1. Which African country's national coach was banned from football for life by the king after the team were eliminated from the 1998 World Cup qualifiers by Kenya?
2. Who topped the Republic of Ireland's qualifying group for the 1994 World Cup?
3. Who scored West Germany's goals when they went down 3–2 to Argentina in the 1986 final?
4. Which nation's 1930 World Cup team was selected by the king?
5. Who are the only World Cup winners not to defend their title?
6. Who were West Germany's first opponents in the 1966 World Cup?
7. And what was the score?
8. Who did the Germans beat 2–1 in the 1966 semi-finals?
9. Which is the only World Cup to have been won by a team from the Americas in Europe or vice versa?
10. How many host nations have won the World Cup?
11. Whose players prepared for a 1998 World Cup tie with a three-hour session of mourning in memory of a seventh-century saint?
12. What nationality was the coach of the 1998 Jamaican World Cup squad?
13. Who scored the first 'golden goal' at the 1998 finals?
14. Who was Argentina's triumphant captain at the 1986 World Cup?
15. How many times have Paraguay reached the World Cup finals?
16. Who was Italy's winning coach in the 1982 World Cup?

Answers to page 598

MANCHESTER CITY 1: **1.** Costa Rica **2.** David White, Paul Stewart and Tony Adcock **3.** Harry Dowd **4.** Bury **5.** 24 **6.** Nicky Summerbee **7.** Chelsea **8.** Bolton Wanderers **9.** Plymouth Argyle **10.** John Bond **11.** Denis Law **12.** Steve Daley **13.** Shaun Goater **14.** One **15.** Kevin Reeves **16.** Bermuda

Brazil 1

Answers on page 599

1. Which Brazilian star had to be stretchered to the dressing room after collapsing under the weight of fans following the 1970 World Cup triumph?
2. Who is the only player to have been a member of three World Cup winning sides?
3. Which Brazilian is the only player to score in every match in a World Cup final tournament?
4. Who did Brazil play in their first-ever World Cup match?
5. How many international goals did Pele score?
6. Which 17-year-old was the youngest player ever to earn a World Cup winners' medal?
7. Which Brazilian player was ordered by law in 1998 to remove an outsize caricature of coach Mario Zagallo from the toilet door of a bar he owned?
8. For which European team does Rivaldo play?
9. Which Brazilian ace was sold to Inter Milan for £18 million in 1997?
10. Who was Brazil's victorious captain at the 1994 World Cup?
11. With which German club was he a player at the time?
12. Which South American rivals did Brazil beat 4–1 at the 1998 World Cup?
13. Which Brazilian was known as 'the White Pele'?
14. In which year did Ronaldo win his first Brazil cap?
15. Which goalscoring landmark did Pele reach in November 1969?
16. For which French club did Jairzinho play in 1972?

Answers to page 599

TRANSFER TRAIL 10: **1.** Emmanuel Petit **2.** Nantes **3.** Barcelona **4.** Tony Cascarino **5.** Celtic **6.** Mark Draper **7.** Silvinho **8.** Peter Rodrigues **9.** Thomas Radzinski **10.** Sampdoria **11.** Bob Latchford **12.** Bordeaux **13.** Jamie Redknapp **14.** Portsmouth **15.** Romario **16.** Andy Townsend

Manchester City 1

Answers on page 596

1. For which country does City's Paulo Wanchope play international football?
2. Which three City players scored hat-tricks in the 10–1 win over Huddersfield in 1987?
3. Who kept goal for City in the 1969 FA Cup final?
4. From which club did City sign Colin Bell?
5. How many managerial changes have City made since the war?
6. Which son of a former player did City sign from Swindon for £1.5 million in 1994?
7. Behind whom were City Division Two runners-up in 1988–9?
8. Who did City beat in the 1904 FA Cup final?
9. From which club did City sign Tony Book?
10. Who succeeded Malcolm Allison as manager in 1980?
11. Which Scottish international moved from Huddersfield to Maine Road for £55,000 in 1960?
12. Whose transfer from Wolves to City for £1.4 million in September 1979 smashed the British record fee?
13. Who was City's top scorer in 1998–9?
14. How many League games did Nicky Weaver play for his previous club, Mansfield Town?
15. Which Norwich City striker cost City £1.25 million in March 1980?
16. On which island was Shaun Goater born?

Answers to page 596

WORLD CUP 6: **1.** Algeria **2.** Spain **3.** Kark Heinz Rummenigge and Rudi Völler **4.** Romania **5.** Uruguay (after winning in 1930 they refused to travel to Italy for the 1934 tournament) **6.** Switzerland **7.** West Germany 5 Switzerland 0 **8.** Soviet Union **9.** 1958 (when Brazil won in Sweden) **10.** Six **11.** Iran **12.** Brazilian **13.** Laurent Blanc **14.** Diego Maradona **15.** Five **16.** Enzo Bearzot

Transfer Trail 10

Answers on page 597

1. Which French World Cup winner moved from Barcelona to Chelsea in the summer of 2001?
2. From which French club did Rangers sign Mo Johnston?
3. Which Spanish club did Gary Lineker join in 1986?
4. Which Republic of Ireland international left Millwall for Aston Villa in March 1990?
5. From which club did Nottingham Forest sign Pierre Van Hooijdonk in 1997?
6. Which former Notts County midfielder moved from Leicester City to Aston Villa for £3.25 million in July 1995?
7. Who moved from Corinthians to Arsenal for £4 million in 1999?
8. Which Welsh international full-back joined Leicester from Cardiff for £40,000 in 1965?
9. Which Canadian international moved from Anderlecht to Everton for £4.5 million in July 2001?
10. From which other Italian club did Juventus sign Gianluca Vialli in June 1992?
11. Which Birmingham City striker cost Everton a British record fee of £350,000 in 1974?
12. Which French club did Clive Allen join in May 1988?
13. Who moved from Bournemouth to Liverpool for £350,000 in 1991?
14. With which club did Kevin Russell make his League debut?
15. Which Brazilian joined Valencia from Flamenco for £5 million in 1996?
16. Which international joined Chelsea from Norwich for £1.2 million in 1990?

Answers to page 597

BRAZIL 1: **1.** Roberto Rivelino **2.** Pele **3.** Jairzinho (1970) **4.** Yugoslavia **5.** 77 **6.** Pele (in 1958) **7.** Romario **8.** Barcelona **9.** Ronaldo **10.** Dunga **11.** VfB Stuttgart **12.** Chile **13.** Zico **14.** 1993 **15.** His 1,000th senior goal **16.** Marseille

Rangers 2

Answers on page 602

1. Which 6ft 4in Rangers goalkeeper was nicknamed 'The Girvan Lighthouse'?
2. Which Yugoslav team knocked Rangers out of the European Cup in 1990–1?
3. In which year did Brian Laudrup join Rangers?
4. Who knocked Rangers out of the Scottish FA Cup in 1994–5?
5. Which Rangers player scored in both legs of the European Cup victory over Leeds in 1992?
6. From which Italian club did Rangers sign Lorenzo Amoruso?
7. Who joined Rangers from Utrecht in June 1999 for £4 million?
8. Who scored Rangers' winner in the 1936 Scottish FA Cup final?
9. Which now defunct club did they beat?
10. Who managed Rangers from 1954 to 1967?
11. Which Scottish international defender joined Rangers from Tottenham in 1987?
12. Which Rangers star was suspended *sine die* in 1954 after being sent off five times?
13. Who was top scorer for Rangers in 1974–5?
14. In which year did Terry Butcher make his debut for Rangers?
15. From which Spanish club did Rangers sign Oleg Salenko?
16. Who did Rangers beat 4–1 in a replay to lift the Scottish FA Cup in 1981?

Answers to page 602

SHARPSHOOTERS 6: **1.** Neil Martin **2.** Jack Balmer **3.** Lee Hughes **4.** Dundee United **5.** Jimmy Hill **6.** Malaysia **7.** Turkey **8.** Australian **9.** Ted Drake **10.** Darlington **11.** Alan Shearer **12.** Belgium **13.** Boavista **14.** Louis Saha **15.** Peter McParland **16.** Gerd Müller

Which Year in Football? 7

Answers on page 603

1. When were Swindon Town demoted a division after being found guilty of making irregular payments to players?
2. When did Paul Ince make his England debut?
3. In which year was a full Football League programme of matches last staged on Christmas Day?
4. In which year did the first floodlit FA Cup match take place?
5. In which year did Kettering Town become the first English club to carry shirt sponsorship?
6. In which year were ten players jailed (and banned for life by the FA) for match-fixing?
7. In which year was the Burnden Park tragedy when 33 people lost their lives?
8. When did Bob Paisley retire?
9. In which year did Nottingham Forest win the last Littlewoods Cup final?
10. In which year did a foreign manager win the Premiership for the first time?
11. In which year was Terry Venables appointed England coach?
12. In which year did Arsenal become the first London club to win the League Championship?
13. In which year were English clubs first allowed to use three substitutes per match?
14. In which year did George Graham win a League Championship medal as a player?
15. In which year did Aston Villa do the League and Cup double?
16. In which year did Manchester United move to Old Trafford?

Answers to page 603

ENGLAND 5: **1.** 1996 **2.** Nine **3.** United States **4.** 1963 **5.** Graham Taylor **6.** Bulgaria **7.** 1999 **8.** Portugal **9.** 61 **10.** Nobby Stiles (28) **11.** 15 **12.** Denmark **13.** Jimmy Greaves **14.** Graham Shaw **15.** Hungary **16.** Republic of Ireland

Sharpshooters 6

Answers on page 600

1. Who was the first player to score 100 goals in both the Scottish and English Leagues?
2. Which Liverpool player scored hat-tricks in three successive First Division matches in November 1946?
3. Who was West Bromwich Albion's leading marksman for 1998–9?
4. For which Scottish club did Danish striker Finn Dossing score in 15 consecutive matches in 1964–5?
5. Which TV pundit once scored all five goals for Fulham in a 5–1 win at Doncaster?
6. In which country was Tony Cottee playing before he returned to England with Leicester City?
7. For which country does Hakan Sukur play?
8. What nationality is John Aloisi?
9. Who scored all seven of Arsenal's goals when the Gunners won at Aston Villa in 1935?
10. From which Third Division club did Bradford City sign Robbie Blake?
11. Which Blackburn Rovers player was Footballer of the Year in 1994?
12. For which country did Luc Nilis play?
13. From which Portuguese club did Leeds sign Jimmy Floyd Hasselbaink?
14. Who was Fulham's leading scorer in 2000–1?
15. Who scored twice for Aston Villa in the 1957 FA Cup final?
16. Which German ace made his international debut against Turkey in 1966?

Answers to page 600

RANGERS 2: **1.** Peter McCloy **2.** Red Star Belgrade **3.** 1994 **4.** Hearts **5.** Ally McCoist **6.** Fiorentina **7.** Michael Mols **8.** Bob McPhail **9.** Third Lanark **10.** Scot Symon **11.** Richard Gough **12.** Willie Woodburn **13.** Derek Parlane **14.** 1986 **15.** Valencia **16.** Dundee United

England 5

Answers on page 601

1. When did Peter Beardsley win the last of his 59 England caps?
2. How many goals did he score for his country?
3. With echoes of 1950, by which team were England humiliated 2–0 in 1993?
4. In which year did Alf Ramsey become England manager?
5. Which England manager awarded Carlton Palmer his first international cap?
6. Against which country did Glenn Hoddle make his international debut?
7. When did Glenn Hoddle step down as England boss?
8. Against which country – semi-finalists in Euro 2000 – did England win 10–0 away from home in 1947?
9. How many England caps did Ray Clemence win?
10. Which of the 1966 World Cup winning team went on to win the fewest number of international caps?
11. England's Euro 2000 victory was their first over Germany for how many years?
12. Against which country did Des Walker make his England debut in 1989?
13. Who scored 44 goals in 57 appearances for England?
14. Which Sheffield United full-back won the first of his five England caps in 1959?
15. To whom did England lose 7–1 in 1954?
16. Who were England's first opponents at the 1990 World Cup finals?

Answers to page 601

WHICH YEAR IN FOOTBALL? 7: **1.** 1990 **2.** 1993 **3.** 1957 **4.** 1955 **5.** 1976 **6.** 1965 **7.** 1946 **8.** 1983 **9.** 1990 **10.** 1998 (Arsène Wenger) **11.** 1994 **12.** 1931 **13.** 1995 **14.** 1971 **15.** 1897 **16.** 1910

General Knowledge 141

Answers on page 606

1. Which fake was 'discovered' by Charles Dawson in East Sussex in 1913?
2. Which horror movie actor's real name was William Pratt?
3. The tiny rock hyrax – a rat-like creature from central Africa – is the closest living relative of which mammal?
4. Which nation's people eat more bread per person than anyone else in the world?
5. Which series was the successor to *That Was The Week That Was*?
6. Which New Zealand-born scientist was awarded the Nobel Prize for chemistry in 1908?
7. About which cathedral did The New Vaudeville Band sing in 1966?
8. What was the name of the woodpecker in *Bagpuss*?
9. Which capital city means 'elephant's trunk'?
10. The Rye House Plot was a conspiracy against which English monarch?
11. Who led the Sioux onslaught against General Custer at the Battle of Little Big Horn?
12. What was U2's first UK number one single?
13. Which flowers have varieties called hybrid teas and floribundas?
14. What is the connection between dynamite and the Nobel Peace Prize?
15. What is the spiny anteater otherwise known as?
16. Which country owns Easter Island?

Answers to page 606

GENERAL KNOWLEDGE 143: **1.** Vulture **2.** Timothy McVeigh **3.** Dover **4.** Melanie Chisholm **5.** Alexander Dubcek **6.** Australia **7.** Medway **8.** They've all had hip replacements **9.** Marlene Dietrich **10.** Belgium **11.** Four **12.** Mrs Strickland **13.** Canadian **14.** Pacific **15.** Pandora **16.** An antelope-like mammal of the USA

General Knowledge 142

Answers on page 607

1. What was the name of Jed Clampett's daughter in *The Beverly Hillbillies*?
2. What wrecked the opening night of BBC2 in 1964?
3. In which year did Muhammad Ali first become World Heavyweight Boxing Champion?
4. Which novelist created detective Albert Campion?
5. The name of which Sixties pop group means 'far from these things'?
6. What does the computer programme language BASIC stand for?
7. Of which family of freshwater fish is the chub a member?
8. In soccer, which country staged the 1982 World Cup finals?
9. Which famous playboy was seen as a pipe-smoking ancient Roman in Mel Brooks' *History of the World – Part 1*?
10. Who invented the electric light bulb?
11. Who scored against his namesake in the 2001–2 Merseyside derby at Goodison Park?
12. Which American politician has a wife called Tipper?
13. Which spirit is the basic ingredient in the liqueur benedictine?
14. Which former TV weathergirl presented the game show *Dog Eat Dog* in 2001?
15. Which London building housed the Great Exhibition of 1851?
16. In which century did Cyrano de Bergerac live?

Answers to page 607

GENERAL KNOWLEDGE 144: **1.** Ewan McGregor **2.** Michael Owen **3.** Madonna **4.** A fear of chins **5.** France **6.** Quintin Hogg **7.** Crow **8.** Tobey Maguire **9.** Ferdinand Magellan **10.** Danish **11.** 9,000 **12.** Blue, black and white **13.** Table tennis **14.** A bat **15.** Jennifer Aniston **16.** Paul Gauguin

General Knowledge 143

Answers on page 604

1. What breed of bird led zoo keepers a merry dance in Norfolk in 2001?
2. Who was executed for the Oklahoma City bombing?
3. Which state capital of Delaware shares its name with a Kentish port?
4. Which Spice Girl recorded 'When You're Gone' with Bryan Adams?
5. Which liberalising Czechoslovak leader was arrested by Soviet troops during the 1968 invasion and subsequently expelled from the Communist Party?
6. Adam Gilchrist is a Test cricketer for which country?
7. Which river flows through the towns of Chatham, Gillingham and Rochester?
8. What do Murray Walker, Elizabeth Taylor and Jimmy Young have in common?
9. Which Hollywood legend once said: 'I acted vulgar, Madonna IS vulgar'?
10. In which country is the town of Oudenaarde?
11. How many gold medals did Jesse Owens win at the 1936 Berlin Olympics?
12. Which *Emmerdale* headmistress was killed by a car in September 2001?
13. What nationality is the singer Joni Mitchell?
14. In which ocean is the island of Nauru?
15. According to Greek mythology, who opened her box of evils?
16. What is a pronghorn?

Answers to page 604

GENERAL KNOWLEDGE 141: **1.** Piltdown man **2.** Boris Karloff **3.** Elephant **4.** Greece **5.** *Not So Much a Programme, More a Way of Life* **6.** Ernest Rutherford **7.** Winchester **8.** Professor Yaffle **9.** Khartoum **10.** Charles II **11.** Sitting Bull **12.** 'Desire' **13.** Roses **14.** Dynamite was first devised by Alfred Nobel **15.** Echidna **16.** Chile

General Knowledge 144

Answers on page 605

1. Who starred in *Trainspotting* and *A Life Less Ordinary*?
2. Which footballer scored a hat-trick for England against Germany in 2001?
3. Who presented the award at the 2001 Turner Prize ceremony?
4. What is geniophobia?
5. In which country is Strasbourg?
6. Which British politician became Lord Hailsham?
7. The jay is a member of which family of birds?
8. Which actor played Spiderman in the 2002 film?
9. Which Portuguese navigator discovered the Philippines in 1521, only to be killed by natives?
10. What nationality is Whigfield?
11. To the nearest 100 miles, how far is Perth, Australia, from London?
12. Which three colours feature on the national flag of Estonia?
13. At which sport was actor Paul Shane a junior champion?
14. What is a noctule?
15. Which Friend inspired a hair craze in 1994?
16. Who painted *Women of Tahiti*?

Answers to page 605

GENERAL KNOWLEDGE 142: **1.** Elly May **2.** A power cut **3.** 1964 **4.** Margery Allingham **5.** Procol Harum **6.** Beginner's All-purpose Symbolic Instruction Code **7.** Carp **8.** Spain **9.** Hugh Hefner **10.** Thomas Edison **11.** Steven Gerrard (against Paul Gerrard) **12.** Al Gore **13.** Brandy **14.** Ulrika Jonsson **15.** Crystal Palace **16.** 17th

General Knowledge 145

Answers on page 610

1. Who wrote the screenplay of *Four Weddings and a Funeral*?
2. Who was the only man who could ever reach Dusty Springfield?
3. Which Liverpool couple had sextuplets in 1983?
4. Which Beatle played a lavatory attendant in a sketch on *Not Only...But Also* With Peter Cook and Dudley Moore?
5. Which Football League club left the Manor Ground for good in 2001?
6. Jonathan and Jennifer were which Seventies crime-fighting husband-and-wife team?
7. On which of the Great Lakes is Chicago a port?
8. In Greek legend, which king was granted the gift of converting all he touched to gold?
9. Which planet is closest to the Sun?
10. Who went from drinking Gold Blend to starring in *Buffy the Vampire Slayer*?
11. Paul Jones was replaced by Mike D'Abo as singer with which Sixties band?
12. What is the capital of Saxony?
13. Which city used to be called Constantinople?
14. In 2001, which country won the Eurovision Song Contest for the first time?
15. Which James Bond used to work as a French polisher for a coffin-maker?
16. What were the names of aviation pioneers the Wright brothers?

Answers to page 610

GENERAL KNOWLEDGE 147: **1.** Arthur Daley **2.** Fulham **3.** Frederick Forsyth **4.** A small bird **5.** The inert gases **6.** Rita Hayworth **7.** *Bob the Builder* **8.** James I **9.** Dennis **10.** Algeria **11.** Slade **12.** Toaster **13.** New York **14.** Yellow **15.** Portuguese **16.** Violin

General Knowledge 146

Answers on page 611

1. Which US President was known as 'The Bull Moose'?
2. Which Miss Teenage Memphis 1966 went on to star in her own TV sitcom?
3. Which Hollywood heartthrob of the 1930s was listed on his birth certificate as a girl?
4. In which country is the Tysee waterfall?
5. Where will the 2004 Olympic Games be held?
6. Who wrote *Gulliver's Travels*?
7. Which US actor was born Bernard Schwarz?
8. What did Kim Cotton become in 1985?
9. Which band used to be called Seymour?
10. As whom is Edson Arantes do Nascimento better known?
11. Who was known as the Iron Duke?
12. Who was the runner-up in *Celebrity Big Brother* in 2001?
13. What is the currency of Thailand?
14. What is Margaret Thatcher's middle name?
15. Who became US President following the assassination of Kennedy?
16. In which car did Damon Hill win the Formula One World Drivers' Championship?

Answers to page 611

GENERAL KNOWLEDGE 148: **1.** 1839 **2.** Hertfordshire **3.** Identikits **4.** Tara King **5.** Bette Davis **6.** A poisonous plant **7.** Edward II **8.** The Kilshaws **9.** Ethiopia **10.** Travis **11.** Suva **12.** Henry Fielding **13.** Red **14.** Sloths **15.** Lily **16.** Ontario

General Knowledge 147

Answers on page 608

1. Who promised: 'The world is your lobster'?
2. The owner of Harrods is also the chairman of which Premiership football club?
3. Who wrote *The Day of the Jackal*?
4. What is a dunnock?
5. Helium, neon, argon, krypton, xenon and radon are collectively known as what?
6. Which Hollywood star of the 1940s was born Margarita Carmen Cansino?
7. Wendy, Scoop, Muck and Dizzy are friends of whom?
8. Who was the first Stuart King of England?
9. Which boy's name is derived from Dionysus, the Greek god of wine?
10. DZ is the international vehicle index mark for which country?
11. Don Powell was the drummer with which Seventies band?
12. Which kitchen appliance was invented by the American Charles Strite in 1927?
13. In which city would you cross the Verrazano Narrows Suspension Bridge?
14. What colour are the flowers of a forsythia?
15. What nationality was the footballer Eusebio?
16. With what musical instrument is Stephane Grappelli primarily associated?

Answers to page 608

GENERAL KNOWLEDGE 145: **1.** Richard Curtis **2.** 'Son Of A Preacher Man' **3.** The Waltons **4.** John Lennon **5.** Oxford United **6.** *Hart to Hart* **7.** Michigan **8.** Midas **9.** Mercury **10.** Anthony Head **11.** Manfred Mann **12.** Dresden **13.** Istanbul **14.** Estonia **15.** Sean Connery **16.** Orville and Wilbur

General Knowledge 148

Answers on page 609

1. In which year was the Grand National first run?
2. In which county is Hemel Hempstead?
3. What were introduced for the first time by Scotland Yard in 1961?
4. Which of Steed's sidekicks in *The Avengers* was played by Linda Thorson?
5. Who said: 'The best time I ever had with Joan Crawford was when I pushed her down the stairs in *Whatever Happened to Baby Jane*'?
6. What is henbane?
7. Which English king was murdered in Berkeley Castle?
8. Which British couple were at the centre of a storm in 2000 over their attempts to procure a baby over the Internet?
9. Of which country did Haile Selassie become emperor in 1930?
10. Which band released the album 'The Man Who'?
11. What is the capital of the Republic of Fiji?
12. Which English novelist's best-known work was *Tom Jones*?
13. According to Dutch superstition, people with what colour hair bring bad luck?
14. Which animals move so slowly that algae grow in their hair?
15. The onion is a member of which family?
16. The Niagara Falls are located in which Canadian province?

Answers to page 609

GENERAL KNOWLEDGE 146: **1.** Theodore Roosevelt **2.** Cybill Shepherd **3.** Clark Gable **4.** Norway **5.** Athens **6.** Jonathan Swift **7.** Tony Curtis **8.** Britain's first commercial surrogate mother **9.** Blur **10.** Pele **11.** The Duke of Wellington **12.** Claire Sweeney **13.** Baht **14.** Hilda **15.** Lyndon B. Johnson **16.** Williams

General Knowledge 149

Answers on page 614

1. What is an oryx?
2. Which composition by Ravel was performed on ice by Torvill and Dean?
3. As whom was Grigory Efimovich better known in early 20th-century Russia?
4. Which TV soap is set in Charnham?
5. Which band released the Seventies albums 'A Question Of Balance', 'Every Good Boy Deserves Favour' and 'Seventh Sojourn'?
6. Which film studios in West London were renowned for their post-war comedies, often starring Alec Guinness?
7. On which racecourse is the St Leger run?
8. What unit is used to measure the fineness of yarns, as in nylon stockings?
9. Which English king was known as 'the Unready'?
10. Which star of *Red River* and *From Here to Eternity* was disfigured in a car crash in 1957?
11. Which 14-year-old Romanian gymnast won three gold medals at the 1976 Montreal Olympics?
12. Which former British Prime Minister died on 29 December 1986?
13. The theme from which TV series gave Nick Berry a number two hit in 1992?
14. Which actress won the Miss Italy title in 1946?
15. Which brothers played for Australia's victorious cricketers against England in the summer of 2001?
16. Which American state is nicknamed 'the Sooner State'?

Answers to page 614

GENERAL KNOWLEDGE 151: **1.** Neil Morrissey (the voice of Bob the Builder played Texas Ranger Rocky in the TV series *Boon*) **2.** Eddie Kelly (for Arsenal in 1971) **3.** Six – Belgium, Luxembourg, Germany, Switzerland, Italy and Spain **4.** *Home and Away* **5.** Wye **6.** Norgay **7.** Jeff Goldblum **8.** Patricia Highsmith **9.** *About a Boy* **10.** Dolls **11.** Lyndon B. Johnson **12.** Gary Player **13.** California **14.** Dire Straits **15.** Mama Cass Elliot and Keith Moon **16.** Vincent Price

General Knowledge 150

Answers on page 615

1. What word featured in both of Art Garfunkel's solo number ones?
2. Which continent does the fierce snake come from?
3. Which actor, born Michael Dumble-Smith, took his stage name from a passing biscuit lorry?
4. Which antiseptic takes its name from trichlorophenol?
5. Which board game was invented by solicitor's clerk Anthony E. Pratt?
6. Which artist appeared in a crowd scene in Jean Cocteau's 1962 film *The Testament of Orpheus*?
7. Which was the 50th state to join the United States?
8. What was the name of the cow in *The Woodentops*?
9. Brian Horton managed which Football League club at the start of season 2001–2?
10. What is another name for the clavicle?
11. The gharial is a species of which reptile?
12. In which country is Krakow?
13. What is the largest island in the Caribbean?
14. What is the second book in the Old Testament?
15. What is the name for a plant which completes its life cycle in two years?
16. What was first erected in 1961?

Answers to page 615

GENERAL KNOWLEDGE 152: **1.** The Outlaws **2.** Belgium **3.** 17 March **4.** Trafalgar **5.** Gardener/botanist **6.** Bruce Willis **7.** Captain and Tennille **8.** Suffragette Emily Davison died after throwing herself in front of the king's horse **9.** Maureen Connolly **10.** Lynmouth **11.** Bakelite **12.** Louis Blériot **13.** Dorset **14.** A bird **15.** Sir Galahad **16.** Four

General Knowledge 151

Answers on page 612

1. Who links Bob the Builder with The Texas Rangers?
2. Who was the first substitute to score in an FA Cup Final?
3. How many countries border France?
4. Which Australian soap returned to Britain on Channel 5 in 2001?
5. On which river does High Wycombe stand?
6. What was Sherpa Tenzing's surname?
7. Who starred in *The Tall Guy* and *Jurassic Park*?
8. Which Patricia wrote *The Talented Mr Ripley*?
9. Hugh Grant starred in a film adaptation of which Nick Hornby book in 2002?
10. Pediophobia is a fear of what?
11. Which American President had a wife named Ladybird?
12. Which veteran golfer is known as 'the man in black'?
13. Pasadena is a city in which American state?
14. Which band's best-selling album of the 1980s was titled 'Brothers In Arms'?
15. Which two rock stars died separately in the same London apartment owned by Harry Nilsson?
16. Which horror movie actor co-starred with Elvis Presley in *The Trouble With Girls*?

Answers to page 612

GENERAL KNOWLEDGE 149: **1.** A large antelope **2.** *Boléro* **3.** Rasputin **4.** *Family Affairs* **5.** The Moody Blues **6.** Ealing **7.** Doncaster **8.** Denier **9.** Ethelred **10.** Montgomery Clift **11.** Nadia Comaneci **12.** Harold Macmillan **13.** *Heartbeat* **14.** Gina Lollobrigida **15.** Steve and Mark Waugh **16.** Oklahoma

General Knowledge 152

Answers on page 613

1. What is the nickname of Nottinghamshire's Norwich Union League cricket team?
2. In which country is Passchendaele?
3. What date is St Patrick's Day?
4. At which battle was Admiral Nelson mortally wounded?
5. In which field did John Tradescant make his name?
6. Who shaved his head for the film *Twelve Monkeys*?
7. Which married couple had a hit with 'Do That To Me One More Time'?
8. What incident marred the 1913 Epsom Derby?
9. Which tennis player was known as 'Little Mo'?
10. Which North Devon town was devastated by a freak flood in August 1952?
11. Which commercial plastic was invented by Leo Baekeland?
12. Who made the first flight across the English Channel?
13. In which county is Corfe Castle?
14. What is a chough?
15. In Arthurian legend, who was the son of Sir Lancelot?
16. How many stomachs does a cow have?

Answers to page 613

GENERAL KNOWLEDGE 150: **1.** 'Eyes' ('I Only Have Eyes For You' and 'Bright Eyes') **2.** Australia **3.** Michael Crawford **4.** TCP **5.** Cluedo **6.** Pablo Picasso **7.** Hawaii **8.** Buttercup **9.** Port Vale **10.** Collar bone **11.** Crocodile **12.** Poland **13.** Cuba **14.** Exodus **15.** Biennial **16.** The Berlin Wall

General Knowledge 153

Answers on page 618

1. Which English city had the Roman name 'Aquae Sulis'?
2. Which 11-year-old qualified for the National Chess Championships in 1977?
3. Which European country held its first democratic election for 41 years in June 1977?
4. What was the name of Regan and Carter's boss in *The Sweeney*?
5. Which US sitcom star provided the voice of Sideshow Bob on *The Simpsons*?
6. Who said: 'I think for the life span he's lasted, Chuck Berry's productivity has been nil, more or less'?
7. Who was the first British footballer to be paid £100 a week?
8. What is 15 squared?
9. Why were parts of Britain temporarily plunged into darkness on 11 August 1999?
10. Gomera and Hierro are part of which group of islands?
11. How many hours are New Zealand ahead of Britain?
12. What colour are the flowers of the dogwood?
13. What animal lives in a lodge?
14. Which mountain did Horace Saussure make the first ascent of in 1787?
15. William the Silent was the ruler of which country from 1572–84?
16. Who gave thanks for the Aintree Iron?

Answers to page 618

GENERAL KNOWLEDGE 155: **1.** Lincoln City **2.** Edwina Currie **3.** They were all once librarians **4.** The Prince Regent **5.** Contact lens **6.** Bob Carolgees **7.** David Gray **8.** Shipping areas **9.** Mark Knopfler (Dire Straits) **10.** *Shakespeare In Love* **11.** It was the first dog in space **12.** Algeria **13.** Mike Tyson **14.** Ian Smith **15.** Suffolk **16.** Argentine

General Knowledge 154

Answers on page 619

1. Who sang about 'Sunshine On A Rainy Day' in 1991?
2. Under which pseudonym did French architect Charles Edouard Jeanneret work?
3. In which city were the 1996 Olympics held?
4. Who discovered the mouth of the River Amazon in 1499?
5. Barbara Windsor succeeded Jo Warne in which role?
6. What is Bono's real name?
7. Which actor's contract with MGM in the 1920s forbade him from smiling on screen?
8. The Maledicta Society caters for people who like to do what?
9. Who directed *Gregory's Girl*?
10. In which year did Concorde make its first flight?
11. The Dalai Lama is the spiritual head of which country?
12. What is the nickname of Leicester's rugby team?
13. On which river does Derby stand?
14. Who wrote the spy thriller *The Ipcress File*?
15. Who was the first golfer to win two successive US Masters titles?
16. What was the Christian name of the English scientist Faraday?

Answers to page 619

GENERAL KNOWLEDGE 156: **1.** A tittle **2.** Ag **3.** Vladimir Putin **4.** 'The Ballad Of John And Yoko' **5.** Charles I **6.** Daisy **7.** Yellow **8.** Sunshine Desserts **9.** Chlorophyll **10.** Dodecanese **11.** Elizabeth I **12.** Baseball **13.** 17th **14.** *Twelfth Night* **15.** Thomas Hearns **16.** Grampians

General Knowledge 155

Answers on page 616

1. Which was the first Football League club to be relegated to the Conference?
2. Which junior health minister resigned in 1988 following a row about the presence of salmonella in eggs?
3. What did Mao Tse-Tung, Casanova and Anthea Turner have in common?
4. Who ordered the building of the Royal Pavilion in Brighton?
5. Which optical aid was invented by the German Adolph E. Fick in 1887?
6. Who has a dog named Spit?
7. Who released the album 'White Ladder'?
8. What are Dogger, Fastnet and German Bight?
9. Which leader of a popular Eighties band has the middle name Freuder?
10. Which Guy Madden movie won an Oscar for Best Film in 1998?
11. What was Laika's claim to fame in the story of space travel?
12. In which country was the writer Albert Camus born?
13. In 1986, which boxer became the youngest World Heavyweight Champion?
14. Which Rhodesian leader declared his country's unilateral independence from Britain in 1965?
15. In which county is Bury St Edmunds?
16. What nationality is tennis player Gabriela Sabatini?

Answers to page 616

GENERAL KNOWLEDGE 153: **1.** Bath **2.** Nigel Short **3.** Spain **4.** Frank Haskins **5.** Kelsey Grammer **6.** Sir Elton John **7.** Johnny Haynes **8.** 225 **9.** Total solar eclipse **10.** Canary Islands **11.** 12 **12.** White **13.** Beaver **14.** Mont Blanc **15.** The Netherlands **16.** Scaffold

General Knowledge 156

Answers on page 617

1. What is the name for the dot over the letter 'i'?
2. What is the chemical symbol for silver?
3. Who succeeded Boris Yeltsin as Russian President?
4. What was The Beatles' last UK number one single?
5. Which English king was beheaded in 1649?
6. *Bellis perennis* is more commonly known as which wild flower?
7. What colour jersey is worn by the leader in the Tour de France cycle race?
8. For which food manufacturing company did Reggie Perrin work?
9. What is the name of the green pigment that is present in most plants?
10. Rhodes and Kos are part of which group of islands?
11. To whom was the poem *The Faerie Queene* dedicated?
12. What sport do the Atlanta Braves play?
13. In which century did the dodo become extinct?
14. Sir Toby Belch and Sir Andrew Aguecheek are characters in which Shakespearean play?
15. In 1988 which American became the first boxer to win world titles at five different weight classes in five separate fights?
16. Which range of mountains separates the Highlands and Lowlands of Scotland?

Answers to page 617

GENERAL KNOWLEDGE 154: **1.** Zoe **2.** Le Corbusier **3.** Atlanta **4.** Amerigo Vespucci **5.** *EastEnders*' Peggy Mitchell **6.** Paul Hewson **7.** Buster Keaton **8.** Swear **9.** Bill Forsyth **10.** 1969 **11.** Tibet **12.** Tigers **13.** Derwent **14.** Len Deighton **15.** Jack Nicklaus **16.** Michael

General Knowledge 157

Answers on page 622

1. Which former England football manager was born on the same day as Yoko Ono – 18 February 1933?
2. Which American state is nicknamed the 'Wolverine State'?
3. Which French playwright died on stage while playing a hypochondriac in his own play *Le Malade Imaginaire*?
4. Which TV detective had the Christian name 'Endeavour'?
5. Who had a number one album in 2001 titled 'A Funk Odyssey'?
6. What was the first James Bond film?
7. What took place in Londonderry on 30 January 1972?
8. At the 1980 Olympics, who became the first Briton since Harold Abrahams to win the men's 100 metres?
9. Which acid is contained in vinegar?
10. Who was President of Ireland between 1959 and 1973?
11. Who was the Roman goddess of the Moon?
12. In which country is the Chihuahuan Desert?
13. Which planet is furthest from the Sun?
14. What is the golfing term for a score of three under par at a hole?
15. What was the name of the bridge in Buckinghamshire where the Great Train Robbery took place?
16. In which ship did the Pilgrim Fathers sail?

Answers to page 622

GENERAL KNOWLEDGE 159: **1.** David Livermore (Millwall) **2.** Boston **3.** Stringed **4.** The leaves **5.** Elbe **6.** Thanksgiving **7.** *Up for Grabs* **8.** Edward G. Robinson **9.** Anton Chekhov **10.** All are qualified pilots **11.** Fender Broadcaster **12.** Thomas **13.** Milan **14.** Harold Macmillan **15.** The Police **16.** The watt (James Watt)

General Knowledge 158

Answers on page 623

1. Which Spice Girl was once an extra in *Emmerdale*?
2. Who played Fred Flintstone in the movie version of *The Flintstones*?
3. Which swimmer was the first woman to win the BBC Sports Personality of the Year Award?
4. Who was found dead in her bed on 5 August 1962?
5. Why were Donald Duck comics once banned in Finland?
6. What nationality was the composer Grieg?
7. Warkworth Castle is situated in which English county?
8. Which member of Hear'Say left the band in 2002?
9. What was sent to attack England in 1588?
10. Who retained the Formula One World Drivers' Championship in 2001?
11. What is the name given to the side opposite the right angle of a triangle?
12. The Phantom Flan Flinger wreaked havoc on which Saturday morning TV show?
13. Who wrote *King Solomon's Mines*?
14. Which football team are nicknamed the Baggies?
15. Which BBC reporter ousted Neil Hamilton as MP for Tatton at the 1997 General Election?
16. Who stuck to his principles at the Diet of Worms?

Answers to page 623

GENERAL KNOWLEDGE 160: **1.** Pope John Paul II **2.** Australia **3.** St Anne's **4.** Gerry and The Pacemakers **5.** Twiggy **6.** Creighton-Ward **7.** Gary Cooper **8.** George III **9.** All were born on Christmas Day **10.** Vincent Van Gogh **11.** Freddie Starr **12.** Verdi **13.** Julius **14.** Annapolis **15.** Hungary **16.** Sodor

General Knowledge 159

Answers on page 620

1. Which player scored the last Football League goal of the 20th century?
2. In which American city was *Cheers* set?
3. What kind of musical instrument is a lute?
4. What parts of the rhubarb plant are poisonous?
5. On which river is the city of Hamburg?
6. What national holiday do Americans celebrate on the fourth Thursday in November?
7. What was the name of the play in which Madonna made her West End debut in 2002?
8. Which Hollywood tough guy of the 1930s was born Emanuel Goldenberg?
9. Who wrote *Uncle Vanya* and *The Three Sisters*?
10. What do John Travolta, Gary Numan and Nicholas Lyndhurst have in common?
11. What was the first solid-body electric guitar?
12. What was the Christian name of the English landscape painter Gainsborough?
13. Which horse – bearing the name of an Italian city – won the 2001 St Leger?
14. Which former British Prime Minister became the first Earl of Stockton?
15. Which band released the album 'Reggatta de Blanc'?
16. Which unit of power is named after the Scottish engineer who developed early models of the steam engine?

Answers to page 620

GENERAL KNOWLEDGE 157: **1.** Bobby Robson **2.** Michigan **3.** Molière **4.** *Inspector Morse* **5.** Jamiroquai **6.** *Dr No* **7.** Bloody Sunday **8.** Allan Wells **9.** Acetic acid **10.** Eamon de Valera **11.** Luna **12.** Mexico **13.** Pluto **14.** Albatross **15.** Bridego Bridge **16.** *Mayflower*

General Knowledge 160

Answers on page 621

1. Who was the most famous goalkeeper in the history of Polish amateur club Wotsyla?
2. The Gulf of Carpentaria lies off the coast of which country?
3. What is the capital of the Channel Island of Alderney?
4. Who were the first Merseybeat group to have a UK number one single?
5. Which model was named Woman of the Year for 1966?
6. What was Lady Penelope's surname in *Thunderbirds*?
7. Who turned down the role of Rhett Butler in *Gone With The Wind* because he was convinced it would be a flop?
8. Who was the longest reigning King of England?
9. What do Sir Isaac Newton, Kenny Everett and Annie Lennox have in common?
10. Who was sacked from his job as assistant to a Paris art dealer for sneaking off to Holland at Christmas and for being rude to customers?
11. Which comedian owned the 1994 Grand National winner, Minnehoma?
12. Who composed the operas *Rigoletto* and *La Traviata*?
13. What was Groucho Marx's real name?
14. What is the state capital of Maryland?
15. The forint is the standard currency of which country?
16. On which fictitious island does *Thomas the Tank Engine* operate?

Answers to page 621

GENERAL KNOWLEDGE 158: **1.** Melanie Brown **2.** John Goodman **3.** Anita Lonsborough **4.** Marilyn Monroe **5.** Because he doesn't wear pants **6.** Norwegian **7.** Northumberland **8.** Kym Marsh **9.** Spanish Armada **10.** Michael Schumacher **11.** Hypotenuse **12.** *Tiswas* **13.** Rider Haggard **14.** West Bromwich Albion **15.** Martin Bell **16.** Martin Luther

Comedy 18

Answers on page 626

1. Which impressionist's athlete father represented Britain at the 1948 and 1952 Olympics?

2. What is Caroline's surname in *Caroline in the City*?

3. Which resident of 52 Acacia Avenue used to ramble on about Aunty and Tiddles?

4. Which real-life problem-page writer co-devised *Agony*?

5. Who created the celebrated actor Sir Norbert Smith?

6. In *The Brittas Empire*, who kept her baby in a drawer?

7. At which pub did Sid Abbott vent his frustrations in *Bless This House*?

8. Which comic cops were played by Stephen Frost and Mark Arden?

9. Who was the youngest of *My Three Sons*?

10. What is Nana's name in *The Royle Family*?

11. Which Seventies sitcom featured a relationship between a white man and a black woman?

12. Who was the child-hating Punch and Judy man in *Hi-De-Hi!*?

13. What is Miss Titley's Christian name in *The Grimleys*?

14. Which of *The Golden Girls* hailed from St Olaf, Minnesota?

15. What is the theme song to *Absolutely Fabulous*?

16. Who plays Douglas in *Kiss Me Kate*?

Answers to page 626

EASTENDERS 4: **1.** Eddie Royle **2.** Harris **3.** Kenny **4.** June **5.** Dot Cotton **6.** At a children's nursery **7.** Grant Mitchell **8.** Geoff Barnes **9.** Diane Butcher **10.** The Dagmar **11.** Sanjay **12.** Saskia Duncan **13.** Annie **14.** Louise Raymond (Tiffany's mum) with Grant Mitchell **15.** The Jacksons **16.** Carol Jackson

Cop Shows 10

Answers on page 627

1. Which series was shown in the US under the title *My Partner the Ghost*?
2. Who had an informant by the name of Ozzie the Answer?
3. Which detective series featured a state-of-the-art computer known as Baby?
4. To which country did Don Beech flee in *The Bill*?
5. Joe Beck and George Parrish were dependable sergeants in which series?
6. What was Robert McCall better known as?
7. Which female cop had an autistic sister named Cheryl?
8. Inspector Jim Oulton features in which 2001 police series?
9. Which former *EastEnder* played PC Terry Sydenham in *City Central*?
10. Which unorthodox Mountie had a deaf wolf as a partner?
11. How did *Hamish Macbeth*'s TV John acquire his nickname?
12. In which Sixties series did Chief Inspector Rose first appear?
13. What was 'Sonny' Crockett's real name?
14. Who replaced Inspector Steve Keller on *The Streets of San Francisco*?
15. How much did Jim Rockford charge for a day's work?
16. What was the name of Broderick Crawford's character in *Highway Patrol*?

Answers to page 627

TV POT LUCK 16: **1.** Andrew Sachs **2.** Ardal O'Hanlon **3.** Chris Beardshaw **4.** *Watchdog* **5.** Majorca **6.** Channel 5 **7.** *Gardening Club* **8.** Alan Whicker **9.** Dennis Pennis **10.** *Sex and the City* **11.** Clive Dunn **12.** *Shillingbury Tales* **13.** David Hatcher and Helen Phelps **14.** Russ Conway **15.** *Children In Need* **16.** Gyles Brandreth

EastEnders 4

Answers on page 624

1. Who was stabbed to death in Albert Square in 1991?
2. What was Pat Evans' maiden name?
3. Which member of the Beale family emigrated to New Zealand?
4. What was the name of Frank Butcher's first wife?
5. Who won £10,000 at bingo in 1990?
6. Where did Ruth Fowler work?
7. Who vanished from Walford in October 1999?
8. Which university tutor enjoyed extra-curricular activities with Michelle Fowler?
9. Which character was played by Sophie Lawrence?
10. Where did James Wilmott-Brown rape Kathy Beale?
11. Who was Gita Kapoor's husband?
12. Who did Steve Owen kill with a blow from an ashtray?
13. What was the name of George Palmer's hard-nosed daughter?
14. Who had sex with her son-in-law after her daughter's birthday party?
15. Which family went into hiding after their youngest member witnessed a building society robbery?
16. Who had four children by four different fathers?

Answers to page 624

COMEDY 18: **1.** Bobby Davro **2.** Duffy **3.** Harry Worth **4.** Anna Raeburn **5.** Harry Enfield **6.** Carole **7.** The Hare and Hounds **8.** *Lazarus and Dingwall* **9.** 'Chip' **10.** Norma **11.** *Mixed Blessings* **12.** Mr Partridge **13.** Geraldine **14.** Rose Nylund **15.** 'This Wheel's On Fire' **16.** Chris Langham

TV Pot Luck 16

Answers on page 625

1. Which *Fawlty Towers* actor narrates *Children's Hospital*?
2. Who found that life outside Craggy Island was a *Big Bad World*?
3. Who was TV's *Flying Gardener* in 2001?
4. Alice Beer made her name on which consumer series?
5. Which island did Nadia Sawalha visit on her *Passport to the Sun*?
6. Which channel screened *Bedroom Confidential* in 2001?
7. Which BBC programme was interrupted in 1960 to announce the engagement of Princess Margaret?
8. Who obtained an interview with the notorious dictator of Haiti, Papa Doc Duvalier, in 1968?
9. Who is Paul Kaye's irreverent alter-ego?
10. Which US comedy series stars Sarah Jessica Parker?
11. Which actor famed for his ageing roles played Old Johnson in *Bootsie and Snudge*?
12. *Cuffy* was a spin-off from which series?
13. Who were the first two police officers to make regular appeals on *Crimewatch UK*?
14. Which pianist on *The Billy Cotton Band Show* was born Trevor Stanford?
15. Which major TV appeal was first held in 1980?
16. Which former Tory MP co-wrote *Dear Ladies* for Hinge and Bracket?

Answers to page 625

COP SHOWS 10: **1.** *Randall & Hopkirk (Deceased)* **2.** *Mike Hammer* **3.** *Matt Houston* **4.** Australia **5.** *Juliet Bravo* **6.** *The Equalizer* **7.** 'Pepper' Anderson (*Police Woman*) **8.** *Mersey Beat* **9.** Paul Nicholls **10.** Benton Fraser **11.** He had the first set in the village **12.** *The Odd Man* **13.** James **14.** Dan Robbins **15.** $200 plus expenses **16.** Dan Mathews

Quiz & Game Shows 8

Answers on page 630

1. Which quiz featured a 'Welsh special' in 2001?
2. Which newsreader was the first host of *The People Versus*?
3. What was the top prize on *Double Your Money*?
4. In which country did *The Golden Shot* originate?
5. Who hosted *Mother Knows Best*?
6. Who was the resident organist on *Double Your Money*?
7. What was the name of the big baby on *Shooting Stars*?
8. Who was the chairman on *That's Showbusiness*?
9. Which Irish presenter was one of the team captains on *That's Showbusiness*?
10. Which ex-*EastEnder* presents the ITV multiple choice quiz *It's Not the Answer*?
11. Which channel showed *Kryptogram*?
12. Who shouted 'Come on Down' on *The Price Is Right*?
13. To whom did *The Generation Game*'s Bruce Forysth address the question: 'What's on the board, Miss Ford?'
14. Who presented *Every Second Counts*?
15. The climax to which quiz is the 'Gold Run'?
16. Which long-running quiz incorporated a dummy keyboard?

Answers to page 630

SPORT 4: **1.** John Fashanu **2.** Terry Wogan **3.** Fred Dinenage **4.** Eddie Waring **5.** Frank Bough **6.** Clive Everton **7.** Henry Cooper **8.** *Sportsview* **9.** 1954 **10.** Horse racing **11.** Bob Wilson **12.** Darts **13.** David Coleman **14.** 50,000 **15.** A cat **16.** Bobby Moore

Dramas 14

Answers on page 631

1. Which series introduced a new task force in 2000, codenamed Indigo?
2. Who was president of Cicely Chamber of Commerce in *Northern Exposure*?
3. Who was plucked from reading the news with Scottish TV to star in *Dr Finlay's Casebook*?
4. What was *Dr Kildare*'s Christian name?
5. Which actor refused to carry a gun and bed beautiful women on *Danger Man*?
6. Peter Strauss and Nick Nolte played the Jordache brothers in which 1976 epic?
7. Which actor bared his bottom on *The Singing Detective*?
8. Which medical field was Dr Doug Ross's speciality in *ER*?
9. Which Yorkshire squire did Jennifer Caldwell marry?
10. What was Sylvia Sands' nickname in *The Hello Girls*?
11. Which US actor was voted Most Courteous Boy in Class upon graduating from high school in 1952?
12. In which Catherine Cookson story did Robson Green play Rory Connor?
13. What kind of firm did *The Brothers* run?
14. What was the name of Tom Howard's yacht in *Howard's Way*?
15. Which actress submitted the idea for *Nanny* under the pen-name of Jonathan Marr?
16. Who played the title role in *Lillie*?

Answers to page 631

CATCHPHRASES 4: **1.** *South Park* **2.** *Play Your Cards Right* **3.** Hylda Baker **4.** Pop Larkin (*The Darling Buds of May*) **5.** *The Prisoner* **6.** *Blue Peter* **7.** Louis Balfour **8.** Gladys Pugh (*Hi-De-Hi!*) **9.** Eric Morecambe **10.** *Star Trek* **11.** Arthur Askey **12.** *Monty Python's Flying Circus* **13.** Bruce Forsyth (*The Generation Game*) **14.** The Scousers **15.** *The Cisco Kid* **16.** Basil Brush

Sport 4

Answers on page 628

1. Which ex-footballer was the first male presenter of *Gladiators*?
2. Who presents *Auntie's Sporting Bloomers*?
3. Who occasionally stood in for Dickie Davies as front man on *World of Sport*?
4. Who was the BBC's colourful Rugby League commentator for many years?
5. Who took over as presenter of *Grandstand* in 1968?
6. Which Clive is a BBC snooker commentator?
7. Who was the first person to win the BBC Sports Personality of the Year twice?
8. Which was the first regular sports series on British television?
9. In which year did it start?
10. Brough Scott presents coverage of which sport on Channel 4?
11. Which goalkeeper-turned-TV presenter left the BBC for ITV in 1994?
12. On which sport does Sid Waddell commentate?
13. Who was chairman of *A Question of Sport* from 1979 to 1997?
14. Approximately how many viewers watched the very first edition of *Match of the Day*?
15. What ran on to the pitch during that opening game on *Match of the Day*?
16. Who was the first footballer to be voted BBC Sports Personality of the Year?

Answers to page 628

QUIZ AND GAME SHOWS 8: **1.** *The Weakest Link* **2.** Kirsty Young **3.** £1,000 **4.** Germany **5.** Ulrika Jonsson **6.** Robin Richmond **7.** George Dawes **8.** Mike Smith **9.** Gloria Hunniford **10.** Nadia Sawalha **11.** Channel 5 **12.** Leslie Crowther **13.** Rosemarie Ford **14.** Paul Daniels **15.** *Blockbusters* **16.** *Face the Music*

Catchphrases 4

Answers on page 629

1. Which show's catchphrase is 'Oh my God, they killed Kenny!'?

2. On which game show did Bruce Forsyth say: 'You get nothing for a pair – not in this game'?

3. Which comedienne used to say: 'She knows you know'?

4. Which character introduced 'Perfick' to the national vocabulary?

5. Who used to repeat: 'I am not a number'?

6. Which children's programme developed the phrase: 'Here's one I made earlier'?

7. Which *Fast Show* character thought all that jazz was 'nice'?

8. Who greeted holidaymakers with the call; 'Hello, campers'?

9. Who asked: 'What do you think of it so far? Rubbish!'?

10. 'Beam me up, Scotty' became a catchphrase for which sci fi series?

11. Which comedian had the catchphrase: 'Before your very eyes'?

12. 'And now for something completely different' was the introduction to which show?

13. Who used to say: 'Let's see the scores on the doors'?

14. Which Harry Enfield characters would urge: 'Calm down. Calm down'?

15. Whose parting words were always: 'Adios amigos'?

16. Which puppet's catchphrase was 'Boom! Boom!'?

Answers to page 629

DRAMAS 14: **1.** *The Knock* 2. Maurice Minnifield **3.** Bill Simpson **4.** James **5.** Patrick McGoohan **6.** *Rich Man, Poor Man* **7.** Patrick Malahide **8.** Paediatrics **9.** *Hadleigh* **10.** 'Fruity' **11.** Richard Chamberlain **12.** *The Gambling Man* **13.** Transport **14.** *The Flying Fish* **15.** Wendy Craig **16.** Francesca Annis

Comedy 19

Answers on page 634

In which series would you find the following characters?

1. Thelma Chambers
2. Blanche Devereaux
3. Joy Merryweather
4. Lukewarm
5. Mickey Pearce
6. Clive Gibbons
7. Woody Boyd
8. Rev. Timothy Farthing
9. Kate Starling
10. Louie De Palma
11. Sam Tyler
12. Charlie Burrows
13. Joey Tribbiani
14. Sharon Theodopolopoudos
15. PC Kevin Goody
16. Johnny Cyclops

Answers to page 634

LOCATIONS 7: **1.** Greenwich Village **2.** Billy Bunter **3.** Hinge and Bracket (*Dear Ladies*) **4.** *Petrocelli* **5.** Windy Miller (*Camberwick Green*) **6.** Truro **7.** Brooksmead **8.** KJCM, San Francisco **9.** Annie Oakley **10.** *Preston Front* **11.** Roy Rogers **12.** Crimpton-on-Sea **13.** *To the Manor Born* **14.** Australia **15.** Holland Park **16.** *Fury*

Soaps 14

Answers on page 635

1. Who was the sheriff in *Flamingo Road*?
2. In *Brookside*, who supplied Ron Dixon with the gun to shoot Clint Moffat?
3. Which Ramsay Street resident is head teacher at Erinsborough High?
4. Which *Coronation Street* wife won a second honeymoon in 1977?
5. Which two magistrates had an affair in *Brookside*?
6. Which Ewing left *Dallas* to star in *Knots Landing*?
7. Which *Home and Away* character shared the same name as a former Australian cricket captain?
8. Who was kidnapped by aliens in *The Colbys*?
9. Which grandson of Dot Cotton was killed in a motorbike crash?
10. In *Compact*, who pretended she was called Mary because she hated her own name?
11. Which sinister businessman led 'The Cartel' in *Falcon Crest*?
12. Who got married in the first episode of *Dallas*?
13. How many different actors have played Mike Baldwin's son Mark Redman in *Coronation Street*?
14. Who was *Eldorado*'s local handyman?
15. What was the name of Luke Warrington's troubled sister in *Family Affairs*?
16. Who were Brian Jarvis's parents in *Crossroads*?

Answers to page 635

CHILDREN'S TV 10: **1.** Bill Salmon **2.** Roger Whittaker **3.** Little Ron **4.** Murgatroyd **5.** Sylvester McCoy **6.** The Thompson Twins **7.** Ding-a-Ling **8.** Jack Wild **9.** Mr Onion **10.** 'Time for Tubby Bye-Bye' **11.** *Rag, Tag and Bobtail* **12.** Sir Topham Hatt **13.** *SM:TV Live* **14.** *The Flowerpot Men* **15.** Eric **16.** Mike Reid

Locations 7

Answers on page 632

1. In which district of New York is *Friends* set?
2. Which schoolboy attended Greyfriars?
3. Who lived in the village of Stackton Tressel?
4. Which Seventies lawyer operated out of San Remo?
5. Which children's TV character lived at Colley's Mill?
6. In which Florida town was *Flamingo Road*?
7. In which road did the Bryces live in *Ever Decreasing Circles*?
8. For which radio station did Jack Killian work in *Midnight Caller*?
9. Which Western heroine kept the peace in Diablo County, Arizona?
10. Which light drama was set in Roker Bridge, Lancashire?
11. Who lived in Mineral City?
12. At which fictional resort was *Hi-De-Hi!* set?
13. Which sitcom was set at Grantleigh?
14. Which country was the setting for *The Thorn Birds*?
15. In which district of London does Edina live in *Absolutely Fabulous*?
16. Which equine hero was based near Capitol City?

Answers to page 632

COMEDY 19: **1.** *Whatever Happened to the Likely Lads* **2.** *The Golden Girls* **3.** *Drop the Dead Donkey* **4.** *Porridge* **5.** *Only Fools and Horses* **6.** *My Good Woman* **7.** *Cheers* **8.** *Dad's Army* **9.** *The Marriage Lines* **10.** *Taxi* **11.** *Three Up, Two Down* **12.** *The Upper Hand* **13.** *Friends* **14.** *Birds of a Feather* **15.** *The Thin Blue Line* **16.** *Whoops Apocalypse*

Children's TV 10

Answers on page 633

1. Who was the Australian question master on *Transworld Top Team*?
2. Who presented the music show *Whistle Stop*?
3. Who was the midget in *Maid Marian and Her Merry Men*?
4. What was the name of *Magpie*'s large mascot?
5. Who was a *Tiswas* presenter before becoming *Doctor Who*?
6. Which Tintin characters gave their names to an Eighties band?
7. Who was Hokey Wolf's sidekick?
8. Who starred in *HR Pufnstuf*?
9. Who was the schoolteacher in *The Herbs*?
10. What is it at the end of each edition of *Teletubbies*?
11. Which programme made up the Thursday strand of *Watch With Mother*?
12. What is the real name of the Fat Controller in *Thomas the Tank Engine and Friends*?
13. 'Wonky Donkey' is a popular segment on which show?
14. Which *Watch With Mother* favourites made a comeback in 2001?
15. Who was the unseen studio crane operator on *Multi-Coloured Swap Shop*?
16. Which future *EastEnder* tried to keep order on *Runaround*?

Answers to page 633

SOAPS 14: **1.** Titus Semple **2.** Tim O'Leary **3.** Susan Kennedy **4.** Hilda Ogden **5.** Annabelle Collins and Brian Lawrence **6.** Gary **7.** Bobby Simpson **8.** Fallon **9.** Ashley **10.** Gussie Brown **11.** Gustav Riebmann **12.** Pam Barnes and Bobby Ewing **13.** Four **14.** Snowy White **15.** Sara **16.** Dick and Kitty

TV Pot Luck 17

Answers on page 638

1. Who presented the Channel 5 revival of *It's a Knockout*?
2. Which John Sullivan comedy/drama was set in a minicab firm?
3. Which travel series began in 1969?
4. Who presented *Find a Fortune*?
5. Who travelled around Britain in search of eccentrics for the 1969 series *One Pair of Eyes*?
6. Who lasted just one show as host of the Seventies science series *Don't Ask Me*?
7. Which designer hosts *House Invaders*?
8. Which actress conducts *Watercolour Challenge*?
9. Which sitcom stars Robert Lindsay and Zoë Wanamaker as Ben and Susan?
10. Who narrated *The Herbs*?
11. In which year did ITV begin?
12. Which Seventies detective series originated from a pilot show called *Smile Jenny, You're Dead*?
13. What was the name of Wilfred Pickles' wife?
14. On which satellite link-up programme did the Beatles perform 'All You Need Is Love'?
15. *Alas Smith and Jones* was a spin-off from which series?
16. Which Saturday evening show featured the Gotcha Oscars?

Answers to page 638

COP SHOWS 11: **1.** Frankie Wharton **2.** Robbie **3.** Sgt Joe Friday (*Dragnet*) **4.** Howard Rollins **5.** Jack Killian **6.** Johnny the Snitch **7.** *Perry Mason* **8.** William Edward **9.** Troy Kennedy Martin **10.** Johnny Briggs **11.** Judith **12.** Eddie Fitzgerald **13.** Diane Russell **14.** *T.J. Hooker* **15.** Jessica Fletcher **16.** *Miami Vice*

Docusoaps 2

Answers on page 639

1. *Motorway Life* followed events on which road?
2. Who narrated *Motorway Life*?
3. Which Channel 5 series chronicles the work of the Endell Veterinary Group in Salisbury?
4. Which 1983 docusoap focused on training for the parachute regiment?
5. Which force were featured in *Police*?
6. Which series about the PDSA in New Cross is ITV's answer to *Animal Hospital*?
7. Who narrates *Airport*?
8. Which Channel 5 fly-on-the-wall series follows a police helicopter patrol?
9. Chamonix mountain rescue team were the subject of which Channel 5 series?
10. Which country was the setting for Channel 5's *Vets Abroad*?
11. Which raunchy ITV series looks at the Jamaican adult resorts of Hedonism II and III?
12. Which docusoap featured British expats in Benidorm?
13. And who narrated it?
14. Which docusoap was set in a shopping mall?
15. Who filmed *The Family*?
16. Who was the manager of *Pleasure Beach*?

Answers to page 639

WHICH YEAR IN TV? 9: **1.** 1989 **2.** 1983 **3.** 1958 **4.** 1966 **5.** 1975 **6.** 1990 **7.** 1983 **8.** 1966 **9.** 1989 **10.** 1973 **11.** 1984 **12.** 1981 **13.** 1965 **14.** 1956 **15.** 1963 **16.** 1955

Cop Shows 11

Answers on page 636

1. What is the name of the pathologist in *Waking the Dead*?
2. What was Lewis's Christian name in *Inspector Morse*?
3. Whose first partner was Ben Romero?
4. Who played Virgil Tibbs in the TV version of *In the Heat of the Night*?
5. Who had a glamorous boss called Devon King?
6. Who was Frank Drebin's chief informant on *Police Squad*?
7. Whose chief adversary was Ham Burger?
8. What are 'Jack' Frost's real forenames?
9. Who created *Z Cars*?
10. Which *Coronation Street* regular had to wear lifts in his shoes to play DS Russell in *No Hiding Place*?
11. In *Cracker*, what was the name of Fitz's long-suffering wife?
12. And what was Fitz's full name?
13. Which detective was Bobby Simone's girlfriend in *NYPD Blue*?
14. On which William Shatner cop show did the Beach Boys make a guest appearance?
15. *The Corpse Danced at Midnight* was which author/sleuth's first bestseller?
16. Which Eighties cop show rejected George Bush's request to play a cameo role?

Answers to page 636

TV POT LUCK 17: **1.** Keith Chegwin **2.** *Roger Roger* **3.** *Holiday* **4.** Carol Vorderman **5.** Patrick Moore **6.** Adrienne Posta **7.** Anna Ryder Richardson **8.** Hannah Gordon **9.** *My Family* **10.** Gordon Rollings **11.** 1955 **12.** *Harry O* **13.** Mabel **14.** *Our World* **15.** *Not the Nine O'Clock News* **16.** *Noel's House Party*

Which Year in TV? 9

Answers on page 637

In which year did the following programmes first appear on British TV

1. *Home and Away*

2. *Knight Rider*

3. *The Black and White Minstrel Show*

4. *It's a Knockout*

5. *The Sweeney*

6. *Waiting For God*

7. *Widows*

8. *Camberwick Green*

9. *The Wonder Years*

10. *The Wombles*

11. *Miss Marple*

12. *A Fine Romance*

13. *Not Only...But Also*

14. *Hancock's Half-Hour*

15. *Burke's Law*

16. *I Love Lucy*

Answers to page 637

DOCUSOAPS 2: **1.** The M25 **2.** Mariella Frostrup **3.** *Animal ER* **4.** *The Paras* **5.** Thames Valley **6.** *The People's Vets* **7.** John Nettles **8.** *Chopper Coppers* **9.** *Alpine Rescue* **10.** India **11.** *Pleasure Island* **12.** *Escape to the Sun* **13.** Stephen Tompkinson **14.** *Lakesiders* **15.** Paul Watson **16.** Jim Rowland

Emmerdale 4

Answers on page 642

1. What was the name of Jackie Merrick's dog?
2. Who deliberately ran her over?
3. Which royal was guest of honour at the 1,000th episode celebrations of the series but admitted she had never even heard of *Emmerdale Farm*?
4. Which mild-mannered farmer was accused of murder in 1986?
5. Which detective failed to nail Kim Marchant?
6. What is the name of Zak Dingle's first wife?
7. How did Pat Sugden die?
8. Who dumped his wife and child in favour of Sandie Merrick?
9. Who looked on callously as Frank Tate suffered a fatal heart attack?
10. Who was sent to prison for pulling down a fence as part of a protest against dumping nuclear waste?
11. Which future *EastEnder* played Dolly Skilbeck's adopted army deserter son, Graham Lodsworth?
12. Who was Jason Kirk's Australian boyfriend?
13. What are the names of Kathy Glover's parents?
14. With which member of the nobility did Sean Reynolds have an affair?
15. For which newspaper was Amos Brearly the local correspondent?
16. Which villager is played by Dominic Brunt?

Answers to page 642

COMEDY 20: **1.** *The Legacy of Reggie Perrin* **2.** Schoolteacher **3.** Piglet **4.** Timothy Lumsden **5.** *Valentine Park* **6.** *Down the 'Gate* **7.** Bill Maynard **8.** *Second Thoughts* **9.** The Batley Townswomen's Guild **10.** Hetty Prout **11.** Truffles **12.** Robert **13.** Ethel Mertz **14.** 1950s **15.** Manchester City **16.** Wayne

Dramas 15

Answers on page 643

1. What was the name of Beverly's put-upon husband in *Abigail's Party*?
2. Which *Kiss Me Kate* actress appears in *Hearts and Bones*?
3. Which local in *Northern Exposure* had an IQ of 180?
4. Whose trilogy of spy novels was adapted for television in *Game, Set and Match*?
5. Which member of the Redgrave family starred in *Bramwell*?
6. Kate Winslet, Minnie Driver and Robert Carlyle have all played patients in which medical series?
7. Who succeeded Michael Praed as the hero of *Robin of Sherwood*?
8. Which comedy double act played *Jeeves and Wooster* in the 1990 version of P.G. Wodehouse's tales?
9. The schooner *Charlotte Rhodes* featured in which seafaring series?
10. Who committed suicide in the final episode of *Upstairs, Downstairs*?
11. Which Hollywood star played the title role in *Moses the Lawgiver*?
12. What was the name of the all-girl group in *Rock Follies*?
13. In *Roger Roger*, which aspiring rock star had daughters called Cher and Madonna?
14. Which veteran comedy actor played Uncle Tom in *Rumpole of the Bailey*?
15. Which series was retitled *Edward the King* when shown in the US?
16. Who played *Casanova* in the 1971 series?

Answers to page 643

SCI FI 7: **1.** Major Kira Nerys **2.** Martin Landau and Barbara Bain **3.** Mike Donovan **4.** *Seaview* **5.** Virgil Tracy **6.** Security chief **7.** Gan Olag **8.** Melody, Harmony, Symphony, Rhapsody and Destiny **9.** Francis Matthews **10.** Summers **11.** Patrick Troughton **12.** The Cylons **13.** Dr Rudy Wells **14.** Jaime Sommers **15.** Green **16.** Mars

Comedy 20

Answers on page 640

1. What was the title of the 1996 sequel to *The Fall and Rise of Reginald Perrin*?
2. What was John's job in *Dear John…*?
3. As played by Nicholas Lyndhurst, what was Peter Chapman's code-name in a 1990 ITV sitcom?
4. Who did Ronnie Corbett play in *Sorry!*?
5. Which park did Ken Jones look after in a 1987 ITV sitcom?
6. Which series saw Reg Varney as a porter at Billingsgate Fish Market?
7. Who played Selwyn Froggitt?
8. *Faith in the Future* was the sequel to which series?
9. In *Monty Python's Flying Circus*, who staged a re-enactment of Pearl Harbour?
10. Who was the nosy next-door neighbour to *The Larkins*?
11. What was the name of Mildred's Yorkshire Terrier in *George and Mildred*?
12. Who did Beryl marry in *The Liver Birds*?
13. In *I Love Lucy*, who was Lucy Ricardo's best friend?
14. In which decade was *Foxy Lady* set?
15. Which football team did Winston Platt support in *The Dustbinmen*?
16. Who was Dailey's partner on *Who Do You Do*?

Answers to page 640

EMMERDALE 4: **1.** Tess **2.** Harry Mowlam **3.** Princess Michael of Kent **4.** Matt Skilbeck **5.** DI Spalding **6.** Nellie **7.** In a hit-and-run **8.** Phil Pearce **9.** His wife Kim **10.** Jack Sugden **11.** Ross Kemp **12.** Joe Fisher **13.** Caroline and Malcolm **14.** Lady Tara Oakwell **15.** The *Hotten Courier* **16.** Paddy Kirk

Sci Fi 7

Answers on page 641

1. Who was the First Officer on *Star Trek: Deep Space Nine*?
2. Which husband and wife starred in *Space: 1999*?
3. Which TV journalist fought against the aliens in *V*?
4. Which submarine did Admiral Harriman Nelson command in *Voyage to the Bottom of the Sea*?
5. Who piloted Thunderbird 2?
6. What is Michael Garibaldi's position on *Babylon 5*?
7. Which muscular member of *Blake's 7* had an electronic device fitted to his brain to stop him killing?
8. Who were the five Angel pilots in *Captain Scarlet and the Mysterons*?
9. Which actor provided the voice of Captain Scarlet?
10. What is Buffy's surname in *Buffy the Vampire Slayer*?
11. Which *Doctor Who* had Victoria Waterfield as an assistant?
12. Which race waged war on humanoids in *Battlestar Galactica*?
13. Which scientist rebuilt Steve Austin?
14. Which girlfriend of Steve Austin became *The Bionic Woman*?
15. What colour was Mr Spock's blood?
16. From which planet did Husky originate in *Space Patrol*?

Answers to page 641

DRAMAS 15: **1.** Laurence **2.** Amanda Holden **3.** Ed Chigliak **4.** Len Deighton **5.** Jemma **6.** *Casualty* **7.** Jason Connery **8.** Fry and Laurie **9.** *The Onedin Line* **10.** Capt. James Bellamy **11.** Burt Lancaster **12.** The Little Ladies **13.** Phil **14.** Richard Murdoch **15.** *Edward the Seventh* **16.** Frank Finlay

Eighties 5

Answers on page 646

Which artists had UK hits in the Eighties with the following tracks?

1. '(Something Inside) So Strong'
2. 'Only When You Leave'
3. 'Owner Of A Lonely Heart'
4. 'Everything Must Change'
5. 'Fantastic Day'
6. 'Causing A Commotion'
7. 'Ain't Nothin' Goin' On But The Rent'
8. 'Wonderful Life'
9. 'Why Can't This Be Love'
10. 'This Charming Man'
11. 'The Land Of Make Believe'
12. 'New Moon On Monday'
13. 'My Baby Just Cares For Me'
14. 'Doctor Doctor'
15. 'Here Comes The Rain Again'
16. 'I Want To Know What Love Is'

Answers to page 646

MUSIC POT LUCK 18: **1.** God **2.** Jeff Beck **3.** Stray Cats **4.** The Strawbs **5.** John Peel **6.** Hank Marvin **7.** Cyndi Lauper **8.** Robert Palmer **9.** The Rumour **10.** Steve Tyler and Joe Perry **11.** A French exchange student **12.** The Teardrop Explodes **13.** Ruth, Anita, Bonnie and June **14.** Barry Manilow **15.** The Sunshine Band **16.** Ringo Starr

Cover Versions 6

Answers on page 647

1. Which song links Anthony Newley and Donny Osmond?
2. Who had the original hit with 'Guantanamera', revived in 1997 by Wyclef Jean featuring Refugee Allstars?
3. Which Detroit Emeralds song did Shakin' Stevens cover in 1988?
4. Which Survivor number one was covered by Frank Bruno in 1995?
5. Which teen band covered Neil Sedaka's 'Breaking Up Is Hard To Do' in 1972?
6. David Whitfield, Frankie Laine and Barbara Dickson have all had hits with which song?
7. Who covered The Searchers hit 'Needles And Pins' in 1977?
8. Who had a hit with 'Somewhere' 33 years before the Pet Shop Boys?
9. Who had the original hit with The Hollies' 'Searchin''?
10. Which Beatles song did David Cassidy cover in 1974?
11. Which Lesley Gore hit from the Sixties became a number one for Dave Stewart and Barbara Gaskin in 1981?
12. Which TV cop had a number one by speaking his way through a Bread song?
13. Bobby Darin and The Four Tops both had hits with which song in the Sixties?
14. Who recorded the original version of 'I'm Doing Fine Now', a hit for The Pasadenas in 1992?
15. What song links Chaka Khan and Whitney Houston?
16. Sam Cooke and Johnny Nash both had hits with which song in the Sixties?

Answers to page 647

DUOS 2: **1.** The Korgis **2.** Michael and Janet Jackson **3.** Marcella Detroit **4.** Alisha's Attic **5.** 'True Love Ways' **6.** Asher and Waller **7.** 'Don't Stay Away Too Long' **8.** German **9.** 'Little Man' **10.** 1975 **11.** Esther and Abi Ofarim **12.** 'Cinderella Rockefella' **13.** 'Letter From America' **14.** Cilla Black **15.** Patti Labelle and Michael McDonald **16.** Three

Music Pot Luck 18

Answers on page 644

1. To whom did Prince dedicate his debut album?
2. Who replaced Eric Clapton in The Yardbirds?
3. Brian Setzer, Lee Rocker and Slim Jim Phantom were better known as which rockabilly trio?
4. Who had a top twenty hit with 'Part Of The Union'?
5. Which long-serving DJ was born John Ravenscroft?
6. Who was the first British guitarist to own a Fender Stratocaster?
7. Which American singer was described as 'The deranged First Lady of kookie pop'?
8. Who was the original singer with Power Station?
9. What was the name of Graham Parker's backing band?
10. Which two members of Aerosmith featured on Run D.M.C.'s version of 'Walk This Way'?
11. For what did Curt Smith mistake his future Tears For Fears partner Roland Orzabal when they first met at the age of 13?
12. Which band were named after a caption in *Marvel* comic?
13. What were the names of the four Pointer Sisters?
14. Which singer/songwriter used to work in the CBS-TV mailroom in Manhattan?
15. What was the name of KC's band?
16. Which Beatle went to school with Billy Fury?

Answers to page 644

EIGHTIES 5: **1.** Labi Siffre **2.** Spandau Ballet **3.** Yes **4.** Paul Young **5.** Haircut 100 **6.** Madonna **7.** Gwen Guthrie **8.** Black **9.** Van Halen **10.** The Smiths **11.** Bucks Fizz **12.** Duran Duran **13.** Nina Simone **14.** The Thompson Twins **15.** Eurythmics **16.** Foreigner

Duos 2

Answers on page 645

1. Which duo had a 1980 hit with 'Everybody's Got To Learn Sometime'?
2. Which brother and sister duetted on 'Scream' in 1995?
3. With whom did Elton John duet on his version of 'Ain't Nothing Like The Real Thing'?
4. Which duo are the daughters of Brian Poole, former leader of The Tremeloes?
5. Which Buddy Holly song was a 1965 hit for Peter and Gordon?
6. What were Peter and Gordon's respective surnames?
7. What did Peters and Lee advise in 1974?
8. What nationality were Modern Talking who had a 1986 UK hit with 'Brother Louie'?
9. After 'I Got You Babe', what was Sonny and Cher's second UK top ten hit?
10. In which year were Sonny and Cher divorced?
11. Which Israeli husband and wife had a number one UK hit in 1968?
12. And what was the title of the song?
13. What was The Proclaimers' first hit single?
14. Who did the UK cover of The Righteous Brothers' 'You've Lost That Lovin' Feelin''?
15. Which duo had a number two hit with 'On My Own' in 1986?
16. How many UK number ones did Robson and Jerome have?

Answers to page 645

COVER VERSIONS 6: **1.** 'Why' **2.** The Sandpipers **3.** 'Feel The Need In Me' **4.** 'Eye Of The Tiger' **5.** The Partridge Family **6.** 'Answer Me' **7.** Smokie **8.** P.J. Proby **9.** The Coasters **10.** 'Please Please Me' **11.** 'It's My Party' **12.** Telly Savalas ('If') **13.** 'If I Were A Carpenter' **14.** New York City **15.** 'I'm Every Woman' **16.** 'Cupid'

Dire Straits 1

Answers on page 650

1. What was the title of Dire Straits' 1984 live double album?
2. Which band did Dire Straits support on their first UK tour, in 1978?
3. What was Dire Straits' first single?
4. Who was Dire Straits' bass guitarist?
5. Which Tina Turner hit was written by Mark Knopfler?
6. Who left the band before the recording of 'Making Movies'?
7. For which Bill Forsyth film starring Burt Lancaster and Denis Lawson did Mark Knopfler write the score?
8. Which group did Mark Knopfler form in 1990?
9. What was the title of Dire Straits' second album?
10. From which album was 'Private Investigations' taken?
11. Which track from *Rocky III* kept 'Private Investigations' off the number one spot in the UK singles chart?
12. Which 14-minute track featured on the 'Love Over Gold' album?
13. Who did Terry Williams replace as drummer in 1982?
14. For how many weeks did the 'Brothers In Arms' album stay at the top of the UK charts?
15. Who co-wrote 'Money For Nothing'?
16. Which five tracks from 'Brothers In Arms' were released as singles?

Answers to page 650

ROCK 'N' ROLL 2: **1.** 'School Day' and 'No Particular Place To Go' **2.** Dion **3.** His voice broke **4.** 'Oh, Boy' **5.** 'The Purple People Eater Meets The Witch Doctor' **6.** 1959 **7.** Bill Haley **8.** Eddie Cochran **9.** 'Blue Suede Shoes' **10.** 'Hound Dog' **11.** 'Poor Me' **12.** Marty Wilde and Craig Douglas **13.** 'Move It' **14.** 'Why Do Fools Fall In Love' **15.** Alligator ('See You Later, Alligator') **16.** Chuck Berry and Jerry Lee Lewis

Chart Toppers 8

Answers on page 651

1. In which year did David Bowie reach number one in the UK with 'Ashes To Ashes'?
2. Who got to number one in 1982 with 'Goody Two Shoes'?
3. Which father and daughter had separate UK number ones in 1966?
4. Andy Fairweather-Low was the singer with which 1969 chart toppers?
5. And what was the title of their number one?
6. Which 1969 chart topper had already seen his brother have a UK number one, but with a different surname?
7. Who had a 1998 number one with 'Gym And Tonic'?
8. Which was the best-selling UK single of 1998?
9. Which boy band had a number one hit in 2001 with 'Let's Dance'?
10. Which 1958 chart topper was promoted as a full-blooded Cherokee Indian?
11. Who reached number one in 1959 with 'The Day The Rains Came'?
12. Which 1982 hit was based on a Zulu folk tune?
13. Whose camera never lied in 1982?
14. Which old Marvin Gaye B-side topped the UK charts in 1983 with a new singer?
15. Who topped the charts in 1977 with 'So You Win Again'?
16. Which charity record gave Wet Wet Wet their first UK number one?

Answers to page 651

VIDEOS 1: **1.** 'Dancing In The Dark' **2.** Neil Kinnock **3.** Claudia Schiffer **4.** 'Rio' **5.** 'Sledgehammer' **6.** 'Bohemian Rhapsody' **7.** Madonna (her brother Christopher) **8.** Michael Jackson ('Thriller') **9.** 'Fat Bottomed Girls' **10.** Diana Dors **11.** 'Take On Me' **12.** Christie Brinkley **13.** '(You Drive Me) Crazy' **14.** Brian May **15.** 'It's Only Love' **16.** 'Black And White'

Rock 'n' Roll 2

Answers on page 648

1. Which two Chuck Berry songs have the same tune but different lyrics?
2. Whose hits included 'Runaround Sue' and 'The Wanderer'?
3. Which natural development brought a temporary halt to Frankie Lymon's singing career in 1959?
4. Which Crickets hit of 1957 became a number one for Mud 18 years later?
5. The Big Bopper's 'Chantilly Lace' began as the B-side to which novelty number parodying two chart hits of the time?
6. In which year did Eddie Cochran have a UK hit with 'C'mon Everybody'?
7. Which rock 'n' roll star started out with the Downhomers?
8. Who sang 'Twenty Flight Rock' in the 1956 Jayne Mansfield film *The Girl Can't Help It*?
9. Which Carl Perkins song, covered by Elvis, was based on a true incident observed at a gig?
10. Which Elvis hit was originally recorded by Big Mama Thornton?
11. Which of his song titles did Adam Faith borrow for the title of his early autobiography?
12. Which two British acts had 1959 hits with 'A Teenager In Love'?
13. Which song started on the B-side of 'Schoolboy Crush' but went on to become Cliff Richard's first hit?
14. What was Frankie Lymon and The Teenagers' 1956 UK number one?
15. Which reptile was Bill Haley looking forward to meeting again in 1956?
16. Which two US artists had UK hits with 'Sweet Little Sixteen'?

Answers to page 648

DIRE STRAITS 1: **1.** 'Alchemy' **2.** Talking Heads **3.** 'Sultans Of Swing' **4.** John Illsley **5.** 'Private Dancer' **6.** David Knopfler **7.** *Local Hero* **8.** The Notting Hillbillies **9.** 'Communique' **10.** 'Love Over Gold' **11.** 'Eye Of The Tiger' **12.** 'Telegraph Road' **13.** Pick Withers **14.** Three **15.** Sting **16.** 'So Far Away', 'Money For Nothing', 'Brothers In Arms', 'Walk Of Life' and 'Your Latest Trick'

Videos 1

Answers on page 649

1. In which Bruce Springsteen video did future *Friends* star Courteney Cox climb on stage?
2. Which British politician appeared in a Tracey Ullman video?
3. Which supermodel was in the video for Westlife's version of 'Uptown Girl'?
4. Which Duran Duran video showed the band sailing on the high seas?
5. Which award-winning Peter Gabriel video featured claymation and stop-motion?
6. Which was the first song to have a genuine promo video?
7. The brother of which international artist appeared in the video for Soft Cell's 'Tainted Love'?
8. Who announced in his 1983 video: 'Due to my strong personal convictions, I wish to stress that this film in no way endorses a belief in the occult'?
9. Which Queen video featured semi-nude female cyclists?
10. Which Fifties film star appeared in the video for Adam and The Ants' 'Prince Charming'?
11. Which a-ha video won five prizes at the 1986 MTV Video Music Awards?
12. Which supermodel appeared in the video for Billy Joel's 'Uptown Girl'?
13. Melissa Joan Hart appeared in which Britney Spears video?
14. Which member of Queen was in the video for Five's 'We Will Rock You'?
15. Which Bryan Adams song won Best Stage Performance at the 1986 MTV Video Awards?
16. Which 1991 Michael Jackson video was withdrawn and re-edited after complaints about its violent content?

Answers to page 649

CHART TOPPERS 8: **1.** 1980 **2.** Adam Ant **3.** Frank Sinatra ('Strangers In The Night') and Nancy Sinatra ('These Boots Are Made For Walkin'') **4.** Amen Corner **5.** '(If Paradise Is) Half As Nice' **6.** Peter Sarstedt (brother of Eden Kane) **7.** Spacedust **8.** 'Believe' by Cher **9.** Five **10.** Marvin Rainwater **11.** Jane Morgan **12.** 'The Lion Sleeps Tonight' **13.** Bucks Fizz **14.** 'Wherever I Lay My Hat (That's My Home)' (Paul Young) **15.** Hot Chocolate **16.** 'With A Little Help From My Friends'

Beatles 2

Answers on page 654

1. Which Paul McCartney composition was originally written for – but rejected by – Billy J. Kramer?
2. Who is the subject of 'Hey Jude'?
3. In which year was 'Sgt. Pepper' released?
4. Which Beatles track ended with an ultrasonic whistle audible only to dogs and recorded by Paul McCartney especially for his Shetland sheepdog?
5. Which closing track on 'Revolver' featured the use of backward tapes?
6. Which 'Sgt. Pepper' track did the BBC ban in 1967 in the belief that it might encourage drug-taking?
7. Which pop artist created the album cover for 'Sgt. Pepper'?
8. Who were the first act signed by Apple Music?
9. How many weeks did 'Hey Jude' stay at number one in the US?
10. Who appeared on TV's *Dee Time* in 1968 to say that her relationship with Paul McCartney was over?
11. What role did Police Inspector Carl Bear play in Beatles history?
12. What premiered on ABC TV on 25 September 1965?
13. Who are the only two singers featured on the sleeve of 'Sgt Pepper'?
14. Which veteran actress initially refused to allow her photo to be used on the 'Sgt. Pepper' cover, on the grounds that she would never be in a lonely hearts club?
15. Which Beatles anthem was transmitted worldwide in 1967 as part of the first global TV link-up?
16. What was voted Song of the Year at the 1967 Grammy Awards?

Answers to page 654

NINETIES 5: **1.** TLC **2.** Boyz II Men **3.** Ian Brown **4.** Gabrielle **5.** 'The Division Bell' **6.** Celine Dion **7.** '36D', a song about topless models **8.** 15 **9.** Kurt Cobain **10.** Eels **11.** The Lemonheads **12.** Suede **13.** Meat Loaf **14.** Alisha's Attic **15.** 'The Only Living Boy In New York' **16.** Spin Doctors

Albums 7

Answers on page 655

Which artists released the following albums?

1. 'The Song Remains The Same' (1976)
2. 'Auberge' (1991)
3. 'Misplaced Childhood' (1985)
4. 'Blue Moves' (1976)
5. 'Growing Up In Public' (1992)
6. 'By Request' (1999)
7. 'No Jacket Required' (1985)
8. 'Some Other Sucker's Parade' (1997)
9. 'On The Waters' (1970)
10. 'Adrenalize' (1992)
11. 'Discovery' (1979)
12. 'His 'N' Hers (1994)
13. 'The Seeds Of Love' (1989)
14. 'No Angel' (2001)
15. 'Present Arms' (1981)
16. 'The Summoner's Tales' (1993)

Answers to page 655

MUSIC POT LUCK 19: **1.** Manfred Mann **2.** Viv Stanshall **3.** Leather jacket **4.** Jack Anglin **5.** Sheryl Crow **6.** David Crosby **7.** The Bee Gees **8.** 'From Russia With Love' **9.** Pulp **10.** Travis **11.** Jamiroquai **12.** Cat Stevens **13.** Gerry Rafferty **14.** The Strawbs **15.** 14 **16.** The Rutles

Nineties 5

Answers on page 652

1. Lisa 'Left Eye' Lopes, Rozanda 'Chilli' Thomas and T-Boz make up which trio?
2. Who had a number one single in 1992 with 'End Of The Road'?
3. Who was lead singer with The Stone Roses?
4. Who took 'Dreams' to number one in 1993?
5. Which 1994 release gave Pink Floyd their first number one UK album for 11 years?
6. Which singer married her 52-year-old manager, René Angelil, in 1994?
7. In protest at the lyrics of which song did singer Briana Corrigan leave The Beautiful South?
8. How many weeks did Wet Wet Wet's 'Love Is All Around' spend at number one in the UK?
9. Whose suicide note said: 'It's better to burn out than to fade away'?
10. Which Los Angeles band had a drummer called Butch?
11. Which band released a cover of Simon and Garfunkel's 'Mrs Robinson' in 1992?
12. Whose 1996 number one album was titled 'Coming Up'?
13. Who had the biggest-selling UK single and album of 1993?
14. Which girl duo's first UK hit was 'I Am I Feel'?
15. Which Simon and Garfunkel song was covered in 1993 by Everything But The Girl?
16. In 1994, Anthony Krizan replaced Eric Shenkman as guitarist with which US band?

Answers to page 652

BEATLES 2: **1.** 'Yesterday' **2.** Julian Lennon **3.** 1967 **4.** 'A Day In The Life' **5.** 'Tomorrow Never Knows' **6.** 'A Day In The Life' **7.** Peter Blake **8.** Grapefruit **9.** Nine **10.** Jane Asher **11.** He stopped a 1964 Beatles show in Cleveland, Ohio, after screaming fans invaded the stage **12.** The Beatles cartoon series **13.** Bob Dylan and Dion **14.** Mae West **15.** 'All You Need Is Love' **16.** 'Michelle'

Music Pot Luck 19

Answers on page 653

1. In 1974, who gave away deeds to a square foot of land on a Welsh mountain to anyone who bought his environment-friendly record 'The Good Earth'?
2. Which eccentric singer once put raw meat into Ringo Starr's drum kit in a bid to wreck the sound?
3. Which 30-year-old item of John Lennon's clothing was sold for £24,200 in 1992?
4. Which country star was killed in a car crash on his way to Patsy Cline's funeral?
5. Who released an album in 2002 entitled 'C'Mon, C'Mon'?
6. Which American was jailed in 1983 for possession of drugs and carrying a gun into a bar?
7. Who wrote Marbles' 1968 hit 'Only One Woman'?
8. Which James Bond film theme gave Matt Monro a hit in 1963?
9. Who were 'Sorted For E's & Wizz' in 1995?
10. Whose 2001 album was titled 'The Invisible Band'?
11. Jay Kay is associated with which band?
12. Which Sixties and Seventies artist returned to music in 1995 under the name of Yusef Islam?
13. Who was the future solo star singer with Steelers Wheel?
14. 'Lay Down' was the first UK top twenty single for which Seventies band?
15. How old was Helen Shapiro when she had a top three hit with 'Don't Treat Me Like A Child'?
16. Which Eric Idle-inspired band were a spoof of The Beatles?

Answers to page 653

ALBUMS 7: **1.** Led Zeppelin **2.** Chris Rea **3.** Marillion **4.** Elton John **5.** Jimmy Nail **6.** Boyzone **7.** Phil Collins **8.** Del Amitri **9.** Bread **10.** Def Leppard **11.** ELO **12.** Pulp **13.** Tears For Fears **14.** Dido **15.** UB40 **16.** Sting

Name Changes 8

Answers on page 658

1. As which heavyweight rock star is Marvin Lee Aday better known?
2. Which backing group to a Fifties Italian/American singer used to be called The Timberlanes?
3. What were Dave Dee, Dozy, Beaky, Mick and Tich previously known as?
4. Which heavy metal band used to be called Earth?
5. Which rap artist started life as Kevin Donovan?
6. What is Babyface's real name?
7. To what did Cherilyn Sarkasian La Piere decide to shorten her name?
8. Which British star of the Fifties was originally Tommy Hicks?
9. What is Jay Kay's real Christian name?
10. As whom was dog-lover Kent Lavoie better known in the Seventies?
11. Who used his imagination when changing his name from John Leslie McGregor?
12. Which enduring star was born Annie Mae Bullock?
13. Which UK singer of the Fifties looked for something more romantic than Richard Bryce?
14. What was Harry Casey better known as initially?
15. Which saxophonist's full name is Kenny Gorelick?
16. Which diminutive Sixties performer was born Eva Narcissus Boyd?

Answers to page 658

a1 1: **1.** Ben **2.** 'Be The First To Believe' **3.** 'Here We Come' **4.** 'Like A Rose' **5.** Spanish **6.** 'I Still Believe' **7.** Columbia **8.** 6 **9.** 'Ready Or Not' **10.** 'Summertime Of Our Lives' **11.** Nine **12.** 'The A List' **13.** 'Take On Me' **14.** Paul **15.** Christian **16.** Ben

Rod Stewart 1

Answers on page 659

1. Which member of Jefferson Starship played piano on 'Maggie May'?
2. Who originally recorded 'Reason To Believe'?
3. For which band did Rod Stewart sing on the 1972 hit 'In A Broken Dream'?
4. Which band had a hit with 'Handbags and Gladrags' at the end of 2001?
5. From which country was the teenage Stewart deported for vagrancy?
6. Which band did Stewart join in 1965?
7. Who played mandolin on the record of 'Maggie May'?
8. What was Stewart's first UK number one album?
9. Who originally recorded 'Angel'?
10. From which album was 'Sailing' taken?
11. In which year did The Faces split?
12. With whom did Stewart duet on the 1990 hit 'It Takes Two'?
13. What was Stewart's last UK number one single?
14. Which Stewart-penned single was about the death of a gay friend in New York?
15. Which album contained the single 'D'Ya Think I'm Sexy'?
16. Why did Stewart refuse to leave the airport international departure lounge on a visit to Britain in 1975?

Answers to page 659

R & B 3: **1.** The Hoochie Coochie Men **2.** Destiny's Child **3.** Jennifer Lopez **4.** 'She's Got That Vibe' **5.** Little Feat **6.** Janis Joplin **7.** 'Let The Heartaches Begin' **8.** 'I Feel Free' **9.** 'With A Little Help From My Friends' **10.** Jennifer Lopez **11.** 'Love II Love' **12.** *Notting Hill* **13.** 'Be Alone No More' **14.** Phil Collins **15.** Cream **16.** Matthew Marsden

a1 1

Answers on page 656

1. Who is the youngest member of a1?
2. What was a1's first UK hit?
3. What was the title of the band's first album?
4. What was the title of the track, later released as a single, written by Ben on the first album?
5. What nationality is Paul's grandfather?
6. Which track on the debut album was written by Mark?
7. What was a1's first record label?
8. What number in the UK charts did 'Be The First To Believe' get to?
9. What was the other track on the double A-side of 'Everytime'?
10. Which September 1999 single reached number five in the UK charts?
11. How many weeks did 'Be The First To Believe' stay in the UK charts?
12. Which album featured 'Same Old Brand New You'?
13. Which single from that album was a cover version of an a-ha hit?
14. Who was the only band member not to have contributed to the writing of 'Forever In Love'?
15. Which member of a1 plays the guitar?
16. Which member of a1 has the surname Adams?

Answers to page 656

NAME CHANGES 8: **1.** Meat Loaf **2.** The Belmonts **3.** Dave Dee and The Bostons **4.** Black Sabbath **5.** Afrika Bambaataa **6.** Kenneth Edmonds **7.** Cher **8.** Tommy Steele **9.** Jason **10.** Lobo **11.** Leee John **12.** Tina Turner **13.** Dickie Valentine **14.** KC **15.** Kenny G **16.** Little Eva

R & B 3

Answers on page 657

1. Which band did Long John Baldry form in 1964?
2. Which R & B band released the album 'Survivor' in 2001?
3. Who had a hit in 2001 with 'Ain't It Funny'?
4. Which was R. Kelly's first top ten single in the UK?
5. Lowell George, Roy Estrada, Bill Payne and Richie Hayward comprised which Californian band of the Seventies?
6. Which R & B singer died of a heroin overdose at her Hollywood hotel in October 1970?
7. With which song did Long John Baldry have a UK number one in 1967?
8. What was Cream's first UK top twenty hit?
9. Which Beatles song did Joe Cocker take to number one in 1968?
10. Whose 1999 album was titled 'On The 6'?
11. What was Damage's first UK top twenty single?
12. Which film featured Another Level's 'From The Heart'?
13. Which Another Level hit featured Jay-Z?
14. Who sang backing vocals on Eric Clapton's 'Bad Love'?
15. Who had a 1967 album called 'Disraeli Gears'?
16. Which former *Coronation Street* actor teamed up with Destiny's Child for the 1998 single 'She's Gone'?

Answers to page 657

ROD STEWART 1: **1.** Pete Sears **2.** Tim Hardin **3.** Python Lee Jackson **4.** The Stereophonics **5.** Spain **6.** Steampacket **7.** Lindisfarne's Ray Jackson **8.** 'Every Picture Tells A Story' **9.** Jimi Hendrix **10.** 'Atlantic Crossing' **11.** 1976 **12.** Tina Turner **13.** 'Baby Jane' **14.** 'The Killing Of Georgie (Parts 1 and 2)' **15.** 'Blondes Have More Fun' **16.** He reportedly owed the UK taxman £750,000 and didn't want to set foot in this country

Sixties 5

Answers on page 662

1. What was the nickname of Small Faces' bass guitarist Ronnie Lane?
2. What did Paul McCartney's younger brother call himself when he was a member of Scaffold?
3. Which bespectacled Cambridge undergraduate got to number four in the charts in 1965 with 'Everyone's Gone To The Moon'?
4. What was the name of Tony Rivers's backing group?
5. Mike Smith was the keyboard player with which successful Sixties band?
6. Who was the female singer with Chicken Shack before joining Fleetwood Mac?
7. Which singer invited listeners to 'Come Back And Shake Me' in 1969?
8. Which bird gave Manfred Mann a 1966 number one?
9. In which song did Ray Davies of The Kinks complain about 'my poor rheumatic back'?
10. Whose Singing Orchestral Circus had a 1968 hit with 'Quick Joey Small (Run Joey Run)'?
11. Whose backing band were The Rebel Rousers?
12. Whose Trinity was fronted by Julie Driscoll?
13. Davey Jones and The King Bees was the first musical venture for which international artist?
14. Hilton Valentine and John Steel were members of which band?
15. Which group had hits with 'He's In Town' and 'Poor Man's Son'?
16. Whose first UK chart action was with 'Arnold Layne' in 1967?

Answers to page 662

FLEETWOOD MAC 1: **1.** 'Tusk' **2.** Peter Green **3.** Jeremy Spencer **4.** Bob Weston **5.** Their manager assembled a bogus Fleetwood Mac to fulfil the dates **6.** Lindsey Buckingham and Stevie Nicks **7.** Stevie Nicks **8.** Peter Green **9.** Ten **10.** 'Rumours' **11.** Christine McVie **12.** Stevie Nicks **13.** Peter Green **14.** 1987 **15.** 'Little Lies' **16.** Stevie Nicks

Punk 3

Answers on page 663

1. Which punk band took their name from a gang in the David Carradine movie *Bound For Glory*?
2. Which punk icon was once a Playboy bunny waitress?
3. Who went to 'Echo Beach' in 1980?
4. Budgie was the drummer with which punk band?
5. Which album did 'Never Mind The Bollocks – Here's The Sex Pistols' knock off the top of the UK chart?
6. Which Clash album was originally going to be called 'The New Testament'?
7. What was Generation X's only UK top twenty hit?
8. Whose 1978 album was titled 'Love Bites'?
9. 'If The Kids Are United' was a hit for which band?
10. Which town did The Stranglers drop from their original name?
11. Which punk band recorded 'Gary Gilmore's Eyes', a reference to the death-row murderer who offered to donate his eyes to science?
12. Which band's biggest hit was 'Into The Valley'?
13. Jello Biafra was the singer with which controversially named US punk band?
14. Why were The Damned fired as support act for The Sex Pistols' 'Anarchy In The UK' tour?
15. Who quit his day job as a computer operator at an Elizabeth Arden cosmetics factory in 1977 to become a full-time musician?
16. Who was the singer with Eddie and The Hot Rods?

Answers to page 663

NOVELTY NUMBERS 3: **1.** The Monks **2.** Frankie Howerd **3.** Mike Reid **4.** Bob the Builder **5.** Orville **6.** Kermit's nephew Robin **7.** None **8.** Terry Wogan **9.** Keith Michell **10.** Hissing Sid **11.** Jimmy Savile **12.** Chelsea **13.** Rod Stewart **14.** 'We Have A Dream' **15.** Splodgenessabounds **16.** Spinal Tap

Fleetwood Mac 1

Answers on page 660

1. What was Fleetwood Mac's follow-up album to 'Rumours'?
2. Which guitarist appeared on stage in 1969 in a long white robe to reflect his new religious beliefs?
3. Who told the rest of the band on a 1971 US tour that he was 'just popping out for a bit to buy newspapers' and wasn't seen again for two years?
4. Which band member was sacked in 1973 for having an affair with Mick Fleetwood's wife?
5. What happened when Fleetwood Mac pulled out of a 1973 tour?
6. Which pair joined the band in 1974?
7. Who wrote 'Rhiannon'?
8. Which former band member was committed to a mental hospital in 1977?
9. How many different line-ups did Fleetwood Mac have between 1967 and 1974?
10. What was named Album of the Year at the 1978 Grammy Awards?
11. Who penned 'Don't Stop'?
12. Which band member wrote and sang 'Dreams'?
13. Who worked as a gravedigger and hospital porter after leaving Fleeetwood Mac?
14. In which year was the album 'Tango In The Night' released?
15. Which single gave Fleetwood Mac their first UK top five hit since 'Albatross' 14 years earlier?
16. Who released a solo album titled 'The Wild Heart'?

Answers to page 660

SIXTIES 5: **1.** 'Plonk' **2.** Mike McGear **3.** Jonathan King **4.** The Castaways **5.** The Dave Clark Five **6.** Christine Perfect **7.** Clodagh Rodgers **8.** 'Pretty Flamingo' **9.** 'Autumn Almanac' **10.** Kasenetz-Katz **11.** Cliff Bennett **12.** Brian Auger **13.** David Bowie **14.** The Animals **15.** The Rockin' Berries **16.** Pink Floyd

Novelty Numbers 3

Answers on page 661

1. Which band had a 1979 hit with the politically incorrect 'Nice Legs Shame About Her Face'?
2. Which comedian sang about the 'Three Little Fishes'?
3. Which ex-*EastEnder* reached number ten in the charts in 1975 with the tale of 'The Ugly Duckling'?
4. Which children's TV character topped the charts with a cover of 'Mambo No. 5'?
5. Which large green duck in a nappy got to number four in the charts in 1982?
6. Which Muppet croaked 'Halfway Down The Stairs'?
7. How many UK number one singles did The Wombles have?
8. Which disc jockey had a 1978 hit with 'The Floral Dance'?
9. Who narrated the adventures of Captain Beaky?
10. Which snake went on trial in the further adventures of Captain Beaky?
11. Which DJ sang out 'Ahab The Arab' in the Sixties?
12. Which football team enjoyed a top five hit with 'Blue Is The Colour' in 1972?
13. Which fan led the Scottish World Cup Squad for 'Ole Ola' in 1978?
14. Which Scottish World Cup Squad song of 1982 teamed up such diverse talents as B.A. Robertson, Miss Scotland and Willie Carson?
15. Who requested 'Two Pints Of Lager And A Packet Of Crisps Please'?
16. Which spoof heavy metal band released a 1992 album 'Break Like The Wind'?

Answers to page 661

PUNK 3: **1.** The Boomtown Rats **2.** Debbie Harry **3.** Martha and The Muffins **4.** Siouxsie and The Banshees **5.** '40 Golden Greats' by Cliff Richard and The Shadows **6.** 'London Calling' **7.** 'King Rocker' **8.** The Buzzcocks **9.** Sham 69 **10.** Guildford (They were The Guildford Stranglers) **11.** The Adverts **12.** The Skids **13.** The Dead Kennedys **14.** For agreeing to play in private for Derby councillors who wanted to assess the band's suitability **15.** Elvis Costello **16.** Barrie Masters

Leicester City 1

Answers on page 666

1. In which season did Leicester City first compete in Europe?
2. Who knocked them out of that competition?
3. After scoring seven goals on the road to Wembley, which Welsh international was surprisingly omitted from the 1961 FA Cup final team?
4. Who took his place?
5. Who managed City from 1958 to 1968?
6. From which club did Leicester sign Gerry Taggart?
7. Against which club in the 1994 First Division play-offs did Leicester end their record of six defeats in six appearances at Wembley?
8. Which team pipped Leicester for the 1928–9 League Championship by a single point?
9. Who scored Leicester's only goal in the 1963 FA Cup final defeat by Manchester United?
10. Who did Leicester beat in the semi-finals of the 1969 FA Cup?
11. Which future England international scored the decisive goal?
12. From which club did Leicester buy both Neil Lennon and Robbie Savage?
13. Which defender did Leicester sell to Derby for £250,000 in 1972?
14. Which forward moved from Leicester to Everton for £1.1 million in 1989?
15. Who played on the left-wing in Leicester's beaten 1961 Cup final team?
16. Which Scot managed Leicester from 1978 to 1982?

Answers to page 666

EUROPEAN CHAMPIONSHIP 3: **1.** Jürgen Klinsmann **2.** Luxembourg **3.** Alan Shearer **4.** Czech Republic **5.** USSR **6.** Munich **7.** Holland **8.** Spain **9.** 1964 **10.** Madrid **11.** Michael Laudrup **12.** Sepp Maier **13.** Paolo Maldini **14.** 651 **15.** Sweden **16.** Josef Hickersberger

The World Game 11

Answers on page 667

1. Which country won their first-ever match in the Copa America by beating Bolivia 2–0 in 2001?
2. Which German international striker helped Inter Milan win the Italian League title in 1989?
3. How many caps did Ruud Gullit win for Holland?
4. Felix Magath became coach of which German club in October 1998?
5. After being sent off in the 1962 World Cup semi-finals, which Brazilian star was allowed to play in the final following a personal plea by the country's president?
6. For which Italian club did Oliver Bierhoff play in 2000–1?
7. Which German was voted Player of the Tournament at the 1990 World Cup?
8. Which future French captain played for his country in the 1976 Olympic Games?
9. Jozef Jankech was dismissed as which country's national coach in 1998?
10. Which former holders of the European Cup-Winners' Cup were relegated from the top division of the Spanish League in 2000?
11. Who won the Greek title in 2000?
12. Which Italian international joined Perugia for a world record £3.5 million in 1979?
13. Who captained Brazil at the 1986 World Cup finals?
14. Who is the only Danish player to have been named European Footballer of the Year?
15. For which club did Luigi Riva top the Serie 'A' scoring charts in 1967, 1969 and 1970?
16. In 1997, who became the first player to win 100 caps for Colombia?

Answers to page 667

FOOTBALL LEAGUE 10: **1.** Bolton Wanderers **2.** Notts County **3.** 1970 **4.** 1983 **5.** Burnley **6.** Darwen **7.** Ipswich Town **8.** 1930 **9.** Queens Park Rangers **10.** Watford **11.** Carlisle United **12.** 1951 **13.** Brentford **14.** Burnley **15.** Barnsley **16.** Preston North End

European Championship 3

Answers on page 664

1. Who was the first player to score at three European Championship finals tournaments?
2. Which minnows knocked Holland out of the European Championship in 1963?
3. Who scored England's goal in the Euro 96 semi-final against Germany?
4. Which country inflicted Scotland's first defeat for 12 years in a home qualifying tie when they won 2–1 at Celtic Park in March 1999?
5. Which nation featured in the first two European Championship finals?
6. In which city was the 1988 final held?
7. And who defeated USSR in the final that year?
8. Who knocked the Republic of Ireland out of the 1964 European Championship at the quarter-final stage?
9. In which European Championship did Spain record their only success in a major international competition?
10. And where was that year's final played?
11. Who captained Denmark at Euro 96?
12. Who kept goal for West Germany in the 1976 final?
13. Who was the captain of Italy at Euro 96?
14. To the nearest hundred, how many spectators turned up to watch Greece entertain Hungary in a European Championship qualifier in 1983?
15. In which neutral country did the Faroe Islands humble Austria in 1990?
16. Which Austrian coach resigned in the wake of the defeat?

Answers to page 664

LEICESTER CITY 1: **1.** 1961–2 **2.** Atletico Madrid **3.** Ken Leek **4.** Hugh McIlmoyle **5.** Matt Gillies **6.** Bolton Wanderers **7.** Derby County **8.** (Sheffield) Wednesday **9.** Ken Keyworth **10.** West Bromwich Albion **11.** Allan Clarke **12.** Crewe Alexandra **13.** David Nish **14.** Mike Newell **15.** Albert Cheesebrough **16.** Jock Wallace

Football League 10

Answers on page 665

1. Which club used to play at Burnden Park?
2. For which club did eccentric goalkeeper Albert Iremonger make 564 League appearances between 1904 and 1926?
3. When did Swansea change their club name from Town to City?
4. And when did Chester add a 'City' to their name?
5. Which former League champions were relegated to Division Four in 1985?
6. Which Lancashire club conceded 141 Second Division goals in 1898–9?
7. Which club was relegated in 1964 just two years after being crowned League champions?
8. In which year did Merthyr Tydfil leave the Football League?
9. Which club that has never won the League championship finished runners-up in 1976?
10. Which club scored just 24 Second Division goals in 1971–2?
11. For which club did goalkeeper Allan Ross make 466 League appearances from 1963–79?
12. In which year did Rotherham United gain promotion for the first time in their history?
13. Who won the Third Division title in 1998–9?
14. Who were Second Division runners-up to Preston North End in 1999–2000?
15. Who beat Birmingham City in the First Division play-offs in 1999–2000?
16. And who eliminated Birmingham City from the First Division play-offs in 2000–1?

Answers to page 665

THE WORLD GAME 11: **1.** Honduras **2.** Jürgen Klinsmann **3.** 65 **4.** Werder Bremen **5.** Garrincha **6.** Milan **7.** Lothar Matthäus **8.** Michel Platini **9.** Slovakia **10.** Atletico Madrid **11.** Olympiakos **12.** Paolo Rossi **13.** Socrates **14.** Allan Simonsen **15.** Cagliari **16.** Carlos Valderrama

Charlton Athletic 1

Answers on page 670

1. From which club did Charlton sign Mike Flanagan?
2. In which year did Charlton return to The Valley?
3. Who scored Charlton's winner in the 1947 FA Cup final?
4. Who scored 153 League goals for Charlton, 1953–62?
5. From which club did Charlton sign Mark Kinsella?
6. Who managed Charlton from 1967 to 1970?
7. Which namesake scored twice against Charlton on his Manchester United debut in 1956?
8. From whom did Charlton sign Alan Curbishley as a player?
9. Which best-selling author was Charlton's top scorer in 1993–4?
10. From which club did Charlton sign Phil Chapple?
11. In which competition were Charlton runners-up in 1987?
12. Who beat them in the final?
13. Behind which club did Charlton finish second in Division Two in 1986?
14. Who made his Charlton debut at the age of 16 against Oxford United in 1997?
15. Who were Charlton's first opponents in a Football League match?
16. With which club did Graham Stuart begin his League career?

Answers to page 670

FA CUP 9: **1.** West Bromwich Albion **2.** Bob Paisley **3.** Bradford City **4.** Wimbledon **5.** Burnley **6.** Stoke City **7.** Hugh Ferguson **8.** Derby County **9.** Billy Bonds **10.** Ian Wright **11.** Mick McGrath **12.** Oxford United **13.** Preston North End **14.** One **15.** Rev. Kenneth Hunt who scored for Wolverhampton Wanderers in the 1908 final **16.** Gordon Smith

Celtic 2

Answers on page 671

1. Which famous Celtic fan officially opened the new North Stand in 1995?
2. Who did Celtic sign from Bayer Leverkusen for £2.3 million in 1995?
3. Who did Celtic crush 11–0 in a First Division match in 1895?
4. Who was Celtic's top scorer in the League in 1981–2?
5. Who became Celtic manager in 1991?
6. Who joined Celtic in 1967 and played 204 games for the club, scoring 112 goals?
7. How many League titles did Jimmy Johnstone win with Celtic?
8. In which year did Billy McNeill make his Celtic debut?
9. From 1969, in how many successive Scottish FA Cup finals did Celtic appear?
10. Who was Celtic's two-goal hero in the 1988 final against Dundee United?
11. Which centre-back did Celtic sell to Chelsea for £1.4 million in 1991?
12. Which manager was sacked after Celtic were sensationally knocked out of the Scottish FA Cup by Inverness Caledonian Thistle in 2000?
13. Who did Celtic sign from Hibernian for £900,000 in July 1990?
14. Which Celtic forward came on as a substitute for Scotland in the two Euro 2000 play-off matches with England?
15. Which Midlands club did he later join on loan?
16. Which French team knocked Celtic out of the 2000 UEFA Cup?

Answers to page 671

NORTHERN IRELAND 2: **1.** Joe Bambrick **2.** France **3.** 2–2 **4.** 1988 **5.** Lawrie McMenemy **6.** 1964 **7.** Brazil **8.** Scotland **9.** Sammy McIlroy **10.** France **11.** Norman Whiteside **12.** 1986 **13.** Jimmy McIlroy **14.** Distillery **15.** 64 **16.** Nigel Worthington

FA Cup 9

Answers on page 668

1. In 1991, who became Marlow's first League opponents after over a century of FA Cup competition?
2. Which future Liverpool manager scored in the club's FA Cup semi-final victory over Everton in 1950?
3. Which club's only FA Cup win came in 1911?
4. In 1975, who became the first non-League side since the First World War to beat a First Division team away from home in the FA Cup?
5. Who were their victims?
6. Which Second Division team were knocked out of the Cup by Blyth Spartans in 1977–8?
7. Who scored Cardiff City's winner in the 1927 FA Cup final?
8. Who did Bury beat 6–0 in the 1903 FA Cup final?
9. Who captained West Ham to victory in the 1980 FA Cup final?
10. Which substitute scored twice against Manchester United in the 1990 final?
11. Which Blackburn player put through his own goal in the 1960 final?
12. Which Fourth Division team reached the quarter-finals in 1964?
13. For which club did Frederick Dewhurst score in successive finals in 1888 and 1889?
14. How many First Division sides did Liverpool meet on their way to winning the FA Cup in 1992?
15. Who is the only clergyman to have collected an FA Cup winners' medal?
16. Whose glaring last-minute miss in the 1983 final deprived Brighton of Cup glory?

Answers to page 668

CHARLTON ATHLETIC 1: **1.** Tottenham Hotspur **2.** 1992 **3.** Chris Duffy **4.** Stuart Leary **5.** Colchester United **6.** Eddie Firmani **7.** Bobby Charlton **8.** Brighton & Hove Albion **9.** Garry Nelson **10.** Cambridge United **11.** Full Members' Cup **12.** Blackburn Rovers **13.** Norwich City **14.** Paul Konchesky **15.** Exeter City **16.** Chelsea

Northern Ireland 2

Answers on page 669

1. Who scored six times for Northern Ireland against Wales in 1930?
2. In 1951, who became Northern Ireland's first continental opponents?
3. What was the score?
4. In which year did Northern Ireland first play the Republic?
5. Who became Northern Ireland manager in 1998?
6. In which year did Pat Jennings make his international debut?
7. Against which country did he win his last cap, on his 41st birthday?
8. To whom did Northern Ireland lose 8–2 in their first-ever World Cup tie?
9. Who took over as manager of Northern Ireland in 2000?
10. Who ended Northern Ireland's heroics at the 1982 World Cup?
11. During that tournament which Northern Ireland player became the youngest ever to appear in a World Cup match?
12. When did Northern Ireland last reach the World Cup finals?
13. Which Burnley and Stoke City inside-forward won 55 caps from 1952 to 1966?
14. As a player with which Irish club did Martin O'Neill make his international debut in 1972?
15. How many caps did he go on to win?
16. Which former Sheffield Wednesday defender won the first of his 66 caps against Wales in 1984?

Answers to page 669

CELTIC 2: **1.** Rod Stewart **2.** Andreas Thom **3.** Dundee **4.** George McCluskey **5.** Liam Brady **6.** Kenny Dalglish **7.** Eight **8.** 1959 **9.** Seven **10.** Frank McAvennie **11.** Paul Elliott **12.** John Barnes **13.** John Collins **14.** Mark Burchill **15.** Birmingham City **16.** Lyon

Oddballs 11

Answers on page 674

1. Which League club's groundsman accidentally sprayed the pitch with concentrated weedkiller in 1986, forcing the cancellation of pre-season friendlies?
2. Which Linfield and Northern Ireland keeper was beaten twice in the space of eight months by clearances from opposing goalkeepers?
3. Against which opponents did Manchester United change their grey strip at half-time because they couldn't see each other?
4. For which club did Stuart Taylor make 546 League appearances?
5. Which League club were formed from the St Mark's Young Men's Friendly Society?
6. Bob Lord was the outspoken chairman of which League club?
7. Which hard-up League club surrendered their goalposts to bailiffs in 1986?
8. Which club staged a chimps tea-party before kick-off against West Ham in 1976?
9. Who bought Chris Coleman from Blackburn for £2.1 million in 1997?
10. Which League club used to have a full-back called Tommy Cooper?
11. And which Midlands team once had a goalkeeper called Charlie Chaplin?
12. Which Scottish club's first overseas tour ended with them being shipwrecked off the Canary Islands?
13. In which city was the 2000 UEFA Cup final held?
14. Harry the Hornet is the mascot of which club?
15. Which club does politician Peter Mandelson support?
16. Which League club used to have the suffix 'Ramblers'?

Answers to page 674

MANAGERS 10: **1.** Egil Olsen **2.** Tele Santana **3.** Cesar Luis Menotti **4.** Peter Eustace **5.** Zdenek Zeman **6.** Nevio Scala **7.** Ottmar Hitzfeld **8.** Chris Nicholl **9.** Bristol City **10.** Brentford **11.** Trevor Cherry **12.** Ebbe Skovdahl **13.** Exeter City **14.** 1970 **15.** Wolverhampton Wanderers **16.** Mark McGhee

Non-League 4

Answers on page 675

1. Which London club were Conference champions in 1985?
2. Who were relegated from the Conference in 1989 despite finishing out of the bottom three?
3. Which club earned a temporary reprieve at Barrow's expense?
4. Which Conference team plays at Bucks Head?
5. Which future England international joined Crystal Palace from Greenwich Borough in 1985?
6. With which Northamptonshire side did million-pound man Steve Daley finish his career?
7. Which future Newcastle, Tottenham and England man started out with Tow Law Town?
8. From which club did Derby County sign Malcolm Christie?
9. Which outspoken non-League forward of the 1970s was christened 'The Leatherhead Lip'?
10. And with which League club did he subsequently enjoy a brief career?
11. Which Wimbledon, Chelsea and Nottingham Forest keeper started out with Edgware Town?
12. Which Isthmian League team reached round four of the 1980–1 FA Cup?
13. What is Morecambe's nickname?
14. Who finished Conference runners-up to Rushden & Diamonds in 2001?
15. Which Midlands team have the suffix 'Dynamo'?
16. And which Kent club have the suffix 'Invicta'?

Answers to page 675

MIDDLESBROUGH 1: **1.** 1903 **2.** 1994 **3.** 1997 **4.** FC Porto **5.** Paul Gascoigne **6.** Oxford United **7.** Tim Williamson **8.** 15 **9.** Queens Park Rangers **10.** Atletico Madrid **11.** Fulham **12.** Chelsea **13.** Stuart Ripley **14.** Crystal Palace **15.** Stan Anderson **16.** Paul Wilkinson

Managers 10

Answers on page 672

1. Which Norwegian took charge of Wimbledon from July 1999?
2. Who coached Brazil at the 1982 and 1986 World Cup finals?
3. Who coached Argentina to victory at the 1978 World Cup?
4. Who succeeded Howard Wilkinson as Sheffield Wednesday manager in 1988?
5. Which Roma coach sold Paul Gascoigne to Lazio?
6. Who became coach of Parma in 1989?
7. Who took over as coach of Bayern Munich in summer 1998?
8. Who was manager of Southampton from 1985 to 1991?
9. Swede Benny Lennartsson was appointed manager of which English team in 1998?
10. Fred Callaghan, Frank McClintock and Steve Perryman all managed which London club in the 1980s?
11. Which former Leeds player guided Bradford City to the Third Division title in 1985?
12. Under whose guidance did Brondby become the first Danish side to qualify for the UEFA Champions' League, in 1998?
13. Which West Country club did Terry Cooper manage from 1988 to 1991?
14. In which year did Freddie Goodwin become Birmingham City boss?
15. Major Frank Buckley was manager of which club from 1927 to 1944?
16. Who took over as Reading manager in 1991?

Answers to page 672

ODDBALLS 11: **1.** Reading **2.** George Dunlop **3.** Southampton **4.** Bristol Rovers **5.** Swindon Town **6.** Burnley **7.** Hartlepool United **8.** Bristol City **9.** Fulham **10.** Liverpool **11.** Wolverhampton Wanderers **12.** Raith Rovers **13.** Copenhagen **14.** Watford **15.** Hartlepool United **16.** Stoke

Middlesbrough 1

Answers on page 673

1. When did Middlesbrough move to Ayresome Park?
2. When did Bryan Robson take over as Middlesbrough manager?
3. In which year did Middlesbrough reach their first FA Cup final?
4. From which club did Middlesbrough sign Emerson?
5. Who joined Middlesbrough from Rangers for £3.4 million in March 1998?
6. From which club did Middlesbrough sign Robbie Mustoe?
7. Which Middlesbrough goalkeeper always used to wear a number of jerseys to make himself look bigger to opposing forwards?
8. By how many points did Middlesbrough win the Second Division title in 1974?
9. Behind which club did Middlesbrough finish runners-up in Division Three in 1967?
10. To which Spanish club did Middlesbrough sell Juninho in 1997?
11. Who did Middlesbrough beat in the 1976 Anglo-Scottish Cup final?
12. Who defeated 'Boro in the 1990 Zenith Data Systems Cup final?
13. Which winger moved from Middlesbrough to Blackburn for £1.3 million in 1992?
14. From which club did Middlesbrough sign Dean Gordon?
15. Who was Middlesbrough manager from 1966 to 1973?
16. Who was Middlesbrough's top scorer in 1993–4?

Answers to page 673

NON-LEAGUE 4: **1.** Wealdstone **2.** Barrow (the club were unable to guarantee their future) **3.** Welling United **4.** Telford United **5.** Ian Wright **6.** Kettering Town **7.** Chris Waddle **8.** Nuneaton Borough **9.** Chris Kelly **10.** Millwall **11.** Dave Beasant **12.** Enfield **13.** 'The Shrimps' **14.** Yeovil **15.** Shepshed **16.** Folkestone

Italy 1

Answers on page 678

1. Which was the only year that Italy failed to qualify for the World Cup finals?
2. Who did Italy beat 11–3 in 1928 – their record international score?
3. Who coached Italy's victorious World Cup teams of 1934 and 1938?
4. Which goalkeeper won 112 caps for Italy?
5. Who is Italy's record goalscorer with 35?
6. Who captained Italy at the 1982 World Cup?
7. In which year did Paolo Rossi make his final international appearance?
8. Who marked his international debut in 1995 with a goal in the 4–1 win over Estonia?
9. Who scored both goals in Italy's semi-final victory over Bulgaria at the 1994 World Cup?
10. Which AC Milan defender captained Italy at the 1990 World Cup?
11. How many caps did successful national coach Enzo Bearzot win as a player?
12. Who made his international debut in a 3–0 win against Brazil in 1963?
13. Who were Italy's first opponents at the 1994 World Cup finals?
14. Which Italian goalkeeper was sent off in the Group E match with Norway at the 1994 World Cup finals?
15. Who scored Italy's winner in that match?
16. Who did Italy beat in the semi-finals of Euro 2000?

Answers to page 678

THE WORLD GAME 12: **1.** Valencia **2.** Peter Møller **3.** Finnish **4.** Marco Van Basten **5.** Andoni Zubizarreta **6.** Lev Yashin **7.** Spain **8.** Patrick Kluivert **9.** 1966 **10.** Daniel Passarella **11.** Haarlem **12.** Dynamo Kiev **13.** Paris St Germain **14.** Croatia **15.** Roberto Carlos **16.** Roger Lemerre

Premiership 7

Answers on page 679

1. Who was Newcastle's leading scorer in 1999–2000?
2. Which Sheffield Wednesday player was given a 12-match ban in 1998?
3. Who were the only team to win a League game at Old Trafford in 1998–9?
4. Which Australian was voted Young Player of the Year for 2000?
5. Who was sacked as Tottenham manager in 2000–1?
6. Which reigning League champions went the entire Premiership season without an away win in 1992–3?
7. Which Queens Park Rangers player was the third highest Premiership marksman in 1994–5?
8. Who were the only team to win at Newcastle in 1994–5?
9. Who conceded four goals in their first game back in the Premiership in 2000–1?
10. Which two defenders were ever present for Aston Villa in their 1998–9 Premiership campaign?
11. Who finished third in the inaugural season of the Premiership?
12. In which year was the Premiership reduced from 22 clubs to 20?
13. Which club ended Nottingham Forest's unbeaten run of 25 Premiership matches in 1995?
14. What was the score?
15. Who went 15 matches without a win at the start of 1993–4?
16. Which London club lost eight Premiership matches in a row in 1997–8?

Answers to page 679

TRANSFER TRAIL 11: **1.** Carl Cort **2.** Martin Peters **3.** Barcelona **4.** Sampdoria **5.** Mark Hughes **6.** Alf Ramsey **7.** Brian Talbot **8.** Morton **9.** Notts County **10.** Matt Lawrence **11.** Torquay United **12.** Kingsley Black **13.** Nigel Winterburn **14.** Bradford City **15.** Jonathan Greening **16.** Queen's Park

The World Game 12

Answers on page 676

1. For which Spanish club did Gaizka Mendieta play in 2000–1?
2. Which Danish World Cup striker joined Real Oviedo from PSV Eindhoven in August 1998?
3. What nationality is Jari Litmanen?
4. Which Ajax striker won the European Golden Boot for 1985–6?
5. Which Spanish international goalkeeper joined Valencia on a free transfer from Barcelona in 1994?
6. Which goalkeeper won the last of his 78 caps for the USSR in 1967?
7. For which country does Luis Enrique play?
8. Which Dutch international striker moved from Milan to Barcelona in 1998?
9. In which year did Ferenc Puskas retire from playing?
10. Who became Argentine national coach after the 1994 World Cup?
11. With which Dutch club did Johan Neeskens make his League debut in 1968?
12. Which club was expelled from the 1995–6 UEFA Champions' League following a match-fixing scandal?
13. To which French club was Ossie Ardiles loaned by Tottenham during the Falklands conflict?
14. For which country does Robert Prosinecki play?
15. Which Brazilian international left-back made his League debut in 1991 with Uniao Sao Joao?
16. Who was appointed French national boss after the 1998 World Cup?

Answers to page 676

ITALY 1: **1.** 1958 **2.** Egypt **3.** Vittorio Pozzo **4.** Dino Zoff **5.** Luigi Riva **6.** Dino Zoff **7.** 1986 **8.** Fabrizio Ravanelli **9.** Roberto Baggio **10.** Franco Baresi **11.** One **12.** Sandro Mazzola **13.** Republic of Ireland **14.** Gianluca Pagliuca **15.** Dino Baggio **16.** Holland

Transfer Trail 11

Answers on page 677

1. Which striker moved from Wimbledon to Newcastle for £7 million in 2000?
2. Which England World Cup winner joined Tottenham from West Ham for £200,000 in 1970?
3. From which Spanish club did Chelsea sign Albert Ferrer in 1998?
4. Which Italian club did Trevor Francis join in 1982?
5. Who rejoined Manchester United from Barcelona for £1.8 million in 1988?
6. Which future England manager cost Tottenham £21,000 as a player from Southampton in 1949?
7. Which midfielder moved from Ipswich to Arsenal for £450,000 in 1979?
8. Which Scottish club sold Neil Orr to West Ham for £350,000?
9. From which club did Walsall sign goalkeeper Jimmy Walker?
10. Which full-back moved from Wycombe to Millwall for £250,000 in 2000?
11. With which club did Matt Elliott makes his League debut?
12. Which Northern Ireland winger joined Nottingham Forest from Luton for £1.5 million in 1991?
13. Which long-serving Arsenal full-back signed for West Ham in 2000?
14. From which club did Bristol City sign Brian Tinnion?
15. Who did York City sell to Manchester United for £1 million in 1998?
16. From which Scottish club did Leeds United sign Willie Bell in the 1960s?

Answers to page 677

PREMIERSHIP 7: **1.** Alan Shearer **2.** Paolo Di Canio **3.** Middlesbrough **4.** Harry Kewell **5.** George Graham **6.** Leeds United **7.** Les Ferdinand **8.** Leeds United **9.** Manchester City **10.** Alan Wright and Gareth Southgate **11.** Norwich City **12.** 1995 **13.** Blackburn Rovers **14.** 7–0 **15.** Swindon Town **16.** Crystal Palace

Chelsea 2

Answers on page 682

1. With which Italian club – a town more famous for its association with another sport — did Pierluigi Casiraghi begin his career?
2. How many games did Casiraghi play for Chelsea before injury struck?
3. Who knocked Chelsea out of the FA Cup in their Championship-winning season of 1954–5?
4. Which 1970s player was famed for his long throws?
5. Which England international did Chelsea sell to Birmingham City for £55,000 in 1966?
6. Who scored a club record 41 League goals for Chelsea in 1960–1?
7. Who scored Chelsea's goal in the 1967 FA Cup final?
8. Which Australian-born full-back did Chelsea sell to Leeds in 1991?
9. Who was Chelsea's first £100,000 signing?
10. When did Gianluca Vialli become Chelsea manager?
11. Who scored five times in the 13–0 demolition of Jeunesse Hautcharage in 1971?
12. And who scored a hat-trick in the same match?
13. From which club did Chelsea sign goalkeeper Kevin Hitchcock?
14. Which Chelsea player scored in seven successive Premiership matches in 1993–4?
15. Who did Chelsea beat in the semi-finals of the 1969–70 FA Cup?
16. Which midfielder joined Chelsea from Crystal Palace for a club record £170,000 in 1971?

Answers to page 682

SCOTTISH SCENE 9: **1.** David Hay **2.** Paisley **3.** 'The Jambos' **4.** St Johnstone **5.** Queen of the South **6.** Alloa Athletic **7.** Clyde and Alloa Athletic **8.** Airdrie **9.** Albion Rovers **10.** Sheffield Wednesday **11.** John Duncan **12.** Colin Stein **13.** Hibernian **14.** Hamilton Academicals **15.** Kilmarnock **16.** Bobby Lennox

European Cups 6

Answers on page 683

1. In July 2001, who became the first League of Wales club to reach the second qualifying round of the Champions' League?
2. Who did they beat in the first qualifying round?
3. Which Italian club knocked Rangers out of the 1998–9 UEFA Cup?
4. Who were the first French team to reach a European Cup final?
5. In which city were the 1990 and 1995 European Cup finals held?
6. Which team featured in both finals?
7. Which Englishman scored in the final of the 1999–2000 Champions' League?
8. For which team was he playing?
9. Which English team were beaten in the 1976 European Cup-Winners' Cup final?
10. Which Belgian club defeated them 4–2 in the final?
11. In which city did Tottenham win the 1963 European Cup-Winners' Cup final?
12. Which two players each scored twice for Spurs in the final?
13. Which Hungarian team reached the 1964 European Cup-Winners' Cup final?
14. Which German team beat Inter Milan on penalties in the 1997 UEFA Cup final?
15. In 1976, who became the first French team for 17 years to reach the European Cup final?
16. Who beat them 1–0 in the final?

Answers to page 683

NOTTINGHAM FOREST 1: **1.** Twice **2.** Nacional **3.** 1975 **4.** 11 **5.** Ajax **6.** Nigel Jemson **7.** Hull City **8.** Lee Chapman **9.** Stan Collymore **10.** Jack Lester **11.** Bob McKinlay **12.** Grantham Town **13.** 1949 **14.** Allan Brown **15.** Chris Bart-Williams **16.** Swansea City

Scottish Scene 9

Answers on page 680

1. Which future Celtic manager moved from Parkhead to Chelsea for £225,000 in 1974?
2. In which Scottish town do St Mirren play?
3. What is Hearts' nickname?
4. For which club did Drew Rutherford make 298 League appearances?
5. Who escaped relegation to Division Three in 2000 because of Hamilton's points deduction?
6. Who knocked Dundee out of the Scottish League Cup in 1998–9?
7. Which two teams were promoted from the Second Division in 1999–2000?
8. Which club that has never won the Scottish League Championship finished runners-up to Rangers in four successive years in the 1920s?
9. Which club won their first title for 55 years when topping the Second Division in 1989?
10. To which English club did Rangers sell Chris Woods in 1991?
11. Which Dundee striker joined Tottenham for £150,000 in 1974?
12. Who was Rangers' first £100,000 signing?
13. From which Scottish club did they sign him?
14. John Blackley, Bertie Auld and John Lambie have all managed which Scottish League club?
15. Behind Queen's Park, which of the current Scottish League clubs is the oldest?
16. Who scored 168 League goals for Celtic between 1962 and 1980?

Answers to page 680

CHELSEA 2: **1.** Monza **2.** 15 **3.** Notts County **4.** Ian Hutchinson **5.** Barry Bridges **6.** Jimmy Greaves **7.** Bobby Tambling **8.** Tony Dorigo **9.** Tony Hateley **10.** 1998 **11.** Peter Osgood **12.** Tommy Baldwin **13.** Mansfield Town **14.** Mark Stein **15.** Watford **16.** Steve Kember

Nottingham Forest 1

Answers on page 681

1. How many times have Forest won the FA Cup?
2. Which Argentinian club beat Forest in the 1980 World Club Championship?
3. In which year did Brian Clough become Forest manager?
4. How many trophies did Forest win in his 18-year reign?
5. Who did Forest beat in the semi-finals of the 1980 European Cup?
6. Who scored Forest's winner in the 1990 League Cup final?
7. From which club did Forest sign Garry Parker?
8. Which striker joined Forest from French club Niort for £400,000 in 1988?
9. Who was Forest's leading scorer in 1993–4?
10. Which forward did Forest sign from Grimsby Town for £250,000 in 2000?
11. Who made 614 League appearances for Forest between 1951 and 1970?
12. From which non-League club did Forest sign Gary Crosby?
13. In which year were Forest relegated to the Third Division for the only time in their history?
14. Who was Brian Clough's predecessor as Forest boss?
15. Which midfielder was Forest's top scorer in 2000–1?
16. From which club did Forest sign Christian Edwards?

Answers to page 681

EUROPEAN CUPS 6: **1.** Barry Town **2.** FC Shambir of Azerbaijan **3.** Parma **4.** Rheims **5.** Vienna **6.** AC Milan **7.** Steve McManaman **8.** Real Madrid **9.** West Ham United **10.** Anderlecht **11.** Rotterdam **12.** Jimmy Greaves and Terry Dyson **13.** MTK Budapest **14.** FC Schalke **15.** St Etienne **16.** Bayern Munich

General Knowledge 161

Answers on page 686

1. With which football team was Des O'Connor once a lively winger?
2. Which chat show host had a cameo role as a postman in *Neighbours*?
3. What does herbicide destroy?
4. What was the nickname of 11th-century English rebel Hereward?
5. What does a udometer measure?
6. Who sang about the 'Best Years Of Our Lives' in 1982?
7. What does a hermaphrodite possess?
8. The Baader-Meinhof gang were a group of terrorists from which country?
9. Which is the largest Mediterranean island?
10. How many wooden pins are arranged in a game of skittles?
11. What is the chemical name for quicklime?
12. In which English county are Slapton Sands?
13. What is the capital of the United Arab Emirates?
14. From which country does snooker player James Wattana come?
15. Who directed the film *Gandhi*?
16. Which couple warbled 'Sing Little Birdie' for the UK in the 1959 Eurovision Song Contest?

Answers to page 686

GENERAL KNOWLEDGE 163: **1.** 1,500 metres **2.** Basil d'Oliveira **3.** Teeth **4.** Pricey **5.** French **6.** Wildebeest **7.** 1980 **8.** His first solo UK number one hit **9.** Marmite **10.** *West Side Story* **11.** Rio de Janeiro **12.** Barrels **13.** Didier Six **14.** Hungary **15.** Gull **16.** *Space Patrol*

General Knowledge 162

Answers on page 687

1. Which 1970s TV comedy series was originally going to be called *Super-Chaps Three* ?
2. What was John Merrick otherwise known as?
3. What is a zinnia?
4. In which county is Kenilworth Castle?
5. On which English river is Washington?
6. Which group of Pacific islands used to be known as the Sandwich Islands?
7. Who was deputy leader of the Labour Party from 1983–92?
8. According to Greek mythology, drinking from which underworld river made you forget the past?
9. Which Yorkshire village was home to the Brontë family?
10. Margaret Thatcher was MP for which constituency?
11. Kyalami is a motor-racing circuit in which country?
12. Who had a number one hit in 1995 with 'Fairground'?
13. Who composed *The Barber of Seville*?
14. In which century was rounders first played?
15. What does RSPB stand for?
16. *Solanum tuberosum* is more commonly known as which vegetable?

Answers to page 687

GENERAL KNOWLEDGE 164: **1.** Medway **2.** John Reid **3.** Along the Welsh border **4.** Oxymorons **5.** North Yorkshire **6.** Mr Spooner **7.** It turns white **8.** Suede **9.** Quartz **10.** The Keystone Cops **11.** Its tail **12.** She was the world's first female Prime Minister **13.** Time **14.** Mediterranean **15.** Amsterdam **16.** Eiffel Tower

General Knowledge 163

Answers on page 684

1. What was the longest running race for women at the 1980 Olympic Games?
2. Which cricketer's inclusion in the MCC party to tour South Africa in 1968 led to the tour being cancelled?
3. What do frogs have in their mouths that toads don't?
4. What was the name of the sports teacher in *Please, Sir!* ?
5. What nationality was the artist Paul Gauguin?
6. A gnu is another name for which animal?
7. In which year did war break out between Iran and Iraq?
8. What did Elton John have to wait until 1990 to achieve?
9. Which food product takes its name from the French for cooking pot?
10. In 1961 George Chakiris and Rita Moreno won Oscars for Best Supporting Actor and Actress for their roles in which musical film?
11. Which city is home to the Copacabana Beach?
12. What does a cooper make?
13. Which number was a French footballer?
14. Magyars come from which country?
15. What type of sea bird is sometimes called a mew?
16. Captain Larry Dart was the hero of which TV series?

Answers to page 684

GENERAL KNOWLEDGE 161: **1.** Northampton Town **2.** Clive James **3.** Plants **4.** 'The Wake' **5.** Rain **6.** Modern Romance **7.** Both male and female sex organs **8.** Germany **9.** Sicily **10.** Nine **11.** Calcium oxide **12.** Devon **13.** Abu Dhabi **14.** Thailand **15.** Sir Richard Attenborough **16.** Teddy Johnson and Pearl Carr

General Knowledge 164

Answers on page 685

1. On which river does Maidstone stand?
2. Who rode Dr Devious to victory in the 1992 Epsom Derby?
3. Where would you find the remains of Offa's Dyke?
4. 'Bittersweet' and 'cruel to be kind' are examples of what?
5. In which county is Pickering?
6. Who replaced Mr Lucas in *Are You Being Served*?
7. What happens to the rock ptarmigan's plumage in winter?
8. Brett Anderson is the singer with which band?
9. What is the crystalline form of silica?
10. Which police force did Mack Sennett create?
11. What is particularly long about the male quetzal bird of Central America?
12. What was notable about Sirimavo Bandaranaike, Prime Minister of Sri Lanka from 1960?
13. What does a chronometer measure?
14. Elba is an island in which sea?
15. TV detective *Van Der Valk* solved crimes in which city?
16. Which monument was designed for the Paris Exhibition of 1889?

Answers to page 685

GENERAL KNOWLEDGE 162: **1.** *The Goodies* **2.** The Elephant Man **3.** A flower **4.** Warwickshire **5.** Wear **6.** Hawaii **7.** Roy Hattersley **8.** Lethe **9.** Haworth **10.** Finchley **11.** South Africa **12.** Simply Red **13.** Rossini **14.** 18th **15.** Royal Society for the Protection of Birds **16.** Potato

General Knowledge 165

Answers on page 690

1. Who asked: 'Does Your Chewing Gum Lose Its Flavour (On The Bedpost Overnight)'?
2. How many Epsom Derby winners did Lester Piggott ride?
3. Which 11th-century wizard became stranded in the 20th century?
4. Iago featured in which Shakespeare play?
5. Which horse won the 2002 Grand National?
6. How many court cards are there in a pack of cards?
7. Which legislation banned alcohol in the United States during the 1920s?
8. Which sound indicated a Rank Organisation film?
9. What did the sisters Stheno, Euryale and Medusa have for hair?
10. Who painted *The Supper at Emmaus*?
11. Which phrase means 'through my fault' in Latin?
12. Which TV medical series is a spin-off from *Casualty*?
13. Which band a 1978 hit with 'Airport'?
14. How many points are there on a backgammon board?
15. Which county's coastline includes Pegwell Bay?
16. Which club were promoted to the Football League in 2001?

Answers to page 690

GENERAL KNOWLEDGE 167: **1.** Rome **2.** Agate **3.** Operation Overlord **4.** Frown **5.** Pink **6.** A type of antelope **7.** *Lady Chatterley's Lover* **8.** Washington **9.** *News at Ten* **10.** Valéry **11.** Giles **12.** Annie Lennox **13.** Lauren Bacall **14.** 'Little Green Apples' **15.** 12th **16.** Robert Burns

General Knowledge 166

Answers on page 691

1. Which is the deepest canyon in North America?
2. Which religious order was founded by Ignatius Loyola?
3. Septime is a position in which sport?
4. What is the capital of Trinidad and Tobago?
5. Which is the second largest English county?
6. Which island is also known as Lindisfarne?
7. Which girl band had three UK number one singles in 1998?
8. Juneau is the capital of which American state?
9. What links William Shakespeare, Ingrid Bergman and former England football manager Joe Mercer?
10. Who was the local butcher in *Dad's Army*?
11. Which horse won the Grand National for the third time in 1977?
12. Who played Himmler in the film *The Eagle Has Landed*?
13. Which title did Austria's Eva Rueber-Staier win in 1969?
14. Which brand of disinfectant took its name from London sanitary engineer Harry Pickup?
15. Which English king reigned from 1272 to 1307?
16. Which much-married American actor's real name is Joe Yule Jnr?

Answers to page 691

GENERAL KNOWLEDGE 168: **1.** Venus **2.** All are former policemen **3.** Transport and General Workers' Union **4.** *As Good as It Gets* **5.** Melinda Messenger **6.** Yachting **7.** Ambrosia **8.** Peter Benchley **9.** *HMS Victory* **10.** Toni Collette **11.** Spain **12.** Sweep with it – it's a kind of broom **13.** Tomatoes **14.** Edward VIII **15.** Desert rat **16.** Timmy

General Knowledge 167

Answers on page 688

1. Which city was sacked in 410?
2. What is the birthstone for the month of June?
3. What was the codename for the D-Day landings?
4. Which requires the use of more facial muscles – a smile or a frown?
5. What colour is yak's milk?
6. What is a gemsbok?
7. Which D.H. Lawrence novel was banned until November 1960?
8. In which American state is Mount St Helens?
9. Which TV news programme began in 1967?
10. What was the Christian name of the French President Giscard d'Estaing?
11. Which newspaper cartoonist created a family built around the formidable Grandma?
12. Which singer's 1992 album was titled 'Diva'?
13. Which Hollywood actress was Miss Greenwich Village of 1942?
14. Which fruit did Roger Miller sing about in 1968?
15. In which century did beavers become extinct in the UK?
16. Which Scottish poet wrote two poems about his pet ewe called Poor Mailie?

Answers to page 688

GENERAL KNOWLEDGE 165: **1.** Lonnie Donegan **2.** Nine **3.** *Catweazle* **4.** *Othello* **5.** Bindaree **6.** 12 **7.** Prohibition **8.** Gong **9.** Snakes **10.** Caravaggio **11.** Mea culpa **12.** *Holby City* **13.** The Motors **14.** 24 **15.** Kent **16.** Rushden and Diamonds

General Knowledge 168

Answers on page 689

1. Which planet has the longest day?
2. What job links Christopher Dean, Geoff Capes and Dave Dee?
3. What does TGWU stand for?
4. Jack Nicholson and Helen Hunt both won Oscars in 1997 for their performances in which film?
5. Which model presents *Fort Boyard*?
6. In which sport do countries compete for the America's Cup?
7. Which food of the Greek gods was supposed to confer eternal life upon all who ate it?
8. Who wrote the novel of *Jaws* ?
9. Which flagship of Nelson's sits in dock at Portsmouth?
10. Which actress starred as Muriel in the film *Muriel's Wedding*?
11. Vigo is a port in which country?
12. What would you do with a besom?
13. Which fruits used to be known as 'love apples'?
14. Which English king abdicated in 1936?
15. Which creature has sex up to 122 times per hour?
16. What was the name of the dog in Enid Blyton's *Famous Five* books?

Answers to page 689

GENERAL KNOWLEDGE 166: **1.** Hell's Canyon **2.** The Jesuits **3.** Fencing **4.** Port of Spain **5.** Cumbria **6.** Holy Island **7.** B*Witched **8.** Alaska **9.** All died on their birthdays **10.** Corporal Jones **11.** Red Rum **12.** Donald Pleasence **13.** Miss World **14.** Harpic **15.** Edward I **16.** Mickey Rooney

General Knowledge 169

Answers on page 694

1. Who lampooned Dickens with the words: 'One must have a heart of stone to read the death of Little Nell without laughing'?
2. In which city is the newspaper *Dagbladet* published?
3. How many points are scored for a field goal in American football?
4. What is South Africa's unit of decimal currency?
5. What was the title of Sherlock Holmes' first adventure?
6. Which London department store first opened its doors to the public in 1909?
7. Who played *The Scarlet Pimpernel* in the 1998 TV adaptation?
8. Which American state is known as the Garden State?
9. What is the official language of Argentina?
10. Which team are the only non-English winners of the FA Cup?
11. Who was 'French Kissin' In The USA' in 1986?
12. Which magazine introduced Billy the Fish?
13. Which British cathedral has three spires?
14. Which projectile was originally called Morrison's Flyin' Saucer?
15. Which sport is played with a shuttlecock?
16. Which high-kicking girls stepped to fame on *Sunday Night at the London Palladium*?

Answers to page 694

GENERAL KNOWLEDGE 171: **1.** 21 **2.** Richard Gordon **3.** Cindy Bear **4.** 1,500 metres **5.** Switzerland and Italy **6.** *A Beautiful Mind* **7.** *Aladdin* **8.** Frank Leboeuf **9.** Zurich **10.** Dorset **11.** Komodo dragon **12.** Pips **13.** Czechoslovakia **14.** Patty Hearst **15.** Richard Marx **16.** An Indian cart

General Knowledge 170

Answers on page 695

1. In an average lifetime, a person will walk the equivalent of how many times around the equator?
2. From which London station would you catch a direct train to Doncaster?
3. Which puppet owl created havoc on *Five O'Clock Club*?
4. What does Goat Island separate?
5. What nationality was Marshal Ney?
6. Whose first UK number one single was 'The Most Beautiful Girl In The World'?
7. Which is the largest planet in the solar system?
8. Which Shakespeare play begins: 'If music be the food of love, play on'?
9. What type of tree is a linden?
10. What is a hinny?
11. In which county was artist John Constable born?
12. Which athletics competition was first held in Helsinki in 1983?
13. Which British-born director was responsible for *Alien*?
14. Which actress of *Straw Dogs* fame appeared in *EastEnders* in 2001?
15. St Agnes and Bryher are islands in which group?
16. Which crime writer created Mike Hammer?

Answers to page 695

GENERAL KNOWLEDGE 172: **1.** *Pride and Prejudice* **2.** Morocco **3.** A belt **4.** Richard and Judy **5.** Jim Carrey **6.** Bradford **7.** Solomon **8.** Her Majesty's Stationery Office **9.** Barbra Streisand **10.** A marmoset **11.** Ethiopia **12.** Space **13.** Ingemar Johansson **14.** Cowslip **15.** Canadian **16.** William Thackeray

General Knowledge 171

Answers on page 692

1. What is the key number in the card game pontoon?
2. Who wrote the *Doctor* books?
3. Who was Yogi Bear's southern sweetheart?
4. What is the final event in the decathlon?
5. Which two countries are linked by the Simplon Pass?
6. Which film won the Best Film Oscar in 2002?
7. Jafar was the villain in which Disney film?
8. In football, which French defender moved from Chelsea to Marseille in July 2001?
9. Which is the largest city in Switzerland?
10. In which county is Weymouth?
11. Which is the biggest lizard in the world?
12. What are missing from a navel orange?
13. Who did Brazil's footballers beat in the 1962 World Cup Final?
14. Which heiress turned bank robber in 1974?
15. Which American singer was 'Right Here Waiting' in 1989?
16. What is an ekka?

Answers to page 692

GENERAL KNOWLEDGE 169: **1.** Oscar Wilde **2.** Oslo **3.** Three **4.** Rand **5.** *A Study in Scarlet* **6.** Selfridges **7.** Richard E. Grant **8.** New Jersey **9.** Spanish **10.** Cardiff City **11.** Debbie Harry **12.** *Viz* **13.** Lichfield **14.** Frisbee **15.** Badminton **16.** The Tiller Girls

General Knowledge 172

Answers on page 693

1. Which Jane Austen novel revolved around the Bennet sisters?
2. The dirham is the currency of which African country?
3. What is a baldric?
4. Which husband and wife left *This Morning* in 2001?
5. Who starred in the movie *Liar Liar*?
6. Which English city houses the National Museum of Photography, Film and Television?
7. In the Old Testament, who was the third king of Israel?
8. What does HMSO stand for?
9. Who starred in and directed *Yentl*?
10. What is a tamarin?
11. In which country is Lake Tana?
12. In 1996, which band reckoned that the female of the species was more deadly than the male?
13. Which Swedish boxer fought for the World Heavyweight title in the early 1960s?
14. *Primula veris* is the Latin name for which plant?
15. What nationality is Jim Carrey?
16. Which English novelist had the middle name Makepeace?

Answers to page 693

GENERAL KNOWLEDGE 170: **1.** Five **2.** King's Cross **3.** Ollie Beak **4.** The two halves of the Niagara Falls **5.** French **6.** Prince **7.** Jupiter **8.** *Twelfth Night* **9.** Lime tree **10.** The offspring of a female ass by a stallion **11.** Suffolk **12.** World Championships **13.** Ridley Scott **14.** Susan George **15.** Isles of Scilly **16.** Mickey Spillane

General Knowledge 173

Answers on page 698

1. Which Bruce Channel hit was a number one for DJ Otzi in 2001?
2. Which national newspaper replaced the *Daily Herald*?
3. In which year was Prince Edward born?
4. Which animal is the national emblem of Canada?
5. Which country's inclusion in 2000 turned the Five Nations' Rugby Championship into the Six Nations?
6. Who composed the *Ring* cycle?
7. Which is the second-longest river in Africa?
8. What are you afraid of if you suffer from ichthyophobia?
9. Who brought the teas in *Acorn Antiques*?
10. On which river does Toulouse stand?
11. Who was married to Michael in *thirtysomething*?
12. Lake Maracaibo is the largest lake on which continent?
13. What is the common abbreviation for deoxyribonucleic acid?
14. What is fumitory?
15. Fatima Whitbread was a champion at which athletics field event?
16. Which gardens adjoin Hyde Park?

Answers to page 698

GENERAL KNOWLEDGE 175: **1.** An old-fashioned name for a golf club **2.** Maundy Thursday **3.** *The Fast Show* **4.** Aston Villa **5.** Newport Pagnell **6.** 13 **7.** D **8.** Dundalk **9.** Helmut Schmidt **10.** Zambezi **11.** Narwhal **12.** Tangelo **13.** Polish **14.** Orange **15.** Wo Fat **16.** Del Shannon

General Knowledge 174

Answers on page 699

1. Who beat Steffi Graf in 1987 to win her sixth Wimbledon women's singles title in a row?
2. At whom did Marcus Sargeant fire blank shots on 30 June 1981?
3. In which stadium did Liverpool's footballers retain the European Cup in 1978?
4. In which city is the Doge's Palace?
5. Io, Europa, Ganymede and Callisto are moons of which planet?
6. In which room in the house did Jim Morrison, Elvis Presley and Judy Garland all die?
7. In Roman mythology, who was Jupiter's wife?
8. What did two women claim to have seen in the Irish village of Knock in 1897?
9. Who played Claude Jeremiah Greengrass in *Heartbeat*?
10. Who was the first man to appear on the cover of *Playboy*?
11. What does 'karaoke' mean literally?
12. In Australia, what is the state capital of Victoria?
13. Who succeeded Zoë Ball as the female presenter of *Live and Kicking*?
14. Which American state is known as the 'Peach State'?
15. Which musical duo took their name from a David Lynch film?
16. What pre-fame job linked Marlon Brando and Dr David Owen?

Answers to page 699

GENERAL KNOWLEDGE 176: **1.** Fish **2.** Wind **3.** They died on stage **4.** Carol Smillie **5.** John Updike **6.** Francis Bacon **7.** Elizabeth I **8.** Fijian **9.** San Francisco **10.** Jack Dempsey **11.** Desert Storm **12.** Marquess **13.** Clarksville **14.** A North American mammal **15.** Three points were awarded for a win instead of two **16.** Harry Enfield

General Knowledge 175

Answers on page 696

1. What is a brassie?
2. In the Christian Church, what is the name given to the Thursday before Easter?
3. On which show might you have met the 13th Duke of Wymbourne?
4. Which club were the first winners of the Football League Cup?
5. Where was Britain's first motorway restaurant?
6. How many were present at the Last Supper?
7. What is the Roman numeral for 500?
8. What town is the administrative centre of County Louth?
9. Which Helmut became Chancellor of Germany in 1974?
10. On which river in Africa are the Victoria Falls?
11. Which species of whale has a distinctive single tusk which can reach up to three metres long?
12. Which fruit is sometimes called ugli?
13. What nationality was Marie Curie?
14. From which fruit is the liqueur Curaçao made?
15. Who was Steve McGarrett's arch enemy on *Hawaii Five-O* ?
16. Which American singer changed his name from Charles Westover?

Answers to page 696

GENERAL KNOWLEDGE 173: **1.** 'Hey Baby' **2.** *The Sun* **3.** 1964 **4.** Beaver **5.** Italy **6.** Richard Wagner **7.** The Zaire **8.** Fish **9.** Mrs Overall **10.** Garonne **11.** Hope **12.** South America **13.** DNA **14.** A plant **15.** Javelin **16.** Kensington Gardens

General Knowledge 176

Answers on page 697

1. What is bouillabaisse primarily made from?
2. What does the Beaufort scale measure?
3. What do Tommy Cooper, Sid James and Leonard Rossiter have in common?
4. Which TV presenter once carried the title of Miss Parallel Bars?
5. Which American novelist wrote *Rabbit is Rich* and *The Witches of Eastwick*?
6. Which eminent 17th-century scientist died of a chill after trying to stuff a chicken with snow?
7. Anthony Babington hatched a plot to assassinate which queen of England?
8. What nationality is golfer Vijay Singh?
9. Which American city was named after St Francis of Assisi?
10. Who was world heavyweight boxing champion from 1919 to 1926?
11. What was the codename of the military operation to eject the Iraqi army from Kuwait in 1991?
12. Which title of the peerage is below a duke but above an earl?
13. Where did The Monkees catch the last train to?
14. What is a pekan?
15. What change was made to the Football League points system in 1981?
16. Who waved about Loadsamoney?

Answers to page 697

GENERAL KNOWLEDGE 174: **1.** Martina Navratilova **2.** The Queen **3.** Wembley **4.** Venice **5.** Jupiter **6.** The bathroom **7.** Juno **8.** A vision of the virgin with two saints **9.** Bill Maynard **10.** Peter Sellers **11.** 'Empty orchestra' **12.** Melbourne **13.** Emma Ledden **14.** Georgia **15.** Erasure (*Eraserhead*) **16.** Sewage worker

General Knowledge 177

Answers on page 702

1. What is Reuters?
2. Which flowers did Queen Elizabeth I have a phobia about?
3. Which actor was born Michael Shalhoub?
4. Which American state is called the Show Me State?
5. Which country conceded 57 goals in their four qualifying matches for the 2002 World Cup?
6. Which Dutch artist painted no fewer than 64 self-portraits?
7. What could be spotted on the ground in the Western *Stagecoach*?
8. Who drove the Varoom Roadster in *Wacky Races*?
9. How old was Drew Barrymore when she starred in *E.T.*?
10. What four tournaments comprise the Grand Slam in tennis?
11. Whose debut novel was entitled *White Teeth*?
12. What did the Queen launch at Clydebank on 20 September 1967?
13. Who was King of France at the outbreak of the French Revolution?
14. Who created *Yogi Bear*?
15. In which country are the Trossachs?
16. What was the world's first theme park?

Answers to page 702

GENERAL KNOWLEDGE 179: **1.** Apples **2.** French **3.** Pudding Lane **4.** Korea and Japan **5.** *Deliverance* **6.** Ear **7.** 'Crusher' **8.** San Diego **9.** T'Pau **10.** Scrabble **11.** L.S. Lowry **12.** York **13.** Huyton **14.** Two **15.** Leslie Crowther **16.** Henry Cooper

General Knowledge 178

Answers on page 703

1. What did Oscar Wilde, Peter O'Toole and General Douglas MacArthur have in common as children?
2. From what country does the word 'sauna' originate?
3. Which boxer was nicknamed the 'Ambling Alp'?
4. Which actress starred in *Platinum Blonde* and *Bombshell*?
5. Which Sixties group sang about a 'Dedicated Follower Of Fashion'?
6. What is the capital of Slovakia?
7. Who wrote the play *Waiting For Godot*?
8. Which sign of the zodiac covers the period from 23 September to 23 October?
9. In *Dallas*, what was Sue Ellen's favourite tipple?
10. On which street in London is Hamley's toy shop?
11. For how long can an ant survive underwater?
12. On which day of the week do nearly half of all American bank robberies take place?
13. In which sport did Britain win its only gold medal at the 2002 Winter Olympics?
14. What is the common name for rubella?
15. Which member of the Brontë family wrote *Agnes Grey*?
16. In TV commercials, what were Humphreys likely to steal?

Answers to page 703

GENERAL KNOWLEDGE 180: **1.** *Beyond the Fringe* **2.** Red **3.** Battle of Copenhagen **4.** Christopher Marlowe **5.** Kansas **6.** 32 **7.** Portugal **8.** Longchamp **9.** An ice cream dessert **10.** Polar bears live at the north pole, penguins at the south **11.** Will Smith **12.** Eight **13.** Ho Chi Minh **14.** A small bobsled **15.** Liverpool **16.** Dow Jones average

General Knowledge 179

Answers on page 700

1. Calvados brandy is distilled from which fruit?
2. What nationality is racing driver Jean Alesi?
3. In which street did the Great Fire of London start?
4. Where were the 2002 World Cup Finals held?
5. Which James Dickey novel about a tragic canoe trip was turned into a chilling movie starring Burt Reynolds and Jon Voight?
6. Where in the human body are the semi-circular canals?
7. What was the nickname of *Coronation Street* pub landlord Duggie Ferguson in his Rugby League-playing days?
8. Which city is served by Lindbergh Airport?
9. Which band released the 1987 album 'Bridge Of Spies'?
10. Which board game was devised by unemployed New York architect Alfred Butts?
11. Which artist was the subject of Brian and Michael's 'Matchstalk Men And Matchstalk Cats And Dogs'?
12. In which English city is Clifford's Tower?
13. What was Harold Wilson's Parliamentary constituency?
14. How many of Henry VIII's wives were beheaded?
15. Who was the original presenter of *Stars in Their Eyes*?
16. Which British boxer fought Muhammad Ali for the world heavyweight title in 1966?

Answers to page 700

GENERAL KNOWLEDGE 177: **1.** An international news agency **2.** Roses **3.** Omar Sharif **4.** Missouri **5.** American Samoa **6.** Rembrandt **7.** Tyre tracks **8.** Peter Perfect **9.** Eight **10.** Wimbledon, US Open, French Championships and Australian Championships **11.** Zadie Smith **12.** The *QE2* **13.** Louis XVI **14.** William Hanna and Joseph Barbera **15.** Scotland **16.** Disneyland

General Knowledge 180

Answers on page 701

1. Which satirical revue featured Peter Cook, Dudley Moore, Alan Bennett and Jonathan Miller?
2. What colour beak does a moorhen have?
3. At which battle did Nelson defeat the Danish fleet in 1801?
4. Who wrote *Doctor Faustus*?
5. In which American state is Dodge City?
6. How many human teeth are there in a permanent full set?
7. In which country is the Algarve?
8. On which racecourse is the Prix de l'Arc de Triomphe run?
9. What is baked Alaska?
10. Why don't polar bears hunt penguins?
11. Who starred as Muhammad Ali in the 2002 film *Ali*?
12. How many reindeer pull Santa's sleigh?
13. Which former world leader once worked as a pastry assistant in the kitchens of London's Carlton Hotel?
14. What is a luge?
15. Albert Dock is a renovated area of which English city?
16. What is the name of the New York Stock Exchange index?

Answers to page 701

GENERAL KNOWLEDGE 178: **1.** They were all dressed as girls in their early years **2.** Finland **3.** Primo Carnera **4.** Jean Harlow **5.** The Kinks **6.** Bratislava **7.** Samuel Beckett **8.** Libra **9.** Vodka **10.** Regent Street **11.** Two weeks **12.** Friday **13.** Curling **14.** German measles **15.** Anne Brontë **16.** Milk